DAVID O. MCKAY LIBRARY
3 1404 00777 7474
SEP 2 9 2004
D1165459
PROPERTY OF:
DAVID O. McKAY LIBRARY
BYU-IDAHO
REXBURG ID 83460-0405

I CHRONICLES
1–9

VOLUME 12

THE ANCHOR BIBLE is a fresh approach to the world's greatest classic. Its object is to make the Bible accessible to the modern reader; its method is to arrive at the meaning of biblical literature through exact translation and extended exposition, and to reconstruct the ancient setting of the biblical story, as well as the circumstances of its transcription and the characteristics of its transcribers.

THE ANCHOR BIBLE is a project of international and interfaith scope: Protestant, Catholic, and Jewish scholars from many countries contribute individual volumes. The project is not sponsored by any ecclesiastical organization and is not intended to reflect any particular theological doctrine. Prepared under our joint supervision, THE ANCHOR BIBLE is an effort to make available all the significant historical and linguistic knowledge which bears on the interpretation of the biblical record.

THE ANCHOR BIBLE is aimed at the general reader with no special formal training in biblical studies; yet it is written with the most exacting standards of scholarship, reflecting the highest technical accomplishment.

This project marks the beginning of a new era of cooperation among scholars in biblical research, thus forming a common body of knowledge to be shared by all.

William Foxwell Albright
David Noel Freedman
GENERAL EDITORS

THE ANCHOR BIBLE

I CHRONICLES 1–9

◆

A New Translation
with Introduction and Commentary

GARY N. KNOPPERS

THE ANCHOR BIBLE
Doubleday
New York London Toronto Sydney Auckland

THE ANCHOR BIBLE
PUBLISHED BY DOUBLEDAY
a division of Random House, Inc.
1745 Broadway, New York, New York 10019

THE ANCHOR BIBLE, DOUBLEDAY, and the portrayal of an anchor
with the letters A and B are registered trademarks of Doubleday,
a division of Random House, Inc.

LIBRARY OF CONGRESS CATALOGING-IN-PUBLICATION DATA
Bible. O.T. Chronicles I–IX, 1st. English. Knoppers. 2004.
I Chronicles 1–9: a new translation with introduction and commentary /
Gary Knoppers.—1st ed.
p. cm. (The Anchor Bible; v. 12)
Includes bibliographical references and indexes.
1. Bible. O.T. Chronicles, 1st—Commentaries. I. Title: 1 Chronicles.
II. Title: First Chronicles. III. Knoppers, Gary N., 1956– . IV. Title.
V. Bible. English. Anchor Bible. 1964; v. 12.
BS192.2.A1 1964 .G3 vol. 12
[BS1345.53]
222'.63077—dc22 2003055813

ISBN 0-385-46928-4

Copyright © 2003 by Doubleday, a division of Random House, Inc.

All Rights Reserved
Printed in the United States of America
July 2004

First Edition

10 9 8 7 6 5 4 3 2 1

To my daughter Theresa and
my son David (Prov 17:1)

CONTENTS

◆

Preface

◆

In writing a commentary on Chronicles at the end of the twentieth century and at the beginning of the twenty-first century C.E., I stand in a very privileged position. The scholarly world has devoted much closer attention to the Persian era (538–332 B.C.E.) in the past three decades than in any other modern period that I am aware of. The bibliography in this volume attests to the keen interest contemporary scholars have exhibited in the Neo-Babylonian, Achaemenid, and Hellenistic eras. Scholars have come to view these periods, rightly in my judgment, to be more formative in the composition and editing of many biblical works than previous generations recognized. The careful attention devoted to the Persian period also holds true for the book of Chronicles. Long neglected by commentators, this work is finally being given its due. I would like to acknowledge the work of several influential scholars in particular. Sara Japhet, Thomas Willi, and Hugh Williamson have provided the scholarly community with insightful and stimulating treatments of the Chronicler's distinctive compositional technique. It is not too much of an exaggeration to say that these scholars have changed the way that we perceive the nature and theological relevance of the Chronicler's work. Pat Graham and Kai Peltonen have performed a real service in providing the scholarly community with detailed histories of Chronicles' interpretation and its relevance to the interpretation of the Pentateuch and the Former Prophets. Isaac Kalimi has compiled a comprehensive bibliography and provided an incisive analysis of the Chronicler's literary craft. The Chronicles-Ezra-Nehemiah section of the Society of Biblical Literature has always proved to be an exciting and supportive context to try out new ideas. John Wright, Steven McKenzie, and Tyler Williams kindly read earlier versions of my introduction and excursus on the genealogies. Ehud Ben Zvi and Bernie Levinson have always been willing to critique anything I write. Francis Andersen drew up a convenient computer-generated Hebrew concordance of Chronicles for my work, while Dean Forbes furnished me with a detailed word count for every chapter in the book.

Other scholars have directly and indirectly contributed to the preparation of this volume. Ray Dillard first piqued my interest in the Chronicler's writing during an end session course he taught at Gordon-Conwell Seminary in the early 1980s. Frank Cross, Tom Lambdin, Bill Moran, Paul Hanson, Michael Coogan, and James Kugel were excellent teachers and mentors during my graduate training at Harvard. I am especially indebted to Frank Cross for his invaluable guidance during the course of writing my dissertation. My current colleagues at Penn

State have been very helpful in aiding my research. John Betlyon, Baruch Halpern, and Paul Harvey supplied me with helpful critiques of my introduction. Ann Killebrew has been a valuable resource for my work with material remains. Don Redford has proved to be a handy consultant on all matters Egyptological, while Phil Baldi, Deborah Beck, David Engel, Garrett Fagan, Stephen Wheeler, and Mark Munn have been handy consultants on all matters Classical. For help in the New Testament and the Patristics, I always turn to my colleagues Bill Petersen and Paul Harvey. Three graduate students, Eugene Shaw Colyer, Deirdre Fulton, and Jeffrey Veenstra, proofread parts of the manuscript.

The completion of the first installment of a two-volume set on 1 and 2 Chronicles is an appropriate time to express one's sincere gratitude to those institutes and libraries that have made the research for this book possible. The Institute for the Arts and Humanities and the Research and Graduate Studies Office of the College of the Liberal Arts (both at Penn State) awarded me with timely travel to collection grants to aid my studies. The Oxford Centre for Hebrew and Jewish Studies graciously bestowed upon me a fellowship during my sabbatical year of 1995–96. The kind support of the staff and faculty of the Centre were of enormous help to me as I conducted the research for this commentary. At Penn State, Roberta Astroff and Daniel Mack have made tremendous strides in improving the quality of the library's collections. At Anchor Doubleday, Andrew Corbin has enthusiastically pushed this project to publication. I am also appreciative of the work of Siobhan Dunn, John Kohlenberger, and Leslie Phillips on this project. The general editor of the Anchor Bible, David Noel Freedman, represents an extraordinary combination of creativity and sensitivity to detail. I have never worked with an editor of his caliber, and I doubt that I shall ever again. Over the course of writing this volume, Noel provided me with over three hundred pages of commentary on my commentary. For this studious attention to matters both large and small in my work, I am truly grateful.

Finally, I would like to express my thanks to family members for their positive influence upon my work. During the course of my upbringing, my parents, Ms. Barthie Maria Boon Knoppers and Rev. Nicolaas Bastiaan Knoppers, communicated a profound love for the Old Testament within the larger context of the Dutch Reformed tradition. My wife, Laura, and our children, Theresa and David, have always encouraged my studies. When I began writing this commentary over nine years ago, I could scarcely imagine how much time and labor would be needed to complete the project. My family's patience, understanding, and unfailing support were invaluable as I slowly worked my way through the genealogies as well as the rest of my work on one of the longest books in the Hebrew Bible.

Gary Knoppers
University Park, Pa.

ABBREVIATIONS

◆

REFERENCE WORKS in biblical and ancient Near Eastern studies dealing with grammar, lexicon, and primary sources. In the text citations, most are organized by paragraph or section, rather than by page number.

Aharoni	Yohanan Aharoni, *Arad Inscriptions.* JDS. Jerusalem: Israel Exploration Society, 1981.
AP	A. Cowley, *Aramaic Papyri of the Fifth Century B.C.* Oxford: Clarendon Press, 1923. Repr. Osnabrück: Otto Zeller, 1967.
ARAB, I (II)	Daniel David Luckenbill, *Ancient Records of Assyria and Babylonia.* Vol. 1: *Historical Records of Assyria from the Earliest Times to Sargon. Ancient Records of Assyria and Babylonia.* Vol. 2: *Historical Records of Assyria from Sargon to the End.* Chicago: Chicago University Press, 1926–1927.
ARI	A. K. Grayson, *Assyrian Royal Inscriptions.* 2 vols. Records of the Ancient Near East 2. Wiesbaden: Otto Harrassowitz, 1972–1976.
ARM(T)	*Archives royales de Mari (Textes)*, Paris, 1946– .
BBSt	L. W. King, *Babylonian Boundary-Stones and Memorial Tablets in the British Museum.* London: Oxford University Press, 1912.
Beckman	Gary M. Beckman, *Hittite Diplomatic Texts.* Writings from the Ancient World 7. Atlanta: Scholars Press, 1996.
BP	E. G. Kraeling, *The Brooklyn Museum Aramaic Papyri: New Documents of the Fifth Century B.C. from the Jewish Colony at Elephantine.* New Haven: Yale University Press, 1953.
Cole and Machinist	Stephen Cole and Peter Machinist, *Letters from Priests to the Kings Esarhaddon and Assurbanipal.* SAA 13. Helsinki: Helsinki University Press, 1998.
CTA	A. Herdner, *Corpus des tablettes en cunéiformes alphabétique découvertes à Ras Shamra-Ugarit de 1929 à 1939.* Mission de Ras Shamra 10, 2 vols. Paris: Imprimerie Nationale, 1963.
CTU	Manfred O. Dietrich, O. Loretz, and J. Sanmartín, *The Cuneiform Alphabetic Texts from Ugarit, Ras Ibn Hani and Other Places.* 2nd ed. Münster: Ugarit-Verlag, 1995.
Davies	G. I. Davies, *Ancient Hebrew Inscriptions: Corpus and Concordance.* Cambridge: Cambridge University Press, 1991.
DNWSI	J. Hoftijzer and K. Jongeling, *Dictionary of the Northwest Semitic Inscriptions.* 2 vols. Leiden: Brill, 1995.
EA	J. A. Knudtzon, *Die El-Amarna Tafeln mit Einleitung und Erläuterungen.* Leipzig: Hinrichs, 1908–15. Reprint, Aalen, 1964. Continued in A. F. Rainey, *El-Amarna Tablets*, 359–79. 2nd revised ed. Kevelaer, 1978.

EDSS	Lawrence S. Schiffman and J. VanderKam, (eds.), *Encyclopedia of the Dead Sea Scrolls.* New York: Oxford University Press, 2000.
FGrH	Felix Jacoby, ed., *Die Fragmente der griechischen Historiker*, vols. 1–3. Leiden: Brill, 1954–1964.
Frame	Grant Frame, *Rulers of Babylonia: From the Second Dynasty of Isin to the End of Assyrian Domination (1157–612 B.C.).* RIMB 2. Toronto: University of Toronto Press, 1995.
Friedrich	Johannes Friedrich, *Staatsverträge des Ḫatti-Reiches in hethitischer Sprache*, Vol. 1: MVAeG 31 (1926). Vol. 2: MVAeG 34 (1930).
Grayson	Albert Kirk Grayson, *Assyrian Rulers of the Early First Millennium B.C., I (858–745 B.C.).* RIMA 3. Toronto: University of Toronto Press, 1996.
HAE	Johannes Renz and Wolfgang Röllig, *Handbuch der althebräischen Epigraphik.* Darmstadt: Wissenschaftlishe Buchgesellschaft, 1995– .
Hinke	W. J. Hinke, *Selected Babylonian Kudurru Inscriptions.* Semitic Study Series 14. Leiden: Brill, 1911.
Horbury and Noy	William Horbury and David Noy, (eds.), *Jewish Inscriptions of Graeco-Roman Egypt.* Cambridge: Cambridge University Press, 1992.
IBoT	Istanbul Arkeoloji Müzelerinde Bulunan Boğazköy Tableteri(nden Seçme Metinler). Istanbul, 1944, 1947, 1954; Ankara, 1988.
Jastrow	Morris Jastrow, A *Dictionary of the Targumim, the Talmud Babli and Yerushalmi, and the Midrashic Literature.* Brooklyn: Traditional, 1903.
Joüon	Paul Joüon, *Grammaire de l'hébreu biblique.* Rev. ed. Rome: Pontifical Biblical Institute, 1923.
KAI	Herbert R. Donner and W. Röllig, *Kanaanäische und aramäische Inschriften.* 3 vols. Wiesbaden: Otto Harrassowitz, 1964–1968.
KBo	*Keilschrifttexte aus Boghazköi.* Leipzig/Berlin: Gebr. Mann Verlag, 1916– .
Kropat	Arno Kropat, *Die Syntax des Autors der Chronik Vergleichen mit der seiner Quellen: Ein Beitrag zur historischen Syntax des Hebräischen.* BZAW 16. Giessen: Töpelmann, 1909.
KTU	Manfred O. Dietrich, O. Loretz, and J. Sanmartín, *Die Keilalphabetischen Texte aus Ugarit.* AOAT 24/1. Neukirchen-Vluyn: Neukirchener Verlag, 1976.
KUB	*Keilschrifturkunden aus Boghazköi.* Berlin: Akademie Verlag, 1912– .
Lambdin	Thomas O. Lambdin, *An Introduction to Biblical Hebrew.* New York: Scribners, 1971.
TAD	Bezalel Porten and Ada Yardeni, *Textbook of Aramaic Documents from Ancient Egypt. Newly Copied, Edited and Translated into Hebrew and English; Vol. 1: Letters* (1986). *Vol. 2: Contracts* (1989). *Vol. 3: Literature, Accounts, Lists* (1993). *Vol. 4: Ostraca and Assorted Inscriptions* (1999). Jerusalem: The Hebrew University, Department of the History of the Jewish People.
VTE	Donald J. Wiseman, The Vassal Treaties of Esarhaddon. *Iraq* 20 (1958), 1–99.
Waltke and O'Connor	Bruce K. Waltke and M. O'Connor, *An Introduction to Biblical Hebrew Syntax.* Winona Lake: Eisenbrauns, 1990.
WDSP	Douglas M. Gropp, *Wadi Daliyeh II: The Samaria Papyri from Wadi Daliyeh.* DJD 28. Oxford: Oxford University Press, 2001.
Weidner	E. F. Weidner, *Politische Dokumente aus Kleinasien: Die Staatsverträge in akkadischer Sprache aus dem Archiv von Boghazköi.* Boghazköi-Studien, 8–9. Leipzig: J. C. Hinrichs, 1923 [rpt. Hildesheim: Georg Olms, 1970].

Williams	Ronald J. Williams, *Hebrew Syntax*. 2nd ed. Toronto: University of Toronto Press, 1976.

SOURCE ABBREVIATIONS

AASF	Annales Academiae scientiarum fennicae
AASOR	Annual of the American Schools of Oriental Research
AB	Anchor Bible
ABAW	Abhandlungen der Bayerischen Akademie der Wissenschaften
ABD	*Anchor Bible Dictionary*. Edited by D. N. Freedman. 6 vols. New York, 1992
ABRL	Anchor Bible Reference Library
ADPV	Abhandlungen des Deutschen Palästinavereins
AfO	*Archiv für Orientforschung*
AGJU	Arbeiten zur Geschichte des antiken Judentums und des Urchristentums
AHw	*Akkadisches Handwörterbuch*. W. von Soden. 3 vols.
AJBI	*Annual of the Japanese Biblical Institute*
AJSL	*American Journal of Semitic Languages and Literature*
AJT	*American Journal of Theology*
ALBO	Analecta lovaniensia biblica et orientalia
AnBib	Analecta biblica
ANET	*Ancient Near Eastern Texts Relating to the Old Testament*. Edited by J. B. Pritchard. 3rd. ed. Princeton, 1969.
AnOr	Analecta orientalia
AOAT	Alter Orient und Altes Testament
AOS	American Oriental Series
ARAB	*Ancient Records of Assyria and Babylonia*. Daniel David Luckenbill. 2 vols. Chicago, 1926–1927.
ArBib	The Aramaic Bible
AS	Assyriological Studies
ASOR	American School of Oriental Research
Asp	*Asprenas: Rivista di scienze teologiche*
ATANT	Abhandlungen zur Theologie des Alten und Neuen Testaments
ATD	Das Alte Testament Deutsch
Aug	*Augustinianum*
AUSS	*Andrews University Seminary Studies*
BA	*Biblical Archaeologist*
BAR	*British Archaeological Reports*
BARev	*Biblical Archaeology Review*
BARIS	Biblical Archaeological Report International Series
BASOR	*Bulletin of the American Schools of Oriental Research*
BBB	Bonner biblische Beiträge
BBET	Beiträge zur biblischen Exegese und Theologie
BBR	*Bulletin for Biblical Research*
BCH	*Bulletin de correspondance hellénique*
BDB	Brown, F., S. R. Driver, and C. A. Briggs. *A Hebrew and English Lexicon of the Old Testament*. Oxford, 1907.
BEATAJ	Beiträge zur Erforschung des Alten Testaments und des antiken Judentum
BeO	*Bibbia e oriente*

Ber	*Berytus*
BETL	Bibliotheca ephemeridum theologicarum lovaniensium
BHAch	Bulletin d'histoire achéménide
BHK	*Biblia Hebraica.* Edited by R. Kittel. Stuttgart, 1905–1906; 2nd ed., 1925; 3rd ed., 1937; 4th ed., 1951; 16th ed., 1973.
BHS	*Biblia Hebraica Stuttgartensia.* Edited by K. Elliger and W. Rudolph. Stuttgart, 1983.
BHT	Beiträge zur historischen Theologie
Bib	*Biblica*
BibInt	*Biblical Interpretation*
BibS(F)	Biblische Studien (Freiburg, 1895–).
BIOSCS	*Bulletin of the International Organization for Septuagint and Cognate Studies*
BJ	*Bonner Jahrbücher*
BJRL	*Bulletin of the John Rylands University Library of Manchester*
BJS	Brown Judaic Studies
BKAT	Biblischer Kommentar, Altes Testament. Edited by M. Noth and H. W. Wolff.
BLit	*Bibliothèque liturgique*
BN	*Biblische Notizen*
BMes	Bibliotheca mesopotamica
BR	*Biblical Research*
BTB	*Biblical Theology Bulletin*
BWANT	Beiträge zur Wissenschaft vom Alten und Neuen Testament
BZ	*Biblische Zeitschrift*
BZAW	Beihefte zur Zeitschrift für die alttestamentliche Wissenschaft
CahRB	Cahiers de la Revue biblique
CAD	*The Assyrian Dictionary of the Oriental Institute of the University of Chicago.* Chicago, 1956– .
CANE	*Civilizations of the Ancient Near East.* Edited by J. Sasson. 4 vols. New York, 1995.
CAT	Commentaire de l'Ancien Testament
CBC	Cambridge Bible Commentary
CBET	Contributions to Biblical Exegesis and Theology
CBQ	*Catholic Biblical Quarterly*
CBQMS	Catholic Biblical Quarterly Monograph Series
CHJ	*Cambridge History of Judaism.* Edited by W. D. Davies and Louis Finkelstein. Cambridge, 1984– .
CIS	*Corpus inscriptionum semiticarum*
ConBOT	Coniectanea biblica: Old Testament Series
COS	*The Context of Scripture.* Edited by W. W. Hallo and K. L. Younger, Jr. 3 vols. Leiden, 1997–2002.
CRBS	*Critical Review: Biblical Studies*
CRINT	Compendia rerum iudaicarum ad Novum Testamentum
CTM	*Concordia Theological Monthly*
CTU	*The Cuneiform Alphabetic Texts from Ugarit, Ras Ibn Hani, and Other Places.* Edited by M. Dietrich, O. Loretz, and J. Sanmartín. Münster. 2nd ed., 1995.
DJD	Discoveries in the Judaean Desert
DSD	*Dead Sea Discoveries*
EB	Echter Bibel

EBib	*Etudes bibliques*
EdF	Erträge der Forschung
EI	*Eretz Israel*
EncJud	*Encyclopaedia Judaica.* 16 vols. Jerusalem, 1972.
ErIsr	*Eretz-Israel*
ETL	*Ephemerides theologicae lovanienses*
ETR	*Etudes théologiques et religieuses*
ExpT	*Expository Times*
FAT	Forschungen zum Alten Testament
FB	Forschung zur Bibel
FoiVie	*Foi et vie*
FOTL	Forms of the Old Testament Literature
FRLANT	Forschungen zur Religion und Literatur des Alten und Neuen Testaments
GAT	Grundrisse zum Alten Testament
GBS	Guides to Biblical Scholarship
GCS	Die griechische christliche Schriftsteller der ersten Jahrhunderte
GKC	*Gesenius' Hebrew Grammar.* Edited by E. Kautzsch. Translated by A. E. Cowley. 2nd ed. Oxford, 1910.
GTA	Göttinger theologischer Arbeiten
HALOT	Koehler, L., W. Baumgartner, and J. J. Stamm. *The Hebrew and Aramaic Lexicon of the Old Testament.* Translated and edited under the supervision of M. E. J. Richardson. 4 vols. Leiden, 1994–1999.
HAR	*Hebrew Annual Review*
HAT	Handbuch zum Alten Testament
HBT	*Horizons in Biblical Theology*
Hen	*Henoch*
HeyJ	*Heythrop Journal*
Hok	*Hokhma*
HS	*Hebrew Studies*
HSAT	*Die Heilige Schrift des Alten Testaments.* Edited by E. Kautzsch and A. Bertholoet. 4th ed. Tübingen, 1922–1923.
HSM	Harvard Semitic Monographs
HSS	Harvard Semitic Studies
HTR	*Harvard Theological Review*
ICC	International Critical Commentary
IDB	*The Interpreter's Dictionary of the Bible.* Edited by G. A. Buttrick. 4 vols., Nashville, 1962.
IDBSup	*The Interpreter's Dictionary of the Bible: Supplementary Volume.* Edited by K. Crim. Nashville, 1976.
IEJ	*Israel Exploration Journal*
Int	*Interpretation*
IOSCS	International Organization for Septuagint and Cognate Studies
Iraq	*Iraq*
JANES	*Journal of the Ancient Near Eastern Society of Columbia University*
JAOS	*Journal of the American Oriental Society*
JAOSSup	Journal of the American Oriental Society: Supplement Series
JB	Jerusalem Bible
JBL	*Journal of Biblical Literature*
JCS	*Journal of Cuneiform Studies*

JDS	Judean Desert Studies
JESHO	*Journal of the Economic and Social History of the Orient*
JET	*Jahrbuch für Evangelische Theologie*
JETS	*Journal of the Evangelical Theological Society*
JJS	*Journal of Jewish Studies*
JNES	*Journal of Near Eastern Studies*
JNSL	*Journal of Northwest Semitic Languages*
JPOS	*Journal of the Palestine Oriental Society*
JPS	Jewish Publication Society
JQR	*Jewish Quarterly Review*
JR	*Journal of Religion*
JRAS	*Journal of the Royal Asiatic Society*
JSJ	*Journal for the Study of Judaism in the Persian, Hellenistic, and Roman Periods*
JSNTSup	Journal for the Study of the New Testament: Supplement Series
JSOT	*Journal for the Study of the Old Testament*
JSOTSup	Journal for the Study of the Old Testament: Supplement Series
JSP	*Journal for the Study of the Pseudepigrapha*
JSS	*Journal of Semitic Studies*
JTS	*Journal of Theological Studies*
Judaica	*Judaica: Beiträge zum Verständnis des jüdischen Schicksals in Vergangenheit und Gegenwart*
Judaism	*Judaism*
KAT	Kommentar zum Alten Testament
KBL	Koehler, L., and W. Baumgartner. *Lexicon in Veteris Testamenti libros.* 2nd ed. Leiden, 1958.
KJV	King James Version
LD	Lectio divina
LEC	Library of Early Christianity
LS	*Louvain Studies*
LTQ	*Lexington Theological Quarterly*
LUÅ	Lunds universitets årsskrift
MdB	*Le Monde de la Bible*
MDOG	Mitteilungen der Deutschen Orient-Gesellschaft
MIOF	*Mitteilungen des Instituts für Orientforschung*
MGWJ	*Monatschrift für Geschichte und Wissenschaft des Judentums*
MVAeG	Mitteilungen der Vorderasiatisch-ägyptischen Gesellschaft, vols. 1–44, 1896–1939.
NAB	New American Bible
NCB	New Century Bible
NEAEHL	*The New Encyclopedia of Archaeological Excavations in the Holy Land.* Edited by E. Stern. 4 vols. Jerusalem, 1993.
NEchtB	Neue Echter Bibel
NIV	New International Version
NJB	New Jerusalem Bible
NJBC	*The New Jerome Biblical Commentary.* Edited by R. E. Brown et al. Englewood Cliffs, 1990.
NJPS	New Jewish Publication Society
NovT	*Novum Testamentum*

NRSV	New Revised Standard Version
OBO	Orbis biblicus et orientalis
ÖBS	Österreichische biblische Studien
OBT	Overtures to Biblical Theology
OCD	*Oxford Classical Dictionary.* Edited by S. Hornblower and A. Spawforth. 3rd ed. Oxford, 1996.
OEANE	*The Oxford Encyclopedia of Archaeology in the Near East.* Edited by E. M. Meyers. New York, 1997.
OLA	Orientalia lovaniensia analecta
OLP	Orientalia lovaniensia periodica
Or	*Orientalia* (NS)
OTG	Old Testament Guides
OTL	Old Testament Library
OTP	*Old Testament Pseudepigrapha.* Edited by J. H. Charlesworth. 2 vols. New York, 1983.
OTS	*Oudtestamentische Studiën*
OTS	Old Testament Studies
PEFQS	Palestine Exploration Fund Quarterly Statement
PEQ	*Palestine Exploration Quarterly*
PIBA	Proceedings of the Irish Biblical Association
PJ	*Palästina-Jahrbuch*
PRU	*Le palais royal d'Ugarit*
RANE	Records of the Ancient Near East
RB	*Revue biblique*
REB	Revised English Bible
REJ	*Revue des études juives*
RelSoc	*Religion and Society*
ResQ	*Restoration Quarterly*
RevQ	*Revue de Qumran*
RIMA	The Royal Inscriptions of Mesopotamia, Assyrian Periods
RIMB	The Royal Inscriptions of Mesopotamia, Babylonian Periods
RivB	*Rivista biblica italiana*
RS	Ras Shamra
RSV	Revised Standard Version
RTP	*Revue de théologie et de philosophie*
SAA	State Archives of Assyria
SBB	Stuttgarter biblische Beiträge
SBLABS	Society of Biblical Literature Archaeology and Biblical Studies
SBLDS	Society of Biblical Literature Dissertation Series
SBLEJL	Society of Biblical Literature Early Judaism and Its Literature
SBLMS	Society of Biblical Literature Monograph Series
SBLSCS	Society of Biblical Literature Septuagint and Cognate Studies
SBLSymS	Society of Biblical Literature Symposium Series
SBLTT	Society of Biblical Literature Texts and Translations
SBLWAW	Society of Biblical Literature Writings from the Ancient World
SBT	Studies in Biblical Theology
SBTS	Sources for Biblical and Theological Study, Eisenbrauns.
Schol	*Scholastik*
ScrHier	Scripta hierosolymitana

SE	*Studia evangelica I, II, III* (= TU 73 [1959], 87 [1964], 88 [1964], etc.)
Sem	*Semitica*
SFSHJ	University of Southern Florida Studies in the History of Judaism
SHANE	Studies in the History of the Ancient Near East
SHCANE	Studies in the History and Cultures of the Ancient Near East
SJLA	Studies in Judaism in Late Antiquity
SJOT	*Scandinavian Journal of the Old Testament*
SNTSMS	Society for New Testament Studies Monograph Series
SP	Sacra pagina
SR	*Studies in Religion*
SSN	Studia semitica neerlandica
SSS	Semitic Study Series
ST	*Studia theologica*
STDJ	*Studies on the Text of the Desert of Judah*
TA	*Tel Aviv*
Tarbiz	*Tarbiz*
TBC	Torch Bible Commentaries
TCS	Texts from Cuneiform Sources
TDOT	*Theological Dictionary of the Old Testament.* Edited by G. Kittel and G. Friedrich. Translated by G. W. Bromiley. Grand Rapids, 1974– .
Text	*Textus*
Them	*Themelios*
TLOT	*Theological Lexicon of the Old Testament.* Edited by E. Jenni, with assistance from C. Westermann. Translated by M. E. Biddle. 3 vols. Peabody, Mass., 1997.
TLZ	*Theologische Literaturzeitung*
TOTC	Tyndale Old Testament Commentaries
TQ	*Theologische Quartalschrift*
Transeu	*Transeuphratène*
TRE	*Theologische Realenzyklopädie.* Edited by G. Krause and G. Müller. Berlin. 1977– .
TRu	*Theologische Rundschau*
TSK	*Theologische Studien und Kritiken*
TU	Texte und Untersuchungen
TynBul	*Tyndale Bulletin*
TZ	*Theologische Zeitschrift*
UF	*Ugarit-Forschungen*
USQR	*Union Seminary Quarterly Review*
VAB	Vorderasiatische Bibliothek
VT	*Vetus Testamentum*
VTSup	Vetus Testamentum Supplements
WBC	Word Biblical Commentary
WO	*Die Welt des Orients*
WTJ	*Westminster Theological Journal*
WUNT	Wissenschaftliche Untersuchungen zum Neuen Testament
WVDOG	Wissenschaftliche Veröffentlichungen der deutschen Orientgesellschaft
ZAH	*Zeitschrift für Althebräistik*
ZAW	*Zeitschrift für die alttestamentliche Wissenschaft*
ZDPV	*Zeitschrift des deutschen Palästina-Vereins*

GENERAL ABBREVIATIONS

abs.	absolute
acc.	accusative
Akk.	Akkadian
Ann.	Annal(s)
Arab.	Arabic
Aram.	Aramaic
Arm.	Armenian
Assyr.	Assyrian
BH	biblical Hebrew
Bibl. Aram.	biblical Aramaic
Boh.	Bohairic
CH	classical Hebrew
Chr^{1,2,3,MPR}	Chronicles editors
const.	construct
D	Deuteronomy or the old Deuteronomic law code
DN	divine name
E	the Elohist
Eg.	Egyptian
ET	English translation
Eth.	Ethiopic
f.	feminine
Gk.	Greek
gen.	genitive
GN	geopolitical or geographic name
H	the Holiness Code
HB	Hebrew Bible
Heb.	Hebrew
Hitt.	Hittite
inf.	infinitive
impv.	imperative
J	the Yahwist
Jer C	a series of texts in the Book of Jeremiah with affinities to Deuteronomy and the Deuteronomistic History
LBH	late biblical Hebrew
Liv. Pro.	*Lives of the Prophets*
LXX	Septuagint
LXX^{A}	Codex Alexandrinus of the Septuagint
LXX^{B}	Codex Vaticanus of the Septuagint
LXX^{L}	the Lucianic recension or the majority of the Lucianic manuscripts of the Septuagint
LXX^{N}	Codex Venetus of the Septuagint
LXX^{S}	Codex Sinaiticus of the Septuagint
masc.	masculine
ms(s)	manuscript, manuscripts
MT	the Masoretic Text of the Hebrew Bible
Nab.	Nabatean
NT	New Testament

Off. Aram.	official Aramaic
OL	Old Latin
OSA	Old South Arabic
OT	Old Testament
P	the Priestly writer(s)
pass.	passive
pers.	person
Phoen.	Phoenician
Pl.	plate
pl.	plural
PN	personal name
prep.	preposition
pres.	present
pron.	pronoun
ptc.	participle
Pun.	Punic
RH	Rabbinic Hebrew
RN	regal name
sg.	singular
SP	Samaritan Pentateuch
sub ast.	*sub asteriscus*
subj.	subject
suf.	suffix
Summ.	Summary
Syr.	Syrian/Syriac
T.	Tel or Tell
Tg.	*Targum*
Tg. Ket.	*Targum of the Writings*
Tg. Neb.	*Targum of the Prophets*
Tg. Neof.	*Targum Neofiti*
Tg. Onq.	*Targum Onqelos*
Tg. Ps.-J.	*Targum Pseudo-Jonathan*
Theodoret	*Quaestiones in Reges et Paralipomena*
Ug.	Ugaritic
Vg.	Vulgate

1 Chronicles: A Translation

A Genealogy of Nations

1:1 Adam, Seth, Enosh; 2 Qenan, Mahalalel, Jared; 3 Enoch, Methuselaḥ, La-
mech, 4 Noaḥ. The sons of Noaḥ: Shem, Ḥam, and Japheth.
5 The sons of Japheth: Gomer, Magog, Madai, Javan, Tubal, Meshech, and
Tiras. 6 And the sons of Gomer: Ashkenaz, Diphath, and Togarmah. 7 The sons of
Javan: Elishah and Tarshish, Kittim and Rodanim.
8 The sons of Ḥam: Cush, Mizraim, Puṭ, and Canaan. 9 The sons of Cush:
Seba, Ḥavilah, Sabta, Raama, and Sabteca. The sons of Raama: Sheba and
Dedan. 10 And Cush sired Nimrod; he was the first to become a warrior in the
land. [11 And Mizraim sired (the) Ludim, the Anamim, the Lehabim, the Naphtuḥim, 12 the Pathrusim, and the Casluḥim who went forth from there, (the)
Philistines and the Caphtorim. 13 And Canaan sired Sidon, his firstborn, Ḥeth,
14 the Jebusites, the Amorites, the Girgashites, 15 the Ḥivites, the Arqites, the
Sinites, 16 the Arvadites, the Zemarites, and the Ḥamathites.]
17 The sons of Shem: Elam, Ashur, Arpachshad, Lud, and Aram. The sons of
Aram: Uz, Ḥul, Gether, and Meshech. 18 And Arpachshad sired Shelaḥ and Shelaḥ sired Eber. 19 Two sons were born to Eber. The name of the first was Peleg, because in his days the land was divided, and the name of his brother was Joqṭan.
20 And Joqṭan sired Almodad, Shaleph, Ḥazarmawet, Jaraḥ, 21 Hadoram, Uzal,
Diqlah, 22 Ebal, Abimael, Sheba, 23 Ophir, Ḥavilah, and Jobab. All these were
sons of Joqṭan. 24 Shem, Arpachshad, Shelaḥ, 25 Eber, Peleg, Reu, 26 Serug, Naḥor,
Taraḥ, 27 Abram, that is, Abraham.
28 The sons of Abraham: Isaac and Ishmael. 29 These are their lineages: the firstborn of Ishmael Nebaioth, Qedar, Adbeel, Mibsam, 30 Mishma, Dumah, Massa,
Ḥadad, Tema, 31 Jeṭur, Naphish, and Qedemah. These were the sons of Ishmael.
32 The sons of Qeṭurah the concubine of Abraham: she gave birth to Zimran, Joqshan, Medan, Midian, Ishbaq, and Shuaḥ. The sons of Joqshan: Sheba and
Dedan. 33 The sons of Midian: Ephah, Epher, Enoch, Abida, and Eldaah. All of
these were descendants of Qeṭurah.
34 And Abraham sired Isaac. The sons of Isaac: Esau and Israel. 35 The sons of
Esau: Eliphaz, Reuel, Jeush, Jalam, and Qoraḥ. 36 The sons of Eliphaz: Teman,
Omar, Zephi, Gatam, Qenaz, Timna, and Amaleq. 37 The sons of Reuel: Naḥath,
Zeraḥ, Shammah, and Mizzah.
38 The sons of Seir: Loṭan, Shobal, Zibeon, Anah, Dishon, Ezer, and Dishan.
39 The sons of Loṭan: Ḥori and Homam. And the sister of Loṭan [was] Timna.
40 The sons of Shobal: Alian, Manaḥath, Ebal, Shephi, and Onam. The sons of
Zibeon: Ayyah and Anah. 41 The sons of Anah: Dishon. The sons of Dishon: Ḥamran, Eshban, Ithran, and Keran. 42 The sons of Ezer: Bilhan, Zaavan, and Jaaqan.
The sons of Dishan: Uz and Aran.
43 These are the kings who reigned in the land of Edom before a king reigned
among the Israelites: Bela son of Beor and the name of his town was Dinhabah.
44 When Bela died, Jobab son of Zeraḥ from Bozrah reigned in his stead. 45 When
Jobab died, Ḥusham from the land of the Temanites reigned in his stead. 46 When
Ḥusham died, Hadad son of Bedad reigned in his stead. He was the one who

struck down Midian in the territory of Moab. The name of his town was Avith. [47]When Hadad died, Samlah from Masreqah reigned in his stead. [48]When Samlah died, Saul from Reḥoboth on the River reigned in his stead. [49]When Saul died, Baal Ḥanan son of Achbor reigned in his stead. [50]When Baal Ḥanan died, Hadad reigned in his stead. The name of his town was Pai.

[51]When Hadad died, the chieftains of Edom were the chieftain of Timna, the chieftain of Alyah, the chieftain of Jetheth, [52]the chieftain of Oholibamah, the chieftain of Elah, the chieftain of Pinon, [53]the chieftain of Q̣enan, the chieftain of Teman, the chieftain of Mibzar, [54]the chieftain of Magdiel, the chieftain of Iram; these were the chieftains of Edom.

[2:1]These are the sons of Israel: Reuben, Simeon, Levi, Judah, Issachar, Zebulun, [2]Dan, Joseph, Benjamin, Naphtali, Gad, and Asher.

The Descendants of Judah, Part I

[2:3]The sons of Judah: Er, Onan, and Shelah; three were born to him by Bath-shua the Canaanite. Although Er was the firstborn of Judah, he did evil in the sight of Yhwh and he killed him. [4]And Tamar his daughter-in-law bore him Perez and Zeraḥ. The sons of Judah were five in all.

[5]The sons of Perez: Ḥezron and Ḥamul. [6]The sons of Zeraḥ: Zimri, Ethan, Heman, Calcol, and Darda; altogether five. [7]The sons of Zimri: Carmi. The sons of Carmi: Achar, the troubler of Israel, who violated the ban. [8]The sons of Ethan: Azariah.

[9]The sons of Ḥezron, who were born to him: Jeraḥmeel, Ram, and Celubai. [10]And Ram sired Amminadab, and Amminadab sired Naḥshon the chieftain of the sons of Judah. [11]And Naḥshon sired Salma and Salma sired Boaz. [12]And Boaz sired Obed and Obed sired Jesse. [13]And Jesse sired Eliab his firstborn, Abinadab the second, Shimea the third, [14]Nethanel the fourth, Raddai the fifth, [15]Ozem the sixth, David the seventh. [16]Their sisters were Zeruiah and Abigail. The sons of Zeruiah: Abshai, Joab, and Asah-el—three. [17]Abigail gave birth to Amasa. The father of Amasa was Jether the Ishmaelite.

[18]Caleb son of Ḥezron sired [children through] Azubah [his] wife and Jerioth. These were her sons: Jesher, Shobab, and Ardon. [19]When Azubah died, Caleb took for himself Ephrath and she bore him Ḥur. [20]Ḥur sired Uri and Uri sired Bezalel.

[21]After Ḥezron had sexual relations with the daughter of Machir, the father of Gilead (he married her when he was sixty years old), she bore him Segub. [22]And Segub sired Jair. He had twenty-three towns in the land of Gilead, [23]but Geshur and Aram took Ḥavvoth Jair from them along with Q̣enath and its dependencies: sixty towns. All these were descendants of Machir the father of Gilead. [24](After the death of Ḥezron, Caleb had sexual relations with Ephrathah.) The wife of Ḥezron was Abijah and she bore him Ashḥur the father of Teqoa.

[25]These were the descendants of Jeraḥmeel the firstborn of Ḥezron: Ram the firstborn, Bunah, Oren, Ozem, and Aḥijah. [26]Jeraḥmeel had another wife whose

name was Aṭarah; she was the mother of Onam. 27 The sons of Ram the firstborn
of Jeraḥmeel: Maaz, Jamin, and Eqer. 28 The sons of Onam: Shammai and Yada.
The sons of Shammai: Nadab and Abishur. 29 The name of the wife of Abishur
was Abiḥail. She bore him Aḥban and Molid. 30 The sons of Nadab: Seled
and Appaim, but Seled died without sons. 31 The son of Appaim: Ishi. The son
of Ishi: Sheshan. The son of Sheshan: Aḥli. 32 The sons of Yada the brother
of Shammai: Jether and Jonathan, but Jether died without sons. 33 The sons of
Jonathan: Peleth and Zaza. These were the descendants of Jeraḥmeel.

34 Sheshan did not have any sons, only daughters, but Sheshan had an Egyptian
servant whose name was Jarḥa. 35 Sheshan gave his daughter to Jarḥa his servant as
[his] wife, and she bore him Attai. 36 Attai sired Nathan and Nathan sired Zabad
37 and Zabad sired Ephlal and Ephlal sired Obed 38 and Obed sired Jehu and Jehu
sired Azariah 39 and Azariah sired Ḥelez and Ḥelez sired Eleasah 40 and Eleasah
sired Sismai and Sismai sired Shallum 41 and Shallum sired Jeqamiah and Jeqamiah sired Elishama.

42 The descendants of Caleb the brother of Jeraḥmeel: Mesha his firstborn, who
was the father of Ziph, and his second son Mareshah the father of Ḥebron. 43 The
sons of Ḥebron: Qoraḥ, Tappuaḥ, Reqem, and Shema. 44 Shema sired Raḥam the
father of Jorqeam and Reqem sired Shammai. 45 The son of Shammai: Maon.
Maon was the father of Beth-zur. 46 Ephah, a concubine of Caleb, bore Ḥaran,
Moza, and Gazez. And Ḥaran sired Gazez. 47 The sons of Jahdai: Regem, Jotham,
Geshan, Peleṭ, Ephah, and Shaaph. 48 A concubine of Caleb, Maacah, gave birth
to Sheber, Tirḥanah, 49 Shaaph the father of Madmannah, Sheva the father of
Machbenah, and the father of Gibea. The daughter of Caleb was Achsah.
50 These were the descendants of Caleb.

The sons of Ḥur the firstborn of Ephrathah: Shobal the father of Qiriath-jearim,
51 Salma the father of Bethleḥem, Ḥareph the father of Beth-gader. 52 Shobal
the father of Qiriath-jearim had sons: Haroeh [and] half of the Manaḥathites.
53 The families of Qiriath-jearim: the Ithrites, the Puthites, the Shumathites, and
the Mishraites. From these came the Zorathites and the Eshtaulites. 54 The sons of
Salma the father of Bethleḥem: the Neṭophathites, Aṭroth-beth-joab, half of the
Manaḥathites, (and) the Zorites. 55 The families of the scribes, inhabitants of
Jabez—the Tirathites, the Shimeathites, the Sucathites—they were Qenites who
came from Ḥammath the father of Beth-rechab.

The Descendants of David

3:1 These are the sons of David who were born to him at Ḥebron. The firstborn was
Amnon by Aḥinoam the Jezreelite, the second Daniel by Abigail the Carmelite,
2 the third Absalom son of Maacah daughter of Talmai king of Geshur, the fourth
Adonijah son of Ḥaggith, 3 the fifth Shephaṭiah by Abiṭal, the sixth Ithream by
Eglah his wife. 4 Six were born to him in Ḥebron. He reigned there for seven years
and six months and he reigned in Jerusalem for thirty-three years. 5 These were
born to him in Jerusalem: Shimea, Shobab, Nathan, and Solomon—four by

Bath-shua daughter of Ammiel. 6 Ibḥar, Elishua, Elipheleṭ, 7 Nogah, Nepheg, Japhia, 8 Elishama, Beeliada, Elipheleṭ—nine. 9 All were sons of David in addition to the sons of (his) concubines. Tamar was their sister.

10 The son of Solomon: Reḥoboam, his son Abijah, his son Asa, his son Jehoshaphaṭ, his son 11 Joram, his son Aḥaziah, his son Joash, his son 12 Amaziah, his son Azariah, his son Jotham, his son 13 Aḥaz, his son Ḥezeqiah, his son Manasseh, his son 14 Amon, (and) his son Josiah.

15 The sons of Josiah: the firstborn Joḥanan, the second Jehoiaqim, the third Zedeqiah, the fourth Shallum. 16 The sons of Jehoiaqim: his son Jeconiah, his son Zedeqiah. 17 The sons of Jeconiah the prisoner: Shealtiel, 18 Malchiram, Pedaiah, Shenazzar, Jeqamiah, Shama, and Nedabiah. 19 The sons of Pedaiah: Zerubbabel and Shimei.

19 The sons of Zerubbabel: Meshullam and Ḥananiah. Shelomith was their sister. 20 The sons of Meshullam: Ḥashubah, Ohel, Berechiah, Ḥasadiah, Jushab-ḥesed—five. 21 The son of Ḥananiah: Pelaṭiah, his son Jeshaiah, his son Rephaiah, his son Arnon, his son Obadiah, his son Shecaniah. 22 The sons of Shecaniah: Shemaiah. The sons of Shemaiah: Ḥaṭṭush, Igal, Bariaḥ, Neariah, and Shephaṭ—six. 23 The sons of Neariah: Elioenai, Ḥizqiah, and Azriqam—three. 24 The sons of Elioenai: Hodaviah, Eliashib, Pelaiah, Aqqub, Joḥanan, Delaiah, and Anani—seven.

The Descendants of Judah, Part II

4:1 The descendants of Judah: Perez, Ḥezron, Caleb, Ḥur, and Shobal.

2 Reaiah son of Shobal sired Jaḥath and Jaḥath sired Aḥimai and Lahad. These were the families of the Zorathites.

3 These are the sons of Eṭam: Jezreel, Ishma, and Idbash. And the name of their sister was Hazlel.

4 Penuel was the father of Gedor and Ezer was the father of Ḥushah. These were the sons of Ḥur, the firstborn of Ephrathah the father of Bethleḥem.

5 Ashḥur father of Teqoa had two wives: Ḥelah and Naarah. 6 Naarah bore him Aḥuzzam, Ḥepher, Temeni, and the Aḥashtarite. These were the sons of Naarah. 7 The sons of Ḥelah were Zereth, Zoḥar, and Ethnan.

8 Qoz sired Annub, Zobebah, the families of the brother of Rechab, and the sons of Harim.

9 Now Jabez was more honored than his brothers. His mother named him Jabez, saying "indeed I have given birth in affliction." 10 And Jabez invoked the God of Israel, saying "Oh, that you would truly bless me, enlarge my territory, and that your hand might stay with me and refrain from evil so as not to afflict me." And God granted what he requested.

11 Celub brother of Shuḥah sired Meḥir. He was the father of Eshton. 12 And Eshton sired Beth-rapha, Paseaḥ, and Teḥinnah the father of the city of Naḥash. These were the men of Recaḥ.

13 The sons of Qenaz: Othniel and Seraiah. The sons of Othniel: Ḥathath and

the Maonathites. 14 The Maonathites sired Ophrah and Seraiah sired Joab the father of Ge-Ḥarashim, [named as such] because they were craftsmen.

15 The sons of Caleb son of Jephunneh: Ir, Elah, and Naam. The sons of Elah: Qenaz.

16 The sons of Jehallelel: Ziph and Ziphah, Tiria and Asarel.

17 The sons of Ezrah: Jether, Mered, Epher, and Jalon. Jether sired Miriam, Shammai, and Ishbah father of Eshtemoa. 18 These are the sons of Bithiah the daughter of Pharaoh, whom Mered wed. She gave birth to Jered the father of Gedor, Ḥeber the father of Soco, and Jequthiel the father of Zanoaḥ. 19 The sons of his Judahite wife, the sister of Naḥam, were the father of Qeilah the Garmite and Eshtemoa the Maacathite.

20 The sons of Shimon: Amnon, Rinnah the son of Ḥanan, and Tilon.

The sons of Ishi: Zoḥeth and the son of Zoḥeth.

21 The sons of Shelah the son of Judah: Er the father of Lecah, Laadah the father of Mareshah, and the families of the house of linen work at Beth-ashbea, 22 Joqim, the men of Cozeba, Joash, and Saraph, who married into Moab. And they resided in Bethleḥem. (The records are ancient.) 23 They were the potters and residents of Netaim and Gederah. With the king in his service they resided there.

The Descendants of Simeon

4:24 The descendants of Simeon: Nemuel, Jamin, Jarib, Zeraḥ, and Saul, 25 Shallum his son, Mibsam his son, Mishma his son. 26 The sons of Mishma: Ḥammuel his son, Zakkur his son, Shimei his son. 27 Shimei had sixteen sons and six daughters. But his kin did not have many descendants. All of their families did not proliferate as much as the Judahites did.

28 They resided in Beer-sheba, Shema, Moladah, Ḥazar-shual, 29 Bilhah, Ezem, Tolad, 30 Bethuel, Ḥormah, Ziqlag, 31 Beth-markabot, Ḥazer-susim, Beth-biri, and Shaaraim. These were their towns and their villages until David became king. 32 Eṭam, Ayin, Rimmon, Tochen, and Ashan—five towns 33 and all their villages which surrounded these towns as far as Baal. Such were their residences.

Their genealogical enrollment: 34 Meshobab, Jamlech, Joshah son of Amaziah, 35 Joel, Jehu son of Joshibiah, son of Seraiah, son of Asiel, 36 Elioenai, Jaaqobah, Jeshoḥaiah, Asaiah, Adiel, Jesimiel, Banaiah, 37 and Ziza son of Shiphi, son of Allon, son of Jedaiah, son of Shimri, son of Shemaiah. 38 These were the ones entered by names—chieftains according to their families and their ancestral houses.

They increased in abundance 39 and went to the approaches of Gerar up to the eastern side of the valley to seek pasture for their flocks. 40 They found rich and fine pasture. The land was spacious on every side—quiet and at ease—although those from Ḥam were residing there before (them). 41 These, the ones written by names, came in the days of Ḥezeqiah king of Judah and attacked the clans of Ḥam, along with the Meunites that were found there, and annihilated them to this day. They resided there in their place, because there was pasture there for their flocks.

[42]From them, that is, from the men of Simeon, five hundred men went to the hill country of Seir with Pelaṭiah, Neariah, Rephaiah, and Uzziel—the sons of Ishi at their head. [43]They struck down the surviving remnant of Amaleq and have resided there to this day.

The Transjordanian Tribes

[5:1]The descendants of Reuben, firstborn of Israel. Indeed, he was the firstborn, but when he defiled the bed of his father his birthright was given to Joseph, the son of Israel, and he could not be registered as having the birthright. [2]Although Judah grew mighty among his brothers and a leader came from him, the birthright belonged to Joseph.

[3]The descendants of Reuben the firstborn of Israel: Enoch, Pallu, Ḥezron, and Carmi. [4]The sons of Joel: Shemaiah his son, Gog his son, Shimei his son, [5]Micah his son, Reaiah his son, Baal his son, [6]Beerah his son—whom Tilgat-pilneser the king of Assyria exiled—he was a chieftain among the Reubenites. [7]His kin, by their families, according to their registration by generations: the head, Jeiel, and Zechariah [8]and Bela son of Azaz, son of Shema, son of Joel. He began to reside in Aroer and as far as Nebo and Baal-meon. [9]To the east he resided as far as the approaches to the wilderness, on this side of the River Euphrates, because their herds had become numerous in the land of Gilead. [10]In the days of Saul they made war with the Hagrites, who fell by their hand, and they resided in their tents throughout the region east of Gilead.

[11]The descendants of Gad resided opposite them in the land of Bashan as far as Salchah. [12]Joel was the head and Shapham the second. And Janai was the officer in Bashan. [13]Their kin according to their ancestral houses: Michael, Meshullam, Sheba, Jorai, Jakan, Zia, and Eber—seven. [14]These are the sons of Abiḥayil, son of Ḥuri, son of Jaroaḥ, son of Gilead, son of Michael, son of Jeshishai, son of Jaḥdo, son of Buz, [15]son of Abdiel, son of Guni, head of the house of their fathers. [16]They resided in Gilead, in Jabesh and its dependencies, and among all of the open spaces of Sharon to their boundaries. [17]All of them were registered in the days of Jotham king of Judah and in the days of Jeroboam king of Israel.

[18]The sons of Reuben, Gad, and the half-tribe of Manasseh had warriors, men who carried the shield and sword, drew the bow, and were well-versed in war—44,760 ready for military service. [19]They made war with the Hagrites, along with Jeṭur, Naphish, and Nodab, [20]and they prevailed over them. The Hagrites and everything with them were delivered into their hands, for they cried out to God in battle and their entreaty was granted, because they trusted in him. [21]They took into (their) possession their livestock—50,000 camels, 250,000 small cattle, 2,000 asses, and 100,000 living persons. [22]Indeed, there were many who fell slain because the battle was from God. They resided (there) in their stead until the exile.

[23]As for the descendants of the half-tribe of Manasseh, they resided in the land from Bashan as far as Baal Ḥermon, Senir, and Mount Ḥermon. And in the Lebanon they became numerous. [24]These are the heads of their ancestral houses:

Epher, Ishi, Eliel, Azriel, Jeremiah, Hodaviah, and Jaḥdiel—men (who were) valiant warriors, men of repute, heads of their ancestral houses.

The Assyrian Exile of the Transjordanian Tribes

[5:25]But they transgressed against the God of their fathers and prostituted themselves to the gods of the peoples of the land whom God had destroyed before them. [26]The God of Israel stirred up the spirit of Pul the king of Assyria, to wit Tilgat-pilneser the king of Assyria, and he exiled them—the Reubenites, the Gadites, and the half-tribe of Manasseh—and he brought them to Ḥelaḥ, Ḥabor, and the river of Gozan (where they are) to this day.

The Priestly Descendants of Levi

[5:27]The sons of Levi: Gershon, Qohath, and Merari. [28]The sons of Qohath: Amram, Izhar, Ḥebron, and Uzziel. [29]The children of Amram: Aaron, Moses, and Miriam. The sons of Aaron: Nadab, Abihu, Eleazar, and Ithamar. [30]Eleazar sired Phineḥas, Phineḥas sired Abishua, [31]Abishua sired Buqqi, Buqqi sired Uzzi, [32]Uzzi sired Zeraḥiah, Zeraḥiah sired Meraioth, [33]Meraioth sired Amariah, Amariah sired Aḥiṭub, [34]Aḥiṭub sired Zadoq, Zadoq sired Aḥimaaz, [35]and Aḥimaaz sired Azariah. It was he who officiated as priest in the temple that Solomon built in Jerusalem. And Azariah sired Joḥanan, [36]Joḥanan sired Azariah, [37]Azariah sired Amariah, Amariah sired Aḥiṭub, [38]Aḥiṭub sired Zadoq, Zadoq sired Shallum, [39]Shallum sired Ḥilqiah, Ḥilqiah sired Azariah, [40]Azariah sired Seraiah, and Seraiah sired Jehozadaq. [41]And Jehozadaq went into exile when Yhwh exiled Judah and Jerusalem at the hand of Nebuchadnezzar.

Other Descendants of Levi

[6:1]The sons of Levi: Gershon, Qohath, and Merari. [2]These are the names of the sons of Gershon: Libni and Shimei. [3]The sons of Qohath: Amram, Izhar, Ḥebron, and Uzziel. [4]The sons of Merari: Maḥli and Mushi. These are the families of the Levites according to their ancestors: [5]belonging to Gershon—Libni his son, Jaḥath his son, Zimmah his son, [6]Joaḥ his son, Iddo his son, Zeraḥ his son, Jeatherai his son; [7]the descendants of Qohath—Amminadab his son, Qoraḥ his son, Assir, [8]Elqanah, and Abiasaph his sons, Assir his son, [9]Taḥath his son, Uriel his son, Uzziah his son, Shaul his son, [10]Elqanah his son, Amasai his son, Maḥath his son, [11]Elqanah his son, Zuphai his son, Naḥath his son, [12]Eliab his son, Jeroḥam his son, Elqanah his son, Samuel his son; [13]the sons of Samuel: Joel the firstborn and Abijah the second; [14]the descendants of Merari—Maḥli, Libni his son, Shimei his son, Uzzah his son, [15]Shimea his son, Ḥaggiah his son, Asaiah his son. [16]It was these whom David appointed to be in charge of song at the House of Yhwh when the Ark came to rest. 17 They were serving before the Tabernacle of the Tent of Meeting with song until Solomon built the Temple of Yhwh in Jerusalem and they stood according to their prescription with respect to their service.

The Levitical Singers

6:18 These were the ones who stood, along with their sons: from the descendants of Qohath-Heman the singer, son of Joel, son of Samuel, 19 son of Elqanah, son of Jeroḥam, son of Eliel, son of Toaḥ, 20 son of Zuph, son of Elqanah, son of Maḥath, son of Amasai, 21 son of Elqanah, son of Joel, son of Azariah, son of Zephaniah, 22 son of Taḥath, son of Assir, son of Abiasaph, son of Qoraḥ, 23 son of Izhar, son of Qohath, son of Levi, son of Israel; 24 his kinsman Asaph—the one stationed at his right—Asaph the son of Berechiah, son of Shimea, 25 son of Michael, son of Maaseiah, son of Malchijah, 26 son of Ethni, son of Zeraḥ, son of Adaiah, 27 son of Ethan, son of Zimmah, son of Shimei, 28 son of Jaḥath, son of Shimei, son of Gershon, son of Levi; 29 the descendants of Merari—their kinsmen on the left—Ethan son of Qishi, son of Abdi, son of Malluch, 30 son of Ḥashabiah, son of Amaziah, son of Ḥilqiah, 31 son of Amzi, son of Bani, son of Shemer, 32 son of Maḥli, son of Mushi, son of Merari, son of Levi. 33 And their kinsmen according to their ancestral houses—the Levites, they were assigned to all the service of the Tabernacle of the House of God.

The Aaronide Priests

6:34 As for Aaron and his sons, they were sacrificing upon the altar of burnt offering and upon the incense altar for every work of the Holy of Holies to atone for Israel according to all that Moses the servant of God had commanded. 35 These are the descendants of Aaron: Eleazar his son, Phineḥas his son, Abishua his son, 36 Buqqi his son, Uzzi his son, Zeraḥiah his son, 37 Meraioth his son, Amariah his son, Aḥiṭub his son, 38 Zadoq his son, Aḥimaaz his son.

The Levitical Places of Residence

6:39 These are their places of residence according to their settlements within their territories. Belonging to the descendants of Aaron who were of the family of the Qohathites, for they received the (first) lot: 40 they gave Ḥebron to them in the land of Judah along with its surrounding open lands, 41 but they gave the territory of the town and its villages to Caleb son of Jephunneh. 42 To the descendants of Aaron they gave the (following) towns of refuge: Ḥebron along with its open land, Libnah along with its open land, Jattir along with its open land, Eshtemoa along with its open land, 43 Ḥilen along with its open land, Debir along with its open land, 44 Ashan along with its open land, Juṭṭah along with its open land, and Beth-

shemesh along with its open land; 45 from the tribe of Benjamin: Gibeon along
with its open land, Geba along with its open land, Alemeth along with its open
land, and Anathoth along with its open land. All of their towns, with their families,
were thirteen.

46 Belonging to the remaining descendants of Qohath: from the families of the
tribe of Ephraim, from the tribe of Dan, and from the half-tribe of Manasseh—ten
towns by lot. 47 Belonging to the descendants of Gershon, by their families: from
the tribe of Issachar, from the tribe of Asher, from the tribe of Naphtali, and from
the tribe of Manasseh in Bashan—thirteen towns. 48 Belonging to the descendants
of Merari, by their families: from the tribe of Reuben, from the tribe of Gad, and
from the tribe of Zebulun—twelve towns by lot. 49 And the descendants of Israel
assigned to the Levites the towns along with their open lands. 50 They assigned
these towns, which they designated by name, by lot from the tribe of the descendants of Judah, from the tribe of the descendants of Simeon, and from the tribe of
the descendants of Benjamin.

51 Some of the families of the descendants of Qohath, the Levites remaining
from the descendants of Qohath, (also) had towns of their territory from the tribe
of Ephraim. 52 They gave to them towns of refuge: Shechem along with its open
land in the hill country of Ephraim, Gezer along with its open land, 53 Joqmeam
along with its open land, Beth-ḥoron along with its open land; 54 from the tribe of
Dan: Elteqe along with its open land, Gibbethon along with its open land,
Ayyalon along with its open land, and Gath-rimmon along with its open land;
55 from the half-tribe of Manasseh: Taanach along with its open land, Ibleam
along with its open land—for the families of the remaining descendants of the Qohathites.

56 Belonging to the sons of Gershon, from the families of the half-tribe of Manasseh: Golan in Bashan along with its open land, and Ashtaroth along with its
open land; 57 from the tribe of Issachar: Qishon along with its open land, Dobrath
along with its open land, 58 Ramoth along with its open land, and Anem along
with its open land; 59 from the tribe of Asher: Mashal along with its open land,
Abdon along with its open land, 60 Ḥuqoq along with its open land, and Reḥob
along with its open land; 61 from the tribe of Naphtali: Qedesh in Galil along with
its open land, Ḥammath along with its open land, and Qiriathaim along with its
open land.

62 Belonging to the remaining descendants of Merari, from the tribe of Zebulun: Joqneam along with its open land, Rimmon along with its open land, Tabor
along with its open land, 63 from across the Jordan, Jericho; to the east of the Jordan, from the tribe of Reuben: Bezer in the wilderness along with its open land,
Jahzah along with its open land, 64 Qedemoth along with its open land, and
Mephaath along with its open land; 65 from the tribe of Gad, Ramoth in Gilead
along with its open land, Maḥanaim along with its open land, 66 Ḥeshbon along
with its open land, and Jaazer along with its open land.

The Descendants of Issachar

7:1 Belonging to the descendants of Issachar: Tola, Puah, Jashub, and Shimron—four. 2 The sons of Tola: Uzzi, Rephaiah, Jeriel, Jaḥmai, Ibsam, Shemuel—heads of their ancestral houses. Belonging to Tola were valiant warriors, according to their lineages; their muster in David's days was 22,600. 3 The sons of Uzzi: Izraḥiah. The sons of Izraḥiah: Michael, Obadiah, Joel, and Isshiah—five. All of them were heads. 4 Together with them, by their lineages according to their ancestral houses, were the detachments of the military campaign: 36,000, for they had many wives and children. 5 And their kinsmen, according to all of the families of Issachar: 87,000 valiant warriors enrolled by their genealogy.

The Descendants of Benjamin

7:6 The descendants of Benjamin: Bela, Becher, and Jediael—three. 7 The sons of Bela: Ezbon, Uzzi, Uzziel, Jerimoth, and Iri—five, heads of ancestral houses, valiant warriors. And their enrollment by their genealogy was 22,034. 8 The sons of Becher: Zemariah, Joash, Eliezer, Elioenai, Omri, Jeremoth, Abijah, Anathoth, and Alameth. All these were the sons of Becher 9 and they were enrolled by their genealogy according to their lineages—heads of their ancestral houses, valiant warriors—20,200. 10 The sons of Jediael: Bilhan. The sons of Bilhan: Jeush, Benjamin, Ehud, Chenaanah, Zethan, Tarshish, and Aḥishaḥar. 11 All these were sons of Jediael, heads of their ancestral houses, valiant warriors—17,200, going out on the military campaign.

The Descendants of Dan

7:12 The descendants of Dan: Ḥushim his son—one.

The Descendants of Naphtali

7:13 The descendants of Naphtali: Jaḥziel, Guni, Jezer, and Shallum, the descendants of Bilhah.

The Descendants of Manasseh

7:14 The descendants of Manasseh: Asriel to whom his Aramaean concubine gave birth; she [also] gave birth to Machir the father of Gilead. The name of his sister was Hammolecheth. 15 And Machir took a wife. The name of the firstborn was Gilead and the name of the second was Zelopheḥad. And Zelopheḥad had daughters. 16 Maacah the wife of Gilead gave birth to a son and she named him Peresh. The name of his brother was Sheresh and his sons were Ulam and Reqem.

17 The sons of Ulam: Bedan. These were the sons of Gilead son of Machir son of Manasseh. 18 And his sister Hammolecheth gave birth to Ishhod, Abiezer, Maḥlah, and Shemida. 19 And the sons of Shemida were Aḥian, Shechem, Ḥeleq, and Aniam.

The Descendants of Ephraim

7:20 The descendants of Ephraim: Shuthelaḥ, his son Bered, his son Taḥath, his son Eleadah, his son Taḥath, 21 his son Zabad, his son Shuthelaḥ. As for Ezer and Elead, the men of Gath, (those born in the land) killed them, because they had gone down to take their cattle. 22 Ephraim their father grieved many days and his brothers came to comfort him. 23 Then he had sexual relations with his wife, who conceived and gave birth to a son. She named him Beriah, because a calamity had occurred in his house. 24 His daughter was Sheerah. She built Lower and Upper Beth-ḥoron and Uzzen-sheerah. 25 His son Rephah, his son Resheph, his son Telaḥ, his son Taḥan, 26 his son Ladan, his son Ammihud, his son Elishama, 27 his son Non, his son Joshua.

28 Their estates and settlements were Bethel and its dependencies, and on the east Naaran, and on the west Gezer and its dependencies, Shechem and its dependencies as far as Ayyah and its dependencies. 29 And under the control of the descendants of Manasseh: Beth-shean and its dependencies, Taanach and its dependencies, Megiddo and its dependencies, Dor and its dependencies. In these resided the descendants of Joseph, son of Israel.

The Descendants of Asher

7:30 The descendants of Asher: Imnah, Ishvah, Ishvi, Beriah—four, and their sister Seraḥ. 31 The sons of Beriah: Ḥeber and Malchiel, who was the father of Birzaith. 32 Ḥeber sired Japhleṭ, Shomer, Ḥotham, and their sister Shua. 33 The sons of Japhleṭ: Pasach, Bimhal, and Ashvath. These were the sons of Japhleṭ. 34 The sons of Shomer his brother: Rohgah, Ḥubbah, and Aram. 35 The sons of Ḥotham his brother: Zophaḥ, Imna, Shelesh, and Amal. 36 The sons of Zophaḥ: Suaḥ, Ḥarnepher, and Shual. The sons of Imna: 37 Bezer, Hod, and Shamma. The sons of Shelesh: Ithran and Beera. 38 The sons of Jether: Jephunneh, Pispa, and Ara. 39 The sons of Amal: Araḥ, Ḥanniel, and Rizia. 40 All of these sons of Asher were heads of their ancestral houses, select men, valiant warriors, heads of the chieftains. They were enrolled by their genealogy as [fit] for the military campaign. Their muster was 26,000 men.

The Descendants of Benjamin

8:1 Benjamin sired Bela, his firstborn, Ashbel the second, Aḥraḥ the third, 2 Noḥah the fourth, and Rapha the fifth. 3 And Bela had sons: Addar and Gera the father of

Ehud. [4]These were the sons of Ehud: Abishua, Naaman, Aḥiah, [5]Gera, Shephuphan, and Ḥuram. [6]These were the ancestral heads of Geba's inhabitants, and they exiled them to Manaḥath. [7]As for Naaman, Aḥiah, and Gera, he was the one who exiled them. Then he sired Uzza and Aḥiḥud.

[8]Shaḥaraim sired [children] in the country of Moab after he had sent them away, his wives Ḥushim and Baara. [9]He sired [children] from Ḥodesh his wife: Jobab, Zibia, Mesha, and Malcam, [10]Jeuz, Sachiah, Mirmah—these were ancestral heads. [11]He sired from Ḥushim: Abiṭub and Elpaal. [12]These were the sons of Elpaal: Eber, Misham, and Shemer. He built Ono and Lud, along with its dependencies.

[13]As for Beriah and Shema, they were the ancestral heads of Ayyalon's inhabitants. They put Gath's inhabitants to flight. [14]Their kinsmen were Shashaq and Jeremoth. [15]Zebadiah, Arad, Ader, [16]Michael, Ishpah, and Joḥa were the sons of Beriah. [17]Zebadiah, Meshullam, Ḥizqi, Ḥeber, [18]Ishmerai, Izliah, and Jobab were the sons of Elpaal. [19]Jachim, Zichri, Zabdi, [20]Elioenai, Zillethai, Eliel, [21]Adaiah, Beraiah, and Shimrath were the sons of Shimei. [22]Ishpan, Eber, Eliel, [23]Abdon, Zichri, Ḥanan, [24]Ḥananiah, Elam, Anthothiah, [25]Iphdeiah, and Penuel were the sons of Shashaq. [26]Shamsherai, Sheḥariah, Athaliah, [27]Jaarshiah, Elijah, and Zichri were the sons of Jeroḥam. [28]These were the ancestral heads by their lineages. These heads resided in Jerusalem.

[29]The father of Gibeon, Jeiel, resided in Gibeon and the name of his wife was Maacah. [30]Her firstborn son: Abdon, Zur, Qish, Baal, Ner, Nadab, [31]Gedor, Aḥio, Zecher, and Miqloth. [32]Miqloth sired Shimeah, and they also resided opposite their kinsmen in Jerusalem. [33]Ner sired Qish, and Qish sired Saul, and Saul sired Jonathan, Malchi-shua, Abinadab, and Eshbaal. [34]The son of Jonathan was Merib-baal, and Merib-baal sired Micah. [35]The sons of Micah were Pithon, Melech, Taarea, and Aḥaz. [36]Aḥaz sired Jehoadah, and Jehoadah sired Alemeth, Azmaveth, and Zimri. Zimri sired Moza, [37]and Moza sired Binea; Raphaiah his son, Eleasah his son, Azel his son. [38]Azel had six sons and these were their names: Azriqam his firstborn, Ishmael, Sheariah, Azariah, Obadiah, and Ḥanan. All of these were sons of Azel. [39]The sons of Esheq his brother: Ulam, Jeush the second, Elipheleṭ the third. [40]The sons of Ulam were valiant warriors, archers, producers of many children and grandchildren—150. All these were from the descendants of Benjamin.

Genealogical Summary

[9:1]So all Israel was genealogically registered and their [records] were written in the book of the kings of Israel and Judah.

Exile and Return

And as for Judah, they were exiled to Babylon on account of their transgression.

[2]The first residents who (settled) in their properties within their towns were

Israel, the priests, the Levites, and the Temple servants. [3]In Jerusalem resided
some of the descendants of Judah, some of the descendants of Benjamin, and
some of the descendants of Ephraim and Manasseh.
[4]From the sons of Judah: Uthai son of Ammihud son of Omri son of Imri son of
Bani from the sons of Perez son of Judah. [5]Of the Shelanites: Asaiah the firstborn
and his sons. [6]From the sons of Zeraḥ: Jeuel and their kinsmen—690. [7]From the
Benjaminites: Sallu son of Meshullam son of Hodaviah son of Senaah, [8]Ibneiah
son of Jeroḥam, Elah son of Uzzi son of Machir, and Meshullam son of Shephaṭiah son of Reuel son of Ibnijah; [9]and their kinsmen according to their lineages—
956. All of these men were heads of their ancestral houses.
[10]From the priests: Jedaiah, Jehoiarib, Jachin, [11]and Azariah son of Ḥilqiah son
of Meshullam son of Zadoq son of Meraioth son of Aḥiṭub, ruler of the House of
God,[12]and Adaiah son of Jeroḥam son of Pashḥur son of Malchiah, and Maasai
son of Adaiel son of Jaḥzerah son of Meshullam son of Meshillemoth son of
Immer; [13]and their kinsmen, heads of their ancestral houses—1,760, men of substance for the work of the service of the House of God. [14]From the Levites: Shemaiah son of Ḥashub son of Azriqam son of Ḥashabiah, of the sons of Merari;
[15]and Baqbaqqar, Ḥeresh, Galal, and Mattaniah son of Mica son of Zichri son of
Asaph, [16]and Obadiah son of Shemaiah son of Galal son of Jeduthun, and
Berechiah son of Asa son of Elqanah, who resided in the villages of the Neṭophathites.

The Levitical Gatekeepers

9:[17]The gatekeepers: Shallum, Aqqub, Ṭalmon; and their kinsman Shallum was
the head [18]up until now in the King's Gate in the east—these were the gatekeepers belonging to the camps of the sons of Levi. [19]Shallum son of Qore son of Abiasaph son of Qoraḥ, and his kinsmen belonging to his ancestral house, the
Qoraḥites, were in charge of the work of the service, guardians of the thresholds of
the Tent. Their ancestors were in charge of the camp of Yhwh (as) guards of the
entrance. [20]Phineḥas son of Eleazar was the officer in charge of them in times
past. Yhwh was with him. [21]Zechariah son of Meshelemiah was the gatekeeper at
the entrance of the Tent of Meeting. [22]All of them, the ones selected as gatekeepers at the thresholds, were 212. They were registered by their genealogies in their
villages. They were appointed by David and Samuel the seer in their position of
trust.
[23]They and their descendants were in charge of the gates of the House of Yhwh,
that is, the House of the Tent, by guard units. [24]On four sides there were gatekeepers: to the east, the west, the north, and the south. [25]And their kinsmen in
their villages had to come for the seven days at regular intervals (to be) with them.
[26]Indeed, there were four chief gatekeepers in a position of trust who were
Levites, and they were in charge of the chambers and the treasuries of the House
of God. [27]They spent the night around the House of God, because they had guard
duty and were responsible for opening (the Temple) every morning. [28]Some of
them were in charge of the service utensils, for they had to be counted when they

brought them in and when they took them out. [29] Some of them were appointed to be in charge of the utensils and to be in charge of all the holy utensils, the choice flour, the wine, the oil, the frankincense, and the spices. [30] Some of the sons of the priests prepared the mixture of spices. [31] As for Mattithiah of the Levites, he was the firstborn of Shallum the Qoraḥite in a position of trust, responsible for making the flat cakes. [32] Some of the sons of the Qohathites, their kinsmen, were in charge of the rows of bread, to prepare them for each sabbath. [33] These are the singers, the heads of the Levitical ancestral houses, in the chambers set free from other responsibility, because they were on duty day and night. [34] These were the heads of the ancestral houses of the Levites by their lineages; these heads resided in Jerusalem.

The Descendants of Benjaminite Jeiel

[9:35] The father of Gibeon, Jeiel, resided in Gibeon and the name of his wife was Maacah. [36] Her firstborn son: Abdon, Zur, Qish, Baal, Ner, Nadab, [37] Gedor, Aḥio, Zechariah, and Miqloth. [38] Miqloth sired Shimeah, and they also resided opposite their kinsmen in Jerusalem. [39] Ner sired Qish, and Qish sired Saul, and Saul sired Jonathan, Malchi-shua, Abinadab, and Eshbaal. [40] The son of Jonathan was Merib-baal, and Merib-baal sired Micah. [41] The sons of Micah were Pithon, Melech, Taḥarea, and Aḥaz. [42] Aḥaz sired Jadah, and Jadah sired Alemeth, Azmaveth, and Zimri. Zimri sired Moza, [43] and Moza sired Binea; Raphaiah his son, Eleasah his son, Azel his son. [44] Azel had six sons and these were their names: Azriqam his firstborn, Ishmael, Sheariah, Azariah, Obadiah, and Ḥanan. All of these were sons of Azel.

The Fall of King Saul

[10:1] Now the Philistines made war with Israel and the men of Israel fled from before the Philistines. The slain fell on Mount Gilboa. [2] The Philistines pursued Saul and his sons and the Philistines struck down Jonathan, Abinadab, and Malchi-shua, the sons of Saul. [3] The battle weighed upon Saul and the archers found him with the bow. He was wounded by the archers and [4] so Saul said to his arms bearer, "Unsheath your sword and run me through with it lest these uncircumcised come and abuse me." Nevertheless, his arms bearer was unwilling, because he was very frightened. Saul then took the sword and fell upon it. [5] When his arms bearer saw that Saul was dead, he also fell upon the sword and died. [6] So Saul died along with his three sons. All of his house died together. [7] When all the men of Israel who were in the valley saw that they fled and that Saul and his sons died, they abandoned their towns and fled. Then the Philistines came and occupied them. [8] When, on the next day, the Philistines came to strip the slain, they found Saul and his three sons, fallen on Mount Gilboa. [9] They stripped him and carried off his head and his armor and sent them to the surrounding territory of the

Philistines to herald the news to their idols and people. [10]They set his armor in the temple of their gods and his skull they impaled in the Temple of Dagon. [11]When all of the inhabitants of Jabesh-gilead heard all that the Philistines did to Saul and to Israel, [12]all of the warriors arose and carried off the corpse of Saul along with the corpses of his sons and brought them to Jabesh. They interred their bones under the oak in Jabesh and fasted for seven days.

[13]Saul died in his transgression by which he transgressed against Yhwh concerning the word of Yhwh, which he did not observe, even consulting a necromancer to seek (counsel). [14]He did not seek Yhwh and so he put him to death and turned the kingdom over to David, son of Jesse.

David Is Acclaimed King by All Israel and Endorsed by the Armed Forces

[11:1]And all Israel gathered to David at Ḥebron, saying, "We are your bone and your flesh. [2]Even formerly, when Saul was king, you were the one who led Israel out and led Israel in. And Yhwh said to you, 'As for you, you will shepherd my people Israel and you, you will become ruler over Israel.' " [3]When all the elders of Israel came to the king at Ḥebron, David cut a covenant with them before Yhwh. And they anointed David as king over Israel, according to the word of Yhwh through the hand of Samuel.

[4]And David and all Israel went to Jerusalem—that is, Jebus, where the Jebusites were the inhabitants of the land. [5]And they told David, "You will not enter here," but David captured the fortress of Zion, that is, the City of David. [6]David said, "Whoever strikes a Jebusite first will become commander in chief." When Joab son of Zeruiah was the first to go up, he became commander. [7]David resided in the fortress; hence, they called it "the City of David." [8]And he built up the city on all sides, from the millo to the surrounding area, while Joab restored the rest of the city. [9]David grew more and more important and Yhwh Sebaoth was with him.

[10]These are the commanders of David's warriors, who continually strengthened him in his kingship, along with all Israel, to make him king, according to the word of Yhwh concerning Israel.

[11]And this is the muster of David's warriors: Jashobeam son of Ḥachmon, commander of the Three. He brandished his spear over three hundred slain on one occasion. [12]And after him, Eleazar son of Dodai the Aḥoḥite. He was among the three warriors. [13]He was with David at Pas Dammim. The Philistines were gathered there for battle and there was a section of the field full of barley. When the people fled from before the Philistines, [14]they took their stand in the middle of the section, held it, and routed the Philistines. Thus, Yhwh achieved a great victory.

[15]Three of the thirty commanders went down by the rock to David, to the cave of Adullam, the force of the Philistines being encamped in the Valley of Rephaim. [16]At that time David was in the fortress, while at the same time a garrison of the Philistines was in Bethleḥem. [17]And David said wishfully, "Who would give me a drink of water from the cistern at Bethleḥem that is inside the gate?" [18]The Three

broke through the Philistine camp and drew water from the cistern at Bethleḥem
that is inside the gate. They carried it and brought it to David, but he was unwilling to drink it. He poured it to Yhwh, 19 saying, "Far be it from me before my God
that I should do this! Shall I drink the blood of these men with their lives? For by
(risk of) their lives they have brought it." Hence, he was unwilling to drink it. Such
were the deeds of the three warriors.

20 As for Abshai the brother of Joab, he became commander of the Thirty. He
brandished his spear over three hundred slain. He did not attain a name among the
Three. 21 Of the Thirty, he was the most honored and functioned as their leader.
But he did not attain to the Three. 22 Benaiah son of Jehoiada from Qabzeel was a
valiant man who accomplished many deeds. He struck down the two sons of Ariel
of Moab. He went down and struck a lion in the midst of a pit on a snowy day.
23 He also struck down the Egyptian man, a giant five cubits tall. In the hand of the
Egyptian was a spear like a weavers' beam. Yet he went down to him with a staff,
wrenched the spear out of the Egyptian's hand, and killed him with his spear.
24 Such were the deeds of Benaiah son of Jehoiada. He did not attain a name
among the three warriors. 25 He was honored among the Thirty, though he did not
attain to the Three, and David appointed him over his bodyguard.

The Valiant Warriors Who Rallied to David

11:26 The valiant warriors:
Asah-el brother of Joab;
Elḥanan son of Dodai from Bethleḥem;
27 Shammoth the Ḥarodite;
Eliqa the Ḥarodite;
Ḥelez the Pelonite;
28 Ira son of Iqqesh the Teqoaite;
Abiezer the Anathothite;
29 Sibbekai the Ḥushathite;
Ilai the Aḥoḥite;
30 Mahrai the Neṭophathite;
Ḥeled son of Benaiah;
31 Ittai son of Ribai from Gibeah of the Benjaminites;
Benaiah the Pirathonite;
32 Ḥurai from the wadis of Gaash;
Abiel the Arbathite;
33 Azmaveth the Baḥarumite;
Eliaḥba the Shaalbonite;
34 Jashen the Gunite;
Jonathan son of Shageh the Hararite;
35 Aḥiam son of Sakar the Hararite;
Eliphal son of Ur;
36 Ḥepher the Mecherathite;

Aḥijah the Pelonite;
37 Ḥezro the Carmelite;
Naarai son of Ezbai;
38 Joel brother of Nathan;
Mibḥar son of Hagri;
39 Zeleq the Ammonite;
Naḥrai the Berothite, the arms bearer for Joab son of Zeruiah;
40 Ira the Ithrite;
Gareb the Ithrite;
41 Uriah the Hittite;
Zabad son of Aḥlai;
42 Adina son of Shiza the Reubenite, a commander among the Reubenites, and thirty with him;
43 Ḥanan son of Maacah;
Jehoshaphaṭ the Mithnite;
44 Uzziah the Ashterothite;
Shama and Jeiel the sons of Ḥotam the Aroerite;
45 Jedaiel son of Shimri;
Joḥa his brother the Tizite;
46 Eliel the Maḥavite;
Jiribai and Joshaviah the sons of Elnaam;
Ithmah the Moabite;
47 Eliel;
Obed;
and Jaasiel the Mezobite.

The Israelite Tribes Mobilize to Support David

12:1 The following came to David at Ziqlag while he was still a refugee from Saul
the son of Qish. They were among the warriors who lent support in battle. 2 Armed
with the bow, capable of using either the right hand or the left hand to sling stones
and to shoot arrows with the bow, they were kinsmen of Saul from Benjamin. 3 At
the head were Aḥiezer and Joash the son of Shimeah the Gibeathite, Jeziel and
Peleṭ the sons of Azmaveth, Berechiah and Jehu the Anathothite, 4 Ishmaiah the
Gibeonite, a warrior among the Thirty and in charge of the Thirty, 5 Jeremiah, Jaḥaziel, Joḥanan, and Jozabad the Gederathite, 6 Eluzai, Jerimoth, Baaliah, Shem-
ariah, and Shephaṭiah the Ḥariphite, 7 Elqanah, Isshiah, Azarel, Joezer, and
Jashobeam the Qoraḥites, 8 Joelah and Zebadiah the sons of Jeroḥam.

9 Some of the Gadites withdrew to David at the wilderness fortress, valiant warriors, men of the army (trained) for battle, armed with shield and lance. Their face
was the face of a lion and they were swift as gazelles upon the hills: 10 Ezer the
commander, Obadiah the second, Eliab the third, 11 Mishmanah the fourth,
Jeremiah the fifth, 12 Attai the sixth, Eliel the seventh, 13 Joḥanan the eighth,
Elzabad the ninth, 14 Jeremiah the tenth, Machbannai the eleventh. 15 These

were from the descendants of Gad, commanders of the army. One to a hundred the least and the greatest to a thousand. [16]They were the ones who crossed over the Jordan in the first month, when it was flooding all of its banks, rendering the lowlands impassable to the east and to the west.

[17]Some of the Benjaminites and Judahites came up to the fortress, to David. [18]When David went out before them, he answered and said to them, "If you have come in peace to me to help me, then my heart shall be one with yours, but if (you have come) to betray me to my enemies, even though there is no violence in my hands, may the God of our fathers see and judge." [19]Then a spirit enveloped Amasai, commander of the officers:

"We are yours, O David,
We are with you, O Son of Jesse.
Peace, peace be to you,
and peace to the one who supports you,
for your God supports you."

So David received them and appointed them as commanders of the brigade.

[20]Some of the people of Manasseh defected to David when he came with the Philistines against Saul for battle. But he did not help them, because upon taking counsel the Philistine lords sent him away saying, "At the cost of our heads, he will defect to his master Saul." [21]When he went to Ziqlag, the following defected to him from Manasseh: Adnaḥ, Jozabad, Jediael, Michael, Elihu, and Zillethai, commanders of the thousands of Manasseh. [22]It was they who supported David against the raid, for they were valiant warriors, all of them, and they became officers in the army. [23]Indeed, from day to day they came to David to support him so that his camp became immense, like the camp of God.

Military Musters

[12:24]These are the musters of the commanders of those equipped for military service who came to David at Ḥebron to turn the kingdom of Saul over to him, according to the word of Yhwh:

[25]the descendants of Judah, carrying shield and lance, 6,800 equipped for military service;

[26]from the descendants of Simeon, valiant warriors of the army, 7,100;

[27]from the descendants of Levi, 4,600; [28]also Jehoiada the leader of Aaron and with him 3,700; [29]Zadoq, a valiant young warrior, along with his ancestral house, 22 officers;

[30]from the descendants of Benjamin, kinsmen of Saul, 3,000; hitherto, their great number were keeping the watch of the house of Saul;

[31]from the descendants of Ephraim, 20,800 valiant warriors, men of repute by their ancestral houses;

[32]from the half-tribe of Manasseh, 18,000 who were enlisted by name to come and make David king;

[33]from the descendants of Issachar, those understanding the times, knowing

what Israel should do, 200 of their commanders and all of their kinsmen, according to their word;

34 from Zebulun, those going out on the campaign, in battle formation with all kinds of weapons, 50,000, to assist David with single-mindedness;

35 from Naphtali, 1,000 officers accompanied by 37,000 with shields and lances;

36 from the Danites, 28,600 in battle formation;

37 from Asher, those going out on the campaign in battle formation, 40,000;

38 from across the Jordan—from the Reubenites, the Gadites, and the half-tribe of Manasseh—with all kinds of military weapons, 120,000.

39 All these men of war—helping with the battle line, wholly dedicated—came to Ḥebron to make David king over all Israel.

Even all the rest of Israel was of one heart to make David king. 40 They were there with David three days, eating and drinking, because their kinsmen provided for them. 41 Even those near to them (and) as far away as Issachar, Zebulun, and Naphtali were bringing food by asses, by camels, by mules, and by oxen—provisions of flour, cakes of figs, raisin cakes, wine, oil, cattle, and sheep in abundance, because there was joy in Israel.

Israel's First Attempt to Escort the Ark to the City of David

13:1 And David took counsel with the officers of the thousands and of the hundreds—with every commander. 2 Then David said to the entire assembly of Israel, "If it seems good to you and if it is from Yhwh our God, let us send out far and wide to our kin, to those remaining in all the regions of Israel, and with them the priests and the Levites in the towns of their open lands that they may gather themselves to us. 3 Let us bring back the Ark of our God to us, for we did not seek it in the days of Saul." 4 And all (the members) of the assembly said to do so, because the word was right in the eyes of all of the people.

5 Then David assembled all Israel, from Shiḥor of Egypt to Lebo-ḥamath, to bring the Ark of God from Qiriath-jearim. 6 Then David and all Israel went up to Baalah, to Qiriath-jearim, which belongs to Judah, to bring back from there the Ark of God, which is invoked by the name "Yhwh enthroned upon the cherubim." 7 They transported the Ark of God upon a new cart from the house of Abinadab. Uzza and Aḥio were guiding the cart 8 while David and all Israel were performing before God with all their strength—with songs, lyres, harps, drums, cymbals, and trumpets. 9 When they came by the threshing floor of Kidon, Uzza extended his hand to steady the Ark because the oxen had let it slip. 10 The anger of Yhwh was kindled against Uzza and he struck him down, because he set his hand upon the Ark. And he died there before God. 11 Then David became angry, because Yhwh had created a breach against Uzza—and that place is called Perez-uzza to this day.

12 And David became fearful of God on that day, saying, "How can I bring the Ark of God (home) to me?" 13 So David did not take the Ark away with him to the

City of David, but redirected it to the house of Obed-edom the Gittite. 14 The Ark
of God remained with the house of Obed-edom for three months and Yhwh
blessed the house of Obed-edom and all that he had.

David Enjoys Success and Military Victory

14:1 Ḥuram king of Tyre sent messengers to David with cedar timber, masons, and
carpenters to construct a palace for him. 2 Then David knew that Yhwh had established him as king over Israel (and) that his kingship was highly exalted for the
sake of his people Israel.

3 David took more wives and concubines in Jerusalem and David sired more
sons and daughters. 4 And these are the names of those who were born to him in
Jerusalem: Shammua, Shobab, Nathan, Solomon, 5 Ibḥar, Elishua, Elpaleṭ,
6 Nogah, Nepheg, Japhia, 7 Elishama, Beeliada, and Eliphaleṭ.

8 When the Philistines heard that David had been anointed as king over all of
Israel, all the Philistines went up to seek David. When David heard, he went out
before them. 9 And the Philistines came and raided the Valley of Rephaim.
10 Then David inquired of God saying, "Shall I go up against the Philistines? Will
you deliver them into my hand?" And Yhwh said to him, "Go up, for I shall deliver
them into your hand." 11 When they went up at Baal-perazim, David defeated
them there. And David said, "God has broken through my enemies by my hands,
like a breakthrough of waters." Therefore they called the name of that place Baal-
perazim. 12 And they abandoned their gods there. Then David gave the word and
they were consigned to fire.

13 But the Philistines again raided the valley 14 and David again inquired of
God. And God told him, "Do not go up after them. Encircle them and engage
them in front of the Bacas. 15 When you hear the sound of the marching in the
tops of the Bacas, then you will go out into battle because God will go out before
you to defeat the Philistine forces."

16 When David did as God commanded him, they defeated the Philistine forces
from Gibeon to Gezer. 17 And the reputation of David spread throughout all of the
lands and Yhwh brought the fear of him on all of the nations.

The Assembling and Preparations of the Levites and Priests

15:1 When he [David] constructed dwellings for himself in the City of David, he
established a place for the Ark of God and pitched a tent for it. 2 Then David said,
"No one is to carry the Ark of God except the Levites, because Yhwh chose them
to carry the Ark of Yhwh and to minister to him forever."

3 David assembled all Israel to Jerusalem to carry the Ark of Yhwh to the
place that he established for it. 4 And David gathered the sons of Aaron and the
Levites:

5 the descendants of Qohath, Uriel the officer and his kinsmen—120;

[6]the descendants of Merari, Asaiah the officer and his kinsmen—220;
[7]the descendants of Gershon, Joel the officer and his kinsmen—130;
[8]the descendants of Elizaphan, Shemaiah the officer and his kinsmen—200;
[9]the descendants of Ḥebron, Eliel the officer and his kinsmen—80;
[10]the descendants of Uzziel, Amminadab the officer and his kinsmen—112.
[11]David called for Zadoq and Abiathar, the priests, and for the Levites—Uriel,
Asaiah, Joel, Shemaiah, Eliel, and Amminadab, [12]saying to them, "You are the
heads of the Levitical houses. Consecrate yourselves, you and your kinsmen, and
you will carry the Ark of Yhwh, the God of Israel, to (the place) I have established
for it. [13]Indeed, when at first you did not carry (it), Yhwh our God created a breach
against us because we did not seek it according to the convention."
[14]Then the priests and the Levites consecrated themselves to carry the Ark of
Yhwh, the God of Israel. [15]And the Levites carried the Ark of God as Moses commanded in accordance with the word of Yhwh, by means of poles upon their
shoulders.
[16]And David told the Levitical officers to appoint their kinsmen, the singers,
with musical instruments—harps, lyres, and cymbals—making themselves heard
by raising a joyful sound.
[17]So the Levites appointed:
Heman son of Joel;
from his kinsmen: Asaph son of Berechiah;
from the descendants of Merari their kinsmen: Ethan son of Qishaiah;
[18]with them their kinsmen of the second rank: Zechariah, Uzziel, Shemiramoth, Jeḥiel, Unni, Eliab, Benaiah, Maaseiah, Mattithiah, Eliphalah, Miqneiah, Obed-edom, Jeiel, and Azaziah—the gatekeepers;
[19]the singers—Heman, Asaph, Ethan to sound the bronze cymbals;
[20]Zechariah, Uzziel, Shemiramoth, Jeḥiel, Unni, Eliab, Maaseiah, Benaiah
with harps set to (the voice of) young women;
[21]Mattithiah, Eliphalah, Miqneiah, Obed-edom, Jeiel, and Azaziah to lead
with lyres, set to the *šĕmînît;*
[22]Chenaniah, officer of the Levites, to wield authority in the porterage, because
he was an expert in it;
[23]Berechiah and Elqnanah—gatekeepers for the Ark;
[24]Shebaniah, Joshaphaṭ, Nethanel, Amasai, Zechariah, Benaiah, and Eliezer
the priests—sounding the trumpets before the Ark of God;
Obed-edom and and Jeḥiah—gatekeepers for the Ark.

The Procession of the Ark to the Tent of David

[15:25]Then David, together with the elders of Israel and the officers of the thousands, went forth joyfully to carry the Ark of the Covenant from the house of
Obed-edom. [26]And God helped the Levites, those carrying the Ark of the
Covenant of Yhwh. They sacrificed seven bulls and seven rams. [27]David was
clothed in a robe of fine linen as were all the Levites, those carrying the Ark and

those singing. David also wore a linen ephod. 28 Thus David and all Israel were
carrying the Ark of the Covenant of Yhwh with acclaim, with the blast of the horn,
with trumpets, with cymbals sounding, with harps, and with lyres.

29 As the Ark of the Covenant of Yhwh entered the City of David, Michal
daughter of Saul gazed through the window and saw King David, dancing and
performing, and she despised him in her heart.

16:1 When they brought up the Ark of God, they stationed it in the midst of the
tent that David had pitched for it. Then they brought near burnt offerings and offerings of well-being before God. 2 When David finished sacrificing the burnt offerings and the offerings of well-being, he blessed the people in the name of
Yhwh. 3 He also apportioned to every Israelite person—male and female alike—a
loaf of bread, a roll, and a raisin cake.

Celebrating the Ark in Jerusalem

16:4 And he [David] stationed some of the Levites as ministers before the Ark of
Yhwh to commemorate, to give thanks, and to give praise to Yhwh, the God of Israel: 5 Asaph the head; Zechariah his second in command; Jeiel, Shemiramoth,
Jeḥiel, Mattithiah, Eliab, Benaiah, Obed-edom, and Uzziel with harps and with
lyres; and Asaph sounding the cymbals; 6 and Benaiah and Jaḥaziel the priests
with trumpets regularly before the Ark of the Covenant of God.

7 Then, on that day, David first put Asaph and his kinsmen in charge of giving
thanks to Yhwh.

8 Give thanks to Yhwh;
call upon his name;
make known his deeds among the peoples.
9 Sing to him; laud him;
muse about all his wonderful deeds.
10 Boast in his holy name;
let the heart of those seeking Yhwh rejoice.
11 Seek Yhwh and his strength;
search out his presence regularly;
12 Remember his wonders that he has accomplished;
his signs and the judgments of his mouth.
13 O seed of Israel his servant,
O sons of Jacob, his elect ones,
14 he is Yhwh our God;
his judgments are throughout the land.
15 Remember his covenant forever,
the word he commanded to the thousandth generation,
16 that which he cut with Abraham,
his oath to Isaac;
17 he confirmed it as a statute to Jacob,
to Israel as an everlasting covenant,

18 saying, "To you I shall give the land of Canaan,
the territory of your inheritance."
19 When you were scant in number,
a few and sojourning in it,
20 wandering from nation to nation,
from one kingdom to another people,
21 he did not permit anyone to oppress them;
he disciplined kings on their account:
22 "Do not strike my anointed ones;
do not mistreat my prophets."
23 Sing to Yhwh all the earth;
proclaim his deliverance from day to day.
24 Recount his glory among the nations,
his wonders among all the peoples,
25 for great is Yhwh and greatly praised;
feared he is above all the gods.
26 Indeed, all the gods of the peoples are nonentities,
but Yhwh made the heavens.
27 Thanksgiving and majesty are before him;
strength and joy are in his place.
28 Ascribe to Yhwh, O families of the peoples,
ascribe to Yhwh honor and strength.
29 Ascribe to Yhwh the honor due his name;
carry tribute and come before him;
worship Yhwh, majestic in holiness.
30 Tremble, all the earth, before him;
the world is established; it cannot be shaken.
31 Let the heavens rejoice and the earth give cheer;
let them say among the nations, "Yhwh reigns!"
32 Let the sea and its fullness thunder;
let the fields and everything within them exult.
33 Then let the trees of the forest shout for joy
from before Yhwh,
because he comes to judge the earth.
34 Give thanks to Yhwh, for he is good,
for his loyalty endures forever.
35 Say, "Deliver us, O God of our deliverance;
gather us and liberate us from the nations,
to give thanks to your holy name,
to boast in your praise.
36 Blessed is Yhwh, the God of Israel,
from ages past to forevermore."
And all the people said, "Amen" and "Praise Yhwh!"

37 And he [David] left Asaph and his kinsmen there before the Ark of the Covenant of Yhwh to serve regularly before the Ark of Yhwh as each day required:

38 Obed-edom, Jeḥiel, and their kinsmen—68; Obed-edom son of Jeduthun and Ḥosah—gatekeepers.

Assignments for the Tabernacle in Gibeon

16:39 [He left] Zadoq the priest and his kinsmen the priests before the Tabernacle of Yhwh, at the high place that is in Gibeon, 40 to sacrifice burnt offerings to Yhwh upon the altar, the regular morning and evening burnt offering according to all that was written in the Torah of Yhwh, which he enjoined upon Israel; 41 with them were Heman and Jeduthun and the rest of the select who were designated by name to give thanks to Yhwh, for his loyalty endures forever; 42 with them trumpets and cymbals for sounding, instruments of the song of God; the sons of Jeduthun to be at the gate. 43 Then all the people departed, each to his own house, and David returned to bless his house.

The Divine Promises to David

17:1 After David settled in his house, David said to Nathan the prophet, "Here I am, living in the cedar house, but the Ark of the Covenant of Yhwh is under curtains." 2 Nathan said to David, "Do all that is in your heart, because God is with you."

3 But during that very night the word of God came to Nathan, saying,

> 4 "Go and say to David my servant: 'Thus Yhwh said, As for you, you will not build the House for me to reside (in). 5 Indeed, I have not resided in a house from the day I brought up Israel until this very day, but have gone about from tent to tent and from tabernacle to tabernacle. 6 In all of my traveling with all Israel, did I ever speak to one of the chieftains of Israel whom I commanded to shepherd my people, saying, "Why have you not built a house of cedars for me?" '
>
> 7 "But now, thus will you say to my servant David, 'Thus said Yhwh Sebaoth, I, I took you from the pasture, from behind the flock, to be ruler over my people Israel. 8 I have been with you wherever you went and have cut off all your enemies from before you. Moreover, I shall make a name for you like the name of the greatest in the land. 9 I shall make a place for my people Israel and I shall plant them so that they will reside in it and be disturbed no longer. Evildoers will no longer wear them down as in the past, 10 ever since the days I commanded chieftains over my people Israel. I shall humble all your enemies and make you great. As for a house, Yhwh will build one for you. 11 When your days are full (and you) go to be with your fathers, I shall establish your seed after you, one of your own sons, and I shall establish his kingship. 12 As for him, he will build a house for me and I shall establish his throne forever. 13 I, I shall be a father to him and he will be a son to me and I shall not withdraw my loyalty from him as I withdrew it from your predecessor. 14 I shall appoint him in my house and in my kingship forever. His throne will be established forever."

15 According to all these words and according to all this vision did Nathan speak to
David.

The Davidic Prayer

17:16 When King David came in and took his seat before Yhwh, he said,
"Who am I, O Yhwh God, and what is my house that you have brought me
so far? 17 And if this were too little in your eyes, O God, you have spoken
about the house of your servant from a long time ago and you have caused
me, someone of human stature, to see into the future, O Yhwh God. 18 What
more can David add to you for honor? As for you, you have known your servant. 19 O Yhwh, for the sake of your servant and according to your heart, you
have done this entire great deed to make known all the great deeds. 20 O
Yhwh, there is no one like you and there is no God except for you, according
to everything that we have heard with our ears. 21 And who is like your people
Israel, a unique nation on the earth, whom God went forth to redeem as a
people for himself to make for himself a great and marvelous name, driving
out nations from before your people, whom you redeemed from Egypt.
22 And you appointed your people Israel as your own people forever. And you,
O Yhwh, you have become their God. 23 And now, O Yhwh, as for the word
that you have spoken about your servant and his house, may it be confirmed
forever. Do according to what you have promised. 24 May it be confirmed and
may your name be magnified forever, saying, 'Yhwh Sebaoth is God of Israel.' And may the house of David your servant be established before you.
25 Indeed, you are Yhwh my God; you have disclosed to your servant that you
will build for him a house. Therefore, your servant has found courage to pray
before you. 26 And now, O Yhwh, you are the God, and your words will come
true, and you have promised this good thing concerning your servant. 27 And
now you have been pleased to bless the house of your servant to abide forever
before you. Indeed, you, O Yhwh, you have blessed and are blessed forever."

"A Time for War": The Beginning of David's Foreign Campaigns

18:1 Sometime after this, David defeated the Philistines, humbled them, and captured Gath and its dependencies from the control of the Philistines. 2 He also defeated the Moabites so that the Moabites became tribute-bearing vassals of David.
3 And David defeated Hadadezer, the king of Zobah toward Ḥamath, when he was
on his way to set up his stela at the Euphrates River. 4 And David captured from
him 1,000 chariots, 7,000 cavalry, and 20,000 foot soldiers. Then David ham-
strung all of the chariot horses, except for 100 chariot horses, which he retained.
5 When the Aramaeans of Damascus came to support Hadadezer, the king of
Zobah, David struck down 22,000 Aramaean men. 6 David stationed garrisons in
Aram-damascus and the Aramaeans became David's tribute-bearing vassals. And
Yhwh gave victory to David wherever he went.

7 Then David took the golden bow-and-arrow cases that belonged to the retainers of Hadadezer and brought them to Jerusalem. 8 And from Ṭibḥath and Kun, cities of Hadadezer, David captured a very large amount of bronze. With it Solomon made the bronze sea, the columns, and the bronze furnishings. 9 When Tou, the king of Ḥamath, heard that David had struck down all of the forces of Hadadezer, the king of Zobah, 10 he sent Hadoram his son to King David to sue for peace and to congratulate him for fighting against Hadadezer and defeating him, because Tou had often fought against Hadadezer. And (with Hadoram) were all kinds of gold, silver, and bronze objects. 11 King David also consecrated them to Yhwh, along with the silver and the gold that he exacted from all of the nations—from Edom, from Moab, from the Ammonites, from the Philistines, and from Amaleq.

12 Moreover, Abshai son of Zeruiah defeated the Edomites in the Valley of Salt—18,000. 13 He stationed garrisons in Edom and all of the Edomites became vassals of David. Yhwh gave victory to David wherever he went.

Royal Administration

18:14 And David reigned over all Israel, exercising justice and equity for all of his people. 15 Joab son of Zeruiah was in charge of the army; Jehoshaphaṭ son of Aḥilud was registrar; 16 Zadoq son of Aḥiṭub and Aḥimelek son of Abiathar were priests; Shawsha was scribe; 17 Benaiah son of Jehoiada was in charge of the Cherethites and the Pelethites; and the first sons of David were at the king's side.

Israelite Successes against the Ammonites and the Aramaeans

19:1 Sometime after this, Naḥash the king of the Ammonites died, and his son Ḥanun reigned in his stead. 2 And David thought, "I shall show loyalty to Ḥanun the son of Naḥash, because his father showed loyalty to me." So David sent messengers with condolences to him concerning his father. When David's servants went to the land of the Ammonites with his condolences to Ḥanun, 3 the Ammonite leaders said to Ḥanun, "Is David honoring your father in your sight because he is sending you those offering condolences? Is not the purpose to explore the town, to overthrow [it], and to search out the land that his servants have come to you?" 4 And Ḥanun took David's servants and shaved them, cutting their garments in half up to the hip, and then he sent them away. 5 When they went and reported to David concerning the men, he sent (others) to meet them, because the men were greatly humiliated. And the king said, "Stay in Jericho until your beards grow back and then return."

6 When the Ammonites saw that they had made themselves odious to David, Ḥanun and the Ammonites sent 1,000 talents of silver to hire chariots and cavalry for themselves from Aram-naharayim, Aram-maacah, and Zobah. 7 They hired for

themselves 32,000 chariots, as well as the king of Maacah and his army. And they
came and encamped before the waters of Rabbah. As for the Ammonites, they
were mobilized from their towns and arrived for battle.
8 When David heard (of this), he dispatched Joab and the entire army of warriors. 9 And the Ammonites went forth and drew up for battle at the entrance of the
town, while the kings who had come were alone in the field. 10 When Joab saw
that the battle line was in front of him and in back of him, he made a selection of
all the elite troops in Israel and drew up to meet the Aramaeans. 11 As for the rest of
the army, he placed (it) under the command of Abshai his brother. When they
drew up to meet the Aramaeans, 12 he said, "If the Aramaeans prove too strong for
me, you will be my deliverance, and if the Ammonites prove stronger than you, I
shall deliver you. 13 Be strong and let us show ourselves strong for the sake of our
people and for the sake of the towns of our God. And may Yhwh do what is right in
his eyes."
14 When Joab and the army that was with him advanced before the Aramaeans
for battle, they fled from before him. 15 When the Ammonites saw that the Aramaeans had fled, they also fled from before Abshai his brother and (re)entered the
town. And Joab returned from (attacking) the Ammonites and came to Jerusalem.
16 When the Aramaeans realized that they had been defeated by Israel, they sent
messengers who brought out the Aramaeans living beyond the river. Shophach,
the commander of Hadadezer's army, led them. 17 When this news was reported to
David, he mobilized all Israel, crossed the Jordan, and came to Ḥelam. And
David drew up (his forces) to meet the Aramaeans in battle.
Then they battled against him. 18 But the Aramaeans fled from before Israel and
David killed 7,000 Aramaean charioteers as well as 40,000 foot soldiers. As for
Shophach, the commander of the army, he put (him) to death. 19 When the
clients of Hadadezer saw that they had been defeated by Israel, they made peace
with David and served him. As for the Aramaeans, they were no longer willing to
rescue the Ammonites.

The Completion of David's Foreign Military Campaigns

20:1 When it was the turn of the year, the time when kings go forth (into battle),
Joab led out the elite of the army and razed the land of the Ammonites. He also
came and besieged Rabbah, while David was staying in Jerusalem. When Joab attacked Rabbah, Joab sent messengers to David saying, "You go capture Rabbah,
lest I capture it and my name be invoked there." Then David mobilized the army,
went to Rabbah, captured it, and tore it down. 2 And David seized Milcom's crown
from his head and found the weight to be a talent of gold. On it was a precious
stone, and it was set on David's head. And the booty that he brought out of the
town was very great. 3 After he brought out the people who were in it, he tore (it)
asunder with a saw, iron picks, and axes. Thus David did to all the towns of the
Ammonites. Then David and the whole army returned to Jerusalem.
4 And sometime after this, war broke out with the Philistines in Gezer. Then

Sibbekai the Ḥushathite struck down Sippai, one of the descendants of the Rephaim, and they were humbled. [5]And there was war again with the Philistines. And Elḥanan the son of Jair struck down Laḥmi the brother of Goliath the Gittite. The shaft of his spear was like a weavers' beam. [6]And there was war once again in Gath. There was a man of (great) stature. His digits were twenty-four—six (on each hand) and six (on each foot). He too was descended from Rapha. [7]Although he harrassed Israel, Jonathan the son of David's brother Shimea struck him down. [8]These were descended from Rapha in Gath and they fell at the hand of David and at the hand of his aides.

The Census and Plague: David as Repentant Sinner

[21:1]An adversary took his stand against Israel and incited David to take a census of Israel. [2]Then David said to Joab and the officers of the army, "Go number Israel from Beer-sheba to Dan and then bring back (the outcome) to me so that I may know their number." [3]But Joab responded, "May Yhwh add to his people one hundred times! Is not my lord the king? All of them are servants of my lord. Why does my lord seek this? Why should there be guilt upon Israel?" [4]But the command of the king prevailed upon Joab. So Joab set forth and traveled through all Israel and came (back) to Jerusalem. [5]Then Joab provided the tally, the muster of the people, to David. All Israel had 1,100,000 men who drew the sword, while Judah had 470,000 men who drew the sword. [6]But Levi and Benjamin he did not count among them, because the command of the king was abhorrent to Joab. [7]This thing was evil in the sight of God and so he struck Israel.

[8]Then David said to God, "I have sinned greatly in doing this thing. Forgive the transgression of your servant, because I have acted very foolishly." [9]And Yhwh spoke to Gad (the) seer, [10]"Go and speak to David saying, 'Thus said Yhwh: I am extending three (choices) to you. Choose one of them for yourself and I shall do it to you.' " [11]When Gad came to David, he said to him, "Thus said Yhwh, 'Choose one of the following for yourself: [12]a three-year famine, three months of your succumbing to your foes, with the sword of your enemy overtaking (you), or three days of the sword of Yhwh accompanied by a plague in the land and a messenger of Yhwh wreaking destruction in every territory of Israel.' Now decide with what word I shall return to my sender." [13]And David replied to Gad, "I am in great distress. Let me fall into the hand of Yhwh, because his compassion is exceedingly great. But into the hand of man let me not fall."

[14]Then Yhwh set a plague in Israel and there fell from among the Israelites 70,000 people. [15]And God sent a messenger to Jerusalem to destroy it; but, as he was about to destroy (it), Yhwh saw and repented of the evil. Then he said to the destroying messenger, "Enough! Now stay your hand!" And the messenger of Yhwh was standing by the threshing floor of Ornan the Jebusite. [16]And David lifted his eyes and saw the messenger of Yhwh standing between the earth and the heavens with his sword drawn in his hand, outstretched against Jerusalem. Then David and the elders, dressed in sackcloth, fell on their faces. [17]And David said to

God, "Was it not I, I who said to number the people? I was the one who sinned and did great evil. But as for these sheep, what have they done? O Yhwh my God, may your hand be upon me and upon the house of my father. But as for your people, let (them) not be subject to a plague."

A Site for the Future Temple

21:18 Then the messenger of Yhwh said to Gad to say to David that David should go up to establish an altar to Yhwh on the threshing floor of Ornan the Jebusite. 19 So David went up in accordance with the command of Gad, who spoke in the name of Yhwh. 20 When Ornan turned and saw the king, his four sons with him hid themselves, covering themselves with sackcloth. Meanwwhile, Ornan continued threshing out the wheat. 21 Then David came to Ornan. When Ornan looked and saw David, he went forth from the threshing floor and bowed before David, nose to the ground. 22 And David said to Ornan, "Give me the place of the threshing floor that I may build upon it an altar to Yhwh. At the full price give it to me so that the plague upon the people will end." 23 Ornan replied to David, "Take (it) for yourself and may my lord the king do what is good in his own eyes. See I give the oxen for the burnt offerings, the threshing sledges for wood, and the wheat for the cereal offering—all of these I give." 24 But King David said to Ornan, "No, I shall indeed buy them at full price, for I shall not lift up to Yhwh what is yours nor offer the burnt offerings for nothing." 25 Then David gave 600 shekels of gold to Ornan for the place.

26 David built there an altar to Yhwh and lifted up burnt offerings and offerings of well-being. He called upon Yhwh and he answered him with fire from the heavens upon the altar of burnt offering and consumed it the burnt offering. 27 Then Yhwh spoke to the messenger and he returned his sword to its sheath. 28 At that time, when David saw that Yhwh answered him at the threshing floor of Ornan the Jebusite and he sacrificed there, 29 the Tabernacle of Yhwh that Moses had made in the wilderness, and the altar of the burnt offering were at that time at the high place in Gibeon. 30 But David was not able to go before it to seek God, because he was terrified on account of the sword of the messenger of Yhwh.

22:1 And David said, "This will be the House of Yhwh God and this will be the altar of the burnt offering for Israel."

Materials, Artisans, and a New King for the Temple

22:2 David gave orders to gather the resident aliens who were in the land of Israel and appointed masons for cutting hewn stones to build the House of God. 3 Iron in abundance for nails for the doors of the gates and for the clasps David provided, as well as bronze in abundance beyond weighing 4 and innumerable cedar logs, because the Sidonians and the Tyrians brought cedar logs in abundance to David. 5 And David thought, "My son is an inexperienced youth, and the House that is to be built for Yhwh must be exceedingly great to win fame and glory throughout all lands. Let me provide, therefore, for it." So David provided (materials) in abundance before his death.

6 Then David called for his son Solomon and commanded him to build a house for Yhwh, the God of Israel. 7 And David said to Solomon, "My son, I myself had it in mind to build a house for the name of Yhwh my God, 8 but the word of Yhwh came to me saying, 'Much blood you have shed and great wars you have waged. You will not build a house for my name, because you have shed much blood to the earth before me. 9 A son has been born to you; he, he will be a man of rest. I shall give him rest from all of his surrounding enemies; indeed, Solomon will be his name and peace and quiet I shall give to Israel in his days. 10 As for him, he will build a house for my name. He, he will become my son and I shall become his father. And I shall establish the throne of his dominion over Israel forever.'

11 "Now, my son, may Yhwh be with you so that you will become very prosperous and build the House of Yhwh your God as he promised concerning you. 12 Only may Yhwh give you insight and understanding so that when he puts you in command over Israel you may observe the Torah of Yhwh your God. 13 Then you will become very prosperous, if you are careful to carry out the statutes and the judgments, that Yhwh commanded Moses concerning Israel. Be strong and resolute; neither fear nor be dismayed. 14 In my humility, I have provided for the House of God: 100,000 talents of gold and 1,000,000 talents of silver, as well as bronze and iron beyond weighing, because there was so much of it. I have also provided wood and stones and you will add to them. 15 And with you in abundance are artisans—masons, stonecutters, and carpenters—with every kind of skill in every kind of work 16 pertaining to gold, silver, bronze, and iron without number. Arise and act and may Yhwh be with you."

17 Then David commanded all the officers of Israel to help Solomon his son. 18 "Is not Yhwh your God with you? He has given you rest on every side. Indeed, he has given all the inhabitants of the land into my hand. The land is subdued before Yhwh and before his people. 19 Now dedicate your hearts and your lives to seeking Yhwh your God. Arise and build the sanctuary of Yhwh God to bring the Ark of the Covenant of Yhwh and the holy furnishings of God into the House that is to be built for the name of Yhwh."

Levitical Census

23:1 When David was old and replete with days, he appointed his son Solomon to reign over Israel. 2 And he gathered together all of the officers of Israel along with the priests and the Levites.

3 And the Levites were numbered from the age of thirty years and up. Their head count was 38,000 men. 4 Out of these, 24,000 were overseeing the work of the Temple of Yhwh, 6,000 were officials and judges, 5 4,000 were gatekeepers, and 4,000 were praising Yhwh with instruments he made for offering praise.

The Three Levitical Divisions

23:6 Then David partitioned them into divisions corresponding to the sons of Levi:
Gershon, Qohath, and Merari.

7 Belonging to the Gershonites: Laadan and Shimei. 8 The sons of Laadan: the
head was Jeḥiel, and Zetham and Joel—three. 9 The sons of Jeḥiel: Shelomoth,
Ḥaziel, and Haran—three. These were the ancestral heads of Laadan. 10 The sons
of Shimei: Jaḥath, Ziza, Jeush, and Beriah. These were the sons of Shimei—four.
11 Jaḥath was the head and Ziza was the second, but Jeush and Beriah did not produce many sons and so they became one ancestral house, according to one enrollment.

12 The sons of Qohath: Amram, Izhar, Ḥebron, and Uzziel—four. 13 The sons of
Amram: Aaron and Moses. And Aaron was set apart so that he could consecrate the
most sacred objects, he and his sons forever, to make offerings before Yhwh, to
serve him, and to pronounce blessings in his name forever. 14 As for Moses, the
man of God, his sons were reckoned among the tribe of Levi. 15 The sons of Moses:
Gershom and Eliezer. 16 The sons of Gershom: Shubael the head. 17 The sons of
Eliezer: Reḥabiah the head. Eliezer had no other sons, but the sons of Reḥabiah
increased abundantly. 18 The sons of Izhar: Shelomoth the head. 19 The sons of
Ḥebron: Jeriah the head, Amariah the second, Jeḥaziel the third, and Jeqameam
the fourth. 20 The sons of Uzziel: Micah the head and Isshiah the second.

21 The sons of Merari: Maḥli and Mushi. The sons of Maḥli: Eleazar and Qish.
22 But Eleazar died without having any sons, only daughters, so the sons of Qish,
their kinsmen, married them. 23 The sons of Mushi: Maḥli, Eder, and Jeremoth—
three.

24 These were the sons of Levi by their ancestral houses, the ancestral heads according to their enrollments by their head count of names, the ones doing the
work for the service of the Temple of Yhwh from the age of twenty and up. 25 For
David said, "Yhwh the God of Israel has given rest to his people and has taken up
residence in Jerusalem forever 26 and so the Levites no longer need to carry the
Tabernacle along with all of its furnishings for its service." 27 For among the last
commands of David, this was the census of the sons of Levi from the age of twenty
years and up.

Levitical Duties

23:28 Indeed, their appointment was to be at the side of the sons of Aaron for the service of the Temple of Yhwh, (to be responsible) for the outer courts, the chambers,
the purity of all sacred objects, and the work for the service of the Temple of God;
29 and for the rows of bread, the choice flour for the cereal offering, the unleavened wafers, the griddle, the well-mixed (cakes), and all measures of capacity and
length; 30 also to stand every morning to give thanks and to praise Yhwh, and likewise in the evening, 31 and whenever burnt offerings are offered to Yhwh for the
sabbaths, new moons, and festivals, with the number (being set) according to the

prescription concerning them, perpetually before Yhwh. 32 They were also to keep
the watch of the Tent of Meeting, the watch of the sacred objects, and the watch
of the sons of Aaron, their kinsmen, for the service of the Temple of Yhwh.

The Twenty-four Priestly Courses

24:1 And as for the descendants of Aaron: their divisions. The sons of Aaron: Nadab
and Abihu, Eleazar and Ithamar. 2 Nadab and Abihu died before their father without having any sons, so Eleazar and Ithamar served as priests. 3 And David partitioned them, along with Zadoq from the sons of Eleazar and Aḥimelek from the
sons of Ithamar, by their duty in their service according to their ancestral houses.
4 When the sons of Eleazar were found to be more numerous as head warriors
than the sons of Ithamar, they partitioned them: of the sons of Eleazar sixteen
heads of ancestral houses and of the sons of Ithamar eight ancestral houses. 5 They
partitioned them by lots, one like the other, because they were officers of the sanctuary and officers of God—from the sons of Eleazar and from the sons of Ithamar.
6 And Shemaiah son of Nethanael, the scribe from the Levites, registered them in
the presence of the king, the officers, Zadoq the priest, Aḥimelek son of Abiathar,
and the heads of the ancestral houses of the priests and the Levites. One ancestral
house was picked out for Eleazar and one (ancestral house) was picked out for
Ithamar.

7 The first lot fell to Jehoiarib,
the second to Jedaiah,
8 the third to Ḥarim,
the fourth to Seorim,
9 the fifth to Malchijah,
the sixth to Mijamin,
10 the seventh to Haqqoz,
the eighth to Abijah,
11 the ninth to Jeshua,
the tenth to Shecaniah,
12 the eleventh to Eliashib,
the twelfth to Jaqim,
13 the thirteenth to Ḥuppah,
the fourteenth to Ishbaal,
14 the fifteenth to Bilgah,
the sixteenth to Immer,
15 the seventeenth to Ḥezir,
the eighteenth to Happizzez,
16 the nineteenth to Pethaḥiah,
the twentieth to Jeḥezqel,
17 the twenty-first to Jachin,
the twenty-second to Gamul,
18 the twenty-third to Delaiah,
the twenty-fourth to Maaziah.

[19]These were their duties corresponding to their service: to enter the House of Yhwh according to their custom at the directive of Aaron their ancestor as Yhwh the God of Israel had commanded him.

The Remaining Levites

[24:20]As for the rest of the descendants of Levi:
belonging to the sons of Amram: Shubael;
belonging to the sons of Shubael: Jeḥdeiah;
[21]belonging to Reḥabiah: belonging to the sons of Reḥabiah, Isshiah was the head;
[22]belonging to the Izharites: Shelomoth;
belonging to the sons of Shelomoth, Jaḥath;
[23]the sons of Ḥebron: Jeriah the head, Amariah the second, Jeḥaziel the third, and Jeqameam the fourth;
[24]the sons of Uzziel: Micah;
belonging to the sons of Micah: Shamir;
[25]the brother of Micah: Isshiah;
belonging to the sons of Isshiah: Zechariah;
[26]the sons of Merari: Maḥli and Mushi;
the sons of Jaaziah: Bani;
[27]the sons of Merari—belonging to Jaaziah: Bani, Shoham, Zakkur, and Ibri;
[28]belonging to Maḥli: Eleazar and Ithamar, but Eleazar died and did not have any sons;
[29]belonging to Qish: the sons of Qish, Jeraḥmeel;
[30]the sons of Mushi: Maḥli, Eder, and Jerimoth.

These were the descendants of the Levites by their ancestral houses. [31]They also cast lots exactly as their kin the sons of Aaron (did) in the presence of King David, Zadoq, Aḥimelek, and the heads of the ancestral houses of the priests and Levites, the ancestral head exactly as his youngest kinsman.

The Twenty-four Courses of Choristers

[25:1]And David and the army officers set apart the sons of Asaph, Heman, and Jeduthun for service, those prophesying to the accompaniment of lyres, harps, and cymbals. Their census by their headcount of working men, according to their service, was:
[2]belonging to the sons of Asaph: Zakkur, Joseph, Nethaniah, and Asarelah—the sons of Asaph under the command of Asaph, who prophesied under the command of the king;
[3]belonging to Jeduthun: the sons of Jeduthun—Gedaliah, Izri, Jeshaiah, Shimei, Ḥashabiah, Mattithiah—six, under the command of their father Jeduthun, who, to the accompaniment of the lyre, prophesied in thanksgiving and praise to Yhwh;

4 belonging to Heman: the sons of Heman—Buqqiah, Mattaniah, Uzziel,
Shubael, Jerimoth, Ḥananiah, Ḥanani, Eliathah, Giddalti, Romamti-
ezer, Joshbeqashah, Mallothi, Hothir, Maḥazioth— 5 all of these were
sons of Heman, the seer of the king, in divine matters to exalt his cause.
So he gave to Heman fourteen sons and three daughters. 6 All of these
were under the command of their father for the singing in the House of
Yhwh, to the accompaniment of cymbals, harps, and lyres for the service
of the House of God, under the command of the king.

Asaph, Jeduthun, and Heman: 7 their census with their kin—trained in singing
to Yhwh, all (of whom were) skillful—was 288. 8 And the lots fell duty corresponding to duty, the small the same as the great, the skillful along with the apprentice.
9 The first lot fell to Asaph—to Joseph: he and his brothers and his sons—12;
the second (to) Gedaliah: he and his brothers and his sons—12;
10 the third, Zakkur: his sons and his brothers—12;
11 the fourth, Izri: his sons and his brothers—12;
12 the fifth, Nethaniah: his sons and his brothers—12;
13 the sixth, Buqqiah: his sons and his brothers—12;
14 the seventh, Jesarelah: his sons and his brothers—12;
15 the eighth, Jeshaiah: his sons and his brothers—12;
16 the ninth, Mattaniah: his sons and his brothers—12;
17 the tenth, Shimei: his sons and his brothers—12;
18 the eleventh, Uzziel: his sons and his brothers—12;
19 the twelfth, Ḥashabiah: his sons and his brothers—12;
20 the thirteenth, Shubael: his sons and his brothers—12;
21 the fourteenth, Mattithiah: his sons and his brothers—12;
22 the fifteenth, Jerimoth: his sons and his brothers—12;
23 the sixteenth, Ḥananiah: his sons and his brothers—12;
24 the seventeenth, Joshbeqashah: his sons and his brothers—12;
25 the eighteenth, Ḥanani: his sons and his brothers—12;
26 the nineteenth, Mallothi: his sons and his brothers—12;
27 the twentieth, Eliathah: his sons and his brothers—12;
28 the twenty-first, Hothir: his sons and his brothers—12;
29 the twenty-second, Giddalti: his sons and his brothers—12;
30 the twenty-third, Maḥazioth: his sons and his brothers—12;
31 the twenty-fourth, Romamti-ezer: his sons and his brothers—12.

The Levitical Gatekeepers

26:1 As for the divisions of the gatekeepers: belonging to the Qoraḥites: Meshelemiah son of Qore, of the sons of Abiasaph. 2 Meshelemiah's sons were
Zechariah the firstborn, Jediael the second, Zebadiah the third, Jathniel the
fourth, 3 Elam the fifth, Jehoḥanan the sixth, Elioenai the seventh; 4 belonging to
the sons of Obed-edom: Shemaiah the firstborn, Jehozabad, Joaḥ, Sakar, Nethanael, 5 Ammiel, Issachar, Peullethai—for God blessed him. 6 To his son She-

maiah were born sons who ruled their ancestral house because they were valiant warriors. 7 The sons of Shemaiah: Othni, Rephael, Obed, Elzabad; and his kinsmen, warriors, Elihu and Semachiah. 8 All of these were among the descendants of Obed-edom; they, their sons, and their kinsmen were warriorlike in strength for the service—62 belonging to Obed-edom. 9 Meshelemiah had sons and brothers, warriors—18. 10 Ḥosah of the sons of Merari had sons: Shimri was the head (even though he was not the firstborn, his father appointed him as head), 11 Ḥilqiah the second, Ṭebaliah the third, Zechariah the fourth. All the sons and brothers of Ḥosah—13. 12 These were the divisions of the gatekeepers by head warriors (with) duties corresponding to those of their kinsmen to serve at the House of Yhwh.

The Casting of Lots for Guard Duty

26:13 And they cast lots by ancestral houses, small and great alike, gate by gate. 14 The lot for the east (gate) fell for Shelemiah. Now Zechariah his son was an insightful counselor. When they cast lots for him, his lot came out to be the north (gate). 15 For Obed-edom, the south (gate), and for his sons, the storehouses; 16 and for Ḥosah, the west (gate), the chamber gate by the ascending road, watch corresponding to watch. 17 At the east there were six daily; at the north, four daily; at the south, four daily; and at the storehouses, two; 18 at the west, four; at the road, two; at the colonnade, two. 19 These were the divisions of the gatekeepers pertaining to the sons of the Qoraḥites and the sons of the Merarites.

The Levitical Supervisors

26:20 And the Levites, their kinsmen, were in charge of the treasuries of the House of God and the treasuries of the dedicated gifts. 21 The sons of Laadan the Gershonite. Belonging to Laadan the Gershonite: Jeḥiel. 22 The sons of Jeḥiel, Zetham and Joel, were in charge of the treasuries of the House of Yhwh. 23 Belonging to the Amramites, the Izharites, the Ḥebronites, the Uzzielites: 24 Shubael, a descendant of Gershom the son of Moses, was commander over the treasuries. 25 And his kinsmen, belonging to Eliezer: his son Reḥabiah, his son Jeshaiah, his son Joram, his son Zichri, and his son Shelomoth. 26 This Shelomoth and his brothers were in charge of the treasuries of all the dedicated gifts that King David, the clan chiefs, the officers of the thousands and of the hundreds, and the officers of the army dedicated. 27 That which they took from the war spoils they dedicated to strengthen the House of Yhwh. 28 All that Samuel the seer dedicated, as well as Saul son of Qish, and Abner son of Ner, and Joab son of Zeruiah—everything that someone dedicated was under the charge of Shelomoth and his brothers.

29 Belonging to the Izharites: Chenaniah and his sons were responsible for the outlying work with respect to Israel as officials and judges. 30 Belonging to the Ḥebronites: Ḥashabiah and his kinsmen, warriors, 1,700 in charge of the supervision

of Israel beyond the Jordan westward for all matters of Yhwh and for the service of
the king. 31 Of the Ḥebronites, Jeriah was the head of the Ḥebronites. The genealogical lines of his ancestors were sought out in the fortieth year of the reign of
David and among them were found valiant warriors in Jaazer of Gilead. 32 As for
his kinsmen, warriors, 2,700 ancestral heads, King David appointed them to be in
charge of the Reubenites, the Gadites, and the half-tribe of Manassites, for every
matter of God and for (every) matter of the king.

Military Officers Appointed for Each Month in the Calendar

27:1 The sons of Israel by their census: the ancestral heads, the officers of thousands and of the hundreds, and the officials—those serving the king for every matter of the rotating divisions, month by month throughout all of the months of the year. Each division had 24,000.

2 In charge of the first division for the first month: Jashobeam son of Zabdiel
3 from the sons of Perez and the head of all of the army officers for the first month. [2 His division had 24,000.]

4 In charge of the division of the second month: Dodai the Aḥoḥite. His division had 24,000.

5 The third army officer for the third month: Benaiah son of the chief priest Jehoiada. His division had 24,000. 6 That one, Benaiah, was a warrior of the Thirty and in command of the Thirty. His son Ammizabad was in command of his division.

7 The fourth for the fourth month: Asah-el brother of Joab, and after him Zebadiah his son. His division had 24,000.

8 The fifth for the fifth month: the officer Shammoth the Zeraḥite. His division had 24,000.

9 The sixth for the sixth month: Ira son of Iqqesh the Teqoaite. His division had 24,000.

10 The seventh for the seventh month: Ḥelez the Pelonite, of the sons of Ephraim. His division had 24,000.

11 The eighth for the eighth month: Sibbekai the Ḥushathite, of the Zeraḥites. His division had 24,000.

12 The ninth for the ninth month: Abiezer the Anathothite, of the Benjaminites. His division had 24,000.

13 The tenth for the tenth month: Mahrai the Neṭophathite, of the Zeraḥites. His division had 24,000.

14 The eleventh for the eleventh month: Benaiah the Pirathonite, from the sons of Ephraim. His division had 24,000.

15 The twelfth for the twelfth month: Ḥeldai the Neṭophathite, of Othniel. His division had 24,000.

Thirteen Tribal Officers

27:16 In charge of the tribes of Israel:
for the Reubenites: the commander was Eliezer son of Zichri;
for the Simeonites: Shephaṭiah son of Maacah;
17 for the Levites: Ḥashabiah son of Qemuel;
for Aaron: Zadoq;
18 for Judah: Eliab, of the brothers of David;
for Issachar: Omri son of Michael;
19 for Zebulun: Ishmaiah son of Obadiah;
for Naphtali: Jerimoth son of Azriel;
20 for the sons of Ephraim: Hoshea son of Azaziah;
for the half-tribe of Manasseh: Joel son of Pedaiah;
21 for the half-tribe of Manasseh in Gilead: Iddo son of Zechariah;
for Benjamin: Jaasiel son of Abner;
22 for Dan: Azarel son of Jeroḥam.

These were the officers of the tribes of Israel. 23 But David did not take a census
of those less than twenty years of age, because God had promised to make Israel as
numerous as the stars of the heavens. 24 Joab son of Zeruiah began to number
(them), but he did not finish. Wrath came upon Israel on account of this and the
census was not entered into the book of the chronicles of King David.

Royal Overseers and Civil Servants

27:25 In charge of the royal storehouses: Azmaveth son of Adiel;
in charge of the storehouses in the country—in the towns, villages, and towers:
Jonathan son of Uzziah;
26 in charge of the country laborers in agricultural work: Ezri son of Chelub;
27 in charge of the vineyards: Shimei the Ramathite;
for the wine cellars: Zabdi the Shiphmite;
28 in charge of the olive trees and the sycamores in the Shephelah: Baal-ḥanan
the Gederite;
in charge of the storehouses of oil: Joash;
29 in charge of the cattle pasturing in the Sharon: Shiṭrai the Sharonite;
in charge of the cattle in the valleys: Shephaṭ son of Adlai;
30 in charge of the camels: Obil the Ishmaelite;
in charge of the she-asses: Jeḥdeiah the Meronothite;
31 in charge of the flocks: Jaziz the Hagrite.
All of these were officers of King David's property.

Royal Advisors and Adjutants

27:32 Jonathan, David's uncle, was a counselor, a man of understanding and
a scribe. He, along with Jeḥiel the Ḥachmonite, was with the king's sons.

[33]Aḥithophel was counselor to the king. Ḥushai the Archite was the friend of the king. [34]And after Aḥithophel was Jehoiada son of Benaiah, counselor to the king, and his priest was Abiathar. The leader of the king's army was Joab.

David Charges the National Assembly and Solomon

[28:1]David assembled all of Israel's officers—the tribal officers, the officers of the divisions, those serving the king, the officers of the thousands, the officers of the hundreds, and the officers in charge of all the property and livestock for the king and for his sons—along with the eunuchs, warriors, and every valiant warrior to Jerusalem.

[2]Then King David rose to his feet and said:

"Hear me, my kinsmen and my people. I myself had it in mind to build a house of rest for the Ark of the Covenant of Yhwh and for the footstool of the feet of our God. So I set out to build. [3]But God said to me, 'You will not build a house for my name, because you are a man of wars and have shed blood.' [4]And Yhwh the God of Israel chose me out of all of the house of my father to become king over Israel forever. Indeed, he chose Judah as leader, and within the house of Judah (he chose) the house of my father, and among the sons of my father he has been pleased with me to make (me) king over all Israel. [5]And from all of my sons—for Yhwh has granted me many sons—he has chosen my son Solomon to sit upon the throne of the kingdom of Yhwh over Israel. [6]So he said to me, 'Solomon your son, he, he will build my house and my courts, for I have chosen him to be a son to me and I, I shall be a father to him. [7]And I shall establish his kingdom forever, if he is resolute to perform my commandments and judgments as is the case today.' [8]Now, in the sight of all of the assembly of Yhwh, and in the hearing of our God, observe and seek out the commandments of Yhwh your God so that you may possess the good land and bequeath it to your children forever after you."

[9]"As for you, Solomon my son, know the God of your father and serve him with a whole heart and a willing soul, for Yhwh searches every heart and understands every form of thought. If you seek him, he will let himself be found by you; but, if you abandon him, he will reject you in perpetuity. [10]Now, take note that Yhwh has chosen you to build for him a house as the sanctuary. Be strong and act."

The Temple Plans Are Handed Over to Solomon

[28:11]Then David gave to Solomon his son the plan for the entrance hall (of the Temple) and its buildings, its storerooms, its upper chambers, its rooms, its inner chambers, and the house of the (ark) cover; [12]and the plan for all that he had by the spirit: for the courts of the House of Yhwh and for all of the surrounding chambers, for the treasuries of the House of God and the treasuries of the dedicated gifts, [13]for the divisions of the priests and the Levites, for every work of the service

of the House of Yhwh, and for all of the furnishings of the service of the House of Yhwh; [14]for all kinds of golden furnishings, by weight, for furnishings of every sort of service; for all kinds of silver furnishings, by weight, for all furnishings of every sort of service; [15]and (for) the weight for the golden lampstands and their golden lamps, by the weight of each lampstand and its lamps; and for the silver lampstands, by weight, for each lampstand and its lamps, according to the service of each lampstand; [16]and the gold, by weight, for the tables of the row bread, for each table; and (for) the silver, by weight, for the silver tables; [17]and (for) the flesh hooks, the basins, and the jars of pure gold; for the golden bowls, by weight, for each bowl; and for the silver bowls, by weight, for each bowl; [18]and for the altar of incense, refined gold, by weight; and for the plan of the chariot—the cherubim in gold spreading out (their) wings and protecting the Ark of the Covenant of Yhwh.
[19]"Everything in writing (has come) to me from the hand of Yhwh. He made (me) understand all the pieces of the plan."

Concluding Invocation Delivered to Solomon

[28:20]Then David said to Solomon his son:

"Be strong, be courageous, and act. Neither fear nor be dismayed, for Yhwh my God is with you. He will neither fail you nor abandon you until every work of the service of the House of Yhwh is completed. [21]Here are the divisions of the priests and the Levites for every kind of service for the House of Yhwh. And with you in all of the work will be all sorts of volunteers, with skill for every kind of service. The officers and all of the people are at your every command."

David Rallies the National Assembly before his Death

[29:1]And King David said to all of the assembly,

"My son Solomon, (the) one whom God chose, is an inexperienced youth and the work is great because the citadel is not for man, but for Yhwh God.
[2]Commensurate with all of my ability, I have set aside for the House of my God gold for all kinds of gold objects, silver for all kinds of silver objects, bronze for all kinds of bronze objects, iron for all kinds of iron objects, and wood for all kinds of wooden objects; onyx stones, stones for setting, stones of antimony, colorful stones, every kind of precious stone, and marble in abundance.
[3]Moreover, in my solicitude for the House of my God, I have my own private possession of gold and silver that I have dedicated to the House of my God, above and beyond all that I set aside for the Holy House:
[4]3,000 talents of gold, of the gold from Ophir, 7,000 talents of silver, refined for overlaying the walls of the rooms,
[5]for all kinds of gold objects, for all kinds of silver objects, and for all of the work to be done by the artisans. Who, then, who is going to make a freewill offering to consecrate himself this day to Yhwh?"

[6]Then the officers of the ancestral houses, the officers of the Israelite tribes, the

officers of the thousands and of the hundreds, and the officers of the royal work made freewill offerings. [7]They donated to the service of the House of God 5,000 talents of gold, 10,000 darics, 10,000 talents of silver, 18,000 talents of bronze, and 100,000 talents of iron. [8]Whoever had (precious) stones donated them to the treasury of the House of Yhwh under the care of Jeḥiel the Gershonite. [9]And the people rejoiced about their voluntary giving, because they made freewill offerings to Yhwh with a whole heart. And King David also rejoiced greatly.

The Blessing of David

29:10 Then King David blessed Yhwh in the presence of all the assembly. And David said,

"Blessed are you, O Yhwh,
God of our ancestor Israel,
from eternity to eternity.
11 To you, O Yhwh, are the greatness and the power,
the distinction, the glory, and the majesty,
indeed, all that is in the heavens and on the earth.
To you, O Yhwh, belong the kingship
and the exaltation over everything as head.
12 Riches and honor come from before you,
and you rule over everything;
in your hand are strength and power,
and it is in your hand to magnify and to strengthen all.
13 And now, our God, we give thanks to you,
and we praise your glorious name.
14 Indeed, who am I
and who are my people
that we should have the means
to make a freewill offering such as this?
For everything is from you,
and from your hand have we given back to you.
15 Indeed, we are resident aliens before you,
and transients as all of our ancestors were;
like a shadow are our days upon the earth,
and there is no hope.

16 "O Yhwh, our God, all this abundance, which we have set aside to build
you a house for your holy name, stems from your hand, and to you it all belongs.
17 I know, my God, that you test the heart and desire justice. As for me,
with a just heart I have freely offered all these things. Now, your people, those
who are present here, I have seen joyfully make a freewill offering to you.
18 O Yhwh, God of Abraham, Isaac, and Israel our ancestors, keep such forms
of thought in the mind of your people forever and direct their hearts toward
you.
19 And grant to Solomon my son a whole heart to keep your command-

ments, your decrees, and your statutes, to practice all (of them) and to build
the citadel that I have prepared."

The Enthronement of Solomon

29:20 Then David said to all of the assembly, "Bless Yhwh your God." Then all of
the assembly blessed Yhwh the God of their ancestors, bowed down and worshiped before Yhwh and before the king, 21 and sacrificed sacrifices to Yhwh. And
they offered up burnt offerings to Yhwh the very next day—1,000 bulls, 1,000
rams, 1,000 lambs, and their libations—sacrifices in abundance for all Israel.
22 They ate and they drank before Yhwh on that day with great joy, and they made
Solomon son of David king. They anointed him before Yhwh as ruler and Zadoq
as priest. 23 Then Solomon sat on the throne of Yhwh as king instead of David his
father. He prospered, and all Israel paid heed to him. 24 The officers, the warriors,
and the sons of King David lent their hand in support of Solomon the king. 25 And
Yhwh made Solomon exceedingly great in the sight of all Israel and endowed him
with a regal majesty that no king over Israel before him ever had.

Summary of David's Reign

29:26 So David son of Jesse ruled over all Israel. 27 And the time which he ruled over
Israel was forty years, in Ḥebron seven years and in Jerusalem thirty-three. 28 He
died at a ripe old age, full of days, riches, and honor and Solomon his son reigned
in his stead. 29 The acts of King David, former and latter, are written in the records
of Samuel the seer, in the records of Nathan the prophet, and in the records of
Gad the visionary, 30 together with (the accounts) of all his kingship, his power,
and the events that befell him, Israel, and all the kingdoms of the lands.

INTRODUCTION

I. Titles

◆

> The seventh book [of the Writings] is Dabreiamin, that is "Words of the days," which we are able to call more specifically a chronicle (χρονικόν) of all divine history; this book is entitled among us *Paralipomenon* One and Two. (St. Jerome, from the preface to his translation of Samuel–Kings [Fischer 1984: 365])

Like many other works from the ancient Near East, the book known to us as Chronicles was originally untitled and anonymously authored. The various titles given to the book by early interpreters provide fascinating glimpses into how the ancients viewed this work. In the Hebrew (rabbinic) tradition, cited by St. Jerome, the book is called "the book of the events [literally: words] of the days" *(sēper dibrê hayyāmîm)*.[1] It is uncertain when the work acquired this title. This title is also found in the Peshiṭta (Bacher 1895: 306). In ascribing the name *sēper dibrê hayyāmîm* to Chronicles, the early interpreters were probably influenced by biblical tradition itself. The authors of Kings occasionally cite lost works entitled "the book of the events of the days of the kings of Israel" (*sēper dibrê hayyāmîm lĕmalkê yiśrā'ēl*; e.g., 1 Kgs 14:19) and "the book of the events of the days of the kings of Judah" (*sēper dibrê hayyāmîm lĕmalkê yĕhûdâ*; e.g., 1 Kgs 14:29; 15:7, 23). Similar names appear in Esther: "the book of the events of the days of the kings of Media and Persia" (*sēper dibrê hayyāmîm lĕmalkê māday ûpārās*; 10:2) and "the book of the records, the events of the days" (*sēper hazzikrōnôt dibrê hayyāmîm*; 6:1). In one case, the book of Chronicles refers to "the book of the events of the days of King David" (*sēper dibrê hayyāmîm lammelek dāwîd*; 1 Chr 27:24). There is no scholarly consensus about the nature of such lost works. Some think of royal annals, the official records of a given king's reign (e.g., Montgomery 1951: 43–44; Jepsen 1956: 54–60; Mettinger 1971: 38–40), while others think of historiographical works or surveys that may have been based, in part, on official records or annals.[2]

One should also call attention to an unparalleled reference in 1 Esdras to "the

---

[1] See, for example, *m. Yoma* 1:6; *b. Meg.* 13a; *b. B. Bat.* 14b–15a; and *Midr. Exod.* 38:5; *Midr. Lev.* 1:3; *Midr. Ruth* 2:1.

[2] E.g., Noth (1957: 66–67, 72–75; 1968: 327); Eissfeldt (1965: 49); Van Seters (1983: 292–302); Cogan (1999: 78–83; Haran (1999: 162). Haran (1999: 156–57) provides a useful survey.

book of the histories concerning the kings of Judah" (*tē bibliō tōn historoumenōn peri tōn basileōn tēs Ioudaias;* 1 Esd 1:31 [ET 1:33]). As van der Kooij (1998: 108–9) points out, the author is referring his readers to material relating to the circumstances of King Josiah's death, including the laments of Jeremiah for Josiah, that are found in Chronicles (not in Kings). Later in the same verse, when the author refers his readers to other actions of the king, he includes a reference to "the book of the kings of Israel and Judah" (*tō bibliō tōn basileōn Israēl kai Iouda;* 1 Esd 1:31 [ET 1:33]). This latter reference is also found at the end of the Chronicler's narration of Josiah's reign, "the book of the kings of Israel and Judah" (ספר מלכי־ישׂראל ויהודה; MT 2 Chr 35:27) and in the translation of LXX 2 Chr 35:27, "the book of the kings of Israel and Judah" *(bibliō basileōn Israēl kai Iouda).* The suggestion that the first reference in 1 Esd 1:31 (to "the book of the histories concerning the kings of Judah") is to Chronicles has merit, because Chronicles, unlike Kings, focuses attention upon the southern Judahite monarchy and not upon the northern Israelite monarchy. One cannot eliminate the possibility, of course, that the notation pertains to some lost historiographical writing assumed by the author. Nevertheless, the wording of the reference seems to be carefully chosen. In their source citations, the authors of Kings regularly speak of "the book of the kings of Israel" (2 Kgs 1:18; 10:34; 13:8, 12; 14:15, 28; 15:11, 15, 21, 31) and of "the book of the kings of Judah" (2 Kgs 8:23; 12:20; 14:18; 15:6, 36; 16:19; 20:20; 21:17, 25; 23:28; 24:5). But the situation in Chronicles is different. The authors of Chronicles speak of "the book of the kings of Judah and Israel" (2 Chr 16:11; 24:27; 25:26; 28:26; 32:32) and of "the book of the kings of Israel and Judah" (2 Chr 27:7; 35:27; 36:8). In one case a reference is made to "the book of the kings of Israel" (2 Chr 20:34; TEXTUAL NOTE to 9:1). A source reference to "the book of the kings of Judah" does not appear, to my knowledge, anywhere in Chronicles. In other words, the author of 1 Esdras is not copying formulaic language from a source citation found somewhere else in Chronicles. If the reference in 1 Esd 1:31 is to the book of Chronicles, specifically the Chronicler's account of the Judahite monarchy, the source citation anticipates the titles given to Chronicles in Codex Alexandrinus of the LXX and in the Peshiṭta (see below).

Aside from works whose titles resemble that given to the book of Chronicles, there are works that refer to its precise name. Both Esth 2:23 and Neh 12:23 mention "the book of the events of the days" *(sēper dibrê hayyāmîm).* Whether the citation in Nehemiah refers to the biblical book of Chronicles is highly disputed. The Rabbis may have thought so, given the context in Nehemiah (referring to the registration of the Levites—a typical theme in Chronicles), but most modern commentators understand "the book of the events of the days" to refer to an otherwise lost historiographical or chronographic work.[3] It is interesting to observe that by the time of the Neo-Babylonian period, historical writings were being composed (e.g., the Babylonian Chronicle series) that drew upon a variety of sources, such as king lists and memorial inscriptions. In the late Persian or early Hellenistic period, works such as "the book of the records, the events of the days"

[3] In this respect, Cross (1975: 8) is an exception in thinking the title does refer to Chronicles.

(Esth 6:1) and "the book of the records" (*sĕpar dokrānayyā'*; Ezra 4:15) could well have been understood as historiographic works (Van Seters 1983: 292–301). The same could be true of "the book of the events of the days" *(sēper dibrê hayyāmîm)* in Neh 12:23. But whatever the precise referent for the work cited in Neh 12:23, the title *sēper dibrê hayyāmîm* is itself significant, indicating that Chronicles is a book dealing in some fashion with the past.

There is another title associated with Chronicles in the Babylonian Talmud: "the book of the genealogies" (*sēper yôḥāsîn*; *b. Pesaḥ.* 62b). This nomenclature may refer, however, to a commentary on Chronicles.[4] The genealogies in Chronicles and in other biblical books were popular in Late Antiquity because the names contained within these lineages were thought to be fraught with meaning (Peltonen 1996: 18–21; Kalimi 1998a). Such names and patterns of names were interpreted symbolically, homiletically, or allegorically (e.g., *Midr. Ruth* 2:1–2). Indeed, according to one rabbinic view, the book of Chronicles was only to be interpreted midrashically (*Midr. Lev.* 1:3). In discussing the Sages' extensive comments on the Benjaminite lineages beginning with "And Azel had six sons" (1 Chr 8:38) and ending with "these were the sons of Azel" (1 Chr 9:44), Mar Zuṭra declared that they "were laden with four hundred camels of exegetical interpretations" (*b. Pesaḥ.* 62b). In this context, it is certainly relevant that *Targum Chronicles* begins with the introduction, "This is the book of the genealogies, the events of the days from antiquity." Both *Pesaḥim* 62b and the Targum thus call attention to one of the work's distinctive, and perhaps most infamous, features: Its first nine chapters consist almost entirely of genealogies.

The standard nomenclature for Chronicles in the Septuagint (LXX), *Paraleipomena* (τὰ Παραλειπόμενα), "the things left out," testifies to another early understanding of the work. Chronicles was written to record the events left out of earlier biblical history. In this, the LXX is followed by the Ethiopic (Grébaut 1932) and the pseudo-Athanasian treatise "Synopsis scripturae sacrae." This line of interpretation also supposes that the book was indeed written to record the events left out of earlier biblical history. Chronicles is understood to parallel, in some sense, Genesis through Kings. Bishop Theodoret of Cyrus (ca. 455 C.E.) represents this tradition, when he comments:

> The beginning of the book of *Paraleipomena* makes the subject clear. What the royal scribe [the redactor of Samuel and Kings] omitted, the author who took up this specific task set down, using many of the books of prophecy as sources. Much of what was written in those books he harmonized with these events [in 1–2 Chronicles], so that he might demonstrate historical consistency. He starts at the beginning with a genealogy, thus to show concisely how all the groups of mankind arose from one man. (Fernández Marcos and Busto Saiz 1984: 244)

The title of Chronicles in Codex Alexandrinus is more expansive: "The Things Omitted regarding the Kings of Judah." Codex Alexandrinus is followed by the

[4] *Pesaḥim* 62b speaks of this book as having been "hidden," a surprising assertion to make about the book of Chronicles itself.

Peshiṭta, which reads the title as "The Book of Chronicles, Namely the Book Remembering the Days of the Kings of Judah" (W. Barnes 1897: 1). It is interesting to observe that St. Augustine (*Doctr. chr.* 2.13.26) understood the title *Paraleipomena* in the Septuagint similarly when he speaks of "four books of Kings and two of Chronicles, which are not consecutive to Kings, but relate events parallel to Kings." Codex Alexandrinus, St. Augustine, and the Peshiṭta thus evince another distinctive feature of Chronicles. In depicting the era of the dual monarchies, the Chronicler, unlike the Deuteronomist (the author of Joshua through 2 Kings), concentrates his attention on Judah. The work does not relate any of the internal events occurring in the northern realm unless those events somehow impinge upon events in the southern realm. In concentrating on Judah, Chronicles presents many incidents not found in Kings. By employing these descriptive titles, the LXX translators, followed by Theodoret, St. Augustine, the Peshiṭta, and others, attempt to explain the existence of two parallel literary works—Genesis through Kings (or simply just Kings) and Chronicles. What the former omits, the latter supplies.

The stance of the LXX fails to do justice, however, to another aspect of the Chronicler's work: his rewriting of earlier biblical works (VII.A below). In addition to providing information not included in previous biblical books, Chronicles rearranges, reworks, and comments on select portions of these works. This may help to explain why St. Jerome provides an alternate designation to that of the LXX. Unfortunately, Jerome's comment about *Paraleipomena* as a "chronicle" has not been generally well understood. Jerome recognized that "the book of the events of the days" manifested both synoptic and nonsynoptic features. The synoptic portions of Chronicles sometimes abbreviate or excerpt earlier biblical texts.[5] The work provides a continuous register of people and events, without either a considered statement of authorial purpose or great ornamental embellishment. While the Hexateuch depicts cycles, lawgiving, peregrinations, and conquests, Chronicles contains only lineages and anecdotes. Some of the genealogies are excerpted from earlier biblical sources, while others are not. The book lacks the graphic tales of David's private life found in Samuel and the many prophetic legends found in Kings. The narrative portions of the Chronicler's work focus, for the most part, on the public actions of monarchs residing in Jerusalem.

In speaking of "the things of the days" as a chronicle, Jerome identified the book with a certain genre of historiography known to him in his own historical context (Knoppers and Harvey 2002). Jerome's classification was undoubtedly informed by his knowledge of a contemporary work, the *Chronicle (chronicon)*, written by the church historian Eusebius, a work Jerome himself had embellished and updated.[6] Eusebius designed his chronicle to be a synchronistic summary of

---

[5] For example, 1 Chr 1:1–2:2 consists of a universal genealogy (in both linear and segmented forms), extending from the first person, Adam, to Israel and his twelve sons (2:2). Most of this material is drawn from Genesis.

[6] Eusebius's *chronicon* (χρονικὰ κανονες), which only survives in Jerome's reworked version (Helm 1956), was itself based upon earlier classical models; note especially the *Chronographies* of Julius Africanus (d. ca. 240 C.E.).

the ancient Near Eastern, Greek, Roman, and biblical past from the birth of Abraham to approximately 325 C.E., the twentieth year of Constantine's reign (J. Kelly 1975: 72–75; Mosshammer 1979). Drawing upon the earlier work of Suetonius, as well as other sources, Jerome extended this historical outline to the latter part of the fourth century (378 C.E.).[7] Considering that Chronicles begins with Adam and continues to the Babylonian Exile (586 B.C.E.) and the decree of Cyrus (538 B.C.E.), Jerome's choice of terminology was apt. His description of the book as a "chronicle of all divine history" attempts to do justice to the scope of the book's coverage. It is interesting to observe that the condensed nature of the work was also recognized by Isidore of Seville (ca. 602–36 C.E.):

> What is called *Paraleipomenon* in Greek we are able to call [the books] of omitted or remaining matters, since those things which were omitted or not fully reported in the Law or the books of Kings are in this book set out concisely and briefly. (*Origin.* 6.2.12)

Jerome's description of *Paraleipomena* also implicitly recognizes a distinction between the biblical work and that of Eusebius. Unlike the *chronica* of Eusebius and Jerome, which synchronize sacred and secular history until the time of Darius I, the biblical book summarizes divine history. The title St. Jerome gave to *sēper dibrê hayyāmîm—Chronicon*—endured, but did not prevail until more recent times (Knoppers and Harvey 2002). The work known in Hebrew tradition as "the book of the events of the days" is now known in modern translations as the book of Chronicles.

The division of Chronicles into two books, 1 and 2 Chronicles, is not original. The marginal *(Masora)* notation to 1 Chr 27:25 identifies this verse as the midpoint of the book of Chronicles. The end of 2 Chronicles (and not 1 Chronicles) contains the final Masoretic annotations. The distinction between 1 and 2 Chronicles was introduced by the translators of the LXX. As Freedman (personal communication) points out, the division into two parts may have been occasioned by the book's length. Like Samuel (24,302 words) and Kings (25,424 words), which were each partitoned into two books, Chronicles (24,058 words) is one of the longest books in the Bible.[8] Presumably with the expansion in spelling (Greek uses a full vowel system) and the expansion in words (to convey the sense of the Hebrew), it may have been convenient to divide these long Hebrew works into two. In any case, the partition the translators introduced was sensitive to the content and organization of the work. The Alexandrian translators ended the first part of Chronicles with the concluding notices to David's reign (1 Chr 29:26–30) and began the second part with the reign of Solomon, David's son and successor (2 Chronicles 1). The LXX division between 1 and 2 Chronicles eventually proved to be influential. It was maintained by other, later translations. In the fifteenth century C.E., the division of the book into two parts began to be introduced in Hebrew editions of the Bible.

---

[7] Later writers would extend, in turn, Jerome's chronicle to their own time (Knoppers and Harvey 2002).

[8] These word counts are from Dean Forbes (personal communication). They represent a slight revision of the tallies in Andersen and Forbes (1989).

II. The Relevance of Textual Criticism

◆

Fundamental to the study of any literary work, especially an ancient literary work, is the collation of manuscripts and textual traditions. When working through this commentary, readers will notice that significant attention has been given to variants among the textual witnesses. This careful consideration to textual criticism is intentional. We do not possess the original Hebrew text of any biblical book; we only have later copies. Moreover, Chronicles, like other biblical books, was also translated and transmitted in a number of other languages. In this respect, the text of Chronicles comes to us in a variety of later forms—Greek, Latin, Aramaic, Arabic, Bohairic, Ethiopic, Armenian, and Syriac. There are also multiple and varying manuscript traditions within a given version (e.g., the LXX). Hence, the collation, comparison, and evaluation of extant manuscripts and textual traditions are foundational to writing a commentary. Establishing a text is a prerequisite for the critical study of that text. The issue of textual criticism is especially acute in the case of a late work, such as Chronicles, which reuses earlier biblical writings, because the many texts the author(s) employed of those earlier books sometimes do not match the received Masoretic text of those books (III.B and C below).

A. The Impact of the Dead Sea Scrolls

Before assessing the value of each of the major versions of Chronicles, it will be useful to survey major developments in textual criticism, specifically the effect of manuscript finds in the Judean desert on how scholars view variants among the witnesses to the biblical text. In his helpful survey, Tov (1992b: 11–47, 155–63) makes a pre-1947 and a post-1947 distinction in the history of scholarship. Such a distinction recognizes the great importance of the Dead Sea Scrolls for biblical criticism. Prior to this monumental discovery, scholarship had been divided between two major perspectives on the relationship between the Hebrew and Greek witnesses to the biblical text. Much of the debate focused on the nature and history of the LXX.

As with the textual criticism of other biblical books, the study of Chronicles has been dominated by two fundamentally different approaches to the LXX. One approach, epitomized in the work of Paul Kahle (1915; 1959), treats the Greek witnesses as essentially targums or midrashes of the Hebrew Scriptures. The Hebrew text, although originally deriving from many different manuscripts and exhibiting many variants, is viewed as having stabilized well before the time of the medieval Masoretes.[9] In this influential reconstruction, the versions—the Old Greek, Old Latin, Aramaic, Syriac, Armenian, Arabic, and Ethiopic—are considered to be useful primarily for two reasons. First, they provide variant readings that illumine enigmatic or problematic Hebrew words and phrases. Second, the versions disclose the history of interpretation of biblical books. Many specialists on Chronicles have been sympathetic to Kahle's basic approach. In fact, it may not be too much of an exaggeration to say that almost all recent commentators on Chronicles share his perspective toward the versions.

The most famous proponent of the alternative approach, Paul Anton de Lagarde (1863; 1882), laid far greater stress on the contributions of the versions for textual criticism and for understanding the recensional history of biblical books. Lagarde contended that one could reconstruct archetypes of recensions in the Old Greek text from the mass of Greek witnesses. Having achieved an identification of the *Trifaria varietas* mentioned by Jerome, one could ultimately aspire to reconstructing the original Old Greek translation. From there one could make meaningful comparisions with the MT. For those who have subscribed to Lagarde's theory, the LXX is important not simply because it occasionally supplies alternate readings to the MT and provides information about the history of exegesis but also because it provides evidence for Hebrew (and Aramaic) biblical texts that differ from those preserved in the MT.

The study of the biblical manuscripts from Qumran—in particular 4QExod[B], 4QpalaeoExod[m] (Sanderson 1986), 4QNum[b] (Jastram 1992), 4QJosh[a] (Ulrich 1994; 1995), 4QJudg[a] (Trebolle Barrera 1992b; 1995), 4QSam[a] (Cross 1964; Ulrich 1978), 4QSam[b], 4QSam[c] (Ulrich 1979), 4QKgs (Trebolle 1992bc; 1995), 4QXII[c] (Fuller 1992), and 4QJer[bd] (Janzen 1973; 1989; Tov 1976)—has furnished telling evidence for the validity of Lagarde's basic approach.[10] In this respect, scholars in the early twenty-first century are in a much more privileged position than their counterparts a century earlier. The manuscript finds at Qumran—the Dead Sea Scrolls—have furnished scholars with unprecedented insight into the development of the biblical text in the last centuries B.C.E. and the first centuries C.E.[11] To be sure, the picture is more complicated than Lagarde envisioned because of the different text types represented in the rabbinic selection of biblical manuscripts. It is now evident that at least some of the oldest Greek texts for certain biblical books were translated from a Hebrew text that differed from the

[9] There are some notable exceptions. Those scholars who have charted significant growth within the proto-rabbinic text include Mulder (1988: 87–135), Orlinsky (1941; 1974: 363–81), Rofé (1982; 1985; 1990; 1997); Talmon (1954; 1961; 1970; 1975), and Tov (1992b: 22–79).

[10] Tov's recent work (1987; 1992a; 1997) emphasizes the pluriformity and diversity of witnesses to the biblical text. The many variations among manuscripts may not tell against basic text types (Ulrich 1984: 613–36; 1999), but they do significantly complicate the text-types theory.

[11] Albright (1955); Chiesa (1992); Cross (1964; 1966b; 1972; 1979a; 1992); Jellicoe (1973: xxi–liv); Tov (1978a; 1992b); Trebolle Barrera (1980); Ulrich (1978; 1984; 1989a; 1992a; 1999).

textual base of the later rabbinic recension. Analysis of a number of the Qumran biblical manuscripts has also supported the view that the Old Greek underwent a series of recensions to bring it into closer conformity with a parallel development in the Hebrew text.

Unfortunately, the Qumran discoveries did not include multiple copies of Chronicles. Only one fragmentary text of the book was found among the Dead Sea Scrolls. This fragment from Cave 4 (4QChr) has recently been published by Trebolle Barrera (2000). It pertains to 2 Chr 28:27–29:3 and contains only eleven completely legible words. The text supplies a few variants to the MT and at least one variant to both the MT and the LXX of Chronicles and Kings (TEXTUAL NOTES to 2 Chr 28–29). The discoveries pertaining to the text of Ezra were a little more extensive. Fragments of Ezra 4:2–6, 9–12, and 5:17–6:5 were found in Cave 4 (4QEzra). In a preliminary publication of these fragments, Ulrich (1992b) demonstrates that their readings are very close to the MT. There are few variants between these texts and their canonical counterparts. Despite the paucity of manuscript finds at Qumran directly relating to the texts of Chronicles and Ezra, the larger insights afforded by the Dead Sea Scrolls into the history of the biblical text provide scholars with more precise tools in dealing with the array of variants that were already known to exist in the Greek, Hebrew, and Latin witnesses of Chronicles. By analyzing new manuscripts, reanalyzing old manuscripts, and recognizing the existence of distinct textual traditions, textual critics are considerably aided in their primary tasks of recension *(recensio)*, examination *(examinatio)*, and emendation *(emendatio)*.[12]

The study of the Dead Sea Scrolls has ramifications that go far beyond the discipline of textual criticism. Many biblical critics have traditionally distinguished between two different kinds of biblical study: higher criticism and lower criticism. Higher criticism has included historical study, redaction criticism, source criticism, and form criticism, among others. In contrast with these complex and necessarily speculative attempts to reconstruct the development of a text along with its historical and literary contexts, lower criticism has simply denoted textual criticism—the attempt to recover a biblical text as close as possible to the original autographs. The major assumption of many textual critics that variations among the Hebrew and the versions were to be explained simply by changes in the transmission of an established text—inadvertent copyist errors, paraphrase, carelessness, assimilation, inexactness in translation, theological emendations—has now been called into question. Variations among the witnesses to a given book could also reflect different stages in the book's composition.

With the realization that the textual witnesses provide significant evidence for the development of the biblical text itself, the categories of higher criticism and lower criticism have become blurred, if not obsolete. Firm and fixed boundaries between the work of authors, editors, and scribes are sometimes difficult to discern (A. Brooke 1992). The shorter (LXX, 4QJer^{bd}) and longer (MT, 2QJer, 4QJer^{ac}) texts of Jeremiah provide, for instance, important clues to the redactional history

[12] On the principles involved in textual criticism, see the convenient studies by Ralph Klein (1974), McCarter (1986), Tov (1992b), and Albrektson (1994).

of this book (Janzen 1973: 127–35; 1989; Goldman 1992; Tov 1992b: 319–27). Many of the variants between the longer and shorter Jeremiahs do not constitute sporadic or tendentious alterations of a standard and fixed text, but form genuine witnesses in their own right to different textual traditions in the history of the book of Jeremiah. The shorter readings of the LXX and 4QJer[bd] reflect an earlier stage in the process of editing and redacting the biblical text than is reflected in either the received rabbinic text (the MT) or the other Jeremiah fragments (2QJer; 4QJer[a]) from Qumran.

Study of the Dead Sea Scrolls and of the LXX has provided scholars with another perspective on the history of biblical texts. The diversity of readings within a given manuscript tradition of a particular book may clarify the history of the composition of that text. The MT and the LXX of Daniel, for example, may belong to the same textual tradition but manifest some important variants, especially in Daniel 4–6. In Daniel 4 and 6 the MT is considerably shorter than the LXX, but in Daniel 5 the LXX is considerably shorter than the MT. In this case, the most compelling explanation of the variants between the MT and the LXX is that each version has incorporated its own set of secondary readings.[13] In other words, the MT and the LXX have each expanded an earlier common edition of Daniel in two different directions (Ulrich 1992a: 283–91). Hence, the discrepancies between textual witnesses testify to secondary developments within both textual traditions. In different ways Jeremiah and Daniel both furnish empirical proof for growth within biblical books in the centuries before the Common Era. Or to put it differently, one must contend with a plurality of biblical texts before the Common Era.

B. THE VARIOUS WITNESSES TO THE TEXT OF CHRONICLES

It may be appropriate to begin with a discussion of the versions and their value for reconstructing the text of Chronicles. A later section (III) will deal with how study of the witnesses (the versions and certain manuscripts from Qumran) to other biblical texts can shed light on synoptic texts in Chronicles. Over the course of the past century, text-critical studies have clarified many features of the versions of Chronicles. Nevertheless, much work remains to be done; comprehensive critical editions of *Paraleipomena* (the Greek Chronicles), the Syriac Peshiṭta, the Armenian, and other versions of Chronicles have either not been executed or are not yet available. Some available editions are more reliable than others.[14] Basic infor-

---

[13] The Qumran fragments of Daniel from Cave 4—4QDan[abcde]—belong to the same general textual tradition as the MT (Ulrich 1987; 1989b). The same could be said for the scrolls from Cave 1—1QDan[ab]—and the scroll from Cave 6—pap6QDan—(Hartman and Di Lella 1978: 72–73; Collins 1993: 2–3). 1QDan[b] and 4QDan[d] do not contain the prayers that are found in the other versions of Daniel 3.

[14] Hanhart's edition of 1 Esdras (1974) is, for instance, first-rate. The publication of the Brooke-McLean-Thackeray apparatus (1932) for Chronicles was a major advance, but is limited and contains numerous mistakes. There is an edition of the Ethiopic Chronicles by Grébaut (1932), but it must be used cautiously.

mation about the specific contributions that some of the versions could make to our understanding of Chronicles is therefore incomplete. Some progress has been made, however, in elucidating the nature and date of the two LXX translations of Chronicles. Since the LXX is generally thought to be the most important witness to the text of Chronicles, aside from the MT itself, it may be helpful to begin by discussing the two forms of Chronicles in the LXX—the Greek Chronicles and the book of 1 Esdras (*Esdras* α). The nature and value of the other versions will then be briefly addressed.

The apocryphal work of 1 Esdras contains 2 Chr 35:1–36:23, Ezra (including 1:21–22 and 3:1–5:6), and Neh 7:73–8:12 in continuous fashion. Except for a fragment at its close, 1 Esdras completes the Ezra narrative found in Neh 8:13–18. The ancient Jewish historian Josephus (*Ant.* 11.1–158) follows the order of 1 Esdras through Nehemiah 8 (including the celebration of *Sukkôt*, the Feast of Tabernacles), thereby bearing witness to the use of 1 Esdras in antiquity. The other translation of Chronicles, the Greek Chronicles or *Paraleipomena*, largely follows the sequence and content of the Hebrew, though it lacks (in Codex Vaticanus: Uncial B) 1 Chr 1:11–16, 17b–24a, 27b (TEXTUAL NOTES). LXX Chronicles also contains a number of additions, clustered near its end (2 *Paraleipomenon* 35:19a-d; 36:2a-c, 5a-d).[15] These additions differ from MT Chronicles and only resemble LXX Chronicles in part. Scholars dispute whether these additions were in the translator's Hebrew *Vorlage* (R. W. Klein 1967; 1968) or were taken from a Lucianic witness to the Greek book of Reigns (Allen 1968; 1974a: 214–17). In any case, the additions, like those to the book of Daniel, provide evidence of secondary developments within a single textual tradition.

The two major Greek translations differ in style. Whereas 1 Esdras is written in elegant and idiomatic Greek, the LXX^B of Chronicles, Ezra, and Nehemiah is a literal translation, written in nonidiomatic Greek (Torrey 1910: 11–36, 82–87; Attridge 1984; Z. Talshir 1999). This extremely literal translation, when retroverted into Hebrew, is often close to the MT. Scholars have long debated the relationships between the two Greek versions to the MT and to each other.[16] There are basically three positions. Some scholars believe that 1 Esdras represents the oldest and most reliable translation of Chronicles, Ezra, and Nehemiah. Howorth (1893b: 13–14) suggests, for instance, that 1 Esdras represents the true (Alexandrine) LXX. Thackeray (1909: 13) largely agrees: 1 Esdras is "the first attempt to present the story of the Return in a Greek dress." For these commentators, 1 Esdras, as a fragment of a larger work, is of primary importance for recovering the Old Greek of Chronicles, Ezra, and Nehemiah.[17]

A second group of commentators advances a markedly different assessment of 1 Esdras. Fritzsche (1851), Keil (1873), Samuel Driver (1914: 553–54), and Eissfeldt

---

[15] Ralph Klein (1967) would add 2 *Paraleipomenon* 35:20; 36:3B–4A, 4a, 5B, 5a-d, 8.

[16] Pohlmann (1970: 15–26), Myers (1974: 5–16), Böhler (1997: 1–18), and Zipora Talshir (1999: 1–6) provide convenient overviews.

[17] The works of Ralph Klein (1966), Pohlmann (1970), Cross (1975; 1998), Schenker (1991), and Böhler (1997) are more recent representatives of this general viewpoint.

(1965: 574–76) cite the free style of 1 Esdras as well as its pluses (e.g., the story of the three youths in 1 Esd 3:1–4:57) to contend that 1 Esdras is a compilation of biblical texts extracted from Chronicles, Ezra, and Nehemiah. This theory has been revived by Williamson (1977b: 12–36; 1996), Eskenazi (1986), Gardner (1986: 18–27), Blenkinsopp (1988: 70–71), van der Kooij (1991ab), Zipora Talshir (1984; 1999), and McKenzie (1999a) in new form.[18] A third group of scholars presents a modified version of the second group's view. Torrey (1896; 1906: 116–41; 1907abc; 1945: 395–410), Bayer (1911: 13–29), Walde (1913: 108–9), Bewer (1922), Tedesche (1928: 12–13), Rudolph (1949: xi–xiii), and Mowinckel (1964: 7–28) view 1 Esdras as a literary work that is itself based upon an earlier Greek version of Chronicles, Ezra, and Nehemiah. This theory assumes the existence of an earlier Greek translation, the *Vorlage* of 1 Esdras, which is otherwise lost (Jellicoe 1968: 291).

A commentary on Chronicles is not the proper place to try to settle all of the highly complicated issues involved with the composition of 1 Esdras. It may be useful, however, to make some observations about the contours of the current debate. First, viewing 1 Esdras simply as a compilation (or as a rewritten Bible) is unsatisfactory, because its contents cannot all be derived from Chronicles, Ezra, and Nehemiah. The story of the three youths and the return to Jerusalem (1 Esd 3:1–5:6), a major feature of the work, is unparalleled in Chronicles, Ezra, and Nehemiah.[19] To sustain the theory, proponents have to acknowledge that the author drew material from Chronicles, Ezra, and Nehemiah, rearranged some sections, rewrote others, and added a significant amount of new material.

Second, both MT Ezra-Nehemiah and 1 Esdras show signs of secondary development.[20] Like MT and LXX Ezra-Nehemiah, 1 Esdras is characterized by a number of pluses and conflations.[21] Like MT (and LXX) Ezra, 1 Esdras exhibits some disorder in its sequence of pericopes.[22] Both 1 Esdras and Chronicles-Ezra-Nehemiah, as they stand, are developed collocations. In its order of pericopes and in its content, 1 Esdras differs more often than one might initially suppose from

---

[18] Eskenazi contends, however, that 1 Esdras was written by a member of the Chronistic school. McKenzie's earlier work (1985) defended the fragmentary hypothesis.

[19] There is, however, considerable debate about whether this story is an original part of 1 Esdras. Some believe that it is (In der Smitten 1972; Talshir and Talshir 1992; Z. Talshir 1999). Others have argued that the tale of the three youths is a secondary insertion (Pohlmann 1970; Cross 1975; 1998; Böhler 1997).

[20] Scholars have long noticed that the text of Ezra-Nehemiah exhibits some disorder, both in its sequence of pericopes and in some of its readings, which make Ezra and Nehemiah contemporaries. For the editors of Ezra-Nehemiah, there may have been theological advantages to making these two leaders contemporaneous (Clines 1984; Williamson 1985: xlviii–lii; Eskenazi 1988ab). Nevertheless, most scholars do not think that Ezra and Nehemiah were contemporary leaders in Jerusalem.

[21] This is not to say that these pluses are all secondary or are worthless for reconstruction. For instance, 1 Esdras mentions the return of Zerubbabel in the second year of Darius (5:1–6) after the return of Sanabassar in the days of Cyrus (2:11ff.). In contrast, Ezra 1–2 (cf. the Aramaic account in Ezra 5:14–16) presents a confusing picture of the relationship between Sheshbazzar and Zerubbabel. MT Ezra 2 leaves the impression that both Sheshbazzar and Zerubbabel returned to Jerusalem in the time of Cyrus.

[22] Compare 1 Esd 2:16–30 with Ezra 4:7, 11–24 and 1 Esd 5:63–70 with Ezra 4:1–5.

Ezra.[23] This makes determining the original relationship between these works a highly complex endeavor. Because of their incorporation of secondary pericopes and their occasional disorder, both Ezra-Nehemiah and 1 Esdras present formidable challenges for interpretation.

Third, some participants in the debate have all but collapsed literary and textual considerations. Even if the compilation theory represents the best explanation of the literary evidence, this does not mean that 1 Esdras has no textual value for reconstructing the original text of Chronicles, Ezra, and Nehemiah. Detailed comparison of 1 Esdras, LXX Chronicles, and MT Chronicles, Ezra, and Nehemiah demonstrates the value of some readings in 1 Esdras. In those sections in which 1 Esdras is parallel to the Hebrew of Chronicles, Ezra, and Nehemiah, 1 Esdras is shorter by more than four hundred words (R. Klein 1966: 3). Corroborative support for many of the minuses in 1 Esdras is found in the Greek Chronicles, the Syriac, and the synoptic portions of 2 Kings (R. Klein 1966: 23–76). Moreover, the translation of 1 Esdras, when retroverted into Hebrew, does not always approximate the MT. There are important variants between the two (Tedesche 1928: 22–25). It seems unlikely that 1 Esdras is simply abbreviating its (MT) *Vorlage*. Nor can one safely argue, given the differences between the Greek Chronicles and 1 Esdras, that 1 Esdras is a translation of LXX Chronicles. Ralph Klein (1969) also shows, over against Walde (1913: 142–48) and Allrik (1954a), that 1 Esdras 5 often preserves an older form of the list in Ezra 2 than is manifest in either the Hebrew (MT) or the Greek (*Esdras* ß) form of Ezra. In short, 1 Esdras has text-critical value, regardless of one's view of its creation.

Fourth, one of the major arguments by proponents of the fragmentary hypothesis is weak, namely that the beginning and ending of 1 Esdras bear marks of being excerpted from a much longer work. Literary treatments of 1 Esdras have succeeded in demonstrating that the work has an integrity and a coherence of its own (Eskenazi 1986; 1988b; Gardner 1986; van der Kooij 1991ab; Z. Talshir 1999). This even seems to be true of the final phrase of 1 Esdras (*kai epistynēchthēsan*; van der Kooij 1991a), long thought to be too abrupt to signal the original end of the work. If proponents of the fragmentary hypothesis are to succeed, they will have to make their case on other grounds.

Fifth, the assumption that one can resolve all of the larger questions concerning the original relationship between Chronicles and Ezra-Nehemiah by recourse to 1 Esdras needs to be questioned. Even if 1 Esdras were a fragment of a longer translation, this would not in and of itself prove that Chronicles, Ezra, and Nehemiah were originally a single work. Conceivably, Chronicles could have been added to Ezra-Nehemiah (or vice versa) prior to the time when the writer(s) of 1 Esdras worked. Similarly, if 1 Esdras was compiled, in part, from sections of Chronicles, Ezra, and Nehemiah, this would not entirely remove 1 Esdras from having any bearing on discovering an older relationship between these scrolls. By the time the authors/translators of 1 Esdras wrote, it seems evident that Chronicles, Ezra, and Nehemiah were regarded, at least by some, as a consecutive narra-

[23] For a helpful list of the differences and similarities, see Myers (1974: 1–19).

tive. The very phenomenon of 1 Esdras indicates that Chronicles, Ezra, and Nehemiah were read as a continuity already in antiquity. In other words, 1 Esdras has critical value not only as a textual witness to the concluding chapters of Chronicles and portions of Ezra-Nehemiah, but also as an indication of the early interpretation of these books. In this respect, each work is an important, albeit involved, witness to the history of the biblical text.

Given the complexity of the evidence, it may be helpful for scholars to revisit some old questions and explore new possibilities beyond those offered by traditional theories. It may well have been the case, for example, that the writer of 1 Esdras was selecting, rearranging, and supplementing parts of Chronicles, Ezra, and Nehemiah, but his *Vorlage* may have been less disturbed than the present form of MT Chronicles, Ezra, and Nehemiah is (McKenzie 1999a). The version of Chronicles, Ezra, and Nehemiah used by the writer(s) of 1 Esdras may have preserved (in certain sections) an older, less corrupt sequence of pericopes. It may be observed, in this context, that the sequence of sections within the shorter Jeremiah of the LXX is now thought to reflect an older order than that found in the longer MT (II.A above).

In light of our discussion of the relationship between 1 Esdras and Chronicles, Ezra, and Nehemiah, some comments on the relationship of 1 Esdras to LXX Chronicles are in order. Questions pertaining to the nature of this relationship are best considered in the context of the evidence provided by the LXX, the MT, and the Dead Sea Scrolls for different textual traditions. Comparisons between the Greek witnesses suggest that 1 Esdras belongs to a textual tradition different from that of the Greek Chronicles, reflecting a shorter, sometimes more primitive text than the text type found in MT Chronicles, MT Ezra, 4QEzra, and LXX Chronicles. As we have noted earlier, 1 Esdras occasionally manifests a superior sequence of pericopes (in synoptic passages) than that offered by MT Chronicles, Ezra, and Nehemiah.

If scholars have disagreed widely on the nature, purpose, and date of 1 Esdras, then this is hardly less true of the other Greek translations of Chronicles. Torrey (1910: 18–36; 1945: 395–410) extends Howorth's thesis (1893b: 13–14) about 1 Esdras to argue that the LXX of Chronicles is not the original LXX at all. Like Hugo Grotius and William Whiston, who wrote centuries before him, Torrey maintains that the LXX of Chronicles is the work of the second-century (C.E.) writer Theodotion.[24] Although Torrey's position has been largely adopted by Curtis and Madsen (1910: 38–40), Tedesche (1928: 12), and Jellicoe (1968: 292–94), it has deservedly not won a wide following. Gerleman (1946: 3–13), R. Klein (1966), and Allen (1974a: 6–17, 141) have refuted Torrey's claim about the Theodotionic nature of this work, demonstrating, on somewhat different grounds, that both of the major Greek witnesses of Chronicles (1 Esdras and LXX Chronicles) antedate the rabbinic Bible. There are too many variants between MT and LXX Chronicles to see the latter simply as a translation of the former.

As the TEXTUAL NOTES to individual chapters demonstrate, *Paraleipomena* belongs to the same textual tradition as the MT. This means that the value of *Para-*

[24] For a more complete history of scholarship, see the survey by Allen (1974a: 6–17).

leipomena for reconstructing the earliest text does not approximate the textual value of the LXX for certain other books, such as Joshua, Samuel, and Jeremiah. As to the relationship between *Paraleipomena* and the Old Greek, *Paraleipomena* is generally thought to be a mixed text, a witness of uneven value. The recensional history of the Greek Chronicles is, however, a matter of continuing debate. Most scholars see Uncial B (Codex Vaticanus) and miniscule c_2 as the oldest extant textform of *Paraleipomena*.[25] Howorth (1893b: 60) and Torrey's arguments (1910: 91–96) for the priority of Uncial A have been soundly rejected.[26] Nevertheless, the nature and extent of revision in B (Codex Vaticanus) are in dispute. According to Barthélemy (1963: 31–80), the LXX of Chronicles (i.e., B) evinces the same kind of *kaige* revision that can be discerned in other biblical books, such as Samuel and Kings. Barthélemy dates this Palestinian revision toward the developing MT to the first century C.E. Whatever the value of Barthélemy's hypothesis of a *kaige* revision in other biblical books, his view of a *kaige* revision in Chronicles has not withstood critical scrutiny. Recent scholarship has shown that there is no compelling evidence for a *kaige* revision in LXX Chronicles. Both Ralph Klein (1966: 317–18) and Allen (1974a: 137–41) point out that LXX Chronicles only rarely displays the characteristics normally associated with the *kaige* recension.[27] "Most of the rest of the key Hebrew words [associated with *kaige*] occur relatively frequently in Chronicles, but they are systematically translated in a non-*kaige* fashion" (R. Klein 1966: 318). Moreover, as Shenkel (1969) points out, not one of the translation characteristics of the *kaige* recension is found in *Paraleipomena* in synoptic passages in which Reigns exhibits the *kaige* recension.[28]

Barthélemy's other suggestion (1963: 41–42, 47)—that the Lucianic witnesses, including the miniscules be_2y, comprise the Old Greek—has more merit, but must be carefully qualified.[29] According to Allen (1974a: 65–72) and Fernández Marcos (1991: 304–5), miniscules $be_2(y)$ definitely comprise an Antiochene, "clearly revised text."[30] Hence, these miniscules cannot be viewed simply as the Old Greek. There are, however, some definite links between these witnesses and Bc_2. In this context, it should be noted that there are numerous agreements between $b(y)e_2$ and Theodoret's quotations of *Paraleipomena* (Fernández Marcos

[25] See, for instance, Kittel (1902: 24), Rehm (1937: 13), and Allen (1974a: 101–6). Uncial S (Codex Sinaiticus) is also a regular member of this group. Unfortunately, S is only extant from 1 Chr 9:27 τὸ πρωί to 1 Chr 19:17.

[26] Exceptions are Curtis and Madsen (1910: 40–41) and Jellicoe (1968: 293). The corollary to Torrey's high opinion of Uncial A was that Uncial B was practically worthless for textual criticism. This position is also mistaken (see below).

[27] Whether this phenomenon should be called a recension or a tradition (Brock 1968: 176–81) need not detain us.

[28] The many agreements between *Paraleipomena* and Reigns in synoptic passages are generally ascribed to the phenomenon of parallel assimilation (Allen 1974a:183–218). It appears that the translators of *Paraleipomena* borrowed from Reigns, but from a copy that had not undergone *kaige* revision (Shenkel 1969: 85).

[29] Allen (1974a: 65) argues that while miniscule y is Lucianic until 1 Chr 11:14, from 1 Chr 11:15 forward it is Hexaplaric.

[30] Allen (1974a: 65) would also include Catena manuscript #350 in this group.

and Busto Saiz 1984: lviii–lx). The text of Chronicles employed in Josephus's *Jewish Antiquities* is also far closer to the Antiochene witnesses than it is to the Old Greek (Allen 1974a: 73–74; Spottorno 1997).

In Chronicles, Bc_2 form the basic text of the be_2 revision. Allen (1974a: 72) even believes that because Bc_2 have undergone their own revisions toward the MT, be_2(y) attest, in certain instances, Bc_2 at an earlier stage. Whenever Bc_2 and be_2 agree, there is a probability that the text approximates an early form of *Paraleipomena.*[31] In dealing with this material, the recently published edition of Fernández Marcos and Busto Saiz (1996) is of considerable help, as it contains many corrections of the so-called Antiochene text of LXX Chronicles as represented in the earlier Cambridge edition of Brooke, McLean, and Thackeray (1932).[32]

In addition to be_2(y), there are two other groups of witnesses to LXX Chronicles that represent recensions of a text similar to Bc_2. Vannutelli (1931), Rehm (1937), and Allen (1974a) see miniscules dpqtz as a group that exhibits two tendencies: approximation toward the MT and departures from the MT to produce a smoother, more comprehensible Greek.[33] Uncials A (Codex Alexandrinus) and N (Codex Venetus) and miniscules aceghn are regular members of another group of witnesses that also form a recension.[34] Like the group composed of dpqtz, this group tends to approximate the MT and to improve the rugged Greek style of its base (Rehm 1937; Allen 1974a: 85–89). Judging by the number of its agreements with the Syro-Hexapla, this group is the closest witness to the Hexaplaric recension in *Paraleipomena.* The base-text of this group is therefore pre-Hexaplaric. Unlike the group of dpqtz, the ANaceghn group does not consistently take liberties with its *Vorlage.* In other words, this group displays less diligence in repairing its basic text than does the group of dpqtz.

We have seen that the textual history of the Greek Chronicles has been the subject of avid debate. The evidence of 1 Esdras bears on this question. Although extreme positions have been taken on the relationship of LXX Chronicles to 1 Esdras, approaching either the Greek Chronicles or 1 Esdras as primary and dismissing the other as late, such views promote a false dichotomy. The relationship between the two is more complex. Neither the Greek Chronicles nor 1 Esdras need be viewed as late in its basic form. There is good reason to believe, in fact, that both stem from the second century B.C.E. (Gerleman 1946: 3–13; R. W. Klein 1966: 308–23; Allen 1974a: 6–17, 168). As we have seen, both 1 Esdras and LXX Chronicles provide useful textual variants to the MT. As to which Greek version provides the earlier or better manuscript evidence, I am inclined to follow the judgment of R. W. Klein (1966: 16–19), who argues that 1 Esdras is, typologically

---

[31] Allen (1974a: 71–72) puts it much more strongly. He thinks that when Bc_2 and be_2 agree, the text is the Old Greek.

[32] The distinction made by Fernández Marcos and Busto Saiz (1996: xvii–xviii) between b′ (MS #19) and *b* (MS #108) will be observed in this commentary.

[33] Manuscripts #74, 144, 236, 321, and 346 exhibit close affinities with these miniscules (Allen 1974a: 75–76).

[34] ANh sporadically display readings that are also found in Bc_2. Torrey's position (1910: 97), that N occupies an intermediary position between A and B has been adopted by Allen (1974a: 103–5).

at least, an earlier (second century) work than are LXX Chronicles and *Esdras* ß. When compared with the MT, LXX Chronicles has significantly fewer minuses than 1 Esdras does. Some of these minuses suggest a shorter *Vorlage* than the MT, but others may be attributed to haplography. Klein (1966: 77–184) describes LXX Chronicles as a highly expansionary, proto-rabbinic text type, probably Palestinian in nature, dating to the second century B.C.E.[35] Gerleman (1946: 8–13) and Allen (1974b: 167–68) also see the Greek Chronicles as stemming from the second century B.C.E. but they locate its provenance as Egypt (Gerleman 1946: 14–29; Allen 1974a: 21–26).

The usefulness of the Old Latin (OL) for recovering the Old Greek has been the subject of considerable debate. Weber's study (1945) of 2 Chronicles in the OL suggests that this text contains a variety of revisions. Nevertheless, he argues that the OL is, at its base, a translation of Theodotion (Weber 1945: xlviii–li). As such, the OL would be of little value for textual criticism.[36] Carmignac (1981) is closer to the mark, however, when he speaks of *Complutensis* as a mixed text.[37] Fernández Marcos (1991; 1997) and Allen (1974a: 107) point out that the OL sometimes shares readings with Hexaplaric materials, other times shares readings with the "Three" (Aquila, Theodotion, and Symmachus), often sides with the Antiochene text, and frequently diverges from the Antiochene text, agreeing with the LXX or going its own way. Fernández Marcos (1991: 306) comments that the textual pluralism exhibited by the OL of Chronicles is greater than that found in either the Greek or the Hebrew witnesses to Chronicles. Both Fernández Marcos and Allen (1974a: 106–8) emphasize that the OL sheds valuable light on an early text-form of *Paraleipomena*. Hence, the OL can be, in many instances, a very useful witness, especially for recovering the Old Greek. Finally, the OL to 1 Esdras should be mentioned. It has been described as an eclectic text, which should be used with some caution in reconstructing the Old Greek (York 1910: 258–76).

The base of *Targum Chronicles* resembles the MT and seems to be Palestinian in nature (Le Déaut and Robert 1971a: 16–18; McIvor 1994: 16–17). The editors of this work made use of other targums in their work, especially *Targum Jonathan to the Former Prophets* and *Targum Pseudo-Jonathan to the Pentateuch*. Le Déaut and Robert (1971a: 24–27) believe that *Tg. Chr.* contains an ancient core, but was composed gradually from the fourth through eighth centuries C.E. As with the other *Targumim* (Alexander 1985), *Tg. Chr.* integrates its exposition and explication of the text into its translation. Both Le Déaut and Robert (1971a: 28–32) and McIvor (1994: 18–24) show how the Targum updates, explicates, specifies, and harmonizes. The Targum is quite helpful in understanding how Chronicles was interpreted in medieval times, but it should be used rather cautiously for text-critical purposes.

---

[35] As the TEXTUAL NOTES to individual chapters demonstrate, LXX Chronicles is also prone to occasional cases of haplography.

[36] Weber's low estimation of the Old Latin has been followed by Curtis and Madsen (1910: 42) and Japhet (1993a: 30).

[37] Nevertheless, as Fernández Marcos (1991: 309) observes, the Old Latin of Chronicles does not exhibit any signs of influence from a putative *kaige* recension.

Like *Tg. Chr.*, the Vulgate is heavily dependent upon the MT. As such, the Vulgate's overall importance for textual criticism is not great. Curtis and Madsen (1910: 42) consider the Vulgate as serving at least one useful purpose, however. They argue that the Vulgate, despite its many similarities to the MT, is important for interpreting the Hebrew consonantal text. Curtis and Madsen believe that the Hebrew *Vorlage* of the Vulgate preserves, in some instances, a text that predates the MT. Whereas the Vulgate version of Chronicles greatly resembles the MT, the Ethiopic of Chronicles is an important witness to the Lucianic recension of the Old Greek. The Ethiopic translation is quite literal in character, "to a very great extent word for word, based on narrow segmentation of the text" (Knibb 1999: 60). Clear (1972: 13) notes that of nine extant manuscripts of the Ethiopic to 2 *Paraleipomenon*, two represent the Old Ethiopic and are based on the Antiochene text, while the remainder consists of a series of inner-Ethiopic revisions. The question of revisions is an important one, because although the original translation from Greek into Ethiopic occurred in the fourth or fifth centuries C.E., revisions of this base text continued through the medieval period and into the beginning of the early modern era. Although the revisions were apparently based on earlier, authoritative Ethiopic texts, they complicate the nature of the Ethiopic version. One such revision, influenced by the Arabic version, may be dated to the fourteenth century, while another, based on the Hebrew text, may be dated to the fifteenth or sixteenth century (Knibb 1999: 40, 109). The occasional Hebraisms found in the Ethiopic version should not be attributed, therefore, to the original translation. Rather, they seem to belong to a late revision of this translation.

The value of the Syriac Peshiṭta and the Arabic of Chronicles is disputed. According to William E. Barnes (1897: x–xiii), the Peshiṭta of Chronicles is midrashic in character and poorly preserved. Similarly, Curtis and Madsen (1910: 43) declare the Peshiṭta to be "practically worthless" for critical purposes. It should be noted, in this context, that the books of Chronicles and Ezra-Nehemiah are lacking in the Edessene (early Syriac) canon (Nestle 1893: 170). Noble (1943: 32–37) contends, however, that the variants of the Peshiṭta over against both the MT and the LXX, including omissions and additions, demonstrate its value. He argues that the Peshiṭta of Chronicles is an independent translation, one that is superior in certain respects to other Peshiṭta translations. Influenced by the Targum of Chronicles, the Peshiṭta of Chronicles nevertheless features its own distinct principles of translation (Noble 1943: 2–9).

Since the Arabic is a translation of the Peshiṭta, the following remarks will focus on the Peshiṭta. Although some have assumed that the Peshiṭta was based on a Targum or on an earlier Aramaic translation, recent studies (e.g., Weitzman 1999) have argued that the Peshiṭta was based on a Hebrew *Vorlage*. The Peshiṭta often exhibits a close correspondence to the MT. Only occasionally does the Peshiṭta evince consultation with the LXX. In many respects, the Peshiṭta of Chronicles is a special case. It deviates from the MT more often than the Peshiṭta to any other biblical book (Tov 1992b: 151–52). Nevertheless, in most cases the Peshiṭta of Chronicles aligns itself with MT in contrast with the other versions. The LXX and the Peshiṭta, for example, share very few common readings over against the MT.

Compared with the MT, the Peshiṭta (or some of its major witnesses) sometimes lacks groups of verses (e.g., 1 Chr 2:47–49; 4:7–8, 34–37; 5:12b–13; 7:34–39a; 8:15b–22; 2 Chr 4:11–17, 19–22; 24:13–14) or even larger sections of chapters (1 Chr 26:13–27:34). Conversely, it occasionally contains substantial additions (e.g., 1 Chr 12:1ff.; 29:18ff.) and at least one major substitution (selecting 1 Kgs 12:25–30ff.; 1 Kgs 14:1–9 instead of 2 Chr 11:5–12:12). The division among scholars reflects differing judgments about how best to explain the Peshiṭta's unusual features. In a series of detailed studies, Weitzman (1994; 1999) has argued that the author of the Peshiṭta to Chronicles was working with a defective Hebrew *Vorlage*. This would account for the close parallels with the MT, the many omissions in his text, and those instances in which he substituted texts from Kings for those in Chronicles. If the writer of the Peshiṭta for Chronicles was working with a poorly preserved text, great caution should be exercised in employing the Peshiṭta to reconstruct a shorter Hebrew text.

In his discussion of the Armenian version of Chronicles, Allen (1974a: 85) argues that this version mainly follows the Hexaplaric recension but occasionally exhibits Lucianic readings. This version is being reexamined by Cowe (1990–91ab). His analysis of four manuscripts within the Armenian tradition suggests that they have escaped revision almost completely. Hence, the Armenian version is an excellent witness to the Lucianic text.[38] In fact, because miniscule e_2 falls away in the final chapters of Chronicles (2 Chr 32:26ff.), the Armenian becomes the only witness to support miniscule b readings (Fernández Marcos 1991: 307).

Finally, some comments should be made about the MT itself. Many of those Qumran manuscripts that resemble the MT (e.g., 4QChr and 4QEzra) testify to the fidelity with which medieval Masoretic scribes reproduced the textual witnesses available to them. Hence, the publication of biblical manuscripts from the Judean desert has generated new appreciation for the antiquity of readings preserved in the MT. Indeed, the MT is the best witness for reconstructing the Chronicler's original text. Despite this renewed regard for the MT, the Qumran discoveries have led to somewhat of a "decentralization" of the MT (Ulrich 1989a: 223–24). The MT represents a collection of texts of varying value. In this respect, the MT is a critical witness to the development of biblical texts before the Common Era, but is best studied in conjunction with other manuscript traditions.

The centralization of the MT, very much in evidence in commentaries on Chronicles, reflects some methodological confusion. To begin from the base of the MT to explain the testimony of the versions is a flawed approach (Zipor 1980). Such a stance privileges the MT and inevitably skews the investigation. Upon comparing 1 Esdras with the MT of Chronicles, Ezra, and Nehemiah, for instance, one is struck by the superiority of some readings in 1 Esdras. As R. W. Klein (1966: 308) points out, the MT is "marked by conflation, expansion of names and titles, the addition of כל, and scores of other additions." Moreover, in those rare instances in which Chronicles preserves two forms of the same text (e.g., 1 Chr

[38] Cowe's analysis would seem to be largely confirmed by the recent edition of Fernández Marcos and Busto Saiz (1996).

8:29–38//9:35–44), one may find important variants within the MT. Finally, when the MT of Chronicles is compared with the MT of other biblical books (III.B and C below), one can sometimes detect corruption in the MT of Chronicles (dittography, expansion, haplography, metathesis, etc.). By the same token, MT Chronicles may be gainfully employed, in certain instances, to recover an older form of those biblical texts extensively used by the Chronicler (e.g., Genesis, Joshua, Samuel-Kings, Psalms).

The stance toward textual criticism in this commentary is, therefore, eclectic. In synoptic passages, the witnesses to Chronicles will be examined and compared at some length with the extant witnesses for other relevant biblical books. In attempting to recover an older text of Chronicles in nonsynoptic texts, the witnesses of the MT, *Paraleipomena*, LXX Chronicles, 1 Esdras, and the rest of the versions will be considered. This is not to say that all of these witnesses are of equal value. As we have seen, the Peshiṭta and the Targum are far less important for textual reconstruction than are the MT and the LXX. Nevertheless, each of the major witnesses supplies variants in varying quantity and quality that have value for reconstructing the history of the biblical text.

III. The Chronicler's Use of Earlier Biblical Books

◆

Discussions about the importance of the Dead Sea Scrolls and the versions for the textual criticism of Chronicles could be paralleled by discussions about the value of these materials for the textual criticism of other biblical books. But the textual criticism of Chronicles differs from the textual criticism of most other biblical books in at least one important respect. By the time the author of Chronicles wrote, much of the literature that we associate with the Hebrew Bible was already written. Chronicles draws extensively upon these rich literary traditions. Given the Chronicler's indebtedness to a variety of older biblical writings, one could make the case that his own work synthesizes several traditional perspectives (Albertz 1994). The dependence upon Genesis, Exodus, Numbers, and Joshua is evident in the genealogies (1 Chr 1–9), the dependence upon Samuel is patent in the narration of Saul's demise and of David's reign (1 Chr 10–29), and the dependence upon Kings is unmistakable in the narration of Solomon and the kingdom of Judah (2 Chr 1–36). In each case, the book quotes extensively from earlier materials.

A. SHARED SOURCE(S) OR REUSED TEXTS?

The dependence of Chronicles on a number of earlier biblical books has recently been challenged. Since this important issue very much influences how most read the Chronicler's work (Mitchell 1999), it bears some discussion. Auld (1992; 1994; 1996; 1999) and Ho (1995; 1999) contend that both Samuel-Kings and Chronicles represent alternate or competing appropriations of an earlier and briefer story of Judah's kings. Both the author(s) of Chronicles and the author(s) of Samuel-Kings, working in the Persian period, expand this older, shared material in distinctive ways. Auld (1978; 1979; 1998) also questions whether the list of Levitical towns in 1 Chr 6:39–66 stems from Joshua and whether the legislation of Deuteronomy is presupposed by Samuel-Kings. Auld and Ho thus seek to overturn a scholarly consensus that is commonly associated with the work of de Wette (1806–7), namely that Joshua-Kings presuppose Deuteronomy and that Chronicles presupposes the Former Prophets. In Auld's and Ho's bold theories, Chronicles is an independent work that is based upon the same source as that underlying

Samuel-Kings.[39] As for the Levitical town list, Auld turns the older theory on its head, arguing that the Chronicles list, although composed in stages, predates the Joshua list.

The theories of Auld and Ho have a number of merits. First, they draw attention to the importance of the textual discoveries at Qumran for exploring basic issues of composition in the books of the Former Prophets and of Chronicles. Second, they disestablish Samuel-Kings, reminding scholars that Chronicles is an integral work in its own right and worthy of careful scrutiny. In dealing with the historical books of the Hebrew Bible, there has been a predilection of scholars to begin with Samuel-Kings as a base in any cross-biblical comparison with Chronicles. Such comparative studies have often worked to the detriment of Chronicles, because many of the differences between Samuel-Kings and Chronicles are thought to represent tendentious alterations of an authoritative *Vorlage* on the part of the Chronicler. This tilts the weight of the comparison against the testimony of the Chronicler's work. He sometimes alters his *Vorlage,* but comparative studies should pursue broader questions as well. What do the differences between these works say about the compositional technique, historiographical assumptions, and ideology of each of the respective authors? What do the similarities between the texts say about the composition of history in monarchic Judah and Achaemenid Yehud? If comparisons are used simply to reflect upon Chronicles, they mystify the Deuteronomistic History—effectively treating this work as history itself, rather than as one particular narration and explanation of the past. Whatever one believes about the compositional history of the Chronicler's work, it clearly offers a distinctive approach to inner-Israelite relationships and identity. Third, Auld and Ho raise important issues about the relationship of books, such as Joshua, Samuel, Kings, and Chronicles, to collections of biblical law, such as Deuteronomy.

Nevertheless, the cogency of their central theses is doubtful. As I have written more extensively elsewhere (Knoppers 1995d; forthcoming [d]), some passages in the Chronicler's narration of Judahite history presuppose texts known from Kings dealing with the northern kingdom, even though the Chronicler does not include these texts within his own narration.[40] This would be unlikely, even impossible, if the author had no access to a text of Kings. In the view of Auld, the high theology of Solomon's visions (1 Kings 3; 9) and prayer (1 Kings 8) is part of the shared source. But given the preponderance of Deuteronomistic expressions and themes found in these texts, it seems more convincing to see the passages as heavily edited by the Deuteronomist (Knoppers 1995c). The recourse given to the witness of the LXX and the texts from Qumran in the work of Auld and Ho is most welcome, but one wonders whether this same evidence militates against some of their foundational claims. To be sure, proponents of the dependence of Chronicles upon the

[39] When the issue is framed in this way, one is reminded of Eichhorn's theory about common sources being used by the authors of both Chronicles and Samuel-Kings. Graham (1990) and Peltonen (1996: 56–64) provide helpful discussions of this eighteenth-to-nineteenth century debate.

[40] The reader is also referred to the comments of Kartveit (1989), Ben Zvi (1992), Schmitt (1995), McKenzie (1999a), Nihan and Römer (1999), and Talshir (2000). The most recent publications of Auld (1978; 1979; 1998) respond to earlier criticisms.

Former Prophets have had difficulty explaining the discrepancies between them in synoptic passages, especially the minuses in Chronicles. Why would the Chronicler randomly, it seems, omit certain words, phrases, or groups of sentences from his *Vorlage*? In this context, one can readily understand the criticisms leveled by Auld and Ho against modern biblical scholarship. If one grants, however, in the wake of the discoveries at Qumran, that the Chronicler's *Vorlagen* of certain books (esp. Joshua and Samuel) differed in some important respects from the MT of these books (III.B and C below), the criticisms largely fall away. The fact that Chron-icles sometimes offers a shorter, more primitive text than the parallel texts in Joshua, Samuel, and Kings can be readily explained by recognizing that the Chronicler was working with older (sometimes shorter, less corrupt) versions of these books.

We have been discussing the author's indebtedness to antecedent biblical literature. It should be pointed out that the Chronicler's dependence upon older writings is not confined to his selective reuse of Joshua and Samuel-Kings. His work is also informed by a variety of earlier biblical texts. Citations from or allusions to Genesis, Exodus, Numbers, Leviticus, Deuteronomy, Isaiah, Jeremiah, Ezekiel, Zechariah,[41] and the Psalms appear in Chronicles.[42] Moreover, what are apparently discrete sources in the Pentateuch—"D" (the Deuteronomic document) and "P" (the Priestly texts found in portions of Genesis, Exodus, Leviticus, and Numbers)—are occasionally harmonized in Chronicles. The author's control over a wide variety of earlier biblical writings is impressive[43] and was recognized already in antiquity. The author's erudition led St. Jerome to comment, "The book of Chronicles, the epitome [ἐπιτομή] of the old dispensation, is of such quality and importance that if anyone wishes to claim knowledge of the Scriptures apart from it, he should laugh at himself" (*Epist.* 53.8).

[41] The Chronicler's dependence on Zechariah, although often asserted (e.g., Willi 1972: 177; Williamson 1982b: 274–75; Japhet 1993a: 735), is not entirely secure. The text quoted, Zech 4:10, "These are the eyes of Yhwh; they are roaming through all of the land" (אלה עיני יהוה המה משוטטים בכל-הארץ), is said to reappear in the prophetic speech of 2 Chr 16:9, "Indeed, Yhwh's eyes roam through all of the land to strengthen those with a blameless heart" (כי יהוה עיניו משטטות בכל-הארץ להתחזק עם-לבבם שלם). The phraseology varies and the contexts of the two lemmata differ (Zech 4:1–6; cf. 2 Chr 16:7–8). It is possible that the Chronicler is adapting the saying of Zechariah to suit his own purposes, but it is also possible that each author is drawing on a popular phrase for his own purposes.

[42] There are also parallels between some of the Judahite lineages and the genealogy that appears in Ruth (e.g., 1 Chr 2:9// Ruth 4:18; 1 Chr 2:10–17// Ruth 4:19b–22), but most think that Chronicles was the source of the genealogical material in Ruth (SOURCES AND COMPOSITION to 1 Chr 2:1–55 and 4:1–23). Some have also seen Neh 11:3–19 as a source for 1 Chr 9:2–17 (or vice versa), but such theories are problematic. It seems more likely that the lists in both of these passages represent extended, largely independent developments from a common source (Knoppers 2000c).

[43] This facet of the Chronicler's writing has received excellent study in recent years (e.g., Willi 1972; 1991; Fishbane 1985; Japhet 1989; Kalimi 1990b; 1993ab; 1995a; Strübind 1991; Brettler 1995; Schniedewind 1994a; 1995; 1999a; Johnstone 1997ab). See further, below (VIII).

B. QUOTATION, REINTERPRETATION, AND THE CHRONICLER'S METHOD

Since Chronicles not only quotes but also rephrases, alludes to, and reinterprets older texts, textual criticism is of great consequence for understanding both the Chronicler's method and his purpose. On occasion, the Chronicler's citation of earlier works differs from the source itself; his quotations sometimes appear to be misquotations. In the past, many commentators assumed that whenever the quotation differs from the source text as we have it in the Hebrew Bible, the Chronicler must be rephrasing or changing the earlier text. But given the multiplicity of textual traditions manifest in the history of any given biblical book, how does one know when the writer is consciously deviating from the text before him (his *Vorlage*) and when he is faithfully quoting his source? If the Chronicler's *Vorlage* of Genesis was, for example, closer to the LXX's version of Genesis than to the MT's (the Hebrew version as it appears in our Bible), we would be guilty of a basic misinterpretation of the Chronicler's craft if we assumed that he was rewriting Genesis whenever his quotations of Genesis differ from the MT.

The textual criticism of Chronicles involves, therefore, not only a comparative study of the various versions of Chronicles, but also a careful study of the various versions to the biblical books from which the author quotes. Such analysis has a double benefit. First, we gain a better understanding of the source texts themselves. Since the Chronicler's edition of a biblical text may be older than the edition of that text embedded in our Hebrew Bible, Chronicles may be critically employed to recover the original text of that book. The study of Chronicles is essential to any study of those books from which the Chronicler amply quotes: Genesis, Exodus, Numbers, Deuteronomy, Joshua, Samuel-Kings, and the Psalms. In this respect, Curtis and Madsen (1910: 37) shortchange the significance of the author's citation of earlier biblical sources when they state that "the goal of the textual criticism of Chronicles is to restore the original Chronicles reading not the original source reading." Chronicles is clearly valuable for both. Second, by determining the kind of text used in a citation of a given book (e.g., whether the text of that book was closer to the LXX or to the MT), we may gain greater sophistication in addressing the debate about the Chronicler's creativity in employing sources.[44]

C. THE NATURE OF THE BIBLICAL TEXTS USED BY THE CHRONICLER

Recent text-critical studies of Chronicles have tempered scholarly attitudes toward the Chronicler's use of earlier biblical literature. Some modern treatments of

[44] Gaining such precision has another advantage. By seeing how the Chronicler uses earlier sources, we may better speculate about how he used other nonbiblical sources that may have been available to him.

Chronicles have been indiscriminate in detecting ideological nuances whenever the text of Chronicles differed even slightly from that of Genesis, Samuel, or Kings. In light of studies on the LXX and the Qumran literature, a more complicated picture emerges. Podechard (1916: 363–86), Gerleman (1946: 22–29), and Allen (1974a: 57–59) contend that the translator of *Paraleipomena* used LXX Genesis as both a commentary and a dictionary. Gerleman (1948: 9–12), Waltke (1965: 266–69), and VanderKam (1978: 47) also suggest that the Chronicler's *Vorlage* for Genesis was more akin to the Samaritan Pentateuch than it was to the MT.

Although more work needs to be done to determine the precise features of the Pentateuchal texts employed by the Chronicler, much study has been devoted to discerning the relationships between the textual witnesses for Chronicles and those for Samuel-Kings. Lemke (1963; 1965) has examined the textual affiliations between Chronicles and Samuel-Kings. Ulrich (1978) has compared the Old Greek, the Old Latin, the Hebrew (MT), the Samuel scrolls from Qumran, and synoptic parallels between Samuel and Chronicles. Traditionally it had been assumed that the Chronicler's *Vorlage* was virtually identical with the present MT. Lemke (1965: 362) and Ulrich suggest, however, that the Chronicler's *Vorlage* was not of the proto-rabbinic type. The text of Samuel that the Chronicler used was an Old Palestinian text type, the type to which 4QSam^a belongs, the type from which the Greek translation of Samuel was made, and the type cited by Josephus (see also Brock 1996: 303). In many respects, the Chronicler's text of Samuel was closer to 4QSam^a than it was to MT Samuel. In those instances in which the Chronicler quotes Samuel, his text is often a better witness to an early form of the text of Samuel than the MT of Samuel is.

McKenzie's study (1985) of the Chronicler's use of the Deuteronomistic History focuses on the nature of the text of Kings used by the Chronicler. McKenzie agrees with Ulrich and Lemke that the text type of Samuel used by the Chronicler was of a different text type than the MT of Samuel, but his study reveals that the text of Kings used by the Chronicler was proto-rabbinic in character. Independent studies by Sugimoto (1990; 1992) have reached similar conclusions. Moreover, there is every indication both in his citation of Samuel and in his citation of Kings that the author has generally followed his *Vorlage* closely. In other words, when studying synoptic passages, the Chronicler's deviations from MT Kings may be more safely ascribed to his creativity than his deviations from MT Samuel may be.[45]

Text-critical studies do not free us from speculation about the Chronicler's use of earlier biblical materials, but they do provide scholars with more precise tools with which to examine the respective textual traditions. On the one hand, caution is dictated in attributing tendentious intention to a Chronicles text whenever it differs from Genesis or Samuel, as the alleged change may be due either to the tex-

[45] McKenzie's further claim, that the Chronicler ceased to use Kings with the report of Josiah's death, has been seriously challenged (Williamson 1987cd; R. Klein 1992). McKenzie (1985: 206) himself concedes that Chronicles is not a completely objective criterion, because the book may include redactional material from different times. In any case, some caution is warranted when examining the last chapters of Chronicles. There one must consider the different textual witnesses to 2 Kings 24–25, Jeremiah 52, and 1 Esdras, and the evidence provided by the Greek Chronicles.

tual tradition represented by the Chronicler's *Vorlage* or to textual corruption. On the other hand, when neither of these two options seems likely, especially in dealing with the text of Kings, one can with confidence more clearly recognize those instances in which the Chronicler consciously made a change in his text.[46] Employing the insights gained by text-critical studies of the Chronicler's sources affords scholars greater control over the available data and, hence, more precision and accuracy in determining the compositional technique and ideology of the Chronicler.

[46] Lemke (1965: 361–63) and McKenzie (1985: 34) also stress the need to check if such an alleged alteration accords with a consistent theological interest of the Chronicler.

IV. The State of the Field: Recent Studies on Chronicles

◆

In his influential *Überlieferungsgeschichtliche Studien* Martin Noth (1943) devoted considerable attention to promoting the view that the Deuteronomistic History (the books of Joshua through 2 Kings) was a carefully unified work, the product of one author. Incorporating the old Deuteronomic law code into the beginning of his work, the Deuteronomist framed this work with speeches of Moses and proceeded to depict Israel's history in the land. In the second part of the same book Noth considered the basic unity of the Chronicler's work (Chronicles, Ezra, and Nehemiah) to be so obvious that he felt little need to defend it at any length. Noth simply proceeded to discuss matters of compositional technique, later additions, and ideology. Noth's facile approach to the authorship of Chronicles, Ezra, and Nehemiah was commonplace in the last century, but it would be highly unlikely today. If there has been some acceptance that Deuteronomy through Kings form a basic unity, the opposite is true of recent treatments of Chronicles, Ezra, and Nehemiah.[47]

Most commentators since antiquity have assumed that the books of Chronicles and Ezra-Nehemiah were in some fashion related to one another.[48] According to some, Chronicles and Ezra-Nehemiah were written by the same author. In the Babylonian Talmud, for instance, Ezra is presented as responsible for Chronicles and Ezra-Nehemiah (*b. B. Bat.* 15a).[49] For others, in modern times, Chronicles and Ezra-Nehemiah were thought to be related, because they manifested a unity in language, style, and content. On these grounds, the nineteenth century scholars Zunz (1832: 13–36) and Movers (1834) argued for the unity of Chronicles, Ezra, and Nehemiah.[50] According to this theory, Chronicles, Ezra, and Nehemiah are a single work that happened to appear in two (or three) pieces during the process of

---

[47] The agreement about the Deuteronomistic work, never unanimous, has encountered more opposition in recent years. See the entries in the volume edited by Römer (2000) and the references listed there.

[48] Japhet (1989: 4; 1991b: 298–99) lists some early and modern exceptions.

[49] There is also a minority tradition (*b. Sanh.* 93b) that Nehemiah authored Ezra. Even this point of view recognizes, however, that Ezra was commonly viewed as the author of the book bearing his name (D. Talshir 1988b). In explaining how Nehemiah follows Ezra in the work ascribed to Ezra, the aforementioned tractate (*b. B. Bat.* 15a) concedes that Nehemiah must have finished the book.

[50] Graham (1990) and Peltonen (1996) provide detailed overviews. See also the detailed bibliography of Kalimi (1990a).

canonization. In the past decades, however, Japhet (1968; 1983; 1991abc; 1994; 1996b), Williamson (1977b: 5–70; 1982b: 5–12; 1983a; 1988b; 1989; 1991b), and others have forcefully challenged this reigning scholarly consensus.[51]

The critique of unified authorship is more radical than many of the criticisms leveled at Noth's hypothesis about the Deuteronomistic History. Whereas some scholars have transformed the notion of one exilic edition of the Deuteronomistic History into two, three, or more editions, Japhet and Williamson propose to sever Chronicles completely from Ezra-Nehemiah. According to Japhet, Chronicles presents "a vigorous antithesis" to the outlook of Ezra-Nehemiah (1983: 118; cf. 1991b: 312–13). Similarly, De Vries (1989: 8) claims that Chronicles and Ezra-Nehemiah comprise "two literary complexes that have been more or less accidentally drawn together without any organic connection, unifying literary design, or common authorship." Williamson's stance on authorship is more complex and nuanced, yet he too argues for "diversity of authorship" (1977b: 70). These scholars do not deny that a few affinities exist between Chronicles and Ezra-Nehemiah but they ascribe such similarities to Chronicles and Ezra-Nehemiah being written in the same historical period and social milieu.

The separate authorship theory has already had a substantial effect on the field, but it is unclear what its long-term impact will be. Some remain unconvinced and have steadfastly defended the idea of single authorship on traditional or innovative grounds (e.g., Blenkinsopp 1988; Gunneweg 1985; 1987; Im 1985; Haran 1986; Shaver 1989; Koch 1996; cf. Bogaert 1999). Some have viewed Chronicles and Ezra-Nehemiah as two different works by the same author (Willi 1972; Welten 1973). Some have spoken of a Chronistic school or tradition as responsible for the production of Chronicles, Ezra, and Nehemiah (Mowinckel 1960; Ackroyd 1967; 1987; 1991; Eskenazi 1986; 1988ab; Riley 1993). Other scholars, such as Freedman (1961), Cross (1975; 1998), Braun (1979; 1986: xix–xxi), Pohlmann (1970; 1991), Becker (1986; 1990; 1998), and Gelston (1996), have advanced multipleredaction theories of Chronicles-Ezra-Nehemiah to account for both the congruities and the incongruities in this literary corpus. Since the question of authorship has profound implications for how one interprets Chronicles, it will be necessary to pursue this question at length.

A. THE UNITY AND EXTENT OF THE CHRONICLER'S WORK

The debate about authorship has involved at least five major issues.[52] One of these, the evidence of 1 Esdras, has already been discussed in our treatment of textual criticism (II.B above).

---

[51] Newsome (1975: 205–17); Throntveit (1982: 201–16; 1987: 1–5); Dillard (1987: xix); Eskenazi (1988a: 14–36); De Vries (1989: 8–10); Kalimi (1993a; 1995a); Talmon (1993); Johnstone (1997a); McKenzie (1999a). Eskenazi (1993), Kleinig (1994), Graham (1998), and Peltonen (2001) provide helpful discussions of recent scholarship.

[52] For good overviews, see Braun (1979), Throntveit (1982), and more recently Steins (1995) and Peltonen (2001). Another topic occasionally mentioned as favoring single authorship is the pattern of

1. Style and characteristic language
2. The doublet in 2 Chr 36:22–23 and Ezra 1:1–3a
3. Ideology
4. Compositional technique

1. *Style and Characteristic Language*

Until recently most commentators followed the classical arguments offered by Kropat (1909), S. R. Driver (1914: 535–40), and Curtis and Madsen (1910: 27–36) that Chronicles, Ezra, and Nehemiah exhibit a common style, phraseology, and diction. Japhet and Williamson have vigorously questioned the grounds for this judgment. Employing the categories of linguistic opposition, technical terms, and stylistic peculiarities, Japhet (1968: 330–71; 1977: 7–15) points to orthographic, linguistic, and stylistic differences between Chronicles and the narrative portions of Ezra-Nehemiah. Williamson (1977b: 37–59) argues that some of the characteristic phrases that appear in both Chronicles and Ezra-Nehemiah are common to Late Biblical Hebrew (LBH).[53] If so, the uniformity in the use of some expressions cannot be used to prove single authorship for Chronicles, Ezra, and Nehemiah.

Japhet's and Williamson's arguments have not escaped criticism. The corpus of available writings is small, a fact that qualifies the accuracy of any purely linguistic or stylistic approach.[54] Cross (1975: 14n) has criticized the conclusions Japhet draws from her orthographic analysis as unwarranted. Croft (1979), Polzin (1976: 81n), Mosis (1973: 215n), Blenkinsopp (1988: 49–54), and Mason (1989) have pointed to the use of sources and variant topics to explain differences between Chronicles and Ezra-Nehemiah. David Talshir's critique (1988a) strikes at the heart of Japhet's and Williamson's linguistic arguments, contending that there is substantial overlap in linguistic usage between Chronicles and much of Ezra-Nehemiah. Moreover, this overlap cannot simply be explained by recourse to a common historical and social setting. D. Talshir (1988a: 192–93) demonstrates that the linguistic features shared solely by Chronicles and Ezra-Nehemiah

---

reform and renewal in Chronicles, Ezra, and Nehemiah. Whereas some scholars (e.g., Blenkinsopp 1988; cf. Pohlmann 1991) see this as an argument for unified authorship, others (e.g., D. McCarthy 1982b) see such major differences between Chronicles and Ezra-Nehemiah in how this pattern is structured that they incline toward separate authorship. Because the relevance of this motif is debated, we need not discuss it here.

[53] LBH is commonly understood as a phase in the history of the Hebrew language between Classical Hebrew and Mishnaic Hebrew. In fact, Chronicles usually appears as representative of LBH in scholarly studies (Kropat 1909; Driver 1914; Hurvitz 1974; 1982; 1988; 1995; Kutscher 1974; Polzin 1976; Rendsburg 1980; Thorion 1983; D. Talshir 1988a; Rooker 1990). To what extent at least some of the features of LBH should be attributed to dialectal differences, as opposed to diachronic development, is debated (e.g., Rendsburg 1980; Sarfatti 1982; P. Davies 1992b; 1998; Lemche 1993).

[54] In this regard, Polzin's linguistic analysis (1976: 54, 71–74) of LBH yields starkly different results from the analyses of Japhet and Williamson. Polzin sees Chronicles, Ezra, and Nehemiah as belonging to the same linguistic substratum. Polzin's main objective is, however, a typological analysis of the language of the P stratum. Hence, the question of the unity of Chronicles, Ezra, and Nehemiah is only indirectly addressed in his book.

(minus the Nehemiah memoir) are much more numerous than those shared solely by Esther and Chronicles or by the Nehemiah memoirs and Chronicles. Talshir's study does not prove single authorship, but it does call into question any severing of Chronicles from Ezra-Nehemiah on purely linguistic or stylistic grounds.

It may well be, as one scholar has put it, that the whole linguistic discussion is at "something of a standstill" (R. Braun 1979: 53), but the debate itself has made scholars much more cautious in their approach to the question of authorship. Most no longer proceed under the assumption that these books are the product of a single editor or writer. The conclusions drawn from the debate about style and language should not be greater than the evidence warrants, however. The arguments for dissimilarity on linguistic grounds fail to prove that Chronicles and Ezra-Nehemiah are unrelated to one another. One must not be content to point out differences; one must also convincingly explain the similarities.

Further complicating things, the linguistic and stylistic studies have not addressed the parameters of Chronicles, Ezra, and Nehemiah. The arguments advanced typically assume the canonical divisions between Chronicles and Ezra-Nehemiah. They neither address the relationship between the last chapters of Chronicles and the first chapters of Ezra nor the relationship between Ezra and Nehemiah.[55] It is by no means to be assumed that the book of Ezra-Nehemiah stems from a single hand.[56] VanderKam (1991) contends, for example, that Ezra and Nehemiah comprise two separately authored works, each with its distinctive point of view. Such issues have yet to be addressed, if indeed they can be addressed, from a purely stylistic or linguistic point of view.[57]

2. *The Doublet in 2 Chronicles 36:22–23 and Ezra 1:1–3a*

The doublet ending Chronicles and beginning Ezra, narrating Cyrus's decree allowing a return of the exiles to their homeland, has been subject to a variety of ex-

---

[55] Williamson recognizes some authorial diversity within Ezra-Nehemiah (1983a; 1985: xxi–xxxvi). He posits three stages of development: (1) the composition of sources (e.g., the Ezra memoir); (2) the combination of most of the Ezra and Nehemiah materials (Ezra 7:1–Neh 11:20; 12:27–13:31) around 400 B.C.E.; and (3) the addition of Ezra 1–6 around 300 B.C.E. Williamson sees this last stage as a link between Chronicles and Ezra-Nehemiah. A pro-Priestly redactor who belonged to the same school as the putative pro-Priestly redactor of Chronicles composed Ezra 1–6.

[56] This consideration obtains whether one thinks of an "author" or an "editor" who incorporated a variety of sources. In all fairness to Japhet and Williamson, this is not a major concern in their studies, which interrogate the common authorship of Chronicles and Ezra-Nehemiah. Nevertheless, the issue should be pursued, given the questions raised by Pohlmann (1970), Cross (1975; 1998), VanderKam (1991), Kraemer (1993), Gelston (1996), Koch (1996), Becking (1998; 1999), and others before them.

[57] It seems unlikely that a purely linguistic analysis could achieve precise results in dealing with such small units as Ezra 1–3, 7–10, and Nehemiah 1–7, 8–10, 11–13, given the apparent incorporation and editing of sources within these sections. Another question involves authorial overlap between certain portions of Ezra-Nehemiah and certain portions of Chronicles. Torrey (1910: 238–48) contends, for instance, that the Ezra narrative and the Ezra memoir reflect the characteristic language and style of the author of Chronicles. David Talshir's study (1988a) points in the same direction. Becker (1998) contends that the Nehemiah memoir exhibits some of the same linguistic features as do the narrative portions in Chronicles.

planations. Many have viewed this doublet as evidence of a secondary division between the two works. Haran (1982a; 1985a; 1986) cites the practice known from the archives of Mesopotamia of catch lines serving as a compositional technique connecting two segments of a literary work.[58] Haran argues that the Cyrus edict plays an important role for the proper understanding of both 2 Chronicles 36 and Ezra 1, noting that the Chronicles citation of the Cyrus edict is stopped in midsentence, "Let him go up" (ויעל), a sentence Ezra 1:3 completes, "Let him go up to Jerusalem, which is in Judah" (ויעל לירושלם אשר ביהודה). Hence, it is fruitless to debate whether the edict originally belonged to the end of Chronicles or to the beginning of Ezra: the Cyrus edict is integral to both.

Williamson (1987a: 56–59) stresses that the doublet can be interpreted differently. The author of Chronicles could have borrowed the reading from Ezra, or a later editor could have added it to ensure that Chronicles ended on a hopeful note.[59] There is some validity to this rejoinder. The doublet could have arisen either from a division of originally unified material or by borrowing between originally distinct works. Indeed, as Freedman points out (personal communication), the creation of the doublet could represent the work of the compiler of the Writings (the third section of the Hebrew Bible). The compiler may have created this doublet to remind readers that Ezra-Nehemiah is a continuation of the story told in Chronicles. It should be remembered in this context that in the most complete manuscript of the Hebrew Bible dating to medieval times (the Leningrad Codex, ca. 1008 C.E.), Chronicles appears at the beginning of the Writings and Ezra-Nehemiah at the end. The situation with the earlier Aleppo Codex (ca. 900 C.E.) is a little more complicated, because it lacks most of the Torah (its extant text begins with Deut 28:17) as well as the last books of the Writings (Goshen-Gottstein 1976). Nevertheless, within the Aleppo Codex, Chronicles appears as the first book in the Writings, followed by the Psalms, Job, Proverbs, Ruth, and Song of Songs.[60] The position of Chronicles in the Aleppo and Leningrad Codices contrasts with the arrangement of books favored in printed editions of the Hebrew Bible since the sixteenth century (replicated in both *BHK* and *BHS*), which places Chronicles after Ezra-Nehemiah at the end of the Writings (Freedman 1990).

Whatever position one adopts on the doublet, one is left with the larger issue that the Cyrus edict culminates the narrative in 2 Chronicles 36 and initiates the narrative of Ezra 1. Moreover, it is unusual for books in the Hebrew Bible to begin with the conjunction *wāw*, "and in the first year of King Cyrus of Persia" (ובשנת אחת לכורש מלך פרס; Ezra 1:1a). The use of the conjunction presupposes an antecedent (Kartveit 1999). Those books that do begin this way (Exodus,

---

[58] One should also note the overlap between the end of Luke and the beginning of Acts. The beginning of the latter (Acts 1:1–2) clearly refers, however, to the former (Luke 1:1–4). Haran (1985a: 8–11) cites additional examples of catch lines from the Greco-Roman world.

[59] Williamson (1977b: 7–10; 1987a: 59) follows the latter option. Japhet (1993a: 18) thinks that the Chronicler borrowed the quotation from Ezra 1.

[60] Hence, most think that the Aleppo Codex reflects the same basic order and structure as the Leningrad Codex.

Leviticus, Numbers, Joshua, Judges, Samuel, Kings) are usually, albeit not always (Ezekiel, Esther), regarded as resuming a previous narrative. In this respect, a preoccupation with the doublet obscures the fact that 2 Chronicles 36 and Ezra 1 naturally form a continuous story. To deny this point is to deny the obvious. That a connection exists between the books is, of course, corroborated by the testimony of 1 Esdras, which begins with the Passover of Josiah (1 Esd 1:1–20//2 Chr 35:1–19), narrates the Babylonian Exile (1 Esd 1:41–55//2 Chr 36:9–21), continues with the decree of Cyrus (1 Esd 2:1–6//2 Chr 36:22–23//Ezra 1:1–4), and ends with Ezra's reading of the Torah (1 Esd 9:37–55//Neh 7:73–8:12).

It is important to demonstrate specific parallels between the early history of the return in Ezra and the narration of earlier Israelite history in Chronicles to clarify the point about continuity.[61] In my judgment, many of the allusions in the opening chapters of Ezra to earlier events are written with a view to the arrangements narrated in Chronicles.[62] Twice Chronicles mentions Jeremiah in narrating the demise of Judah (2 Chr 36:12, 21–22), but references to Jeremiah are lacking in the closing chapters of Kings (Pohlmann 1979). In the first instance, Chronicles indicates that Zedeqiah "did not humble himself before Jeremiah, [who spoke] from the mouth of Yhwh." In the second instance, the writer declares that the exile occurred "to fulfill the word of Yhwh [spoken] through the mouth of Jeremiah" (2 Chr 36:21). Similarly, in the doublet occurring at the end of Chronicles and the beginning of Ezra, the decree of Cyrus allowing Jews to return home, is cited as completing the word of Yhwh from the mouth of Jeremiah.[63]

The recourse to Jeremiah to attribute the return to divine providence is but one parallel between Chronicles and Ezra. The theme of the Temple furnishings is another. The loss of sanctuary furnishings in 2 Kings (24:13; 25:13–17) occurs in both of the major Babylonian captivities (597 and 587/6 B.C.E.). In Kings it is not entirely clear precisely what is sent away, what is stripped, and what is destroyed.[64] In Chronicles (2 Chr 36:7, 10, 18–19), however, "all of the furnishings of the Temple of Yhwh, large and small" are sent to Babylon. The dispatching of the Temple furnishings to Babylon narrated in Chronicles is redressed by their return narrated in Ezra 1:7–11 (Ackroyd 1987; Kalimi and Purvis 1994a; Knoppers 1999e).

---

[61] Graham (1985) sees a clear connection between 2 Chr 24:26 and Ezra 9–10. Steins (1995: 167–211, 231–36, 332–35, 355–59) argues that there is also a series of connections between certain texts in Chronicles and certain texts in Ezra-Nehemiah (1 Chr 28:12–19; 29:1–22a; cf. Ezra 2:68ff.; 8:24–34; 2 Chronicles 29–35; cf. Ezra 6:16–22; 2 Chronicles 31; cf. Neh 10:31–40; 12:44–13:14). These suggest some sort of relationship between the books, even if they do not entail common authorship of the works themselves.

[62] A number of these parallels have also been recognized by Ryle (1893: 1–49), Batten (1913: 55–125), Rudolph (1949: 2–32), Noordtzij (1951: 40–72), Galling (1954: 186–93), R. Braun (1979: 61–64), Williamson (1983a: 8–15, 23–29), Blenkinsopp (1988: 73–104), and others.

[63] 2 Chr 36:22//Ezra 1:1//1 Esd 2:1. This citation also alludes to the prophecies concerning Cyrus in Deutero-Isaiah (Williamson 1983a: 12; Blenkinsopp 1988: 74–75).

[64] MT Jer 27:19–22 and 28:6 are clearer. In these texts, the Temple furnishings are sent to Babylon. But much of MT Jer 27:19–22 is lacking in the LXX (Janzen 1973: 46, 69–75; W. Holladay 1989: 113–14).

The first chapters of Ezra stress the continuity between the preparations for building the Second Temple and the preparations for building the First Temple. The establishment of "the altar upon its foundations" (Ezra 3:3) alludes to the original choice of the threshing floor of Ornan the Jebusite for the site of the Temple and to David's establishment of an altar there (1 Chr 21:18–22:1). The parallel in 2 Samuel 24 mentions both the threshing floor of Araunah (vv. 18–25) and David's construction of an altar, but it does not identify this location as the future site of the Temple and the future site of "the altar of the burnt offerings for Israel" (1 Chr 22:1). In both Chronicles and Ezra the altar is established before the Temple is constructed. The celebration of the Feast of Tabernacles along with its burnt offerings, the provision of regular burnt offerings for the new moons, and the provision of regular burnt offerings for all the sacred appointed times of Yhwh (Ezra 3:3–6) are introduced with explicit reference to legal authority, "as (it) is written" (*kakkātûb*; Ezra 3:4). At first glance, this citation seems only to refer to Pentateuchal legislation (cf. Lev 23:34; Num 29:12–39; Deut 16:13–17). But the configuration and locus of these rites suggest otherwise. The practice of regular sacrifices *(tāmîd)*, the observance of the morning and evening burnt offerings, and the celebration of the festivals in accordance with earlier legal precedent is a consistent emphasis of Chronicles. More to the point, both Ezra and Chronicles manifest a concern that these rites and rituals should be performed at the Jerusalem Temple.[65] Similarly, the description of freewill offerings at the Jerusalem altar (Ezra 3:5) recalls the freewill offerings made by David, the officers, and the people prior to Solomon's construction of the First Temple (1 Chr 29:5–9). Whereas Kings mentions only the royal endowment of the Temple, both Chronicles and Ezra-Nehemiah depict endowments by heads of the ancestral houses as well (2 Kgs 12:18; cf. 1 Chr 26:26; 29:6; Ezra 2:68).

When preparing to build the Temple, King Solomon provides wheat,[66] barley, wine, and oil for those servants of Ḥuram (= Ḥiram) of Tyre who will help with construction (2 Chr 2:9, 14). Solomon also obtains Lebanon cedar, cypress, and algum wood from Ḥuram to build the sanctuary (2 Chr 2:7–8, 15).[67] In Ezra, the preparations are more briefly described. The exiles pay food, drink, and oil to the Tyrians and the Sidonians to bring them cedar from Lebanon for rebuilding the Temple (Ezra 3:7). In accordance with the explicit precedent established by

---

[65] E.g., 1 Chr 23:31; 2 Chr 2:3, 5; 8:13; 13:8–11; 31:3. The laws pertaining to sacrifices originally involve local altars (Exod 20:22–25), but the Chronicler, like the authors of Deuteronomy (ch. 12), sees one central site as the proper locus for animal sacrifice. Like the Deuteronomist (1 Kings 8), the Chronicler views the Jerusalem Temple as the divinely mandated central sanctuary. More so than Samuel-Kings, Chronicles addresses whether the proper observance of feasts and sacrifices occurs during the reigns of individual kings.

[66] These preparations for Temple bulding are paralleled in Kings. First Kgs 5:23 mentions food *(lḥm)*, while 1 Kgs 5:25 mentions Solomon's payment of wheat as food (*ḥṭym mklt* = *m'klt* [GKC, § 23f]) and beaten oil *(šmn ktyt)*. MT 2 Chr 2:9 reads *ḥṭym mkwt* ("crushed wheat"), while LXX 2 Chr 2:9 adds εἰς βρώματα ("for food"). Similarly, both *Tg. 2 Chr* 2:9 and *Tg. 1 Kgs* 5:25 have *prnws* ("food").

[67] As Williamson (1983a: 24) observes, the bracketing together of the Sidonians and Tyrians is found also in 1 Chr 22:4. The Sidonians and Tyrians provide cedar to King David in preparation for the construction of the First Temple.

David (1 Chr 23:24, 27), Zerubbabel and Jeshua appoint Levites who are at least twenty years old "to oversee the work of the house of Yhwh" (Ezra 3:8).[68] The claim has also been made that the timing of this appointment is significant (Williamson 1985: 48; Blenkinsopp 1988: 100–101), but this is less certain. Solomon begins to build the Temple in the second month of the fourth year of his reign (1 Kgs 6:1; 2 Chr 3:2), while Zerubbabel and Jeshua's laying of the foundation is associated with the second month of the second year following their return (Ezra 3:8–10).[69]

When the builders lay the foundation of the Second Temple, the vested priests with trumpets, accompanied by the Levites, the sons of Asaph, with cymbals, are stationed to praise Yhwh "as King David of Israel had ordained" (על-ידי דויד מלך-ישׂראל; Ezra 3:10). Descriptions of the priests with trumpets and of the Levites with musical instruments are common in Chronicles (e.g., 1 Chr 6:1–33; 15:1–28; 16:4–42; 2 Chr 5:11–14; 7:6; 35:10–19). The reference for an explicit Davidic mandate to the sons of Asaph is found only in Chronicles. David and the army officers set the sons of Asaph apart to prophesy to the accompaniment of lyres, harps, and cymbals (1 Chr 25:1–2; cf. 1 Chr 6:24–27; 16:5, 7, 37; 25:6ff.). In the same chapter, the Asaphites are described as "trained in singing to Yhwh" (1 Chr 25:7). In Ezra both the appearance of the priests and Levites and their ascription of praise to Yhwh, "for he is good, his fidelity to Israel is everlasting" (Ezra 3:11), recall three festive occasions in Chronicles. The priests and Levites sing the identical psalmic refrain (e.g., Ps 106:1; 136) when the Ark is brought into Zion (1 Chr 16:34), when the Ark is placed in the Temple (2 Chr 5:11–13), and when Solomon offers innumerable sacrifices at the Temple dedication (2 Chr 7:6–7). There are, of course, other occasions in Chronicles (1 Chr 29:10–19; 2 Chr 2:11; 6:4–11; 9:9; 20:5–12), Ezra (7:27–28), and Nehemiah (9:5–6) when such liturgical prayers and psalms are used (Blenkinsopp 1988: 53). The common typology of Chronicles and Ezra becomes all the more remarkable, given the absence of any comparable references in Samuel-Kings.

In sum, Ezra 1–3 quite logically resumes where 2 Chr 36 ends. We have also seen that the narrative portions of Ezra 1–3 resonate with a variety of features in the Chronicler's account of the monarchy. One can argue whether the connections between Ezra 1–3 and Chronicles are authorial (possibly the work of a common author or the work of a later author basing his writing upon an earlier work) or editorial (possibly the result of an attempt to bring the story of the return into conformity with Chronicles, the result of an attempt to shape David's actions in Chronicles to conform to the claims made for him in Ezra, or the result of an editor who has shaped both works), but the connections themselves seem to be incontrovertible. These texts do display aspects of a "unifying literary design" (contra De Vries 1989: 8). In describing the events of the return—the fulfillment

---

[68] In contrast, 1 Chr 23:3, which draws upon Num 4:1–4, mentions a minimum age of thirty years (see SOURCES AND COMPOSITION to 1 Chr 23).

[69] There is a dittography in MT 2 Chr 3:2, בחדש השני בשני בשנת. A few Heb. MSS and many of the versions lack בשני.

of Jeremiah's prophecy, the reestablishment of the Jerusalem altar, the rites associated with this altar, the preparations for rebuilding the Temple, and the conduct of the officiants—the editor of Ezra 1–3 makes a series of studied references to earlier precedent. To be sure, the allusions in the early chapters of Ezra are not only to events described in Chronicles. Events depicted in other works are also alluded to.[70] But whatever the nature and extent of the references to other biblical contexts, the resonance between the opening chapters of Ezra and Chronicles seems patent. The doublet between the end of Chronicles and the beginning of Ezra is not, in and of itself, indubitable evidence for literary unity. But the occurrence of the doublet in the context of a continuous narrative that repeatedly underscores the parallels between the preparations for the Second Temple and the preparations for the First Temple demonstrates a link between the two texts.

The question that needs to be addressed, then, is not whether Chronicles is related to Ezra-Nehemiah, but how. Is the unity between Chronicles and Ezra original or secondary? If the latter, where did the Chronicler's work originally end: 2 Chr 36:21 (Williamson 1982b: 412–19; De Vries 1989: 12–13), 2 Chr 36:23 (Newsome 1975; Japhet 1993a), Ezra 3:13 (Cross 1975), Ezra 6:22 (Freedman 1961; Becker 1986; 1990; Gelston 1996), or Neh 8:18 (Pohlmann 1970: 146; Mosis 1973: 215–31)? Our discussion of parallels between the opening chapters of Ezra and Chronicles has accentuated similarities between them. By its very nature, such an approach does not seek out differences. An exploration of ideology and compositional technique may elucidate, however, whether portions of Ezra were authored or edited by the same person who authored or edited portions of Chronicles.

3. *Ideology*

In positing a common authorship of Chronicles-Ezra-Nehemiah, scholars have traditionally cited similar interests in genealogies, lists, the primacy of Jerusalem, the centrality of the Temple, and the details of cultic affairs (e.g., sacrifices, feasts and festivals, the relations between the priests and Levites). Japhet and Williamson argue the contrary: Chronicles exhibits a fundamentally different theological orientation from that of Ezra-Nehemiah. The major topics at issue include the doctrine of immediate retribution, the emphasis (or lack thereof) on the Exodus and Conquest, Moses and the Mosaic law, David and the Davidic promises, the attitude toward northerners, prophecy, and the role of the so-called Levitical sermons.[71] To delve into every one of these major issues in the context of an

[70] Rudolph (1949: 2–4); Koch (1974: 184–89); Ackroyd (1976: 149–52); Japhet (1983: 115); Williamson (1985: 16–20); Blenkinsopp (1988: 73–105).

[71] Wellhausen (1885: 171); Curtis and Madsen (1910: 27–36); von Rad (1930); Welch (1935: 242–44; 1939: 1–9); Freedman (1961: 436–42); Michaeli (1967); Newsome (1975); Japhet (1977: 7–15; 1991b); Welten (1973: 1–6; 1991); Williamson (1977b: 60–69; 1982b: 5–11, 24–33; 1987a); R. L. Braun (1971; 1973; 1977); Mosis (1973); Cross (1975; 1998); Seeligmann (1978); Gunneweg (1985; 1987); Hanson (1986: 300–11); Jenni (1980); Im (1985); Throntveit (1987); Dillard (1984b; 1987: 3–4, 44–53); De Vries (1988; 1989); Kartveit (1989); Becker (1986; 1990; 1998); Oeming (1990); Strübind (1991); Riley (1993); Albertz (1994); Dörrfuß (1994); Kleinig (1994); Selman (1994a); Steins (1995); Gelston (1996); Brian Kelly (1996); Koch (1996); Weinberg (1996); Dyck (1998); Bogaert (1999).

introduction goes beyond the scope of this commentary. It may be appropriate to begin with a brief discussion of a few issues in the arguments for separate authorship—the Exodus and Conquest, Moses and the Mosaic law, David and the Davidic promises, and the stance toward northerners. This survey will be followed by another dealing with the arguments for single authorship, especially the oft-cited common interest in genealogies and lists. It is my contention that while some of the differences in perspective between Chronicles and Ezra-Nehemiah have been overstated, others can be underscored.

a. SEPARATE AUTHORSHIP

In the speeches found in Deuteronomy and the Deuteronomistic History, the Exodus and Conquest are presented as definitive acts by which Israel becomes God's own people.[72] In contrast, Chronicles neither stresses the Exodus and Conquest nor ties these events to the founding of Israel as a nation.[73] It would be an exaggeration to say that the Chronicler deliberately ignores Israel's liberation from Egypt, because the Chronicler reproduces some passages from his *Vorlage* in which the Exodus is mentioned (1 Chr 17:21; 2 Chr 6:5; 7:22) and directly alludes to the Exodus himself (2 Chr 20:7–11). Nevertheless, he does not associate the Exodus with the crystalization of Israel's corporate identity. There are also only a few instances in which the Exodus and Conquest are explictly mentioned in Ezra (9:11) and Nehemiah (8:17; 9:9–25). Mention is made of the Feasts of Passover, Unleavened Bread (Ezra 6:19–22), and Tabernacles (Ezra 3:3–5; Neh 8:14–18). There does not seem to be a major tension between the two works on this issue.[74]

Williamson contrasts what he perceives to be the emphasis upon David and the Davidic covenant in Chronicles with the great importance attached to Moses and the Sinaitic covenant in Ezra-Nehemiah. According to Williamson, the author of Chronicles engineered a shift away from the emphasis of the Deuteronomist on Exodus and Sinai by emphasizing the Davidic promises instead. Ezra-Nehemiah offers a "position which takes no account of this development" (Williamson 1982b: 10). Exodus and Sinai purportedly play a far more prominent role in the narratives of Ezra-Nehemiah than they do in Chronicles.[75] Even a cursory reading

---

[72] E.g., Deut 5:15; 7:6, 8; 9:26; 13:6; 15:15; 16:12; 21:8; 24:18; 26:18–19; 2 Sam 7:23; 1 Kgs 8:51, 53; Weinfeld (1972a: 326–31; 1991: 60–62).

[73] Von Rad (1930: 65); Noth (1957: 175); Rudolph (1955: ix); Brunet (1959); North (1963: 377–78); Japhet (1979; 1989: 96–124); Weinberg (1996: 277–90).

[74] One could argue that the return in Ezra is presented, typologically at least, as a second Exodus and Conquest (Williamson 1977b); nevertheless, it is very interesting that with the exception of the speech in Nehemiah 9, the author(s) of Ezra-Nehemiah do not lay much stress on the Exodus and Conquest. The stress on exile in Ezra and Nehemiah is, of course, another matter.

[75] Although the significance of David in Chronicles has been the subject of much discussion, my own research leads me to agree with von Rad (1930: 119–32), Botterweck (1956), Brunet (1959), Stinespring (1961), North (1963), Williamson (1977a; 1983b), Wright (1989; 1990; 1991), B. E. Kelly (1995; 1996), and others in seeing a substantial role for David and the Davidic covenant in Chronicles. The work upholds the importance of the Davidic promises not only during the United Kingdom, the time in which the promised Temple is built, but also during the Judahite monarchy. The Chronicler's historiography of the dual monarchies, his decison to concentrate attention on the Judahite kingdom, is very much affected by his understanding of the divine promises to David (Knoppers 1988; 1990; 1993a; 1998).

of Chronicles, Ezra, and Nehemiah verifies the more prominent position of David in Chronicles compared to Ezra-Nehemiah. In assessing the significance of this feature, one should take into account, however, the periods depicted in each work. Since Chronicles extensively cites Samuel-Kings, in which the Davidic promises play a crucial role, one can easily understand why much attention is given to David and the Davidic promises. Conversely, the authors of Ezra-Nehemiah employ different sources and depict a period when the monarchy was no longer in existence.[76] One can readily understand why frequent reference to David is not made in the latter work. As in Chronicles (e.g., 2 Chr 8:14; 11:17; 29:25), Davidic authority is cited in Ezra (3:10) and Nehemiah (12:24, 36, 45). Israel's revered king appears as a cult founder in both books (Japhet 1989: 467–78; De Vries 1988; Blenkinsopp 1988: 51).

The parallels end there, however. If David's role in Ezra-Nehemiah is that of a cult founder, he is much more than that in Chronicles: a gifted and successful warrior (1 Chr 14; 18–20), the recipient of dynastic promises (1 Chr 17), a repentant sinner (1 Chr 21), and an astute administrator (1 Chr 22–29). The writer does not simply mention these royal achievements; he clearly considers them to be critical features of the Davidic legacy. The contrast with Ezra-Nehemiah is stark. Even in that portion of Ezra-Nehemiah in which the (apparent) descendants of David—Sheshbazzar and Zerubbabel—play an important role (Ezra 1–6), they do not enjoy the same significance accorded to Davidic kings in Chronicles. Jeshua and Zerubbabel may form a dyarchy in Ezra, but dyarchy is not the standard form of government in Chronicles. Even when one accounts for differences in sources and coverage, one must acknowledge a difference in how each work construes David's significance.

The legislation associated with Moses is more prominent in Chronicles than some commentators have acknowledged.[77] First, the author of Chronicles does not dispense with the occasions in which Moses is mentioned in his *Vorlage* (e.g., 2 Chr 5:10; 25:4; 33:8). Second, in the material peculiar to Chronicles, such as the genealogies and lists, the figure of Moses again appears (e.g., 1 Chr 5:29; 6:34; 23:13–15; 26:24). Finally, in depicting the monarchy, the Chronicler explicitly rates royal performance with reference to Mosaic precedent or Sinaitic legislation

---

[76] The argument has been made that Sheshbazzar and Zerubbabel were, in fact, Davidic monarchs in Yehud (Sacchi 1989; 2000; Bianchi 1994: 163). In this reconstruction, these members of the royal Davidic line were vassal kings (clients) of the Persian emperor. While it is possible that some in Yehud wished to regard Sheshbazzar and Zerubbabel as their kings, clear evidence for their actual being such in the Persian period literature is lacking. See further the nuanced comments of Lemaire (1996b: 49–54).

[77] The importance of the law code used by Ezra has been much discussed (Grabbe 1992: 94–98). Shaver's study (1989) focuses on the nature of the Pentateuch used in the Chronicler's work (i.e., Chronicles, Ezra, and Nehemiah). Other studies have debated the nature and extent of Ezra's law book and the possible authorization of Ezra's law book by the Persian crown (e.g., Blum 1990; Albertz 1994; Berquist 1995; Frei 1996; Koch 1996; Crüsemann 1996; Watts 1999). This scholarly inquiry is certainly valuable, but more attention needs to be paid to the role of law in Chronicles. In this context, see Willi (1980: 102–5, 148–51), Fishbane (1985), Auld (1994: 126–46), Dörrfuß (1994: 119–283), Knoppers (1994b), and Schniedewind (1999a).

on at least thirty occasions.[78] In contrast, Kings only refers to Mosaic precedent or legislation nineteen times.[79] The Chronicler deliberately introduces an emphasis in his narrative which did not figure as prominently in his *Vorlage*.[80] Were earlier legislation not such a prominent and consistent motif in Chronicles, de Wette (1806–7), Vatke (1886), and Wellhausen (1885; 1889) would never have privileged Chronicles with such extensive historical criticism.[81] To prove the tenability of the Documentary Hypothesis, these scholars found it necessary to discredit Chronicles as a trustworthy source for reconstructing preexilic history, specifically the use of law as an ancient criterion for evaluating monarchical conduct. Far from receding in importance after the introduction of the Davidic promises (1 Chr 17), Mosaic legislation consistently occupies an important place in Chronicles and should not be overlooked in any study of Chronistic theology. Even when the matter of sources is taken into consideration, our brief comparison of Chronicles with Ezra-Nehemiah reveals that Mosaic precedent and law play a foundational role in both books. Recourse to earlier legislation as the community's standard of conduct is a unifying feature of both Chronicles and Ezra-Nehemiah.

A third ideological concern cited in the debate about authorship is the treatment of northerners. Many have seen Chronicles and Ezra-Nehemiah as manifesting an unfavorable attitude toward the residents of the former northern kingdom.[82] Whether Chronicles should be lumped together with Ezra-Nehemiah on this issue has been assiduously questioned, however. Japhet, followed by Williamson and Braun, has, in fact, turned the issue of northerners into an argument for separate authorship. Williamson (1987a: 56) characterizes Ezra-Nehemiah as manifesting a "very harsh, negative view of the inhabitants of the former northern kingdom of Israel." The author of Ezra 4:1–3 "did not consider these northerners any longer to be true Israelites, but were descendants of 'foreigners' " (Williamson 1987a: 57). As opposed to the very negative stance found in Ezra-Nehemiah, the Chronicler promotes a very conciliatory attitude toward the north.[83] Although they differ on details, Japhet, Williamson, and Braun depict the writer as insisting that the inhabitants of the north are bona fide Israelites. For

[78] 1 Chr 15:15; 16:40; 21:29; 22:12, 13; 2 Chr 1:3; 5:10; 6:16; 8:13; 12:1; 14:3; 15:3; 17:9; 19:10; 23:18; 24:6, 9; 25:4; 30:5, 16; 31:3, 4, 21; 33:8; 34:14, 15, 19; 35:6, 12, 26. On one occasion an Aaronic precedent (itself attributed to a divine command), "according to their custom at the directive of Aaron their ancestor, as Yhwh the God of Israel had commanded him" (כמשפטם ביד אהרן אביהם כאשר צוהו יהוה אלהי ישראל), is cited as determinative of how the priests are to enter the Temple (1 Chr 24:19).

[79] 1 Kgs 2:3; 8:9, 53, 56; 21:8; 2 Kgs 10:31; 14:6; 17:13, 34, 37; 18:4, 6, 12; 21:8; 22:18; 23:24; 23:25.

[80] The scroll of the Torah only plays a limited role in the overall presentation of the dual monarchies in Kings (Knoppers 1994e: 120–69).

[81] On the history of Chronicles interpretation in the nineteenth century, see Japhet (1985), Graham (1990), and Wright (1991). The recent study of Peltonen (1996) is the most thorough.

[82] De Wette (1850: 253–316); Wellhausen (1885: 172–73, 187–89); William E. Barnes (1896–97b: 17–18); von Rad (1930: 18–37); Pfeiffer (1948); Galling (1954: 14–15); Rudolph (1955: viii–ix); Noth (1957: 178); Rowley (1955–56: 191); Eissfeldt (1965: 531); Mosis (1973: 169–72, 200–204); Becker (1986: 9–10); Oeming (1990: 47); Albertz (1994: 545–56).

[83] Japhet (1977: 228–77); Williamson (1977b: 66–67, 87–140); Roddy Braun (1977; 1979: 56–59).

the Chronicler, Israel consists of twelve (or more) tribes over against any schematic political or administrative divisions (Japhet 1977: 237). In accentuating this pan-Israel theme, the writer points to the integral role each tribe plays, whatever its geographical location, within the one nation of Israel. Williamson points to the overtures made toward northerners during the reigns of Ḥezeqiah (2 Chr 30:1–9) and Josiah (2 Chr 35:1–19) as indicating the Chronicler's hope for reconciliation with the north. The Chronicler painstakingly calls attention to the ways in which "Hezekiah and Josiah go out of their way to woo back northerners" (Williamson 1987a: 58). It is safe to say that Japhet and Williamson regard the attitude toward northerners as one of the greatest contrasts, if not the greatest contrast, between Chronicles and Ezra-Nehemiah.

Japhet, Williamson, and Braun have insightfully questioned scholarly dogma on this issue, but some questions remain. That Ezra 4:1–3 refers to opposition against allowing the descendants of the former settlers of the north to participate in the building of the Temple does not in and of itself indicate a hostile attitude toward the descendants of the Israelite tribes.[84] Coggins (1976: 26–27) argues that because Ezra 4:2 mentions Esarhaddon having brought them to this land, "the Samaritans," or preferably, "the Samarians," are in fact not the intended referent.[85] This is but one indication of the complex problems that exist in discerning who the "enemies" are and what attitude the editor has toward the north (Coggins 1975: 63–74).

In spite of the considerable attention given to the Chronicler's perspective toward northerners, important dimensions of his perspective await to be explored. I would phrase the question somewhat differently from its traditional formulation. Unlike some scholars, I do not think this matter was the primary concern for the Chronicler. In my judgment, the contrast lies in Ezra and Nehemiah being much more limited in their definitions and concerns than the author of Chronicles is. Like the author(s) of Chronicles, the author(s) of Ezra and Nehemiah display a keen interest in genealogy and descent in determining the ancestral roots of a person, family, or group. But the author(s) of Ezra-Nehemiah also display a preoccupation with maintaining proper seed and with safeguarding the people's distinctiveness in the midst of opposition. The impression gained from Ezra-Nehemiah is that of a community whose very survival is at stake. Chronicles evinces a much more sweeping and comprehensive agenda. Throughout his portrayal of the past, the author promulgates a vision for the present and the future, a program that highlights the establishment of the Davidic state, the Jerusalem Temple, and its cult. The matter of northerners is but one element within this larger perspective. In this context, it is important to recognize that the Chroni-

[84] Williamson's exegesis (1985: 49–50) assumes either that the author lumps all of the northerners together, whatever their origin, and brands them as descendants of Assyrian settlers or that the author purposely ignores them. Other scholars have proffered different explanations, for example, that the people in question were descendants of Judahites, who remained in the land during the Babylonian exile (Cogan 1974: 103–10).

[85] *Pace m. Šeqal.* 1.5. The usage of the term "Samaritan" to denote the residents of the north during this period is anachronistic (Cross 1966a; Coggins 1975; Purvis 1968; 1981; 1988; Hoglund 1992).

cler's work also has an edge to it. The author not only lauds the initiatives by Ḥezeqiah and Josiah toward northerners, but he also praises those kings—Abijah (2 Chr 13:2–21), Asa (2 Chr 15:8), Jehoshaphaṭ (2 Chr 17:2–6), and Josiah (2 Chr 34:1–7)—who incorporate northern territory into the domain of Judah. In Chronicles, such acquisition of northern land is a sign of divine blessing (Knoppers 1989). Moreover, the author not only includes material in his *Vorlage* mentioning contacts with the north, but when these contacts include some sort of assent on Judah's part to cooperate with Israel, they receive negative commentary (2 Chr 19:1–3; 20:35–36, 37; 22:2–7; 25:7–12; Knoppers 1996c). Inasmuch as the overture by Ḥezeqiah is indicative of the Chronicler's attitude toward the north, should not the actions of these other kings also be considered as illustrative of his ideology?

b. SINGLE AUTHORSHIP

We have been discussing ideological differences between Chronicles and Ezra-Nehemiah. To be fair to the single-authorship theory, we should also discuss a few of the arguments for unity in Chronicles-Ezra-Nehemiah. One should begin by acknowledging that the two books share some foundational assertions. In the depiction of the divided monarchy and the depiction of the return, only the leadership of Jerusalem receives divine sanction. For the authors of both Chronicles and Ezra-Nehemiah, only the Jerusalem Temple cultus receives divine affirmation. In both Chronicles and Ezra-Nehemiah, Judah/Yehud upholds and carries on the legacy of ancient Israel. In both cases, a variety of tribes belong to Israel, but Judah, Levi, and Benjamin are pivotal to achieving the goals set for Israel.

There also can be little doubt that both Chronicles and Ezra-Nehemiah take a keen interest in genealogy, in tracing the bloodlines of key individuals and groups into the past. Present status and authority are very much linked to pedigree in both works. The question that must be addressed in this context is to what effect are the genealogies used? Lineages can have many functions ("Excursus: The Genealogies"). They may be employed to posit links to a variety of groups or, in a more restrictive sense, to posit exclusive bloodlines. Precisely how are lineages used to define the author's community in each work? Here, one finds a contrast between Chronicles and Ezra-Nehemiah on the question of self-definition. The very explanation of Judah's identity in the genealogies of Chronicles differs from the understanding of Judah evident in Ezra-Nehemiah (Knoppers 2000a). Both works take a keen interest in ancestry, but they exploit such interests in different ways. The genealogy of Judah (1 Chr 2:3–4:23), a collection of segmented lineages, undercuts a critical premise of the position found in Ezra-Nehemiah. In the latter, Israel is identified with the Diaspora group and divorces are mandated for the wives (and children) of those exiles who intermarried with autochthonous peoples (Ezra 3:3; 9:1–2, 11–15; 10:2–44; Neh 9:30; 10:29, 31–32; 13:23–28; Williamson 1977b: 60–61; Knoppers 1994d; Dyck 1996; Brett 2000). But in the Judahite lineages groups that seem to be non-Israelites or distant relations of the Israelites in other biblical contexts—the Calebites, Jeraḥmeelites, and Qenizzites—are incorporated into Judah's lineages. Members of other peoples such as the Canaanites and

Qenites appear within Judah. Intermarriage with Canaanites, Ishmaelites, Aramaeans, Egyptians, and Moabites leads to the growth and expansion of the Judahite tribe (Knoppers 2001c). The multilayered depiction of Judah's development underscores ethnic and social diversity within the larger sodality. Some groups are well-integrated into the tribe, while others are only loosely affiliated. The intimations of links not only with Canaanites, but also with a variety of other peoples stand in sharp contrast with the strictures of Ezra and Nehemiah. In fact, two out of the four peoples added to the Pentateuchal list of autochthonous nations in Ezra 9—the Egyptians and the Moabites—appear within the Judahite lineages involving mixed marriages. Connections with a third—the Edomites—are also intimated. If in Ezra (9:10–15) the people's fragile existence in the land is threatened by the phenomenon of intermarriage, in Chronicles the phenomenon of intermarriage is one means by which Judah expands and develops within the land.

It is certainly true that both works exhibit an interest in and a propensity for list making.[86] The inclusion of such detailed catalogues leaves readers with impressions of exactitude and specificity (Eskenazi 1988a; Scolnic 1995). From a literary point of view, lists may be skillfully employed to authenticate and structure surrounding narratives. Nevertheless, one has to acknowledge that lists may be edited, supplemented, and structured in a variety of ways within the two books. A prime example is a register of Jerusalem's residents that appears in both 1 Chr 9:2–18 and MT Neh 11:3–19.[87] Scholars have long debated the relationship between the two—whether one is earlier, whether one has been borrowed from or reused by the other, whether the two lists stem from a common source, or whether one (or both) of the lists is a later addition. In my judgment, the many incidental, but not insignificant differences between the registers in Nehemiah and Chronicles make it very difficult to derive one list from the other. It seems more likely that each catalogue represents a major revision of and a development from an older source (Knoppers 2000c). Examining the differences between the catalogues enables one to see how the editors of each work have each gone their own way with earlier material. Each has contextualized, edited, and supplemented the catalogue according to his own interests.[88] To take one example, Chronicles, consistent with the interests it manifests elsewhere, provides an extended list of gatekeepers and singers (9:17–34) and labels both groups as Levites (9:14ff.). Given the significant dissimilarities between the two registers in content and in

[86] E.g., 1 Chr 6:39–66(//Josh 21:3–42); 15:4–11, 16–24; 23:6–27:34; 2 Chr 17:14–19; 31:12–18; Ezra 1:9–11; 2:1–70(//Neh 7:6–72); 8:1–20; 10:16–43; Neh 3:1–32; 10:1–30; 12:1–26.

[87] The version in LXX Nehemiah is significantly shorter than that of the MT and probably represents an earlier edition of the list appearing in MT Nehemiah (Knoppers 2000c).

[88] Williamson (1985: 129–46); Blenkinsopp (1988: 320–27); Kartveit (1989: 151–52); Japhet (1993a: 206–19); De Vries (1989: 88–93). Because the lists in both Chronicles and Nehemiah betray some of the language and typical concerns of these works, it is doubtful that the catalogues are late additions to these books. Indeed, most of the writers who have dismissed one or both of the lists as later interpolations have held to a common-authorship view for Chronicles, Ezra, and Nehemiah and presumed that a single author would not produce two somewhat different versions of the same source within one literary work. This is not a problem, of course, if one holds to a view of separate authorship.

development, it is unlikely that the editors (or authors) of the two works were identical.

4. Compositional Technique

Scholars have long pointed out that there are some similarities in compositional technique between Chronicles and Ezra-Nehemiah. Both books incorporate long lists, genealogies, and descriptions of cultic assemblies (Zunz 1832: 22; Wellhausen 1885: 220). The technique of chronological displacement (the narrating of an episode out of historical sequence) is evident in both works (Glatt 1993: 55–74, 113–42). So for example, the editor(s) of Ezra-Nehemiah cite a letter of Artaxerxes I during the reign of Darius I (Ezra 4:6–24) and has Ezra make a sudden appearance during Nehemiah's first stint as governor (Neh 8:1–18). In Chronicles David conquers Jerusalem as his first official act upon being made king (1 Chr 11:4–9).

Some have contended, however, that Ezra-Nehemiah also reveals different compositional techniques from those employed in Chronicles.[89] The author(s) of Chronicles delights in the use of hyperbolic numbers (NOTE to 1 Chr 12:38) and in portraying spectacular national victories, whereas the author(s) of Ezra-Nehemiah stress modest community gains in the midst of strife. The authors of Ezra and Nehemiah also call attention to sources, such as royal decrees, lists, and letters. Reading Ezra-Nehemiah, one gains the impression that the editors have presented certain source materials intact. One can argue whether some or all of the cited sources in Ezra-Nehemiah are genuine or authorial creations, but the citation of such real or invented sources is overt.[90] In contrast, the author of Chronicles is much more likely to integrate sources into his narrative. He routinely omits, inserts, and supplements material from Samuel-Kings without calling attention to the fact that he is using material from his *Vorlage*.

In discussing the composition of Ezra 1–6, Halpern (1990) calls attention to another important issue: The editor of Ezra 1–6 employs a dual chronology. On one level, the writer provides the reader with detailed information about the early Persian period such as the names of Achaemenid kings, the names of early community leaders, and the difficulties in rebuilding the Temple. On another level, however, the editor complicates this chronological information with a theological chronology, which entangles, but does not entirely supplant, the historical chronology. For instance, the theological chronology makes Sheshbazzar (Ezra 1:8) and Zerubabbel (Ezra 2:2) appear as near contemporaries, even though the text elsewhere makes clear that they were not (Ezra 5:14–16). The use of dual chronology may not be, however, unique to Ezra. In presenting the early reign of David, the Chronicler has all Israel immediately endorse David following Saul's

[89] Willi (1972); Talmon (1976); Williamson (1983a; 1985); Japhet (1983; 1991b); Eskenazi (1988ab); Hoglund (1992).

[90] Torrey (1896); Noth (1957); In der Smitten (1972; 1973); Kellerman (1967); Clines (1984); Eskenazi (1988a).

death (1 Chr 11:1–3). This acclamation is followed by the conquest of Jerusalem (11:4–9), the mention of assorted warriors who strengthened David's position (11:10–47), and the rallies of Benjaminites, Gadites, Judahites, and Benjaminites to David at various locales (12:1–19). It would seem that the Davidic kingdom only grows stronger with such defections. But a close reading of 1 Chr 11–12 reveals that those defections occurred earlier in David's career, either before he became king (e.g., at his fortress; in Ziqlag) or when he resided in Ḥebron. On one level, the author has David become king and immediately enjoy support from various sectors of Israel. The capture of Jerusalem at the very beginning of David's kingly career underscores Jerusalem's critical status to Israel. On another level, the author alludes to a series of events narrated in Samuel to acknowledge that David's rise was a protracted affair, albeit still a glorious one. The elaborate technique of dual chronology, like the closely related technique of chronological displacement, is found in both Chronicles and Ezra-Nehemiah.

Williamson (1985) argues for a different kind of contrast between the composition of Chronicles and the composition of Ezra-Nehemiah. The editors of Ezra-Nehemiah structure postexilic history according to a consistent typology: project, opposition, and eventual success. This dialectical construction of the past, in which one problem (rebuilding Jerusalem's walls) after another (making the Torah scroll the constitution of the community) after another (rebuilding Jerusalem's sanctuary) is engaged and surmounted, is not characteristic of Chronicles. The work begins with an extensive genealogical introduction, continues with a glorious portrait of the Davidic-Solomonic monarchy, and ends with a mixed picture of the Judahite kingdom. In many respects, this observation is much more telling than the use of chronological displacement, because the technique of chronological displacement is found in a variety of biblical and ancient Near Eastern writings (Glatt 1993). One could still argue that a single author changed styles between presenting the monarchy and the Persian period. But if so, the result is two quite different works.

5. *Summation*

In our review of a few select issues, we have seen that some arguments for disunity are more convincing than others. In neither Chronicles nor Ezra-Nehemiah are the Exodus and Conquest emphasized. One of the putative contrasts between the two works—Moses and Sinai—is not really a contrast. Chronicles and Ezra-Nehemiah share similar interests in upholding the importance of Mosaic law. In other cases, such as David and the Davidic promises, the use of genealogy to define the community, and compositional style, one would be hard pressed to explain the differences between Chronicles and Ezra-Nehemiah merely on the basis of a variation in sources and coverage. It is on certain issues of ideology that one finds the most glaring of contrasts between Chronicles and Ezra-Nehemiah. In this respect, the differences between the two are more telling than are the similarities. Chronicles evinces a much broader and more inclusive concept of the Israelite community than does Ezra-Nehemiah. The author's agenda in Chronicles appears to be much more extensive than that of Ezra-Nehemiah. On the issue of the treatment of northerners, we noted an insular and preservationist perspective as opposed to an optimistic and comprehensive program. The perspective of Ezra-Nehemiah is oriented toward maintaining the "holy seed" in the midst of opposition, while the author of Chronicles wishes to see a unique community realize a decidedly more optimistic and far-reaching program. Finally, we have stressed that in comparative analysis, one should not lose sight of the fundamental postulates all three books share about matters such as the primacy of Jerusalem, the exclusive status of the Jerusalem Temple, the importance of supporting the priests and Levites, and the critical role that Judah, Levi, and Benjamin have in upholding the legacy of ancient Israel.

Our discussion of select areas of contention between those who advocate separate authorship and those who assert common authorship has led to inconclusive results. The cumulative weight of these considerations would suggest that Chronicles has some points of connection with Ezra and Nehemiah, but that it is quite unlikely that one individual is responsible for both works. It is improbable that the author(s) of the narrative portions of Ezra and Nehemiah are also responsible for Chronicles. The position espoused in the Talmud *(b. B. Bat. 15a)* and revived by Albright (1921: 120) that Ezra was basically responsible for Chronicles-Ezra-Nehemiah is historically improbable. Given the overlap between the ending of Chronicles and the beginning of Ezra, one has to inquire further as to the relationship between the two works. We are dealing with more than two literary complexes that have been "accidentally drawn together," because the building of the Second Temple, as portrayed in the early chapters of Ezra, seems to have been modeled after the building of the First Temple, as portrayed in Chronicles (IV.A.2 above). Has an editor shaped the beginning of Ezra to accord with certain features of Chronicles (or vice versa)? Or are theories of multiple editions of Chronicles, Ezra, and Nehemiah best able to account for all of the evidence?

V. Theories of Multiple Editions

◆

Two related issues inform the debate about multiple editions: the relationship of Chronicles to Ezra and to Nehemiah and the possibility of redactional activity within Chronicles (or within Chronicles-Ezra-Nehemiah). In the former case, scholars often employ block models *(Blockmodelle)* of recensional activity within Chronicles, Ezra, and Nehemiah to contend for the existence of different sections of material (dating to various periods) within a particular literary corpus. In the latter case, scholars employ layer models *(Schichtenmodelle)* of recensional activity to contend for the existence of two or more levels of redactional activity within the Chronicler's work. Obviously, there can be significant overlap between the two approaches, but for the sake of convenience, we will discuss them separately.

A. EDITIONS WITHIN 1 AND 2 CHRONICLES?

One of the major ways of configuring redactional activity, represented by the work of Rothstein and Hänel (1927: xliv), is to posit two redactions of the Chronicler's work (i.e., Chronicles-Ezra-Nehemiah), the first Priestly and the second Deuteronomistic.[91] In this conception, the Chronicler's work is to be aligned with the Priestly source of the Pentateuch.[92] Insofar as major Deuteronomistic influence can be found in certain passages, such texts are attributed to the later Deuteronomistic editor. The work of von Rad (1930: 88–115; 1962b: 347–54) represents another major approach to the issue of redactional activity. He contends that some Levitical (i.e., Levitical and Priestly) texts in Chronicles are later additions. While von Rad agrees with Rothstein and Hänel that the Chronicler was influenced by earlier Priestly material, von Rad stresses the Chronicler's debt to Deuteronomy and the Deuteronomistic History. This basic stance is extended by Noth (1957: 110–23), Rudolph (1955: 1–5), and more recently Roddy Braun (1986: xix,

---

[91] For 1 Chr 22–27, Rothstein and Hänel contend for the existence of a third editor (Chr^M), who wrote in the interval between the work of the two major editors (Chr^P and Chr^R).

[92] Without recourse to a theory of multiple editions, Curtis and Madsen (1910: 8–10) also contended that the Chronicler wrote to promote a Priestly view of history.

187–88, 228), who argue for many such additions. Similarly, recent scholars such as Willi (1972: 195–204), Mosis (1973: 44–45), Throntveit (1987: 6–7), and Welten (1991: 371) view some of the so-called Levitical portions of Chronicles (e.g., parts or all of 1 Chr 1–9, 15–16, 23–27; 2 Chr 29–31) as the product of later redaction(s).

A few scholars go a step further in arguing for the existence of Levitical or Priestly redactions. Kittel (1902) posits three such Levitical levels in Chronicles. Galling (1954: 8–12) conceives of an original Chronicler, who is greatly influenced by Deuteronomy, and a later redactor, who displays a special interest in Levitical (i.e., Priestly and Levitical) matters.[93] According to Welch (1935: 172–84, 217–44; 1939: 55–96), the first edition of Chronicles was decisively pro-Levitical in character. A second pro-Priestly redaction modified and expanded this earlier edition. Here, one encounters a problem with terminology. Some scholars employ the adjective *Levitical* in a broad sense to designate all sorts of cultic interests, while others employ it more narrowly to distinguish between Levitical and Priestly positions (and groups) and their respective roles in worship. In line with the latter understanding, Williamson (1982b; 1983a; 1985), De Vries (1989: 191–96), and Dirksen (1995a; 1996a; 1998ab) also believe that Chronicles has been subject to some pro-Priestly redaction.

In the main, then, commentators view the Chronicler as falling into one of two major camps: Deuteronomic/Deuteronomistic or Priestly. Both positions acknowledge that the book contains texts with other points of view, but attribute such texts to the work of later editors or interpolators. In this fundamental disagreement, one is left with two disparate constructions of the author's work. In one conception, the Chronicler was profoundly influenced by Deuteronomy and the Deuteronomistic History, while in the other, the Chronicler was profoundly influenced by the Priestly work.

Recently, two scholars have tried to break out of the mold set by older studies. Dörrfuß (1994: 119ff.) explores the role and references to Moses in Chronicles. This is, in and of itself, a service to the study of the postexilic literature (Knoppers 1996d). Dörrfuß observes that of the twenty-one direct references to Moses in the book, many are concerned with cultic regulations, practices, and sacrifices. Since Moses is associated with the Exodus, Sinai, and the desert wanderings, motifs not particularly conspicuous in Chronicles, Dörrfuß hypothesizes a Moses redaction of Chronicles, one that challenges the idealization of the Davidic kingdom and Jerusalem Temple in favor of Moses' authority and the Sinaitic institutions associated with him. Yet of the many references to Moses in Chronicles only a few can conceivably be said to criticize David by recourse to Moses' authority. Moreover, because the Levites and priests are active during a variety of periods, including the Mosaic and the Davidic eras, texts critical of the priests or the Levites cannot be taken as necessarily critical of David and the Jerusalem Temple. Hence, the existence of a Moses redaction is doubtful.

In many respects, the recent work of Steins (1995) represents the most complex

---

[93] Welten (1973: 189–91) provides an incisive critique of Galling's theory.

example of redactional theories. In his view, Chronicles not only manifests many layers of composition but also layers within layers. Three major levels of composition beyond the primary work itself are traced within certain sections of the book:

1. a cultic personnel level (itself containing a Levitical layer, two musician layers, and a musician-gatekeeper layer)
2. a community level
3. a cultic level (itself containing a cult layer and a northern layer).[94]

A series of other later additions rounded off the work. Steins's research exhibits a keen understanding of earlier scholarship, as well as a profound appreciation for the manner in which the authors/editors of Chronicles reinterpreted earlier biblical writings.[95] The literary heterogeneity within Chronicles makes it unlikely that a single author composed the entire work. Even when one allows for the use of sources, Chronicles occasionally speaks with more than one voice.

Yet, I find myself among those scholars who are skeptical that Chronicles underwent one or more major Priestly, Levitical, or Deuteronomistic redactions.[96] Arguments for pervasive disunity fail to come to full grips with the distinctive features of the Chronicler's compositional technique: his adroitness in drawing upon originally disparate lemmata, his ability to acknowledge and negotiate different ideological perspectives, and his capacity for pursuing his own agenda as he engages a variety of earlier biblical traditions. There is no question that one encounters both pro-Priestly and pro-Levitical passages in Chronicles. Nor is there any doubt that the work draws from Priestly tradition in certain contexts, but from Deuteronomic tradition in others. Rather than an indelible mark of literary disunity, these passages evince the author's concern to mediate different perspectives within the context of the late Persian period or early Hellenistic age.[97] No writer works in a vacuum. The Chronicler is heir to and interpreter of a variety of older texts. Living in the late Achaemenid or early Hellenistic period, he feels it necessary to authorize his own position and those of major characters in his work by recourse to prestigious older writings. That the Chronicler alludes to earlier precedent to validate or criticize the behavior of characters within his story carries a number of benefits. First, it establishes his own position as an exegete and tradent of older traditions. The author writes to establish his own point of view as he reveals his erudition by quoting, paraphrasing, and alluding to earlier biblical traditions. Second, by citing older texts, he creates the impression of a continuity from ancient times to the monarchy. The Chronicler's claims for a variety of links

---

[94] Steins mainly limits his study to 1 Chr 11–29; 2 Chr 1–9, 29–32, 34–35, but hypothesizes that his analysis could be extended to other sections of the work.

[95] The work of Steins also seriously revisits the question of literary connections between certain texts in Chronicles and others in Ezra-Nehemiah (IV.A.2 above).

[96] Knoppers (1999a). See also Myers (1965ab); Japhet (1968; 1977; 1993a); Dillard (1987); Marshall Johnson (1988); Wright (1989; 1990; 1991); Duke (1990); Ralph Klein (1992); Kleinig (1993); Selman (1994a); Ben Zvi (1995; 1997); Brettler (1995); Weinberg (1996); Graham (1998); Kalimi (1993a; 1995a); Schniedewind (1994a; 1999b); Brian Kelly (1996); McKenzie (1999a).

[97] In this context, see also the comments of Liver (1987), Ackroyd (1991), Fishbane (1985), Japhet (1989: 7–10), and Hanson (1987).

between the Tabernacle and the Temple is one example (Van Seters 1997a). King Abijah's oration delivered in the midst of a conflict with Jeroboam and the northern kingdom (2 Chr 13:4–12) is another example. This speech stresses the continuity, if not identity, between the cult of the Judahite monarchy and that of Mosaic legislation (Knoppers 1993a: 521). Third, the citation of older precedent in Pentateuchal texts can be used to authorize later innovations.[98] Given that the texts in Exodus, Leviticus, Numbers, and Deuteronomy ostensibly deal with the earliest periods of Israel's national history, the author is able to justify departures from those texts by recourse to the inevitable changes involved in transforming ancient Israel to a Jerusalem-based, Temple-centered society during the monarchy. Positing such practices in the course of First Temple history allows the Chronicler (by implication) to authorize such practices in Second Temple times.

Nevertheless, it has to be acknowledged that the very quotation of older texts creates its own difficulties, because the sources quoted are neither the product of a single author nor a seamless whole. The citation of different strands of biblical law, for instance, results in some disunity within the Chronicler's presentation. The Pentateuch is, after all, a combination of disparate documents produced by a variety of authors from different historical and social settings. Deuteronomy itself, of course, involves the reworking of earlier biblical law. To complicate matters further, the Chronicler is also heir to both the reworking of Deuteronomic law in the Deuteronomistic History and the reworking of Priestly law in Ezekiel. One should not be surprised that some of the writer's citations of earlier works do not mesh with each other. Given that his biblical sources speak with more than one voice, it could not be otherwise. This is, of course, not to say that there are no additions, glosses, or embellishments to the original text of Chronicles. From a text-critical perspective alone, we can be fairly certain there were such additions. But these interpolations and glosses seem to display the character of random additions rather than of systematic redactions.

B. EDITIONS WITHIN CHRONICLES-EZRA-NEHEMIAH?

We have been discussing layer models *(Schichtenmodelle)* that involve positing different levels of redactional activity within the Chronicler's work. Many commentators apply, however, block models *(Blockmodelle)* to Chronicles, Ezra, and Nehemiah. This involves isolating different blocks of literary material within the Chronicler's work (however one defines it). To be sure, it is not the task of this commentary to settle all of the complex questions about the composition of Ezra-Nehemiah. Nevertheless, it will be useful to review major hypotheses about the

---

[98] Willi (1980); Fishbane (1985: 380–407); Knoppers (1991; 1994b); Kalimi (1995a); Levinson (1991; 1992; 1997).

editorial history of Chronicles, Ezra, and Nehemiah to clarify the major issues at stake.[99]

To begin, one should point out that some scholars observe the canonical boundaries between Chronicles and Ezra-Nehemiah, even though they see some connections between the two works. Newsome (1975: 201–17), for example, limits the Chronicler's work to an early edition of Chronicles.[100] He sees the first layer of the Chronicler's work as comprising 1 Chr 10–22, 28 through 2 Chr 36. Roddy Braun (1971; 1979; 1986: xxix) and Throntveit (1987: 1–5; 1992: 8–10) also date Chronicles early and observe the canonical divisions between Chronicles and Ezra-Nehemiah as representing the original boundaries between these works. Halpern (1990) separates Chronicles from Ezra 1–6 and argues for multiple editions of Ezra-Nehemiah.

Other scholars see the Chronicler's work as extending into Ezra or into Ezra-Nehemiah. Freedman (1961; 1992: 93–97; 1993: 75–93) contends that Chronicles-Ezra-Nehemiah are composed of two main strata, the first extending from 1 Chr 10 through Ezra 6, dating to 515 B.C.E, and a second stratum that brought this earlier history up to date in the late fifth century. According to Freedman (1961: 437), the author of the first stratum wrote to legitimate the Davidic dynasty, the Zadoqite priesthood, and the Jerusalem Temple. In this reconstruction, the celebration of Passover and the Feast of Unleavened Bread by the returned exiles and others who had separated themselves from the uncleanness of the nations (Ezra 6:19–22) served as an appropriate climax to the story of the Exile, the return, and the efforts to rebuild the Temple. If the first Chronicler was a monarchist, the second Chronicler was a "clericalist, i.e., a scribe" (Freedman 1961: 442). Not displaying any of the royalist hopes of his predecessor, the second Chronicler wrote to confirm the struggling Jerusalem community in the midst of its enemies.[101]

Like Freedman, Pohlmann (1970: 146) and Mosis (1973: 215–34) see the original conclusion of the Chronicler's work as signaling a high point in the history of the return. Pohlmann, followed by Mosis, associates this climax, however, with the reading of the law and the celebration of the Festival of Tabernacles *(Sukkôt)* in Neh 8:18. A more complex theory of multiple authorship has been propounded by Cross (1975: 4–18; 1998: 151–72), who contends for an original edition that included portions of 1 Chr 1–9*, 1 Chr 10–2 Chr 34, and the *Vorlage* of 1 Esd 1:1–5:65 (= Ezra 3:13).[102] Written shortly after 520 B.C.E., this first edition

[99] Some scholars (e.g., Mowinckel 1960: 4–5; Ackroyd 1967; 1991; Eskenazi 1986; 1988b; Oeming 1990: 41–47; Riley 1993: 25) recognize evidence for authorial diversity in Chronicles-Ezra-Nehemiah, but prefer to speak of a Chronistic school rather than formulate a precise editorial history.

[100] Like Freedman, Newsome advocates an early date for the Chronicler. Welch (1939) assigns an even earlier date (525 B.C.E.) for the composition of Chronicles. Dörrfuß (1994: 9–14) also limits the original Chronicler's work to an earlier form of Chronicles (see V.A above).

[101] Gelston (1996) also contends that the original version of the Chronicler's work extends to Ezra 6:22. He points out that Pavloský (1957: 280–82) may have been the first modern scholar to espouse this theory.

[102] This *Vorlage* did not include the story of the three bodyguards (1 Esd 3:1–4:63). In the period since the publication of his article (1975) Cross has modified his views on the genealogies contained in 1 Chr 1–9. He (1998: 165) now holds that some of these stem from the Chronicler's own hand.

supported the program for the restoration of the kingdom under the dyarchy of Zerubbabel and Jeshua and ended with the founding of the Second Temple (Ezra 3:13). A second edition was completed shortly after Ezra's mission in 458 B.C.E. (1 Chr 1–2 Chr 34 plus the *Vorlage* of 1 Esd). This second edition ended with Neh 8:13–18.[103] Cross sees the reference in Neh 12:23 to the "book of Chronicles" *(sēper dibrê hayyāmîm)* as assuming the existence of an earlier edition of the Chronicler's History (= Chr²). The final edition was composed around 400 B.C.E. or shortly thereafter (1 Chr 1–2 Chr 36 plus Hebrew Ezra-Nehemiah).[104] In this reconstruction, the entire Ezra narrative was originally separate from the Nehemiah materials. The missions of Ezra and Nehemiah did not overlap.[105] The third editor of Chronicles-Ezra-Nehemiah (Chr³) created the confusion now evident in Hebrew Ezra-Nehemiah by reordering and editing some of the material he found in the second edition. Chr³ interpolated part of the Ezra narrative into the Nehemiah narrative. In accordance with his "anti-monarchic, theocratic views," Chr³ suppressed the wisdom tale of 1 Esd 3:1–5:6.

The proposals for a series of redactions in Chronicles, Ezra, and Nehemiah have some attractions. First, in contrast to the positions of separate authorship and unified authorship, the theories of multiple authorship account for both the similarities and the dissimilarities between these books. Second, the proposals for multiple authorship accord to some degree with the history of interpretation evident in 1 Esdras for a link between Chronicles and Ezra. Of the various proposals for the ending of the Chronicler's work, I am inclined toward those who observe the canonical boundary between Chronicles and Ezra. In spite of the literary connections between Chronicles and the early chapters of Ezra (IV.A.2), there are also significant disparities between the two. These involve not only the dyarchy upheld in the early chapters of Ezra but also the classification of cultic personnel. In Ezra the returnees are categorized as Israelites (2:2), priests (2:36, 61, 70), Levites (2:40, 70), singers (2:41, 65, 70), gatekeepers (2:42, 70), Temple servants (2:43, 58, 70), and sons of Solomon's servants (2:55, 58). In Chronicles, Israelites do not normally appear in a separate category. The priests, Levites, singers, and gatekeepers all fall under the Israelite rubric. Moreover, in Chronicles the priests, Levites, singers, and gatekeepers are all classified, broadly speaking, as Levites.

There are other complications in reconciling the classifications found in Ezra with those in Chronicles. When David organizes the administration of the king-

[103] Neh 8:13–18 does not appear at the end of 1 Esd 9, but Cross believes that they were part of the edition of 1 Esdras available to Josephus, because Josephus includes this material in his history. Cross contends, in fact, that Josephus did not have an edition of the Chronistic History in which the Nehemiah memoirs were an integral part. Rather, the Nehemiah memoirs "were composed and circulated independently of the Chronicler's work" (Cross 1975: 9).

[104] Chr¹ or "the Chronicler" signifies the first edition of this work dating to ca. 520–515 B.C.E. Chr² stands for the second edition of the Chronicler's work dating to ca. 450 B.C.E. Chr³ signifies the third edition of the Chronicler's work stemming from 400 B.C.E. or shortly thereafter. For an intelligent critique of Cross's theory, see McKenzie (1999a: 72–78).

[105] 1 Esd 9:49 (= Neh 8:9) does not mention Nehemiah, only the 'Ατθαράτης (= *tiršātā'*). The appearance of Ezra in Neh 12:36 and the appearance of both Ezra and Nehemiah in Neh 12:25 may well be later additions to the text.

dom in anticipation of his son's succession, he summons all of the Israelite officers, the priests, and the Levites (1 Chr 23:2). His staff are configured as Levites (23:2–31; 24:20–30), priests (24:1–19), singers (23:5; 25:6–31), gatekeepers (23:5; 26:1–19), army officers (27:1–25), and so forth. Missing from the lists of 1 Chr 23–27 are the Temple servants *(nĕtînîm)* and the sons of Solomon's servants. There are, in fact, no references in Chronicles to the sons of Solomon's servants. Only one reference is made to the *nĕtînîm* in Chronicles (1 Chr 9:2), whereas in Ezra (2:43, 58, 70; 7:7; 8:17 [Qere], 20) and Nehemiah (3:26, 31; 7:46, 60, 72; 10:29; 11:3, 21) such references are common.[106] It could be objected that the editor of Ezra 2 is simply quoting from a list, but the very classification of personnel is not a neutral activity. In the context of the Persian and Hellenistic periods, making distinctions within and without the Levitical ranks was a value-laden enterprise. The matter may be put somewhat differently. If the editor made no modifications to a (hypothetical) list, that would say something in itself about the nature of this editor and his handling of sources (III.A.4). In any case, many of the distinctions made in Ezra 2 are not unique to this list, but are found elsewhere in Ezra-Nehemiah.[107] My argument is not that the early chapters of Ezra lack any connections with Chronicles. Clearly, they do. Nevertheless, it seems implausible that these chapters and Chronicles were authored by the same person.

C. SEPARATE AUTHORSHIP AND THE CONNECTIONS BETWEEN CHRONICLES AND EZRA-NEHEMIAH

The early chapters of Ezra were, in all likelihood, edited by someone who wished to link the Chronicler's work with the materials in Ezra depicting the early Persian period.[108] This editor developed a series of ties between the two works by resuming the preexilic story, which ended in Chronicles with a story of the return and the struggles to rebuild the Temple. The writer presented the activities of the early leaders as a restoration and modeled his narratives about the return and

[106] The translation of *nĕtînîm*, the relationship of the *nĕtînîm* to the *nĕtûnîm* (Num 3:9; 8:17; 1 Chr 6:33), and the function of the *nĕtînîm* are disputed (Levine 1963; Blenkinsopp 1988: 89–91). The reference in 1 Chr 9:2 parallels the reference in Neh 11:3. See further the commentary on 1 Chr 6:33 and 9:2.

[107] Although it has to be acknowledged that Ezra-Nehemiah does not speak with one voice on these issues (Gese 1963).

[108] In this, I am in agreement with Williamson (1983a). Nevertheless, I hesitate to label this editor as pro-Priestly, because his interests seem to be broader than that designation implies. Another question involves the extent of his work. I do not see any clear signs that he heavily reworked the materials found in Ezra 4–6 with a view to the arrangements in Chronicles. The dedication of the Second Temple presented the editor with a splendid opportunity to draw a series of parallels with Solomon's Temple dedication (1 Kgs 8; 2 Chr 5–7), but there is little evidence that he chose to do so. Most of the allusions to older biblical literature in this account are to legal materials. To be sure, Ezra 6:18 mentions the appointment of the priests in their courses and the Levites in their divisions (cf. 1 Chr 23–26), but employs the authorization formula "as it was written in the book of Moses." Given the testimony of 1 Chr 23–26, one would have expected the reference to be to David. There is no mention of Zerubbabel at either the dedication (Ezra 6:13–18) or the following Passover (6:19–22).

the efforts to reestablish the Temple in reference to a number of earlier works, but especially in reference to earlier biblical law and the arrangements found in Chronicles.[109]

That the writer chose Chronicles and not Kings as the base of his work should not be too surprising. The Chronicler's writing, unlike the Deuteronomistic History, exhibits a great interest in the details of the Jerusalem cult. Both the Deuteronomistic work and the Chronicler's work extol the primacy of the Jerusalem Temple, but Chronicles provides much more coverage to the actual system of worship found at the Temple—the system of sacrifices, the observance of the festivals, the activities of the priests, the Levites, the gatekeepers, and the singers. Like Chronicles, Ezra-Nehemiah stresses continuity between the preexilic and the postexilic communities. Like Chronicles, Ezra-Nehemiah portrays the Jerusalem leadership as charged with the major, if not exclusive, responsibility of carrying on the institutional legacy of ancient Israel.[110] To be sure, differences between the two works are still visible. There is no clear evidence that the editor of the early chapters of Ezra overwrote major portions of the Chronicler's work. Nevertheless, the conjoining of these two writings (Chronicles and Ezra-Nehemiah) was not a literary accident. The editor of the early chapters in Ezra brought together two literary works that already shared a number of common interests. One effect of his labors was to create a long history, beginning with the first person in the ancient past (Adam) and extending to the reform efforts of Nehemiah in the Persian period. The combined work underscored the parallels between the preexilic and the postexilic communities without providing any significant coverage of the Exile itself. In this respect, both Chronicles and Ezra-Nehemiah underscore the ties between the people and the land.

Another effect of joining the two works was to orchestrate, if not commend, the transition in leadership from the Davidic monarchy in preexilic times to the Jerusalem theocracy in postexilic times. To be sure, Chronicles itself takes a great interest in David and Solomon's efforts on behalf of Jerusalemite worship. But in Ezra-Nehemiah, Davidic patronage is replaced by Persian imperial patronage. In the early transition, the governors Sheshbazzar (Ezra 1:8, 11; 5:14–16) and Zerubbabel (Ezra 2:2; 3:2, 8; 4:2–3; 5:2; Neh 7:7; 12:1, 47) are critical to the reestablishment of the Jerusalem Temple.[111] Both are subject to and sponsored by the Persian authorities. Neither in the case of Sheshbazzar nor in the case of Zerubbabel does the author invoke the Davidic covenant as a basis for their rule (cf. 1 Chr 17:4–15, 16–27; 22:7–13; 28:2–7; 2 Chr 6:7–17; 7:17–18; 13:5–8; 21:7).

---

[109] One could argue the contrary, that the Chronicler's work was written as an introduction to the story of the return, but this seems less likely. The force of making studious allusions to the Davidic arrangements for the establishment of the First Temple would be lost if there were no such arrangements found in any earlier work.

[110] The situation with the Deuteronomist's portrayal of Israel and Judah during the dual monarchies is more complex in that he recognizes the legitimacy of the northern kingdom (Knoppers 1993c; 1994e).

[111] Whether Sheshbazzar is the Shenazzar mentioned in the Davidic lineages is debated (2nd NOTE to 3:18).

Sheshbazzar receives, in fact, little attention at all. Zerubbabel is mentioned more prominently, but the editor provides no clear hint that the rebuilding of the Temple will lead somehow to the full reconstitution of the Davidic monarchy.[112] After Zerubbabel mysteriously exits the stage, the editors of Ezra-Nehemiah do not express any clear interest in or preference for the reestablishment of the Davidic line. A few later references to David occur in Nehemiah, but these references deal with the City of David (Neh 3:16) and David's legacy as a musician and a cult founder (Neh 12:24, 36, 45, 46). They do not mention larger political concerns, such as the Davidic promises. Insofar as Solomon is cited at all, his most prominent mention is as a negative example of intermarriage (Neh 13:26; Williamson 1977b: 60–61). In short, Davidic royalist concerns in Chronicles largely give way to theocratic and clerical concerns in Ezra-Nehemiah.

To this reconstruction of the original Chronicler's work, which largely observes the canonical boundaries of Chronicles and Ezra-Nehemiah, it may be objected that the ending of Chronicles, the decree of Cyrus, is a strange way to end a book. Assuming, for the sake of argument, that these verses (2 Chr 36:21–23) represent the book's original ending, one can still make the case why the book ends on a decidedly optimistic note. The dissimilarity with the presentation of the two Babylonian Exiles (598 and 586 B.C.E.) in Kings represents, in all likelihood, a deliberate narrative strategy. The Deuteronomistic presentation details massive deportations, the plunder and destruction of the Temple, and the dismal end of the Davidic kingdom.[113] In contrast with the somber ending of the story in 2 Kgs 24–25, the ending of 2 Chr 36 offers clear hope for the future. The concluding lines present one version of Cyrus's decree, announcing the return of the Babylonian deportees to the land of Judah (2 Chr 36:22–23). This is not the only indication of an exile-return motif in Chronicles. Both the Assyrian Exile and the Babylonian Exile are repeatedly mentioned in the genealogies (1 Chr 5:6, 21–22, 26, 41; 8:6, 7; 9:1). The genealogies also include a list of those who returned from the Babylonian Exile (1 Chr 9:2ff.). A return from captivity is repeatedly anticipated in King Solomon's Temple prayer (2 Chr 6:36, 37, 38; cf. 1 Kgs 8:46, 47, 48, 50). The description of the land's needing its sabbaths (2 Chr 36:20–21) also indirectly points toward repatriation. Drawing on both Priestly theology and the

[112] In this respect, it is helpful to distinguish the perspective found in Ezra 1–3 from those found in other works, such as Ḥaggai (1:1, 12, 14; 2:2, 4, 21, 23) and Zechariah (4:6, 7, 9, 10).

[113] Some scholars have found a measure of clear hope in the notice of Jehoiachin's release (2 Kgs 25:27–30). But the precise significance of this note, which does not appear in Chronicles, is not readily transparent. While some think that 2 Kgs 25:27–30 was written to herald a new age of messianic promise (von Rad 1962b: 344–46; 1966b: 219–21) or predict a restoration (Janssen 1956: 76; Seitz 1989: 218–21), others argue that the text is simply a historical footnote to the Deuteronomistic History (Noth 1957: 108; Wolff 1975: 85–86, 99–100). The passage does not mention Yhwh, David, the people, fulfillment, or repentance (Begg 1986: 50–52). A few scholars argue that 2 Kgs 25:27–30 demonstrates that the future of the Davidic line runs through Jehoiachin and not Zedekiah (Purvis 1988: 152–53; Seitz 1989: 214–21). This is possible, but one wonders why 2 Kgs 25:27–30 does not mention any of Jehoiachin's sons (1 Chr 3:17–18). Becking (1990: 286–90) contends that Jehoiachin's release is a goodwill measure, an act of amnesty implemented at Amel-Marduk's accession in 561 B.C.E.

prophecies of Jeremiah, the text portrays the exile as allowing the land a seventy-year respite from Judahite occupation.[114] The very notion of a temporary (seventy-year) exile presumes, however, an eventual return. Finally, scholars have pointed to the recurrence of an exile-restoration motif within the Chronicler's account of the monarchy, a *topos* which adumbrates a favorable outcome to the Babylonian Exile.[115]

The ending of Chronicles also performs an important structural function within the context of the Chronicler's larger account of Israel and Judah. Beginning with the emergence of the Israelite people within the land, Chronicles closes with the exile of this people and the announcement of their return. The author underscores the importance of the land by ending his version of Cyrus's decree in midsentence, "Whoever is among you from his people, may Yhwh his God be with him, and let him go up" (2 Chr 36:23). Considering that Judaism was already an international religion in the Persian period, the rhetorical ploy is strategic. Not only does it summon Jews from the Diaspora to return home, but it also reaffirms the importance of land and Temple for Jews within the land of Israel.

Two further objections may be raised against this hypothesis. First, it may be argued that the writer would relate events up to his or her own time (e.g., Cross 1975; Gelston 1996). Yet there are notable counterexamples within biblical literature (the Yahwist, the Elohist, the Deuteronomic writers, the Priestly writers) to such a practice. Moreover, the Chronicler, upholding the Davidic monarchy as the normative polity for all of Israel, may have considered the Persian-period theocracy as less than an ideal system of governance (Japhet 1996b; 1999). If so, he would have resisted drawing a continuous line from the preexilic Judahite monarchy to the situation in his own time. Second, some see 1 Esdras as implying an original unity between Chronicles and Ezra. But 1 Esdras testifies to a linkage between Chronicles and Ezra in the second century B.C.E. This unity is only a problem for those scholars who deny any connections whatsoever between Chronicles and Ezra-Nehemiah. Those who hold either to an editorial bridge between the works or to multiple redaction theories affirm that by the second century Chronicles had become linked to Ezra-Nehemiah (II.B; IV.A.2).

It may be useful to end this section with a more general comment. Whichever of the aforementioned views one adopts on the composition of Chronicles-Ezra-Nehemiah—separate authorship, two books by the same author, a Chronistic school, multiple editions—each hypothesis has a similar effect on interpretation. To a greater or lesser extent, every one of these approaches distances Chronicles from Ezra-Nehemiah. Because these approaches do not posit Chronicles, Ezra, and Nehemiah as a single, original work, they do not examine the ideology of

---

[114] Steins (1995) observes that the final verses in Chronicles contain references to both legal material (= the Torah) and Jeremiah (= the Prophets). Steins contends that Chronicles ends the Writings (in one version of the canon) by referring back to the two earlier sections of the Bible.

[115] Mosis (1973: 17–43); Ackroyd (1977). In particular, note 2 Chr 14:14; 21:17; 25:12; 28:5, 8, 11, 13, 14, 15, 17; 29:9; 30:9.

Chronicles from the vantage point of Ezra-Nehemiah.[116] Interpreting Chronicles without primary reliance upon Ezra-Nehemiah also has indirect consequences for any comparison between Chronicles and Samuel-Kings. Because Chronicles is no longer being viewed as inseparable from Ezra-Nehemiah, its characteristic concerns are no longer being forced into the mold of Ezra or Nehemiah.

[116] Hence, even those recent authors (e.g., Kartveit 1989; Strübind 1991) who are noncommittal about the question of separate authorship proceed to treat Chronicles as a distinct work.

VI. The Debate over Authorship and Date

◆

Like many biblical books, Chronicles is an anonymous work. The formulation of a theory of authorship is, therefore, inseparably bound up with an understanding of the setting and nature of the book. The major themes and theology of Chronicles will be explored in the introduction to the second volume of this commentary. The focus of this section will be the many complicated questions concerning the work's authorship and time of composition.

A. THE MANY PROBLEMS IN DATING CHRONICLES

Many scholars agree that the final edition of the Hebrew-Aramaic book of Daniel was edited sometime during the second century B.C.E. Would that such unanimity existed in dating the Chronicler's work. A range of over three hundred and fifty years (from the late sixth to the mid-second century B.C.E.) has been suggested for Chronicles! Each of the proposed theories of dating, whether early or late, has its strengths and weaknesses. Indeed, the range of proposals testifies to the difficulty in dating the book. It is not as if progress has been lacking in documenting the history and sociopolitical context of Persian-period Judah. Only a little more than two decades ago, one prominent scholar referred to the period from 400 to 200 B.C.E. as Judaism's "Dark Ages" (Stone 1980: 23–25). Things do not look quite so bleak now. Many contemporary biblical scholars have come to the conclusion that the Persian and Hellenistic periods were much more important in the editing of the Hebrew Scriptures than earlier generations had imagined. Whereas a few decades ago it was common to find scholars searching the Hebrew Bible for the earliest oral and written layers of composition, it is now common for scholars to be examining the extent to which the Persian period was the formative period for the composition of many biblical writings.

The archaeological finds from the Persian period are much more plentiful and better analyzed than they were a few decades ago (e.g., Stern 1982b; 1984a; 2001; Betlyon 1991; Hoglund 1992; Lemaire 1989; 1994b; 1995; Ofer 1993ab; 1997; Berquist 1995; Carter 1994; 1999; Lipschits 2001). Recourse to the material remains of ancient Palestine for establishing a context for the composition of

Chronicles is both desirable and necessary, but this new information has not been of direct consequence for dating the book in question. The discovery of hundreds of Edomite inscriptions written in Aramaic has furnished scholars with unprecedented insight into the growth and expansion of various groups in the southern Levant during the Persian period (Lemaire 1996a; 2000a; Eph'al and Naveh 1996). Thanks to the discovery of hundreds of ancient bullae, coins, and other artifacts, our knowledge of Samaria in the fourth and third centuries B.C.E. has increased exponentially.[117] Careful study of the art, inscriptions, and material remains from the Phoenician states have added considerably to our understanding of developments in the coastal region.[118]

Nevertheless, such welcome advances in epigraphy, art history, and archaeology have not materially affected the debates about the date of the Chronicler's work. Chronicles is a postexilic work that depicts the preexilic period. There are no specific references, no absolute synchronisms, and no extrabiblical citations that could definitively situate the work within a given decade or century. Recourse to the linguistic features of Chronicles for purposes of dating is also desirable and necessary. But the classification of Late Biblical Hebrew (LBH) only provides scholars with a broad range of dates to associate with the writing of the work. Hence, those who wish to see the date of Chronicles pinpointed to a specific decade or year are faced with an impossible challenge.

In this context, one should take issue with a common criterion to establish a *terminus ante quem* for the Chronicler's work. Some scholars contend that because Chronicles (purportedly) does not betray any Greek or Hellenistic influence, it cannot date to a time later than the fourth century.[119] The employment of this criterion is predicated on two faulty premises. The first is that there are no significant comparisons that can be made between the Chronicler's work and those of classical authors, while the second is that Alexander's conquest of Judea (332 B.C.E.) marks the beginning of contacts with the west. Both of these assumptions need to be questioned. As to the first issue, a number of historiographical writings from ancient Greece have been compared with Genesis and the Deuteronomistic History even though almost all scholars date Genesis and the Deuteronomistic History significantly earlier than the Chronicler's history.[120] Problems of chronology and geographical distance have not prevented scholars from undertaking such cross-cultural studies with either the Pentateuch or the Former Prophets. Given such precedents, it is surely ironic that the chronological boundary of 332 B.C.E.—Alexander's conquest of Palestine—has inhibited most scholars from

---

[117] M. Tadmor (1988); Zertal (1990; 1999); Meshorer and Qedar (1991; 1999); Machinist (1994a); Cross (1988a; 1998: 173–202); Eph'al (1998); Naveh (1998); Uehlinger (1999).

[118] Elayi (1980; 1986a; 1987; 1988; 1994); Betlyon (1982); Lund (1990); Stager (1991b); Stern (1994b; 2001); Elayi and Sayegh (1998); Nunn (2000); Lemaire (2001).

[119] Recent examples include Ackroyd (1970b: 7), Williamson (1982b: 16), and Japhet (1993a: 25–26).

[120] E.g., Van Seters (1983: 8–54, 209–321; 1988: 1–22; 1992); West (1985; 1997); Ackerman (1991); Lemche (1993; 2001); Mandell and Freedman (1993); J. P. Brown (1995; 2000); F. A. J. Nielsen (1997); Noegel (1998); Wesselius (1999); Carroll (2001); Grabbe (2001ab).

doing the same with the Chronicler's work.[121] There are, however, a number of features in the Chronicler's work that may be fruitfully compared with both classical writings and with Jewish Hellenistic writings. These areas include the development of local histories,[122] the idealization of certain characters, the use of *imitatio* (the conscious reuse of an earlier work's style or content as a means by which to identify one's own work), the excerpting or condensation of older works, and the employment of highly segmented systems of genealogies to identify and define a people (see "Excursus: The Genealogies").

Turning to the second assumption, the material remains from ancient Palestine do not support the use of 332 B.C.E. (Alexander's conquest of Judea) as the threshold for western influence upon the southern Levant. Alexander's campaigns in the east were clearly signal military and political events. Yet archaeological and historical evidence for Greek contacts with the eastern Mediterranean world predates the Macedonian conquest by centuries.[123] Stern (1982b: 283–86) points out that material remains in the Persian period from the Galilee region and the coastal plain are basically western, evincing Greek, Cypriot, and Athenian influence. The Judean hills, the Transjordan, and, to a lesser degree, Samaria are more eastern, evincing traditional culture as well as Assyrian, Babylonian, and Egyptian influences (Stern 1994a). It may well be, as some have suggested, that Yehud was initially isolated from western influence, but it would seem hazardous to deny any contacts whatsoever, especially among traders, the military, and the elite. As the centuries passed, the material remains in the Judean hills, the Transjordan, and Samaria become more and more imitative of western types. That the process of Hellenization preceded the conquest by Alexander is also suggested by the Zenon papyri[124] and to a lesser extent by the Samaria papyri.[125] Taking note of transfor-

---

[121] A few scholars (e.g., Kegler 1993: 481–97; Steins 1997: 90–92), who date Chronicles late, have viewed the Chronicler's work, at least in part, as a reaction to Hellenism. Welten (1973: 195–206) does see some Hellenistic influence on the Chronicler's descriptions of military matters. For a helpful review of the literature on the engagement of Judaism with Hellenism, see Grabbe (1992: 147–70).

[122] It seems preferable to see the Chronicler's work as focusing on Judah (within the context of the other tribes) than to see it as consisting of a series of royal biographies with a genealogical introduction (*pace* Weinberg 1996: 284–87). The genealogical consideration of all of the tribes, the attention paid to the Temple, the Levites, and the priests, and the interest in presenting the participation of the people in important events all suggest that the Chronicler was interested in more than the careers of David and his descendants.

[123] Auscher (1967); Stern (1984a; 1989a; 1995; 2001); Wenning (1990); Hoglund (1992: 97–205); Waldbaum (1994; 1997); Elayi and Sayegh (1998); Nunn (2000). Contacts are also attested in preexilic times; see, for example, Sass's (1990) and Naveh's discussion (1977: 862–63) of the seventh-century material remains from Meṣad Ḥashavyahu and Arad ostraca #1, 2, 4, 7, 8 (Aharoni 1981), as well as the recent treatments of Boardman (2001) and Niemeier (2001).

[124] A body of reports written in Greek beginning in 259 B.C.E. by Zenon, a steward of Apollonius, the financial officer of Ptolemy II Philadelphus (Edgar 1925–40). The reports focus on Zenon's trips to and experiences in Palestine.

[125] A group of mostly legal documents dating approximately to 375 through 335 B.C.E. The texts were left in a cave in the Wâdī ed-Dâliyeh north of Jericho by Samarian refugees fleeing from the army of Alexander the Great in 331 B.C.E. (Cross 1966a; 1969; 1974; 1985; 1988a; Gropp 1992; 2001). Note especially the study of Leith (1997) on the remarkably varied Greek and Persian imagery found on the seal impressions affixed to these documents.

mations in sculpture, painting, architecture, town planning, coinage, and seals, some recent scholars have begun to speak of a pre-Alexandrine *oikumene* during the fourth century in western portions of the Persian empire (e.g., Hornblower 1982; 1983; Elayi 1980; 1988; Leith 1997; Boardman 1999; 2000).

In short, Alexander's conquest should be discontinued as a benchmark to establish a *terminus ante quem* for the composition of the Chronicler's work. Ironically, jettisoning this criterion does not entail that Chronicles must be a late work. Quite the contrary, as we have seen, the contacts between east and west predate Alexander by centuries. The point is understanding the larger context in which the Chronicler worked. Recent studies of ancient history and trade suggest that major literary works stemming from Yehud may be best understood in their broader ancient Mediterranean contexts. During the Persian period one can chart the meeting of a variety of ancient cultures.

We have been discussing some of the problematic assumptions that scholars have brought to the issue of dating the Chronicler's work. Other complications include the simplistic notions employed by biblical scholars about how to date an anonymous work. One such erroneous assumption is that a composition mirrors the mood and tenor of a certain period. Two examples come to mind. Myers sees the Chronicler (i.e., the author of Chronicles-Ezra-Nehemiah) as very much concerned with the proper operation of cult. In discussing the Chronicler's "exclusivistic" orientation, Myers (1966: 265) states:

> But it must be remembered that in his time the Jewish community as an entity was at stake. Many hostile forces were beating against its flimsy and shaky tent. Social and economic conditions led many of the golah to compromise with their neighbors. The guiding voice of prophecy had ceased; the instruction of the wise men were [sic] no longer in evidence—or at best ineffective, so that the only protection against complete submersion in a sea of syncretism was the cultus.

Myers dates Chronicles in the fourth century, a period in which he believes the concern with insularity was paramount in Judah.

Other scholars, who see the Chronicler as much more of a royalist, situate Chronicles within historical contexts characterized by renewed nationalism. For some, the late sixth century (the time in which the Temple is rebuilt) holds the key to explaining the Chronicler's emphasis on the Davidic promises, Solomon's Temple, and David's ordering of its personnel.[126] The Chronicler's great interest in the monarchy purportedly matches the era when Ḥaggai and Zechariah (3:8) championed Zerubbabel as the rightful heir of the Davidic dynasty and Jeshua as the legitimate high priest. This was also a time of considerable unrest in the Achaemenid empire (Olmstead 1948: 107–18; J. M. Cook 1983: 44–66; Grabbe 1992: 124–26; Kuhrt 1995: 667–70; Briant 1996: 119–50). The great turmoil in Babylon precipi-

[126] See, for instance, Welch (1935: 241–42; 1939: 155–60); Freedman (1961: 436–42; 1993: 75–100); Cross (1975: 4–18); Newsome (1975: 216); Petersen (1977: 58–60); Roddy Braun (1986: xix); Dillard (1987: xix); Throntveit (1987: 2–5). I also held to this view in my dissertation (Knoppers 1988: 57–62), but I no longer consider such an early date to be the most likely context for the Chronicler's writing.

tated by the revolts of Nebuchadnezzar III (522 B.C.E.) and Nebuchadnezzar IV (521 B.C.E.) and by the economic crisis that followed may have helped to fuel nationalism in Judah. While some scholars associate the Chronicler's nationalism with events of the late sixth century, others correlate it with events in the fourth century. Williamson (1982b: 16–17) sees the Chronicler as very much a monarchist, but associates the composition with the Tennes rebellion in the mid-fourth century B.C.E. This revolt, although sponsored by the Sidonians, probably affected portions of Judah.[127] In Williamson's view, Chronicles was written not so much to support these rebellions as to encourage people in the wake of their failure.

The aforementioned attempts to situate Chronicles within a specific historical context are commendable, but their presumption of a direct correlation between a text and a given context needs to be rethought. Authors can respond to or even react against their circumstances.[128] To be sure, a literary work may betray its historical milieu in spite of itself. There may be hints—anachronisms, references, citations—that are important for dating.[129] Nevertheless, the literary products need not exactly mirror the conditions—whether dreary or ebullient—in which their authors lived. Writers are not only shaped by their circumstances, they can also seek to shape those circumstances. One should allow some latitude in dating a literary work, recognizing the complex relationships between authors and the social conditions in which they live.

B. THE WEIGHT OF RELATIVE CONSIDERATIONS: HOW LATE A DATE?

Given the absence of verifiable ties between Chronicles and particular historical events in the Persian and Hellenistic periods, theorizing about a date of composition becomes a matter of weighing relative considerations—archaeological, textual, and epigraphic. This does not mean that any proposed date is as viable as any other—the available evidence sets temporal limits and renders certain contexts less plausible than others—but it does mean that any proposal that tenders a spe-

[127] There were actually two fourth-century rebellions against the Persians. The first revolt (ca. 370–362 B.C.E.) was lead by the Sidonian Tennes and supported by Cypriot monarchs. The second (ca. 352–347 B.C.E.) was led by the Sidonians, Tyrians, and Egyptians (Josephus, *Ant.* 11.297–301; Diodorus Siculus, *Bibl.* 16.40–46). My dates follow those proposed by Betlyon (1986: 633–42). On the relevant Jewish and Phoenician coinage of the period, see Mildenberg (1979; 1998), Meshorer (1982), and Betlyon (1982). The extent to which either of these events involved the active participation of Judah is debated (Barag 1966: 6–12; Widengren 1977: 499–503; Stern 1982b: 236–55; M. Smith 1987: 43–45; Grabbe 1992: 99–100, 140–41; Briant 1996: 675–709). That one or both of these rebellions had an impact on people living in Judah should not be in doubt.

[128] As we have seen, this is very much the way Williamson understands the Chronicler's purpose.

[129] First Maccabees is clearly imitative of earlier biblical historiography, but it evinces its own historical context and interpretive stance through, among other things, the avoidance of direct references to the deity, the absence of miracles, and the absence of prophecies (Goldstein 1976: 12–13; 1983). Many argue that 2 Maccabees belongs to the Greek genre of "pathetic" or "tragic" history (Bickerman, 1937: 147; Goldstein 1976: 33–34; Momigliano 1978: 8; cf. Polybius 2.56; Plutarch, *Them.* 32).

cific date of composition must be regarded as speculative. It will be helpful to discuss the extreme limits that can be set for the composition of the basic form of Chronicles within the Persian and Hellenistic ages. The absolute *terminus a quo* is 538 B.C.E., the decree of Cyrus presented in 2 Chr 36:22–23. The *terminus ante quem* is the mid-third century B.C.E. The *terminus a quo* is obvious, but the *terminus ante quem* requires some defense.[130] I posit the mid-third century as the latest reasonable time for composition to explain the second- and first-century reuse of Chronicles. To begin with, one must allow some time for Chronicles or Chronicles-Ezra-Nehemiah to be brought to Egypt and translated into at least two different works: 1 Esdras (*Esdras* α) and *Paraleipomena*. To this it may be added that *Paraleipomena* is cited by Eupolemus, a Jewish-Hellenistic writer living in the second century B.C.E.[131] In the case of Eupolemus's work, one not only has to allow for Chronicles to be translated into Greek but also for this translation to become established.

Very much affecting what *terminus ante quem* one should assign to the Chronicler's work is the fact that portions of Chronicles are cited, reused, or alluded to in the second and first centuries B.C.E. Many of these references are not well known, so they require some discussion. For the sake of convenience, the relevant works will be divided according to the following categories:

1. Biblical and Apocryphal (or Deuterocanonical) Works
2. Pseudepigraphic Works
3. Dead Sea Scrolls

My concern in what follows is to trace the possible reuse or reinterpretation of the Chronicler's work in later writings. The question of authority (whether later writers considered Chronicles to be an authoritative work) is a related but distinct issue (Ben Zvi 1988; Crawford 2000).

1. *Biblical and Apocryphal (or Deuterocanonical) Works*

One may begin this brief survey with a relatively minor feature in Judith, a book commonly dated to the Hasmonean period (e.g., Moore 1985: 67–70). The author of Judith is apparently acquainted with some of the Simeonite lineages in Chronicles. In discussing Judith's various ancestors, the writer mentions a leader of Simeon named *Rhaphaein* (Jdt 8:1; LXX^{A} *Raphain*; Vg. *Raphaim*). This text seems to allude, in slightly corrupted form, to "Rephaiah" (MT רפיה; LXX *Rhaphaia*) one of "the men of Simeon," who "journeyed to the hill country of Seir" (1 Chr 4:42). The author(s) of the introductory chapters of Daniel are familiar with at least part of the Chronicler's work. In referring to the circumstances and aftermath of the Babylonian Exile, the writer of Dan 1:1–2 draws upon 2 Chr 36:6b–7, a text unparalleled in 2 Kgs 24, which relates that Nebuchadnezzar had

---

[130] Especially so, because the Maccabean hypothesis has been revived in recent years (e.g., Steins 1995; 1997: 84–92).

[131] Eupolemus's quotation of certain texts dealing with David and Solomon is preserved in Eusebius (*Praep. ev.* 9.30.1–34.18) and discussed by Gerleman (1946: 11–13). Carl Holladay (1983), Attridge (1984), and especially Wacholder (1974) provide detailed reconstructions of Eupolemus's work.

Jehoiaqim bound in chains and brought to Babylon. There is no account in Kings of Nebuchadnezzar's exile of Jehoiaqim to Babylon.[132] The Chronicler also makes an important claim about the Temple furnishings: "As for some of the furnishings of the Temple of Yhwh, Nebuchadnezzar brought [them] to Babylon and deposited them in his temple in Babylon" (ומכלי בית יהוה הביא נבוכדנאצר לבבל ויתנם בהיכלו בבבל; 2 Chr 36:7).[133] Again, this assertion finds no parallel in Kings. Indebted to the account found in Chronicles, the author of Daniel declares that "The Lord[134] delivered Jehoiaqim king of Judah into his hand and some of the furnishings of the Temple of God[135] over to Nebuchadnezzar, and he [Nebuchadnezzar] brought them to the land of Shinar" (Dan 1:2).[136] The author of Daniel, like the Chronicler himself, takes a keen interest in the fate of the Temple vessels, "And the furnishings he brought to the treasury of his god" (ואת-הכלים הביא בית אוצר אלהיו; Dan 1:2). In brief, it is clear that Daniel draws from Chronicles in its account of Jehoiaqim's Babylonian exile.

Ben Sira also seems to know parts of the Chronicler's work. Ben Sira alludes to the description of David's cultic policies in Chronicles when he speaks of David's establishing singers before the altar to provide sweet melody with their voices, his giving beauty to the festivals, arranging their times to completion, "causing his [God's] holy name to be praised and the sanctuary to resound from daybreak" (47:9–10).[137] Some knowledge of Chronicles is evident in the composition of 1 Maccabees. The author of 1 Macc 2:1 is familiar with the priestly rota described in 1 Chr 24:1–19, because he traces the ancestry of Mattathias the Maccabee to one of the priestly families who were awarded lots (SOURCES AND COMPOSITION to 1 Chr 24:1–19). The 1 Maccabees account has, in fact, an edge to it. The author privileges Mattathias by linking him to Jehoiarib, who was awarded the very first lot (1 Chr 24:7a). If Chronicles was unknown or had just been written, it is implausible that the authors of Daniel, 1 Maccabees, and Sirach would use it as a source upon which to construct their own accounts.

---

[132] The first part of 2 Chr 36:6 draws upon 2 Kgs 24:1, but there is no parallel in 2 Kgs 24 to 2 Chr 36:6b–7. According to 2 Kgs 24:6, Jehoiaqim died and lay with his ancestors (in Jerusalem). There is no record of Jehoiaqim's death and burial in Chronicles.

[133] As we have seen (IV.A.2), the fate of the Temple furnishings is a continuity theme in Chronicles and the early chapters of Ezra. On the passage in Daniel, see Koch (1986: 27–31) and Collins (1993: 130–34). Kalimi (1998a: 9–10) points out that the reuse of the material from Chronicles fits well into the narrative agenda established by the author(s) of Daniel.

[134] So MT (אדוני). A few Heb. MSS יהוה.

[135] So MT (אלהים). LXX *Kyrios*.

[136] For "Shinar," LXX reads "Babylon." MT adds "house of his god" (בית אלהיו). I am following LXX$^{O'}$, which lacks the phrase *lectio brevior*.

[137] It may be that the author of Sir 47:8–10 knew of other texts (Ezra 3:10; Neh 12:24) that allude to David's appointment of temple singers (Ben Zvi 1988: 61–62). Nevertheless, there do not seem to be any compelling reasons to distance Ben Sira's description of David's organization of cultic worship from the detailed descriptions found in Chronicles (1 Chr 15:16–29; 16:4–6, 37–42; 23:3–5, 24–32; 25:1–7; 2 Chr 5:11–14). The Chronicler's work remains the most complete and clearest source for Ben Sira's assertions about David's role in appointing musicians and ordering the festivals associated with the sanctuary. See further Skehan and Di Lella (1987: 522–26) and Kalimi (1998a: 12–13).

2. *Pseudepigraphic Works*

Among the Pseudepigrapha, the *Prayer of Manasseh* is clearly dependent upon the account of King Manasseh's repentance found in 2 Chr 33:12–13, 18–19. The Deuteronomistic portrayal of Manasseh makes him out to be Judah's worst king (2 Kgs 21:1–18). The Manasseh of Kings never repents. The *Prayer of Manasseh* is interesting as it fills a significant gap within the Chronicler's text—a notorious sinner utters an efficacious prayer, but the prayer itself is not given. It is also relevant to observe that the author of this long Jewish prayer has partially modeled its contents after the account of Manasseh's misdeeds and repentance in 2 Chr 33:2–12 (Charlesworth 1985: 628–29). The date and language of the work's original composition are much disputed. Most estimates of the work's date range between the second century B.C.E. and the end of the first century C.E.[138]

Mention should also be made in this context of an important superscription in the noncanonical psalms collection found at Qumran relating to Manasseh (4Q381 frg. 33, 1.8–11; Schuller 1986; 1992; 1997). The superscription mentions a "prayer of Manasseh, king of Judah, when the king of Assyria imprisoned him" (תפלה למנשה מלך יהודה בכלו אתו מלך אשור; 4Q381 33 1.8), but the accompanying psalm does not resemble the *Prayer of Manasseh* in the Pseudepigrapha.[139] Nor, for that matter, does the noncanonical psalm show a clear dependence on the account of Manasseh's reign in 2 Chr 33:1–19. Hence, the title is the clearest tie between the lament and 2 Chr 33. On the basis of language, style, and orthography, the collection of noncanonical psalms (of which 4Q381 33 is a part) is dated by Schuller (1986; 1997) and Tov (1986: 56) to the late Persian or early Hellenistic period. How does one explain the association with Manasseh? Schniedewind (1991; 1996) suggests that the prayer of Manasseh at Qumran represents an early tradition that may predate the Chronicler's work. This is certainly possible, as the Chronicler may have used an extrabiblical source in composing his distinctive account of Manasseh's reign. Alternatively, Schuller suggests that a traditional (noncanonical) psalm became associated with Manasseh. Presumably, this occurred sometime after the Chronicler wrote his work. In this understanding, the psalm predates its superscription. If this reconstruction has merit, one has to reckon with two independent prayers of Manasseh dating to antiquity, both of which explicate an intriguing feature of the Chronicler's presentation.

Ben Zvi (1988: 63–64) points out that the history of the divided monarchy presented in the *Testament of Moses* (2.5–9) reflects some aspects of the Chronicler's distinctive portrayal of this period. The numerical details about those Judahite kings who made fortifications, those who rebelled against God, and those who were protected by the deity all seem to reflect a reading of monarchical history in Chronicles. Kings, by contrast, reflects different numbers and supplies little information about the building activities of Judahite monarchs. Dates for the composi-

---

[138] The prayer is dated by Charlesworth (1985: 627) to the second or first century B.C.E., even though he acknowledges and cites a wide range of opinion.

[139] Schuller thinks that another fragment (4Q381 45) may also be related to this psalm.

tion of this pseudepigraphic work vary widely, ranging from the second century B.C.E. to the second century C.E., but many date it to the first century C.E. (Priest 1983: 920–21). The contention that Pseudo-Philo's *Liber Antiquitatum Biblicarum* (*LAB*; "Book of Biblical Antiquities") was written to supplement the Chronicler's account of the period extending from the first person (Adam; 1 Chr 1:1) through the time of Saul (1 Chr 10:1–14; Kalimi 1998a: 14–15), while certainly interesting, is less relevant in this context. The argument is predicated on demonstrating that all of the details found in the *LAB* about the Exodus, wilderness journeys, Conquest, and so forth are designed to be a counterpoint or a corollary to the presentation of the same period in Chronicles. To be sure, if the argument holds, it presupposes the existence of the first ten chapters of Chronicles. But since the *LAB* explicitly draws from other biblical books (and not from Chronicles), its evidence is of an indirect, rather than of a direct, nature. As with many pseudepigraphic works, there is no consensus about the original date for the composition of the *LAB*. Harrington (1985: 297–300) dates it to the first century C.E.

3. The Dead Sea Scrolls

Certain documents from Qumran show a familiarity with, if not a dependence upon, texts in Chronicles. The *Temple Scroll* (11QT[a]), dating from the early second century B.C.E. (Puech 1997: 63; García Martínez 1999: 444; Crawford 2000: 26) or the very beginning of the first (Yadin 1983: 1.386–90), draws heavily upon a variety of Pentateuchal texts. But especially in those contexts in which the writers are describing the Temple, they draw upon other texts as well, such as Kings, Ezekiel, and Chronicles.[140] The portions of the *Temple Scroll* depicting the sanctuary, its chambers, courts, furnishings, and stoas (cols. 2.1–13.8; 30.3–47.18) are indebted to the biblical texts describing Solomon's Temple. Indeed, Yadin (1983: 1.82–83, 177) and others argue that the texts of Exod 25:1–9 and 1 Chr 28:11–19, describing a plan *(tabnît)* from God for the sanctuary, are an essential starting point for understanding the context of the scroll itself. The *Temple Scroll* seems to present itself as a Temple plan, a realization of the pattern(s) handed over earlier to Moses and David, even though the work draws upon a range of earlier texts and supplements them with its own regulations and architectural details. The composition of this material in the *Temple Scroll* has relevance for the dating of Chronicles, because the scroll seems to draw upon and reuse parts of older works (e.g., 4QRP; 4Q524). If this is so, the earlier dates proposed for the composition of the *Temple Scroll* (see above) become more likely and the composition of Chronicles has to be pushed back to at least some time in the early to mid-third century B.C.E.[141]

---

[140] Stegemann (1989: 146) contends that the author(s) of the *Temple Scroll* only knew some of the traditions that may have been used in the composition of Chronicles, but see Swanson (1992; 1995).

[141] Steins (1995: 373–93) makes the interesting claim that sections dealing with Solomon's Temple building in 2 Chr 3–4 are indebted to an extrabiblical document that was perhaps a precursor of the

Sections of the *War Scroll* (1QM), "The Sons of Light against the Sons of Darkness," dealing with the organization of army divisions reveal an indebtedness to the system of divisions attributed to David in Chronicles (1.2.7–10; Yadin 1962: 80–86). In Yadin's view, the organization of twelve rotating military divisions in the *War Scroll* does not exactly duplicate, but is very much informed by the system of twelve rotating military courses of 24,000 troops described in Chronicles, each of which was to serve one month per year (1 Chr 27:1–15). In both cases, the divisions are directed by single individuals. Similarly, in both cases, the twelve military divisions draw upon the various Israelite tribes, but are not organized according to the tribal principle. It has also been argued that the typology of the forty-year war described in this work (1QM) is dependent on the forty-year Davidic reign in Chronicles (Sweeney 1990), but this is much less certain.

Various calendrical scrolls at Qumran (e.g., 4Q320–30), show a dependence on the system(s) of twenty-four courses described in 1 Chr 24–27, especially those found in 1 Chr 24 (Talmon 1989; Beckwith 1996; Glessmer 1998; VanderKam 1998; Talmon, Ben Dov, and Glessmer 2001). The authors of these elaborate and important documents coordinated the observance of festivals and Sabbaths with the litany of successive priestly divisions found in Chronicles. The number, names, and sequence of priestly courses in many of these works match those of 1 Chr 24:1–19. Because the twenty-four priestly courses served in a regular succession, as defined by the model presented in Chronicles, weeks and days could be designated by recourse to these sacerdotal divisions.

The connections among David's successful military campaigns (2 Chr 18–20), David's construction of an altar, and the future site of the Temple appear in a fragmentary text (4Q522) from Qumran, sometimes called the *Prophecy of Joshua* (Puech 1992; 1998). This fascinating text, which forms part of the larger *Apocryphon of Joshua* (Qimron 1994), has God explain to Joshua why he should refrain from taking Jerusalem. Among other things, the document predicts David's taking of "the rock of Zion" (את סלע ציון; line 4), his laying aside of gold and silver for the Temple (line 5), and his importation of cedar and cyprus from Lebanon for the Temple's construction (line 6). In the depiction of David's reign, the author is clearly drawing from Chronicles. In 1 Kgs 5–7 Solomon both prepares for and constructs the Temple that David was forbidden to build (2 Sam 7), but in 1 Chr 21–22 and 28–29 David himself makes elaborate plans for the Temple to be constructed by his son. David's actions include the construction of an altar at the future site of the sanctuary (1 Chr 21:18–22:1), the securing of massive amounts of cedar from the Sidonians and Tyrians (22:4–5), and the dedication of a hundred thousand talents of gold and a million talents of silver for the Temple (22:14; cf. 29:2–5). The *Prophecy of Joshua* is dated by Puech (1992: 689–91) to the second century B.C.E.

Temple Scroll (or a text like it). If this argument were to be sustained (it has yet to undergo critical scrutiny), it would not only tie one edition of Chronicles more closely to the tradition behind the *Temple Scroll*, but it would also reverse the direction of dependence.

In another text, the *Commentary on Genesis* A (4Q252), an allusion is made to the text of 2 Chr 20:7. The *Commentary on Genesis* A identifies the "tents of Shem" (Gen 9:27) as the land given to "Abraham his beloved" (4Q252 2.7–8). Finally, one should mention the evidence provided by the fragment of Chronicles among the Dead Sea Scrolls. Trebolle Barrera's preliminary edition (1992a: 528) of Chronicles (4Q118) assigns this text to between 50 and 25 B.C.E. and debates whether this text is a citation of Chronicles or a fragment of a Chronicles scroll. Given the date assigned to this work, it is of less value for dating the original Chronicler's work than is some of the other textual evidence stemming from Qumran.

The evidence supplied by biblical, deuterocanonical, and pseudepigraphical works is not of equal value for determining a *terminus ante quem* for the composition of the Chronicler's work. The evidence supplied by the Pseudepigrapha is not altogether helpful because the dates assigned to its works are so disputed. Similarly, the partial reuse of the Simeonite genealogy in Judith would be a meager basis upon which to establish a *terminus ante quem* for Chronicles. But the testimony of Daniel, 1 Maccabees, Ben Sira, and the Dead Sea Scrolls is clearly more helpful. When taken together with the Septuagintal evidence for two translations of (at least parts of) Chronicles, Ezra, and Nehemiah (1 Esdras and *Paraleipomena*) and the citation of *Paraleipomena* in Eupolemus, the collective evidence points to a mid-third-century date as the latest reasonable time for composition. The Chronicler's work was clearly not as influential in early Judaism as were some other biblical writings, such as Deuteronomy and the Psalms. Nevertheless, in accounting for the reuse and citation of Chronicles in the second and first centuries B.C.E., one has to allow some time for the text to become established. In the case of the Septuagintal evidence and Eupolemus, one has to allow both for Chronicles to be translated into Greek and for this translation to be cited by a Jewish-Hellenistic author.

C. THE WEIGHT OF RELATIVE CONSIDERATIONS: HOW EARLY A DATE?

We have seen that the content of Chronicles and its relationship to Ezra-Nehemiah indicate that the date of its composition is unlikely to be later than the mid-third century. Another set of considerations suggests that an early (sixth century) date for its composition is also unlikely. First, if the Second Temple was under construction when the Chronicler wrote, one would have expected him to devote much greater attention to the specifications and construction of Solomon's sanctuary (Dillard 1987: 31). He substantially abbreviates, however, the Deuteronomistic narration of Temple building and Temple furnishings (2 Chr 3:1–5:1; cf. 1 Kgs 6:1–7:51). This suggests that the Temple was already standing when the author wrote. The great attention the writer devotes to other matters, such as the staffing and rota of the shrine, indicates that he was more concerned with buttressing the Temple's legitimacy and addressing its polity than he was in commenting on the actual dimensions of the structure itself.[142]

In any event, the early Achaemenid period was undoubtedly not the only time in which a Judean author would consider it important to compose a work that promoted the Jerusalem Temple. The Jerusalem sanctuary was not without rivals. The claim has been made (Blenkinsopp 1998; 2003) that the sanctuary near or at Bethel, along with its priestly cultus, survived into Neo-Babylonian times. Apart from the Jerusalem Temple, another Jewish sanctuary is known to have existed at Elephantine (Vincent 1937; Porten 1968; 1984; Bolin 1995). Whether there were also Jewish shrines at Casiphia[143] and Lachish is disputed.[144] In the second century B.C.E., Jews would build a temple at Leontopolis in Egypt (Josephus, *Ant.* 12.388ff.; *J.W.* 7.436; Jerome, *Expl. Dan.* 3.11.14; Delcor 1968; Bohak 1996: 19–40). For their part, the Samarians built a temple on Mt. Gerizim (Josephus, *Ant.* 11.346–347; Purvis 1981; 1988). In short, the reconstruction of the House of God in Jerusalem did not put an end to all other sanctuary construction. In the context of the Persian and Hellenistic periods, the exclusive authority and privilege of the Jerusalem Temple should not be taken for granted. Its supporters had to argue and promote their case. What is more, the Jerusalem sanctuary, unlike most other temples in the Achaemenid empire, does not seem to have had its own extensive lands to support it (Dandamaev and Lukonin 1989: 360–66). This meant that the Jerusalem Temple was dependent on the goodwill of patrons for its maintenance. Persian period texts paint an uneven picture of support for the Temple within Yehud. The author of Isa 66:1–2 casts aspersions on the legitimacy of the Second Temple, questioning whether transcendent Yhwh really needed this earthly house (Hanson 1979: 170–86). The prophet Ḥaggai (2:3) complains that the people of Yehud were not always generous in either the quantity or the quality of their Temple offerings. One wonders whether the enthusiasm and whole-

---

[142] E.g., 1 Chr 5:27–41; 6:1–66; 23:1–26:32; 2 Chr 8:14–16; 13:4–12; 29:3–31:21. See most recently Dyck (1996; 1998).

[143] Whether the references to "the place" *(ham-māqôm)* in Casiphia (Ezra 8:17) and to the "sanctuary" *(miqdāš)* in Ezek 11:16 constitute evidence for the existence of a Jewish sanctuary in Babylonia is textually uncertain (Purvis 1988:158–60; *pace* Browne 1916: 400–401; Ackroyd 1968: 34–35; 1970b: 25–27; Chong 1996). Blenkinsopp (1992: 238) speaks of Casiphia as a "cultic establishment . . . a center of worship and learning." On the construction, *bĕkāsipyāʾ ham-māqôm,* see Williamson (1985: 116–17).

[144] Aharoni (1975: 5–11) and Widengren (1977: 557) believe that the shrine was Yahwistic. Disputing that the sanctuary at Lachish was Judean, Stern (1984ab) argues that the Lachish sanctuary was Edomite. Actually, Aharoni points to the existence of two successive but architecturally similar shrines at Lachish, the first (building 10) dating to the Persian age and the second (building 106), the so-called Solar-Shrine, constructed at the end of the third century. On the basis of both architectural evidence (e.g., similarities between the plan of the Lachish shrines and those of the Arad temple) and epigraphic evidence (the Aramaic inscription on a Persian period altar), Aharoni argues for the Yahwistic orientation of both sanctuaries. In my judgment, Aharoni's argument from architecture is stronger than his argument from epigraphy. Aharoni's analysis of the Aramaic inscription is much disputed (e.g., Lemaire 1974; 1994b; Lipiński 1975: 143–45). Further weakening Widengren's and Aharoni's arguments is the fact that according to most recent archaeological studies, Lachish lay outside the boundaries of Yehud.

hearted support with which all the people greeted both the Temple construction and later reform efforts in Chronicles are meant to address similar concerns.

Similarly, the age of Zerubbabel and Jeshua seems to be only one of a number of historical contexts in which an author would underscore the unity of Israel, the perpetual ties between God, people, and land, and the legitimacy of the institutions established during the United Monarchy. There is no reason to believe, for example, that Jews in the Persian period would uniformly advocate the reinstitution of the Davidic monarchy. Aside from the practical consideration that the Jews were under foreign domination and unlikely to regain their independence, there were those who saw no need, conditions permitting, to revitalize the Davidic monarchy. During the Babylonian Exile, Deutero-Isaiah announced a new dispensation in Yhwh's dealing with his people. In his vision, there is no warrant to reestablish a Davidic monarchy. Yhwh was democratizing the Davidic promises (Isa 55:3–5). The people themselves now had a Davidic role to play among the nations. The authors of Trito-Isaiah extend and revise these same themes (e.g., Isa 60–62). Given this creative reapplication of the Davidic promises, those Judeans who believed in a more traditional understanding of the Davidic covenant would have ample justification to compose a text, which would underscore the ongoing validity of Yhwh's commitment to David's descendants (e.g., 2 Chr 13:4–5).

Moreover, if the troubles attending the beginning of the rule of Darius I contributed to renewed royalism and nationalism in Yehud, the same could be said for the Egyptian revolts of the fifth century. The first revolt occurred at the end of the reign of Darius I and the beginning of the reign of Xerxes I (486 B.C.E.).[145] The second revolt, led by Inaros, occurred early in the reign of Artaxerxes I (ca. 460 B.C.E.).[146] These rebellions were serious, albeit temporary, threats to Achaemenid rule in the eastern Mediterranean. To compound matters for the Persians, the second insurrection was accompanied by the intervention of armed forces from the Delian League on the side of the Egyptians.[147] Some in Yehud may have seen in either of these revolts an opportunity for new autonomy and independence. In any case, one need not look for a specific crisis or conflict as the occasion for the composition of the Chronicler's writing. By the late sixth century Judaism was already an international religion. Jewish communities existed in both Babylon and Egypt. Despite having permission to return home, many Jews in Babylon apparently saw no need to leave.[148] Nehemiah (7:4–5; 11:1–2) found it necessary to in-

---

[145] Olmstead (1948: 227–36); Dandamaev (1989: 178–83). The assertion of Aharoni (1979: 412) and Stern (1982b: 253–55; 1984a:114) that there is archaeological evidence of widespread destruction in Benjamin and in southern Samaria dating to around 480 B.C.E. is contested by Hoglund (1992: 62–69).

[146] Herodotus (*Hist.* 3.12, 15; 7.7); Thucydides (*Hist. Pelop.* 1.104, 109–10); Ctesias (*Persika* 14–15); *FGrH* (3c, 688); Diodorus Siculus (*Bibl.* 2.32.4; 11.71, 74–75, 77; 12.3).

[147] Olmstead (1948: 262–71); Cook (1983: 127–31); Miller and Hayes (1986: 462–64); Dandamaev (1989: 238–43); Grabbe (1992: 129–31); Hoglund (1992: 97–164).

[148] Note, in this context, the recent publication of a late-sixth-century cuneiform tablet from Babylonia, bearing the inscription ^{uru}*ia-a-ḫu-du*, normalized by Joannès and Lemaire (1999) as ^{al}*Yâhûdû*, "the town of Judah." The tablet contains twelve Hebrew names.

crease Jerusalem's population by approximately 10 percent.[149] The everlasting ties that the Chronicler posits between God, king, people, and land underscore the centrality of land to Jewish identity. Indeed, the people inhabiting the land have a pivotal role to play in the well-being of those in other territories. Solomon speaks of popular prayers directed at the Jerusalem Temple having positive effects on those in exile.[150] Ḥezeqiah speaks of the abandonment of the Jerusalem Temple as a reason for the exile of many Judahites during the reign of his predecessor, Aḥaz (2 Chr 29:5–11). The Chronicler's Ḥezeqiah, unlike the Deuteronomist's Ḥezeqiah, also sends a remarkable message to the people "throughout Israel, from Beer-sheba to Dan," inviting them to worship at the House of God and to participate in a national Passover. He informs them that the return of their kin and children from captivity is linked to their repentance (2 Chr 30:1–9). Given the nature and extent of the Diaspora, one is hard-pressed to pinpoint a specific date, much less a particular century, for the Chronicler's stress on the importance of the people, city, Temple, and land to those outside the land.

Second, the Chronicler's very indebtedness to a wide variety of biblical texts makes it unlikely that he wrote so early as 525–515 B.C.E. In the last few decades, scholars have become much more cognizant of the importance of the Persian period for the shaping and editing of various biblical writings. One must allow sufficient time for disparate works, such as Isaiah, the Yahwistic work, Deuteronomy, Joshua, and the Priestly writing to be written and become established in the community. One must also allow, as Japhet (1993a: 27) points out, a certain chronological distance between the Chronicler and his Deuteronomistic predecessors. The Chronicler is heavily dependent upon Samuel-Kings for his account of the monarchy, but he also exhibits an adroitness in departing from his *Vorlage* whenever he sees fit. The Chronicler's conservatism in quoting the Deuteronomistic History coupled with his use of omission, supplementation, and recontexualization to create his own distinctive composition suggests that the Deuteronomistic History enjoyed a certain currency in his time. Yet the very same features of the

[149] The population estimates for postexilic Judah have varied wildly. Yamauchi (1980: 196–97) provides a convenient survey of opinion. Meyer's estimate (1896: 185) is only 10,000. According to Albright (1963: 87), the population of the territory of Yehud in 522 B.C.E. can scarcely have been more than 20,000. Happily, a series of site surveys have brought a measure of control to the investigation (Ofer 1993a; 1997; Carter 1994; 1999; 2003). When seen against the evidence furnished by the material remains, Weinberg's total (1972; cf. 1992: 34–48) of over 200,000 pre–458 B.C.E. Judeans, based primarily upon a series of inferences from Kings and Ezra-Nehemiah, is untenable. Carter estimates the fourth-century population of Judah to be close to Albright's estimate for the late sixth century. Lipschits (2003) would put the estimate a little higher (about 30,000). See also the more general remarks of Ahlström (1993: 831–35).

[150] The Chronicler basically duplicates this petition from his *Vorlage* (2 Chr 6:36–39; cf. 1 Kgs 8:46–53; McKenzie 1985: 199–205; Knoppers 1993c: 106–8). The Chronicler's placement of and additions to Solomon's prayer generate new meanings. Note three important additions that he makes to his *Vorlage*: first, the reuse of Ps 132: 8–10 to climax Solomon's prayer (2 Chr 6:41–42), second, the unparalleled divine affirmation of Solomon's prayer in the form of fire (2 Chr 7:1–3; cf. Lev 9:24; Judg 13:19, 20; 1 Kgs 18:38), and third, the Chronicler's positive rewrite of the second divine theophany to Solomon (2 Chr 7:12–22; cf. 1 Kgs 9:1–9). See Pratt (1987: 198–273) and the commentary (vol. 2) to 2 Chr 6 and 7.

Chronicler's compositional technique indicate something else as well. Sufficient time had elapsed from the writing of the Deuteronomistic historical work that the Chronicler did not see this older literary corpus as meeting the needs of his own time.

Third, the book's depiction of cultic institutions is complex and not at all rudimentary.[151] Among the reasons some commentators date Chronicles late (e.g., the late fourth century) is the developed nature of the Chronicler's cultic institutions. To be sure, this hypothesis presumes that portions of Chronicles dealing with these matters (e.g., 1 Chr 9; 15–16; 23–27) are original and that Temple polity became more complex over time. If the sacerdotal orders are more developed in Chronicles than they are in Ezra-Nehemiah, the former must postdate the latter. Admittedly, this criterion is of somewhat limited value, because the order and number of Temple personnel may have expanded or contracted according to varying political, cultic, and economic conditions.[152] Finally, the use of some technical terms and rosters in Chronicles seems to belie a late-sixth-century date. The persuasiveness of the arguments based on these terms and lists vary, however. Each passage occurs in a disputed context. The anachronistic use of darics in 1 Chr 29:7 (TEXTUAL NOTE) is problematic for an early date of the Chronicler's History (Williamson 1977a: 123–26; Bivar 1985: 617–21). Darius I did not issue this coin until 515 B.C.E. and one must allow some time for its dissemination in Palestine. Mosis (1973: 105–6) and Throntveit (1987: 89–96) claim, however, that this text is part of a secondary expansion. These authors point to a number of peculiarities in the vocabulary and placement of 1 Chr 29:1–9, but these traits may not be sufficiently jarring to justify assigning this pericope to the work of a later redactor (SOURCES AND COMPOSITION to 1 Chr 29).

The genealogy of Jehoiachin (1 Chr 3:17–24) is also an obstacle to an early date of composition. To be sure, this lineage is text-critically, grammatically, and syntactically fraught with difficulties (Rothstein 1902). The number of generations recounted varies from five to fourteen according to different interpretations (TEXTUAL NOTES to 1 Chr 3:20–21). But by any reckoning, the line of descent extends at least two generations beyond that of Zerubbabel (3:19–24), effectively ruling out a 525–515 date of composition. Despite this fact, the genealogical argument has not been terribly influential, because the compositional history of the lineages in Chronicles has been subject to such avid debate. Scholars typically see 1 Chr 1–9, of all the major sections in Chronicles, as the most subject to later additions and glosses.[153] Even among those scholars who see a core of 1 Chr 1–9 as original

---

[151] See Gese (1974: 147–58), Williamson (1979a; 1982b: 120–22), and Japhet (1993a: 26–27), although I do not agree with all of their conclusions.

[152] One could also argue that the writer wrote his work paradigmatically. Rather than a reflection of priestly orders in the writer's own time, the work may simply reflect the writer's preferred configuration of priestly polity. Nevertheless, it seems more likely, in this case, that the author is justifying postexilic institutions, however transformed and idealized by the writer, by recourse to Davidic policies many centuries earlier.

[153] E.g., Welch (1935; 1939); Noth (1943); Rudolph (1955); Newsome (1975). See further, V.A (above).

to the Chronicler's work, there are some who doubt that all or part of 1 Chr 3:17–24 is original.[154]

The list in 1 Chr 9:2–17, paralleled in Neh 11:3–19, has also been cited as relevant for dating. Some scholars (e.g., Japhet 1993a: 18; Weinberg 1996: 281–84) have claimed that the Chronicler borrowed this material from Nehemiah, but the significance of the parallel is uncertain. The Chronicler's indebtedness to Nehemiah is only one possible explanation of the data. The lists contain more variant readings than they do parallels. The account in Chronicles is generally shorter, the account in Nehemiah more expansive. To complicate matters further, the list in LXX Neh 11 is substantially shorter than that of MT Neh 11. In my judgment, it seems more likely that the editors of Chronicles and Nehemiah reworked and expanded an older source in very distinctive ways (Knoppers 2000c). Hence, the existence of a partial parallel in Neh 11 to 1 Chr 9 is not of great help for dating the Chronicler's work.

The genealogy in 1 Chr 3:17–24, the list in 1 Chr 9:2–17, and the mention of darics in 1 Chr 29:7 vary in their value for dating Chronicles. To press the case for an early time of composition, one has to jettison at least part of 1 Chr 3:19–24 and 1 Chr 29:7. The genealogy of Jehoiachin is text-critically problematic, but I see no compelling grounds to excise this lineage simply because of its difficult features. Finally, the inadvertent appearance of darics in 1 Chr 29:7 speaks against dating Chronicles in the age of Zerubbabel and Jeshua.

D. SUMMARY

Given the limited amount of evidence directly bearing on the composition of Chronicles, this commentary allows a range of dates, from the late fifth century through the mid-third century. My own inclination is toward a date in the late fourth or early third century.[155] The *terminus a quo* is contingent upon the date of composition of Ezra 1–3 and its relationship to the rest of the Ezra materials. Due to editorial work, Ezra-Nehemiah became appended to the Chronicler's work (1–2 Chronicles). First Esdras, followed by Josephus, bears witness to this larger unity, even if it differs from MT Chronicles-Ezra-Nehemiah in some of its contents and sequence of pericopes. If one assumes both that the initial chapters of

[154] Rudolph (1955: 26); Myers (1965a: 19); Ackroyd (1973a: 34–35); De Vries (1989: 41–44); Kartveit (1989: 48–49, 108). For different perspectives, see Kittel (1902: 21–27); Osborne (1979: 228–33); Oeming (1990: 103–4); Japhet (1993a: 92–94); Knoppers (2001b).

[155] Similarly, Albertz (1994) opts for either the late fourth century or the first half of the third century. Most scholars date Ezra-Nehemiah (or Chronicles-Ezra-Nehemiah) to the fourth century. See, for instance, Curtis and Madsen (1910: 5–6); Albright (1950: 71); Myers (1965a: lxxxvii–lxxxix); Eissfeldt (1965: 540); Rudolph (1955: x); Japhet (1972: 533; 1993a: 27); Williamson (1982b: 15–17; 1985: xxxv–xxxvi); Gabriel (1990: 2); North (1990); Oeming (1990: 4–47); Kalimi (1993a: 228–33); Kleinig (1993: 24–26); Riley (1993: 26); Selman (1994a: 69–71); Brian Kelly (1996: 26–28); Dyck (1998: 33). Some date the work to the third century (e.g., Noth 1957: 150–55; Welten 1973: 199–200; Strübind 1991: 23–25; Ruffing 1992: 301–2).

Ezra presuppose the existence of some form of Chronicles and that these chapters were one of the last sections composed within Ezra-Nehemiah (Williamson 1983a; Halpern 1990), this pushes the *terminus a quo* to at least the end of the fifth century. In any case, the primary composition of Chronicles should be separated from that of Ezra-Nehemiah. The advantage to this reconstruction is that it accounts for the testimony of Chronicles, the connections between Chronicles and Ezra, and the evidence of 1 Esdras. Given the differences among these works, it will be helpful to be consistent in describing them. In this commentary, "the Chronicler's work," "the Chronicler's history," and "the Chronistic history" all refer to Chronicles.

VII. The Issue of Extrabiblical Sources

◆

Over the past two centuries the issue of whether the Chronicler employed extrabiblical sources has exercised the imaginations of many commentators.[156] The issue has attracted intense scrutiny not only from those scholars directly concerned with Chronicles (and Ezra-Nehemiah) but also from those concerned with the composition of the Pentateuch and the Former Prophets. Given that historical criticism has dominated biblical studies in general and Chronicles studies in particular during the modern era, the scholarly preoccupation with sources is not surprising. But the concern with source-critical theory takes on an added dimension when it is applied to the Chronicler's work. In the case of Chronicles, source criticism has been intimately tied to questions of history writing and of genre.[157] Those commentators who have presented Chronicles as an example of ancient historiography have often done so on the basis of arguments that the Chronicler selectively used one or more extrabiblical sources in composing his writing. But others have adamantly argued the opposite position, namely that the Chronicler did not use preexilic noncanonical materials in preparing his work. Several recent studies have shown, in fact, that the usefulness of the Chronicler's work has been measured in the modern era to no small degree by the criterion of whether the Chronicler employed authentic preexilic sources and thus presents a historically credible picture of Israel's past.[158] Because of the great attention given to the subject, it is impossible to do justice to all of the different scholarly theories within the context of one section in a commentary introduction. The following treatment, necessarily limited, will begin with a review of the major stances taken on the issue of noncanonical sources. Following a discussion of the Chronicler's use (and nonuse) of source citations, we will revisit the issue of what role source criticism should play in historical reconstruction.

In the nineteenth century a series of scholars, most prominently de Wette

---

[156] For a discussion of the Chronicler's use of biblical sources, see III.A above.

[157] The operative assumption at work in this traditional point of view is that historians, whether modern or ancient, can be distinguished from other sorts of writers by their critical use of sources. To be sure, this is not the only distinction made in these sorts of discussions, but it is one of them.

[158] Emblematic of this subject's importance is the fact that a variety of major studies (Willi 1972: 12–47; Japhet 1985; Wright 1991; Peltonen 1999) and books (Graham 1990; Peltonen 1996) have been devoted to it.

(1806–7) and Wellhausen (1885), sought to discredit the value of Chronicles for reconstructing Israelite history by presenting the Chronicler's work as late and historically untrustworthy. In this period, the criticism of the Chronicler's work was very much tied to the establishment of the documentary hypothesis. Wellhausen (1885: 171–227) used the witness of Chronicles to surmount a major obstacle to a late dating of the Priestly work (one of the major sources or strands of the Pentateuch). If pro-Priestly Chronicles could be shown to be both late and historically unreliable, the Chronicler's claims for monarchical adherence to Priestly law could be safely ignored as simply reflecting the author's own circumstances in the postexilic period. With the testimony of Chronicles set aside, Wellhausen (1885: 222–27) believed that he could safely date P to the exile or later. While Wellhausen affirmed that the Chronicler had recourse to extrabiblical sources, he thought these were relatively few in number and as unreliable as the Chronicler himself.[159]

A second group of scholars present a modified version of the first position. These commentators contend that the Chronicler had access to an expanded version of Samuel-Kings or to an early commentary on it.[160] They point, for example, to the concluding regnal formulas for certain monarchs that vary from those employed in Kings. Whereas the writer of 2 Kgs 15:6 refers readers to "the book of the events of the days of the kings of Judah" *(sēper dibrê hayyāmîm lĕmalkê yĕhûdâ)*, the writer of 2 Chr 13:22 refers readers to the "midrash of the prophet Iddo" *(midraš hannābîʾ ʿiddô)*. Similarly, for King Jehoash 2 Kgs 12:20 supplies the standard reference to "the book of the events of the days of the kings of Judah" *(sēper dibrê hayyāmîm lĕmalkê yĕhûdâ)*, but 2 Chr 24:27 refers readers to a "midrash of the book of Kings" *(midraš sēper hammĕlākîm)*. The two citations pertaining to midrash (an exposition or commentary) are taken to suggest that the Chronicler had access to an expansion of or midrash on Samuel-Kings. Because the source cited was not an official annalistic source, but an explication of an earlier work, its historical value was largely limited to shedding light on the time in which it was written.[161] The subject of the Chronicler's source citations is more complicated than this analysis might initially suggest. But whatever one thinks of this position, the issue raised about the nature of the Chronicler's sources is quite important.

[159] In this context, the works of Kuenen (1887–92), Stade (1887), Torrey (1896; 1910), and Pfeiffer (1948) are relevant. More recent examples include North (1974), Becker (1986: 5–7), and Van Seters (1983: 48). The work of Welten (1973) is more nuanced, but admits to only a paucity of sources. Noth (1932; 1934; 1943; 1960) is sometimes grouped with these figures, but his statements on the subject are inconsistent (Knoppers 2000a).

[160] E.g., Curtis and Madsen (1910: 22); Ackroyd (1967: 506); Michaeli (1967: 10–11). Wellhausen (1885: 226–27) raised the possibility of a midrash or commentary himself. Halpern (1990) suggests that both the Deuteronomist and the Chronicler had access to a common source, dating to the time of Ḥezeqiah, upon which the Chronicler relied more heavily than the Deuteronomist did.

[161] But a few in this group think that the expanded source or midrash contained valuable information. Taking "midrash" to refer to an essay or study, Eissfeldt (1965: 531–35) contends that the midrash employed by the Chronicler could be used for reconstructing some preexilic facts. Willi (1972: 52–53) and Peltonen (1996: 365–70) furnish helpful discussions.

The question is not simply the possibility of noncanonical sources, but the date and nature of those sources. We will have occasion to return to this matter below.

Scholars belonging to a third tradition have trenchantly defended the notion that the Chronicler had access to both written and oral sources.[162] These scholars point to the Chronicler's source citations, the large portions of nonsynoptic texts in his work, the historical details about the Judahite monarchy, the historical anecdotes in the genealogies, the references to scribes and writings,[163] and the knowledge of historical geography to argue that the writer must have had access to some noncanonical materials. The appeal to extrabiblical sources serves two complementary functions. First, the supposition of the author's access to such documents—either unused or unavailable to earlier biblical writers—explains his nonsynoptic material. Second, because the Chronicler used such putative sources, his work is a legitimate witness to preexilic realities. To be sure, recent defenders of this stance are much more measured and cautious than many were in the early nineteenth century. Even among proponents of this point of view, there is an acknowledgment that the Chronicler's work is very much the product of its own age. What these scholars defend is the notion that in certain contexts the book incorporates sources that shed some light on preexilic history. In this respect, Chronicles reflects not simply its own time but also occasionally some details about preexilic life.

A. WHAT SORTS OF NONCANONICAL SOURCES?

In my judgment, de Wette, Wellhausen, and others have been overly skeptical about noncanonical sources. The quest to discredit the Chronicler's historical veracity in dealing with the age of the monarchy ("the Judaising of the past"—Wellhausen [1885: 223]) may have been one factor that contributed to the formulation of a minimalistic approach toward explaining the existence of the nonsynoptic portions of the Chronicler's work. To be sure, some of this additional material may be attributed to the Chronicler's interpretation of his biblical sources (see below). But the unparalleled material in Chronicles is variegated and massive. Arguments that most or even all of this unique material represents the Chronicler's exposition of his *Vorlagen* have not been successful. If the later library at Qumran is any indication at all of the sorts of written documents that were available in earlier times, the Chronicler, living in Jerusalem, may have had access to a variety of materials. The pertinent questions that need to be addressed have to do with the nature, origins, and date of such sources. Were they mostly, if not exclusively, Persian period materials or were there also a few that hailed back somehow to the monarchy?

---

[162] Some recent examples include Goettsberger (1939: 6–11); Albright (1950); Galling (1954: 8–12); Rudolph (1955: xii–xiii); Myers (1965a: xlvi–xlvii); Michaeli (1967: 10–12); de Vaux (1970; 1978); Weinberg (1979: 181; 1981: 91–114; 1996); Williamson (1982b: 17–23); Japhet (1989: 8–9; 1993a: 14–23); Dillard (1987); Edelman (1988); Na'aman (1980a; 1991b); Halpern (1990); Schniedewind (1991; 1995); Jones (1993; 1994); Kalimi (1995a; 1997); Rainey (1997).

[163] E.g., 1 Chr 2:55; 4:41; 5:17; 24:6; 27:24; 2 Chr 25:4; 29:30; 35:4, 12, 13.

One also has to deal with a series of other considerations. To what extent did the Chronicler employ postexilic sources to depict preexilic conditions? It is entirely possible, for example, that the Chronicler had access to a Temple-based source in writing about the staffing and rota of the Temple. But if so, the source was likely a Persian period source that was exploited to depict David's arrangements for Solomon's Temple (cf. the lists in 1 Chr 23–26). The Chronicler's writing is a highly stylized, didactic work. To what extent did he project into the distant past his present conditions and wishes for the future? To what extent did he abridge, rearrange, rewrite, amplify, or transform his sources? Acknowledging, for the sake of argument, that the Chronicler had access to some preexilic extrabiblical materials, were they complete, internally consistent, and credible? Did the author always understand their origins and proper contexts?

Two examples may suffice to underscore the larger point. First, many scholars agree that the list of fifteen fortified towns built by Reḥoboam in Judah and Benjamin (2 Chr 11:5–10) reflects the use of an extrabiblical source (most recently, Japhet 1993a: 663–67). But commentators debate whether the listed fortifications should be attributed to Reḥoboam, Ḥezeqiah, or Josiah.[164] Second, one of the few texts in Chronicles that explictly deals with the Persian period (1 Chr 9:2–18) is partially paralleled by Neh 11:3–19. Both passages list various residents of Jerusalem, mention assorted genealogical connections of Judahites, Benjaminites, priests, and Levites, and follow a similar order. A common source seems to underlie both accounts (Knoppers 2000c). Yet close study of 1 Chr 9, MT Neh 11, and LXX Neh 11 (which is considerably shorter than MT Neh 11) reveals the extent to which the editors of these materials have provided their own comments, added or altered kinship relationships, supplemented genealogies, added administrative functions, added numerical totals for a particular group or subgroup, and expanded the list in new directions. In Chronicles the list appears as a catalogue of returnees to Jerusalem, whereas in Nehemiah the list is associated with the results of Nehemiah's efforts to repopulate Jerusalem. Examining the similarities and differences between the catalogues enables one to see how editors have each gone their own way with earlier material.[165] Each has contextualized, edited, and supplemented the catalogue according to his own interests. One is reminded of the comment by Williamson (1982b: 23) that "overall the Chronicler shows himself as the master, not the servant, of his sources."

Another relevant consideration is rarely, if ever, brought forward in discussions of sources. The Chronicler, by all accounts, lived in Jerusalem during the Persian or Hellenistic age and was not restricted from traveling to different sites and villages. How much is his presentation of geographical details and topography informed by his own journeys into the countryside? To what extent did he rely on

---

[164] Reḥoboam (J. Miller 1987; Hobbs 1994); Ḥezeqiah (Na'aman 1986b; 1988a; cf. Garfinkel 1988); Josiah (Fritz 1981). The Chronicler's larger contextualization of this material is also important (Knoppers 1990).

[165] In the case of LXX vs. MT Neh 11, one can see how a shorter list was expanded within a particular tradition. In this respect, LXX and MT Neh 11 represent two stages in the growth of a single literary unit. The lists in Neh 11 and 1 Chr 9 represent, however, two distinct literary editions.

personal travel and oral sources for at least some of the details he provides about buildings and fortifications at various sites in Judah? Modern discussions of biblical historiography focus attention on the issue of written sources. In this, they follow the lead of the relevant biblical texts themselves. Such written sources have been construed as both authoritative and reliable.[166] Nevertheless, the possibility that the Chronicler also depended to some extent on oral sources and personal excursions cannot be dismissed. Certainly, this would help to explain the wealth of geographical detail that informs his work. Classical historians were wont to rely heavily on oral sources in composing their works.[167] In contrast to historiographic works within the Hebrew Bible, written sources do not figure prominently in their accounts.[168] If the Chronicler depended, at least in part, on oral sources for some genealogical, geographical, or historical claims, these sources have to be subjected to the same sorts of questions as those asked of written sources. How accurate were these sources about centuries-old sites, artifacts, and events? To what degree did the Chronicler shape their testimony in accordance with his own judgments and theological outlook?

There is yet another critical issue with respect to the Chronicler's use of sources. Unlike the authors of Ezra-Nehemiah, who show a propensity to call attention to written sources (letters, documents, royal decrees, etc.) included within their text, the Chronicler does not (IV.A.4). We know that the Chronicler borrows heavily from earlier biblical books, but he never explicitly draws attention to this fact. In the genealogical prologue, the reader is never informed that the author is quoting from Genesis, Exodus, Numbers, Joshua, and other books. Similarly, in the narration of the monarchy, the author never explicitly discloses to his readers that he is quoting extensively from Samuel-Kings. The Chronicler sometimes uses the book of the Torah, the Torah of Moses, or the Torah of Yhwh as a cipher by which to judge the actions of major characters within his work (IV.A.3). In this respect, he refers his readers to written sources outside his own work. Another example is his reference to the laments of Jeremiah composed following the death of Josiah (2 Chr 35:25). But in these cases, the Chronicler is referring his audience to literary compositions that are not included within his own work. As for those compositions he includes within his work, he rarely, if ever, directly cites them. It may well be that the Chronicler, like a number of other authors in the ancient Mediterranean world, employed the literary technique of mimesis (μίμησις) or *imitatio*, the conscious reuse of the content, form, or style of an older literary work to define and bring recognition to one's own work.[169] The deployment of *imitatio*

[166] The supposition, very common in modern biblical scholarship, needs to be critically reexamined (see VII.C below).

[167] E.g., Herodotus (*Hist.* 1.1, 2, 3, 5; 2.29, 99, 147, 154; 3.38, 140; 4.81; 5.59; 6.2, 137; 7.152.3); Thucydides (*Hist. Pelop.* 1.1.1; 22.3); Xenophon (*Anab.* 5.3.5).

[168] Thucydides refuses, in fact, to write about the ancient past, because he cannot personally check (oral) references to events in centuries past (*Hist. Pelop.* 1.20–21). His focus is thus on contemporary history (1.1.1). Note also the comment by Herodotus about the starting point of his own history (*Hist.* 1.5).

[169] The phenomenon was widespread in Classical antiquity (Auerbach 1953; Cairns 1972; 1979: 121–34; Russell 1979; 1981). On its use among biblical writers, see the insightful treatment of Van Seters (2000), although I do not agree with all of his conclusions.

was very common in the classical world and connoted an author's admiration for older established literary works (Conte 1986). In an age that prized continuity with the past, the careful use of *imitatio* was a mark of erudition and distinction.[170] The writer employing literary imitation could benefit in different ways from exploiting this form of composition. The unschooled might be awed by what they mistakenly saw as the originality of the writer's work, while the literate would see the emulation of an earlier work and appreciate its studied reuse. In this context, the learned reader would recognize those instances in which an author was replicating the style, tropes, or content of an older work and those instances in which the author was producing his own material.[171] In any case, the use of *imitatio* shows that ancient authors need not always have overtly cited their sources to employ them within their own works.

B. "AS IT IS WRITTEN": THE CHONICLER'S SOURCE CITATIONS

The question thus becomes how one can tell when the Chronicler is using a noncanonical source? Does one determine the presence of a source by recourse to a shift in style, vocabulary, and theme? But given that the author shows a propensity to integrate his sources within his own composition, the standard tools of source criticism are not always applicable or helpful. To this line of reasoning it may be objected that a casual reading of Chronicles suggests both that the author had access to a wide variety of writings and that he cited them. Especially in narrating the course of the monarchy, the author repeatedly refers his readers to what appear to be a whole range of noncanonical materials.[172] Moreover, the notations within the Chronicler's source citations are often much more extensive than those found in Kings. But the Chronicler's source citations are not nearly as clear cut as they first appear to be. In narrating the dual monarchies, the authors of Kings consistently refer to "the book of the events of the days of the kings of Israel" (*sēper dibrê hayyāmîm lĕmalkê yiśrā'ēl*; 1 Kgs 14:19; 15:31; 16:5, 14, 20, 27; 22:39; 2 Kgs 1:18; 10:34; 13:8, 12; 14:15, 28; 15:11, 15, 21, 31) and to "the book of the events of the days of the kings of Judah" (*sēper dibrê hayyāmîm lĕmalkê yĕhûdâ*; 1 Kgs 14:29; 15:7, 23; 22:46; 2 Kgs 8:23; 12:20; 14:18; 15:6, 36; 16:19; 20:20; 21:17, 25; 23:28; 24:5). The use of these two titles comports with the Deuteronomist's synchronistic method of dealing with the history of Israel and Judah. The former title refers to

---

170 Given that many biblical writings were anonymous, it would seem that they readily lent themselves to imitation.

171 But the use of creative imitation also had its dangers as the boundary between the appropriation of an older work and outright plagiarism was not always clear. At least some of the literate might deem that reuse of an older composition as improper. What might be viewed by one ancient critic as a brilliant *imitatio* might be condemned by another critic as derivative copying or theft (κλοπή) of another author's writing. See Aristophanes, *Nub.* 553–54, 559; Isocrates 5.94; Seneca the Elder, *Suas.* 3.7; Horace, *Ars* 131; Longinus, *Subl.* 13–14; Quintilian, *Inst.* 10.1, 2, 3, 10; Seneca the Younger, *Ep.* 114; Terence, *Eun.* 23; *Ad.* 6; Eusebius, *Praep. ev.* 10.3.12.

172 1 Chr 9:1; 29:29; 2 Chr 9:29; 12:15; 13:22; 16:11; 20:34; 24:27; 25:26; 26:22; 27:7; 28:26; 32:32; 33:18, 19; 35:27; 36:8.

records pertaining to northern kings, while the latter refers to records pertaining to southern kings.

In Chronicles the citations vary. In some cases, the text speaks of "the book of the kings of Judah and Israel" (*sēper hammĕlākîm lîhûdâ wĕyiśrāʾēl/sēper malkê-yĕhûdâ wĕyiśrāʾēl*; 2 Chr 16:11; 25:26; 28:26; 32:32) and of "the book of the kings of Israel and Judah" (*sēper malkê yiśrāʾēl wîhûdâ*; 1 Chr 9:1; 2 Chr 27:7; 35:27; 36:8).[173] Only in one case is reference made to "the book of the kings of Israel" *sēper malkê yiśrāʾēl*; (2 Chr 20:34). In no instance is there a reference made to "the book of the kings of Judah." The information included in the source citations found in Chronicles sometimes varies from the standard formulas found in Kings. We have already seen that the book refers on one occasion to a "midrash of the prophet Iddo" (2 Chr 13:22) and on another occasion to a "midrash of the book of Kings" (2 Chr 24:27). The most common variations from the source citations in Kings are the references to a variety of (mostly unknown) prophetic materials. Precisely because they exhibit such variety, the prophetic source citations need to be carefully scrutinized. In David's case, the writer refers his readers to "the acts of Samuel the seer, the acts of Nathan the prophet, and the acts of Gad the visionary" (*dibrê šĕmûʾēl hārōʾeh wĕʿal-dibrê nātān hannābîʾ wĕʿal-dibrê gād haḥōzeh*; 1 Chr 29:29). In the case of Reḥoboam, the writer refers his readers to "the acts of Shemaiah the prophet and Iddo the seer" (*dibrê šĕmaʿyāh hannābîʾ wĕʿiddô haḥōzeh*; 2 Chr 12:15). Such citations of prophetic works are, in fact, quite common in the narration of the Judahite monarchy (2 Chr 12:15; 13:22; 20:34; 26:22; 32:32; 33:19; cf. 35:25). The references to these prophetic sources are a subject in and of themselves (Micheel 1983; Schniedewind 1995; 1997; Glatt 2001). Yet even when such additional citations are found in the regnal formulas (over and beyond those given in Kings), this may not entail that the Chronicler possessed additional (noncanonical) sources. Williamson (1982b: 18, 236–37) argues, for instance, that the Chronicler employed only his *Vorlage* of Kings to portray the reign of Solomon, even though the concluding formulas for Solomon's reign, in contradistinction from 1 Kgs 11:41, mention prophetic sources pertaining to Nathan, Aḥijah, and Iddo (2 Chr 9:29). To this may be added another consideration. If the Chronicler had access to additional sources for Solomon's reign, aside from the book of Kings, how likely is it that they would be prophetic sources related to Nathan, Aḥijah, and Iddo? Most of the material the Chronicler adds to the presentation of Solomon in Kings has to do with the furnishings and staffing of the Temple, topics not normally associated with the Hebrew prophets.

The Chronicler's references to prophets and prophetic figures in his source citations seem to fall into a larger pattern. Such references almost always occur for rulers whom the Chronicler appraises positively: David (1 Chr 29:29), Solomon (2 Chr 9:29), Abijam (2 Chr 13:22), Jehoshaphaṭ (2 Chr 20:34), Uzziah (2 Chr 26:22), and Ḥezeqiah (2 Chr 32:32).[174] Only in two instances does the author pro-

---

[173] The first reference (1 Chr 9:1) is disputed (see TEXTUAL NOTE).

[174] Note as well the reference in the Chronicler's concluding remarks about Josiah to Jeremiah's laments sung after this reformer king's death (2 Chr 35:25).

vide such a prophetic-source citation for monarchs whom he seems to rate negatively: Reḥoboam (2 Chr 12:14) and Manasseh (2 Chr 33:18–19).[175] In both cases, the Chronicler provides more complex and temperate accounts of their careers than are found in Kings and in both cases, prophecies or prophetic figures play major roles in turning around negative segments of their reigns (2 Chr 11:2–4; 12:7; 33:10, 18). In other words, the prophetically attributed sources attested in Chronicles are not extraneous to the author's larger compositional technique. Rather, the prophetic-source citations seem to be one means by which the author configures particular reigns (Glatt 2001). In so doing, the author may be aligning himself with a prophetic view of history, a perspective that sermonizes about the past and holds people, priests, and potentates accountable to a higher authority. Such a prophetic perspective, which has been traditionally attributed to the books of Joshua through Kings (the Former Prophets), has also been attributed to Chronicles (e.g., Schniedewind 1995; 1997). To be sure, in two cases the prophetic writings are said to be contained within the "book of the kings of [Judah and] Israel" (2 Chr 20:34; 32:32). But in these two cases the author may be alluding to the (biblical) book of Kings (Williamson 1982b: 18), which includes, of course, many prophetic stories and speeches. If so, the author is pointing not toward an extrabiblical source, but to prophetic accounts within his major biblical source.

How the Chronicler composes and distributes the prophetic-source citations may offer some clues about the other variations found within his source citations. Almost all of the source citations seem to be at least partially adapted from the Chronicler's *Vorlage* of Samuel-Kings.[176] The citations appear precisely at the same point in the narration of a monarch's reign as they appear in Kings. Indeed, in those instances in which the source citations in Kings appear anomalously (not at the end of a monarch's reign), Chronicles follows suit (2 Chr 16:11; 20:34; 25:26). With the exception of 1 Chr 9:1 and 29:29, the Chronicler does not add new source citations to those already found in Kings. In the book of Kings the reigns of Aḥaziah, Athaliah, Jehoaḥaz, Jehoiachin, and Zedeqiah all lack source citations.[177] Similarly, these monarchs also lack source citations in Chronicles.[178]

As we have seen, the standard titles attributed to the Chronicler's sources differ from the titles employed in Kings—"the book of the events of the days of the kings of Israel" (for northern monarchs) and "the book of the events of the days of the kings of Judah" (for southern monarchs). Interestingly enough, the references in Chronicles to "the book of the kings of Israel and Judah" and to "the book of the kings of Judah and Israel" are all found in discussions of southern kings. Unlike

[175] In the latter case, there are no final judgment formulas in Chronicles. In Kings, Manasseh is the most harshly condemned Judahite monarch (2 Kgs 21:2–18).

[176] 1 Chr 29:29; 2 Chr 9:29; 12:15; 13:22; 16:11; 20:34; 24:27; 25:26; 26:22; 27:7; 28:26; 32:32; 33:18, 19; 35:27; 36:8.

[177] In the case of Queen Athaliah (2 Kgs 11:1–16), regnal formulas are entirely lacking, because the Deuteronomist presents her reign as an interregnum.

[178] In one case, a standard source citation appears in Kings for Jehoram (2 Kgs 8:23), while Chronicles lacks any source citation at all (2 Chr 21:20).

the Deuteronomistic portrayal of the dual monarchies, the Chronicler focuses on narrating Judahite history to the virtual exclusion of (northern) Israelite history. The adaptations of the source citations found in Kings are consistent with the Chronicler's own theology. In Chronicles, the use of the term "Israel" is deliberately complex (Danell 1946; Willi 1972; 1995; Japhet 1977; Williamson 1977b). In his account of the Judahite monarchy, the Chronicler acknowledges the existence of the northern kingdom (e.g., 2 Chr 10:1–19; 11:1–4, 13–17; 13:4–12; 18:1–34; 20:35–37). The repeated references to both Israel and Judah in the source references for the accounts of monarchs in the southern kingdom are further testimony to this fact. Nevertheless, the Chronicler maintains that Judah, Benjamin, and Levi continue the legacy of ancient Israel. In this respect, the Chronicler can refer his readers to the "book of the kings of Israel" in the context of his discussion of King Jehoshaphaṭ of Judah (2 Chr 20:34).[179] The nation of Israel contains a variety of tribes, but these three particular tribes are critical to carrying on the ideals established during the United Monarchy (Knoppers 1988; 1989; 1990). Hence, even though the Chronicler focuses on the Judahite monarchy, his source citations reveal to his readers that he was aware of the larger picture of which Judahite history was one part.

To sum up, the Chronicler's source citations are helpful in ascertaining relevant features of his theology, his historiographic method, and his interpretation of older biblical books, but they are not particularly helpful in determining what extrabiblical sources he may have had at his disposal. The author's use of sources and source citations constitutes a paradox. He cites sources in a variety of contexts—for theological reasons, to validate his judgments about a character's actions, or when he excludes such putative sources from his own narration. But the Chronicler does not normally cite his (biblical) sources, when he includes them within his own narration.

C. RETHINKING THE LINK BETWEEN SOURCE CRITICISM AND HISTORICAL RECONSTRUCTION

Readers will observe that this commentary does not show the keen interest in (extrabiblical) source criticism that has characterized many previous commentaries. In my judgment, the methodology of source criticism needs to be distanced from the discipline of historical reconstruction. The two are related but discrete enterprises. Even though the techniques of source criticism have become very refined within the past few decades, source criticism remains a profoundly subjective enterprise. Arguments for the existence of an underlying source for a given text can be examined on a case-by-case basis. But even if one is able to isolate a source embedded within a given narrative, that source, like the narrative itself, is but a secondary witness to history. The task of historical reconstruction remains.

[179] Given the context, "Israel" refers either to Judah or to the larger entity of which Judah was one part.

Moreover, as we have seen, such a putative source has to be subject to its own set of questions relating to its date, origins, *Tendenz*, editing, reuse, and recontextualization.

If one is interested in historical reconstruction, it seems more promising and relevant to look to the witness of archaeology and epigraphy than it is to look to the results of source criticism. In the former case, scholars are employing the results of another set of disciplines dealing with the material cultures of the ancient Mediterranean world, whereas in the latter case scholars are involved in one form of literary criticism, that of excavating the text. The former is potentially more productive because one may compare the witness of the Chronicler's narration, whatever his sources may (or may not) have been, with the testimony provided by archaeology and epigraphy. His portrayal of the past, especially his depiction of the Judahite monarchy, may provide some indications of whether his work has any value for reconstructing the past. Does the Chronicler's writing—however much it reflects the ideology of its author, a particular rhetorical structure, and the conditions of its own time—ever engage something beyond itself in Judah's monarchic past? Conversely, what does the Chronicler's writing say, however indirectly, about the conditions of the author's own time? To be sure, the Chronicler's work tells us first of all about the writer's own compositional technique, style, and ideology. What we primarily derive from Chronicles, or for that matter from any writing, is what the author(s) thought about a certain subject at a particular time. Allowing that ancient historiography involves the deployment of certain rhetorical tropes, narrative strategies, and the work of the imagination, one cannot simply assume that Chronicles primarily tells us about either the preexilic period or the postexilic period. The advantage of employing a comparative approach is that it focuses upon the degree to which, if any, the Chronicler's unique claims correspond to our present knowledge of the material remains of monarchic and postmonarchic Judah.

Recourse to archaeology and epigraphy does not deny the role of the Chronicler as either a theologian or an expositor of older biblical writings. Neither should such study proceed in ignorance of the many methodological problems and limitations inherent in the examination of ancient inscriptions and material artifacts. Rather, this approach should seek to determine, insofar as it is possible, the degree to which the author's account of a particular war or set of fortifications coheres (or fails to cohere) with information gleaned from the study of the material remains of the southern Levant. The record of royal reforms in Chronicles may serve as an example. Close study of the pattern of royal reforms in the Judahite monarchy reveals how much more attention the Chronicler gives to a wide range of royal initiatives than the Deuteronomist does (Knoppers 1997a). Moreover, there is a substantial difference in the very conception of what a royal reform involves. In the Deuteronomistic work, kingly reforms are virtually synonymous with cultic reforms. Noncultic reforms are occasionally mentioned, but almost as an afterthought. Kings mentions, for example, the towns that Asa built (1 Kgs 15:23 [MT]), the ivory palace and towns that Aḥab built (1 Kgs 22:39), and how Ḥezeqiah "made the pool and the conduit" (2 Kgs 20:20). But in each case, this information is conveyed in the concluding formulas for these monarchs.[180] The main attention of the Deuteronomist lies elsewhere. Assuming a normative (Deuteronomic) mandate for *Kultuseinheit* (cultic unity) and *Kultusreinheit* (cultic purity), the Deuteronomist constructs an elaborate system of religious regression and reform in the records of the northern and southern monarchies.

In contrast, royal reforms in Chronicles are martial, administrative, judicial, geopolitical, and cultic in nature. Monarchs renew their domain by building fortified towns, fortifying existing towns, appointing officers, amassing armies, stationing garrisons, constructing towers, and rebuilding city walls. This does not mean, of course, that the unique material in Chronicles must somehow comport with preexilic (or postexilic) conditions. In certain cases, the Chronicler's presentation of a royal reform may simply reflect what the author thinks a royal reform should consist of (Knoppers 1994b). Nevertheless, there is a larger principle at stake. Because the Chronicler's work exhibits broader historiographical interests in narrating the performance of Judahite monarchs than the Deuteronomist's work does, the additional reforms the Chronicler ascribes to Judah's kings cannot all be dismissed out of hand for historical reconstruction. This is especially true when one compares both Kings and Chronicles with a variety of ancient Near Eastern royal texts. In exhibiting a keen interest in geopolitical and martial reforms, Chronicles is broadly consistent with the interests of many ancient Near Eastern royal inscriptions and dedicatory texts (Knoppers 1997a). In short, the witness of archaeology and epigraphy offers a productive, even an essential, path to the writing of ancient history. Source criticism has its place among the various literary-critical approaches that modern scholars bring to the biblical text, but it is not nearly as important for historical reconstruction as it has often been touted to be.

[180] In this context, the formulaic introduction to these notices is relevant, "The rest of [all] the deeds of [king's name] . . . , are they not written in the book of the events of the days of the kings of Judah/Israel?" (1 Kgs 15:23; 22:39; 2 Kgs 20:20).

VIII. Chronicles: A Rewritten Bible?

The publication in recent decades of most of the Dead Sea Scrolls provides an excellent opportunity to raise anew the question as to the genre of the Chronicler's work. Among the scrolls published are fascinating works belonging to the broad category of "rewritten Bible," such as the *Genesis Apocryphon* (1QapGen[ar]), the *Temple Scroll* (11QT19), and the *Reworked Pentateuch* (4Q158; 4Q364–367; 4QRP). Study of these works along with other previously known writings, such as the book of *Jubilees*, Josephus's *Jewish Antiquities*, and Pseudo-Philo's *Liber Antiquitatum Biblicarum* ("Book of Biblical Antiquities"), has furnished scholars with new insight into the variety of biblically based literary works in early Judaism. In this line of interpretation, Deuteronomy (which draws on parts of Genesis, Exodus, and Numbers) and Chronicles (which draws on a number of earlier biblical writings) are the prototypes or forerunners of certain types of literary works attested at Qumran, in the Pseudepigrapha, and in Josephus's *Jewish Antiquities*.[181] Indeed, the success of Deuteronomy as a prestigious and authoritative writing may have spurred the creation of new rewritten-Bible texts. That Chronicles shares many traits with rewritten-Bible texts will become clear in the following discussion. Whether Chronicles should be classified simply as a rewritten Bible is a question that deserves careful scrutiny. In pursuing this matter, it will be useful to broaden the base of the discussion. Comparisons with writings from other parts of the ancient Mediterranean world may shed some light on the question of genre.

Unfortunately, scholars do not agree on a precise definition of what a rewritten Bible is. Vermes (1986: 326) speaks of "a narrative that follows Scripture but includes a substantial amount of supplements and interpretative developments." Brooke (2000: 777) refers to "any representation of an authoritative scriptural text that implicitly incorporates interpretive elements, large or small, in the retelling itself." Crawford (1999: 1) thinks that the criteria for inclusion in the genre should specify a "close attachment, either through narrative or through themes, to some book contained in the Jewish canon of Scripture and some type of reworking, whether through rearrangement, conflation, or supplementation, of the present

[181] On the claim that Chronicles is a rewritten Bible text, see, for example, Alexander (1988: 100), Steins (1995: 171; 1996), and Brooke (2000: 778).

canonical biblical text." Nickelsburg (1984: 89) presents a more expansive understanding of the literary form, when he speaks of "literature that is very closely related to the biblical texts, expanding and paraphrasing them and implicitly commenting on them." This loose definition actually allows for the inclusion of a variety of genres: long paraphrases (e.g., *Jubilees*), narrative sections in larger works (e.g., *1 Enoch*), narratives shaped by nonnarrative genres (e.g., the *Apocalypse of Moses*), and poetic versions of biblical stories (e.g., Philo the Elder, Theodotus, Ezekiel the Tragedian; Nickelsburg 1984: 89–156).[182]

In spite of the differences among critics about what qualifies as a rewritten-Bible text, some generalizations are possible. Such works take as a point of departure an earlier biblical book or collection of books. They select from, interpret, comment on, and expand portions of a particular biblical book (or group of books), addressing obscurities, contradictions, and other perceived problems with the source text. Rewritten Bible texts normally emulate the form of the source text and follow it sequentially. The major intention of such works seems to be to provide a coherent interpretive reading of the biblical text. The added comments, interpolated into the sources, are often of a moral, theological, or didactic type. The authors of rewritten biblical texts fuse their own additions, clarifications, and expositions with the base text. They normally follow the narration of events found in their biblical source and do not employ citation formulas to distinguish their own material from that found within the source. The authors may presupppose some familiarity on the part of the readers with the base text, but untrained readers will not find clear demarcations between the base text and the additions made to it.

Viewing these works as belonging to the category of "rewritten Bible" is, of course, anachronistic. There was no one set, universally agreed on, authoritative collection of sacred writings within the Jewish tradition during the period in which the Dead Sea Scrolls were written. As we have seen (II.A), in the last centuries B.C.E., there were multiple textual witnesses to many books. Certain texts, such as the Pentateuch and the Prophets, may have been viewed as canonical among the various early Jewish communities, but the status of a number of works in the Writings is unclear. Moreover, some works that did not make it into the Tanakh may have been considered prestigious and influential by certain communities. Works such as *Jubilees,* which was found in many (fourteen or fifteen) copies at Qumran, may have been viewed as authoritative by some, whereas other writings, such as Esther, which was not found at Qumran, may have not been (Crawford 2000: 1).[183] Nevertheless, there are some advantages to looking at Chronicles with the category of rewritten Bible in view. There are cases in Chronicles in which the author discerns a problem in his biblical sources, for example, whether the Passover lamb is to be boiled (Exod 12:8) or roasted (Deut 16:7) and attempts to solve the problem harmonistically ("they boiled the Passover lamb

[182] In contrast, Alexander (1988: 116–18) provides a much tighter, albeit more elaborate, definition involving some nine principal characteristics.

[183] For a different view, which contends that Chronicles was written to complete the canon, see Steins (1995: 415–44; 1997: 89–90) and Koorevaar (1997).

with fire" ויבשלו הפסח באש; 2 Chr 35:13). In cases in which the author reproduces large sections of Samuel or Kings, he interweaves his own additions with his source texts to produce a continuous work. As we have already seen, the Chronicler does not use citation formulas to distinguish his own additions from the material found within his source.

In some cases, the Chronicler adds commentary to the material he borrows from an earlier biblical source. Note, for instance, the prophetic reprimand of Jehu (2 Chr 19:2–3), following what the Chronicler deems to be an unholy alliance between Aḥab of Israel and Jehoshaphaṭ of Judah (1 Kgs 22:2–35//2 Chr 18:2–34; Knoppers 1996c). In some other cases, he abbreviates, edits, reworks, and supplements the materials in his *Vorlage*. The Chronicler's account of Sennacherib's invasion (2 Chr 32:1–23) stands out as an example of condensation, editing, and occasional supplementation (cf. 2 Kings 18–20). Even though some of the additions the author makes to his biblical sources are large, there is, in many cases, a "centripetal" quality (Alexander 1988: 117) to the Chronicler's work. Whether in the account of the United Monarchy or in the account of the divided monarchy, Chronicles returns again and again to its biblical sources.

In brief, Chronicles may be profitably compared with a number of rewritten Bible texts. In this respect, such comparisons dovetail with some of the earlier classifications of the author's work—Chronicles as midrash, Chronicles as exegesis, and Chronicles as theology. Viewing Chronicles as a work of midrash or exegesis draws attention to the many different literary techniques the author employs to interpret his biblical sources. As Willi (1972), Japhet (1977; 1993a), Seeligmann (1979–80), Fishbane (1985), Strübind (1991), Brettler (1995), Kalimi (1995a), Schniedewind (1999a), and others have shown in impressive detail, these techniques anticipate a number of the very sophisticated interpretive techniques used in rabbinic Judaism. Viewing Chronicles as a work of theology highlights the many paradigmatic elements of his history of the monarchy.[184] Many of the author's stories, even those borrowed from his biblical sources, come to serve theological and didactic ends. Another merit of the theological viewpoint lies in the links it recognizes between the Chronicler's work and the context in which it was written. Some aspects of the Chronicler's coverage, such as his use of incredible numbers, directly relate to his ideology. Yet the exegetical, midrashic, and theological approaches encounter difficulty in explaining the Chronicler's *Sondergut*, the material in Chronicles that is unparalleled in earlier biblical sources. Some of this additional material may be attributed to the author's interpretation or theological reworking of his biblical sources, but much of it cannot be. It is reductive to attribute all of the Chronicler's unique material to exegesis or theological reflection.

Can the rewritten-Bible category, precisely because it allows for the incorpora-

[184] E.g., Swart (1911); von Rad (1930; 1962b); Brunet (1959); North (1963); Ackroyd (1967; 1973ab); Mosis (1973); Goldingay (1975); Dillard (1980b); Saebø (1981); Gabriel (1990); Oeming (1990); Steins (1995); Balentine (1997); Dyck (1998). In Welten's view (1973), Chronicles anticipates certain features of apocalytic writing.

tion of various additions and editorial comments, explain all of Chronicles' distinctive literary features? This seems doubtful. To begin with, the presentation of Israel in the genealogical introduction cannot (or should not) be viewed as a rewritten or reworked Pentateuch, even though the authors draw upon a variety of genealogical materials in the Pentateuch. In citing texts from these books, the writers of Chronicles are highly selective, omitting virtually all narratives and legal sections. Only certain genealogies and anecdotes are taken up and recontextualized in Chronicles. To this material, the authors add their own substantial traditions, as well as material from other books, such as Joshua, Samuel, and Kings. Well over half of the material in the genealogies is not paralleled in earlier biblical writings. Second, the authors do not structure their work to follow the broad outline found in the Pentateuch, which begins with the first persons, narrates the primeval era, the Ancestral period, the Exodus, the giving of law at Sinai, the wilderness journeys, and the various speeches of Moses, and ends with an Israel encamped on the plains of Moab, waiting to enter the promised land. The sequence differs completely in 1 Chr 1–9. The genealogies still begin with the first person (1 Chr 1:1) but concentrate on the progeny of Israel's many sons (2:3–9:1). In accordance with this focus on the Israelite tribes, the lineages continually revert to the Ancestral period (1 Chr 2:3; 4:24; 5:1, 11, 23, 27; 6:1; 7:1, 6, 12 [see TEXTUAL NOTE], 13, 14, 20, 30; 8:1). From a form-critical standpoint, the genealogical introduction to Israel—its identity, lineages, relationships, and settlements—is a very different work from the Pentateuch. The authors have treated the Pentateuch as one resource among others, creating a profoundly new work.

There is, in fact, nothing in earlier biblical literature directly comparable to the intensive and sustained interest in Israel's lineages found in 1 Chr 1–9. The closest analogies that I am aware of stem from the classical world (see "Excursus: The Genealogies"). But within the Bible the form and structure of Chronicles are unparalleled by any other work. To this it may be objected that the Chronicler's account of the monarchy is closely modeled after that of Samuel-Kings. In this respect, the Chronicler's presentation may be labeled a rewritten monarchy. There is some validity to this objection. The Chronicler's account of the monarchy follows the broad outline of Samuel-Kings and borrows extensively from this earlier work. Yet one must ask whether the Chronicler's presentation, with its focus on the Davidides and Judahite history, is a literary embellishment of Samuel-Kings or whether it employs Samuel-Kings, among other sources, to create an alternative story of the monarchy. The Chronicler, by all accounts, composes new material. Well over half of the coverage devoted to David in Chronicles is not found in Samuel.[185] Even the repetition from Samuel can be misleading, if scholars take the part for the whole. When he borrows texts from Samuel, the Chronicler freely

[185] The reign of Solomon (2 Chr 1:1–9:31) more closely follows the pattern of 1 Kgs 1–10, but the Chronicler's coverage of the Judahite monarchy (2 Chr 10–36) features some major differences from the Deuteronomistic presentation of the dual monarchies. Having omitted the independent history of the northern kingdom except when it affects Judah, the Chronicler substantially recontextualizes, reworks, and supplements the coverage found in Kings.

interpolates other material, including selections from the Psalms (1 Chr 16:8–36). The many omissions (over against Samuel), the rearrangements, and the many additions all contribute to a unique portrayal of the past.

The Chronicler's depiction of the monarchy is not simply a commentary on the Deuteronomistic History. A number of his major claims contrast markedly with those of Samuel-Kings. Rather than the beleaguered David of Samuel, who is continually beset by personal, familial, poltical, and military woes, the highly successful David of Chronicles defeats all of his enemies, oversees the founding of a national administration, reorders the priests and Levites, makes grand plans for the new Temple, and studiously prepares his chosen heir for the succession. The new presentation does not simply embellish the old; it substitutes for the old. Whereas, for example, much of 2 Samuel is characterized by a sequence of David's sons making ill-fated bids for the throne, the succession in Chronicles is smooth, well-planned, and without incident. "All of the sons of the king" endorse Solomon as monarch (1 Chr 29:24). This brings to the fore another paradox about the Chronicler's work. It is both profoundly related and profoundly unrelated to Samuel-Kings. He employs the older work as a major source, even as he contests some of its central claims.

If Chronicles as a complete literary work is to be compared with any corpus of biblical writings, it probably should be compared with the primary history (Genesis through Kings). The scope of the two works is similar. Like Genesis, Chronicles takes as a point of departure the first human(s). Both the primary history and the Chronicler's history are sweeping in their coverage, beginning with the first person(s) and ending with the Babylonian Exile.[186] Both incorporate a broad mixture of genres—genealogies, lists, anecdotes, speeches, prayers, poems, and narratives. Both evince a national concern with Israel in its tribal and state forms. To be sure, the Chronicler's work is much shorter than the former and exhibits its own individual traits. Moreover, the Chronicler's work, unlike the primary work, is chiefly focused on one particular period: the monarchy. Both writings manifest a keen interest in the story of Israel within the land.

In this context, there is something to be said for viewing Chronicles as a second national epic. Chronicles was composed not necessarily as a replacement of, but as an alternative to the primary history. The Chronicler's employment of mimesis or *imitatio* (see VII.A above), the deliberate reuse of older works, expresses his respect for and admiration of a variety of older biblical writings. Indeed, the Chronicler's work may have had an effect on how these older works were interpreted by some readers. After reading the Chronicler's composition and its selective incorporation of earlier writings, ancient readers may have understood those earlier writings differently.

By the same token, the author's skillful reuse, reinterpretation, rearrangement, and major supplementation of sections within the primary history all conspire to create a very different work. The parallels position the author's writing, defining and yet bringing recognition to his own work. The new traditions incorporated

[186] When Ezra-Nehemiah was added to Chronicles, the coverage extended to the late fifth century.

within the body of the text, coupled with the reworking of selections from older biblical texts, contribute to the creation of a new literary work that is designed to suit the writer's own times and interests in the Second Commonwealth. Given its unique literary structure and its unparalleled content, Chronicles is more than a paraphrase or literary elaboration of the primary history. Chronicles needs to be understood as its own work.

IX. Chronicles and Canon

◆

The editors of Chronicles-Ezra-Nehemiah designed their work to be a continuous story. Yet they preserved, through the catch lines at the end of Chronicles and the beginning of Ezra, the original division between two earlier editions. In contrast to the partition left between Chronicles and Ezra, the editor of the Nehemiah narrative reworked his *Vorlage*, locating Ezra's reading of the law in the time of Nehemiah (7:72–8:18). The connections between the Ezra and Nehemiah materials are, therefore, stronger than those binding Chronicles (2 Chr 36:22–23) and Ezra (1:1–3). The result is a paradox. Chronicles is both independent of and linked to Ezra-Nehemiah. This linkage has important consequences for (re)interpretation. That the unity and diversity represented by Chronicles and Ezra-Nehemiah are susceptible to a variety of readings is already apparent in the history of early Judaism and Christianity. Linked to but separate from Ezra-Nehemiah, the book of Chronicles could precede Ezra-Nehemiah, follow Ezra-Nehemiah, or take on a life of its own.[187]

In the LXX, Chronicles usually precedes Ezra and Nehemiah and follows other historical books (Joshua through 2 Kings). Its title, *Paraleipomena* ("the things left out"), provides a vital clue about its interpretation. Chronicles complements and supplements the primary history, that is, Genesis through 2 Kings (Freedman 1992: 95–97, 105–6). Both works are profoundly concerned with the land—how Israel emerges in, consolidates its control over, and is finally expelled from the territory Yhwh gave it. The primary history ends with Judah's exile from the land, but the Chronistic History supplements this earlier work by announcing the people's return.

Whereas in the LXX Chronicles, Ezra, and Nehemiah normally find their place among the Historical books, in the Hebrew Bible, Chronicles, Ezra, and Nehemiah find their place among the Writings *(Kethuvim)*, the third and final section of *Tanakh*. But the placement of Chronicles within the Writings is not consistent. Within important medieval codices (the Aleppo Codex and the Leningrad Codex

---

[187] This is especially apparent in the order of the biblical books in patristic and synodical lists of the Eastern Church. Chronicles usually precedes or follows Samuel-Kings, but Ezra-Nehemiah can either immediately follow Chronicles or appear much later in the list, if not last among all of the books; see the discussions of Swete (1914: 203–30) and Leiman (1976: 37–50).

19[A]), Chronicles occurs first among the Writings.[188] Ezra-Nehemiah appears last.[189] In another Hebrew tradition, represented by the Babylonian Talmud (*b. B. Bat.* 14b), Ezra-Nehemiah precedes Chronicles. Ezra-Nehemiah and Chronicles are the last two books of the *Kethuvim*. The assertion of the Masoretic authors of *Adat Devarim* (1207 C.E.) that these differences in sequence reflect the Palestinian and the Babylonian traditions, respectively, is disputed (Curtis and Madsen 1910: 2; cf. Japhet 1993a: 2). Scholars debate which order is original, but each sequence evinces its own logic.[190]

The placement of Chronicles at the beginning of the Writings calls attention to the links between the Chronicler's exemplary David and the David of the Writings. Even before one reads about David's associations with Temple music and the Jerusalem cult in the Psalm superscriptions, one reads detailed descriptions of these activities in Chronicles (S. Driver 1914: 369–70; Childs 1979: 514–15; Freedman 1993: 78–85). The very positive depiction of Solomon in the Writings also coheres with the presentation of Chronicles. To be sure, the Chronicler's depiction of Solomonic wisdom is directly inherited from the presentation in Kings. But the Chronicler's Solomon also differs from the Deuteronomist's Solomon. In describing the United Monarchy, Kings does not refrain from pointing out major failings of David and Solomon (e.g., 1 Samuel 11–12; 1 Kgs 11:1–40). Such sins do not occur in Chronicles. The appearance of Chronicles before Proverbs, Qoheleth (Ecclesiastes), and Song of Songs elucidates the celebrated position Solomon enjoys in these works.

The location of Chronicles at the beginning and Ezra-Nehemiah at the end of the Writings is meaningful for another reason. Chronicles begins with the first human, depicts the totality of Israel in genealogical form, presents the story of Israelite occupation of the land during the monarchy, and concludes with the decree of Cyrus ending the Babylonian Exile. In this manner, Chronicles contains and reverses the tremendous tragedy of the Babylonian destructions and deportations soberly depicted in 2 Kgs 24–25 (Meade 1987: 44–71). Since Ezra-Nehemiah begins with the decree of Cyrus and continues with the resettlement of Yehud, Chronicles and Ezra-Nehemiah form an *inclusio* around the Writings (Freedman 1993: 27). As a frame to the Writings, Chronicles and Ezra-Nehemiah cover practically the entire historical span of the Hebrew Scriptures.

The decree of Cyrus is also a unifying feature of the book order of Ezra-Nehemiah and Chronicles in *Tanakh*. That Ezra-Nehemiah begins with the de-

---

[188] This fact is obfuscated in the modern editions of *BHK* and *BHS*. The editors of the latter work acknowledge that although they place Chronicles at the end of the writings, it does not appear there in Leningrad Codex B 19[A] (*BHS:* xii). They do not justify their rearrangement.

[189] Swete (1914: 198–214); Leiman (1976: 56–72); Beckwith (1985: 183–95, 452–64). The incomplete Aleppo Codex does not contain Ezra-Nehemiah (Goshen-Gottstein 1976). Nevertheless, the order of the surviving Writings suggests that Ezra-Nehemiah came last.

[190] The claim that Matt 23:35 and Luke 11:51 assume that Chronicles is the final book in the canon cannot be proved (*pace* de Wette 1850:17; Japhet 1993a: 2). Matt 23:35 clearly draws upon both Zech 1:1 and 2 Chr 24:20–22 (Gundry 1982: 470–72). But whether Jesus' saying "from the blood of innocent Abel to the blood of Zechariah, son of Berachiah" alludes to the OT canon or to the OT period is uncertain (Eissfeldt 1965: 567–68; Harris 1990: 77–80).

cree of Cyrus and Chronicles ends with the same underscores the importance of the return (Freedman 1993: 76). When seen in historical perspective, the placement of Chronicles at the end of the "Babylonian" canon is quite interesting. The first and last books of *Tanakh* begin with creation.[191] Because the history depicted by Chronicles covers the same period as that of Genesis through Kings, Chronicles brings a sense of closure to the canon (Japhet 1993a: 2; Steins 1995: 507–17; Koorevaar 1997). But one can argue that the agenda of Chronicles, and therefore that of the Hebrew Bible, is incomplete in 2 Chr 36:22–23. The decree of Cyrus, authorizing the rebuilding of the Temple and allowing the exiles to return home, ends with a summons, "Whoever among you from his [Yhwh's] people, may Yhwh be with him and let him go up *(wĕyāʿal).*" At first, the notion that the Hebrew Scriptures should end in midsentence is puzzling. But when one considers the events of the first centuries C.E., the rationale underlying this order becomes clear. The First Jewish Revolt (66–73 C.E.) witnessed the devastation of Jerusalem and the burning of the Second Temple. The destruction of the Temple, never supposed to happen again (Ezekiel), did. This catastrophe constituted a profound crisis in the history of Judaism, but the rabbis, drawing upon the traditions of Pharisaic Judaism, responded to the challenge. Indeed, the Judaism that emerges from the two Jewish wars is formative, hence classical, for medieval and modern Judaism (S. Cohen 1987; Neusner 1988). The ending of *Tanakh* becomes understandable in the context of the emergence of rabbinic Judaism. Even though Jerusalem is deprived of its Temple (66–73 C.E.) and its people (132–35 C.E.), the ending of Chronicles bears witness to hope for restoration. Transformations occur, but the ties binding God, people, land, and city together endure. The final verses of one of the "sources of Judaism" announces the reconstruction of the Jerusalem Temple and beckons the people to return home.

---

[191] A section devoted to the Chronicler's theology will appear in vol. 2.

BIBLIOGRAPHY

SELECT BIBLIOGRAPHY

The abbreviations for works in biblical and ancient Near Eastern studies follow those used in the *SBL Handbook of Style*, ed. P. H. Alexander et al. (Peabody, Mass.: Hendrickson, 1999) and *Old Testament Abstracts* 24 (Washington, D.C.: Catholic Biblical Association, 2001). Abbreviations for additional works in classics follow those used in the *OCD*, ed. S. Hornblower and A. Spawforth (3rd ed.; Oxford: Oxford University Press, 1996). Other abbreviations are included in the abbreviation lists on pages xv–xxiv.

Abadie, Philippe

1994 "Le fonctionnement symbolique de la figure de David dans l'oeuvre du Chroniste." *Transeu* 7: 143–51.

1997 "David innocent ou coupable?" *FoiVie* 96: 73–83.

1999 "La figure de David dans le livre des Chroniques." Pages 157–86 in Desrousseaux and Vermeylen (1999).

Ackerman, Susan

1991 "The Deception of Issac, Jacob's Dream at Bethel, and Incubation on an Animal Skin." Pages 92–120 in Anderson and Olyan (1991).

1992 *Under Every Green Tree: Popular Religion in Sixth-Century Judah.* HSM 46. Atlanta: Scholars Press.

Ackroyd, Peter Runham

1966 "Some Notes on the Psalms." *JTS* 17: 392–99.

1967 "History and Theology in the Writings of the Chronicler." *CTM* 38: 501–15.

1968 *Exile and Restoration.* OTL. Philadelphia: Westminster.

1970a *The Age of the Chronicler.* Supplement to *Colloquium: The Australian and New Zealand Theological Review.* Auckland.

1970b *Israel under Babylon and Persia.* The New Clarendon Bible. Oxford: Oxford University Press.

1973a *Chronicles, Ezra, Nehemiah.* TBC. London: SCM.

1973b "The Theology of the Chronicler." *LTQ* 8: 101–16.

1976 "God and People in the Chronicler's Presentation of Ezra." Pages 145–62 in *La Notion biblique de Dieu.* Edited by J. Coppens. BETL 41. Leuven: Leuven University Press.

1977 "The Chronicler as Exegete." *JSOT* 2: 2–32.

1987 *Studies in the Religious Tradition of the Old Testament.* London: SCM.
1991 *The Chronicler in His Age.* JSOTSup 101. Sheffield: JSOT Press.

Aharoni, Yohanan
1973 Ed. *Beer Sheba I.* Tel Aviv: Institute of Archaeology.
1975 *Investigations at Lachish: The Sanctuary and the Residency (Lachish V).* Tel Aviv: Gateway.
1979 *The Land of the Bible.* Rev. ed. Translated and edited by Anson Rainey. Philadelphia: Westminster.
1981 *Arad Inscriptions.* JDS. Jerusalem: Israel Exploration Society.
1982 *The Archaeology of the Land of Israel.* Philadelphia: Westminster.

Aḥituv, Shmuel
1984 *Canaanite Toponyms in Ancient Egyptian Documents.* Jerusalem: Magnes.

Aḥituv, Shmuel, and Baruch A. Levine.
1993 Eds. *Avraham Malamat Volume. ErIsr* 24. Jerusalem: Israel Exploration Society.

Ahlström, Gösta W.
1959 *Psalm 89: Eine Liturgie aus dem Rituel des leidenden Königs.* Lund: Gleerup.
1971 *Joel and the Temple Cult of Jerusalem.* VTSup 21. Leiden: Brill.
1982 *Royal Administration and National Religion in Ancient Palestine.* SHANE 1. Leiden: Brill.
1993 *The History of Ancient Palestine from the Palaeolithic Period to Alexander's Conquest.* JSOTSup 146. Sheffield: JSOT Press.
1995 "Administration of the State in Canaan and Ancient Israel." *CANE* 1: 587–603.

Albertz, Rainer
1994 *A History of Religion in the Old Testament Period.* 2 vols. OTL. Louisville, Ky.: Westminster John Knox.

Albrektson, Bertil
1981 "*Difficilior Lectio Probabilior*: A Rule of Textual Criticism and Its Use in Old Testament Studies." *OTS* 21: 5–18.
1994 "Translation and Emendation." Pages 27–39 in Balentine and Barton (1994).

Albright, William F.
1921 "The Date and Personality of the Chronicler." *JBL* 40: 104–24.
1924 "The Topography of Simeon." *JPOS* 24: 149–61.
1926 "Notes on Early Hebrew and Aramaic Epigraphy." *JPOS* 6: 75–102.
1929 "New Israelite and Pre-Israelite Sites." *BASOR* 35: 1–14.
1934 *The Vocalization of the Egyptian Syllabic Orthography.* AOS 5. New Haven, Conn.: American Oriental Society.
1942 "King Jehoiachin in Exile." *BASOR* 5: 49–55.
1945 "The List of Levitic Cities." Pages 49–73 in the *Louis Ginzberg Jubilee Volume* (English section). New York: American Academy for Jewish Research.
1950 "The Judicial Reform of Jehoshaphat." Pages 61–82 in the *Alexander*

Marx Jubilee Volume. Edited by S. Lieberman. New York: Jewish Publication Society.
1953 "Dedan." Pages 1–12 in *Geschichte und Altes Testament*. Edited by G. Ebeling. BHT 16. Tübingen: Mohr.
1955 "New Light on Early Recensions of the Hebrew Bible." *BASOR* 140: 27–33.
1956 "The Biblical Tribe of Massa' and Some Congeners." Pages 1–14 in *Studi orientalistici in onore di Giorgio Levi della Vida*. Vol. 1. Rome: Oriental Institute.
1963 *The Biblical Period from Abraham to Ezra*. New York: Harper & Row.
1966 *Archaeology, Historical Analogy, and the Biblical Tradition*. Baton Rouge: Louisiana State University Press.
1968a *Archaeology and the Religion of Israel*. 5th ed. Baltimore: Johns Hopkins University Press.
1968b *Yahweh and the Gods of Canaan*. Garden City: Doubleday. Repr., Winona Lake, Ind.: Eisenbrauns, 1994.

Alexander, Philip S.
1974 *The Toponymy of the Targumim*. Ph.D. diss., University of Oxford.
1982 "Notes on the *Imago Mundi* in the Book of Jubilees." *JJS* 33: 197–213.
1985 "The Targumim and the Palestinian Rules for the Delivery of the Targum." Pages 14–22 in Emerton (1985).
1988 "Retelling the Old Testament." Pages 99–121 in *It Is Written: Scripture Citing Scripture. Essays in Honour of Barnabas Lindars, SSF*. Cambridge: Cambridge University Press.
1992 "Early Jewish Geography." *ABD* 2: 977–88.
1997 "Omphalos of the World." *Judaism* 46: 147–58.

Allan, Nigel
1982 "The Identity of the Jerusalem Priesthood during the Exile." *HeyJ* 23: 259–69.

Allen, Leslie C.
1968 "Further Thoughts on an Old Recension of Reigns in Paralipomena." *HTR* 61: 483–91.
1974a *The Greek Chronicles: The Relation of the Septuagint of I and II Chronicles to the Masoretic Text*. Part 1. VTSup 25. Leiden: Brill.
1974b *The Greek Chronicles: The Relation of the Septuagint of I and II Chronicles to the Masoretic Text*. Part 2. VTSup 27. Leiden: Brill.
1988 "Kerygmatic Units in 1 and 2 Chronicles." *JSOT* 41: 21–36.

Allrik, H. L.
1954a "1 Esdras according to Codex B and Codex A as Appearing in Zerubbabel's List in 1 Esdras 5: 8–23." ZAW 66: 272–92.
1954b "The Lists of Zerubbabel (Nehemiah 7 and Ezra 2) and the Hebrew Numerical Notation." *BASOR* 136: 21–27.

Alt, Albrecht
1934 "Die Rolle Samarias bei der Entstehung des Judentum." Pages 5–28 in *Festschrift Otto Procksch*. Leipzig: Deichert-Hinrichs.
1936 "Zu II Samuel 8,1." ZAW 54: 149–52.

1939 "Sihor und Epha." *ZAW* 57: 147–48.

1951 "Bemerkungen zu einigen judäischen Ortslisten des Alten Testaments." *Beiträge zur biblischen Landes- und Altertumskunde* 68: 193–210.

1953 *Kleine Schriften zur Geschichte des Volkes Israel.* Vols. 1–2. Munich: Beck.

1954 *Der Stadstaat Samaria.* Berichte über die Verhandlungen der sächsischen Akademie der Wissenschaften zu Leipzig, Philosophisch-historische Klasse 101/5. Berlin: Akademie.

1959 *Kleine Schriften zur Geschichte des Volkes Israel.* Vol. 3. Munich: Beck.

1967 *Essays on Old Testament History and Religion.* Garden City: Doubleday.

Alter, Robert, and Frank Kermode

1987 Eds. *The Literary Guide to the Bible.* Cambridge: Belknap.

Anbar, Moshe

1982 "Genesis 15: A Conflation of Two Deuteronomic Narratives." *JBL* 101: 51–55.

1992 " 'Mot en vedette' (Stichwort) en vue d'une correction." *BN* 63: 7–11.

Andersen, Francis I., and A. Dean Forbes

1989 *The Vocabulary of the Old Testament.* Rome: Pontifical Biblical Institute.

Andersen, Francis I., and David N. Freedman

1980 *Hosea.* AB 24. Garden City: Doubleday.

1989 *Amos.* AB 24a. Garden City: Doubleday.

Anderson, A. A.

1989 *2 Samuel.* WBC 11. Waco, Tex.: Word.

Anderson, Gary A.

1991a *A Time to Mourn, a Time to Dance: The Expression of Grief and Joy in Israelite Religion.* University Park, Penn.: Pennsylvania State University Press.

1991b "The Praise of God as a Cultic Event." Pages 15–33 in Anderson and Olyan (1991).

Anderson, Gary A., and Saul M. Olyan

1991 Eds. *Priesthood and Cult in Ancient Israel.* JSOTSup 125. Sheffield: JSOT Press.

Anderson, Robert D.

1995 "Music and Dance in Pharaonic Egypt." *CANE* 4: 2555–68.

Ariel, D. T.

1990 *Excavations at the City of David, 1978–1985.* Qedem 30. Jerusalem: Israel Exploration Society.

Arnold, Patrick M.

1990 *Gibeah: The Search for a Biblical City.* JSOTSup 79. Sheffield: JSOT Press.

Astour, Michael

1965 "Sabtah and Sabteca: Ethiopian Pharaoh Names in Genesis 10." *JBL* 84: 422–25.

Attridge, Harold W.
1984 "Historiography." Pages 157–232 in Stone (1984).
Auerbach, Eric
1953 *Mimesis: The Representation of Reality in Western Literature.* Princeton: Princeton University Press.
Auffret, Pierre
1995 *Merveilles à nos yeux: Etude structurelle de vingt psaumes dont celui de 1 Ch 16, 8–36.* BZAW 235. Berlin: de Gruyter.
Aufrecht, Walter E.
1988 "Genealogy and History in Ancient Israel." Pages 205–35 in *Ascribe to the Lord: Biblical and Other Studies in Memory of Peter C. Craigie.* Edited by L. Eslinger and G. Taylor. JSOTSup 67. Sheffield: JSOT Press.
1989 *A Corpus of Ammonite Inscriptions.* Ancient Near Eastern Texts and Studies 4. Lewiston, N.Y.: Edwin Mellen.
1999a "Ammonite Texts and Language." Pages 163–88 in MacDonald and Younker (1999).
1999b "The Religion of the Ammonites." Pages 152–62 in MacDonald and Younker (1999).
Augustin, Matthias
1990 "The Role of Simeon in the Book of Chronicles and in Jewish Writings of the Hellenistic-Roman Period." Pages 137–44 in *Proceedings of the Tenth World Congress of Jewish Studies.* Vol. 1. Jerusalem: Magnes.
1994 "Neue territorialgeschichtliche Aspekte zu 1 Chronik 1–9 am Beispiel der Rubeniten." Pages 299–309 in *Nachdenken über Israel, Bibel und Theologie: Festschrift für Klaus-Dietrich Schunck zu einem 65. Geburtstag.* Edited by H. M. Niemann, M. Augustin, and W. H. Schmidt. BEATAJ 37. Frankfurt am Main: Lang.
Auld, A. Graeme
1978 "Cities of Refuge in Biblical Tradition." *JSOT* 10: 26–40. Repr., pages 37–48 in Auld (1998).
1979 "The 'Levitical Cities': Texts and History." ZAW 91: 194–207. Repr., pages 25–36 in Auld (1998).
1990 "The Cities in Joshua 21: The Contribution of Textual Criticism." *Text* 15: 141–52. Repr., pages 49–57 in Auld (1998).
1992 "Salomo und die Deuteronomisten—eine Zukunftsvision?" *TZ* 48: 343–54.
1994 *Kings without Privilege: David and Moses in the Story of the Bible's Kings.* Edinburgh: T&T Clark.
1996 "Re-reading Samuel (Historically): 'Etwas mehr Nichtwissen.' " Pages 160–69 in Fritz and Davies (1996).
1998 *Joshua Retold: Synoptic Perspectives.* Edinburgh: T&T Clark.
1999 "What Was the Main Source of the Book of Chronicles?" Pages 91–100 in Graham and McKenzie (1999).
Auscher, Dominique
1967 "Les Relations entre la Grèce et la Palestine avant la Conquète d'Alexandre." *VT* 17: 8–30.

Auwers, Jean-Marie

1999 "Le David des psuames et les psuames de David." Pages 187–224 in Desrousseaux and Vermeylen (1999).

Avigad, Nahman

1976 *Bullae and Seals from a Post-exilic Judean Archive. Qedem 4.* Monographs of the Hebrew University Institute of Archaeology. Jerusalem.

1978 "Baruch the Scribe and Jerahmeel the King's Son." *IEJ* 28: 52–56.

1981 "Jerusalem—'The City Full of People.' " Pages 129–40 in Shanks and Mazar (1981).

1983 *Discovering Jerusalem.* New York: Thomas Nelson.

1986 *Hebrew Bullae from the Time of Jeremiah: Remnants of a Burnt Archive.* Jerusalem: Israel Exploration Society.

1987 "The Contribution of Hebrew Seals to an Understanding of Israelite Religion and Society." Pages 195–208 in Miller, Hanson, and McBride (1987).

1988 "Hebrew Seals and Sealings and Their Significance for Biblical Research." Pages 7–16 in Emerton (1988).

Avigad, Nahman, and Benjamin Sass

1997 *Corpus of West Semitic Stamp Seals.* Jerusalem: Israel Academy of Sciences and Humanities.

Avishur, Yitzhak

2000 *Phoenician Inscriptions and the Bible.* Tel Aviv–Jaffa: Archaeological Center.

Avishur, Yitzhak, and M. Heltzer

2000 *Studies on the Royal Administration in Ancient Israel in the Light of the Epigraphic Sources.* Tel Aviv–Jaffa: Archaeological Center.

Bacher, W.

1895 "Der Name der Bücher der Chronik in der Septuaginta." ZAW 15: 305–8.

Bahat, Dan, and Gila Hurvitz

1996 "Jerusalem—First Temple Period: Archaeological Exploration." Pages 287–306 in *Royal Cities of the Biblical World.* Edited by Joan Westenholz. Jerualem: Bible Lands Museum.

Bailey, Noel

1994 "David's Innocence: A Response to J. Wright." *JSOT* 64: 83–90.

1999 "David and God in 1 Chronicles 21: Edged with Mist." Pages 337–59 in Graham and McKenzie (1999).

Baker, David W., and B.T. Arnold

1999 Eds. *The Face of Old Testament Studies.* Grand Rapids: Baker.

Bal, Mieke

1988 *Death and Dissymmetry: The Politics of Coherence in the Book of Judges.* Chicago: University of Chicago Press.

Balcer, Jack Martin

1984 *Sparda by the Bitter Sea: Imperial Interaction in Western Anatolia.* BJS 52. Chico, Calif.: Scholars Press.

1995 *The Persian Conquest of the Greeks, 545–450 B.C.* Konstanzer Althistorische Vorträge und Forschungen 38. Xenia: Konstanz Universitätsverlag.

Balentine, Samuel E.

1993 *Prayer in the Hebrew Bible: The Drama of Divine-Human Dialogue.* OBT. Minneapolis: Fortress.

1997 " 'You Can't Pray a Lie': Truth *and* Fiction in the Prayers of Chronicles." Pages 246–67 in Graham, Hoglund, and McKenzie (1997).

Balentine, Samuel E., and J. Balentine and Barton

1994 Eds. *Language, Theology, and the Bible: Essays in Honour of James Barr.* Oxford: Clarendon Press.

Baltzer, Klaus

1971 *The Covenant Formulary in Old Testament, Jewish, and Early Christian Writings.* Philadelphia: Fortress.

Barag, Dan

1966 "The Effects of the Tennes Rebellion on Palestine." *BASOR* 183: 6–12.

Barkay, Gabriel

1986 *Ketef Hinnom: A Treasure Facing Jerusalem's Walls.* Jerusalem: The Israel Museum.

1992a "The Iron Age II–III." Pages 302–73 in Ben-Tor (1992).

1992b "The Priestly Benediction on Silver Plaques from Ketef Hinnom in Jerusalem." *TA* 19: 139–92.

1993 "The Redefining of Archaeological Periods: Does the Date 588/586 B.C.E. Indeed Mark the End of Iron Age Culture?" Pages 106–12 in Biran (1993).

Barnes, William Emery

1896 "The Midrashic Element in Chronicles." *The Expositor* 5/4: 426–39.

1896–97a "Chronicles as Targum." *ExpT* 8: 316–19.

1896–97b "The Religious Standpoint of the Chronicler." *AJSL* 13: 14–20.

1897 *An Apparatus Criticus to Chronicles in the Peshitta Version with a Discussion of the Value of Codex Ambrosianus.* Cambridge: Cambridge University Press.

1909 "The David of the Book of Samuel and the David of the Book of Chronicles." *The Expositor* 7/7: 49–59.

Barnes, William H.

1992 "Jeduthun." *ABD* 3: 655–56.

Barr, James

1984 "*migraš* in the Old Testament." *JSS* 29: 15–31.

Barstad, Hans M.

1988 "On the History and Archaeology of Judah during the Exilic Period." OLP 19: 25–36.

1997 *The Babylonian Captivity of the Book of Isaiah.* Instituttet for sammenlignende kulturforskning B/CII. Oslo: Novus.

2003 "After the 'Myth of the Empty Land:' Major Challenges in the Study of Neo-Babylonian Judah." Pages 3–20 in Lipschits and Blenkinsopp (2003).

Barthélemy, Dominique
1963 *Les Devanciers d'Aquila.* VTSup 10. Leiden: Brill.
1982 *Critique textuelle de l'ancien Testament.* Fribourg: Éditions Universitaires.

Bartlett, John R.
1965 "The Edomite King-List of Genesis XXXVI.31–39 and 1 Chron. I.43–50." *JTS* 16: 301–14.
1968 "Zadok and His Successors at Jerusalem." *JTS* 19: 1–18.
1979 "From Edomites to Nabataeans: A Study in Continuity." *PEQ* 111: 53–66.
1989 *Edom and the Edomites.* JSOTSup 77. Sheffield: JSOT Press.
1992 "Biblical Sources for the Early Iron Age in Edom." Pages 13–19 in Bienkowski (1992).
1995 "Edom in the Nonprophetical Corpus." Pages 13–21 in Edelman (1995b).

Barton, John, and David Reimer
1996 Eds. *After the Exile: Essays in Honour of Rex Mason.* Macon, Ga.: Mercer University Press.

Batten, Loring Woard
1913 *A Critical and Exegetical Commentary on the Books of Ezra and Nehemiah.* ICC. Edinburgh: T&T Clark.

Bayer, P. Edmund
1911 *Das dritte Buch Esdras und sein Verhältnis zu den Büchern Esra-Nehemia.* BibS(F) 16/1.

Beck, Astrid B., et al.
1995 Eds. *Fortunate the Eyes That See: Essays in Honor of David Noel Freedman in Celebration of His Seventieth Birthday.* Grand Rapids: Eerdmans.

Becker, Joachim
1986 *1 Chronik.* NEchtB 18. Würzburg: Echter.
1988 *2 Chronik.* NEchtB 20. Würzburg: Echter.
1990 *Esra, Nehemia.* NEchtB 25. Würzburg: Echter.
1998 *Der Ich-Bericht des Nehemiabuches als chronistische Gestaltung.* FB 87. Würzburg: Echter.

Becking, Bob
1990 "Jehojachin's Amnesty, Salvation for Israel? Notes on 2 Kings 25, 27–30." Pages 283–93 in Brekelmans and Lust (1990).
1998 "Ezra on the Move: Trends and Perspectives on the Character and His Book." Pages 154–79 in *Perspectives in the Study of the Old Testament and Early Judaism: A Symposium in Honour of Adam S. van der Woude on the Occasion of His Seventieth Birthday.* Edited by F. García Martinez and E. Noort. VTSup 73. Leiden: Brill.
1999 "Continuity and Community: The Belief System of the Book of Ezra." Pages 256–75 in Becking and Korpel (1999).

Becking, Bob, and Marjo C. A. Korpel
1999 Eds. *The Crisis of Israelite Religion: Transformation of Religious Tradition in Exilic and Post-Exilic Times.* OTS 42. Leiden: Brill.

Beckman, Gary M.

1982 "The Hittite Assembly." *JAOS* 102: 435–42.

1986 "Inheritance and Royal Succession among the Hittites." Pages 53–58 in *Kaniššuwar: A Tribute to Hans G. Güterbock on His Seventy-fifth Birthday.* Edited by H. A. Hoffner and G. M. Beckman. AS 23. Chicago: The Oriental Institute of the University of Chicago.

1992 "Hittite Administration in Syria in the Light of the Texts from Ḫattuša, Ugarit, and Emar." Pages 41–49 in *New Horizons in the Study of Ancient Syria.* Edited by M. K. Chavalas and J. L. Hayes. BMes 25. Malibu: Undena.

1995 "Royal Ideology and State Administration in Hittite Anatolia." *CANE* 1: 529–42.

1996 *Hittite Diplomatic Texts.* Writings from the Ancient World 7. Atlanta: Scholars Press.

Beckwith, Roger T.

1985 *The Old Testament Canon of the New Testament Church and Its Background in Early Judaism.* Grand Rapids: Eerdmans.

1996 *Calendar and Chronology, Jewish and Christian.* AGJU 33. Leiden: Brill.

Beecher, Willis J.

1885 "Note on the Proper Paragraph Division in 1 Chron xxix. 22." *JBL* 5: 73–75.

Beentjes, Pancratius C.

1982 "Inverted Quotations in the Bible: A Neglected Stylistic Pattern." *Bib* 63: 506–23.

1996 "Jerusalem in the Book of Chronicles." Pages 15–28 in Poorthuis and Safrai (1996).

1999 "Identity and Community in the Book of Chronicles: The Role and Meaning of the Verb *jāḥaś*." *ZAH* 12: 233–37.

Begg, Christopher T.

1982 " 'Seeking Yahweh' and the Purpose of Chronicles." *LS* 9: 128–41.

1986 "The Significance of Jehoiachin's Release: A New Proposal." *JSOT* 36: 49–56.

1994 "Josephus' Version of David's Census." *Hen* 16: 199–225.

Beit-Arie, Malachi

1982 "A Lost Leaf from the Aleppo Codex Recovered." *Tarbiz* 171–73.

Beit-Arieh, Itzhaq

1995 *Ḥorvat Qitmit: An Edomite Shrine in the Biblical Negev.* Tel Aviv: Institute of Archaeology.

1996 "Edomites Advance into Judah: Israelite Defensive Fortresses Inadequate." *BARev* 22/6: 28–36.

Bendavid, Abba

1972 *Parallels in the Bible.* Jerusalem: Carta.

Ben-Dov, Jonathan

2001 "4QOtot." Pages 195–244 in Talmon, Shemaryahu, Ben-Dov, and Glessmer (2001).

Bennett, W. J., and J. A. Blakely
1989 *Tell El-Hesi: The Persian Period (Stratum V)*. Winona Lake, Ind.: Eisenbrauns.
Benoît, P., J. T. Milik, and R. de Vaux
1961 *Les Grottes de Murabbaʿat*. DJD 2. Oxford: Clarendon Press.
Ben-Tor, Amnon
1992 Ed. *The Archaeology of Ancient Israel*. New Haven, Conn.: Yale University Press.
1993 "Jokneam." *NEAEHL* 3: 805–11.
Ben-Tor, Amnon, J. C. Greenfield, and A. Malamat
1989 Eds. *Yigael Yadin Memorial Volume*. *ErIsr* 20. Jerusalem: Israel Exploration Society.
Bentzen, Aage
1933 "Zur Geschichte der Sadokiden." *ZAW* 51: 173–76.
1934 "Die Herkunft Ṣadoḳ's." *ZAW* 52: 42–50, 160.
Benz, Frank L.
1972 *Personal Names in the Phoenician and Punic Inscriptions*. Studia Pohl 8. Rome: Biblical Institute Press.
Benzinger, I.
1901 *Die Bücher der Chronik*. KHT 20. Tübingen: Mohr.
Ben Zvi, Ehud
1988 "The Authority of 1–2 Chronicles in the Late Second Temple Period." *JSP* 3: 59–88.
1992 "The List of the Levitical Cities." *JSOT* 54: 77–106.
1993 "A Gateway to the Chronicler's Teaching: The Account of the Reign of Ahaz in 2 Chr 28,1–27." *SJOT* 7: 216–49.
1995 "A Sense of Proportion: An Aspect of the Theology of the Chronicler." *SJOT* 9: 37–51.
1997 "The Chronicler as Historian: Building Texts." Pages 132–49 in Graham, Hoglund, and McKenzie (1997).
1999 "When the Foreign Monarch Speaks." Pages 109–28 in Graham and McKenzie (1999).
2000 "About Time: Observations about the Construction of Time in the Book of Chronicles." *HBT* 22: 17–31.
forthcoming "Shifting the Gaze: Looking at the Lack of Change in Chronicles and Historiographic Constraints in Chronicles and Its Implications." JSOTSup 343. Sheffield: JSOT Press.
Berger, Paul-Richard
1971 "Zu den Namen ששבצר und שנאצר." *ZAW* 83: 98–100.
1973 *Die neubabylonischen Königschriften*. AOAT 4/1. Kevelaer: Butzon & Bercker.
Berquist, Jon L.
1995 *Judaism in Persia's Shadow*. Minneapolis: Fortress.
Bertheau, Ernst
1873 *Die Bücher der Chronik*. 2nd ed. Kurzgefasstes exegetisches Handbuch zum Alten Testament 15. Leipzig: Hirzel.

Betlyon, John Wilson

1982 *The Coinage and Mints of Phoenicia: The Pre-Alexandrian Period.* HSM 26. Chico, Calif.: Scholars Press.

1986 "The Provincial Government of Persian Period Judea and the Yehud Coins." *JBL* 105: 633–42.

1991 "Archaeological Evidence of Military Operations in Southern Judah during the Early Hellenistic Period." *BA* 54: 36–43.

Bewer, Julius A.

1922 *Der Text des Buches Ezra: Beiträge zu einer Wiederherstellung.* Göttingen: Vandenhoeck & Ruprecht.

Bianchi, F.

1991 "Zorobabele re di Giuda." *Hen* 13: 133–50.

1994 "Le rôle de Zorobabel et de la dynastie davidique en Judée du VIe siècle au IIe siècle." *Transeu* 7: 154–65.

Bickerman, Elias J.

1937 *Der Gott der Makkabäer.* Berlin: Schocken.

Biella, Joan Copeland

1982 *Dictionary of Old South Arabic: Sabaean Dialect.* HSS 25. Chico, Calif.: Scholars Press.

Bienkowski, Piotr

1992 Ed. *Early Edom and Moab: The Beginning of the Iron Age in Southern Jordan.* Sheffield Archaeological Monographs 7. Sheffield: J. R. Collis.

1995 "The Edomites: Archaeological Evidence from Transjordan." Pages 41–92 in Edelman (1995b).

Biran, Avraham

1981 Ed. *Temple and High Places in Biblical Times.* Jerusalem: The Nelson Glueck School of Biblical Archaeology.

Biran, Avraham, and Joseph Aviram

1993 Eds. *Biblical Archaeology Today, 1990: Proceedings of the Second International Congress on Biblical Archaeology.* Jerusalem: Israel Exploration Society.

Biran, Avraham, and Joseph Naveh

1993 "An Aramaic Stele Fragment from Tel Dan." *IEJ* 43: 81–98.

1995 "The Tel Dan Inscription: A New Fragment." *IEJ* 45: 1–18.

Biran, Avraham, et al.

1996 Eds. *Archaeological, Historical, and Geographical Studies (Joseph Aviram Volume). ErIsr* 25. Jerusalem: Israel Exploration Society.

Bird, Phyllis A.

1992 "Women (OT)." *ABD* 6: 951–57.

Bivar, D. H.

1985 "Achaemenid Coins, Weights, and Measures." Pages 610–39 in Gershevitch (1985).

Blenkinsopp, Joseph

1988 *Ezra-Nehemiah: A Commentary.* OTL. Philadelphia: Westminster.

1992 *The Pentateuch: An Introduction to the First Five Books of the Bible.* ABRL. Garden City: Doubleday.
1995 *Sage, Priest, Prophet: Religious and Intellectual Leadership in Ancient Israel.* Louisville, Ky.: Westminster John Knox.
1998 "The Judaean Priesthood during the Neo-Babylonian and Achaemenid Periods: A Hypothetical Reconstruction." *CBQ* 60: 25–43.
2000 "A Case of Benign Imperial Neglect and Its Consequences." *BibInt* 8: 129–36.
2001 "The Social Roles of Prophets in Early Achaemenid Judah." *JSOT* 93: 39–58.
2003 "Bethel in the Neo-Babylonian Period." Pages 93–107 in Lipschits and Blenkinsopp (2003).

Blum, E.
1990 *Studien zur Komposition des Pentateuch.* BZAW 189. Berlin: de Gruyter.

Boardman, John
1999 *The Greeks Overseas.* 4th ed. London: Thames & Hudson.
2000 *Persia and the West.* London: Thames & Hudson.
2001 "Aspects of 'Colonization.' " *BASOR* 322: 33–42.

Bogaert, P.-M.
1999 "La Porte Orientale, place de rassemblement du peuple, et l'extension de l'oeuvre du Chroniste." *Transeu* 17: 9–16.

Bohak, Gideon
1996 *Joseph and Aseneth and the Jewish Temple in Heliopolis.* SBLEJL 10. Atlanta: Scholars Press.

Böhler, Dieter
1997 *Die heilige Stadt in Esdras α und Esra-Nehemia: Zwei Konzeptionen der Wiederherstellung Israels.* OBO 158. Freiburg: Universitätsverlag.

Bolin, Thomas M.
1995 "The Temple of יהו at Elephantine and Persian Religious Policy." Pages 127–42 in Edelman (1995a).

Boling, Robert G.
1975 *Judges.* AB 6A. Garden City: Doubleday.
1985 "Levitical Cities: Archaeology and Texts." Pages 23–32 in Kort and Morschauser (1985).

Boling, Robert G., and G. E. Wright
1982 *Joshua: A New Translation with Notes and Commentary.* AB 6. Garden City: Doubleday.

Bonnet, C., E. Lipiński, and P. Marchetti
1986 Eds. *Studia Phoenicia IV: Religio Phoenicia.* Collection d'Études Classiques 1. Namur: Société des Études Classiques.

Bordreuil, Pierre, F. Israel, and D. Pardee
1996 "Deux ostraca paléo-hébreux de la Collection Sh. Moussaïeff." *Sem* 46: 49–76.

Borger, Riekele
1956 "Die Inschriften Asarhaddons, Königs von Assyrien." *AfO* 9. Graz.

1972 "Die Waffenträger des Königs Darius." *VT* 22: 385–98.

Borger, Riekele, and H. Tadmor

1982 "Zwei Beiträge zur alttestamentlichen Wissenschaft aufgrund der Inschriften Tiglatpilesers III." ZAW 94: 244–51.

Borowski, O.

1987 *Agriculture in Ancient Israel: The Evidence from Archaeology and the Bible.* Winona Lake, Ind.: Eisenbrauns.

Botterweck, G. J.

1956 "Zur Eigenart der chronistischen Davidgeschichte." *TQ* 136: 402–35.

Bowra, Cecil Maurice

1961 *Heroic Poetry.* New York: St. Martin's Press.

Boyer, G.

1955 "La Place des textes d'Ugarit dans l'histoire de ancien droit oriental." *PRU* 3: 283–308.

Braun, Joachim

1999 *Die Musikkultur Altisraels/Palästinas.* OBO 164. Freiburg: Universitätsverlag.

Braun, Roddy L.

1971 "The Message of Chronicles: Rally 'Round the Temple." *CTM* 42: 503–16.

1973 "Solomonic Apologetic in Chronicles." *JBL* 92: 503–16.

1976 "Solomon, the Chosen Temple Builder: The Significance of 1 Chronicles 22, 28, and 29 for the Theology of Chronicles." *JBL* 95: 581–90.

1977 "A Reconsideration of the Chronicler's Attitude toward the North." *JBL* 96: 59–62.

1979 "Chronicles, Ezra and Nehemiah: Theology and Literary History." Pages 52–64 in *Studies in the Historical Books of the Old Testament.* Edited by J. A. Emerton. VTSup 30. Leiden: Brill.

1986 *1 Chronicles.* WBC 14. Waco: Word.

1997 "1 Chronicles 1–9 and the Reconstruction of the History of Israel: Thoughts on the Use of Genealogical Data in Chronicles in the Reconstruction of the History of Israel." Pages 92–105 in Graham, Hoglund, and McKenzie (1997).

Brekelmans, C., and J. Lust

1990 Eds. *Pentateuchal and Deuteronomistic Studies: Papers Read at the XIIIth International Organization for the Study of the Old Testament Congress.* BETL 94. Leuven: Leuven University Press.

Bretschneider, Joachim

1993 "Götter im Schreinen: Eine Untersuchung zu den syrischen und levantinischen Tempelmodellen, ihrer Bauplastik und ihren Götterbildern." *UF* 23: 13–32.

Brett, Mark G.

1996 Ed. *Ethnicity and the Bible.* Leiden: Brill.

2000 *Genesis: Procreation and the Politics of Identity.* London: Routledge.

Brettler, Marc Zvi
1995 *The Creation of History in Ancient Israel.* London: Routledge.
Briant, Pierre
1982 *Rois, Tributs et paysans: Études sur les formations tributaires du Moyen-Orient ancien.* Annales littéraires de l'Université de Besançon 269; Centre de recherches d'histoire ancienne 43. Paris: Belles lettres.
1996 *Histoire de l'Empire perse: De Cyrus à Alexandre.* Achaemenid History 10. Paris: Fayard.
1997 "Bulletin d'histoire achéménide *(BHAch)* I." Pages 5–127 in *Recherches récentes sur l'Empire achéménide.* Edited by M.-F. Boussac. *Topoi* Supplément 1. Paris: De Boccard.
Briggs, A., and E. G. Briggs
1907 *The Book of Psalms,* 2. ICC. New York: Scribner's.
Bright, John
1981 *A History of Israel.* 3rd ed. Philadelphia: Westminster.
Brinkman, J. A.
1963 "Provincial Administration in Babylonia under the Second Dynasty of Isin." *JESHO* 6: 233–41.
1968 *A Political History of Post-Kassite Babylonia 1158–722 B.C.* AnOr 43. Rome: Pontifical Biblical Institute.
Broadbent, Molly
1968 *Studies in Greek Genealogy.* Leiden: Brill.
Brock, Sebastian P.
1968 "Lucian *redivivus:* Some Reflections on Barthélemy's 'Les Devanciers d'Aquila.' " *SE* 5: 176–81 (TU 103).
1996 *The Recensions of the Septuagint Version of I Samuel.* Quaderni di Henochi 9. Torino: S. Zamorani.
Brooke, A. E., N. McLean, and H. S. J. Thackeray
1932 *The Old Testament in Greek, Vol. II Part III: I and II Chronicles.* London: Cambridge University Press.
Brooke, George J.
1985 *Exegesis at Qumran: 4QFlorilegium in Its Jewish Context.* JSOTSup 29. Dead Sea Scrolls Project of the Institute for Antiquity and Christianity 2. Sheffield: JSOT Press.
1992 "The Textual Tradition of the *Temple Scroll* and Recently Published Manuscripts of the Pentateuch." Pages 261–82 in *The Dead Sea Scrolls: Forty Years of Research.* Edited by D. Dimant and U. Rappaport. Leiden: Brill.
2000 "Rewritten Bible." *EDSS* 2: 777–81.
Brooke, George J., and Florentino García Martínez
1994 Eds. *New Qumran Texts and Studies: Proceedings of the First Meeting of the International Organization for Qumran Studies.* Leiden: Brill.
Broshi, K. M., and Israel Finkelstein
1992 "The Population of Palestine in Iron Age II." *BASOR* 287: 47–60.

Broshi, Magen, and Ada Yardeni
1995 "On *netinim* and False Prophets." Pages 29–37 in Zevit, Gitin, and Sokoloff (1995).

Broshi, Magen, et al.
1995 Eds. *Qumran Cave 4, XIV: Parabiblical Texts, Part 2*. DJD 19. Oxford: Clarendon Press.

Brown, John Pairman
1995 *Israel and Hellas*. BZAW 231. Berlin: de Gruyter.
2000 *Sacred Institutions with Roman Counterparts*. Vol. 2 of *Israel and Hellas*. BZAW 276. Berlin: de Gruyter.

Brown, Raymond E.
1977 *The Birth of the Messiah*. Garden City: Doubleday.

Brown, Truesdell S.
1973 *The Greek Historians. Civilization and Society: Studies in Social, Economic, and Cultural History*. Lexington, Mass.: D. C. Heath.

Browne, Laurence E.
1916 "A Jewish Sanctuary in Babylonia." *JTS* 17: 400–401.

Bruneau, Phillipe
1982 "Les Israélites de Délos et la juivierìe délienne." *BCH* 106: 465–504.

Brunet, Adrien-Marie
1953 "Les Chroniste et ses sources." *RB* 60: 481–508.
1954 "Les Chroniste et ses sources." *RB* 61: 349–86.
1959 "La theólogie du Chroniste: Théocratie et messianisme." SP 1: 384–97. Paris: Gamblous.

Büchler, Adolf
1899 "Zur Geschichte der Tempelmusik und der Tempelpsalmen." ZAW 19: 96–133, 329–44.
1900 "Zur Geschichte der Tempelmusik und der Tempelpsalmen." ZAW 20: 97–135.

Budde, Karl
1902 *Die Bücher Samuel erklärt*. KHT 8. Tübingen: Mohr.

Bultmann, Christoph
1992 *Der Fremde im antiken Juda: Eine Untersuchung zum sozialen Typenbegriff "ger" und seinem Bedeutungswandel in der alttestamentlichen Gesetzgebung*. FRLANT 153. Göttingen: Vandenhoeck & Ruprecht.

Burford, Alison
1972 *Craftsmen in Greek and Roman Society*. Ithaca, N. Y.: Cornell University Press.

van den Bussche, H.
1948 *Le texte de la prophétie de Nathan sur la dynastie Davidique*. ALBO II/7. Duculot: Gembloux (= *ETL* 24: 354–94).

Butler, Trent C.
1978 "A Forgotten Passage from a Forgotten Era (1 Chr. xvi 8–36)." *VT* 28: 142–50.

Cahill, J. M., and D. Tarler
1994 "Excavations Directed by Yigal Shiloh at the City of David, 1978–1985," in Geva (1994).
Cairns, Francis
1972 *Generic Composition in Greek and Roman Poetry*. Edinburgh: Edinburgh University Press.
1979 *Tibullus: a Hellenistic Poet at Rome*. New York: Cambridge University Press.
Calderone, P. J.
1966 *Dynastic Oracle and Suzerainty Treaty*. Logos 1. Manila: Ateneo University Publications.
Callendar, Dexter E.
2000 *Adam in Myth and History*. HSS 48. Winona Lake, Ind.: Eisenbrauns.
Campbell, Antony F., S.J.
1986 *Of Prophets and Kings: A Late-Ninth-Century Document (1 Samuel 1–2 Kings 10)*. CBQMS 17. Washington, D.C.: The Catholic Biblical Association of America.
Caquot, André
1966 "Peut-on parler de messianisme dans l'oeuvre du Chroniste?" *RTP* 3/16: 110–20.
Caquot, André, and P. de Robert
1994 *Les Livres de Samuel*. CAT 6. Geneva: Labor et Fides.
Carmignac, J.
1981 "Les Devanciers de S. Jerome: Une traduction latine de la Recension *kaige* dans la seconde Livre des Chroniques." Pages 31–50 in *Mélanges Dominique Barthélemy*. Edited by P. Cassetti, O. Kell, and A. Schenker. OBO 38. Göttingen: Vandenhoeck & Ruprecht.
Carroll, Robert P.
1992 The Myth of the Empty Land. *Semeia* 59: 79–93.
2001 "Jewgreek Greekjew: The Hebrew Bible Is All Greek to Me. Reflections on the Problematics of Dating the Origins of the Bible in Relation to Contemporary Discussions of Biblical Historiography." Pages 91–107 in Grabbe (2001c).
Carter, Charles E.
1994 "The Province of Yehud in the Post-Exilic Period: Soundings in Site Distribution and Demography." Pages 106–45 in Eskenazi and Richards (1994).
1999 *The Emergence of Yehud in the Persian Period*. JSOTSup 294. Sheffield: Sheffield Academic Press.
2003 "Ideology and Archaeology in the Neo-Babylonian Period: Excavating Text and Tell." Pages 301–22 in Lipschits and Blenkinsopp (2003).
Cazelles, Henri
1980 "חבר; *chābhar*." *TDOT* 4: 193–98.
1992 "Sacral Kingship." *ABD* 5: 863–66.

Charlesworth, J. H.
1985 "Prayer of Manasseh." *OTP* 2: 625–37.

Chavalas, Mark
1994 "Genealogical History as 'Charter': A Study of Old Babylonian Period Historiography and the Old Testament." Pages 103–28 in Millard, Hoffmeier, and Baker (1994).

Chiesa, Bruno
1992 "Textual History and Textual Criticism of the Hebrew Old Testament." Pages 257–72 in Trebolle Barrera and Vegas Montaner (1992).

Childs, Brevard S.
1971 "Psalm Titles and Midrashic Exegesis." *JSS* 16: 137–150.
1979 *Introduction to the Old Testament as Scripture.* Philadelphia: Fortress.

Chong, Joong Ho
1996 "Were There Yahwistic Sanctuaries in Babylon?" *AJT* 10: 198–217.

Clear, J.
1972 "The Ethiopic Text of II Paralipomenon." *BIOSCS* 5: 13–14.

Clements, Ronald Ernest
1967 *Abraham and David.* SBT 5. Naperville, Ill.: Allenson.
1989 Ed. *The World of Ancient Israel.* Cambridge: Cambridge University Press.

Clines, David J. A.
1984 *Ezra, Nehemiah, Esther.* NCB. Grand Rapids: Eerdmans.

Cody, Aelred
1965 *A History of the Old Testament Priesthood.* AnBib 35. Rome: Pontifical Biblical Institute.

Cogan, Mordecai
1974 *Imperialism and Religion: Assyria, Judah and Israel in the Eighth and Seventh Centuries B.C.E.* SBLMS 19. Missoula, Mont.: Scholars Press.
1979 "The Men of Nebo: Repatriated Reubenites." *IEJ* 29: 37–39.
1995 "The Road to En-dor." Pages 319–26 in Wright, Freedman, and Hurvitz (1995).
1999 "Towards a Definition of ספר דברי הימים למלכי ישׂראל/יהודה" Pages 78–83 in Levine et al. (1999).

Cogan, Mordecai, and Israel Eph'al
1991 Eds. *Ah, Assyria: Studies in Assyrian History and Ancient Near Eastern Historiography Presented to Hayim Tadmor. ScrHier* 33. Jerusalem: Magnes.

Coggins, R. J.
1975 *Samaritans and Jews: The Origins of Samaritanism Reconsidered.* Atlanta: John Knox.
1976 *The First and Second Books of Chronicles.* CBC. Cambridge: Cambridge University Press.

Cohen, Chaim
1999 "Biblical Hebrew-Ugaritic Comparative Philology: The Comparison BH הדר/הדרת = Ug. hdrt." Pages 71–77 in Levine et al. (1999).

Cohen, Shaye J. D.
1987 *From the Maccabees to the Mishnah.* LEC 7. Philadelphia: Westminster.

Cole, Stephen, and Peter Machinist
1988 *Letters from Priests to the Kings Esarhaddon and Assurbanipal.* SAA 13. Helsinki: Helsinki University Press.

Collins, John J.
1993 *Daniel.* Hermeneia. Minneapolis: Fortress.

Conrad, Edgar W.
1985 *Fear Not Warrior: A Study of ʾal tîrāʾ Pericopes in the Hebrew Scriptures.* BJS 75. Chico, Calif.: Scholars Press.

Conte, Gian Biagio
1986 *The Rhetoric of Imitation.* Ithaca, N. Y.: Cornell University Press.

Coogan, Michael David
1976 *West Semitic Names in the Murašu Documents.* HSM 7. Missoula, Mont.: Scholars Press.
1999 "Literacy and the Formation of Biblical Literature." Pages 49–62 in Williams and Hiebert (1999).

Cook, J. M.
1983 *The Persian Empire.* New York: Barnes & Noble.

Cook, Stephen L.
1995 *Prophecy and Apocalypticism: The Postexilic Setting.* Minneapolis: Fortress.

Cooper, Alan M.
1983 "The Life and Times of King David according to the Book of Psalms." HSS 26: 117–31.

Coppens, J.
1968 *Le messianisme royal: Ses origines; son développement; son accomplissment.* LD 54. Paris: Cerf.

Cowe, S. Peter
1990–91a "The Two Armenian Versions of Chronicles, Their Origin and Translation Technique." *Revue des études arméniennes* 22: 53–96.
1990–91b "Tendentious Translation and the Evangelical Imperative: Religious Polemic in the Early Armenian Church." *Revue des études arméniennes* 22: 97–114.

Cowley, A.
1916 "The Meaning of מָקוֹם in Hebrew." *JTS* 17: 174–76.

Cox, Claude E.
1991 Ed. *VII Congress of the International Organization for Septuagint and Cognate Studies, Leuven 1989.* SBLSCS 31. Atlanta: Scholars Press.

Crawford, Sidnie White
1999 "The 'Rewritten Bible' at Qumran: A Look at Three Texts." Pages 1*–8* in Levine et al. (1999).
2000 *The Temple Scroll and Related Texts.* Companion to the Qumran Scrolls 2. Sheffield: Sheffield Academic Press.

Crenshaw, James L.

1988 Ed. *Perspectives on the Hebrew Bible: Essays in Honor of Walter J. Harrelson.* Macon, Ga.: Mercer University Press.

Croft, S. J. L.

1979 Review of H. G. M. Williamson, *Israel in the Books of Chronicles. JSOT* 14: 68–72.

Cross, Frank Moore

1961 "The Development of the Jewish Scripts." Pages 133–202 in *The Bible and the Ancient Near East: Essays in Honor of William Foxwell Albright.* Edited by G. E. Wright. Garden City: Doubleday.

1964 "The History of the Biblical Text in the Light of the Discoveries in the Judaean Desert." *HTR* 57: 281–99.

1966a "Aspects of Samaritan and Jewish History in Late Persian and Hellenistic Times." *HTR* 59: 201–11.

1966b "The Contribution of the Discoveries at Qumran to the Study of the Biblical Text." *IEJ* 16: 81–95.

1969 "Papyri of the Fourth Century B.C. from Dâliyeh: A Preliminary Report on Their Discovery and Significance." Pages 41–62 in *New Directions in Biblical Archaeology.* Edited by D. N. Freedman and J. C. Greenfield. Garden City: Doubleday.

1972 "The Evolution of a Theory of Local Texts." Pages 108–26 in Kraft (1972).

1973 *Canaanite Myth and Hebrew Epic.* Cambridge, Mass.: Harvard University Press.

1974 "The Papyri and Their Historical Implications." Pages 17–29 in *Discoveries in the Wâdī ed-Dâliyeh.* Edited by Paul W. Lapp and Nancy L. Lapp. AASOR 41. Cambridge: ASOR.

1975 "A Reconstruction of the Judean Restoration." *JBL* 94: 4–18 (= *Int* [1975] 29: 187–203).

1979a "Problems of Method in the Textual Criticism of the Hebrew Bible." Pages 31–54 in *The Critical Study of Sacred Texts.* Edited by W. D. O'Flaherty. Berkeley: Graduate Theological Union.

1979b "Two Offering Dishes with Phoenician Inscriptions from the Sanctuary of 'Arad." *BASOR* 235: 75–78.

1981 "The Priestly Tabernacle in Light of Recent Research." Pages 169–80 in Biran (1981).

1983a "The Ammonite Oppression of the Tribes of Gad and Reuben: Missing Verses from 1 Samuel 11 Found in 4QSamuel[a]." Pages 148–58 in Tadmor and Weinfeld (1983).

1983b "The Seal of Miqneyaw, Servant of Yahweh." Pages 55–63 (pls. ix–x) in *Ancient Seals and the Bible.* Edited by L. Gorelick and E. Williams-Forte. Malibu: Undena.

1985 "Samaria Papyrus 1: An Aramaic Slave Conveyance of 335 B.C.E. Found in the Wâdī ed-Dâliyeh." *ErIsr* 18: 1–17.

1986 "A New Aramaic Stele from Taymā." *CBQ* 48: 387–94.

1988a "A Report on the Samarian Papyri." Pages 17–26 in Emerton (1988).
1988b "Reuben, First-Born of Jacob. *ZAW* (suppl.)100: 46–65.
1992 "Some Notes on a Generation of Qumran Studies." Pages 1–14 in Trebolle Barrera and Vegas Montaner (1992).
1995 "A Note on a Recently Published Arrowhead." *IEJ* 45: 188–89.
1998 *From Epic to Canon: History and Literature in Ancient Israel.* Baltimore: Johns Hopkins University Press.

Cross, Frank M., and D. N. Freedman.
1975 *Studies in Ancient Yahwistic Poetry.* SBLDS. Missoula, Mont.: Scholars Press.

Cross, Frank M., and Donald W. Parry
1997 "A Preliminary Edition of a Fragment of 4QSam[b] (4Q52)." *BASOR* 306: 63–74.

Cross, Frank M., and Shemaryahu Talmon
1975 Eds. *Qumran and the History of the Biblical Text.* Cambridge, Mass.: Harvard University Press.

Cross, Frank M., and George E. Wright
1956 "The Boundary and Province Lists of the Kingdom of Judah." *JBL* 75: 202–26.

Crüsemann, Frank
1996 *The Torah: Theology and Social History of Old Testament Law.* Minneapolis: Fortress.

Curtis, Edward Lewis, and Albert Alonzo Madsen
1910 *The Books of Chronicles.* ICC. Edinburgh: T&T Clark.

Dahood, Mitchell
1965 *Psalms I: 1–50.* AB 16. Garden City: Doubleday.

Dalley, Stephanie
1984 *Mari and Karana: Two Old Babylonian Cities.* London: Longman.
1989 *Myths from Mesopotamia.* Oxford: Oxford University Press.

Dandamaev, Muhammad A.
1979 "State and Temple in Babylonia in the First Millennium B.C." Pages 589–96 in Lipiński (1979).
1987 "Free Hired Labor in Babylonia during the Sixth through Fourth Centuries B.C." Pages 271–79 in *Labor in the Ancient Near East.* Edited by M. A. Powell. AOS 68. New Haven, Conn.: American Oriental Society.
1989 *A Political History of the Achaemenid Empire.* Leiden: Brill.
1990 "The Economy of the Uruk Region in the 6–5th Centuries B.C. (Nergal-nāṣir, son of Nanâ-ibni)." Paper presented at the Tenth International Economic History Congress. Leuven, 1990.
1995a "Babylonian Popular Assemblies in the First Millennium B.C." *Bulletin of the Canadian Society for Mesopotamian Studies* 30: 23–29.
1995b "The Neo-Babylonian *tamkārū.*" Pages 523–30 in Zevit, Gitin, and Sokoloff (1995).
1996 "An Age of Privatization in Ancient Mesopotamia." Pages 197–221 in

Privatization in the Ancient Near East and Classical World. Edited by M. Hudson and B. A. Levine. Cambridge, Mass.: Peabody Museum of Archaeology and Ethnology.

1999 "Achaemenid Imperial Policies and Provincial Governments." *Iranica Antiqua* 34: 269–82.

Dandamaev, Muhammad A., and V. Lukonin

1989 *The Culture and Social Institutions of Ancient Iran*. Cambridge: Cambridge University Press.

Danell, Gustaf Adolph

1946 *Studies in the Name Israel in the Old Testament*. Uppsala: Appelsbergs Boktryckeri-A.-B.

Daviau, P. M. Michèle

1997 "Tell Jawa: A Case Study of Ammonite Urbanism during Iron Age II." Pages 156–71 in *Aspects of Urbanism in Antiquity: From Mesopotamia to Crete*. Edited by W. E. Aufrecht, N. A. Mirau, and S. W. Gauley. JSOTSup 244. Sheffield: Sheffield Academic Press.

Davies, Philip R.

1991 Ed. *Second Temple Studies; 1. Persian Period*. JSOTSup 117. Sheffield: JSOT Press.

1992a "Defining the Boundaries of Israel in the Second Temple Period: 2 Chronicles 20 and the 'Salvation Army.' " Pages 43–54 in Ulrich, Wright, et al. (1992).

1992b *In Search of "Ancient Israel."* JSOTSup 148. Sheffield: JSOT Press.

1998 *Scribes and Schools: The Canonization of the Hebrew Scriptures*. Library of Ancient Israel. Louisville, Ky.: Westminster John Knox.

Davies, W. D., and L. Finkelstein

1984 Eds. *The Cambridge History of Judaism*. Vol. 1. Cambridge: Cambridge University Press.

Day, John

2000 *Yahweh and the Gods and Goddesses of Canaan*. JSOTSup 265. Sheffield: Sheffield Academic Press.

Day, John, R. P. Gordon, and H. G. M. Williamson

1995 Eds. *Wisdom in Ancient Israel*. Cambridge: Cambridge University Press.

Day, Peggy L.

1988 *An Adversary in Heaven:* śāṭān *in the Hebrew Bible*. HSM 43. Atlanta: Scholars Press.

Dearman, J. Andrew

1997 "Roads and Settlements in Moab." *BA* 60/4: 205–13.

Deist, Ferdinand E.

1995 "On 'Synchronic' and 'Diachronic': Wie es eigentlich Gewesen." *JNSL* 21: 37–48.

Delcor, Mathias

1968 "Le Temple d'Onias en Égypte." *RB* 75: 189–203.

Demsky, Aaron

1966 "The Houses of Achzib: A Critical Note on Micah 1: 14b." *IEJ* 16: 211–15.

1971 "The Genealogy of Gibeon (I Chronicles 9: 35–44): Biblical and Epigraphic Considerations." *BASOR* 202: 16–23.

1986 "The Clans of Ephratah: Their Territory and History." *TA* 13: 46–59.

2000 "The Chronicler's Description of the Common Border of Ephraim and Manasseh." Pages 8–13 in *Studies in Historical Geography and Biblical Historiography Presented to Zecharia Kallai*. VTSup 81. Leiden: Brill.

Dennerlin, Norbert

1999 *Die Bedeutung Jerusalems in den Chronikbüchern*. BEATAJ 46. New York: Lang.

De Odorico, Marco

1995 *The Use of Numbers and Quantifications in the Assyrian Royal Inscriptions*. SAA 3. Helsinki: Neo-Assyrian Text Corpus Project.

Dequeker, L.

1986 "1 Chronicles XXIV and the Royal Priesthood of the Hasmoneans." Pages 94–105 in van der Woude (1986).

Desrousseaux, Louis, and Jacques Vermeylen

1999 Eds. *Figures de David à travers la Bible: XVIIe congrès de l'ACFEB (Lille, 1er-5 septembre 1997)*. LD 177. Paris: Cerf.

Deutsch, Robert

1999 *Messages from the Past*. Tel Aviv–Jaffa: Archaeological Center.

Deutsch, Robert, and Michael Heltzer

1995 *New Epigraphic Evidence from the Biblical Period*. Tel Aviv–Jaffa: Archaeological Center.

1997a "Abday on Eleventh-Century-B.C.E. Arrowheads." *IEJ* 47: 111–12.

1997b *Windows to the Past*. Tel Aviv–Jaffa: Archaeological Center.

1999 *West Semitic Epigraphic News of the 1st Millennium B.C.E.* Tel Aviv–Jaffa: Archaeological Center.

Dever, William G.

1990 *Recent Archaeological Discoveries and Biblical Research*. Seattle: University of Washington Press.

De Vries, Simon J.

1987 "The Schema of Dynastic Endangerment in Chronicles." *Proceedings, Eastern Great Lakes and Midwest Biblical Societies* 7: 59–78.

1988 "Moses and David as Cult Founders in Chronicles." *JBL* 107: 619–39.

1989 *I and II Chronicles*. FOTL. Grand Rapids: Eerdmans.

Diakonoff, I. M.

1969 Ed. *Ancient Mesopotamia: Socio-Economic History*. Moscow: Central Department of Oriental Literature.

Dick, Michael B.

1999 "Prophetic Parodies of Making the Cult Image." Pages 1–53 in *Born in Heaven, Made on Earth: The Making of the Cult Image in the Ancient Near East*. Edited by Michael B. Dick. Winona Lake, Ind.: Eisenbrauns.

Dicou, Bert

1994 *Edom, Israel's Brother and Antagonist.* JSOTSup 169. Sheffield: JSOT Press.

Dietrich, Walter

1992 *David, Saul, und die Propheten: Das Verhältnis von Religion und Politik nach das prophetischen Überlieferungen vom frühesten Königtum in Israel.* 2nd ed. BWANT 122. Stuttgart: Kohlhammer.

Dietrich, Walter, and Thomas Naumann

1995 *Die Samuelbücher.* EdF 287. Darmstadt: Buchgesellschaft.

Dijkstra, M.

1975 "A Note on 1 Chr IV 22–23." *VT* 25: 671–74.

Dillard, Raymond B.

1980a "The Chronicler's Solomon." *WTJ* 43: 289–300.

1980b "The Reign of Asa (2 Chr 14–16): An Example of the Chronicler's Theological Method." *JETS* 23: 207–18.

1984a "The Literary Structure of the Chronicler's Solomon Narrative." *JSOT* 30: 85–93.

1984b "Reward and Punishment in Chronicles: The Theology of Immediate Retribution." *WTJ* 46: 164–72.

1987 *2 Chronicles.* WBC 15. Waco, Tex.: Word.

Dion, Paul-Eugène

1985 "The Angel with the Drawn Sword (II Chron. 21.16): An Exercise in Restoring the Balance of Text Criticism *and* Attention to Context." ZAW 97: 114–17.

1991 "The Civic-and-Temple Community of Persian Period Judaea: Neglected Insights from Eastern Europe." *JNES* 50: 281–87.

1995 "Aramaean Tribes and Nations of First-Millennium Western Asia." *CANE* 1281–94.

1997 *Les Araméens à l'âge du fer: Histoire politique et structures sociales. EBib* n.s. 34. Paris: Gabalda.

Dirksen, Piet B.

1995a "The Development of the Text of 1 Chronicles, 15: 1–24." *Hen* 17: 267–77.

1995b "What are the m^{e}ḥabb^{e}rôt in 1 Chron. 22: 3?" *BN* 80: 23–24.

1996a "1 Chronicles 16: 38: Its Background and Growth." *JNSL* 22: 85–90.

1996b "1 Chronicles XXVIII 11–18: Its Textual Development." *VT* 46: 429–38.

1996c "Why Was David Disqualified as Temple Builder? The Meaning of 1 Chronicles 22: 8." *JSOT* 70: 51–56.

1998a "The Composition of 1 Chronicles 26: 20–32." *JNSL* 24: 145–55.

1998b "1 Chronicles 9,26–33: Its Position in Chapter 9." *Bib* 79: 91–96.

1999 "Chronistic Tendency in 1 Chr 18:10–11." *Bib* 80: 269–71.

Dombrowski, D. W. W.

1997 "Socio-religious Implications of Foreign Impact on Palestinian Jewry under Achaemenid Rule." *Transeu* 13: 65–89.

Donner, Herbert

1984 *Von den Anfängen bis zur Staatenbildungszeit.* Vol. 1 of *Geschichte des Volkes Israel und seiner Nachbarn in Grundzügen.* GAT 4/1. Göttingen: Vandenhoeck & Ruprecht.

1986 *Von der Königszeit bis zu Alexander dem Großen.* Vol. 2 of *Geschichte des Volkes Israel und seiner Nachbarn in Grundzügen.* GAT 4/2. Göttingen: Vandenhoeck & Ruprecht.

Dörrfuß, Ernst Michael

1994 *Moses in den Chronikbüchern: Garant theokratischer Zukunftserwartung.* BZAW 219. Berlin: de Gruyter.

Dorsey, David A.

1985 "Another Peculiar Term in the Book of Chronicles: מְסִלָּה, 'Highway'?" *JQR* 4: 385–91.

1991 *The Roads and Highways of Ancient Israel.* Baltimore: Johns Hopkins University Press.

Driver, Samuel R.

1892 *A Treatise on the Use of the Tenses in Hebrew and Some Other Syntactical Questions.* 3rd. ed. London: Oxford University Press. Repr., Grand Rapids: Eerdmans, 1998.

1895a *A Critical and Exegetical Commentary on Deuteronomy.* ICC. Edinburgh: T&T Clark.

1895b "The Speeches in Chronicles." *The Expositor* 1: 241–56; 2: 286–308.

1911 *The Book of Exodus in the Revised Version.* CBC. Cambridge: Cambridge University Press.

1912 *Notes on the Hebrew Text of the Books of Samuel.* 2nd ed. Oxford: Clarendon Press.

1913 *The Book of Genesis.* 9th ed. Westminster Commentaries. London: Methuen & Co.

1914 *An Introduction to the Literature of the Old Testament.* New ed. New York: Scribner's.

Duchesne-Guillemin, Jacques

1972 "La Religion des Achéménides." Pages 59–82 in *Beiträge zur Achämenidengeschichte.* Edited by G. Walser. *Historia* 18. Wiesbaden: Franz Steiner.

Duchesne-Guillemin, Marcelle

1981 "Music in ancient Mesopotamia and Egypt." *World Archaeology* 12/3: 287–97.

Duke, Rodney K.

1990 *The Persuasive Appeal of the Chronicler: A Rhetorical Analysis.* JSOTSup 88. Sheffield: Almond.

Dumbrell, William J.

1971 "The Tell el-Maskhuṭa Bowls and the 'Kingdom' of Qedar in the Persian Period." *BASOR* 203: 33–44.

Durand, Jean-Marie

1981 *Textes babyloniens d'époque récente.* Recherche sur les grandes civilisations 6. Paris: Éditions ADPF.

Dyck, Jonathan E.
1996 "The Ideology of Identity in Chronicles." Pages 89–116 in Brett (1996).
1998 *The Theocratic Ideology of the Chronicler.* Biblical Interpretation Series 33. Leiden: Brill.
Ebeling, E.
1953 *Die Akkadische Gebetsserie "Handerhebung."* Berlin: Akademie.
Edelman, Diane Vikander
1988 "The Asherite Genealogy in 1 Chronicles 7: 3–40." *BR* 33: 13–23.
1991 *King Saul in the Historiography of Judah.* JSOTSup 121. Sheffield: JSOT Press.
1995a Ed. *The Triumph of Elohim: From Yahwisms to Judaisms.* CBET 13. Kampen: Kok Pharos.
1995b Ed. *You Shall Not Abhor an Edomite For He Is Your Brother: Edom and Seir in History and Tradition.* SBLABS 3. Atlanta: Scholars Press.
1996 "Saul ben Kish in History and Tradition." Pages 142–59 in Fritz and Davies (1996).
2003 "Gibeon and the Gibeonites Revisited." Pages 153–67 in Lipschits and Blenkinsopp (2003).
Edgar, Campbell Cowen
1925–40 *Catalogue général des antiquités égyptiennes du Musée du Caire: Zenon Papyri.* 5 vols. Cairo: Insitut Français d'Archéologie Orientale. Repr., Hildesheim: Olms, 1971.
Ego, Beate, Armin Lange, and Peter Pilhofer
1999 Eds. *Gemeinde ohne Tempel: Zur Substituierung und Transformation des Jerusalemer Tempels und seines Kults im Alten Testament, antiken Judentums und frühen Christentum.* WUNT 118. Tübingen: Mohr.
Ehrenberg, Victor
1969 *The Greek State.* 2nd ed. London: Methuen & Co.
Ehrlich, Arnold Bogemil
1914 *Randglossen zur hebräischen Bibel.* Vol. 7. Hildesheim: Olms. Repr., 1968.
Ehrlich, Carl S.
1996 *The Philistines in Transition: A History from 1000–730 B.C.E.* Leiden: Brill.
Ehrlich, Carl S., and Marsha White
forthcoming Eds. *Saul in History and Tradition.*
Eisenstadt, Shmuel N.
1986 Ed. *The Origins and Diversity of Axial Age Civilizations.* Albany, N. Y.: State University of New York Press.
Eising, H.
1980 "זָכַר; *zākhar.*" *TDOT* 4: 64–82.
Eissfeldt, Otto
1931 *Die Komposition der Samuelbücher.* Leipzig: Hinrichs.
1965 *The Old Testament: An Introduction.* New York: Harper & Row.

Elayi, Josette

1980 "The Phoenician Cities in the Persian Period." *JNES* 12: 13–28.

1981 "The Relations between Tyre and Carthage during the Persian Period." *JANES* 13: 15–29.

1986a "Le roi et la religion dans la les cités phéniciennes à l'époque perse." Pages 249–61 in Bonnet, Lipiński, and Marchetti (1986).

1986b "Le sceau du prêtre Ḥanan, fils de Ḥilqiyahu." *Sem* 36: 42–46.

1987 *Recherches sur les cités phéniciennes à l'époque perse.* Supplemento 51 agli *Annali* 47/2. Naples: Instituto Universitario Orientale.

1988 *Pénétration grecque en Phénicie sous l'empire perse.* Nancy: Presses Universitaires de Nancy.

1994 "Présence grecque sur la côte palestinienne." Pages 245–60 in Laperrousaz and Lemaire (1994).

Elayi, Josette, and H. Sayegh

1998 *Un quartier du port phénician de Beyrouth au Fer III-Perse. Les objets.* Supplément 6 à *Transeu.* Paris: Gabalda.

Elliger, K.

1935 "Die dreissig Helden Davids." *PJ* 31: 29–75.

1962 "Benjamin." *IDB* 1: 383–84.

Ellis, Maria deJong

1976 *Agriculture and the State in Ancient Mesopotamia: An Introduction to Problems of Land Tenure.* Occasional Publications of the Babylonian Fund 1. Philadelphia: University Museum.

Emerton, J. A.

1962 "Priests and Levites in Deuteronomy." *VT* 12: 129–138.

1982 "New Light on Israelite Religion: The Implications of the Inscriptions from Kuntillet ʿAjrud." ZAW 94: 2–20.

1985 Ed. *Congress Volume: Salamanca, 1983.* VTSup 36. Leiden: Brill.

1988 Ed. *Congress Volume: Jerusalem, 1986.* VTSup 40. Leiden: Brill.

1991 Ed. *Congress Volume: Leuven, 1989.* VTSup 43. Leiden: Brill.

Ephʿal, Israel

1983 "On Warfare and Military Control in the Ancient Near Eastern Empires: A Research Outline." Pages 88–106 in Tadmor and Weinfeld (1983).

1984 *The Ancient Arabs: Nomads on the Borders of the Fertile Crescent, 9th–5th Centuries B.C.* Jerusalem: Magnes.

1991 " 'The Samarian(s)' in the Assyrian Sources." Pages 36–45 in Cogan and Ephʿal (1991).

1998 "Changes in Palestine during the Persian Period in Light of Epigraphic Sources." *IEJ* 48: 106–119.

Ephʿal, Israel, and J. Naveh

1989 "Hazael's Booty Inscriptions." *IEJ* 39: 192–200.

1996 *Aramaic Ostraca of the Fourth Century B.C. from Idumaea.* Jerusalem: Magnes.

Eshel, Hanan, and E. Eshel

2000 "4Q448, Psalm 154 (Syriac), Sirach 48: 20, and 4QpIsa[a]." *JBL* 119: 645–59.

Eshel, Hanan, and H. Misgav
1988 "A Fourth-Century Document from Ketef Yeriḥo." *IEJ* 38: 158–76.

Eskenazi, Tamara Cohn
1986 "The Chronicler and the Composition of 1 Esdras." *CBQ* 48: 39–61.
1988a *In an Age of Prose: A Literary Approach to Ezra-Nehemiah.* SBLMS 36. Atlanta: Scholars Press.
1988b "The Structure of Ezra-Nehemiah and the Integrity of the Book." *JBL* 107: 641–56.
1993 "Current Perspectives on Ezra-Nehemiah and the Persian Period." *CRBS* 1: 59–86.
1995 "A Literary Approach to the Chronicler's Ark Narrative in I Chronicles 13–16." Pages 258–74 in Beck et al. (1995).

Eskenazi, Tamara Cohn, and Kent H. Richards
1994 Eds. *Second Temple Studies 2. Temple and Community in the Persian Period.* JSOTSup 175. Sheffield: JSOT Press.

Eslinger, Lyle
1994 *House of God or House of David? The Rhetoric of 2 Samuel 7.* JSOTSup 164. Sheffield: JSOT Press.

Estes, Daniel J.
1991 "Metaphorical Sojourning in 1 Chronicles 29: 15." *CBQ* 53: 45–49.

Ewald, Heinrich
1870 *Ausführliches Lehrbuch der hebräischen Sprache des alten Bundes.* 8th ed. Göttingen: Dieterichsche Buchhandlung.

Exum, Cheryl
1990 "The Centre Cannot Hold." *CBQ* 52: 410–31.

Fales, Frederick Mario
1981 Ed. *Assyrian Royal Inscriptions: New Horizons.* Orientis Antiqvi Collectio 17. Rome: Oriental Institute.

Fales, Frederick Mario, and J. N. Postgate
1992 Eds. *Imperial Administrative Records I: Palace and Temple Administration.* SAA 7. Helsinki: Helsinki University Press.

Falkenstein A., and W. von Soden
1953 Eds. *Sumerische und akkadische Hymnen und Gebete.* Die Bibliothek der alten Welt. Zürich: Artemis.

Fensham, F. C.
1962 "Widow, Orphan, and the Poor in Ancient Near Eastern Legal and Wisdom Literature." *JNES* 21: 129–39.
1971 "Father and Son as Terminology for Treaty and Covenant." Pages 121–28 in *Near Eastern Studies in Honor of William Foxwell Albright.* Edited by H. Goedicke. Baltimore: Johns Hopkins University Press.

Fernández Marcos, Natalio
1985 Ed. *La Septuaginta en la investigación contemporánea.* V Congreso de la IOSCS. Madrid: Textos y Estudios "Cardenal Cisneros" de la Biblia Poliglota Matritense Instituto "Arias Montano" CSIC.

1991 "The Antiochian Text in I–II Chronicles." Pages 301–11 in *VII Congress of the International Organization for Septuagint and Cognate Studies, Leuven 1989*. Edited by Claude E. Cox. SBLSCS 31. Atlanta: Scholars Press.

1997 "The Old Latin of Chronicles between the Greek and the Hebrew." Pages 123–36 in *IX Congress of the International Organization for Septuagint and Cognate Studies, Cambridge 1995*. Edited by Bernard A. Taylor. SBLSCS 45. Atlanta: Scholars Press.

Fernández Marcos, Natalio, and José Ramón Busto Saiz

1984 Eds. *Theodoreti Cyrensis Quaestiones in Reges et Paralipomena: Editio Critica*. Textos y Estudios "Cardinal Cisneros" 32. Madrid: Consejo Superior de Investigaciones Científicas.

1996 Eds. *El Texto Antioqueno de la Biblia griega III: 1–2 Crónicas*. Textos y Estudios "Cardinal Cisneros" 60. Madrid: Instituto de Filología del CSIC.

Finkelstein, Israel

2001 "The Rise of Jerusalem and Judah: The Missing Link." *Levant* 33: 105–15.

Finkelstein, Israel, and Iṣḥaq Magen

1993 *Archaeological Survey of the Hill Country of Benjamin* (Hebrew). Jerusalem.

Finley, Moses

1982 *Authority and Legitimacy in the Classical City-State*. Det Kongelige Danske Videnskabernes Selskab Historisk-filosofiske Meddelelser 50/3. Copenhagen: Munksgaard.

1985 *Ancient History: Evidence and Models*. New York: Viking.

Fischer, Bonifatius, et al.

1984 Ed. *Biblia sacra iuxta vulgatam versionem*. 3rd ed. Stuttgart: Deutsche Bibelgesellschaft.

Fishbane, Michael

1985 *Biblical Interpretation in Ancient Israel*. Oxford: Clarendon Press.

Fishbane, Michael, and E. Tov

1992 Eds. *"Shaʿarei Talmon": Studies in the Bible, Qumran, and the Ancient Near East Presented to Shemaryahu Talmon*. Winona Lake, Ind.: Eisenbrauns.

Fitzmyer, J. A.

1967 *The Aramaic Inscriptions of Sefîre*. Rome: Pontifical Biblical Institute.

1972 "David, 'being therefore a prophet . . .' (Acts 2: 30)." *CBQ* 34: 332–39.

Flanagan, James W.

1983 "Succession and Genealogy in the Davidic Dynasty." Pages 35–55 in *The Quest for the Kingdom of God: Studies in Honor of George E. Mendenhall*. Edited by H. B. Huffmon, F. A. Spina, and A. R. W. Green. Winona Lake, Ind.: Eisenbrauns.

Flint, Peter W.

1997 *The Dead Sea Psalms Scrolls and the Book of Psalms*. *STDJ* 17. Leiden: Brill.

2000 "David." *EDSS* 1: 178–80.

Forbes, A. Dean

1987 "Syntactic Sequences in the Hebrew Bible." Pages 59–70 in *Perspectives on Language and Text.* Edited by E. W. Conrad and E. G. Newing. Winona Lake, Ind.: Eisenbrauns.

Fornara, Charles

1983 *The Nature of History in Ancient Greece and Rome.* Berkeley: University of California Press.

Fosse, B.

1998 "L'Alliance avec Abraham et les relectures de l'histoire d'Israël en Ne 9, Pss 105–106, 135–136 et 1 Ch 16." *Transeu* 15: 123–35.

Fouts, David M.

1994 "Another Look at Large Numbers in Assyrian Royal Inscriptions." *JNES* 53: 205–11.

1997 "A Defense of the Hyperbolic Interpretation of Large Numbers in the Old Testament." *JETS* 40: 377–87.

Fowler, Jeaneane D.

1988 *Theophoric Personal Names in Ancient Hebrew.* JSOTSup 49. Sheffield: JSOT Press.

Fox, Michael V.

1973 "*Ṭôb* as Covenant Terminology." *BASOR* 209: 41–42.

Fox, Michael V., et al.

1996 Eds. *Texts, Temples, and Traditions: A Tribute to Menahem Haran.* Winona Lake, Ind.: Eisenbrauns.

Frankel, Raphael

1998 The Territory of the Tribe of Asher. Pages 49–76 in *From The Ancient Sites of Israel: Essays on Archaeology, History and Theology in Memory of Aapeli Saarisalo.* Edited by T. Eskola and E. Junkkaala. Helsinki: Theological Institute.

Frankfort, Henri

1948 *Kingship and the Gods: A Study of Ancient Near Eastern Kingship as the Integration of Society and Nature.* Chicago: University of Chicago Press.

Freedman, David Noel

1961 "The Chronicler's Purpose." *CBQ* 23: 432–42.

1987 "Headings in the Books of the Eighth-Century Prophets." *AUSS* 25: 9–26.

1990 "The Formation of the Canon of the Old Testament." Pages 315–31 in *Religion and Law: Biblical-Judaic and Islamic Perspectives.* Edited by E. B. Firmage, B. G. Weiss, and J. W. Welch. Winona Lake, Ind.: Eisenbrauns.

1992 "The Symmetry of the Hebrew Bible." *ST* 46: 83–108.

1993 *The Unity of the Hebrew Bible.* Ann Arbor, Mich.: University of Michigan Press.

Freedman, David Noel, and Bruce E. Willoughby

1989 "I and II Chronicles, Ezra, Nehemiah." Pages 155–71 in *The Books of the Bible, I.* Edited by B. W. Anderson. New York: Scribner's.

Frei, Peter

1996 "Zentralgewalt und Lokalautonomie im Achämenidenreich." Pages 7–131 in Frei and Koch (1996).

Frei, Peter, and Klaus Koch

1984 *Reichsidee und Reichsorganisation im Perserreich.* OBO 55. Göttingen: Vandenhoeck & Ruprecht.

1996 *Reichsidee und Reichsorganisation im Perserreich.* 2nd ed. OBO 55. Göttingen: Vandenhoeck & Ruprecht.

Fretheim, Terence E.

1967 "Psalm 132: A Form-Critical Study." *JBL* 86: 289–300.

1968a "The Ark in Deuteronomy." *CBQ* 30: 1–14.

1968b "The Priestly Document: Anti-Temple?" *VT* 18: 313–29.

Frevel, Christian

1991 "Die Elimination der Göttin aus dem Weltbild des Chronisten." *ZAW* 103: 263–71.

Frick, Frank S.

1971 "The Rechabites Reconsidered." *JBL* 90: 279–97.

Fired, Lisbeth S.

2003 "The Land Lay Desolate: Conquest and Restoration in the Ancient Near East." Pages 21–54 in Lipschits and Blenkinsopp (2003).

Friedman, Richard E.

1981 Ed. *The Creation of Sacred Literature, Composition and Redaction of the Biblical Text.* Near Eastern Studies 22. Berkeley: University of California Press.

1987 *Who Wrote the Bible?* Englewood Cliffs: Prentice Hall.

1992 "Tabernacle." *ABD* 6: 292–300.

Friedman, Richard E., and H. G. M. Williamson

1987 Eds. *The Future of Biblical Studies: The Hebrew Scriptures.* SBLSymS. Decatur: Scholars Press.

Friedrich, Johannes

1959 *Die hethitischen Gesetze.* Documenta et Monumenta Orientis Antiqui 7. Leiden: Brill.

von Fritz, Kurt

1967 *Die griechische Geschichtsschreibung.* Berlin: de Gruyter.

Fritz, Volkmar

1981 "The 'List of Rehoboam's Fortresses' in 2 Chr 11: 5–12—A Document from the Time of Josiah." *ErIsr* 15: 46*–53*.

1990 *Die Stadt im alten Israel.* Munich: Beck. Translated under the title *The City in Ancient Israel.* The Biblical Seminar 29. Sheffield: Sheffield Academic Press, 1995.

Fritz, Volkmar, and Philip R. Davies

1996 Eds. *The Origins of the Israelite States.* JSOTSup 228. Sheffield: JSOT Press.

Fritzsche, O. F.

1851 *Kurzegefasstes exegetisches Handbuch zu den Apokryphen des Alten Testaments.* Erste Lieferung. Leipzig: Weidmann.

Fuller, Russell
1992 "Textual Traditions in the Book of Hosea and the Minor Prophets." Pages 247–56 in Trebolle Barrera and Vegas Montaner (1992).
Gabriel, Ingeborg
1990 *Friede über Israel. Eine Untersuchung zur Friedenstheologie im Chronik I 10–II 36.* ÖBS 10. Klosterneuberg: ÖKB.
Gal, Zvi
1992 *Lower Galilee during the Iron Age.* Winona Lake, Ind.: Eisenbrauns.
Galil, Gershon
1991 "The Chronicler's Genealogies of Ephraim." *BN* 56: 11–14.
Galling, Kurt
1954 *Die Bücher der Chronik, Esra, Nehemia.* ATD 12. Göttingen: Vandenhoeck & Ruprecht.
1964 *Studien zur Geschichte Israels im persischen Zeitalter.* Tübingen: Mohr.
García Martínez, Florentino
1999 "The Temple Scroll and the New Jerusalem." Pages 431–60 in vol. 2 of *The Dead Sea Scrolls after Fifty Years.* Edited by P. Flint and J. VanderKam. Leiden: Brill.
Gardiner, A.
1959 *The Royal Canon of Turin.* Oxford: Oxford University Press.
Gardner, Anne E.
1986 "The Purpose and Date of I Esdras." *JJS* 37: 18–27.
Garelli, Paul
1974 Ed. *Le Palais et la Royauté (Archéologie et Civilisation).* XIX Recontre Assyriologique Internationale. Paris: Paul Geuthner.
Garfinkel, Yosef
1988 "2 Chr 11: 5–10 Fortified Cities List and the *lmlk* Stamps—Reply to Nadav Na'aman." *BASOR* 271: 69–73.
Garr, Randall
1985 *Dialect Geography of Syria-Palestine.* Philadelphia: University of Pennsylvania Press.
Garrone, Daniele, and Felice Israel
1991 Eds. *Storia e Tradizioni di Israele: Scritti in Onore di J. Alberto Soggin.* Brescia: Paideia Editrice.
Gelston, Anthony
1972 "A Note on II Samuel 7^{10}." ZAW 84: 92–94.
1996 "The End of Chronicles." *SJOT* 10: 53–60.
Gerleman, Gillis
1946 *Studies in the Septuagint, II. Chronicles.* LUÅ 43/3. Lund: Gleerup.
1948 *Synoptic Studies in the Old Testament.* LUÅ 44/5. Lund: Gleerup.
Gershevitch, Ilya
1985 Ed. *The Median and Achaemenian Periods.* Vol. 2 of *The Cambridge History of Iran.* Cambridge: Cambridge University Press.
Gerstenberger, Erhard S.
1996 *Leviticus: A Commentary.* OTL. Louisville, Ky.: Westminster John Knox.

Gese, Hartmut
1963 "Zur Geschichte der Kultsänger am zweiten Tempel." Pages 222–34 in *Abraham unser Vater: Juden und Christen im Gespräch über die Bibel (Festschrift für Otto Michel)*. Edited by O. Betz, M. Hengel, and P. Schmidt. Leiden: Brill.
1974 *Vom Sinai zum Zion*. Munich: Kaiser.
Geva, Hillel
1994 Ed. *Ancient Jerusalem Revealed*. Jerusalem: Israel Exploration Society.
Gevirtz, Stanley
1981 "Simeon and Levi in 'The Blessing of Jacob' (Gen. 49: 5–7)." *HUCA* 52: 93–128.
Gibson, J. C. L.
1971 *Hebrew and Moabite Inscriptions*. Vol. 1 of *Textbook of Syrian Semitic Inscriptions*. Oxford: Clarendon Press.
1975 *Aramaic Inscriptions*. Vol. 2 of *Textbook of Syrian Semitic Inscriptions*. Oxford: Clarendon Press.
1982 *Phoenician Inscriptions*. Vol. 3 of *Textbook of Syrian Semitic Inscriptions*. Oxford: Clarendon Press.
Gilbert, Henry L.
1896–97 "The Forms of Names in 1 Chronicles 1–7 Compared with Those in Parallel Passages of the Old Testament." *AJSL* 13: 279–98.
Gitin, Seymour
1995 Ed. *Recent Excavations in Israel: A View to the West*. Archaeological Institute of America Colloquia and Conference Papers 1. Dubuque, Iowa: Kendall/Hunt.
Glatt(-Gilad), David
1993 *Chronological Displacement in Biblical and Related Literatures*. SBLDS 139. Atlanta: Scholars Press.
2001 "Regnal Formulae as a Historiographic Device in the Book of Chronicles." *RB* 108: 184–209.
Glazier-McDonald, Beth
1995 "Edom in the Prophetic Corpus." Pages 23–32 in Edelman (1995b).
Glessmer, Uwe
1998 *Die ideale Kultordnung: 24 Priesterordnungen in den Chronikbüchern, kalendarischen Qumrantexten und in synagogalen Inschriften*. *STDJ* 25. Leiden: Brill.
2001 "4QOrdo." Pages 167–94 in Talmon, Ben-Dov, and Glessmer (2001).
Goettsberger, Johann
1939 *Die Bücher der Chronik oder Paralipomenon*. *HSAT* 4. Bonn: Peter Hanstein.
Goetze, Albrecht
1947 "Critical Review: Bozkurt-Çiğ-Güterbock Istanbul Arkeoloji Müzelerinde Bulunan Boğazköy Tableterinden Seçme Metinler." *JCS* 1: 90–91.

1957 *Kleinasien.* 2nd ed. Handbuch der Altertum Wissenschaft III.1.2.2.1. Munich: Beck.

1960 "The Beginning of the Hittite Instructions for the Commander of the Border Guards." *JCS* 14: 69–73.

1964 "State and Society of the Hittites." Pages 232–33 in *Neuere Hethiterforschung.* Edited by G. Walser. Historia Einzelschriften 7. Wiesbaden: Franz Steiner.

Goldingay, John

1975 "The Chronicler as a Theologian." *BTB* 5: 99–126.

Goldman, Yohanan

1992 *Prophétie et royauté au retour de l'exil.* OBO 118. Göttingen: Vandenhoeck & Ruprecht.

Goldstein, Jonathan A.

1976 *I Maccabees.* AB 41. Garden City: Doubleday.

1983 *II Maccabees.* AB 41A. Garden City: Doubleday.

Gonçalves, Francolino J.

1986 *L'expédition de Sennachérib en Palestine dans la littérature hebraïque ancienne. EBib* n.s. 7. Paris: Librairie Lecoffre.

Goody, Jack

1968 Ed. *Literacy in Traditional Societies.* Cambridge: Cambridge University Press.

Gordon, Robert

1994 "In Search of David: The David Tradition in Recent Study." Pages 285–98 in Millard, Hoffmeier, and Baker (1994).

Goshen-Gottstein, Moshe Henry

1976 *The Aleppo Codex* (in Hebrew). Jerusalem: Magnes.

Gottheil, R. J. H.

1898 "On קושיהו and קישי." *JBL* 17: 199–202.

Gottwald, Norman K.

1979 *The Tribes of Yahweh.* New York: Orbis.

Grabbe, Lester L.

1992 *The Persian and Greek Periods.* Vol. 1 of *Judaism from Cyrus to Hadrian.* Philadelphia: Fortress.

1996 *Priests, Prophets, Diviners, Sages: A Socio-Historical Study of Religious Specialists in Ancient Israel.* Philadelphia: Trinity.

2001a Introduction to Grabbe (2001c).

2001b "Who Were the First Real Historians? On the Origins of Critical Historiography." Pages 156–81 in Grabbe (2001c).

2001c Ed. *Did Moses Speak Attic? Jewish Historiography and Scripture in the Hellenistic Period.* JSOTSup 317. Sheffield: Sheffield Academic Press.

Graham, M. Patrick

1985 "A Connection Proposed between II Chr 24, 26 and Ezra 9–10." ZAW 97: 256–58.

1990 *The Utilization of 1 and 2 Chronicles in the Reconstruction of Israelite History in the Nineteenth Century.* SBLDS 116. Atlanta: Scholars Press.

1993 "Aspects of the Structure and Rhetoric of 2 Chronicles 25." Pages 78–89 in *History and Interpretation: Essays in Honour of John H. Hayes*. Edited by M. Patrick Graham. JSOTSup 173. Sheffield: JSOT Press.

1998 "The 'Chronicler's History': Ezra-Nehemiah, 1–2 Chronicles." Pages 201–35 in *The Hebrew Bible Today*. Edited by S. L. McKenzie and M. P. Graham. Louisville, Ky.: Westminster John Knox Press.

1999 "Setting the Heart to Seek God: Worship in 2 Chronicles 30.1–31.1." Pages 124–41 in Graham, Marrs, and McKenzie (1999).

Graham, M. Patrick, K. G. Hoglund, and S. L. McKenzie

1997 Eds. *The Chronicler as Historian*. JSOTSup 238; Sheffield: JSOT Press.

Graham, M. Patrick, G. N. Knoppers, and S. L. McKenzie

forthcoming Eds. *The Chronicler as Theologian: Festschrift, Ralph W. Klein*. JSOTSup. 371. Sheffield: Sheffield Academic Press.

Graham, M. Patrick, R. R. Marrs, and S. L. McKenzie

1999 Eds. *Worship and the Hebrew Bible: Essays in Honour of John T. Willis*. JSOTSup 284. Sheffield: JSOT Press.

Graham, M. Patrick, and S. L. McKenzie

1999 Eds. *The Chronicler as Author: Studies in Text and Texture*. JSOTSup 263. Sheffield: Sheffield Academic Press.

Grayson, Albert Kirk

1975 *Assyrian and Babylonian Chronicles*. TCS 5. Locust Valley, N.Y.: Augustin. Repr., Winona Lake, Ind.: Eisenbrauns, 2000.

1976 *From Tiglath-pileser I to Ashur-nasir-apli II*. Part 2 of *Assyrian Royal Inscriptions*. RANE 2. Wiesbaden: Otto Harrassowitz.

1980 "Assyria and Babylonia." *Or* 49: 140–94.

1981 "Assyrian Royal Inscriptions: Literary Characteristics." Pages 35–47 in Fales (1981).

1991 *Assyrian Rulers of the Early First Millennium B.C. I (1114–859 B.C.)*. RIMA 2. Toronto: University of Toronto Press.

1995 "Eunuchs in Power: Their Role in the Assyrian Bureaucracy." Pages 85–97 in *Vom Alten Orient zum Alten Testament: Festschrift Wolfram von Soden*. Edited by M. Dietrich and O. Loretz. Neukirchen-Vluyn: Neukirchener Verlag.

1996 *Assyrian Rulers of the Early First Millennium B.C., I (858–745 B.C.)*. RIMA 3. Toronto: University of Toronto Press.

Grébaut, Sylvain

1932 *Les Paralipomenes, Livres I et II: Version éthiopienne éditée et traduite*. *Patrologia Orientalis* 23/4. Paris: Firmin-Didot.

Greenberg, Moshe

1951 "Hebrew sᵉgullā: Akkadian sikiltu." *JAOS* 71: 172–74.

1990 "Three Conceptions of Torah in the Hebrew Scriptures." Pages 365–78 in *Die Hebräische Bibel und ihre zweifache Nachgeshichte: Festschrift Rolf Rendtorff*. Edited by E. Blum et al. Neukirchen-Vluyn: Neukirchener Verlag.

Greenspahn, Frederick E.

1994 *When Brothers Dwell Together: The Preeminence of Younger Siblings in the Hebrew Bible.* New York: Oxford University Press.

Grelot, P.

1961 "*Parwaïm* des Chroniques a l'Apocryphe de la Genèse." *VT* 11: 30–38.

1964 "Retour au *Parwaïm.*" *VT* 14: 155–63.

1972 *Documents araméens d'Égypt.* Paris: Cerf.

van Groningen, Bernhard Abraham

1953 *In the Grip of the Past: An Essay on an Aspect of Greek Thought.* Leiden: Brill.

de Groot, Alon

2001 "The 'Invisible' City of the Tenth Century B.C.E." (Hebrew). Pages 29–34 in *New Studies on Jerusalem.* Edited by A. Faust and E. Baruch. Jerusalem: Ingeborg Rennert Center for Jewish Studies.

Gropp, Douglas M.

1992 "Samaria (Papyri)." *ABD* 5: 931–32.

2001 Ed. *Wadi Daliyeh II: The Samaria Papyri from Wadi Daliyeh.* DJD 28. Oxford: Clarendon.

Grözinger, K. E.

1982 *Musik und Gesang in der Theologie der frühen jüdischen Literatur—Talmud Midrash Mystik.* Tübingen: Mohr.

Gundry, Robert Horton

1982 *Matthew: A Commentary on His Literary and Theological Art.* Grand Rapids: Eerdmans.

Gunkel, Hermann

1926 *Die Psalmen.* 4th ed. Göttinger Handkommentar zum Alten Testament II/2. Göttingen: Vandenhoeck & Ruprecht.

Gunkel, Hermann, and J. Begrich

1933 *Einleitung in die Psalmen: die Gattungen der religiösen Lyrik Israels.* HKAT Abt. 2, Ergänzungsband. Göttingen: Vandenhoeck & Ruprecht.

Gunn David M., and D. N. Fewell

1993 *Narrative in the Hebrew Bible.* Oxford Bible Series. Oxford: Oxford University Press.

Gunneweg, Antonius H. J.

1985 *Esra.* KAT 19/1. Gütersloh: G. Mohn.

1987 *Nehemia.* KAT 19/2. Gütersloh: G. Mohn.

1989 *Geschichte Israels.* 6th ed. Theologisches Wissenschaft 2. Stuttgart: Kohlhammer.

Gunneweg, Antonius H. J., and O. Kaiser

1979 Eds. *Textgemäß. Aufsätze und Beiträge zur Hermeneutik des alten Testaments: Festschrift Ernst Würthwein.* Göttingen: Vandenhoeck & Ruprecht.

Güterbock, Hans G.

1940 "Siegel aus Boğhazköy." *AfO* 5: 1–59.

1954 "Authority and Law in the Hittite Kingdom." Pages 16–24 in *Author-*

ity and Law in the Ancient Orient. Edited by J. A. Wilson et al. JAOS-Sup 17. Baltimore: American Oriental Society.

Güterbock, Hans G., and Theo P. J. van den Hout

1991 *The Hittite Instruction for the Royal Bodyguard.* AS 24. Chicago: University of Chicago Press.

Hackett, Jo Ann

1984 *The Balaam Text from Deir ʿAllā.* HSM 31. Chico, Calif.: Scholars Press.

1987 "Israelite Traditions in Israelite Transjordan." Pages 125–36 in Miller, Hanson, and McBride (1987).

Hadley, Judith M.

1987 "Some Drawings and Inscriptions on Two Pithoi from Kuntillet ʿAjrûd." *VT* 37: 180–211.

Hallo, William W., J. Moyer, and L. Perdue

1983 Eds. *Scripture in Context II: More Essays on the Comparative Method.* Winona Lake, Ind.: Eisenbrauns.

Halpern, Baruch

1981a *The Constitution of the Monarchy in Israel.* HSM 25. Chico, Calif.: Scholars Press.

1981b "Sacred History and Ideology: Chronicles' Thematic Structure—Indications of an Earlier Source." Pages 35–54 in Friedman (1981).

1983 *The Emergence of Israel in Canaan.* SBLMS 29. Chico, Calif.: Scholars Press.

1988 *The First Historians: The Hebrew Bible and History.* San Francisco: Harper & Row.

1990 "A Historiographic Commentary on Ezra 1–6: Achronological Narrative and Dual Chronology in Israelite Historiography." Pages 81–141 in *The Hebrew Bible and Its Interpreters.* Edited by W. H. Propp, B. Halpern, and D. N. Freedman. Biblical and Judaic Studies 1. Winona Lake, Ind.: Eisenbrauns.

1996a "The Construction of the Davidic State: An Exercise in Historiography." Pages 44–75 in Fritz and Davies (1996).

1996b "Sybil or the Two Nations? Archaism, Kinship, Alienation, and the Elite Redefinition of Traditional Culture in the 8th–7th Centuries B.C.E." Pages 291–338 in *The Study of the Ancient Near East in the Twenty-First Century.* Edited by J. S. Cooper and G. M. Schwartz. Winona Lake, Ind.: Eisenbrauns.

2001 *David's Secret Demons.* Grand Rapids: Eerdmans.

Halpern, Baruch, and Jon Levenson

1981 Eds. *Traditions in Transformation: Turning Points in Biblical Faith. Essays Presented to Frank Moore Cross, Jr.* Winona Lake, Ind.: Eisenbrauns.

Hamilton, Gordon J.

1998 "New Evidence for the Authenticity of *bšt* in Hebrew Personal Names and for Its Use as a Divine Epithet in Biblical Texts." *CBQ* 60: 228–50.

Hamp, V.
1986 "חצר; *ḥāṣēr.* " *TDOT* 5: 131–39.

Handy, Lowell K.
1994 *Among the Host of Heaven: The Syro-Palestinian Pantheon as Bureaucracy.* Winona Lake, Ind.: Eisenbrauns.
1997 Ed. *The Age of Solomon: Scholarship at the Turn of the Millennium.* SHANE 11. Leiden: Brill.

Hanhart, Robert
1974 *Esdrae liber I.* Auctoritate Academiae Scientarum Göttingensis 8, 1. Göttingen: Vandenhoeck & Ruprecht.
1982 "Zu den ältesten Traditionen über das Samaritanische Schisma." *ErIsr* 16: 106–115.

Hanson, Paul D.
1979 *The Dawn of Apocalyptic: The Historical and Social Roots of Jewish Apocalytic Eschatology.* Philadelphia: Fortess.
1986 *The People Called: The Growth of Community in the Bible.* San Francisco: Harper & Row.
1987 "Israelite Religion in the Early Postexilic Period." Pages 485–508 in Miller, Hanson, and McBride (1987).
1992 "1 Chronicles 15–16 and the Chronicler's Views on the Levites." Pages 69–77 in Fishbane and Tov (1992).

Haran, Menaḥem
1961a "The Gibeonites, the Nethinim, and the Sons of Solomon's Servants." *VT* 11: 159–69.
1961b "Studies in the Account of the Levitical Cities." *JBL* 80: 45–54, 156–65.
1971 "Priests and Priesthood." *EncJud* 13: 1070–86.
1978 *Temples and Temple-Service in Ancient Israel: An Inquiry into the Character of Cult Phenomena and the Historical Setting of the Priestly School.* Oxford: Oxford University Press. Repr., Winona Lake, Ind.: Eisenbrauns, 1985.
1981 "Temples and Cultic Open Areas as Reflected in the Bible." Pages 31–37 in Biran (1981).
1982a "Book Scrolls at the Beginning of the Second Temple Period." *EI* 16: 86–92.
1982b "Book Scrolls in Israel in Pre-Exilic Times." *JJS* 32: 161–73.
1985a "Book Size and the Device of Catch-Lines in the Biblical Canon." *JJS* 36: 1–11.
1985b "Cult and Prayer." Pages 87–92 in Kort and Morschauser (1985).
1986 "Explaining the Identical Lines at the End of Chronicles and the Beginning of Ezra." *BR* 2: 18–20.
1999 "'The Books of the Chronicles 'of the Kings of Judah' and 'of the Kings of Israel': What Sort of Books Were They?" *VT* 49: 156–64.

Harmatta, J., and G. Komoróczy
1976 Eds. *Wirtschaft und Gesellschaft im Alten Vorderasien.* Budapest: Akadémiai Kiadó.

Harrington, D. J.
1985 "Pseudo-Philo." *OTP* 2: 297–377.
Harris, R. Laird
1990 "Chronicles and the Canon in New Testament Times." *JETS* 33: 75–84.
Hartman, Louis F., and Alexander A. Di Lella
1978 *The Book of Daniel.* AB 23. Garden City: Doubleday.
Hatch, Edwin, and Henry Redpath
1897 *A Concordance to the Septuagint and the Other Greek Versions of the Old Testament.* Vols. 1–2. Suppl. 1906. Oxford: Clarendon Press.
Hauer, Christian E.
1963 "Who Was Zadok?" *JBL* 82: 89–94.
1982 "David and the Levites." *JSOT* 23: 33–54.
Hausmann, Jutta
1987 *Israels Rest: Studien zum Selbstverständnis der nachexilischen Gemeinde.* BWANT 124. Stuttgart: Kohlhammer.
Heinzerling, R.
1999 "Bileams Rätsel: Die Zählung der Wehrfähigen in Numeri 1 und 26." ZAW 111: 404–15.
2000 "On the Interpretation of the Census Lists by C. J. Humphreys and G. E. Mendenhall." *VT* 50: 250–52.
Helm, Rudolf
1956 *Die Chronik des Hieronymus: Eusebius Werke* 7. GCS. Berlin: Akademie.
Heltzer, Michael
1979 "The Royal Economy in Ancient Ugarit." Pages 459–96 in vol. 2 of *State and Temple Economy in the Ancient Near East.* Edited by E. Lipiński. OLA 6. Leuven: Department Oriëntalistiek.
1982 *The Internal Organization of the Kingdom of Ugarit.* Wiesbaden: L. Reichert.
1989a "The Tell el-Mazār Inscription No. 7 and Some Historical and Literary Problems of the Vth Satrapy." *Transeu* 1: 111–18.
1989b "The Royal Economy of King David Compared with the Royal Economy of Ugarit" (in Hebrew). Pages 175–80 in Ben-Tor, Greenfield, and Malamat (1989).
Hengel, Martin
1974 *Judaism and Hellenism.* 2 vols. 2nd rev. ed. Philadelphia: Fortress.
Herr, Larry G.
1992 "Shifts in Settlement Patterns of Late Bronze and Iron Age Ammon." Pages 175–78 in vol. 4 of *Studies in the History and Archaeology of Jordan.* Edited by G. Bisheh. Amman.
1997 "The Iron Age II Period: Emerging Nations." *BA* 60/3: 114–83.
1999 "The Ammonites in the Late Iron Age and Persian Period." Pages 219–37 in MacDonald and Younker (1999).
Hertzberg, Hans Wilhelm
1964 *I & II Samuel.* OTL. Philadelphia: Westminster.

Herzog, Ze'ev
1993 "Tel Beersheba." *NEAEHL* 1: 167–73.

Hess, Richard S.
1990 "The Genealogies of Genesis 1–11 and Comparative Literature." *Bib* 70: 241–54.
1993 *Studies in the Personal Names of Genesis 1–11*. AOAT 234. Kevelaer: Butzon & Bercker.
1994 "Achan and Achor: Names and Wordplay in Joshua 7." *HAR* 14: 89–98.

Hiebert, Theodore
1986 *God of My Victory: The Ancient Hymn in Habakkuk 3*. HSM 38. Atlanta: Scholars Press.
1996 *The Yahwist's Landscape: Nature and Religion in Early Israel*. New York: Oxford University Press.

Hill, Andrew E.
1983 "Patchwork Poetry or Reasoned Verse? Connective Structure in I Chronicles XVI." *VT* 33: 97–101.

Hinke, W. J.
1911 *Selected Babylonian Kudurru Inscriptions*. SSS 14. Leiden: Brill.

Hirsch, Steven W.
1985 *The Friendship of the Barbarians: Xenophon and the Persian Empire*. London: University Press of New England.

Ho, Craig Y. S.
1995 "Conjectures and Refutations: Is 1 Samuel XXXI 1–13 Really the Source of 1 Chronicles X 1–12?" *VT* 45: 82–106.
1999 "The Stories of the Family Troubles of Judah and David: A Study of Their Literary Links." *VT* 49: 514–31.

Hobbs, T. R.
1994 "The 'Fortresses of Rehoboam': Another Look." Pages 41–64 in *Uncovering Ancient Stones: Essays in Memory of H. Neil Richardson*. Edited by L. M. Hopfe. Winona Lake, Ind.: Eisenbruans.

Hoffman, Yair
1988 "The Technique of Quotation and Citation as an Interpretive Device." Pages 71–79 in *Creative Bible Exegesis: Jewish and Christian Hermeneutics through the Centuries*. Edited by B. Uffenheimer and H. G. Reventlow. JSOTSup 59. Sheffield: JSOT Press.

Hoffmann, R. E.
1980 "Eine Parallele zum Rahmenerzählung des Buches Hiob in I Chr. 7.20–29?" *ZAW* 92: 120–32.

Hoffmeier, James
1997 "Canonical Compositions: Historiography." *COS* 1: 68–73.

Hoffner, Harry
1973 Ed. *Orient and Occident: Essays Presented to Cyrus H. Gordon on the Occasion of His Sixty-fifth Birthday*. AOAT 22. Kevelaer: Butzon & Bercker.

Hoffner, Harry, and Gary M. Beckman

1986 Eds. *Kaniššuwar: A Tribute to Hans G. Güterbock on His Seventy-fifth Birthday.* AS 23. Chicago: The Oriental Institute of the University of Chicago.

Hogg, Hope W.

1899 "The Genealogy of Benjamin: A Criticism of 1 Chronicles 8." *JQR* 11: 102–114.

1901 "The Ephraim Genealogy." *JQR* 8: 147–54.

Hoglund, Kenneth G.

1992 *Achaemenid Imperial Administration in Syria-Palestine and the Missions of Ezra and Nehemiah.* SBLDS 125. Atlanta: Scholars Press.

1997 "The Chronicler as Historian: A Comparativist Perspective." Pages 19–29 in Graham, Hoglund, and McKenzie (1997).

Hognesius, Kjell

1987 "A Note on 1 Chr 23." *SJOT* 1: 123–27.

Holladay, Carl R.

1983 *Historians. Vol. 1 of Fragments from Hellenistic Jewish Authors.* SBLTT. Chico, Calif.: Scholars Press.

Holladay, William L.

1986 *Jeremiah 1.* Hermeneia. Philadelphia: Fortress.

1989 *Jeremiah 2.* Hermeneia. Philadelphia: Fortress.

1993 *The Psalms through Three Thousand Years.* Minneapolis: Fortress.

Hölscher, Gustav

1923 *Die Bücher Esra und Nehemia. HSAT.* Tübingen: Mohr.

Hooke, S. H.

1958 Ed. *Myth, Ritual, and Kingship: Essays on the Theory and Practice of Kingship in the Ancient Near East and in Israel.* Oxford: Clarendon Press.

Hornblower, Simon

1982 *Mausolus.* Oxford: Clarendon Press.

1983 *The Greek World.* London: Methuen & Co.

1994 Introduction to *Greek Historiography.* Edited by S. Hornblower. Oxford: Clarendon Press.

Horowitz, Wayne

1993 "Moab and Edom in the Sargon Geography." *IEJ* 43: 151–56.

1998 *Mesopotamian Cosmic Geography.* Winona Lake, Ind.: Eisenbrauns.

van Houten, Christiana

1991 *The Alien in Israelite Law.* JSOTSup 107. Sheffield: JSOT Press.

Howorth, Henry H.

1893a "A Criticism of the Sources and the Relative Importance and Value of the Canonical Book of Ezra and the Apocryphal Book Known as Esdras I." *Transactions of the Ninth International Congress of Orientalists, London,* 68–85.

1893b "The Real Character and the Importance of the Book of 1 Esdras." *The Academy* 43: 13–14, 60, 106, 174–75, 326–27, 524.

Hübner, Ulrich
1992 *Die Ammoniter.* ADPV 16. Wiesbaden: Harrassowitz.

Huffmon, Herbert B.
1966 "The Treaty Background of Hebrew *yādaʿ*." *BASOR* 181: 31–37.
1976 "Prophecy in the Ancient Near East." *IDBSup* 697–700.
1997 "The Expansion of Prophecy in the Mari Archives: New Texts, New Readings, New Information." Pages 7–22 in *Prophecy and Prophets.* Edited by Y. Gitay. SBLSymS. Atlanta: Scholars Press.

Humphreys, Colin J.
1998 "The Number of People in the Exodus from Egypt: Decoding Mathematically the Very Large Numbers in Numbers i and xxvi." *VT* 48: 196–213.

Hurowitz, Victor (Avidor)
1993 "Temporary Temples." Pages 37–50 in *kinattūtu ša dārâti: Raphael Kutscher Memorial Volume.* Edited by A. F. Rainey et al. Tel Aviv–Jaffa: Institute of Archaeology.
1995 "Solomon's Golden Vessels (1 Kings 7: 48–50) and the Cult of the First Temple." Pages 151–64 in Wright, Freedman, and Hurvitz (1995).

Hurvitz, Avi
1974 "The Evidence of Language in Dating the Priestly Code: A Linguistic Study in Technical Terms and Terminology." *RB* 81: 24–56.
1982 *A Linguistic Study of the Relationship between the Priestly Source and the Book of Ezekiel.* CahRB 20. Paris: Gabalda.
1988 "Dating the Priestly Source in Light of the Historical Study of Biblical Hebrew a Century after Wellhausen." ZAW (suppl.) 100: 88–100.
1995 "Terms and Epithets Relating to the Jerusalem Temple Compound in Chronicles: The Linguistic Aspect." Pages 165–83 in Wright, Freedman, and Hurvitz (1995).

Im, Tae-Soo
1985 *Das Davidbild in den Chronikbüchern: David als Idealbild des theokratischen Messianismus für den Chronisten.* Europäische Hochschulschriften 23. Frankfurt am Main: Lang.

Immerwahr, H. R.
1966 *Form and Thought in Herodotus.* Cleveland: Western Reserve University.

In der Smitten, Wilhelm, Th.
1972 "Zur Pagenerzählung im 3.Esra [3 Esr. III 1–V 6]." *VT* 22: 492–95.
1973 *Esra: Quellen, Überlieferung, und Geschichte.* SSN 15. Assen: Van Gorcum.

Irani, K. D., and Morris Silver
1995 Eds. *Social Justice in the Ancient World.* Westport, Conn.: Greenwood.

Ishida, Tomoo
1977a *The Royal Dynasties in Ancient Israel. A Study on the Formation and Development of Royal-Dynastic Ideology.* BZAW 142. Berlin: de Gruyter.

1977b "*nāgîd:* A Term for the Legitimization of the Kingship." *AJBI* 3: 35–51.

1979 "The Structure and Implications of the Lists of PreIsraelite Nations." *Bib* 60: 461–90.

1982 Ed. *Studies in the Period of David and Solomon and Other Essays.* Winona Lake, Ind.: Eisenbrauns.

1985 " 'Solomon Who Is Greater Than David': Solomon's Succession in 1 Kings I–II in the Light of the Inscription of Kilamuwa, King of Y'DY-Sam'al." Pages 145–53 in Emerton (1985).

1991 "The Succession Narrative and Esarhaddon's Apology: A Comparison." Pages 166–73 in Cogan and Eph'al (1991).

Jackson, Kent P.

1983 *The Ammonite Language of the Iron Age.* HSM 27. Chico, Calif.: Scholars Press.

Jacobsen, Thorkild

1939 *The Sumerian King List.* AS 11. Chicago: University of Chicago Press.

1943 "Parerga Sumerologica." *JNES* 2: 119–21.

Jacoby, Felix

1923– *Die Fragmente der griechischen Historiker.* 15 vols. Berlin: Weidmann.

1949 *Atthis: The Local Chronicles of Ancient Athens.* Oxford: Clarendon Press.

1956a *Abhandlungen zur griechischen Geschichtsschreibung.* Leiden: Brill.

1956b *Griechische Historiker.* Stuttgart: Alfred Druckenmüller.

Janssen, Enno

1956 *Juda in der Exilszeit.* FRLANT 69. Göttingen: Vandenhoeck & Ruprecht.

Janzen, J. Gerald

1973 "Studies in the Text of Jeremiah." HSM 6. Cambridge: Harvard University Press.

1989 A Critique of Sven Soderlund, *The Greek Text of Jeremiah. BIOSCS* 22: 16–47.

Japhet, Sara

1968 "The Supposed Common Authorship of Chronicles and Ezra-Nehemiah Investigated Anew." *VT* 18: 330–71.

1972 "Chronicles, Book of." *EncJud* 5: cols. 517–34. Jerusalem: Keter.

1977 *The Ideology of the Book of Chronicles and Its Place in Biblical Thought* (in Hebrew). Jerusalem: Bialik. Translated by Anna Barber in 1989.

1979 "Conquest and Settlement in Chronicles." *JBL* 98: 205–18.

1983 "People and Land in the Restoration Period." Pages 103–25 in *Das Land Israel in biblischer Zeit.* Edited by G. Strecker. GTA 25. Göttingen: Vandenhoeck & Ruprecht.

1985 "The Historical Reliability of Chronicles." *JSOT* 33: 83–107.

1987 "Interchanges of Verbal Roots in Parallel Texts in Chronicles." *HS* 28: 9–50.

1989 *The Ideology of the Book of Chronicles and Its Place in Biblical Thought.* BEATAJ 9. Frankfurt am Main: Lang.

1991a " 'History' and 'Literature' in the Persian Period: The Restoration of the Temple." Pages 174–88 in Cogan and Ephʿal (1991).

1991b "The Relationship between Chronicles and Ezra-Nehemiah." Pages 298–313 in Emerton (1991).

1991c "The Temple in the Restoration Period: Reality and Ideology." *USQR* 44: 195–251.

1992 "The Israelite Legal and Social Reality as Reflected in Chronicles: A Case Study." Pages 79–91 in Fishbane and Tov (1992).

1993a *I and II Chronicles.* OTL. Louisville, Ky.: Westminster John Knox.

1993b "The Prohibition of the Habitation of Women: The Temple Scroll's Attitude toward Sexual Impurity and Its Biblical Precedents." *JANES* 22: 69–87.

1994 "Composition and Chronology in the Book of Ezra-Nehemiah." Pages 189–216 in Eskenazi and Richards (1994).

1996a "The Distribution of the Priestly Gifts according to a Document of the Second Temple Period." Pages 3–20 in Fox et al. (1996).

1996b "L'Historiographie post-exilique: Comment at pourquoi?" Pages 123–52 in de Pury, Römer, and Macchi (1996).

1997 *The Ideology of the Book of Chronicles and Its Place in Biblical Thought.* 2nd ed. BEATAJ 9. Frankfurt am Main: Lang.

1999 "Exile and Restoration in the Book of Chronicles." Pages 33–44 in Becking and Korpel (1999).

Jastram, Nathan

1992 "The Text of 4QNum[b]." Pages 177–98 in Trebolle Barrera and Vegas Montaner (1992).

Jellicoe, Sidney

1968 *The Septuagint and Modern Study.* Oxford: Oxford University Press.

1973 "Prolegomenon." Pages xiii–lxi in *Studies in the Septuagint: Origins, Recensions, and Interpretations.* Edited by H. M. Orlinsky. Library of Biblical Studies. New York: KTAV.

Jenni, Ernst

1980 "Aus der Literatur zur chronistischen Geschichtsschreibung." *TRu* 45: 97–108.

Jepsen, Alfred

1956 *Die Quellen des Königbuches.* 2nd ed. Halle: Max Niemeyer.

1974 "אָמַן." *TDOT* 1: 292–323

Joannès, Francis

1982 *Textes économiques de la Babylonie récente (Études des Textes de TBER-Cahier 6).* Recherche sur les civilisations 5. Paris: Editions ADPF.

Joannès, Francis, and André Lemaire

1999 "Trois tablettes cunéiformes à onomastique ouest-sémitique (collection Sh. Moussaïeff)." *Transeu* 17: 17–34.

Jobling, David

1978 *The Sense of Biblical Narrative.* 2nd ed. JSOTSup 7. Sheffield: Sheffield Academic Press.

Johnson, Aubrey R.

1979 *The Cultic Prophet and Israel's Psalmody.* Cardiff: University of Wales Press.

Johnson, Marshall D.

1988 *The Purpose of the Biblical Genealogies.* 2nd ed. SNTSMS 8. Cambridge: Cambridge University Press.

Johnstone, William

1986 "Guilt and Atonement: The Theme of 1 and 2 Chronicles." Pages 113–38 in *A Word in Season: Essays in Honour of William McKane.* Edited by J. D. Martin and P. D. Davies. JSOTSup 42. Sheffield: JSOT Press.

1996 "The Use of Leviticus in Chronicles." Pages 243–59 in *Reading Leviticus: A Conversation with Mary Douglas.* Edited by J. F. A. Sawyer. JSOTSup 227. Sheffield: JSOT Press.

1997a *1 Chronicles 1–2 Chronicles 9: Israel's Place among the Nations.* Vol. 1 of *1 and 2 Chronicles.* JSOTSup 253. Sheffield: JSOT Press.

1997b *2 Chronicles 10–2 Chronicles 36: Guilt and Atonement.* Vol. 2 of *1 and 2 Chronicles.* JSOTSup 254. Sheffield: JSOT Press.

1998 *Chronicles and Exodus: An Analogy and Its Application.* JSOTSup 275. Sheffield: Sheffield Academic Press.

Jones, Gwilym H.

1990 *The Nathan Narratives.* JSOTSup 80. Sheffield: JSOT Press.

1993 *1 and 2 Chronicles.* OTG. Sheffield: JSOT Press.

1994 "From Abijam to Abijah." ZAW 106: 420–34.

Joüon, Paul

1938 "Notes de lexicographie hebraïque (XV): Racine *'šm.*" *Bib* 19: 454–59.

Judge, H. G.

1956 "Aaron, Zadok, and Abiathar." *JTS* 7: 70–74.

Junge, E.

1937 *Der Wiederaufbau der Heerwesens des Reiches Juda unter Josia.* BWANT 4/23. Stuttgart: Kohlhammer.

Kahle, Paul

1915 "Untersuchungen zur Geschichte des Pentateuchtextes." *TSK* 88: 399–439.

1959 *The Cairo Geniza.* 2nd ed. Oxford: Blackwell.

Kalimi, Isaac

1988 "Three Assumptions about the Kenites." ZAW 100: 386–93.

1990a *The Books of Chronicles: A Classified Bibliography.* Jerusalem: Simor.

1990b "The Land of Moriah, and the Site of Solomon's Temple in Biblical Historiography." *HTR* 83: 345–62.

1993a "Die Abfassungszeit der Chronik: Forschungsstand und Perspectiven." ZAW 105: 223–33.

1993b "The Contribution of the Literary Study of Chronicles to the Solution of Its Textual Problems." *Tarbiz* 62: 471–86.
1993c "Literary-Chronological Proximity in the Chronicler's Historiography." *VT* 43: 318–38.
1995a *Zur Geschichtsschreibung des Chronisten.* BZAW 226. Berlin: de Gruyter.
1995b "Paronomasia in the Book of Chronicles." *JSOT* 67: 27–41.
1997 "Was the Chronicler a Historian?" Pages 73–89 in Graham, Hoglund, and McKenzie (1997).
1998a "History of Interpretation: The Book of Chronicles in Jewish Tradition from Daniel to Spinoza." *RB* 105: 5–41.
1998b "Könnte die aramäische Grabinschrift aus Ägypten als Indikation für die Datierung der Chronikbücher fungieren?" *ZAW* 110: 79–81.
2001 "A Transmission of Tradition: The Number of Jesse's Sons." *TZ* 57: 1–9.

Kalimi, Isaac, and James D. Purvis
1994a "King Jehoiachin and the Vessels of the Lord's House in Biblical Literature." *CBQ* 56: 449–57.
1994b "The Hiding of the Temple Vessels in Jewish and Samaritan Literature." *CBQ* 56: 679–85.

Kallai(-Kleinmann), Zecharia
1958 "The Town Lists of Judah, Simeon, Benjamin and Dan." *VT* 8: 134–60.
1986a *Historical Geography of the Bible: The Tribal Territories of Israel.* Leiden: Brill.
1986b "The Settlement Traditions of Ephraim: A Historiographical Study." *ZDPV* 102: 68–74.
1997 "The Twelve-Tribe Systems of Israel." *VT* 47: 53–89.
1998 *Biblical Historiography and Historical Geography.* BEATAJ 44. Frankfurt am Main: Lang.
1999 "A Note on the Twelve-Tribe Systems of Israel." *VT* 49: 125–27.

Kalluveettil, Paul
1982 *Declaration and Covenant.* AnBib 88. Rome: Pontifical Biblical Institute.

Kang, Sa-Moon
1989 *Divine War in the Old Testament and in the Ancient Near East.* BZAW 177. Berlin: de Gruyter.

Kapelrud, Arvid S.
1963 "Temple Building, a Task for Gods and Kings." *Or* 32: 56–62.

Kartveit, Magnar
1989 *Motive und Schichten der Landtheologie in I Chronik 1–9.* ConBOT 28. Stockholm: Almqvist & Wiksell.
1999 "2 Chronicles 36.20–23 as Literary and Theological Interface." Pages 395–403 in Graham and McKenzie (1999).

Kaster, Robert A.
1996 "Epitome." *OCD.*

Kaufmann, Yeḥezkel

1960 *The Religion of Israel: From Its Beginnings to the Babylonian Exile.* Trans. and abr. by M. Greenberg. Chicago: Chicago University Press.

1961 *The Messianic Idea: The Real and Hidden Son of David.* El Haʿayin 5. Jerusalem: World Jewish Bible Society.

Keel, Othmar

1978 *The Symbolism of the Biblical World.* New York: Seabury. Repr., Winona Lake, Ind.: Eisenbrauns 1985.

Kegler, Jürgen

1993 "Prophetengestalten im Deuteronomistischen Geschichtswerk und in den Chronikbüchern: Ein Beitrag zur Kompositions- und Redaktionsgeschichte der Chronikbücher." ZAW 105: 481–97.

Kegler, Jürgen, and Matthias Augustin

1991 *Synopse zum Chronistischen Geschichtswerk.* 2nd ed. BEATAJ 1. Frankfurt am Main: Lang.

1993 *Deutsche Synopse zum Chronistischen Geschichtswerk.* 2nd ed. BEATAJ 33. Frankfurt am Main: Lang.

Keil, C. F.

1873 *The Books of the Chronicles.* Edinburgh: T&T Clark. Repr., Grand Rapids: Eerdmans 1978.

Kellermann, Diether

1975 "גור; *gûr.*" *TDOT* 2: 439–49.

Kellerman, U.

1967 *Nehemia: Quellen, Überlieferung, und Geschichte.* BZAW 102. Berlin: Töpelmann.

Kelly, Brian E.

1995 "Messianic Elements in the Chronicler's Work." Pages 249–64 in *The Lord's Anointed: Interpretation of Old Testament Messianic Texts.* Edited by P. E. Satterthwaite, R. S. Hess, and G. J. Wenham. Grand Rapids: Eerdmans.

1996 *Retribution and Eschatology in Chronicles.* JSOTSup 211. Sheffield: JSOT Press.

1998 "David's Disqualification in 1 Chronicles 22: 8: A Response to Piet B. Dirksen." *JSOT* 80: 53–61.

Kelly, J. N. D.

1975 *Jerome: His Life, Writings, and Controversies.* New York: Harper & Row.

Kempinski, A.

1974 "Tell el-ʿAjjûl—Beth-Aglayim or Sharuḥen?" *IEJ* 3–4: 145–52.

Kennett, R. H.

1904–05 "The Origin of the Aaronite Priesthood." *JTS* 6: 161–86.

Kent, Roland G.

1953 *Old Persian.* 2nd rev. ed. AOS 33. New Haven, Conn.: American Oriental Society.

Kenyon, Kathleen Mary

1974 *Digging Up Jerusalem.* New York: Praeger.

Kilmer, Anne Draffkorn

1995 "Music and Dance in Ancient Western Asia." *CANE* 4: 2601–13.

King, Philip J.

1999 "The Musical Tradition of Ancient Israel." Pages 84–99 in Williams and Hiebert (1999).

Kitchen, Kenneth A.

1986 *The Third Intermediate Period in Egypt (1100–650 B.C.)*. 2nd rev. ed. Warminster: Aris & Philips.

1997 "Sheba and Arabia." Pages 127–53 in Handy (1997).

Kittel, Rudolf

1895 *The Books of Chronicles: Critical Edition of the Hebrew Text.* The Sacred Books of the Old Testament 20. Edited by Paul Haupt. Leipzig: Hinrichs.

1902 *Die Bücher der Chronik und Esra, Nehemia und Esther.* HAT 1/6. Göttingen: Vandenhoeck & Ruprecht.

Klein, Ralph Walter

1966 "Studies in the Greek Texts of the Chronicler." Ph.D. diss., Harvard University.

1967 "New Evidence for an Old Recension of Reigns." *HTR* 60: 93–105.

1968 "Supplements in the Paralipomena: A Rejoinder." *HTR* 61: 492–95.

1974 *Textual Criticism of the Old Testament: The Septuagint after Qumran.* GBS. Philadelphia: Fortress.

1983a "Abijah's Campaign against the North (2 Chr. 13): What Were the Chronicler's Sources?" *ZAW* 95: 210–17.

1983b *1 Samuel.* WBC 10. Waco, Tex.: Word.

1992 "Chronicles, Book of 1–2." *ABD* 1: 992–1003.

1995 "Reflections on Historiography in the Account of Jehoshaphat." Pages 643–57 in Wright, Freedman, and Hurvitz (1995).

1997 "How Many in a Thousand?" Pages 270–82 in Graham, Hoglund, and McKenzie (1997).

Klein, Samuel

1926 "Die Schreiberfamilien: 1 Chronik 2^{55}." *MGWJ* 70: 410–16.

Kleinig, John W.

1993 *The Lord's Song: The Basis, Function, and Significance of Choral Music in Chronicles.* JSOTSup 156. Sheffield: JSOT Press.

1994 "Recent Research in Chronicles." *CRBS* 2: 43–76.

Kletter, Raz

1991 "The Rujm El-Malfuf Buildings and the Assyrian Vassal State of Ammon." *BASOR* 284: 33–50.

Kloner, Amos

1997 "Underground Metropolis: The Subterranean World of Maresha." *BARev* 23/2: 24–35, 67.

Klostermann, A.

1898 Die Bücher der Chronik. Pages 84–98 in Vol. 4 of *Realencyklopädie für protestantische Theologie und Kirche.* 3rd ed. Leipzig: J. C. Hinrichs.

Knauf, Ernst Axel

1985a "Alter und Herkunft der edomistischen Königsliste Gen 36, 31–39." ZAW 97: 245–53.

1985b "Mu'näer und Meüniter." *WO* 16: 114–23.

1988 *Midian: Untersuchungen zur Geschichte Palastinas und Nordarabiens am Ende des 2. Jahrtausends v. Chr.* ADPV. Wiesbaden: Harrassowitz.

1989 *Ismael: Untersuchungen zur Geschichte Palastinas und Nordarabiens im 1. Jahrtausend v. Chr.* 2nd ed. ADPV. Wiesbaden: Harrassowitz.

1990a "Hesbon, Sihons Stadt." *ZDPV* 106: 135–44.

1990b "The Persian Administration in Arabia." *Transeu* 2: 201–17.

1992a "The Cultural Impact of Secondary State Formation: The Cases of the Edomites and Moabites." Pages 47–54 in Bienkowski (1992).

1992b "Hagar." *ABD* 3: 18–19; "Ishmaelites." *ABD* 3: 513–20; "Ituraea." *ABD* 3: 583–84; "Jetur." *ABD* 3: 821–22; "Manahath. Manahathites." *ABD* 4: 493–94; "Meunim." *ABD* 4: 801–2; "Mibhar." *ABD* 4: 805; "Naphish." *ABD* 4: 1020; "Rekem." *ABD* 5: 665; "Shobal." *ABD* 5: 1224.

1995a "Edom: The Social and Economic History." Pages 93–117 in Edelman (1995b).

1995b "Zum Verhältnis von Esra 1, 1 zu 2 Chronik 36,20–23." *BN* 78: 16–17.

2000 "Jerusalem in the Late Bronze and Early Iron Ages." *TA* 27: 75–90.

Knibb, Michael A.

1999 *Translating the Bible: The Ethiopic Version of the Old Testament.* The Schweich Lectures 1995. Oxford: Oxford University Press.

Knierim, Rolf

1997 "מעל *mʿl* 'to be unfaithful.' " *TLOT* 2: 680–82.

Knights, Chris H.

1987 "The Text of 1 Chronicles iv 12: A Reappraisal." *VT* 37: 375–77.

1993 "Kenites = Rechabites? 1 Chronicles II 55 Reconsidered." *VT* 43: 10–18.

1996 "Who Were the Rechabites?" *ExpT* 107/5: 137–40.

Knohl, Israel

1995 *The Sanctuary of Silence.* Minneapolis: Fortress.

1996 "Between Voice and Silence: The Relationship between Prayer and Temple Cult." *JBL* 115: 17–30.

Knoppers, Gary N.

1988 " 'What Share Have We in David?': The Division of the Kingdom in Kings and Chronicles." Ph.D. diss., Harvard University.

1989 "A Reunited Kingdom in Chronicles?" *Proceedings, Eastern Great Lakes and Midwest Biblical Societies* 9: 74–88.

1990 "Rehoboam in Chronicles: Villain or Victim?" *JBL* 109: 423–40.

1991 "Reform and Regression: The Chronicler's Presentation of Jehoshaphat." *Bib* 72: 500–524.

1992a " 'The God in His Temple': The Phoenician Text from Pyrgi as a Funerary Inscription." *JNES* 51: 105–20.

1992b " 'There Was None Like Him': Incomparability in the Books of Kings." *CBQ* 54: 411–31.

1993a " 'Battling against Yahweh': Israel's War against Judah in 2 Chr 13: 2–20." *RB* 100: 511–32.

1993b "Treaty, Tribute List, or Diplomatic Letter?: KTU 3.1 Re-examined." *BASOR* 289: 81–94.

1993c *The Reign of Solomon and the Rise of Jeroboam*. Vol. 1 of *Two Nations under God: The Deuteronomistic History of Solomon and the Dual Monarchies*. HSM 52. Atlanta: Scholars Press.

1994a "Dissonance and Disaster in the Legend of Kirta." *JAOS* 114: 572–82.

1994b "Jehoshaphat's Judiciary and the Scroll of YHWH's Torah." *JBL* 113: 59–80.

1994c Review of K. Strübind, *Tradition als Interpretation*, *CBQ* 55: 780–82.

1994d "Sex, Religion, and Politics: The Deuteronomist on Intermarriage." *HAR* 14: 121–41.

1994e *The Reign of Jeroboam, the Fall of Israel, and the Reign of Josiah*. Vol. 2 of *Two Nations under God: The Deuteronomistic History of Solomon and the Dual Monarchies*. HSM 53. Atlanta: Scholars Press.

1995a "Aaron's Calf and Jeroboam's Calves." Pages 92–104 in Beck et al. (1995).

1995b "Images of David in Early Judaism: David as Repentant Sinner in Chronicles." *Bib* 76: 449–70.

1995c "Prayer and Propaganda: The Dedication of Solomon's Temple and the Deuteronomist's Program." *CBQ* 57: 229–54. Repr. pages 370–96 in Knoppers and McConville (2000).

1995d Review of A. Graeme Auld, *Kings without Privilege*. *Ashland Theological Journal* 27: 118–21.

1996a "Ancient Near Eastern Royal Grants and the Davidic Covenant: A Parallel?" *JAOS* 116: 670–97.

1996b "The Deuteronomist and the Deuteronomic Law of the King: A Reexamination of a Relationship." *ZAW* 108: 329–46.

1996c " 'Yhwh Is Not with Israel': Alliances as a *Topos* in Chronicles." *CBQ* 58: 601–26.

1996d Review of Ernst Michael Dörrfuß, *Moses in den Chronikbüchern*. *CBQ* 58: 705–7.

1997a "History and Historiography: The Royal Reforms." Pages 178–203 in Graham, Hoglund, and McKenzie (1997). Repr. pages 557–78 in *Israel's Past in Present Research*. Edited by V. Philips Long. SBTS 7. Winona Lake, Ind. Eisenbrauns: 1999.

1997b "The Vanishing Solomon: The Disappearance of the United Monarchy from Recent Histories of Ancient Israel." *JBL* 116: 19–44.

1997c "Solomon's Fall and Deuteronomy." Pages 392–410 in Handy (1997).

1998 "David's Relation to Moses: The Context, Content, and Conditions of the Davidic Promises." Pages 91–118 in *King and Messiah in Israel* and the Ancient Near East: Papers from the Oxford Old Testament Seminar. Edited by J. Day. JSOTSup 270. Sheffield: JSOT Press.

1999a "*Hierodules*, Priests, or Janitors? The Levites in Chronicles and the History of the Israelite Priesthood." *JBL* 118: 49–72.

1999b "The History of the Monarchy: Developments and Detours." Pages 207–35 in *The Face of Old Testament Studies*. Edited by D. W. Baker and B. T. Arnold. Grand Rapids: Baker.

1999c "Jerusalem at War in Chronicles." Pages 57–76 in *Zion, City of Our God*. Edited by R. S. Hess and G. J. Wenham. Grand Rapids: Eerdmans.

1999d Review of Josette Elayi and Jean Sapin, *Beyond the River: New Perspectives on Transeuphratene*. *JBL* 118: 712–14.

1999e "Treasures Won and Lost: Royal (Mis)appropriations in Kings and Chronicles." Pages 181–208 in Graham and McKenzie (1999).

2000a " 'Great among His Brothers,' But Who Is He? Heterogeneity in the Composition of Judah." *Journal of Hebrew Scriptures* 3, 4. Online: http://www.purl.org/jhs.

2000b "The Preferential Status of the Eldest Son Revoked?" Pages 115–26 in McKenzie and Römer (2000).

2000c "Sources, Revisions, and Editions: The Lists of Jerusalem's Residents in MT and LXX Nehemiah 11 and 1 Chronicles 9." *Text* 20: 141–68.

2001a "An Achaemenid Imperial Authorization of Torah in Yehud?" Pages 115–34 in *Persia and Torah: The Theory of Imperial Authorization of the Pentateuch*. Edited by J. W. Watts. SBLSymS. Atlanta: SBL Press.

2001b "The Davidic Genealogy: Some Contextual Considerations from the Ancient Mediterranean World." *Transeu* 22: 35–50.

2001c "Intermarriage, Social Complexity, and Ethnic Diversity in the Genealogy of Judah." *JBL* 120: 15–30.

2001d "Rethinking the Relationship between Deuteronomy and the Deuteronomistic History: The Case of Kings." *CBQ* 63: 393–415.

2003 "The Relationship of the Priestly Genealogies to the History of the High Priesthood in Jerusalem." In Lipschits and Blenkinsopp (2003).

forthcoming (a) "Classical Historiography and the Chronicler's History: A Reexamination of an Alleged Nonrelationship." *JBL* 122.

forthcoming (b) "Israel's First King and 'the Kingdom of Yhwh in the Hands of the Sons of David': The Place of the Saulide Monarchy in the Chronicler's Historiography." In Ehrlich and White (forthcoming).

forthcoming (c) "The Universal and the Particular: The Relationship between the Nations and Israel in the Chronicler's Work." In Graham, Knoppers, and McKenzie (forthcoming).

forthcoming (d) "Projected Age Comparisons of the Levitical Townlists: Divergent Theories and Their Significance."

forthcoming (e) "Changing History: Nathan's Dynastic Oracle and the Structure of the Davidic Monarchy in Chronicles." In *The Sara Japhet Jubilee Volume*. Edited by M. Bar-Asher, D. Rom-Shiloni, E. Tov, and N. Wazana.

forthcoming (f) "In Search of Postexilic Israel: Samaria after the Fall of the Northern Kingdom." In *In Search of Pre-Exilic Israel: Proceedings of the Oxford Old Testament Seminar.* Edited by John Day. Edinburgh: T. & T. Clark.

Knoppers, Gary N., and Paul B. Harvey Jr.

2002 "Things Omitted and Things Remaining: The Name of the Book of Chronicles in Antiquity." *JBL* 121: 227–43.

Knoppers, Gary N., and J. Gordon McConville

2000 Ed. *Reconsidering Israel and Judah: Recent Studies on the Deuteronomistic History.* SBTS 8. Winona Lake, Ind.: Eisenbrauns.

Köberle, J.

1899 *Die Tempelsanger im Alten Testament: ein Versuch zur israelitischen und jüdischen Cultusgeschichte.* Erlangen: Fr. Junge.

Koch, Klaus

1974 "Ezra and the Origins of Judaism." *JSS* 19: 173–97.

1986 *Daniel.* BKAT 22/1. Neukirchen-Vluyn: Neukirchener Verlag.

1992 "Ezra and Meremoth: Remarks on the History of the High Priesthood." Pages 105–10 in Fishbane and Tov (1992).

1996 "Weltordnung und Reichsidee im alten Iran und ihre Auswirlungen auf die Provinz Jehud." Pages 133–337 in Frei and Koch (1996).

Koester, Craig R.

1989 *The Dwelling of God: The Tabernacle in the Old Testament, Intertestamental Jewish Literature, and the New Testament.* CBQMS 22. Washington: The Catholic Biblical Association of America.

van der Kooij, Arie

1991a "On the Ending of the Book of 1 Esdras." Pages 37–49 in Cox (1991).

1991b "Zur Frage des Anfangs des 1. Esrabuches." ZAW 103: 239–52.

1998 "The Death of Josiah According to 1 Esdras." *Text* 19: 97–109.

König, Eduard

1923 *Die messianischen Weissagungen des Alten Testaments.* Stuttgart: C. Belser.

Koorevaar, Hendrik J.

1997 "Die Chronik als intendierter Abschluß des alttestamentlichen Kanons." *JET* 11: 42–76.

Korošec, V.

1931 *Hethitische Staatsverträge: Ein Beitrag zu ihren juristischen Wertung.* Leipziger Rechtswissenschaftliche Studien 60. Leipzig: T. Weicher.

1974 "Les Rois hittites et la formation du droit." Pages 315–21 in *Le Palais et la royauté, archéologie et civilization.* 19e Rencontre Assyriologique Internationale. Edited by P. Garelli. Paris: P. Geuthner.

Kort, Ann, and Scott Morschauser

1985 Eds. *Biblical and Related Studies Presented to Samuel Iwry.* Winona Lake, Ind.: Eisenbrauns.

Kraeling, E. G.

1953 *The Brooklyn Museum Aramaic Papyri.* New Haven, Conn.: Yale University Press.

Kraemer, David
1993 "On the Relationship of the Books of Ezra and Nehemiah." *JSOT* 59: 73–92.

Kraft, Robert A.
1972 Ed. *Proceedings, International Organization for Septuagint and Cognate Studies and the Society of Biblical Literature Pseudepigrapha Seminar.* SBLSCS 2. Missoula, Mont.: Scholars Press.

Krahmalkov, Charles R.
2000 *Phoenician-Punic Dictionary.* OLA 90. Studia Phoenicia 15. Leuven: Peeters.

Kraus, Hans-Joachim
1988 *Psalms 1–59.* Minneapolis: Augsburg.
1993 *Psalms 60–150.* Minneapolis: Augsburg.

Kropat, Arno
1909 *Die Syntax des Autors der Chronik Vergleichen mit der seiner Quellen: Ein Beitrag zur historischen Syntax des Hebräischen.* BZAW 16. Giessen: Töpelmann.

Kruse, Heinz
1983 "Psalm CXXXII and the Royal Zion Festival." *VT* 33: 279–97.
1985 "David's Covenant." *VT* 35: 139–64.

Kuenen, Abraham
1887–92 *Historisch Kritische Einleitung in die Bücher des Alten Testaments.* Leipzig: Otto Schulze.

Kugel, James
1986 "Early Interpretation: The Common Background of Late Forms of Biblical Exegesis." Pages 9–106 in *Early Biblical Interpretation.* Edited by J. L. Kugel and R. A. Greer. LEC 3. Philadelphia: Westminster.
1988 "Topics in the History of the Spirituality of the Psalms." Pages 113–44 in *Jewish Spirituality from the Bible through the Middle Ages.* Edited by Arthur Green. World Spirituality 13. New York: Crossroad.
1993 "Levi's Elevation to the Priesthood in Second Temple Writings." *HTR* 86: 1–63.
1995 "Reuben's Sin with Bilhah in the *Testament of Reuben.*" Pages 525–54 in Wright, Freedman, and Hurvitz (1995).

Kugler, Robert
1996 *From Patriarch to Priest: The Levi-Priestly Tradition from Aramaic Levi to the Testament of Levi.* SBLEJL 9. Atlanta: Scholars Press.

Kuhl, Curt
1952 "Die 'Wiederaufnahme': Ein literarkritische Prinzip?" ZAW 64: 1–11.

Kuhrt, Amélie
1995 *The Ancient Near East c. 3000—330 B.C.* 2 vols. London: Routledge.

Kuntzmann, Raymond
1993 "Le Trône de Dieu dans l'Oeuvre du Chroniste." Pages 19–27 in *Le Trône de Dieu.* Edited by Marc Philonenko. Tübingen: Mohr.

1999 "David, constructeur du Temple?" Pages 139–56 in Desrousseaux and Vermeylen (1999).

Kutscher, Eduard Yeḥezkel

1974 *The Language and Linguistic Background of the Isaiah Scroll (IQ Isa*[a]). Leiden: Brill.

Laato, Antti

1992a *Josiah and David Redivivus: The Historical Josiah and the Messianic Expectations of Exilic and Postexilic Times.* ConBOT 33. Stockholm: Almqvist & Wiksell.

1992b "Psalm 132 and the Development of the Jerusalemite/Israelite Royal Ideology." *CBQ* 54: 49–66.

1992c *The Servant of YHWH and Cyrus: A Reinterpretation of the Exilic Messianic Programme in Isaiah 40–55.* ConBOT 35. Stockholm: Almqvist & Wiksell.

1994a "The Levitical Genealogies in 1 Chronicles 5–6 and the Formation of Levitical Ideology in Post-exilic Judah." *JSOT* 62: 77–99.

1994b "Zechariah 4, 6b–10a and the Akkadian Royal Building Inscriptions." ZAW 106: 53–69.

1997 *A Star Is Rising: The Historical Development of the Old Testament Royal Ideology and the Rise of the Jewish Messianic Expectations.* University of South Florida International Studies in Formative Christianity and Judaism 5. Atlanta: Scholars Press.

LaBianca, Øystein

1999 "Salient Features of Iron Age Tribal Kingdoms." Pages 19–29 in MacDonald and Younker (1999).

LaBianca, Øystein, and R. W. Younker

1995 "The Kingdoms of Ammon, Moab, and Edom: The Archaeology of Society in Late Bronze/Iron Age Transjordan (ca. 1400–500 B.C.E.)." Pages 399–415 in Levy (1995).

Labuschagne, C. J.

1960 "Some Remarks on the Prayer of David in II Sam. 7." Pages 28–35 in *Studies on the Books of Samuel.* Papers Read at the Third Meeting of Die O. T. Werkgemeenskap in Suid-Afrika. Pretoria: University of Stellenbosch.

Laffey, Alice L.

1992 "1 and 2 Chronicles." In *The Women's Bible Commentary.* Edited by C. A. Newsom and S. H. Ringe. London: SPCK.

de Lagarde, Paul

1863 *Anmerkungen zur griechischen übersetzung der Proverbien.* Leipzig: F. A. Brockhaus.

1882 *Ankündigung einer neuen ausgabe der griechischen übersetzung des alten Testaments.* Göttingen: Dieterichsche Buchhandlung.

1883 *Librorum Veteris Testamenti Canonicorum Pars Prior Graece.* Göttingen: Dieterichianis Arnoldi Hoyer.

Lambdin, Thomas O.

1953 "Egyptian Loan Words in the Old Testament." *JAOS* 73: 145–55.

1962 "Shihor." *IDB* 4: 328.
1971 *An Introduction to Biblical Hebrew.* New York: Scribner's.

Lambert, W. G. and S. B. Parker
1966 *Enuma elis: The Babylonian Epic of Creation.* Oxford: Clarendon Press.

Lamberts, E.
1970 *Studien zur Parataxe bei Herodot.* Wien: Notring.

Langston, Scott M.
1998 *Cultic Sites in the Tribe of Benjamin: Benjaminite Prominence in the Religion of Israel.* New York: Lang.

Laperrousaz, Ernest-Marie, and A. Lemaire
1994 Eds. *La Palestine à l'époque perse.* Études annexes de la Bible de Jérusalem. Paris: Cerf.

Lapp, Nancy L.
1997 "Tell el-Ful." *OEANE* 2: 346–47.

Larsen, Mogens Trolle
1979 "The Tradition of Empire in Mesopotamia." Pages 75–103 in *Power and Propaganda. Mesopotamia* 7. Copenhagen: Akademisk.

Layton, Scott C.
1990a *Archaic Features of Canaanite Personal Names.* HSM 47. Atlanta: Scholars Press.
1990b "The Semitic Root **Ǵlm* and the Hebrew Name *ʿĀlemet.*" ZAW 102: 80–94.
1993 "The Hebrew Personal Name Merab: Its Etymology and Meaning." *JSS* 38: 193–207.
1996 "Leaves from an Onomastician's Notebook." ZAW 108: 608–20.

Le Déaut, R., and J. Robert
1971a *Introduction et Traduction.* Vol. 1 of *Targum des Chroniques.* AnBib 51. Rome: Biblical Institute Press.
1971b *Text et Glossaire.* Vol. 2 of *Targum des Chroniques.* AnBib 51. Rome: Biblical Institute Press.

Leiman, Sid Z.
1976 *The Canonization of Hebrew Scripture: The Talmudic and Midrashic Evidence.* Transactions: The Connecticut Academy of Arts and Sciences 47. Hamden, Conn.: Archon.

Leith, Mary Joan Winn
1997 *The Seal Impressions.* Vol. 1 of *Wadi Daliyeh.* Oxford: Oxford University Press.

Leithart, Peter J.
1999 "Attendants of Yahweh's House: Priesthood in the Old Testament." *JSOT* 85: 3–24.

Lemaire, André
1973a "Asriel, Šr'l, Israel et l'origine de la confédération israélite." *VT* 23: 239–43.
1973b "L'ostrokon 'Ramat-Négeb' et la topographie historique du Négeb." *Sem* 23: 11–26

1974 "Un nouveau roi arabe de Qedar dans l'inscription de l'autel à encens de Lakish (*Planche I*)." *RB* 81: 63–72.
1977 *Inscriptions hébraïques, I: les ostraca.* Paris: Cerf.
1988 "Hadad l'Édomite ou Hadad l'Araméen?" *BN* 43: 14–18.
1989 "Les inscriptions palestiniennes d'époque perse: Un bilan provisoire." *Transeu* 1: 87–104.
1994a "Epigraphie palestienne: Nouveaux documents I. Fragment de stèle araméene de Tell Dan (IXe s. av. J.-C.)." *Hen* 16: 87–93.
1994b "Histoire et administration de la Palestine à l'époque perse." Pages 11–53 in Laperrousaz and Lemaire (1994).
1995 "La fin de la première période perse en Égypte et la chronologie judéenne vers 400 av. J. C." *Transeu* 9: 51–61.
1996a *Nouvelles Inscriptions araméennes d'Idumée au Musée d'Israël.* Supplément 3 à *Transeu.* Paris: Gabalda.
1996b "Zorobabel et la Judée à lumière de l'épigraphie (fin du VIe s. av. J.-C.)." *RB* 103: 48–57.
1997a "Les Minéens et la Transeuphratène à l'époque perse: Une première approche." *Transeu* 13: 123–39.
1997b "Nouvelles données épigraphiques sur l'époque royale Israélite." *REJ* 156 (3–4): 445–61.
1999 "Nouveaux sceaux et bulles paléo-hébraïques." Pages 106*–115* in Levine et al (1999).
2000a "L'economie de l'Idumée d'après les nouveaux *ostraca* araméens." *Transeu* 19: 131–43.
2000b "*Tarshish-Tarsisi:* Problème de topographie historique biblique et assyrienne." Pages 44–62 in *Studies in Historical Geography and Biblical Historiography: Presented to Zecharia Kallai.* Edited by G. Galil and M. Weinfeld. VTSup 81. Leiden: Brill.
2001 "Phoenician Funerary Stelae in the Hecht Museum Collection." *Michmanim* 15: 7*–23*.

Lemaire, André, and Hélène Lozachmeur
1987 "Bīrāh/Birtāʾ en araméen." *Syria* 64: 261–66.
1995 "La Birta en Méditerranée orientale." *Sem* 43–44: 75–78.

Lemche, Niels Peter
1993 "The Old Testament—a Hellenistic Book?" *SJOT* 7: 163–93. Rev. and repr. as pages 287–318 in Grabbe (2001c).
1998 *Prelude to Israel's Past.* Peabody, Mass.: Hendricksen.
2001 "How Does One Date an Expression of Mental History? The Old Testament and Hellenism." Pages 200–224 in Grabbe (2001c).

Lemke, Werner E.
1963 "Synoptic Studies in the Chronicler's History." Ph.D. diss., Harvard University.
1965 "The Synoptic Problem in the Chronicler's History." *HTR* 58: 349–63.

Levenson, Jon Douglas

1976 *Theology of the Program of Restoration of Ezekiel 40–48*. HSM 10. Missoula, Mont.: Scholars Press.

1979 "The Davidic Covenant and Its Modern Interpreters." *CBQ* 41: 205–19.

1984a "The Last Four Verses in Kings." *JBL* 103: 353–61.

1984b "The Temple and the World." *JR* 64: 275–98.

1996 "The Universal Horizon of Biblical Particularism." Pages 143–69 in Brett (1996).

Levenson, Jon Douglas, and Baruch Halpern

1980 "The Political Import of David's Marriages." *JBL* 99: 507–18.

Levey, Samson H.

1974 *The Messiah: An Aramaic Interpretation*. Cincinnati: Hebrew Union College–Jewish Institute of Religion.

Levin, Chris

1994 "Die Enstehung der Rechabiter." Pages 301–17 in *"Wer is wie du, HERR, unter den Göttern?" Studien zur Theologie und Religionsgeschichte für Otto Kaiser zum 70. Geburtstag*. Edited by I. Kottsieper et al. Göttingen: Vandenhoeck & Ruprecht.

Levine, Baruch A.

1963 "The Netînîm." *JBL* 82: 207–12.

1973 "Later Sources on the *Netînîm*." Pages 101–107 in Hoffner (1973).

1989 *Leviticus*. The JPS Torah Commentary. Philadelphia: Jewish Publication Society.

1993 *Numbers 1–20*. AB 4. Garden City: Doubleday.

1996 "Farewell to the Ancient Near East: Evaluating Biblical References to Ownership of Land in Comparative Perspective." Pages 223–52 in *Privatization in the Ancient Near East and Classical World*. Edited by M. Hudson and B. A. Levine. Cambridge, Mass.: Peabody Museum of Archaeology and Ethnology.

Levine, Baruch A., et al.

1999 Eds. *Frank Moore Cross Volume*. *ErIsr* 26. Jerusalem: Israel Exploration Society.

Levinson, Bernard M.

1991 "The Hermeneutics of Innovation: The Impact of Centralization upon the Structure, Sequence, and Reformulation of Legal Material in Deuteronomy." Ph.D. diss., Brandeis University.

1992 "The Human Voice in Divine Revelation: The Problem of Authority in Biblical Law." Pages 46–61 in *Innovation in Religious Traditions*. Edited by M. A. Williams, C. Cox, and M. S. Jaffee. *Rel Soc* 31. Berlin: de Gruyter.

1997 *Deuteronomy and the Hermeneutics of Legal Innovation*. New York: Oxford University Press.

Levy, Thomas E.

1995 Ed. *The Archaeology of Society in the Holy Land*. London: Leicester University Press.

Lewis, Theodore J.
1989 *Cults of the Dead in Ancient Israel and Ugarit.* HSM 39. Atlanta: Scholars Press.

Lichtheim, Miriam
1997 "Sinuhe." Pages 77–82 in *Canonical Compositions from the Biblical World.* Vol. 1 of *The Context of Scripture.* Edited by W. W. Hallo and K. L. Younger Jr. Leiden: Brill.

Lidzbarski, Mark
1902–15 *Ephemeris für semitische Epigraphik.* 3 vols. Giessen: J. Ricker.

Lindblom, J.
1962 *Prophecy in Ancient Israel.* Philadelphia: Fortress.

van der Lingen, Anton
1992 "*BWʾ-YṢʾ* ('to go out and to come in') as a Military Term." *VT* 42: 1: 59–66.

Lipiński, Édouard
1967 *Le Poème royal du Psaume lxxxix 1–5. 20–38.* CahRB 6. Paris: Gabalda.
1974a "אשבעל and אשיהו and Parallel Personal Names." *OLP* 5: 5–13.
1974b "*Nāgîd*, der Kronprinz." *VT* 24: 497–99.
1975 Ed. *Studies in Aramaic Inscriptions and Onomastics I.* OLA 1. Leuven: Leuven University Press.
1979 Ed. *State and Temple Economy in the Ancient Near East I–II.* OLA 5–6. Leuren: Department Oriëntalistiek.
1987 Ed. *Studia Phoenicia V: Phoenicia and the East Mediterranean in the First Millennium B.C.* OLA 22. Leuven: Peeters.
1990 "Les Japhétites selon Gen 10, 2–4 et 1 Chr 1, 5–7." *ZAH* 3: 40–53.
1992 "Les Chamites selon Gen 10, 6 et 1 Chr 1, 8–16." *ZAH* 5: 132–62.
1993 "Les Sémites selon Gen 10, 21–30 et 1 Chr 1, 17–23." *ZAH* 6: 193–214.

Lipschits, Oded
1997 "The Origins of the Jewish Population in Modiʿin and Its Vicinity" (in Hebrew). *Cathedra* 85: 7–32.
1998 "Nebuchadnezzar's Policy in 'Ḫattu-Land' and the Fate of the Kingdom of Judah." *UF* 30: 467–87.
1999 "The History of the Benjamin Region under Babylonian Rule." *TA* 26: 155–90.
2001 "Judah, Jerusalem, and the Temple 586–539 B.C." *Transeu* 22: 129–42.
2003 "Demographic Changes in Judah between the Seventh and the Fifth Centuries B.C.E." Pages 323–76 in Lipschits and Blenkinsopp (2003).

Lipschits, Oded, and Joseph Blenkinsopp
2003 Eds. *Judah and the Judeans in the Neo-Babylonian Period.* Winona Lake, Ind.: Eisenbrauns.

Liver, Jacob
1987 *Chapters in the History of the Priests and Levites* (in Hebrew). 2nd ed. Jerusalem: Magnes.

Liverani, Mario

1979 "The Ideology of the Assyrian Empire." Pages 297–317 in Larsen (1979).

Loewenstamm, Samuel E.

1980 "Šopeṭ and Šebaṭ." Pages 270–72 in *Comparative Studies in Biblical and Ancient Oriental Literatures.* AOAT 204. Kevelaer: Butzon & Bercker.

Lohfink, Norbert

1962 "Die deuteronomistische Darstellung des Übergangs der Führung Israels von Moses auf Josue." *Schol* 37: 32–44.

1985 Ed. *Das Deuteronomium: Entstehung, Gestalt, und Botschaft.* BETL 68. Leuven: Leuven University Press.

Long, Burke O.

1987 "Framing Repetitions in Biblical Historiography." *JBL* 106: 385–99 (= *Proceedings of the Ninth World Congress of Jewish Studies* A: 69–76).

1991 *2 Kings.* FOTL 10. Grand Rapids: Eerdmans.

Long, V. Philips

1989 *The Reign and Rejection of King Saul.* Atlanta: Scholars Press.

1999 Ed. *Israel's Past in Present Research.* SBTS 7. Winona Lake, Ind.: Eisenbrauns.

Lorenzin, T.

1996 "L'uso della regola ermeneutica *gezerah shawah* nel Chronista." *RivB* 44: 65–70.

Loretz, Oswald

1961 "The *Perfectum Copulativum* in 2 Sm 7, 9–11." *CBQ* 23: 294–96.

Lund, J.

1990 "The Northern Coastline of Syria in the Persian Period: A Survey of the Archaeological Evidence (Pl. 1)." *Transeu* 2: 13–36.

Maass, F.

1997 "כפר *kpr.*" *TLOT* 624–35.

Macalister, R. A. S.

1905 "The Craftsmen's Guild of the Tribe of Judah." *PEFQS* 243–53, 328–42.

MacDonald, Burton

1999 "Ammonite Territory and Sites." Pages 30–56 in MacDonald and Younker (1999).

2000 *"East of the Jordan": Territories and Sites of the Hebrew Scriptures.* Boston: ASOR.

MacDonald, Burton, and Randall W. Younker

1999 Eds. *Ancient Ammon.* SCANE 17. Leiden: Brill.

MacDonald, John

1976 "The Status and Role of the Naʿar in Israelite Society." *JNES* 35: 147–70.

Machinist, Peter Bruce

1991 "The Question of Distinctiveness in Ancient Israel: An Essay." Pages 196–212 in Cogan and Ephʿal (1991).

1994a "The First Coins of Judah and Samaria: Numismatics and History in the Achaemenid and Early Hellenistic Periods." Pages 365–79 in Sancisi-Weerdenburg, Dijvers, and Root (1994).

1994b "Outsiders or Insiders: The Biblical View of Emergent Israel and Its Contexts." Pages 35–60 in *The Other in Jewish Thought and History: Constructions of Jewish Culture and Identity*. Edited by L. J. Silberstein and R. L. Cohn. New York: New York University Press.

1995a "Fate, *miqreh*, and Reason: Some Reflections on Qohelet and Biblical Thought." Pages 159–75 in Zevit, Gitin, and Sokoloff (1995).

1995b "The Transfer of Kingship: A Divine Turning." Pages 105–20 in Beck et al. (1995).

Macy, Howard Ray

1975 "The Sources of the Books of Chronicles: A Reassessment." Ph.D. diss., Harvard University.

Malamat, Avraham

1968 "King Lists of the Old Babylonian Period and Biblical Genealogies." *JAOS* 88: 168–73.

1973 "Tribal Societies: Biblical Genealogies and African Lineage Systems." *European Journal of Sociology* 14: 126–36.

1975 "The Twilight of Judah: In the Egyptian-Babylonian Maelstrom." Pages 123–45 in *Congress Volume, Edinburgh 1974*. VTSup 28. Leiden: Brill.

1995a "A Note on the Ritual of Treaty Making in Mari and the Bible." IEJ 45: 226–29.

1995b "A Recently Discovered Word for 'Clan' in Mari and its Hebrew Cognate." Pages 177–79 in Zevit, Gitin, and Sokoloff (1995).

1998 *Mari and the Bible*. SCANE 12. Leiden: Brill.

Mandell, Sara, and David Noel Freedman

1993 *The Relationship between Herodotus' History and Primary History*. SFSHJ 60. Atlanta: Scholars Press.

Marböck, J.

1981 "Henoch—Adam—der Thronwagen: Zu frühjüdischen pseudepigraphischen Traditionem bei Ben Sira." *BZ* 25: 103–11.

Marcus, David

1981 "Civil Liberties under Israelite and Mesopotamian Kings." *JANES* 11: 53–60.

Mare, W. H.

1987 *The Archaeology of the Jerusalem Area*. Grand Rapids: Baker.

Margain, J.

1974 "Observations sur *I Chroniques*, XXII: A propos des anachronismes linguistiques dans la Bible." *Sem* 24: 35–43.

Margolis, Max Leopold

1992 *Joshua 19: 39–24: 33*. Part 5 of *The Book of Joshua in Greek*. Philadelphia: Annenberg Research Institute.

Marquart, J.

1902 "The Genealogies of Benjamin (Num 26: 38–40, 1 Chron. 7: 6ff. 8: 1ff.)." *JQR* 14: 343–51.

Martin, W. J.

1969 " 'Dischronologized' Narrative in the Old Testament." Pages 179–86 in *Congress Volume: Rome 1968*. Edited by G. W. Anderson et al. VTSup 17. Leiden: Brill.

Mason, Rex

1989 "Some Chronistic Themes in the 'Speeches' in Ezra and Nehemiah." *ExpT* 101: 72–76.

1990 *Preaching the Tradition: Homily and Hermeneutics after the Exile*. Cambridge: Cambridge University Press.

Masson, Olivier, and M. Sznycer

1972 *Recherches sur les Phéniciens à Chypre*. Geneva-Paris: Droz.

Matson, Frederick R.

1995 "Potters and Pottery in the Ancient Near East." *CANE* 1553–65.

Matthews, Donald

1995 "Artists and Artisans in Ancient Western Asia." *CANE* 455–68.

Mattila, Raija

2000 *The King's Magnates: A Study of the Highest Officials of the Neo-Assyrian Empire*. SAA 11. Helsinki: Helsinki University Press.

Mayes, A. D. H.

1983 *The Story of Israel between Settlement and Exile: A Redactional Study of the Deuteronomistic History*. London: SCM.

Mazar, Amihai

1990 *Archaeology of the Land of the Bible 10,000–586 B.C.E.* ABRL. Garden City: Doubleday.

2001 Ed. *Studies in the Archaeology of the Iron Age in Israel and Jordan*. JSOTSup 331. Sheffield: Sheffield Academic Press.

Mazar, Benjamin

1960 "The Cities of the Priests and the Levites." Pages 193–205 in *Congress Volume, Oxford 1959*. Edited by G. W. Anderson et al. VTSup 7. Leiden: Brill.

1963a "David's Reign in Hebron and the Conquest of Jerusalem." Pages 235–44 in *In the time of Harvest: Essays in Honor of A. H. Silver*. Edited by D. J. Silver. Repr. pages 78–87 in *Biblical Israel: State and People*, by Benjamin Mazar. Jerusalem: Israel Exploration Society, 1992.

1963b "The Military Elite of King David." *VT* 13: 310–20. Repr. pages 83–103 in Benjamin Mazar (1986).

1965 "The Sanctuary of Arad and the Family of Hobab the Kenite." *JNES* 24: 297–303.

1975 *The Mountain of the Lord*. Garden City: Doubleday.

1986 *The Early Biblical Period: Historical Studies*. Jerusalem: Israel Exploration Society.

Mazar, Eilat

1994 "The Royal Quarter of Biblical Jerusalem: The Ophel." Pages 64–72 in Geva (1994).

Mazor, L.
1994 "The Septuagint Translation of the Book of Joshua." *BIOSCS* 27: 29–38.
McCarter, P. Kyle
1980a "The Apology of David." *JBL* 90: 489–504.
1980b *I Samuel*. AB 8. Garden City: Doubleday.
1983 "The Ritual Dedication of the City of David in 2 Samuel 6." Pages 273–77 in Meyers and O'Connor (1983).
1984 *II Samuel*. AB 9. Garden City: Doubleday.
1986 *Textual Criticism: Recovering the Text of the Hebrew Bible*. GBS. Philadelphia: Fortress.
McCarthy, Carmel
1985 "The Davidic Genealogy in the Book of Ruth." PIBA 9: 53–62.
McCarthy, Dennis J.
1965a "Notes on the Love of God in Deuteronomy and the Father-Son Relationship between Yahweh and Israel." *CBQ* 27: 144–47.
1965b "II Samuel 7 and the Structure of the Deuteronomic History." *JBL* 84: 131–38.
1971 "An Installation Genre?" *JBL* 90: 31–41.
1981 *Treaty and Covenant*. AnBib 21A. New ed. Rome: Pontifical Biblical Institute.
1982a "Compact and Royal Ideology: Stimuli for Covenant Thinking." Pages 75–90 in Ishida (1982).
1982b "Covenant and Law in Chronicles-Nehemiah." *CBQ* 44: 25–44.
McConville, J. Gordon
1986a "1 Chronicles 28: 9: Yahweh 'Seeks Out' Solomon." *JTS* 37: 105–8.
1986b "Ezra-Nehemiah and the Fulfillment of Prophecy." *VT* 36: 205–24.
McEwan, Gilbert J. P.
1981 *Priest and Temple in Hellenistic Babylonia*. Freiburger altorientalische Studien 4. Wiesbaden: Franz Steiner.
McIvor, J. Stanley
1994 *The Targum of Chronicles*. ArBib 19. Collegeville, Minn.: Liturgical Press.
McKenzie, Steven Linn
1985 *The Chronicler's Use of the Deuteronomistic History*. HSM 33. Atlanta: Scholars Press.
1999a "The Chronicler as Redactor." Pages 70–90 in Graham and McKenzie (1999).
1999b "Why Didn't David Build the Temple?: The History of a Biblical Tradition." Pages 204–24 in Graham, Marrs, and McKenzie (1999).
McKenzie, Steven Linn, and M. P. Graham
1994 Eds. *The History of Israel's Traditions: The Heritage of Martin Noth*. JSOTSup 182. Sheffield: Sheffield Academic Press.

McKenzie, Steven Linn, and Thomas Römer
2000 *Rethinking the Foundations: Historiography in the Ancient World and in the Bible. Essays in Honour of John Van Seters.* BZAW 294. Berlin: de Gruyter.
Meade, D. G.
1987 *Pseudonymity and Canon.* Grand Rapids: Eerdmans.
Meeks, Theophile James
1929 "Aaronites and Zadokites." *AJSL* 45: 149–66.
Meier, Samuel A.
1984 "Temple Plundering in the Book of Kings." Unpublished paper.
1988 *The Messenger in the Ancient Semitic World.* HSM 45. Atlanta: Scholars Press.
Mendelsohn, I.
1940a "Guilds in Ancient Palestine." *BASOR* 80: 17–21.
1940b "Guilds in Babylonia and Assyria." *JAOS* 60: 68–72.
Mendenhall, George E.
1958 "The Census Lists of Numbers 1 and 26." *JBL* 77: 52–66.
1973 *The Tenth Generation: The Origins of the Biblical Tradition.* Baltimore: The Johns Hopkins University Press.
Merkelbach, R., and M. L. West
1967 *Fragmenta Hesiodea.* Oxford: Clarendon Press.
Meshorer, Yaʿaḳov
1982 *Ancient Jewish Coinage.* Dix Hills, N. Y.: Amphora.
Meshorer, Yaʿaḳov, and Shraga Qedar
1991 *The Coinage of Samaria in the Fourth Century B.C.E.* Beverly Hills: Numismatics Fine Arts International.
1999 *Samarian Coinage.* Numismatics Studies and Researches 9. Jerusalem: Israel Numismatics Society.
Mettinger, Tryggve N. D.
1971 *Solomonic State Officials: A Study of the Civil Government Officials of the Israelite Monarchy.* ConBOT 5. Lund: Gleerup.
1976 *King and Messiah: The Civil and Sacral Legitimation of the Israelite Kings.* ConBOT 8. Lund: Gleerup.
1982 *The Dethronement of Sebaoth: Studies in the Shem and Kabod Theologies.* ConBOT 18. Lund: Gleerup.
Meyer, Eduard
1896 *Die Enstehung des Judentums: Eine historische Untersuchung.* Halle Repr., Hildesheim: G. Olms, 1965.
1906 *Die Israeliten und ihre Nachbarstämme.* Halle.
Meyers, Carol L.
1992 "Jerusalem Temple." *ABD* 6: 350–69.
1997 "מנורה; *mᵉnôrâ.*" *TDOT* 8: 401–6.
1999 "Guilds and Gatherings: Women's Groups in Ancient Israel." Pages 154–84 in Williams and Hiebert (1999).
Meyers, Carol L., and M. O'Connor
1983 Eds. *The Word of the Lord Shall Go Forth: Essays in Honor of David*

Noel Freedman in Celebration of His Sixtieth Birthday. Winona Lake, Ind.: Eisenbrauns.

Meyers, Eric M.

1985 "The Shelomith Seal and the Judean Restoration: Some Additional Considerations." *ErIsr* 18: 33–38.

Michaeli, Frank

1967 *Les Livres des Chroniques, d'Esdras, et de Néhémie.* CAT 16. Neuchâtel: Delachaux & Nestlé.

Michalowski, Piotr

1983 "History as Charter: Some Observations on the Sumerian King List." *JAOS* 103: 237–48.

Micheel, Rosemarie

1983 *Die Seher- und Prophetenüberlieferungen in der Chronik.* BBET 18. Frankfurt am Main: Lang.

Mildenberg, Leo

1979 "Yehud: A Preliminary Study of the Provincial Coinage of Judaea." Pages 183–96 in *Greek Numismatics and Archaeology: Essays in Honor of Margaret Thompson.* Edited by O. Mørkholm and N. M. Waggoner. Wetteren: NR.

1998 *Vestigia Leonis: Studien zur antiken Numismatik Israels, Palästinas und der östlichen Mittelmeerwelt.* Göttingen: Vandenhoeck & Ruprecht.

Milgrom, Jacob

1970 *Studies in Levitical Terminology, I.* Near Eastern Studies 14. Berkeley: University of California.

1976 *Cult and Conscience: The Asham and the Priestly Doctrine of Repentance.* SJLA 18. Leiden: Brill.

1982 "The Levitic Town: An Exercise in Realistic Planning." Pages 185–88 in Vermes and Neusner (1982).

1990 *Numbers.* The JPS Torah Commentary. Philadelphia: Jewish Publication Society.

1991 *Leviticus 1–16.* AB 3. Garden City: Doubleday.

Millard, Alan

1991 "Large Numbers in the Assyrian Royal Inscriptions." Pages 213–22 in Cogan and Ephʿal (1991).

1995 "The Knowledge of Writing in Iron Age Palestine." *TynBul* 46: 207–17.

1999 "Owners and Users of Hebrew Seals." Pages 129*–33* in Levine et al. (1999).

Millard, Alan, J. Hoffmeier, and D. W. Baker

1994 Eds. *Faith, Tradition, and History: Old Testament Historiography in Its Near Eastern Context.* Winona Lake, Ind.: Eisenbrauns.

Miller, James Maxwell

1970 "The Korahites of Southern Judah." *CBQ* 32: 58–68.

1976 *The Old Testament and the Historian.* Philadelphia: Fortress.

1987 "Rehoboam's Cities of Defense and the Levitical City List." Pages 273–86 in Perdue, Toombs, and Johnson (1987).

1989 "The Israelite Journey through (around) Moab." *JBL* 108: 577–95.
1992 "Early Monarchy in Moab?" Pages 77–91 in Bienkowski (1992).
1999 "Notes on Benjaminite Place Names." *JNSL* 25: 61–73.

Miller, James Maxwell, and John H. Hayes
1986 *A History of Ancient Israel and Judah.* Philadelphia: Westminster.

Miller, Patrick D.
1970 "Animal Names as Designations in Ugaritic and Hebrew." *UF* 2: 177–86.
1994 *They Cried to the Lord: The Form and Theology of Biblical Prayer.* Minneapolis: Fortress.

Miller, Patrick D., Paul D. Hanson, and S. Dean McBride
1987 Eds. *Ancient Israelite Religion: Essays in Honor of Frank Moore Cross.* Philadelphia: Fortress.

Miller, Patrick D., and J. J. M. Roberts
1977 *The Hand of the Lord: A Reassessment of the "Ark Narrative" of I Samuel.* Baltimore: Johns Hopkins University Press.

Mitchell, Christine
1999 "The Dialogism of Chronicles." Pages 311–26 in Graham and McKenzie (1999).

Mittmann, Siegfried
1995 "Die Gebietsbeschreibung des Stammes Ruben in Josua 13, 15–23." *ZDPV* 111: 1–27.

Möhlenbrink, Kurt
1934 "Die levitischen Überlieferungen des Alten Testaments." ZAW N.S. 11: 184–231.

Momigliano, Arnaldo
1978 "Greek Historiography." *History and Theory* 17: 1–28.

Montgomery, James A. (and H. S. Gehman)
1951 *A Critical Commentary on the Books of Kings.* ICC. Edinburgh: T & T Clark.

Moore, Carey A.
1985 *Judith.* AB 40. Garden City: Doubleday

Moran, William L.
1963 "The Ancient Near Eastern Background of the Love of God in Deuteronomy." *CBQ* 25: 77–87.
1992 *The El Amarna Letters.* Baltimore: Johns Hopkins University Press.

Mosis, Rudolph
1973 *Untersuchungen zur Theologie des chronistischen Geschichtswerkes.* Freiburg: Herder.
1990 "יָחַשׂ *yāhaś*; יַחַשׂ." *TDOT* 6: 55–59.

Mosshammer, Alden A.
1979 *The Chronicle of Eusebius and Greek Chronographic Tradition.* Lewisburg: Bucknell University Press.

Movers, Frank Karl
1834 *Kritische Untersuchungen über die biblische Chronik: Ein Beitrag zur Einleitung in das alte Testament.* Bonn: T. Habicht.

Mowinckel, Sigmund
1954 *He That Cometh*. New York: Abingdon.
1960 "Erwägungen zum chronistischen Geschichtswerk." *TLZ* 85: 1–8.
1962 *The Psalms in Israel's Worship*. 2 vols. Oxford: Blackwell.
1964 *Die Nachchronistische Redaktion des Buches: Die Listen*. Vol. 1 of *Studien zu dem Buche Ezra-Nehemia*. Oslo: Universitetsforlaget.

Muffs, Yochanan
1969 *Studies in the Aramaic Legal Papyri from Elephantine*. Leiden: Brill.
1979 "Love and Joy as Metaphors of Volition in Hebrew and Related Literatures, Part 2: The Joy of Giving." *JANES* 11: 97–111.
1992 *Love and Joy: Law, Language, and Religion in Ancient Israel*. Cambridge, Mass.: Harvard University Press.

Mulder, Martin J.
1975 "1 Chronik 7, 21b–23 und die Rabbinische Tradition." *JSJ* 6: 141–66.
1988 "The Transmission of the Biblical Text." Pages 87–135 in *Mikra, Text Translation Reading and Interpretation of the Hebrew Bible in Ancient Judaism and Early Christianity*. Edited by Martin J. Mulder. CRINT 2/1. Philadelphia: Fortress.

Mullen, E. Theodore
1980 *The Divine Council in Canaanite and Hebrew Literature*. HSM 24. Chico, Calif.: Scholars Press.
1992 "Crime and Punishment: The Sins of the King and the Despoliation of the Treasuries." *CBQ* 54: 231–48.

Müller, W. W.
1992 "Seba." *ABD* 5: 1064

Muraoka, Takamitsu
1985 *Emphatic Words and Structures in Biblical Hebrew*. Leiden: Brill.

Murray, Donald F.
1990 "*MQWM* and the Future of Israel in 2 Samuel VII 10." *VT* 40: 298–320.
2001 "Under YHWH's Veto: David as Shedder of Blood in Chronicles." *Bib* 82: 457–76.

Mussies, G.
1986 "Parallels to Matthew's Version of the Pedigree of Jesus." *NovT* 28: 32–47.

Myers, Jacob M.
1965a *I Chronicles*. AB 12. Garden City: Doubleday.
1965b *II Chronicles*. AB 13. Garden City: Doubleday.
1966 "The Kerygma of the Chronicler." *Int* 20: 259–73.
1974 *I and II Esdras*. AB 42. Garden City: Doubleday.

Na'aman, Nadav
1980a "The Inheritance of the Sons of Simeon." *TA* 96: 136–52.
1980b "The Shihor of Egypt and Shur That Is before Egypt." *TA* 7: 95–109.
1986a *Borders and Districts in Biblical Historiography*. Jerusalem Biblical Studies 4. Jerusalem: Simor.

1986b "Hezekiah's Fortified Cities and the *LMLK* Stamps." *BASOR* 261: 5–21.

1988a "The Date of 2 Chronicles 11: 5–10: Reply to Y. Garfinkel." *BASOR* 271: 74–77.

1988b "The List of David's Officers (*Šālîšîm*)." *VT* 38: 71–79.

1991a "The Kingdom of Judah under Josiah." *TA* 2: 3–69.

1991b "Sources and Redaction in the Chronicler's Genealogies of Asher and Ephraim." *JSOT* 49: 99–111.

1995a "The Deuteronomist and Voluntary Servitude to Foreign Powers." *JSOT* 65: 37–53.

1995b "Rezin of Damascus and the Land of Gilead." *ZDPV* 111: 105–17.

1999 "Lebo-Hamath, Şubat-Hamath, and the Northern Boundary of the Land of Canaan." *UF* 31: 417–41.

Najjar, Mohammed

1999 " 'Ammonite' Monumental Architecture." Pages 103–12 in MacDonald and Younker (1999).

Naveh, Joseph

1998 "Scripts and Inscriptions in Ancient Samaria." *IEJ* 48: 91–100.

Nelson, Richard D.

1997 *Joshua.* OTL. Louisville, Ky.: Westminster John Knox.

Nestle, Eberhard

1893 *Marginalien und Materialien.* Tübingen: Heckenhauer.

Neusner, Jacob

1988 *From Testament to Torah.* Englewood Cliffs, N. J.: Prentice-Hall.

Newsome, James Dupre

1975 "Toward an Understanding of the Chronicler and His Purposes." *JBL* 94: 201–17.

Nickelsburg, George W. E.

1984 "The Bible Rewritten and Expanded." Pages 89–156 in Stone (1984).

Niehr, Herbert

1999 "Religio-Historical Aspects of the 'Early Post-Exilic' Period." Pages 228–44 in Becking and Korpel (1999).

Nielsen, Flemming A. J.

1997 *The Tragedy in History: Herodotus and the Deuteronomistic History.* JSOTSup 251. Copenhagen International Seminar 4. Sheffield: Sheffield Academic Press.

Nielsen, Kristen

1999 "Whose Song of Praise? Reflections on the Purpose of the Psalm in 1 Chronicles 16." Pages 327–36 in Graham and McKenzie (1999).

Niemann, Hermann Michael

1973 "The Two Genealogies of Japhet." Pages 119–26 in Hoffner (1973).

1985 *Die Daniten: Studien zur Geschichte eines altisraelitischen Stammes.* FRLANT 135. Göttingen: Vandenhoeck & Ruprecht.

1999 "Zorah, Eshtaol, Beth-Shemesh, and Dan's Migration to the South: A

Region and Its Traditions in the Late Bronze and Iron Ages." *JSOT* 86: 25–48.

1997 The Socio-Political Shadow Cast by the Biblical Solomon. Pages 252–95 in Handy (1997).

Niemeier, Wolf-Dietrich

2001 "Archaic Greeks in the Orient: Textual and Archaeological Evidence." *BASOR* 322: 33–42.

Nihan, Christophe, and Thomas Römer

1999 "Une source commune aux récits de Rois et Chroniques?" *ETR* 74: 415–22.

Noble, Joseph S.

1943 "The Syriac Version to the Books of Chronicles." Thesis, Yeshiva University.

Noegel, Scott

1998 "The Aegean Ogygos of Boeotia and the Biblical Og of Bashan: Reflections of the Same Myth." ZAW 110: 411–26.

Noordtzij, Arie

1937 *De Boeken der Kronieken, Erste Deel: 1 Kronieken 1–29*. Korte Verklaring der Heilige Schrift. Kampen: J. H. Kok.

1940 "Les intentions du Chroniste." *RB* 49: 369–81.

1951 *De Boeken Ezra en Nehemia.* Korte Verklaring der Heilige Schrift. Kampen: J. H. Kok.

North, Robert Grady

1963 "Theology of the Chronicler." *JBL* 82: 369–81.

1974 "Does Archaeology Prove Chronicles' Sources?" Pages 375–401 in *A Light unto My Path: Old Testament Studies in Honor of Jacob M. Myer.* Edited by H. N. Bream, R. D. Heim, and C. A. Moore. Philadelphia: Temple University Press.

1990 "The Chronicler: 1–2 Chronicles, Ezra, Nehemiah." *NJBC* 362–98.

Noth, Martin

1928 *Die israelitischen Personennamen im Rahmen der gemeinsemitischen Namengebung.* Stuttgart: Kohlhammer.

1930 *Das System der zwölf Stämme Israels.* BWANT 4/1. Stuttgart: Kohlhammer.

1932 "Eine siedlungsgeographische Liste in 1. Chr. 2 und 4." *ZDPV* 55: 98–124.

1934 "Die Ansiedlung des Stammes Juda auf dem Boden Palästinas." *PJB* 30: 31–47.

1935 "Zur historischen Geographie Süd-Judas." *JPOS* 15: 35–50.

1943 *Überlieferungsgeschichtliche Studien: Die sammelnden und bearbeitenden Geschichtswerke im Alten Testament.* Tübingen: Max Niemeyer.

1953 *Das Buch Josua.* 2nd ed. HAT 1/7. Tübingen: Mohr.

1957 *Überlieferungsgeschichtliche Studien: Die sammelnden und bearbeitenden Geschichtswerke im Alten Testament.* 2nd ed. Tübingen: Max Niemeyer. Noth 1981a, 1987, and 1991 are English translations of parts of this work.

1960 *The History of Israel*. 2nd ed. London: A. & C. Black.
1968 *Könige*. BKAT 9/1. Neukirchen-Vluyn: Neukirchener Verlag.
1971 *Aufsätze zur biblische Landes- und Altertumskunde*. 2 vols. Edited by H. W. Wolff. Neukirchen-Vluyn: Neukirchener Verlag.
1981a *The Deuteronomistic History*. JSOTSup 15. Sheffield: JSOT Press.
1981b *A History of Pentateuchal Traditions*. Chico, Calif.: Scholars Press.
1987 *The Chronicler's History*. JSOTSup 50. Sheffield: JSOT Press.
1991 *The Deuteronomistic History*. 2nd ed. JSOTSup 15. Sheffield: JSOT Press.

Nunn, Astrid
2000 *Der figürliche Motivschatz Phöniziens, Syriens, und Transjordaniens vom 6. bis zum 4. Jahrhundert v. Chr.* OBO Series Archaeologica 18. Freiburg: Vandenhoeck & Ruprecht.

Nurmela, Risto
1998 *The Levites: Their Emergence as a Second-Class Priesthood*. SFSHJ 193. Atlanta: Scholars Press.

O'Brien, Julia M.
1990 *Priest and Levite in Malachi*. SBLDS 121. Atlanta: Scholars Press.

O'Connell, Kevin G.
1984 "The List of Seven Peoples in Canaan: A Fresh Analysis." Pages 221–41 in *The Answers Lie Below: Essays in Honor of Lawrence Edmund Toombs*. Edited by H. O. Thompson. Lanham, Md.: University Press of America.

O'Connor, David
1995 "The Social and Economic Organization of Ancient Egyptian Temples." *CANE* 319–29.

Oeming, Manfred
1990 *Das wahre Israel: Die 'genealogische Vorhalle' 1 Chronik 1–9*. BWANT 128. Stuttgart: Kohlhammer.
1994 "Die Eroberung Jerusalems durch David in deuteronomisticher und chronistischer Darstellung (II Sam 5, 6 und 1 Chr 11, 4–8): Ein Beitrag zur *narrativen Theologie* de beiden Geschichtswerke." ZAW 106: 404–20.

Oesterly, W. O. E.
1959 *The Psalms*. London: SPCK

Oettli, Samuel
1889 *Die Bücher der Chronik, Esra, und Nehemia*. Kurzgefasster Kommentar zu den heiligen Schriften des Alten und Neuen Testamentes A, 8. Edited by D. H. Strack and D. O. Zöckler. Nördlingen: Beck.

Ofer, Avi
1993a "The Highland of Judah during the Biblical Period" (Hebrew with English summary). Ph.D. diss., Tel Aviv University.
1993b "Judean Hills Survey." *NEAEHL* 3: 814–16.
1997 "Judah." *OEANE* 3: 253–57.
2001 "The Monarchic Period in the Judean Highland." Pages 14–37 in Amihai Mazar (2001).

Olávarri-Goicoechea, Emilio
1993 "Aroer." *NEAEHL* 1: 92–93.
Olmstead, Albert Ten Eyck
1948 *History of the Persian Empire.* Chicago: University of Chicago Press.
Olyan, Saul M.
1982 "Zadok's Origins and the Tribal Politics of David." *JBL* 101: 177–93.
1985 "2 Kings 9: 31: Jehu as Omri." *HTR* 78: 203–7.
1996a "Honor, Shame, and Covenant Relations in Ancient Israel and Its Environment." *JBL* 115: 201–18.
1996b "Why an Altar of Finished Stones? Some Thoughts on Ex 20, 25 and Dtn 27, 5–6." *ZAW* 108: 161–71.
1997 "Cult." *OEANE* 2: 79–86.
1998 "Anyone Blind or Lame Shall Not Enter the House." *CBQ* 60: 218–27.
Oppenheim, A. Leo
1961 "The Mesopotamian Temple." *BAR* 1: 158–69.
1969 "Babylonian and Assyrian Historical Texts." *ANET* 265–317, 556–67.
1977 *Ancient Mesopotamia: Portrait of a Dead Civilization.* Rev. ed. by Erica Reiner. Chicago: University of Chicago Press.
Oren, Eliezer D.
1993 "Tel Seraʿ." *NEAEHL* 3: 1329–35. Edited by E. Stern et al. Jerusalem: Israel Exploration Society. New York: Simon & Schuster.
Oren, Eliezer D. and E. Netzer
1974 "Tell Seraʿ (Tell esh-Shariʿa)." *IEJ* 24: 265.
Orlinsky, Harry M.
1941 "On the Present State of Proto-Septuagint Studies." *JAOS* 61: 81–91.
1969 *Notes on the New Translation of the Torah.* Philadelphia: Jewish Publication Society.
1974 *Essays in Biblical Culture and Bible Translation.* New York: KTAV.
Osborne, William L.
1979 "The Genealogies of 1 Chronicles 1–9." Ph.D. diss., Dropsie University.
Otten, H.
1958 "Die altassyrischen Texte aus Boğazköy." *MDOG* 91.
Parker, Simon
1997 *Stories in Scripture and Inscriptions.* New York: Oxford University Press.
Parker, Simon et al.
1992 *Ugaritic Narrative Poetry.* SBLWAW 9. Atlanta: Scholars Press.
Parpola, Simo
1970 *Neo-Assyrian Toponyms.* AOAT 6. Neukirchen-Vluyn: Neukirchener Verlag.
1995 "The Assyrian Cabinet." Pages 379–401 in *Vom Alten Orient zum Alten Testament: Festschrift für Wolfram Freiherrn von Soden.* Edited by M. Dietrich and O. Lorenz. AOAT 240. Neukirchen-Vluyn: Neukirchener Verlag.

Patton, Corrine

1995 "Psalm 132: A Methodological Inquiry." *CBQ* 57: 643–54.

Paul, Shalom M.

1979–80 "Adoption Formulae: A Study of Cuneiform and Biblical Legal Clauses." *Maarav* 2: 173–85.

1991 *Amos*. Hermeneia. Philadelphia: Fortress.

Pavloský, A.

1957 "Die Chronologie der Tätigkeit Esdras: Versuch einer neuen Lösung (I)." *Bib* 38: 275–305.

Payne, J. Barton

1978 "Validity of Numbers in Chronicles." *Near East Archaeological Society Bulletin* 11: 5–58.

Pearce, Laurie E.

1995 "The Scribes and Scholars of Ancient Mesopotamia." *CANE* 2265–78.

Pearson, Lionel I. C.

1939 *Early Ionian Historians*. Oxford: Clarendon Press.

Peckham, J. B.

1968 "Notes on a Fifth-Century Phoenician Inscription from Kition, Cyprus (*CIS* 86)." *Or* 37: 304–24.

Pedersen, Johannes

1940 *Israel: Its Life and Culture*. London: Oxford University Press. Repr., SFSHJ 28. Atlanta: Scholars Press, 1991.

Peltonen, Kai

1996 *History Debated: The Historical Reliability of Chronicles in Pre-Critical and Critical Research*. 2 vols. Publications of the Finnish Exegetical Society 64. Helsinki: The Finnish Exegetical Society.

1999 "Function, Explanation and Literary Phenomena: Aspects of Source Criticism as Theory and Method in the History of Chronicles Research." Pages 18–69 in Graham and McKenzie (ed.).

2001 "A Jigsaw without a Model? The Date of Chronicles." Pages 225–71 in Grabbe (ed.).

Perdue, Leo G., Lawrence E. Toombs, and Gary L. Johnson

1987 Eds. *Archaeology and Biblical Interpretation: Essays in Memory of D. Glenn Rose*. Atlanta: John Knox.

Perles, Felix

1895 *Analekten zur Textkritik des Alten Testaments*. Munich: Ackermann.

Petersen, David L.

1977 *Late Israelite Prophecy: Studies in Deutero-Prophetic Literature and in Chronicles*. SBLMS 23. Missoula, Mont.: Scholars Press.

1991a "Israelite Prophecy: Change versus Continuity." Pages 190–203 in Emerton (1991).

1991b "The Temple in Persian Period Prophetic Texts." Pages 125–44 in Philip Davies (1991).

Pfeiffer, Robert H.
1948 *Introduction to the Old Testament*. 2nd ed. New York: Harper & Brothers.

Pietersma, Albert
2001 "Exegesis and Liturgy in the Superscriptions of the Greek Psalter." Pages 99–137 in *X Congress of the International Organization for Septuagint and Cognate Studies, Oslo, 1998*. Edited by Bernard A. Taylor. SBLSCS 51. Atlanta: Society of Biblical Literature.

Pietersma, Albert, and Claude Cox
1984 Eds. *De Septuaginta: Studies in Honour of John William Wevers on His Sixty-fifth Birthday*. Mississauga, Ont.: Benben.

Pitard, Wayne T.
1987 *Ancient Damascus: A Historical Study of the Syrian City-State from Earliest Times until Its Fall to the Assyrians in 732 B.C.E.* Winona Lake, Ind.: Eisenbrauns.

Plöger, Otto
1957 "Reden und Gebete im deuteronomistischen und chronistischen Geschichtswerk." Pages 35–49 in *Festchrift für Günther Dehn zum 75. Geburtstag*. Edited by W. Schneemelcher. Neukirchen-Vluyn: Neukirchener Verlag. Trans. and repr. pages 31–46 in Knoppers and McConville (2000).
1968 *Theocracy and Eschatology*. Oxford: Blackwell.

Podechard, E.
1916 "Le premier chapître des Paralipomènes." *RB* 13: 363–86.

Pohlmann, Karl-Friedrich
1970 *Studien zum dritten Esra: Ein Beiträg zur Frage nach dem ursprunglichen Schluss des chronistischen Geschichtswerkes*. FRLANT 104. Göttingen: Vandenhoeck & Ruprecht.
1978 *Studien zum Jeremiabuch: Ein Beiträg zur Frage nach der Enstehung des Jeremiabuches*. FRLANT 118. Göttingen: Vandenhoeck & Ruprecht.
1979 "Erwägungen zum Schlußkapitel des deuteronomistischen Geschichtswerkes: Oder Warum wird der Prophet Jeremia in 2. Kön. 22–25 nicht erwähnt?" Pages 94–109 in *Textgemäß: Aufsätze und Beiträge zur Hermeneutik des alten Testaments*. Edited by A. Gunneweg and O. Kaiser. Göttingen: Vandenhoeck & Ruprecht.
1991 "Zur Frage von Korrespondenzen und Divergenzen zwischen den Chronikbüchern und dem Esra/Nehemia-Buch." Pages 314–30 in Emerton (1991).

Polzin, Robert
1976 *Late Biblical Hebrew: Toward an Historical Typology of Biblical Hebrew Prose*. HSM 12. Missoula, Mont.: Scholars Press.

Pomykala, Ken E.
1995 *The Davidic Dynasty Tradition in Early Judaism*. Atlanta: Scholars Press.

Poorthuis, M., and Chana Safrai
1996 Eds. *The Centrality of Jerusalem*. Kampen: Kok Pharos.

Pope, Marvin H.

1977a "Notes on the *Rephaim* Texts." Pages 163–81 in *Essays on the Ancient Near East in Memory of Jacob Joel Finkelstein.* Edited by M. de Jong Ellis. Memoirs of the Connecticut Academy of Arts and Sciences 19. Hamden, Conn. : Archon.

1977b *Song of Songs.* AB 7C. Garden City: Doubleday.

Porten, Bezalel

1968 *Archives from Elephantine.* Berkeley: University of California Press.

1984 "The Jews in Egypt." *CHJ* 372–400.

Porten, Bezalel, and Jonas C. Greenfield

1984 *Jews of Elephantine and Arameans of Syene: Aramaic Texts with Translation.* Jerusalem: The Hebrew University.

Porten, Bezalel et al.

1996 *The Elephantine Papyri in English: Three Millennia of Cross-Cultural Continuity and Change.* Leiden: Brill.

Porter, J. Roy

1963 Anticipation of Subject and Object in Biblical Hebrew. JTS 14: 371–74.

1970 "The Succession of Joshua." Pages 102–32 in *Proclamation and Presence: Old Testament Essays in Honor of Gwynne Henton Davies.* Edited by J. I. Durham and J. R. Porter. Richmond, Va.: John Knox. Repr. pages 139–62 in Knoppers and McConville (2000).

Postgate, J. Nicholas

1994a *Early Mesopotamia: Society and Economy at the Dawn of History.* London: Routledge.

1994b "The Ownership and Exploitation of Land in Assyria in the 1st Millennium B.C." Pages 141–52 in *Reflets des deux fleuves: Volume de mélanges offerts à André Finet.* Akkadica Supplementum 6. Edited by M. Lebeau and P. Talon. Leuven: Peeters.

Pratt, Richard Linwood

1987 "Royal Prayer and the Chronicler's Program." PhD. diss., Harvard Divinity School.

Priest, J.

1983 "Testament of Moses." *OTP* 1: 919–34.

Pritchett, William Kendrick

1974– *The Greek State at War.* Parts 1–4. Berkeley: University of California Press.

Propp, William H. C.

1998 *Exodus 1–18.* AB 2. New York: Doubleday.

Puech, Émile

1986 "The Tell el-Fûl Inscription and the *Nĕtînîm.*" *BASOR* 261: 69–72.

1992 "La pierre de Sion et l'autel des holocaustes d'après un manuscrit hébreu de la grotte 4 (4Q522) (*Planche XIX*)." *RB* 99: 676–96.

1997 "Fragments du plus ancien exemplaire du Rouleau du Temple (4Q524)." Pages 19–64 in *Legal Texts and Legal Issues.* Edited by M.

F. Bernstein, F. García Martínez, and J. Kampen. *STDJ* 23. Leiden: Brill.

1998 *Qumrân Grotte 4 (XVIII) Textes Hébreux (4Q521–4Q528, 4Q576–579)*. DJD 25. Oxford: Clarendon Press.

Purvis, James D.

1968 *The Samaritan Pentateuch and the Origins of the Samaritan Sect*. HSM 2. Cambridge: Harvard University Press.

1981 "The Samaritan Problem: A Case Study in Jewish Sectarianism in the Roman Era." Pages 323–50 in Halpern and Levenson (1981).

1988 "Exile and Return." Pages 151–75 in Shanks (1988).

de Pury, Albert, T. Römer, and J.-D. Macchi

1996 Eds. *Israël construit son histoire: L'historiographie deutéronomiste à la lumière des recherches récentes*. *MdB* 34. Geneva: Labor et Fides.

Qimron, Elisha

1994 "Concerning the 'Joshua Cycle' from Qumran" (in Hebrew) *Tarbiz* 68: 503–8.

Qimron, Elisha, et al.

1994 *Miqṣat Maʿaśe Ha-Torah*. Vol. 5 of *Qumran Cave 4*. DJD 10. Oxford: Clarendon Press.

Rabinowitz, Isaac

1956 "Aramaic Inscriptions of the Fifth Century B.C.E. from a North-Arab Shrine in Egypt." *JNES* 15: 1–9.

Rabinowitz, Jacob J.

1955 "A Clue to the Nabatean Contract from the Dead Sea Region." *BASOR* 139: 11–14.

von Rad, Gerhard

1930 *Das Geschichtsbild des chronistischen Werkes*. Stuttgart: Kohlhammer.

1947 "Das judäische Königsritual." *TLZ* 72/4: 211–16.

1951 *Der heilige Krieg im alten Israel*. Zurich: Zwingli. Von Rad 1991 is the English translation of this work.

1953 *Studies in Deuteronomy*. SBT 9. London: SCM.

1962a *Genesis*. Rev. ed. OTL. Philadelphia: Westminster.

1962b *Old Testament Theology*. Vol. 1. New York: Harper & Row.

1966a *Deuteronomy*. OTL. Philadelphia: Westminster.

1966b *The Problem of the Hexateuch and Other Essays*. New York: McGraw-Hill.

1991 *Holy War in Ancient Israel*. Grand Rapids: Eerdmans.

Rainey, Anson F.

1962 "The Social Stratification of Ugarit." Ph.D. diss., Brandeis University.

1975a "The Identification of Philistine Gath: A Problem in Source Analysis for Historical Geography." *ErIsr* 12: 63*–76*.

1975b "Institutions: Family, Civil, and Military." Pages 71–107 in *Ras Shamra Parallels: The Texts from Ugarit and the Hebrew Bible*. Vol. 2. Edited by L. R. Fisher. AnOr 50. Rome: Pontifical Biblical Institute.

1983 "The Biblical Shephelah of Judah." *BASOR* 251: 1–22.

1997 "The Chronicler and His Sources: Historical and Geographical." Pages 30–72 in Graham, Hoglund, and McKenzie (1997).

Redford, Donald B.

1970 *A Study of the Biblical Story of Joseph.* VTSup 20. Leiden: Brill.

1972 "Studies in Relations between Palestine and Egypt during the First Millennium B.C." Pages 141–56 in *Studies on the Ancient Palestinian World.* Edited by J. W. Wevers and D. B. Redford. Toronto: University of Toronto Press.

1986 *Pharaonic King-Lists, Annals, and Day-Books.* SSEA 4. Mississauga, Ont.: Benben.

1992 *Egypt, Canaan, and Israel in Ancient Times.* Princeton: Princeton University Press.

1995 "Ancient Egyptian Literature: An Overview." *CANE* 4: 2223–41.

Rehm, Martin

1937 *Textkritische Untersuchungen zu den Parallelstellen der Samuel-Königsbücher und der Chronik.* Alttestamentliche Abhandlungen 13/3. Münster: Aschendorff.

1954 *Die Bücher der Chronik.* EB. Würzburg: Echter.

Rendsburg, Gary A.

1980 "Late Biblical Hebrew and the Date of 'P.' " *JANES* 12: 65–80.

1987 "Gen 10: 13–14: An Authentic Hebrew Tradition concerning the Origin of the Philistines." *JNSL* 13: 89–96.

1990a "The Internal Consistency and Historical Reliability of the Biblical Genealogies." *VT* 40: 185–206.

1990b *Linguistic Evidence for the Northern Origin of Selected Psalms.* SBLMS 43. Atlanta: Scholars Press.

Rendtorff, Rolf

1986 *The Old Testament: An Introduction.* Philadelphia: Fortress.

1992 "Some Reflections on Creation as a Topic of Old Testament Theology." Pages 204–12 in Ulrich, Wright, et al. (1992).

Renger, Johannes

1975 "Örtliche und zeitliche Differenzen in der Struktur de Priesterschaft babylonischer Tempel." Pages 108–15 in *Le Temple et le Culte: compte rendu de la vingtième recontre assyriologique Internationale.* Edited by E. Van Donzel et al. Leiden: Nederlands Instituut voor het Nabje Oosten.

Revell, E. J.

1969 "A New Biblical Fragment with Palestinian Vocalization." *Text* 7: 59–75.

Richter, Wolfgang

1963 *Traditionsgeschichtliche Untersuchungen zum Richterbuch.* BBB 18. Bonn: Peter Hanstein.

1965 "Die *nagid*-Formel." *BZ* 9: 71–84.

Riemschneider, Kaspar K.

1958 "Die hethitischen Landschenkungsurkunden." *MIOF* 6: 330–76.

Riley, William
1993 *King and Cultus in Chronicles: Worship and the Reinterpretation of History*. JSOTSup 160. Sheffield: JSOT Press.

Ringgren, Helmer
1986 "טהר; *ṭāhar*." *TDOT* 5: 287–96.

Rivkin, Ellis
1976 "Aaron, Aaronides." *IDBSup* 1–3.

Roberts, J. J. M.
1991 *Nahum, Habakkuk, and Zephaniah*. OTL. Louisville, Ky.: Westminster/John Knox.
1997 "Whose Child Is This? Reflections on the Speaking Voice in Isaiah 9: 5." *HTR* 90: 115–29.

Robertson, John F.
1995 "The Social and Economic Organization of Ancient Mesopotamian Temples." *CANE* 1: 443–54.

Rofé, Alexander
1982 "The End of the Book of Joshua according to the Septuagint." *Hen* 4: 17–36.
1985 "Joshua 20: Historico-Literary Criticism Illustrated." Pages 131–47 in Tigay (1985).
1990 "4QSam[a] in the Light of Historico-Literary Criticism: The Case of 2 Sam 24 and 1 Chr 21. Pages 110–19 in *Biblische und judaistische Studien: Festschrift für Paolo Sacchi*. Edited by A. Vivian. *Judentum und Umwelt* 29. Frankfurt am Main: Lang.
1997 "The Methods of Late Biblical Scribes as Evidenced by the Septuagint Compared with the Other Textual Witnesses." Pages 259–70 in *Tehillah le-Moshe: Biblical and Judaic Studies in Honor of Moshe Greenberg*. Edited by M. Cogan, B. L. Eichler, and J. H. Tigay. Winona Lake, Ind. : Eisenbrauns.

Rofé, Alexander, and Yair Zakovitch
1983 Eds. *Studies in Ancient Narrative and Historiography: Sefer Yitshak Aryeh Zeligman (Isac Leo Seeligmann Anniversary Volume)*. Vol. 3. Jerusalem: Rubenstein.

Rolla, A.
1986 "La Palestina Postesilica alla luce dell'archeologia." *RivB* 34: 111–19.

Römer, Thomas
1990 *Israels Väter: Untersuchungen zur Väterthematik im Deuteronomium und in der deuteronomistischen Tradition*. OBO 99. Göttingen: Vandenhoeck & Ruprecht.
2000 Ed. *The Future of the Deuteronomistic History*. BETL 147. Leuven: Leuven University Press.

Romerowski, Sylvain
1986 "Les régnes de David et de Salomon dans les Chroniques." *Hok* 31: 1–23.
1987a "L'espérance messianique dans les Chroniques." *Hok* 34: 37–63.
1987b "La théologie de la retribution dans les Chroniques." *Hok* 35: 1–34.

Rooke, Deborah W.

2000 *Zadok's Heirs: The Role and Development of the High Priesthood in Ancient Israel.* Oxford: Oxford University Press.

Rooker, Mark

1990 *Biblical Hebrew in Transition: The Language of the Book of Ezekiel.* JSOTSup 90. Sheffield: JSOT Press.

Roschinski, Hans P.

1980 "Sprachen, Schriften, und Inschriften in Nordwestarabien." *BJ* 180: 155–88.

Rose, Martin

1981 *Deuteronomist und Yahwist: Untersuchungen zu den Berührungspunkten beider Literaturwerke.* ATANT 67. Zurich: Theologischer Verlag.

Rosenthal, Franz

1969 "Canaanite and Aramaic Inscriptions." *ANET* 653–62.

Rothstein, Johann Wilhelm

1902 *Die Genealogie des Königs Jojachin und seiner Nachkommen (1 Chron. 3, 17–24): Eine kritische Studie zur jüdischen Geschichte und Litteratur.* Berlin: Reuther & Reichard.

Rothstein, Johann Wilhelm, and Johannes Hänel

1927 *Kommentar zum ersten Buch der Chronik.* KAT 18/2. Leipzig: Deichertsche Verlagsbuchhandlung.

Rowley, H. H.

1939 "Zadok and Nehushtan." *JBL* 58: 113–41.

1955–56 "Sanballat and the Samaritan Temple." *BJRL* 38: 166–98.

1965 "*The Servant of the Lord.* 2nd rev. ed. Oxford: Blackwell.

Rudolph, Wilhelm

1949 *Esra und Nehemia.* HAT 20. Tübingen: Mohr.

1954 Problems of the Books of Chronicles. *VT* 4: 401–9.

1955 *Chronikbücher.* HAT 21. Tübingen: Mohr.

1981 "Lesefrüchte, 1." *ZAW* 93: 291–92.

Ruffing, Andreas

1992 *Jahwekrieg als Weltmetapher: Studien zu Jahwekriegstexten des chronistischen Sondergutes.* SBB 24. Stuttgart: Katholisches Bibelwerk.

Runnalls, Donna

1991 "The *Parwār*: A Place of Ritual Separation?" *VT* 41: 324–31.

Russell, Donald Andrew

1979 *De Imitatione.* Pages 1–16 in *Creative Imitation and Latin Literature.* Edited by D. West and A. J. Woodman. Cambridge: Cambridge University Press.

1981 *Criticism in Antiquity.* London: Duckworth.

Russell, Donald Andrew and Michael Winterbottom

1998 Eds. *Classical Literary Criticism.* Oxford: Oxford University Press.

Ryle, Herbert Edward

1893 *The Books of Ezra and Nehemiah.* The Cambridge Bible for Schools and Colleges. Cambridge: Cambridge University Press.

Sacchi, Paolo
1989 "L'esilio e la fine della monarchia Davidica." *Hen* 11: 131–48.
2000 *The History of the Second Temple Period.* JSOTSup 285. Sheffield: Sheffield Academic Press.

Sack, Ronald J.
1995 "Royal and Temple Officials in Eanna and Uruk in the Chaldean Period." Pages 425–32 in *Vom Alten Orient zum Alten Testament: Festschrift Wolfram von Soden.* Edited by M. Dietrich and O. Loretz. Neukirchen-Vluyn: Neukirchener Verlag.

Saebø, Magne
1980 "Messianism in Chronicles? Some Remarks to the Old Testament Background of the New Testament Christology." *HBT* 2: 85–109.
1981 "Chronistische Theologie/Chronistisches Geschichtswerk." *TRE* 8: 74–87.

Sahlins, Marshall
1985 *Islands of History.* Chicago: University of Chicago Press.

Sancisi-Weerdenburg, Heleen, and J. W. Dijvers
1990 Eds. *Achaemenid History.* Vol. 5. Leiden: Brill.

Sancisi-Weerdenburg, Heleen, J. W. Dijvers, and M. Cool Root
1994 Eds. *Achaemenid History.* Vol. 8. Leiden: Brill.

Sancisi-Weerdenburg, Heleen, and Amélie Kuhrt
1984 Eds. *Achaemenid History.* Vol. 1. Leiden: Brill.
1990 Eds. *Achaemenid History.* Vol. 4. Leiden: Brill.

Sanders, James A.
1967 *The Dead Sea Psalms Scroll.* Ithaca N. Y.: Cornell University Press.

Sanderson, Judith E.
1986 *An Exodus Scroll from Qumran: 4QpalaeoExod^{m} and the Samaritan Tradition.* HSS 30. Atlanta: Scholars Press.

Sarfatti, Gad B.
1982 "Hebrew Inscriptions of the First Temple Period: A Survey and Some Linguistic Comments." *Maarav* 3: 55–83.

Sarna, Nahum M.
1963 "Psalm 89: A Study in Inner Biblical Exegesis." Pages 29–46 in *Biblical and Other Studies.* Edited by A. Altmann. Cambridge, Mass.: Harvard Univiversity Press.
1979 "The Psalm Superscriptions and the Guilds." Pages 281–300 in *Studies in Jewish Religious and Intellectual History Presented to Alexander Altmann.* Edited by S. Stein and R. Loewe. University of Alabama Press.

Sass, Benjamin
1990 "Arabs and Greeks in Late First Temple Jerusalem." *PEQ* 122: 59–61.

Sasson, Jack
1973 "The Worship of the Golden Calf." Pages 151–69 in Hoffner (1973).
1974 "Reflections on an Unusual Practice Reported in ARM X: 4." *Or* 43: 404–10.

1978 "A Genealogical 'Convention' in Biblical Chronography?" ZAW 90: 171–85.

Schams, Christine

1998 *Jewish Scribes in the Second Temple Period*. JSOTSup 291. Sheffield: Sheffield Academic Press.

Schenker, A.

1991 "La relation d'Esdras A' au text massorétique d'Esdras-Néhémie." Pages 218–44 in *Tradition of the Text: Studies Offered to Dominique Barthélemy in Celebration of His 70th Birthday*. Edited by G. J. Norton and S. Pisano. OBO 109. Freiburg: Universitätsverlag.

Schmitt, Götz

1995 "Levitenstädte." *ZDPV* 111: 28–48.

Schneider, Tsvi

1988 "Azariahu Son of Hilkiahu (High Priest?) on a City of David Bulla." *IEJ* 38: 139–41.

Schniedewind, William M.

1991 "The Source Citations of Manasseh: King Manasseh in History and Homily." *VT* 41: 450–61.

1994a "History or Homily: Toward Understanding the Chronicler's Purpose." *Proceedings of the Eleventh World Congress of Jewish Studies*. Pages 91–97.

1994b "King and Priest in the Book of Chronicles and the Duality of Qumran Messianism." *JJS* 45: 71–78.

1995 *The Word of God in Transition: From Prophet to Exegete in the Second Temple Period*. JSOTSup 197. Sheffield: JSOT Press.

1996 "A Qumran Fragment of the Ancient 'Prayer of Manasseh?' " ZAW 108: 105–7.

1997 "Prophets and Prophecy in the Book of Chronicles." Pages 204–24 in Graham, Hoglund, and McKenzie (1997).

1998 "The Geopolitical History of Philistine Gath." *BASOR* 309: 69–77.

1999a "The Chronicler as an Interpreter of Scripture." Pages 158–80 in Graham and McKenzie (1999).

1999b *Society and the Promise to David: The Reception History of 2 Samuel 7: 1–17*. New York: Oxford University Press.

Schorn, Ulrike

1997 *Ruben und das System der zwölf Stämme Israels: Redaktionsgeschichtliche Untersuchungen zur Bedeutung des Erstgeborenen Jakobs*. BZAW 248. Berlin: de Gruyter.

2000 "Rubeniten als exemplarische Aufrührer in Num. 16f*/ Deut. 11." Pages 251–68 in McKenzie and Römer (2000).

von Schuler, Einar

1957 *Hethitische Dienstanweisungen für höhere Hof- und Staatsbeamte*. *AfO* Beiheft 10. Graz: Im Selbstverlage des Herausgebers.

Schuller, Eileen M.

1986 *Non-Canonical Psalms from Qumran: A Pseudepigraphic Collection*. HSS 28. Atlanta: Scholars Press.

1992 "4Q380 and 4Q381: Non-Canonical Psalms from Qumran." Pages 90–99 in *The Dead Sea Scrolls: Forty Years of Research.* Edited by D. Dimant and U. Rappaport. Leiden: Brill.

1997 "Qumran Pseudepigraphic Psalms (4Q380 and 381)." Pages 1–40 in *Pseudepigraphic and Non-Masoretic Psalms and Prayers.* Vol. 4A of *The Dead Sea Scrolls : Hebrew, Aramaic, and Greek Texts with English Translations.* Edited by J. H. Charlesworth et al. Tübingen: Mohr.

Schwartz, Daniel R.

1996 "Temple or City: What Did Hellenistic Jews See in Jerusalem?" Pages 114–27 in Poorthuis and Safrai (1996).

Schwartz, Joshua

1996 "The Temple in Jerusalem: Birah and Baris in Archaeology and Literature." Pages 29–49 in Poorthuis and Safrai (1996).

Scippa, Vincenzo

1989 "Davide e la conquista di Gerualemme: La teologia del Cronista in 1 Cr 11, 4–9." *Asp* 37: 59–73.

Scolnic, Benjamin Edidin

1995 *Theme and Context in Biblical Lists.* SFSHJ 119. Atlanta: Scholars Press.

Seebass, Horst

1978 Erwägungen zum altisraelitischen System der zwölf Stämme. ZAW 90: 196–219.

Seeligmann, Issac Leo

1978 "Die Auffassung von der Prophetie in der deuteronomistischen und chronistischen Geschichtsschreibung." Pages 254–84 in *Congress Volume, Göttingen 1977.* Edited by J. A. Emerton. VTSup 29. Leiden: Brill.

1979–80 "The Beginnings of Midrash in the Book of Chronicles" (Hebrew). *Tarbiz* 49: 14–32.

Segal, J. B.

1983 *Aramaic Texts from North Saqqâra with Some Fragments in Phoenician.* Texts from Excavations. 6th Memoir. London: Egypt Exploration Society.

Seidel, Moshe

1955–56 "Parallels between Isaiah and Psalms." *Sinai* 38: 149–72, 229–40, 272–80, 335–55 (Hebrew). Repr. pages 1–97 in *Hiarei Miara,* by Moshe Seidel. Jerusalem: Mossad ha-Rav Kook, 1978.

Seitz, Christopher R.

1989 *Theology in Conflict.* BZAW 176. Berlin: de Gruyter.

Selman, Martin J.

1994a *1 Chronicles.* TOTC. Leicester: Inter-Varsity Press.

1994b *2 Chronicles.* TOTC. Leicester: Inter-Varsity Press.

1999 "Jerusalem in Chronicles." Pages 43–56 in *Zion, City of Our God.* Edited by R. S. Hess and G. J. Wenham. Grand Rapids: Eerdmans.

Seow, C. L.
1989 *Myth, Drama, and the Politics of David's Dance*. HSM 44. Atlanta: Scholars Press.
1992 "Ark of the Covenant." *ABD* 1: 386–93.
1997 *Ecclesiastes*. AB 18C. New York: Doubleday.

Sérandour, A.
1996 "Les récits bibliques de la construction du second temple: Leurs enjeux." *Transeu* 11: 9–32.

Shanks, Hershel
1988 Ed. *Ancient Israel: A Short History from Abraham to the Roman Destruction of the Temple*. Englewood Cliffs, N. J.: Prentice-Hall.

Shanks, Hershel and Benjamin Mazar
1981 Eds. *Recent Archaeology in the Land of Israel*. Washington, D.C.: Biblical Archaeological Society.

Shaver, Judson R.
1989 *Torah and the Chronicler's History Work: An Inquiry into the Chronicler's References to Laws, Festivals, and Cultic Institutions in Relationship to Pentateuchal Legislation*. BJS 196. Atlanta: Scholars Press.

Shenkel, James D.
1969 "A Comparative Study of Synoptic Parallels in I Paralipomena and I–II Reigns." *HTR* 62: 63–85.

Shiloh, Yigal
1981 "Past and Present in Archaeological Research on the City of David." Pages 149–57 in Shanks and Mazar (1981).

Shipp, R. Mark
1993 " 'Remember His Covenant Forever': A Study of the Chronicler's Use of the Psalms." *ResQ* 35: 29–39.

Shrimpton, Gordon S.
1991 *Theopompus the Historian*. Montreal: McGill–Queen's University Press.

Silverman, Michael H.
1981 "Biblical Name Lists and the Elephantine Onomasticon: A Comparison." *Or* 50: 265–331.
1985 *Religious Values in the Jewish Proper Names at Elephantine*. AOAT 217. Kevelaer: Butzon & Bercker.

Simon, Uriel
1991 *Four Approaches to the Book of Psalms from Saadiah Gaon to Abraham Ibn Ezra*. Albany: State University of New York Press.

Skehan, Patrick W., and Alexander A. Di Lella
1987 *The Wisdom of Ben Sira*. AB 39. Garden City: Doubleday.

Smelik, Klaas A. D.
1991 *Writings from Ancient Israel*. Louisville, Ky.: Westminster.
1992 *Converting the Past: Studies in Ancient Israelite and Moabite Historiography*. OTS 28. Leiden: Brill.

Smick, Elmer B.
1973 "The Jordan of Jericho." Pages 177–79 in Hoffner (1973).

Smith, Daniel L.
1989 *The Religion of the Landless: The Social Context of the Babylonian Exile.* Bloomington, Ind.: Meyer Stone.

Smith, Morton
1987 *Palestinian Parties and Politics That Shaped the Old Testament.* London: SCM.

Snijders, L. A.
1997 "מָלֵא *mālēʾ*." *TDOT* 8: 297–307.

Soggin, J. Alberto
1964 " 'Wacholderholz' 2 Sam VI 5a gleich 'Schlaghölzer', 'Klappern'?" *VT* 14: 374–77.
1981 *Judges.* OTL. Philadelphia: Westminster.
1999 *An Introduction to the History of Israel and Judah.* 3rd ed. London: SCM.

Sollberger, Edmond, and J.-R. Kupper
1971 *Inscriptions royales sumériennes et akkadiennes.* Paris: Cerf.

Sommer, F., and A. Falkenstein
1938 *Die hethitisch-akkadische Bilingue des Ḫattušili I. (Labarna II.).* ABAW, Phil.-hist. Abt., N.F. 16. Munich: Bayerischen Akademie der Wissenschaften.

Spawn, Kevin L.
2002 *"As It is Written" and Other Citation Formulae in the Old Testament.* BZAW 311. Berlin: de Gruyter.

Speiser, E. A.
1963 "Unrecognized Dedication." *IEJ* 13: 69–73.
1969 "Akkadian Myths and Epics." *ANET* 60–119.

Spencer, John R.
1992 "Levitical Cities." *ABD* 4: 310–11.

Sperber, Alexander
1959 Ed. *The Former Prophets according to Targum Jonathan.* Vol. 2 of *The Bible in Aramaic Based on Old Manuscripts and Printed Texts.* Leiden: Brill.

Sperling, S. David
1992 "Blood." *ABD* 1: 761–63.

Spottorno, María Victoria
1997 "The Books of Chronicles in Josephus' *Jewish Antiquities.*" Pages 381–90 in *IX Congress of the International Organization for Septuagint and Cognate Studies, Cambridge 1995.* Edited by Bernard A. Taylor. SBLSCS 45. Atlanta: Scholars Press.
2001 Lexical Variants in the Greek Text of Reigns and Chronicles. Pages 63–80 in *X Congress of the International Organization for Septuagint and Cognate Studies, Oslo, 1998.* Edited by Bernard A. Taylor. SBLSCS 51. Atlanta: Society of Biblical Literature.

Stade, Bernhard
1887 *Geschichte des Volkes Israel.* Erster Band. Berlin: Historischer Verlag Baumgärtel.

Stager, Larry

1985 "The Archaeology of the Family in Ancient Israel." *BASOR* 260: 1–35.

1991a "Eroticism and Infanticide at Ashkelon." *BARev* 17/4: 34–53, 72.

1991b "When Canaanites and Philistines Ruled Ashkelon." *BARev* 17/2: 24–31, 35–37, 40–43.

1999 "Jerusalem and the Garden of Eden." Pages 183*–94* in Levine (1999).

Stamm, J. J.

1965 "Hebräische Ersatznamen." Pages 413–24 in *Studies in Honor of Benno Landsberger.* AS 16. Chicago: University of Chicago Press.

1980 *Beiträge zur hebräischen und altorientalischen Namenkunde.* OBO 30. Freiburg: Universitätsverlag.

Starcky, J.

1954 "Un Contrat nabatéen sur papyrus." *RB* 61: 161–81.

Stegemann, Hartmut

1989 "The Literary Composition of the Temple Scroll and Its Status at Qumran." Pages 123–48 in *Temple Scroll Studies.* Edited by G. Brooke. Sheffield: JSOT Press.

Steiner, Margaret

1994 "Redating the Terraces of Jerusalem." *IEJ* 44: 13–20.

Steiner, Richard C.

1989 New Light on the Biblical Millo from the Hatran Inscriptions. *BASOR* 276: 15–23.

Steins, Georg

1995 *Die Chronik als kanonisches Abschlußphänomen: Studien zur Entstehung und Theologie von 1/2 Chronik.* BBB 93. Weinheim: Beltz Athenäum.

1996 "Die Bücher der Chronik als Schule der Bibellektüre (Teil 2)." *BLit* 69: 105–9.

1997 "Zur Datierung der Chronik: Ein neuer methodischer Ansatz." ZAW 109: 84–92.

Stern, Ephraim

1975 "Israel at the Close of the Monarchy: An Archaeological Survey." *BA* 38: 26–54.

1981 "The Province of Yehud: The Vision and the Reality." *The Jerusalem Cathedra* 9–21.

1982a "A Favissa of a Phoenician Sanctuary from Tel Dor." Pages 35–54 in Vermes and Neusner (1982).

1982b *Material Culture of the Land of the Bible in the Persian Period 538–332 B.C.* Warminster: Aris & Phillips.

1984a "The Archaeology of Persian Palestine." *CHJ* 88–114.

1984b "The Persian Empire and the Political and Social History of Palestine in the Persian Period." *CHJ* 70–87.

1989a "The Beginning of the Greek Settlement in Palestine in the Light of the Excavations at Tel Dor." Pages 107–23 in *Recent Excavations in Is-*

rael: Studies in Iron Age Archaeology. Edited by S. Gitin and W. G. Dever. AASOR 49. Winona Lake, Ind.: Eisenbrauns.

1989b "What Happened to the Cult Figurines?" *BARev* 15/4: 22–29, 53–54.

1994a "Assyrian and Babylonian Elements in the Material Culture of Palestine in the Persian Period." *Transeu* 7: 51–62.

1994b *Dor: Ruler of the Seas.* Jerusalem: Israel Exploration Society.

1995 "Between Persia and Greece: Trade, Administration, and Warfare in the Persian and Hellenistic Periods." Pages 432–45 in Levy (1995).

2001 *The Assyrian, Babylonian, and Persian Periods 732–332 B.C.E.* Vol. 2 of *Archaeology of the Land of the Bible.* ABRL. New York: Doubleday.

Stern, Philip D.

1991 *The Biblical Ḥerem: A Window on Israel's Religious Experience.* BJS 211. Atlanta: Scholars Press.

Sternberg, Meir

1987 *The Poetics of Biblical Narrative: Ideological Literature and the Drama of Reading.* Indiana Studies in Biblical Literature. Bloomington, Ind.: Indiana University Press.

Steussy, Marti J.

1999 *David, Biblical Portraits of Power.* Columbia, S.C.: University of South Carolina Press.

Steve, M.-J.

1974 "Inscriptions des Achéménides à Suse (Fouilles de 1952 à 1965)." *Studia Iranica* 3: 7–28, 135–71.

1975 "Inscriptions des Achéménides à Suse (fin)." *Studia Iranica* 4: 7–26.

Stinespring, William F.

1961 "Eschatology in Chronicles." *JBL* 80: 209–19.

Stoebe, Hans Joachim

1973 *Das erste Buch Samuelis.* KAT 8/1. Gütersloh: Gütersloher Verlagshaus.

1994 *Das zweite Buch Samuelis.* KAT 8/2. Gütersloh: Gütersloher Verlagshaus.

Stolper, Matthew W.

1985 *Entrepreneurs and Empire: The Murašû Archive, the Murašû Firm, and Persian Rule in Babylonia.* Istanbul: Nederlands Historisch-Archaeologisch Institut.

1989 The Governor of Babylon and Across the River in 486 B.C. *JNES* 48: 283–305.

Stone, Michael Edward

1980 *Scriptures, Sects, and Visions: A Profile of Judaism from Ezra to the Jewish Revolts.* Philadelphia: Fortress.

1984 Ed. *Jewish Writings of the Second Temple Period: Apocrypha, Pseudepigrapha, Qumran Sectarian Writings, Philo, Josephus.* CRINT 2. Philadelphia: Fortress.

1996 "The Genealogy of Bilhah." *DSD* 3: 20–36.

Strange, J.

1980 *Caphtor/Keftiu: A New Investigation.* Leiden: Brill.

Strübind, Kim

1991 *Tradition als Interpretation in der Chronik: König Josaphat als Paradigma chronistischer Hermeneutik und Theologie.* BZAW 201. Berlin: de Gruyter.

Sugimoto, Tomotoshi

1990 "The Chronicler's Techniques in Quoting Samuel-Kings." *AJBI* 16: 30–70.

1992 "Chronicles as Independent Literature." *JSOT* 55: 61–74.

Svensson, Jan

1994 *Towns and Toponyms in the Old Testament.* ConBOT 38. Stockholm: Almqvist & Wiksell.

Swanson, Dwight D.

1992 "The Use of the Chronicles in 11QT: Aspects of a Relationship." Pages 290–98 in *The Dead Sea Scrolls: Forty Years of Research.* Edited by D. Dimant and U. Rappaport. Leiden: Brill.

1995 *The Temple Scroll and the Bible: The Methodology of 11QT. STDJ* 14. Leiden: Brill.

Swart, J.

1911 *De Theologie van Kronieken.* Groningen: Gebroeders Hoitsema.

Sweeney, Marvin A.

1990 "Davidic Typology in the Forty Year War between the Sons of Light and the Sons of Darkness." *Proceedings of the Tenth World Congress of Jewish Studies in Jerusalem, August 16–24, 1989* 1: 213–20.

Swete, Henry Barclay

1914 *An Introduction to the Old Testament in Greek.* Cambridge: Cambridge University Press. Repr., Peabody, Mass.: Hendrickson 1989.

Szubin, H. Z., and Bezalel Porten

1982 " 'Ancestral Estates' in Aramaic Contracts: The Legal Significance of the Term *mhḥsn.*" *JRAS* 3–9.

1983 "Testamentary Succession at Elephantine." *BASOR* 252: 35–46.

Tadmor, Hayim

1958 "The Campaigns of Sargon II of Assur: A Chronological-Historical Study." *JCS* 12: 22–40, 77–100.

1965 "The Inscriptions of Nabunaid: Historical Arrangement." Pages 351–63 in *Studies in Honor of Benno Landsberger on His 75th Birthday.* Edited by H. Güterbock and T. Jacobsen. AS 17. Chicago: The Oriental Institute of the University of Chicago.

1971 " 'The People' and the Kingship in Ancient Israel: The Role of Political Institutions in the Biblical Period." Pages 46–68 in *Jewish Society through the Ages.* Edited by H. H. Ben-Sasson and E. Ettinger. New York: Schocken.

1981 "History and Ideology in the Assyrian Royal Inscriptions." Pages 13–32 in Fales (1981).

1982 "Traditional Institutions and the Monarchy: Social and Political Tensions in the Time of David and Solomon." Pages 239–57 in Ishida (1982).

1983 "Autobiographical Apology in the Royal Assyrian Literature." Pages 36–57 in Tadmor and Weinfeld (1983).
1986 "Monarchy and the Elite in Assyria and Babylonia: The Question of Royal Accountability." Pages 203–24 in Eisenstadt (1986).
1994 *The Inscriptions of Tiglath-pileser III King of Assyria*. Jerusalem: Israel Academy of Sciences and Humanities.
1995 "Was the Biblical *sārîs* a Eunuch?" Pages 317–25 in Zevit, Gitin, and Sokoloff (1995).

Tadmor, Hayim, and Mordecai Cogan
1988 *II Kings*. AB 11. Garden City: Doubleday.

Tadmor, Hayim and Moshe Weinfeld
1983 Eds. *History, Historiography, and Interpretation*. Jerusalem: Magnes.

Tadmor, Miriam
1988 "Fragments of an Achaemenid Throne from Samaria." *IEJ* 24: 37–43.

Tallqvist, Knut Leonard
1914 *Assyrian Personal Names*. Helsinki. Repr., Hildesheim: Olms, 1966.

Talmon, Shemaryahu
1953 "The Qumran יחד: A Biblical Noun. *VT* 3: 133–40. Repr. pages 53–60 in Talmon (1989).
1954 "A Case of Abbreviation Resulting in Double Readings." *VT* 4: 206–8.
1960a "Double Readings in the Massoretic Text." *Text* 1: 144–84.
1960b "המה הקינים הבאים מחמת אבי בית-רחב: 1 Chron. ii, 55." *IEJ* 10: 174–80.
1961 "Synonymous Readings in the Textual Traditions of the Old Testament." *ScrHier* 8: 335–83.
1970 "The Old Testament Text." Pages 159–99 in *From the Beginnings to Jerome*. Vol. 1 of *The Cambridge History of the Bible*. Edited by P. R. Ackroyd and C. F. Evans. Cambridge: Cambridge University Press.
1975 "The Textual Study of the Bible: A New Outlook." Pages 321–400 in Cross and Talmon (1975).
1976 "Ezra and Nehemiah: Books and Men." *IDBSup* 317–28.
1989 *The World of Qumran from Within: Collected Studies*. Jerusalem: Magnes.
1993 "Esra und Nehemia: Historiographie oder Theologie?" Pages 329–56 in *Ernton was man sät: Festschrift für Klaus Koch zu einem 65. Geburtstag*. Edited by D. W. Daniels et al. Neukirchen-Vluyn: Neukirchener Verlag.
2001 "Calendrical Documents and Mishmarot." Pages 1–166 in Talmon, Ben-Dov, and Glessmer (2001).

Talmon, Shemaryahu, Jonathan Ben-Dov, and Uwe Glessmer.
2001 Eds. *Calendrical Texts*. Vol. 16 of *Qumran Cave 4*. DJD 21. Oxford: Clarendon Press.

Talmon, Shemaryahu, and Israel Knohl
1995 "A Calendrical Scroll from a Qumran Cave: *Mišmarot* B[a], 4Q321." Pages 267–301 in Wright, Freedman, and Hurvitz (1995).

Talshir, David

1988a "A Reinvestigation of the Linguistic Relationship between Chronicles and Ezra-Nehemiah." *VT* 38: 165–93.

1988b "The References to Ezra and the Books of Chronicles in B. Baba Bathra 15a." *VT* 38: 358–61.

Talshir, Zipora

1984 "The Milieu of 1 Esdras in the Light of Its Vocabulary." Pages 129–47 in Pietersma and Cox (1984).

1999 *I Esdras: From Origin to Translation.* SBLSCS 47. Atlanta: SBL.

2000 "The Reign of Solomon in the Making: Pseudo-Connections between 3 Kingdoms and Chronicles." *VT* 50: 233–49.

Talshir, Zipora, and David Talshir

1992 "The Original Language of the Story of the Three Youths (1 Esdras 3–4)" (in Hebrew). Pages 63*–75* in Fishbane and Tov (1992).

Tedesche, Sidney S.

1928 *A Critical Edition of I Esdras.* Ph.D. diss., Yale University.

Thackeray, Henry St. John

1907 The Greek Translators of the Four Books of Kings. *JTS* 8: 262–78.

1909 *A Grammar of the Old Testament in Greek according to the Septuagint.* Cambridge: Cambridge University Press.

Thomas, Rosalind

1989 *Oral Tradition and Written Record in Classical Athens.* Cambridge Studies in Oral and Literate Culture 18. Cambridge: Cambridge University Press.

1992 *Literacy and Orality in Ancient Greece.* Cambridge: Cambridge University Press.

Thompson, H. O., and F. Zayadine

1973a "The Ammonite Inscription from Tell Siran." *Ber* 22: 115–40.

1973b "The Tell Siran Inscription." *BASOR* 212: 5–11.

Thompson, Thomas L.

1992 *Early History of the Israelite People: From the Written and Archaeological Sources.* SHANE 4. Leiden: Brill.

1997 "Defining History and Ethnicity in the South Levant." Pages 166–87 in *Can a "History of Israel" Be Written?* Edited by L. L. Grabbe. JSOTSup 245. Sheffield: Sheffield Academic Press.

Thorion, Yohanan

1983 "Die Sprache der Tempelrolle und die Chronikbücher." *RevQ* 11: 423–26.

Throntveit, Mark A.

1982 "Linguistic Analysis and the Question of Authorship in Chronicles, Ezra, and Nehemiah." *VT* 32: 201–16.

1987 *When Kings Speak: Royal Speech and Royal Prayer in Chronicles.* SBLDS 93. Atlanta: Scholars Press.

1992 *Ezra-Nehemiah.* Interpretation. Louisville, Ky.: John Knox.

1997 "The Chronicler's Speeches and Historical Reconstruction." Pages 225–45 in Graham, Hoglund, and McKenzie (1997).

Tidwell, N. L.
1995 "No Highway! The Outline of a Semantic Description of *M[e]sillâ*." *VT* 45: 251–69.
Tigay, Jeffrey H.
1985 Ed. *Empirical Models for Biblical Criticism*. Philadelphia: University of Pennsylvania Press.
1986 *You Shall Have No Other Gods: Israelite Religion in the Light of Hebrew Inscriptions*. HSS 31. Atlanta: Scholars Press.
1996 *Deuteronomy*. The JPS Torah Commentary. Philadelphia: Jewish Publication Society.
Tomback, Richard S.
1978 *A Comparative Semitic Lexicon of the Phoenician and Punic Languages*. SBLDS 32. Missoula, Mont.: Scholars Press.
van der Toorn, Karel
1995 "Theology, Priests, and Worship in Canaan and Ancient Israel." *CANE* 2043–58.
1996a "Ancestors and Anthroponyms: Kinship Terms as Theophoric Elements in Hebrew Names." *ZAW* 108: 1–11.
1996b *Family Religion in Babylonia, Syria, and Israel*. SHCANE 7. Leiden: Brill.
1997 Ed. *The Image and the Book: Iconic Cults, Aniconism, and the Rise of Book Religion in Israel and the Ancient Near East*. CBET 21. Leuven: Peeters.
Torrey, Charles C.
1896 *The Composition and Historical Value of Ezra-Nehemiah*. BZAW 2. Giessen: J. Ricker.
1906 "Portions of First Esdras and Nehemiah in the Syro-Hexaplar Version." *AJSL* 23: 65–74.
1907a "The First Chapter of Ezra in Its Original Form and Setting." *AJSL* 24: 7–33.
1907b "The Nature and Origin of 'First Esdras.' " *AJSL* 23: 116–41.
1907c "The Story of the Three Youths." *AJSL* 23: 177–201.
1910 *Ezra Studies*. Chicago: University of Chicago Press.
1945 "A Revised View of First Esdras." Pages 395–410 in the *Louis Ginzberg Jubilee Volume*. Edited by S. Lieberman et al. New York: American Academy for Jewish Research.
1954a *The Chronicler's History of Israel*. New Haven, Conn.: Yale University Press.
1954b "More Elephantine Papyri." *JNES* 13: 149–53.
Torczyner, H.
1949 "A Psalm by the Sons of Heman." *JBL* 68: 247–49.
Tov, Emmanuel
1976 *The Septuagint Translations of Jeremiah and Baruch: A Discussion of an Early Revision of the LXX of Jeremiah 29–52 and Baruch 1: 1–3: 8*. HSM 8. Missoula, Mont.: Scholars Press.
1978a "The Nature of the Hebrew Text Underlying the LXX: A Survey of the Problems." *JSOT* 7: 53–68.

1978b "The Use of Concordances in the Reconstruction of the *Vorlage* of the LXX." *CBQ* 40: 29–36.

1986 "The Orthography and Language of the Hebrew Scrolls Found at Qumran and the Origin of These Scrolls." *Text* 13: 31–57.

1987 "Some Sequence Differences between the MT and LXX and Their Ramifications for the Literary Criticism of the Bible." *JNSL* 13: 151–60.

1992a "Some Notes on a Generation of Qumran Study (by Frank M. Cross): A Reply." Pages 15–21 in Trebolle Barrera and Vegas Montaner (1992).

1992b *Textual Criticism of the Hebrew Bible.* Assen: Van Gorcum.

1994 "Glosses, Interpretations, and Other Types of Scribal Additions in the Text of the Hebrew Bible." Pages 40–66 in Balentine and Barton (1994).

1995 "Excerpted and Abbreviated Biblical Texts from Qumran." *RevQ* 64: 581–600.

1997 *The Text-Critical Use of the Septuagint in Biblical Research.* Rev. ed. Jerusalem Biblical Studies 8. Jerusalem: Simor.

Towner, W. S.

1968 " 'Blessed be Yahweh' and 'Blessed art Thou YHWH': The Modulation of a Biblical Formula." *CBQ* 30: 386–99.

Trebolle Barrera, Julio

1980 *Salomón y Jeroboán: historia de la recensión y redacción de 1 Reyes 2–12, 14.* Institución San Jerónimo 10. Valencia: Investigación Biblica.

1989a *Centena in libros Samuelis et Regum: variantes textuales y composición literaria en los libros de Samuel y Reyes.* Textos y Estudios "Cardinal Cisneros" 47. Madrid: Consejo Superior de Investigaciones Científicas Instituto de Filología.

1989b "The Text-Critical Use of the Septuagint in the Books of Kings." Pages 285–99 in Cox (1991).

1992a "Édition préliminaire de *4Chroniques.*" *RevQ* 60: 523–29.

1992b "Light from 4QJudg[a] and 4QKgs on the Text of Judges and Kings." Pages 315–24 in *The Dead Sea Scrolls: Forty Years of Research.* Edited by D. Dimant and U. Rappaport. Leiden: Brill.

1992c "A Preliminary Edition of 4QKings (4Q54)." Pages 229–46 in Trebolle Barrera and Vegas Montaner (1992).

1995 "4QJudg[a] (Pl. XXXVI); 4QKgs (Pl. XXXVII)." Pages 161–64, 171–83 in Ulrich, Cross, et al. (1995).

2000 "4QChr (P1. XXXVIII)." Pages 295–97 in Ulrich, Cross, et al. (2000).

Trebolle Barrera, Julio, and Luis Vegas Montaner

1992 Eds. *The Madrid Qumran Congress: Proceedings of the International Congress on the Dead Sea Scrolls, Madrid 18–21 March 1991, Vols. 1 and 2.* Leiden: Brill.

Tsevat, Matitiahu

1965 "The House of David in Nathan's Prophecy." *Bib* 46: 353–56.

Tuell, Steven Shawn

1992 *The Law of the Temple.* HSM 49. Atlanta: Scholars Press.

Tuplin, Christopher
1987 "The Administration of the Achaemenid Empire." Pages 109–66 in *Coinage and Administration in the Athenian and Persian Empires.* Edited by I. Carradice. BARIS 343. Oxford: BAR.
1996 *Achaemenid Studies.* Stuttgart: Franz Steiner.

Uehlinger, Christoph
1999 " 'Powerful Persianisms' in Glyptic Iconography of Persian Period Palestine." Pages 134–82 in Becking and Korpel (1999).
2000 *Images as Media: Sources for the Cultural History of the Near East and the Eastern Mediterranean.* OBO 175. Freiburg: Vandenhoeck & Ruprecht.

Ulrich, Eugene C.
1978 *The Qumran Text of Samuel and Josephus.* HSM 19. Missoula, Mont.: Scholars Press.
1979 "4QSam[c]: A Fragmentary Manuscript of 2 Samuel 14–15 from the Scribes of the Serek Hay-yaḥad (IQS)." *BASOR* 235: 1–25.
1984 "Horizons of Old Testament Textual Research at the Thirtieth Anniversary of Qumran Cave 4." *CBQ* 46: 613–36.
1987 "Daniel Manuscripts from Qumran. Part 1: A Preliminary Edition of 4QDan[a]." *BASOR* 268: 17–37.
1989a "The Biblical Scrolls from Qumran Cave 4: An Overview and a Progress Report on Their Publication." *RevQ* 54: 207–28.
1989b "Daniel Manuscripts from Qumran. Part 2: Preliminary Editions of 4QDan[b] and 4QDan[c]." *BASOR* 274: 3–25.
1992a "The Canonical Process, Textual Criticism, and Later Stages in the Composition of the Bible." Pages 267–91 in Fishbane and Tov (1992).
1992b "Ezra and the Qoheleth Manuscripts from Qumran (4QEzra and 4QQoh[a,b])." Pages 139–57 in Ulrich, Wright, et al. (1992).
1994 "4QJoshua[a] and Joshua's First Altar in the Promised Land." Pages 89–104 in Brooke and García Martínez (1994).
1995 "4QJosh[a] (Pls. XXXII–XXXIV)." Pages 143–52 in Ulrich, Cross, et al. (1995).
1996 "Multiple Literary Editions: Reflections toward a Theory of the History of the Biblical Text." Pages 78–105 in *Current Research and Technological Developments of the Dead Sea Scrolls: Conference on the Texts from the Judean Desert, Jerusalem, 30 April 1995.* Edited by D. W. Parry and S. D. Ricks. *STDJ* 20. Leiden: Brill.
1999 *The Dead Sea Scrolls and the Origin of the Bible: Studies in the Dead Sea Scrolls and Related Literature.* Grand Rapids: Eerdmans.
2000 "4QEzra (P1. XXXVIII)." Pages 291–93 in Ulrich, Cross, et al. (2000).

Ulrich, Eugene C., Frank Moore Cross, et al.
1994 Eds. *Genesis to Numbers.* Vol. 7 of *Qumran Cave 4.* DJD 12. Oxford: Clarendon Press.
1995 Eds. *Deuteronomy, Joshua, Judges, Kings.* Vol. 9 of *Qumran Cave 4.* DJD 14. Oxford: Clarendon Press.

2000 Eds. *Psalms to Chronicles*. Vol. 11 of *Qumran Cave 4*. DJD 16. Oxford: Clarendon Press.

Ulrich, Eugene C., J. W. Wright, et al.

1992 Eds. *Priests, Prophets, and Scribes: Essays on the Formation and Heritage of Second Temple Judaism in Honour of Joseph Blenkinsopp*. JSOTSup 149. Sheffield: JSOT Press.

Van Dam, Cornelis

1997 *The Urim and the Thummim: A Means of Revelation in Ancient Israel*. Winona Lake, Ind.: Eisenbrauns.

Van den Branden, A.

1966 "Elenco della spese del tempio di Cition." *BeO* 8: 245–62.

Vanderhooft, David Stephen

1999a "Dwelling beneath the Sacred Place: A Proposal for Reading 2 Samuel 7: 10." *JBL* 118: 525–33.

1999b "The Israelite *mišpāḥâ* in the Priestly Writings: An Elite Reconstruction of Social Organization." Unpublished paper.

1999c *The Neo-Babylonian Empire and Babylon in the Latter Prophets*. HSM 59. Atlanta: Scholars Press.

2003 "Babylonian Strategies of Imperial Control in the West: Royal Practice and Rhetoric." Pages 235–62 in Lipschits and Blenkinsopp (2003).

VanderKam, James C.

1978 "The Textual Affinities of the Biblical Citations in the Genesis Apocryphon." *JBL* 97: 45–55.

1991 "Jewish High Priests of the Persian Period: Is the List Complete?" Pages 67–91 in Anderson and Olyan (1991).

1992 "Ezra-Nehemiah or Ezra and Nehemiah?" Pages 55–75 in Ulrich, Wright, et al. (1992).

1994 "Putting Them in Their Place: Geography as an Evaluative Tool." Pages 46–69 in *Pursuing the Text: Studies in Honor of Ben Zion Wacholder on the Occasion of His Seventieth Birthday*. Edited by J. C. Reeves and J. Kampen. JSOTSup 184. Sheffield: Sheffield Academic Press.

1998 *Calendars in the Dead Sea Scrolls: Measuring Time*. London: Routledge.

Van Driel, G.

1969 *The Cult of Aššur*. Assen: Van Gorcum.

Vannutelli, Primus

1931 *Libri synoptici Veteris Testamenti*. Rome: Pontifical Biblical Institute.

Van Rooy, Harry V.

1994 "Prophet and Society in the Persian Period according to Chronicles." Pages 163–79 in Eskenazi and Richards (1994).

Van Seters, John

1983 *In Search of History*. New Haven, Conn.: Yale University Press.

1988 "The Primeval Histories of Greece and Israel Compared." ZAW 100: 1–22.

1992 *Prologue to History: The Yahwist as Historian in Genesis*. Louisville, Ky.: Westminster John Knox.

1997a "The Chronicler's Account of Solomon's Temple-Building: A Continuity Theme." Pages 283–300 in Graham, Hoglund, and McKenzie (1997).

1997b "Solomon's Temple: Fact and Ideology in Biblical and Ancient Near Eastern Historiography." *CBQ* 59: 45–57.

2000 "Creative Imitation in the Hebrew Bible." *SR* 29: 395–409.

Vansina, Jan

1985 *Oral Tradition as History*. Madison, Wis.: University of Wisconsin Press.

Vargyas, Péter

1988 "Stratification sociale à Ugarit." Pages 110–23 in *Society and Economy in the Eastern Mediterranean (c. 1500–1000 B.C.)*. Edited by M. Heltzer and E. Lipiński. OLA 23. Leuven: Peeters.

Vatke, Wilelm

1886 *Historisch-kritische Einleitung in das Alte Testament*. Bonn: E. Strauss.

Vattioni, Francesco

1991a "ʾAdbeʾel di *Gen* 25,13 = 1 *Cr* 1,29 anche in 1 *Cr* 5,19?" *Aug* 31: 479–82.

1991b "3 (1) *Re* 12,10; 2 *Par* (*Cr*) 10,10 e Teodoreto di Ciro." *Aug* 31: 475–77.

Vaughn, Andrew, and Ann E. Killebrew

forthcoming Eds. *Jerusalem in Bible and Archaelogy*. SBLSymS 18. Atlanta: SBL Press/Leiden: Brill.

de Vaux, Roland Guérin

1964 "Le Roi d'Israël, vassal de Yahvé." Pages 119–33 in *Écriture sainte—ancien Orient*. Vol. 1 of *Mélanges Eugène Tisserant*. Studi e testi 231. Vatican: Biblioteca Apostolica Vaticana.

1965 *Ancient Israel: Its Life and Institutions*. 2 vols. New York: McGraw-Hill.

1969 "Téman, ville ou région d'Édom?" *RB* 76: 379–85.

1970 "The Settlement of the Israelites in Southern Palestine and the Origins of the Tribe of Judah." Pages 108–34 in *Translating and Understanding the Old Testament: Essays in Honor of Herbert Gordon May*. Edited by H. T. Frank et al. Nashville: Abingdon.

1978 *The Early History of Israel*. Philadelphia: Westminster.

Veijola, Timo

1975 *Die ewige Dynastie: David und die Entstehung seiner Dynastie nach der deuteronomistischen Darstellung*. AASF série B, Tom 193. Helsinki: Suomalainen Tiedeakatemia.

1983 "Davidverheißung und Staatsvertrag: Beobachtungen zum Einfluß altorientalischer Staatsverträge auf die biblische Sprache am Beispiel von Psalm 89." *ZAW* 95: 9–31.

1990 *Gesammelte Studien zu den Davidüberlieferungen des Alten Testa-*

ments. Schriften der finnischen exegetischen Gesellschaft 52. Göttingen: Vandenhoeck & Ruprecht.

te Velde, Herman

1995 "Theology, Priests, and Worship in Ancient Egypt." *CANE* 3: 1731–49.

Verbrugghe, Gerald P., and J. M. Wickersham

1996 *Berossos and Manetho: Introduced and Translated*. Ann Arbor, Mich.: Unversity of Michigan Press.

Vermes, Géza

1986 "Biblical Midrash. Pages 308–41 in vol. 3.1 of *The History of the Jewish People in the Age of Jesus Christ* by Emil Schürer. Rev. ed. by G. Vermes, F. Millar, and M. Goodman. Edinburgh: T & T Clark.

1989 Bible Interpretation at Qumran. Pages 184–91 in *Yigael Yadin Memorial Volume*, ed. A. Ben-Tor, J. C. Greenfield, and A. Malamat. *ErIsr* 20. Jerusalem: Israel Exploration Society.

Vermes, Géza, and Jacob Neusner

1982 Eds. *Essays in Honour of Yigael Yadin* (= *JJS* 33). Totowa, N. J.: Allanheld, Osmun, & Co.

Vermeylen, J.

1992 "Le 'table des nations' (Gn 10): Yaphet figure-t-il l'Empire perse?" *Transeu* 5: 113–32.

Vincent, Albert

1937 *La Religion des Judéo-Araméens d'Éléphantine*. Paris: P. Geuthner.

Wacholder, B. Z.

1974 *Eupolemus: A Study of Judeo-Greek Literature*. Monographs of Hebrew Union College 3. Cincinnati: Hebrew Union College–Jewish Institute of Religion.

Wagner, S.

1978 "דרשׁ; *dārash*; מדרשׁ." *TDOT* 3: 293–307.

Waldbaum, Jane C.

1994 "Early Greek Contacts with the Southern Levant, 1000–600 B.C.: The Eastern Perspective." *BASOR* 293: 53–66.

1997 "Greeks in the East or Greeks *and* the East? Problems in the Definition and Recognition of Presence." *BASOR* 305: 1–17.

Walde, Bernhard

1913 *Die Esdrasbücher der Septuaginta: Ihr gegenseitiges Verhältnis untersucht*. Bib S(F) 18/4.

Wallace, Howard N.

1999 "What Chronicles Has to Say about Psalms." Pages 267–91 in Graham and McKenzie (1999).

Waltke, Bruce Kenneth

1965 "Prolegomena to the Samaritan Pentateuch." Ph.D. diss., Harvard University.

Watts, James W.

1992 *Psalm and Story: Inset Hymns in Hebrew Narrative*. JSOTSup 139. Sheffield: JSOT Press.

1999 *Reading Law: The Rhetorical Shaping of the Pentateuch.* The Biblical Seminar 59. Sheffield: Sheffield Academic Press.

2001 Ed. *Persia and Torah: The Theory of Imperial Authorization of the Pentateuch.* SBL Symposium Series. Atlanta: SBL Press.

Weber, Robert

1945 *Les anciennes versions latines du deuxième livre des Paralipomènes.* Collectanea Biblica Latina 8. Rome: Libreria Vaticana.

Weil, Gérard E.

1984 "Nouveau Fragment massoretique de la Massorah du Targum babylonien du pentateuque (5) et de la Massorah magna tiberienne des Chroniques." *Text* 11: 37–87.

Weinberg, Joel P.

1972 "Demographische Notizen zur Geschichte der nachexilischen Gemeinde in Juda." *Klio* 54: 45–59.

1974 "Das *bēit 'ābôt* im 6.–4. Jh. v. u.Z." *VT* 23: 400–414.

1976 "Die Agrarverhältnisse in der Bürger-Tempel-Gemeinde der Achämenidenzeit." Pages 473–85 in Harmatta and Komoróczy (1976).

1978 "Die 'ausserkanonischen Prophezeiungen' in den Chronikbüchern." *Acta Antiqua* 26: 387–404.

1979 "Das Eigengut in den Chronikbüchern." *OLP* 10: 161–81.

1981 "Das Wesen und die funktionelle Bestimmung der Listen in I Chr 1–9." ZAW 93: 91–114.

1992 *The Citizen-Temple Community.* JSOTSup 151. Sheffield: JSOT Press.

1995 "The Word *ndb* in the Bible: A Study in Historical Semantics and Biblical Thought." Pages 365–75 in Zevit, Gitin, and Sokoloff (1995).

1996 *Der Chronist in seiner Mitwelt.* BZAW 239. Berlin: de Gruyter.

1997 "Transmitter and Recipient in the Process of Acculturation: The Experience of the Judean Citizen-Temple Community." *Transeu* 13: 91–105.

Weinfeld, Moshe

1970 "The Covenant of Grant in the Old Testament and in the Ancient Near East." *JAOS* 90: 184–203.

1972a *Deuteronomy and the Deuteronomic School.* Oxford: Clarendon Press.

1972b "Elders." *EncJud* 6: 578–80.

1976 "The Loyalty Oath in the Ancient Near East." *UF* 8: 379–414.

1980 "The Royal Guard according to the Temple Scroll." *RB* 87: 394–96.

1982 "The Counsel of the 'Elders' to Rehoboam and Its Implications." *Maarav* 3: 27–53. Repr. Pages 516–39 in Knoppers and McConville (2000).

1983 "Social and Cultic Institutions in the Priestly Source Against Their Ancient Near Eastern Background." Pages 95–129 in *Proceedings of the Eighth World Congress of Jewish Studies.* Jerusalem: Magnes.

1991 *Deuteronomy 1–11.* AB 5. Garden City: Doubleday.

1993 *The Promise of the Land: The Inheritance of the Land of Canaan by*

the Israelites. The Taubman Lectures in Jewish Studies 3. Berkeley: University of California Press.
1995 *Social Justice in Ancient Israel and in the Ancient Near East*. Jerusalem: Magnes.

Weippert, Helga
1988 *Palästina in vorhellenistischer Zeit*. Handbuch der Archäologie Vorderasien 2, Band 1. Munich: Becksche Verlagsbuchhandlung.

Weippert, Manfred
1972 "'Heiliger Krieg' in Israel und Assyrien: Kritische Anmerkungen zu G. von Rads Konzept des 'Heiligen Kreiges im alten Israel.' " ZAW 84: 460–93.

Weisberg, David B.
1967 *Guild Structure and Political Allegiance in Early Achaemenid Mesopotamia*. New Haven, Conn.: Yale University Press.

Weiser, Artur
1962 *Psalms*. 5th ed. OTL. London: SCM.

Weiss, Raphael
1963 "On Ligatures in the Hebrew Bible." *JBL* 82: 188–94.
1968 "Textual Notes." *Text* 6: 127–31.

Weitzman, Michael Perry
1994 "From Judaism to Christianity: The Syriac Version of the Hebrew Bible." Pages 147–73 in *Jews among Pagans and Christians in the Roman Empire*. Edited by J. Lieu, J. North, and T. Rajak. London: Routledge.
1999 *The Syriac Version of the Old Testament: An Introduction*. University of Cambridge Oriental Publications 56. Cambridge: Cambridge University Press.

Welch, Adam C.
1935 *Post-Exilic Judaism*. London: Blackwood.
1939 *The Work of the Chronicler: Its Purpose and Date*. The Schweich Lectures 1938. London: Oxford University Press.

Wellhausen, Julius
1870 *De Gentibus et Familiis Judaeis*. Göttingen: Officina Academica Dieterichiana.
1871 *Der Text der Bücher Samuelis untersucht*. Göttingen: Vandenhoeck & Ruprecht.
1885 *Prolegomena to the History of Ancient Israel*. Trans. J. Sutherland Black and A. Menzies. Edinburgh: A. & C. Black.
1889 *Die Composition des Hexateuchs und der historischen Bücher des Alten Testaments*. 4th ed. Berlin: de Gruyter. Repr., 1963.

Welten, Peter
1969 *Die Königs-Stempel: Ein Beitrag zur Militärpolitik Judas unter Hiskia und Josia*. Abhandlugen des Deutschen Palästinavereins 1. Wiesbaden: Harrassowitz.
1973 *Geschichte und Geschichtsdarstellung in den Chronikbüchern*. Neukirchen: Neukirchener Verlag.

1979 "Lade-Tempel-Jerusalem: Zur Theologie der Chronikbücher." Pages 169–83 in *Textgemäß: Aufsätze und Beiträge zur Hermeneutik des alten Testaments*. Edited by A. Gunneweg and O. Kaiser. Göttingen: Vandenhoeck & Ruprecht.

1991 "Chronikbücher, Chronist." *NBL* 1: 369–72.

Wenham, Gordon J.

1975 "Were David's Sons Priests?" *ZAW* 87: 79–82.

Wenham, J. W.

1967 "Large Numbers in the Old Testament." *TynBul* 18: 19–53.

Wenning, R.

1990 "Attische Keramik in Palästina: Ein Zwischenbericht." *Transeu* 2: 157–67.

Wente, Edward F.

1995 "The Scribes of Ancient Egypt." *CANE* 2211–21.

Wesselius, Jan-Wim

1999 "Discontinuity, Congruence, and the Making of the Hebrew Bible." *SJOT* 13: 24–77.

West, David, and Tony Woodman

1979 *Creative Imitation and Latin Literature*. Cambridge: Cambridge University Press.

West, M. L.

1966 *Hesiod: Theogony*. Oxford: Clarendon Press.

1985 *The Hesiodic Catalogue of Women: Its Nature, Structure, and Origins*. Oxford: Oxford University Press.

1997 *The East Face of Helicon*. Oxford: Oxford University Press.

Westermann, Claus

1981 *Praise and Lament in the Psalms*. Atlanta: John Knox.

1984 *Genesis 1–11*. Minneapolis: Augsburg.

1985 *Genesis 12–36*. Minneapolis: Augsburg.

1986 *Genesis 37–50*. Minneapolis: Augsburg.

de Wette, Wilhelm Martin Lebrecht

1806–07 *Beiträge zur Einleitung in das Alten Testament*. 2 vols. Halle: Schimmelpfennig.

1850 *A Critical and Historical Introduction to the Canonical Scriptures of the Old Testament*. Vol. 2. 2nd ed. Boston: Little & Brown.

Wevers, John William

1993 *Notes on the Greek Text of Genesis*. SBLSCS 35. Atlanta: Scholars Press.

1995 *Notes on the Greek Text of Deuteronomy*. SBLSCS 39. Atlanta: Scholars Press.

1998 *Notes on the Greek Text of Numbers*. SBLSCS 46. Atlanta: Scholars Press.

White, L. Michael

1987 "The Delos Synagogue Revisited: Recent Fieldwork in the Graeco-Roman Diaspora." *HTR* 80: 133–60.

Whitelam, Keith W.

1979 *The Just King: Monarchical Judicial Authority in Ancient Israel.* JSOTSup 12. Sheffield: JSOT Press.

1986 "The Symbols of Power: Aspects of Royal Propaganda in the United Monarchy." *BA* 49: 166–73.

1992 "King and Kingship." *ABD* 4: 40–48.

Whitt, William

1995 "The Story of the Semitic Alphabet." *CANE* 2379–97.

Widengren, Geo

1977 "The Persian Period." Pages 489–538 in *Israelite and Judaean History.* Edited by J. H. Hayes and J. M. Miller. London: SCM.

Wightman, G. J.

1993 *The Walls of Jerusalem: From the Canaanites to the Mamluks.* Mediterranean Archaeology Supplements 4. Sydney: Meditarch.

Willi, Thomas

1972 *Die Chronik als Auslegung.* FRLANT 106. Göttingen: Vandenhoeck & Ruprecht.

1980 "Thora in den biblischen Chronikbüchern." *Judaica* 36: 102–5, 148–51.

1991 *Chronik.* BK xxiv/1. Neukirchen: Neukirchener Verlag.

1994a "Die alttestamentliche Prägung des Begriffs אֶרֶץ יִשְׂרָאֵל." Pages 387–97 in *Nachdenken über Israel, Bibel, und Theologie: Festschrift für Klaus-Dietrich Schunk zu einem 65. Geburstag.* BEATAJ 37. Frankfurt am Main: Lang.

1994b "Late Persian Period Judaism and Its Conception of an Integral Israel according to Chronicles." Pages 146–62 in Eskenazi and Richards (1994).

1995 *Juda-Jehud-Israel: Studien zum Selbstverständnis des Judentums in persischer Zeit.* FAT 12. Tübingen: Mohr.

1999 "Leviten, Priester, und Kult in vorhellenistischer Zeit: Die chronistische Optik in ihrem geschichtlichen Kontext." Pages 75–96 in Ego, Lange, and Pilhofer (1999).

Williams, P. J.

1998 "The LXX of 1 Chronicles 5: 1–2 as an Exposition of Genesis 48–49." *TynBul* 49: 369–71.

Williams, Prescott H., and Theodore Hiebert

1999 Eds. *Realia Dei: Essays in Archaeology and Biblical Interpretation in Honor of Edward F. Campbell Jr. at His Retirement.* Atlanta: Scholars Press.

Williams, Ronald J.

1976 *Hebrew Syntax.* 2nd ed. Toronto: University of Toronto Press.

Williamson, H. G. M.

1973 "A Note on I Chronicles 7.12." *VT* 23: 375–79.

1976 "The Accession of Solomon in the Books of Chronicles." *VT* 26: 351–61.

1977a "Eschatology in Chronicles." *TynBul* 28: 115–54.

1977b *Israel in the Books of Chronicles.* Cambridge: Cambridge University Press.
1979a "The Origins of the Twenty-four Priestly Courses: A Study of 1 Chronicles xxii–xxvii." VTSup 30: 251–68.
1979b "Sources and Redaction in the Chronicler's Genealogy of Judah." *JBL* 98: 351–59.
1981 " 'We Are Yours, O David': The Setting and Purpose of 1 Chronicles xii 1–23." OTS 21: 164–76.
1982a "The Death of Josiah and the Continuing Development of the Deuteronomic History." *VT* 32: 242–47.
1982b *1 and 2 Chronicles.* NCB. Grand Rapids: Eerdmans.
1983a "The Composition of Ezra i–vi." *JTS* 34: 1–30.
1983b "The Dynastic Oracle in the Books of Cronicles [sic]." Pages 305–18 in Rofé and Zakovitch (1983).
1985 *Ezra, Nehemiah.* WBC 16. Waco, Tex.: Word.
1987a "Did the Author of Chronicles Also Write the Books of Ezra and Nehemiah?" *BR* 3: 56–59.
1987b "Postexilic Historiography." Pages 189–207 in *The Future of Biblical Studies: The Hebrew Scriptures.* Edited by R. E. Friedman and H. G. M. Williamson. Atlanta: Scholars Press.
1987c "Reliving the Death of Josiah: A Reply to C. T. Begg." *VT* 37: 9–15.
1987d Review of S. L. McKenzie, *The Chronicler's Use of the Deuteronomistic History.* VT 37: 107–14.
1988a "The Governors of Judah under the Persians." *TynBul* 39: 59–82.
1988b "History." Pages 25–38 in *It Is Written: Scripture Citing Scripture. Essays in Honour of Barnabas Lindars, SSF.* Cambridge: Cambridge University Press.
1989 "The Concept of Israel in Transition." Pages 141–60 in Clements (1989).
1991a "Ezra and Nehemiah in the Light of the Texts from Persepolis." *BBR* 1: 41–61.
1991b "The Temple in the Books of Chronicles." Pages 15–31 in *Templum Amicitae: Essays on the Second Temple Presented to Ernst Bammel.* Edited by W. Horbury. JSNTSup 48. Sheffield: JSOT Press.
1996 "The Problem with First Esdras." Pages 201–16 in Barton and Reimer (1996).
1998 "Judah and the Jews." Pages 145–63 in *Studies in Persian History: Essays in Memory of David M. Lewis.* Edited by M. Brosius and A. Kuhrt. Achaemenid History 11. Leiden: Nederlands Institut voor het Nabje Oosten.

Wilson, John A.
1969a "Egyptian Historical Texts." *ANET* 227–64.
1969b "An Egyptian Letter." *ANET* 476–79.

Wilson, Robert R.
1975 "The Old Testament Genealogies in Recent Research." *JBL* 94: 169–89.

1977 *Genealogy and History in the Biblical World.* Yale Near Eastern Researches 7. New Haven, Conn.: Yale University Press.

1979 "Between 'Azel' and 'Azel': Interpreting the Biblical Genealogies." *BA* 42: 11–22.

1980 *Prophecy and Society in Ancient Israel.* Philadelphia: Fortress.

Winnett, Frederick Victor

1957 *Safaitic Inscriptions from Jordan.* Near and Middle East Series 2. Toronto: University of Toronto Press.

Winnett, Frederick Victor, and G. Lankester Harding

1978 *Inscriptions from Fifty Safaitic Cairns.* Near and Middle East Series 9. Toronto: University of Toronto Press.

Winnett, Frederick Victor, et al.

1970 *Ancient Records from North Arabia.* Near and Middle East Series 6. Toronto: University of Toronto Press.

Wintermute, O. S.

1985 "Jubilees." *OTP* 2: 35–142.

Wolff, Hans Walter

1971 Ed. *Probleme biblischer Theologie: Festschrift Gerhard von Rad.* Munich: Kaiser.

1975 "The Kerygma of the Deuteronomic Historical Work." Pages 83–100 in *The Vitality of Old Testament Traditions.* Edited by W. Brueggeman and H. W. Wolff. Atlanta: John Knox.

1977 *Joel and Amos.* Hermeneia. Philadelphia: Fortress.

van der Woude, A. S.

1986 Ed. *Crises and Perspectives, Studies in Ancient Near Eastern Polytheism, Biblical Theology, Palestinian Archaeology, and Intertestamental Literature: Papers Read at the Joint British-Dutch Old Testament Conference, Held at Cambridge, 1985.* OTS 24. Leiden: Brill.

1990 Ed. *In Quest of the Past, Studies on Israelite Religion, Literature, and Prophetism: Papers Read at the Joint British-Dutch Old Testament Conference, Held at Elspeet, 1988.* OTS 26. Leiden: Brill.

Wright, D. P., D. N. Freedman, and A. Hurvitz

1995 Eds. *Pomegranates and Golden Bells: Studies in Biblical, Jewish, and Near Eastern Ritual, Law, and Literature in Honor of Jacob Milgrom.* Winona Lake, Ind.: Eisenbrauns.

Wright, John Wesley

1989 "The Origin and Function of 1 Chronicles 23–27." Ph.D. diss., Notre Dame University.

1990 "Guarding the Gates: 1 Chronicles 26.1–19 and the Roles of Gatekeepers in Chronicles." *JSOT* 48: 69–81.

1991 "The Legacy of David in Chronicles: The Narrative Function of 1 Chronicles 23–27." *JBL* 110: 229–42.

1992 "From Center to Periphery: 1 Chronicles 23–27 and the Interpretation of Chronicles in the Nineteenth Century." Pages 20–42 in Ulrich, Wright, et al. (1992).

1993 "The Innocence of David in 1 Chronicles 21." *JSOT* 60: 87–105.

1997 "The Fight for Peace: Narrative and History in the Battle Accounts in Chronicles." Pages 150–77 in Graham, Hoglund, and McKenzie (1997).

1998 "The Founding Father: The Structure of the Chronicler's David Narrative." *JBL* 117: 45–59.

1999 "The Fabula of the Book of Chronicles." Pages 136–55 in Graham and McKenzie (1999).

Würthwein, Ernst

1984 *Die Bücher der Könige: 1 Kön. 17–2 Kön. 25*. ATD 11/2. Göttingen: Vandenhoeck & Ruprecht.

Wyatt, Nicolas

1998 "Arms and the King: The Earliest Allusions to the *Chaoskampf* Motif and Their Implications for the Interpretation of the Ugaritic and Biblical Traditions." Pages 833–82 in *"Und Mose schrieb dieses Lied auf": Studien zum Alten Testament and zum Alten Orient (Festschrift für Oswald Loretz)*. Edited by Manfried Dietrich and I. Kottsieper. Münster: Ugarit Verlag.

Yadin, Yigael

1962 *The Scroll of the War of the Sons of Light against the Sons of Darkness*. London: Oxford University Press.

1963 *The Art of Warfare in Biblical Lands in the Light of Archaeological Study*. 2 vols. New York: McGraw-Hill.

1983 *The Temple Scroll*. 3 vols. Jerusalem: Israel Exploration Society.

Yamauchi, Edwin M.

1980 "The Reverse Order of Ezra/Nehemiah Reconsidered." *Them* 5/3: 7–13.

1990 *Persia and the Bible*. Grand Rapids: Baker.

Yeivin, S.

1971 "The Benjaminite Settlement in the Western Part of Their Territory." *IEJ* 21: 141–54.

York, Harry Clinton

1910 "The Latin Versions of First Esdras." *AJSL* 26: 253–302.

Younger, K. Lawson

1998 "The Deportations of the Israelites." *JBL* 117: 201–27.

Younker, Randall W.

1997a "Moabite Social Structure." *BA* 60/4: 237–48.

1997b "Some Notes on the Identity of Tell Jawa (South) Jordan: Mephaath or Abel Keramim?" Pages 257–63 in *To Understand the Scriptures: Essays in Honor of William H. Shea*. Edited by David Merling. Berrien Springs, Mich.: Andrews University Institute of Archaeology.

1999 "The Emergence of the Ammonites." Pages 189–218 in MacDonald and Younker (1999).

Zaccagnini, Carlo

1983 "On Gift Exchange in the Old Babylonian Period." Pages 189–253 in *Studi orientalistici in ricordo di Franco Pintore*. Edited by Onofrio Carruba, M. Liverani, and C. Zaccagni. Studia Mediterranea. Pavia: GJES.

Zadok, Ran
1976 "Geographical and Onomastic Notes." *JANES* 8: 113–26.
1980 "Notes on the Biblical and Extra-Biblical Onomasticon." *JQR* 71: 107–17.
1982 "Remarks on Ezra and Nehemiah." ZAW 94: 296–98.
1985 "Die nichthebräischen Namen der Israeliten vor dem hellenistischen Zeitalter." *UF* 17: 387–98.
1988a "A Note on *sn'h*." *VT* 38: 483–86.
1988b "Notes on the Prosopography of the Old Testament." *BN* 42: 44–47.
1988c *The Pre-Hellenistic Israelite Anthroponymy and Prosopography.* OLA 28. Leuven: Peeters.
1998 "On the Reliability of the Genealogical and Prosopographical Lists of the Israelites in the Old Testament." *TA* 25: 228–54.

Zakovitch, Y.
1985 "Assimilation in Biblical Narratives." Pages 175–96 in Tigay (1985).

Zalewski, Saul
1989 "The Purpose of the Story of the Death of Saul in 1 Chronicles X." *VT* 39: 449–67.
1997 "Saul in the Eyes of the Author of Chronicles" (in Hebrew). Pages 55–70 in *Studies in Bible and Exegesis 4*. Vol. 4. Edited by B. Kasher, Y. Sefati, and M. Zipor. Ramat Gan: Bar Ilan University.

Zenger, Erich
1968 "Die deuteronomistische Interpretation der Rehabilitierung Jojachins." *BZ* 12: 16–30.

Zeron, A.
1974 "Tag für Tag kam man zu David, um ihm zu helfen, 1 Chr 12: 1–22." *TZ* 30: 257–61.
1978 "Der Platz Benajahaus in der Heldenliste Davids (II Sam 23^{20-23})." ZAW 90: 20–28.

Zertal, Adam
1990 "The Pahwah of Samaria (Northern Israel) during the Persian Period: Types of Settlement, Economy, History, and New Discoveries." *Transeu* 3: 9–30.
1992 "Hepher." *ABD* 3: 138–39.
1995 "Three Iron Age Fortresses in the Jordan Valley and the Origin of the Ammonite Circular Towers." *IEJ* 45: 253–73.
1999 "The Province of Samaria during the Persian and Hellenistic Periods" (in Hebrew). Pages 75*–98* in Avishur and Deutsch (1999). *Michael: Historical, Epigraphical and Biblical Studies in Honor of Prof. Michael Heltzer.* Edited by Y. Avishur and R. Deutsch. Tel Aviv: Archaeological Center.
2001 "The Heart of the Monarchy: Patterns of Settlement and Historical Considerations of the Israelite Kingdom of Samaria." Pages 38–64 in A. Mazar (2001).
2003 "The Province of Samaria (Assyrian *Samerina*) in the Late Iron Age (Iron Age III)." Pages 377–412 in Lipschits and Blenkinsopp (2003).

Zevit, Ziony, S. Gitin, and M. Sokoloff

1995 Eds. *Solving Riddles and Untying Knots: Biblical, Epigraphic, and Semitic Studies in Honor of Jonas C. Greenfield.* Winona Lake, Ind.: Eisenbrauns.

Zimmerli, Walther

1979 *Ezekiel 1.* Hermeneia. Philadelphia: Fortress.

1983 *Ezekiel* 2. Hermeneia. Philadelphia: Fortress.

Zipor, Moshe

1980 "The Greek Chronicles." *Bib* 61: 561–71.

Zöckler, Otto

1877 *The Books of Chronicles Theologically and Homiletically Expounded.* Commentary on the Holy Scriptures 7. New York: Scribner's.

Zorn, Jeffrey R.

1997 "Mizpah: Newly Discovered Stratum Reveals Judah's Other Capital." *BARev* 23/5: 28–38, 66.

2003 "Tell en-Naṣbeh and the Problem of the Material Culture of the Sixth Century." Pages 413–47 in Lipschits and Blenkinsopp (2003).

Zunz, Leopold

1832 *Die gottesdienstlichen Vorträge der Juden, historisch entwickelt.* Berlin: Asher.

Zwickel, Wolfgang

1993 "Die Landnahme in Juda." *UF* 23: 473–91.

Translation, Notes, and Comments

1. The Genealogical Introduction to the People of Israel

◆

EXCURSUS: THE GENEALOGIES

According to Plato, when Socrates asked the famous sophist Hippias, "What are the subjects that the Spartans gladly hear from you?" Hippias replied:

> They listen with the greatest pleasure to the genealogies of their heroes and men, to the settlement of tribes, and how cities were founded of old and, in a word, to everything concerning antiquarian knowledge. (Plato, *Hipp. mai.* 285d)

If one were to take a poll in a contemporary context, requesting respondents to name their favorite subjects, it would be unlikely that listening to rehearsals of long genealogies would be listed as their most preferred leisure activity. Indeed, people in the modern world may find the intense fascination of ancients with the past puzzling. Why would individuals in ancient Mediterranean societies display such an avid interest in the lineages and stories of their predecessors in bygone eras? To be sure, even in our own age, people attempt to trace their family trees or search archives to discover the lawful heir to a property or a title. Moreover, many educated people in Western societies are interested in the origins of their nations and those of the natural world. Nevertheless, genealogies devoted to single persons are mostly of interest only to those individuals, their family members, and perhaps to professional historians.

In the answer of Hippias to Socrates, both the general interest in former times (literally, "archaeology") and the particular interest in the genealogies of heroes and of persons are remarkable. Many of the major genealogical works in ancient Greece date to the sixth and the fifth centuries B.C.E., but the interest in genealogy was neither a new nor a temporary phenomenon. One feature of the Homeric interest in the past is a concern with genealogy (e.g., *Il.* 5.533–60; 20.215–40 [Aeneas]; 6.153–206 [Glaukos]; Hornblower 1994: 9). In pre-Herodotean Greece, writers established lineages for Greek noble families, who claimed descent from heroes and gods in the mythological past (T. Brown 1973: 3–4; West 1985: 8–9). Hecataeus of Miletus is supposed to have been able to trace his family back sixteen generations to a god (Herodotus, *Hist.* 2.143).[1] Two Spartan royal houses

[1] But such long genealogies appear to have been rare. In most cases, genealogies achieve a depth of only a few generations.

were officially said to have descended from Herakles, at least by the time of Tyrtaeus. One version of their genealogies is recorded by Herodotus (*Hist.* 7.204; 8.131). Indeed, Plato's very criticism of the infatuation with and reliance on lineages (*Theaet.* 174e ff.) is itself indicative of the continuing influence of genealogical considerations in his time.[2]

The fascination with establishing connections to the ancient past through genealogy was, of course, not a unique characteristic of ancient Greece. Ancient Mesopotamian and Egyptian scribes had been formulating genealogical registers for centuries, if not millennia, before the ancient Greeks began to do so. Examples from ancient Mesopotamia are found among the royal inscriptions of the Sumerians, Assyrians, and Babylonians (Frame 1995; Grayson 1976; 1980; 1991; 1996) and the king lists from ancient Sumer and Assyria (Jacobsen 1939; Malamat 1968; Sollberger and Kupper 1971; R. Wilson 1977). Examples from ancient Egypt include assorted pharaonic king lists and extensive priestly lineages (Redford 1970; 1986). In the tradition represented by the Turin Canon, scribes connected a dynastic succession of gods and divine spirits to a dynastic succession of monarchs of Upper and Lower Egypt.[3] More proximate examples, geographically speaking, to the Chronicler's use of pedigrees include the genealogies of Darius I in the Old Persian version of the Behistun inscription (§§1.2–3; 2.1.3–6)[4] and the genealogical lists found among the Safaitic inscriptions of ancient Jordan and North Arabia (Winnett 1957; Winnett, et al. 1970; Winnett and Harding 1978).

Before proceeding with a discussion of the importance and place of genealogies in Chronicles, it will be useful to elaborate on what a genealogy is and what types of genealogies may be found in this work. Because genealogies have such a prominent place in Chronicles, occupying the first nine chapters of the book, it will be helpful to survey the presentation of genealogies within other works stemming from the ancient Mediterranean world. Having briefly examined various forms and functions that lineages take, I will go on to discuss some larger questions of organization, theme, and purpose.[5]

I. *"And She Begat": Different Types of Genealogies*

Following Robert Wilson (1977: 9), I understand a genealogy to refer to "a written or oral expression of the descent of a person or persons from an ancestor or ancestors." Most genealogies, whether oral or written, fall into one of two patterns.

[2] Plato's criticism may have more to do with the proposition that the presence of some illustrious figures within one's lineage determines one's present character than it does with the verifiability of the lineage itself (Thomas 1989: 174–75).

[3] See Gardiner (1959); Hoffmeier (1997: 68, 71–73). Written genealogies were especially common in the Persian and Hellenistic periods. They appear in both private inscriptions and in inscriptions of large priestly families (Redford 1970: 5–6; 1986).

[4] The latter, a more complete lineage (DB I, §2.1.3–6), immediately follows the former (DB I, §1.2–3; Kent 1953: 116).

[5] In the context of this excursus, I make no pretensions of being comprehensive. In his survey, Marshall Johnson (1988: 77–78) lists some nine different purposes according to which authors may formulate genealogies.

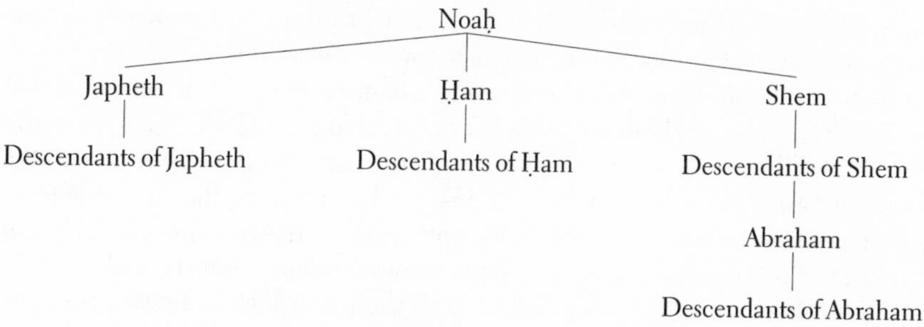

Some genealogies take a segmented form, tracing two or more lines of descent from a single ancestor. Because these lineages are concerned with following the progression of different branches within a single family tree and the relations between those branches, segmented genealogies are sometimes also called horizontal or lateral genealogies. Segmented genealogies relate various members of a single lineage to each other. As such, segmented genealogies can be used to posit complex social and political relationships between clans, peoples, towns, and places. In the universal genealogy, which begins his book, the Chronicler mentions the three sons of Noaḥ: "Shem, Ḥam, and Japheth" (1 Chr 1:4). Each of these three individuals represents one family of peoples in the ancient world known by the writer. Following the pattern set by his source (Genesis), he begins with the descendants of Japheth (1:5–7) and the descendants of Ḥam (1:8–16) and concludes with the descendants of Shem (1:17–27). In this context, it is worthwhile underscoring that the names occurring in ancient genealogies are sometimes toponyms or are directly or indirectly connected to territories. In this case, each family of peoples is implicitly associated with a certain land mass. As befitting the early time period depicted, Noaḥ's three sons represent very large areas. Taking the geographical perspective of Canaan as a starting point, the writer associates Shem with peoples to the east, Ḥam with peoples to the south and southwest, and Japheth with peoples to the north and west. Having traced the descendants of each of Noaḥ's three sons (1:5–27), the author continues his genealogy of nations by focusing on his main interest, the descendants of one descendant of Shem: Abraham (1:27–28). The pattern of the genealogy may be abstracted as shown in the diagram. In this instance, a segmented genealogy is employed both to posit long-distance international relationships and to distinguish the emergence of different peoples. All of the descendants of Shem, Ḥam, and Japheth (1:4) are related to each other through a common ancestor (Noaḥ). Because the emergence of Jacob (almost always called Israel in Chronicles; see Gen 32:29) and his sons does not occur until later in the segmented genealogy (2:1–2), Israel appears as a relative latecomer. Like the authors of Genesis, the Chronicler recognizes the existence of a variety of peoples before his own appears on the world scene.

One can see the advantage of formulating a complex segmented lineage. The author places the emergence of Israel against the background of the emergence of other peoples. He begins his work by listing antediluvians from Adam to Noaḥ's sons, Shem, Ḥam, and Japheth (1:1–4), and by providing a catalogue of the nations (1:5–23; cf. Gen 10:1–32). Hence, the writer takes an interest in the origins of both Israel and its neighbors, observing a continuity from Shem to Abraham (1:24–27) and from Abraham to his various descendants (1:28–34). The twelve sons of Israel (2:1–2) are only dealt with after the genealogist has dealt with the posterity of his older brother Esau (1:35–54). Even among the descendants of Abraham, Israel is but one people among others. The descendants of Israel live in the context of a variety of other peoples to whom they are closely related.

The second form that genealogies take is the linear type. A linear genealogy follows a line of descent from one ancestor to a later descendant. Because a linear genealogy establishes a chain of generations relating a person to a given ancestor, this type of genealogy is also called a vertical genealogy. A clear example occurs within the Davidic genealogy, when the author narrates Solomon's descendants:

> The son of Solomon: Reḥoboam, his son Abijah, his son Asa, his son Jehoshaphaṭ, his son Joram, his son Aḥaziah, his son Joash, his son Amaziah, his son Azariah, his son Jotham, his son Aḥaz, his son Ḥezeqiah, his son Manasseh, his son Amon, [and] his son Josiah. (1 Chr 3:10–14)

In this history of generations, one can see a straight line of descent.

Solomon
|
Reḥoboam
|
Abijah
|
Asa
|
Jehoshaphaṭ
|
Joram
|
Aḥaziah
|
Joash
|
Amaziah
|
Azariah
|
Jotham
|
Aḥaz
|
Ḥezeqiah
|

Manasseh
|
Amon
|
Josiah

Note how the genealogist, extracting information from the book of Kings, chooses not to relate other facts pertaining to brothers, sisters, and (queen) mothers. While economical (the genealogist manages to cover three centuries in only a few lines), the linear genealogy does have its limitations. Whereas segmented lineages can educe relationships between different individuals, families, or peoples by positing a common ancestor, linear genealogies can only educe a relationship between a single individual or people and a single individual or people in the past.

Linear genealogies are not all the same. Most genealogies of the linear type trace lines of descent from one ancestor to a single descendant. Hence, these lineages are more specifically called descending linear genealogies. But there is also a subpattern of the linear type that begins with a given person and traces his forebearers back to an appropriate ancestor. This type of genealogy is called an ascending linear genealogy. So, for example, in the context of narrating David's commission for choral music to the Levitical Gershonite, Qohathite, and Merarite singers (6:16–17), the author comments:

> These were the ones who stood, along with their sons: from the descendants of Qohath—Heman the singer, son of Joel, son of Samuel, son of Elqanah, son of Jeroḥam, son of Eliel, son of Toaḥ, son of Zuph, son of Elqanah, son of Maḥath, son of Amasai, son of Elqanah, son of Joel, son of Azariah, son of Zephaniah, son of Taḥath, son of Assir, son of Abiasaph, son of Qoraḥ, son of Izhar, son of Qohath, son of Levi, son of Israel. (6:18–23)

This ascending linear genealogy, taking the time of David as a starting point, traces Heman's predecessors (father, grandfather, great-grandfather, and so forth) back to the progenitor of the phratry (Qohath), to the original progenitor of the tribe (Levi), and ultimately to the eponymous ancestor of the entire nation (Israel).[6]

At first glance, this may all seem like another collection of dry, abstract, and unfamiliar names. Some of the names are obscure, but the effects of formulating a long, twenty-one-generation ascending linear genealogy for Heman are worth commenting upon. By creating this lineage, the writer is able to claim a measure of cultic continuity from the formative time of the United Monarchy, the time in

[6] A similar genealogical technique is used with respect to the Gershonite and Merarite singers (1 Chr 6:24–33). It should be noted, however, that tying a particular person or group to a specific or formative age in the past is not a necessary feature of genealogizing in the ancient Near Eastern world. In the case of priestly genealogies in first millennium Thebes, for example, Egyptian scribes did not single out a particular bygone age as a special time of origins or seek to link their ancestors to mythical figures and the divine. When Hecataeus of Miletus told the Egyptian priests at Thebes that he could trace his lineage in the sixteenth generation back to a god, the priests countered that they could trace their priestly line back three hundred and forty-five generations and still not discover any connection to a hero or a god (Herodotus, *Hist.* 2.143).

which the Temple was planned and built, back to the age of his nation's very beginnings, the time of the Ancestors. The patronym of Heman represents one of three classes or guilds of singers that receives new appointments during the time of David. Many contemporary scholars believe (rightly or wrongly) that the singers became esconced as a constituent feature of Temple worship only in Achaemenid times. But in Chronicles, David's reign appears as the definitive age for the Levitical singers. In this context, it is fascinating that the genealogist mentions not only Heman, Gershon, and Merari, but also "their sons." In this way, the author is able to hint that the Levitical singers working in the author's own time, the late Achaemenid or early Hellenistic period, have an impeccable pedigree. To be sure, the genealogist does not actually proceed to formulate a long genealogy of Levitical singers stretching from Heman to Neo-Babylonian and Persian times. But given his allusion to "their sons," he may not have felt the compulsion to document a complete genealogy to his own time. Presumably, the three classes of singers were well known in the writer's time and were already functioning as part of temple worship. From the writer's vantage point, it was probably more important to try to establish something else, namely, that the three branches of Levitical singers were already active centuries ago in the time of David (something that the authors of Samuel-Kings do not claim). Moreover, from the author's perspective it was important to claim that each of the three guilds of singers—the Gershonites, Qohathites, and Merarites (cf. 2 Chr 5:12; 29:14; 35:15)—ultimately hailed from the time of national origins. Hence, the genealogy furnishes the singers with a written basis to argue that their roots were as historic as those of the priests (1 Chr 5:27–41; 6:35–38).

We have been discussing different kinds of genealogies (segmented and linear) and their uses. Not all genealogies fall cleanly into either the segmented or linear types. Some genealogies are of a mixed type, combining segmented and linear forms. For example, the priestly genealogy in 1 Chr 5:27–41 begins in segmented form before switching to linear form (5:30–41). The segmented portion of the genealogy (5:27–29) traces a particular line within the Levitical tribe, even as it acknowledges that the members of this line are but one part of a larger whole. The pattern within 5:27–29 may be diagrammed as shown on p. 251. The segmentation allows the genealogist to point out that while he is tracing one particular priestly line from Levi through Qohath, Amram, Aaron, to Eleazar (and on to Phineḥas, etc., in 5:30–41), he acknowledges the existence of broader relationships within the Levitical tribe and the (potential) existence of other priestly lines within the Aaronide branch of the Levitical family tree, most relevantly the descendants of Ithamar (cf. 1 Chr 24:5; Knoppers 2003).

II. The Use of Genealogies to Convey Pedigree, Hierarchy, and Status

The regard of ancient Mediterranean peoples for matters genealogical must be connected to the significance they attributed to origins and the original ancestor in determining the character of future generations. In ancient Greece, prestige, status, even moral character might be derived from the original progenitor, prefer-

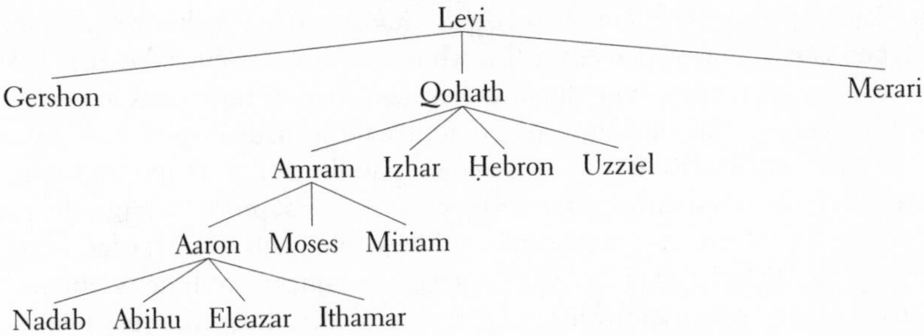

ably legendary, heroic, or divine (van Groningen 1953: 47–61). One's identity was intimately tied to one's roots and social context. Whether one had the credentials to serve in certain public offices was determined to no small extent by one's pedigree. Peisistratus reportedly wrote Solon, the sixth century Athenian politician and poet, that since he (Peisistratus) was a descendant of Codrus, the last king of Athens, he was rightfully tyrant of the Athenians (Diogenes Laertius, *Lives* 1.53). According to Herodotus (*Hist.* 5.22; 8.137–39), Alexander I of Macedon (ca. 498–454 B.C.E.) was not allowed to compete in the Olympic Games until he convinced officials that he was a Hellene by presenting his genealogy in which he descended from Temenos, the Herakleid king of Argos. Within Chronicles, we have already seen a case in point with respect to Heman and the lineages of the Levitical singers. The author traces the ancestry of these figures from his own era back to what he considers to be the classical age of Israel's past—the United Monarchy—and ultimately back to the time of national origins (Levi).

Current social relationships or political hierarchies may be claimed, explained, or ratified by recourse to genealogies. It is certainly relevant, in this context, that when the authors of the Babylonian creation epic *Enūma eliš* set out to explain how the Babylonian god Marduk rose to become king of the gods, they begin their myth with a long theogony (Lambert and Parker 1966). The many generations of the gods and goddesses establish a divine hierarchy and social order or, as the case may be, a divine disorder that is only finally addressed when the gods turn to a most promising younger god (Marduk) to take up their cause and vanquish Tiamat and her cohort. Influenced, either directly or indirectly, by a version of *Enūma eliš*, the Greek poet Hesiod also created a major and far-ranging genealogy of the gods. His *Theogonia*, prefaced by a hymn to the Muses (lines 1–104), deals with the origins and (mostly) segmented genealogies of the goddesses and gods, including the divine world masses, Earth, Sky, and Sea, and the events that eventually led to the kingship of Zeus (West 1966). As with *Enūma eliš*, the genealogies engage questions of divine origins, establish a divine hierarchy, and posit relationships (and degrees of relationships) among the gods and goddesses.

Like other ancient Hebrew writers (as represented in the Hebrew Scriptures), the Chronicler chooses not to tackle the question of divine origins. He assumes the existence of Yhwh and first mentions the God of Israel by name, appropriately enough, in his discussion of the genealogy of Judah (1 Chr 2:3; cf. 4:10). Nevertheless, like the authors of the *Enūma eliš* and the *Theogonia*, the Chronicler is intensely interested in the question of origins. Looking at actual word counts (and not chapter totals or verse summaries), genealogies and lists make up a substantial part (between 25 and 30 percent) of the whole book (Andersen and Forbes 1989). The assumptions made about the links between ancestry and status in postexilic Judah's historiographic literature are not unlike those made in other ancient societies in the first millennium B.C.E. According to the author of the list found in Ezra 2, those priests returning from exile who could not prove their priestly pedigree were barred from serving as priests. These officiants were "exiled [וַיְגֹאֲלוּ] from the priesthood" (Ezra 2:62//Neh 7:64). The concern with ties to the past is also very much evident in the list of the first returnees, those who returned to Jerusalem in the Persian period (1 Chr 9:2–34). Some nineteen allusions in thirty-two verses underscore the links made between these repatriates and their forebearers in the preexilic past. The lineages themselves are short, achieving a depth of only two to three generations, yet the connections claimed—whether direct or indirect—are ancient. Foundational figures include the Patriarchs Levi and Judah, as well as prominent members of their tribes (e.g., Perez and Zeraḥ from Judah; Zadoq, Aḥiṭub, Merari, Asaph, Qoraḥ, Phineḥas, and Eleazar from Levi). Those recent immigrants who settled "in their properties" (9:2) are given the patina of a native pedigree.

Within Chronicles, the concern with pedigree is by no means unique to the genealogies. In a speech of David to the Israelite assembly near the end of his reign, the monarch takes it upon himself to explain why Solomon his son had been chosen to succeed him. The reasons have much to do with genealogy, even though David recognizes that the pattern of divine choice within the ancestral houses of his tribe did not focus on the firstborn male of each household (1 Chr 28:4–5). The pattern of divine election began with the divine choice (בחר) of Judah as leader (נגיד) among his brothers and the house of David's father out of the tribe of Judah (28:4). In neither case does the author claim that Judah or Jesse were firstborn or possessed the birthright within their respective families (1 Chr 2:1, 12; Knoppers 2000b). David asserts that "Yhwh the God of Israel chose (בחר) me out of all of the house of my father to become king over Israel forever" (28:4). As for the future, divine election is again determinative: "from all of my sons . . . he has chosen (בחר) my son Solomon to sit upon the throne of Yhwh over Israel" (28:5).

The same argument, aligned with the principle of pedigree, can also be used negatively to disqualify those who are not eligible, or who should recognize themselves as ineligible, from holding public office. When King Abijah and Judah confront Jeroboam and Israel in battle during the early Divided Monarchy, Abijah delivers a public speech before the troops of both parties, casting aspersions on Jeroboam's kingship and contrasting his lack of a royal pedigree with the long-established credentials of David's descendants in Jerusalem.

> Hear me, O Jeroboam and all of Israel! Do you not know that Yhwh, the God of Israel gave the kingship over Israel forever to David and to his sons with a covenant of salt? Yet Jeroboam, son of Nebaṭ, a servant of Solomon the son of David rose up and rebelled against his master. And worthless men gathered themselves about him, scoundrels who prevailed upon Reḥoboam, the son of Solomon when Reḥoboam was a youth and fainthearted and could not

withstand them. But now do you intend to withstand the kingship of Yhwh in the hands of the descendants of David? (2 Chr 13:4b–8a)

Whereas Jeroboam is an upstart, merely "the son of Nebaṭ, a servant of Solomon," Abijah is the son of Reḥoboam the son of Solomon the son of David, to whom Yhwh awarded dynastic kingship. Playing on the different connotations of "Israel," the Chronicler boldly argues that the kingship held by Abijah represents Yhwh's kingship and stands in continuity with Israel's historic past, whereas Jeroboam and "all" of (northern) Israel have abandoned their own roots.

The importance of pedigree among the elites of ancient Mediterranean societies should not be underestimated, but neither should the stress on lineage be misconstrued. From the perspective of the Chronicler and other ancient authors, a bloodline rendered one eligible to hold certain positions in society. By the same token, bloodline served as a means to disqualify certain individuals from holding a high office. In spite of this emphasis on lineage, the right bloodline did not automatically entitle a person to a high post. There were many descendants of David (3:1–24) who did not ascend to the kingship. Similarly, from the perspective of the Chronicler, there were descendants of Eleazar the son of Aaron (5:30–41) who did not hold the highest priestly office in the Temple (Knoppers 2003).

III. Classical Genealogies and the Segmented Lineages of 1 Chronicles 1–9

Undoubtedly, the most sustained example of the concern with pedigree in Yehud is the genealogies of 1 Chr 1–9.[7] The amount of coverage devoted to the lineages of the Israelite tribes (2:3–8:40; 9:35–44) is extraordinary. Within biblical literature these genealogies are unique, standing apart as an entire section within a book. To be sure, the issue is not simply the presence of genealogy itself. One of the authors of the Pentateuch, the Yahwist (or J source) sporadically employs genealogies within his presentation (R. Wilson 1977; M. Johnson 1988). The Priestly writers (responsible for a variety of other sections within the Pentateuch) incorporate genealogies within their work. The use of such genealogies allows the Priestly writers to enumerate and categorize a variety of peoples in relation to Israel (M. Johnson 1988: 14–36). In fact, the Priestly authors systematically employ lists and genealogical materials to structure entire periods they posit within the past. Similarly, the editors of Ezra-Nehemiah integrate genealogies and lists into the larger framework of their presentation (e.g., Ezra 7:1–5). Homer (e.g., *Il.* 2.653, 734, 740–41, 746, 763, 818, 822) and Herodotus (*Hist.* 7.204; 8.131) also incorporate genealogies within their works. Although the use of genealogies by classical, Near Eastern, and other biblical writers provides parallels to the use of genealogies by the Chronicler, one must still acknowledge that the use of so many

[7] Forbes (1987) points out that 1 Chr 1–9 exhibits the lowest part-of-speech entropy (i.e., is the most syntactically predictable) of any portion of the Hebrew Bible. That this is so should not be surprising, considering the repetitive use of genealogical formulas and locutions in this particular section of the book.

consecutive blocks of lineages to preface a long narrative work is quite remarkable. In Chronicles one finds an entire collection of genealogies, some of which are the longest genealogies one finds anywhere in the Hebrew Bible (Aufrecht 1988), appearing as a daunting prologue to the story of the monarchy (1 Chr 10–2 Chr 36).

Some important features of the Chronicler's genealogical introduction find analogies in classical prose composition.[8] The point is not simply the phenomenon of genealogies per se, because genealogies are found in earlier biblical sources (e.g., J and P), in Mesopotamian sources, in Achaemenid royal inscriptions, and in many other cultures of the ancient world (R. Wilson 1977: 56–136). In this context, one can readily acknowledge the Chronicler's indebtedness to earlier biblical authors, especially to the Priestly source. But the issue needs to be more narrowly defined: Where can one find parallels to the elaborate system of genealogies found in 1 Chr 1–9, that is, to a group of lineages appearing either as a single work by themselves or as a substantial part of a larger literary work? One hastens to add that the genealogies of 1 Chr 1–9 do not comprise a conglomeration of totally unrelated lineages, but reveal a pattern of organization and conscious editing. They begin with the first man Adam (1:1), list his various descendants in prediluvian and postdiluvian times (1:1–54), and focus on the descendants of Israel's twelve sons (2:1–9:1).

A related issue is that of segmentation. Since 1 Chr 1–9 contains both linear and segmented genealogies, one should look for collections of genealogies that contain both linear and segmented genealogies.[9] In this respect, the ancient Near Eastern parallels adduced to the Chronicler's genealogies are not directly germane because these comprise individual lists (or genealogies) and do not represent large collections of multilinear and linear genealogies.[10] In my judgment, the closest counterparts to the phenomenon of 1 Chronicles 1–9 may be found in the works of the Greek genealogists. The mass of ancient Greek genealogical literature was originally quite considerable, but only survives in fragmentary and testi-

[8] I agree with many recent scholars who have argued that the core (however one defines that) of the genealogies in 1 Chr 1–9 are original to the first edition of the Chronicler's work. See, for instance, Japhet (1977; 1979; 1993a); Williamson (1977b; 1982b); Roddy Braun (1986); Marshall Johnson (1988: 55–56); Kartveit (1989: 19–167); Oeming (1990); Wright (1999). For the opposite point of view, see Noth (1943) and Rudolph (1955). The latter scholars posit a very short core text (*Grundschrift*) and a large number of subsequent additions. In the words of Noth (1943: 122), "Die große Masse dessen, was jetzt in 1. Chr. 2–9 steht, ist ein Gewirr von sekundären wilden Textwucherungen" ("The great bulk of that which now stands in 1 Chr 2–9 is a jumble of wild secondary textual growth"). But texts are not plants; they do not grow all by themselves.

[9] Both kinds of genealogies are found in earlier biblical writings (Malamat 1973). But the pertinent issue in this context is the systematic attempt to formulate a segmented genealogical presentation of Israel's many tribes.

[10] On the composite nature of these works, see Robert Wilson (1977). Whether some of these works should be classified as genealogies at all, rather than as lists, has been questioned by Hess (1990: 252–53), who draws formal contrasts between some biblical genealogies and the Sumerian, Babylonian, and Assyrian King Lists. In any case, the Mesopotamian royal lineages are not segmented or multilinear in their present form. Within these lists, in fact, some contemporary dynasties have been made sequential so as to create one continuous lineage.

monial form.[11] In some cases, one finds genealogies pursued for individual lines. The titles for some of the mythographic works associated with Hellanicus of Lesbos—*Deucalioneia, Phoronis,* and *Atlantis*—indicate that this fifth-century writer sought to work out genealogies for individual families from a particular mythological figure (Jacoby 1956b: 262–87). But already in the sixth century, the poet responsible for the Hesiodic *Catalogue of Women* put together a comprehensive collection of heroic genealogies in five books (Merkelbach and West 1967; West 1985).[12] At the end of the sixth century or the beginning of the fifth, Hecataeus of Miletus composed a mythographic work, comprising at least four books, on the genealogies of heroes.[13] Genealogists in the fifth century, such as Acusilaus of Argos and Damastes of Sigaeum, also composed large collections of genealogies involving a number of different lines.[14] Confronting disconnected and heterogeneous local traditions, these writers collated older materials, placed stories in a series, and fixed them within a larger genealogical order. To resolve many of the tensions and contradictions that arose from multiple stories about one hero, genealogists might posit more than one hero by the same name, but living at different times (T. Brown 1973: 3–17 [with reference to Timaeus]). Marital ties (many of which were artificial), migrations, and settlements of Greek heroes were used to link generations together and explain the alliances or enmities of different individuals and groups.

The rationalizing approach employed by these genealogists in reconstructing the history of past generations may be compared with the systematic approach one finds in evidence within 1 Chr 1–9. The author(s) of these chapters string together lineages for a variety of tribes, or portions thereof (e.g., Half-Manasseh in 5:23–24), as well as for certain groups within tribes, such as the descendants of David (3:1–24), the priests (5:27–41; 6:35–38), and the Levitical singers (6:1–33).[15] In spite of the detailed attention given to specific groups and families within Greek and Hebrew traditions, the larger focus is national in both cases. First Chronicles 1–9 situates the appearance of Israel and his sons in the context of the development of other peoples (1 Chr 1), but the text concentrates on the Israelite tribes themselves and their relationships (2:3–8:40). Similarly, the ancient Greek ge-

---

[11] Broadbent (1968); West (1985: 1–11); Thomas (1989: 155–95; 1992). In the view of Fornara (1983), genealogies were one of the earliest types of prose written in ancient Greece.

[12] The work, called the Γυναικῶν Κατάλογος or simply the Ἠοῖαι (literally, "or the ones like," derived from the recurrent refrain ἢ οἵη, "the like," which marked the beginning of a section), was designed as a continuation of Hesiod's *Theogonia* (West 1966), but had its own proem. West dates the completion of the work to between 560 and 525 B.C.E.

[13] The work is variously referred to as the *Genealogies* (Γενεηλογίαι), the *Histories* (Ἱστορίαι), and the *Herology* (Ἡρωλογία). Fewer than forty fragments remain (*FGrH* 1; cf. Herodotus, *Hist.* 5.36, 125–26). On the historical context of Hecataeus and his connections to the aristocratic elite of Miletus, see Pearson (1939: 25–106), Jacoby (1956b: 185–237), and von Fritz (1967).

[14] *FGrH* 5; von Fritz (1967). According to Josephus (Ag. *Ap.* 1–13), Acusilaus lived before the Persian Wars (490–480/79 B.C.E.).

[15] The Chronicler's universal genealogy also contains an Edomite king list (1:43–50) and an Edomite chieftain list (1:51–54) that are borrowed (in edited form) from Gen 36:31–39 and 36:40–43, respectively.

nealogists focused on what they considered to be Greek lines of descent from various heroes and deities. In their work they may have attempted to be pan-Hellenic in their coverage, but they paid little attention to the lineages of barbarian peoples. In this respect, comparison with the work of the Greek genealogists elucidates the configuration of the Chronicler's genealogical prologue. The primary issue at stake is not so much the definition of the *ethnos* over against external groups as it is the relationships of the various groups who make up the *ethnos*.[16]

Because the Greek genealogies were composed of names that were significant and designed to support the nation's traditions and speculations, it is not surprising that they were interlaced with digressions and narrative comments explaining what particular groups did, what battles they fought, or where their descendants settled (West 1985: 29). Again, one can find parallels in the ancient Near East. The Sumerian King List contains comments detailing individual royal accomplishments, regnal markers detailing the length of reigns, titles for certain monarchs, and chronological summaries (Jacobsen 1939; R. Wilson 1977: 73–86). The Assyrian King List incorporates narrative digressions, regnal formulae, titles, and chronological summaries (Oppenheim 1969: 564–66; R. Wilson 1977: 86–101; Chavalas 1994: 114–20). Chronological formulae and narrative summaries in the Sumerian and Assyrian King Lists mark transitions between disparate dynasties and note changes in the location of capital cities. The Seleucid King List even alludes to events in other lands (Oppenheim 1969: 566–67).

The genealogies in Chronicles contain many anecdotes dealing with settlements, invasions, migrations, deportations, and wars.[17] Admittedly, there is also a difference of degree among the sets of Mesopotamian, Israelite, and Greek traditions. The circumstantial tales appear to be much longer and more fabulous in the works of the Greek genealogists than they are in the Mesopotamian king lists and in Chronicles.[18] But the basic pattern of interlacing lineages with stories and explanatory comments is found in each work. Moreover, such narrative excursions can serve a larger purpose by making chronology complement genealogy. An event alluded to in a remark can be made to correlate to a specific point in a particular lineage, which is, after all, a history of generations. So, for example, Hellanicus was one of the first to work out the chronological implications of the genealogies he created (Pearson 1939: 232).[19] In the linear descending ancestry given by Pherecydes of Athens for Philaias we find both topographical and historical markers:

---

[16] A point also stressed by Hoglund (1997: 19–29).

[17] E.g., 1 Chr 1:10; 2:3, 7, 22–23; 4:9–10, 27, 38–43; 5:1–2, 9–10. Based on the comparative evidence, there is no inherent need to excise such comments as later additions and glosses. Indeed, analysis of these digressions reveals many of the same themes found in the Chronicler's coverage of the United Kingdom and of Judah (Dillard 1984b). Oeming (1990: 206–18) goes so far as to say that the genealogies proleptically summarize the Chronicler's thought.

[18] Indeed, the original length of most Greek genealogical works must have been much longer than 1 Chr 1–9.

[19] But whether the chronological interest of Hellanicus is as pronounced as Pearson thinks is questioned by Thomas (1989: 185).

> Philaias the sons of Aias resides in Athens. Of him is born Daiklos, of him Epilykos, of him Akestōr, of him Agēnor, of him O[u]lios, of him Lykēs, of him Tophōn, of him Laios, of him Agamēstōr, of him Tisandros, of him Hippokleidēs, during whose archonship the Panathenaea were established, [of him Kypselos,] and of him Miltiadēs, who colonized the Cherronēsos [Chersonesus]. (Marcellin., *Vit. Thuc.* 2–4 [= *FGrH* 3.2]).

Or to take an example from one of the priestly genealogies found in Chronicles, the reference to Azariah's serving in Solomon's temple (1 Chr 5:35 [TEXTUAL NOTE]) and the reference to the Babylonian exile of Jehozadaq (5:41) punctuate the lineage extending from Levi to Jehozadaq (5:27–41).[20] In this manner, narrative digressions help to define the vague chronology inherent within the genealogies themselves.[21]

In one of his remarks about these earlier authors, Josephus (*Ag. Ap.* 1.16) comments about how often Hellanicus disagrees with Acusilaus about the genealogies and how often Acusilaus corrects Hesiod. Indeed, writers could even disagree about the ancestry of famous persons. According to ancient authorities, the parents of King Agamemnon (Homer, *Il.* 1.12–30, 130–44; 2.1ff., 110–39, 474–81; 3.166–79; 4:339–; 9.114–61; 11.252; 14.80–109; etc.) were Atreus and Aerope (Apollodorus, *Epit.* 3.12), Pleisthenes and Aerope (Pseudo-Apollodorus, *Bibl.* 3.2.2), and Pleisthenes and Eriphyle (scholium on Euripides, *Orest.* 4; Mussies 1986: 43–44). That ancient authors present so many different opinions should not be surprising. Their works did not consist of congeries of facts about remote periods that each writer passively acquired. Notwithstanding their appearance as sober collections of traditional data, genealogies can manifest great creativity.[22] Each writer assembled, arranged, combined, shaped, and augmented traditional materials in line with his own assumptions, preferences, and conceptions. One has to allow the genealogists a fair degree of stylization and literary license. Some genealogical writers, for example, show a marked preference for certain numbers within the generations they posit (the numbers three and seven were popular) or for situating favorite figures in special places within their lineages (Sasson 1978; West 1985: 27–29; Johnstone 1997a). To take one example from Chronicles, the priestly genealogy purports to establish an unbroken succession from the Ancestral era until the Babylonian exile (1 Chr 5:27–41). Taken as a whole, the genealogy has been structured to call attention to the figures appearing at its beginning, center, and end.[23]

---

[20] See also 1 Chr 1:43; 3:4; 4:41, 43; 5:10, 17, 22, 26; 6:16–17; 9:1, 2.

[21] If a (linear) genealogy is basically a history of generations, the synchronization of a known event with a person in a particular lineage defines both the event and the person.

[22] Typical devices included duplicating names and introducing new members into a line of succession. These techniques were used to reconcile contradictory legends and to fill up missing generations (Pearson 1939: 161, 210, 224).

[23] For details on what follows, see Knoppers (2003) and the commentary on 1 Chr 5:27–41.

Qohath
Amram
Aaron
Eleazar
Phineḥas
Abishua
Buqqi
Uzzi
Zeraḥiah
Meraioth
Amariah
Aḥiṭub
Zadoq
Aḥimaaz
Azariah
Joḥanan
Azariah
Amariah
Aḥiṭub
Zadoq
Shallum
Ḥilqiah
Azariah
Seraiah
Jehozadaq

There are twenty-five descendants from Qohath to Jehozadaq. If Qohath is the first pertinent scion of Levi and Jehozadaq the last, the midpoint is Zadoq. Twelve generations of priests precede him (Qohath to Aḥiṭub) and twelve generations of priests succeed him (Aḥimaaz to Jehozadaq). Commentators have called attention to a possible connection to MT 1 Kgs 6:1, which dates the building of the Temple to four hundred and eighty years after the Exodus (12 generations x 40 = 480), but the Exodus is not in view. Rather, the time of Zadoq marks the halfway point between the Ancestral era and the Babylonian exile. In this stylized line of descent, twelve generations (or 480 years) precede Zadoq and twelve generations (or 480 years) follow him.

Whether in the ancient Greek or the early Jewish arena, whether in poetic verse or in prose, each genealogical work represents a particular construction made by a particular author in a particular time from a particular vantage point. In the hands of later tradents, such literary works could be adapted to reflect new social or political conditions. A good example of genealogical variability, documented in great detail by Broadbent (1968: 240–339), is the genealogical claims relating to Kephalos, the eponymous ancestor of the Athenian family of Kephalids. The origins of this family are disputed, but the most obvious explanation is that they originally stemmed from the district of Kephale, southeast of Attica. At one point Kephalos was considered to be a son of Deion (or Deioneus) king of Phokis (Apollodorus, *Bibl.* 1.9.4; 3.15.1). Kephalos is said to have come to Athens, married the princess Prokris, accidently killed her, and was exiled from Athens (Mussies 1986: 44). Many generations later his descendants returned to Athens, took up residence there, and established a cult of the Delphian Apollo (Pausanias, *Descr.* 1.37.6–7). The establishment of a prominent connection to Athens was expressed genealogically in at least two ways. In one tradition, Kephalos was made a prince of the royal house of Athens—whether as a grandson of King Erechtheus (Hyg., *Fab.* 160) or as a son of King Pandion (Hyg., *Fab.* 270; scholium on Dionysius. Per. 509). In another tradition, Kephalos appears as a king himself (Hyg., *Fab.* 48; 189; Serv. ad Verg., *G.* 1.19).

One could make a counterargument to the line of presentation we have been sketching, namely, that the Chronicler was much more conservative than other genealogists. While his Greek counterparts worked with oral traditions, the Chronicler worked with written materials. To be sure, there were some basic data pertaining to the Ancestors in the genealogies found in the Pentateuch that he did not, and perhaps could not, change. These included the number and sequence of many of the early generations of the Patriarchs and Matriarchs (Rendsburg 1990a; Ben Zvi forthcoming). Nevertheless, the larger point remains the same. Each ancient writer was attempting to create an intelligible network of lineages that would fit his own conceptions and reconcile, if not select from, available traditions. Genealogists employed a variety of literary conventions to structure their works. If political or social conditions changed, the genealogy created by one writer in one geopolitical setting might be adjusted by a later writer working in another setting.[24] Or, alternatively, a new genealogy could be fashioned to comport with current social and religious realities.[25]

IV. Genealogy As a Prologue to History?

We have been discussing genealogical works as a whole, collections of lineages whose organization reflects deliberate attempts at rationalization. But genealogy can also be a prelude to story. A system of genealogies need not be an end in and of itself. In ancient biographies, it is only natural for the author to begin with an account of ancestry (Mussies 1986: 33). One could draw a broad parallel with the presentation in Chronicles. The text offers us a genealogical introduction to Israel before it provides us with the story of its life during the monarchy. But biographies relate to individual persons, and the genealogies for such people are relatively short compared with the great attention devoted to the genealogical registers in Chronicles. Is there any parallel to the phenomenon of prefacing major genealogies to the stories of a people or nation in the ancient Mediterranean world? It

---

[24] One of the merits of Robert Wilson's detailed analysis (1977; 1979) of royal Mesopotamian genealogical traditions is his demonstration that these written sources exhibit some of the same fluidity as that characterizing oral sources.

[25] For this and other reasons, Vansina (1985: 182) declares that "genealogies are among the most complex sources in existence."

has to be acknowledged that the juxtaposition of a large system of genealogies with a long sequence of narratives in the context of a single historiographic work is a rarity.[26] The *Troika*, authored by Hellanicus, may offer, however, a broad analogy.[27] As reconstructed by some modern scholars, the *Troika* was an extensive work, perhaps comprising more than two books (*FGrH* 4, 323a, 608a). The first book of the *Troika* apparently contained genealogies of many prominent Greeks and Trojans, while the second book dealt with the Trojan War.[28] These two books may have been followed by (unattested) third and fourth books describing the wanderings of heroes, such as Aeneas and Odysseus (Pearson 1939). Whether there were such third and fourth volumes in Hellanicus's work need not detain us here. What is important is the use of genealogies, as in 1 Chr 1–9, as a prelude to a longer narrative history of a given period or war. One is reminded of Pearson's comment (1939: 176) that a "writer with a taste for genealogy, such as Hellanicus was, could not tell the story of the war without first explaining the ancestry of those who took a prominent part in it." The lines of descent provide vital information to the readers or hearers about the identity of the persons introduced. If so, this would parallel the purpose that may be ascribed to the genealogies in 1 Chr 1–9. These lines of descent introduce readers to the Israelites—their identity, their land, and their internal kinship relationships.[29]

V. Israel's Indivisibility and the Stress on Judah, Benjamin, and Levi

Within his portrayal of a unified Israel, the author accords special attention to what he deems to be pivotal tribes. The particular consideration given to Judah,

[26] In this context, it is not surprising that some modern critics (e.g., Welch 1935; 1939; de Vaux 1965: 390) have thought that the genealogies represent a later addition to the Chronicler's work.

[27] One should also mention the work of Manetho of Heliopolis (*FGrH* 609), the Egyptian priest living in the early Ptolemaic period (ca. 280 B.C.E.). In three books, Manetho wrote a history of Egypt that adapted the older Egyptian tradition, involving a dynastic succession from gods and divine spirits to Egyptian kings, to more of a Greek model by tracing a dynastic succession from mythical times (gods, demigods, heroes, and spirits of the dead) through to the time of fully human rulers. Manetho influentially divided the latter part of his work into some thirty dynasties (Redford 1986). This seems to be a more compelling explanation of Manetho's work than that offered recently by Verbrugghe and Wickersham (1996).

[28] In a number of details, Hellanicus and the author of the *Bibliotheke* (falsely attributed to Apollodorus) seem to agree (Pearson 1939: 181–82).

[29] In this respect, I differ with the important assessment of Japhet (1979; 1989: 278–85; 1993a: 52), who contends that 1 Chr 1–9 presents a history of an autochthonous Israel up to the time of David. In my judgment, the Chronicler's genealogies were written not so much to present an alternative history to that presented in the Hexateuch as they were to situate Israel in the context of other nations and to make assertions about Israel's tribal heritage, its identity, its internal configuration, and its relationship to the land. As such, the genealogies pertain to periods prior to, during, and following the monarchy (see "Excursus" V, below). This is not to say that the Chronicler's surveys of Israel's tribes do not contain any lineages, anecdotes, or narrative digressions whose content is at variance with earlier biblical traditions.

Benjamin, and Levi is readily apparent in the genealogies. The author arranges his material according to a broad chiastic pattern.[30]

a The peoples of the world (1 Chr 1:1–54)
  b Judah (1 Chr 2:3–4:23)
    c Simeon and the Transjordanian tribes (1 Chr 4:24–5:26)
      d The tribe of Levi (1 Chr 5:27–6:66 [ET 6:1–81])
    c′ The northern tribes (1 Chr 7:1–40)
  b′ Benjamin (1 Chr 8:1–40)
a′ The Persian period inhabitants of Jerusalem (1 Chr 9:2–34)

Although the book begins with the first person and provides a universal genealogy, the focus is clearly on the Israelite tribes. Even then, the writer does not provide a continuous set of lineages that would cover (in genealogical form) Israel's entire history up to his time. Instead, he takes Israel's segmentation into sundry tribes as a starting point (2:1–2) and repeatedly returns to this point of origin until he has managed to provide genealogies for all of the tribes.[31] To be sure, narrative digressions and anecdotes appear relating to different periods of history, especially the United and Divided Monarchies. In at least one case (the descendants of David), a lineage is traced well into the late Persian period (TEXTUAL NOTES to 3:19–24). In some cases (e.g., 5:25–26, 41; 9:1), mention is made of exile (whether Assyrian or Babylonian). In a few instances (e.g., 6:1–33, 35–38), genealogies stop with the United Monarchy. The different ending points reveal something important about the author's purpose in writing. His goal was not to be exhaustive, dealing with all of the tribes throughout the entire course of their histories. Rather, he provides readers with a sampling, perhaps what he considers to be a representative sampling, of the lineages for each of the groups that constitute Israel.

That the text repeatedly returns to Israel (Jacob) means that the author privileges the Ancestral age as definitive for the genesis of his people. The orientation toward the time of the Matriarchs and Patriarchs has a major effect on the organization of the lineages and the progression of the book (Wright 1999; Ben Zvi 2000). The Israelite genealogies exhibit a cyclical quality, even though the individual tribal genealogies move forward in time and the genealogies as a whole end with a list of Persian period repatriates (9:2–34). The importance of the Ancestral period can also be seen in the lineages the author provides for individual families or groups. Genealogical registers appear for the priests (5:27–41) and the Levitical singers (6:1–33) as part of the larger presentation of the Levitical tribe, yet each of these lines takes the Patriarch Levi as a starting point. Similarly, the Judahite genealogies contain a lineage for the descendants of David, but David's own pedigree is traced back to Judah (2:3–5, 9–17).[32]

---

[30] Similarly, Oeming (1990: 206–10) sees the genealogies as comprising a system of concentric rings. See also the comments of Noth (1930: 21ff.), Brunet (1953: 485), Williamson (1982b: 38–39), De Vries (1989: 21–26), Kartveit (1989: 110–56), and Willi (1991: 7–9).

[31] 1 Chr 2:3; 4:24; 5:1, 11, 23, 27; 6:1; 7:1, 6, 12 [TEXTUAL NOTE], 13, 14, 20, 30; 8:1. Of all of the sons of Israel listed in 1 Chr 2:1–2, Zebulun does not receive, however, a tribal genealogy.

[32] It may be relevant to observe that the same pattern can be found in other contexts within early Judaism. In the genealogy bestowed upon Judith (Jdt 8:1), for instance, her pedigree is ultimately traced

Particularly interesting, given the time in which the Chronicler wrote, is the coverage devoted to Simeon, the northern tribes, and the Transjordanian tribes. Wellhausen (1885: 212) comments: "But in Chronicles these extinct tribes again come to life—and not Levi alone, which is a special case, but also Simeon and Reuben, with which alone we are to deal—and they exist as independent integral twelfths of Israel." Wellhausen recognizes a most interesting paradox in the Chronicler's presentation.[33] Twelve (or more) sodalities comprise Israel, yet by the time the writer worked many of these groups had disappeared as self-standing entities. Indeed, the author himself admits that some tribes (e.g., 5:25–26) had already been in exile for hundreds of years. Moreover, authorial interest in these groups is not simply ethnographic in nature. The Chronicler's genealogical introduction features not only ethnographic data, but also a variety of geographical notations.[34] Containing toponyms, geographical allusions, and details about population shifts (e.g., 2:23; 7:21; 8:6, 13), the Chronicler's lineages renew ancient ties between groups and territories, as well as add new ones.

The territory and population of Yehud, as reconstructed by modern scholars (Stern 1982b; 2001; Ofer 1997; Carter 1999; 2003; Lipschits 2003), form a stark contrast with the territory and population Chronicles ascribes to the United Monarchy. Given the circumscribed borders of Yehud in the late Achaemenid or early Hellenistic period, the writer could easily have mentioned only Judah, Benjamin, and Levi or restricted himself to certain groups, such as the priests, within these sodalities. Yet he continues to hold on to a larger Israelite ideal. If genealogies can function as charters (Michalowski 1983; Chavalas 1994), one has to acknowledge that the Chronicler's charter for his people is much more comprehensive and ambitious than the geopolitical realities of Yehud might suggest. The author combs Genesis and Joshua for lineal material relating to the various tribes and adds his own contributions (more than half of the total) to present a comprehensive portrait of the fullness of his people. One cannot do justice to the genealogical schema without recognizing that the author both adheres to a pan-Israel ideal and maintains that certain tribes have played major roles in Israel's development.

Within the Chronicler's tribal schema—Judah, Levi, and Benjamin—the dominant tribes of the author's own time, receive privileged positions and the bulk of the attention. Levi, Israel's priestly tribe, occupies the central position, but Judah appears first and receives more coverage than any other sodality. Normally,

---

to Simeon in the Ancestral age (Jdt 9:2; cf. Tob 1:1; *Jub.* 4:1–33; Rom 11:1; Phil 3:4–5; *b. Pesaḥ.* 62b; *b. Qidd.* 69a–79b). In some cases, however, the Sinaitic age is determinative (e.g., Ezra 7:1–5).

[33] Because Wellhausen was primarily interested in demonstrating that the Chronicler's work was a late work, unreliable for reconstructing preexilic history, he did not explore the ramifications of his observation. On the Chronicler's pan-Israelite orientation, see further Danell (1946), Japhet (1977), Williamson (1977b), R. Braun (1977), and Knoppers (1989).

[34] In this I agree with most commentators (e.g., M. Johnson 1988: 57–62; Japhet 1989: 352–63; Williamson 1977b: 76–79; 1982b: 39; Kartveit 1989: 30–152; Oeming 1990: 73–218; Johnstone 1997a: 24–117) over against Rudolph (1955: 6–91). See, for example, 1 Chr 2:42–46, 50–55; 4:11–12, 21–23, 28–33, 39–43; 5:8–10, 11, 16, 23–26; 6:39–66; 7:21, 24, 28–29; 8:6–8, 12–13.

the eldest son of Israel would be listed first (1 Chr 2:1–2), but this privilege goes instead to Judah (2:3–4:23). According to Chronicles, Reuben's demise is directly related to Judah's ascent. Reuben squandered his primogeniture by polluting his father's bed, and Judah sired a ruler (5:1–2; Willi 1991: 46–80). In addition to explaining the primacy of Judah, this rationale sheds some light on the use of Judahite genealogies (2:3–55; 4:1–23) to frame the lengthy genealogy of David's seed (3:1–24).

a Lineages of Judah (1 Chr 2:3–55)
  b Descendants of David (1 Chr 3:1–24)
a′ Lineages of Judah (1 Chr 4:1–23)

The employment of the literary technique of chiasm calls attention to relationships within the Chronicler's genealogical system. If Levi is central to Israel, David is central to Judah (Knoppers 2001b). If one grants that the tribe of Levi has an abiding role to play in Israelite life by virtue of its lineages (Oeming 1990: 142–57), the same must be said of the descendants of David within Judah.[35]

Taking Judah as his starting point the author proceeds to catalogue the other tribes, moving geographically in basically a counterclockwise motion. The Chronicler begins with the Simeonites in the south and the Transjordanian tribes in the east (Reuben, Gad, and the half-tribe of Manasseh; 4:24–5:26). Levi (5:27–6:66 [ET 6:1–81]) is placed at the center of the genealogical system. Levi—composed of Aaronide priests and Gershonide, Qohathite, and Merarite singers—serves all of the other Israelite tribes by orchestrating their worship of Yhwh. Complementing the picture of Simeon in the south and the Transjordanian tribes in the east is a presentation of the Israelite tribes in the north and northwest—Issachar, Dan, Naphtali, Manasseh, Ephraim, and Asher (7:1–40).[36] Corresponding to Simeon's position to the south of Judah is Benajmin's position just to the north of Judah. If Judah's primacy is signaled by its initial position in the tribal genealogies, Benjamin's importance to Israel is underscored by its final position and its extensive lineages (8:1–40; 9:35–44). In this manner, Judah, Levi, and Benjamin occupy the critical positions in the larger schematic depiction of the descendants of Israel's sons.

The Chronicler's keen interest in Judah, Levi, and Benjamin is obviously related to their survival and prominence in his own time. As we have seen in our comparative discussion of genealogies from the ancient Mediterranean world, lines of descent often validate contemporary realities. Even though they construct a past, genealogists are inevitably affected by the present. The same can be said of the great attention given to Judah, Levi, and Benjamin. The literary and chronographic dimensions of the Chronicler's text converge in suggesting that these

[35] Nevertheless, it seems reductive to attribute the genealogical interest in all of these tribes and various lines of descent to an interest in validating the central position of David and his descendants (*pace* Myers 1965a: 6; Osborne 1979: 159; M. Johnson 1988: 74–75). David's line occupies the central position in the genealogy of Judah, but the Chronicler's purposes in composing the genealogies are much broader than either royalistic or messianic interpretations might suggest.

[36] Whether the Benjaminite genealogy of 1 Chr 7:6–11 is original to the Chronicler's text, seems doubtful (SOURCES AND COMPOSITION to 1 Chr 7:1–40).

three tribes were not only destined to play an essential role in maintaining Israel's heritage, but that they had already done so from antiquity. It is, however, too strong a claim to suggest that Judah, Levi, and Benjamin comprise a "true Israel" over against the northern tribes (contra Torrey 1954a: xix; Galling 1954: 19; von Rad 1962b: 348, 354; Plöger 1968: 37–38). If the writer wished to invalidate a Samarian claim to authentic Israelite status, his own presentation of Israel's heritage is self-defeating. Some tribes may play a more central and enduring role than others (see above), but the very scope and structure of the genealogical system underscores the indivisibility of Israel. For the Chronicler, the people's unity is a past, present, and future reality. In this context, it is no accident that the genealogy of the return (9:2–34) mentions repatriates from Judah, Benjamin, Ephraim, Manasseh, and Levi (cf. Neh 11:4; Knoppers 2000c: 155–56).

The Chronicler's outer frame (1:1–54; 9:2–34) says something about his view of larger divine purposes in human history. The *imago mundi* of 1 Chr 1 reveals that Israel is kin to its neighbors, but the following genealogies (1 Chr 2–8) reveal that the descendants of Israel occupy a privileged place among the very nations to whom they are related. The list of those in the restored community (1 Chr 9) creates continuity between postexilic society and the Israel of ages past. Population shifts, war, political turmoil, natural disaster, and exile are part of history, but Yhwh's relationship with his people endures. Because the roster of 1 Chr 9 repeatedly mentions Jerusalem and various temple officials, it accentuates the importance of city and temple to the community of Yehud. The list of 1 Chr 9 serves another important function. If the universal lineage sets the stage for the appearance of Israel (1 Chr 2–8), the tribal lineages set the stage for the reestablishment of an Israel centered around Jerusalem (9:2–34).[37] That the Chronicler's ethnography begins with the primal human and ends with the ethnography of Achaemenid Judah is but one more sign of how much genealogies about the past are related to the times and circumstances of the genealogists who formulate them. Ending with the Persian period community in Jerusalem, the text prepares readers for the concentration of the narrative portions of the book on the state centered in the same city (1 Chr 11–2 Chr 36).

Having looked at the combination of genealogy and history in the Chronicler's work, it is appropriate to explore the implications of their juxtaposition. What is the literary effect of prefacing narratives about the monarchy with lineages of Israel's various tribes? In one sense, the genealogies in Chronicles are both an introduction to the people of Israel—their origins, identity, relationships—and a prologue to the story of their monarchical development in the land. References to individual monarchs and to events during the monarchy are, of course, often found within the genealogies themselves. But in another sense, the Israel discussed in the genealogies outlives the monarchy discussed in the history (Wright 1999). The account of the United Monarchy narrates, among other things, the fall

[37] Keil (1873: 152–68); Galling (1954: 37–38); Rudolph (1949: 181–91; 1955: 83–91); von Rad (1962b: 347); Ackroyd (1973a: 43–47); Osborne (1979: 302–8); R. Braun (1986: 129–46); De Vries (1989: 88–94); Oeming (1990: 180–204); Japhet (1993a: 200–220); Johnstone (1997a: 118–29).

of Saul, the consolidation of the Davidic kingdom, the establishment of Jerusalem as a capital city, and the construction of the Temple. These normative institutions remain during the Judahite monarchy, but come to an end with the Babylonian exile. The people themselves survive, however, and return at a later time to rebuild. In the context of the Persian age, those who call themselves Israelites may find themselves scattered in different lands, but even so, Jerusalem and Yehud are indispensable to their identity and future hopes as a people. In this respect, the genealogical prologue (1 Chr 1–9) and the story of the monarchy (1 Chr 10–2 Chr 36), despite their different genres, reveal similar points of view. Both end with exile (1 Chr 9:1; 2 Chr 36:17–21), charge the deportation to infidelity (1 Chr 9:1; 2 Chr 36:12–16), and announce a return (1 Chr 9:2–34; 2 Chr 36:22–23).

I. From Adam to Esau and Israel: A Genealogy of Nations (1:1–2:2)

The Descendants of Adam

1 Adam, Seth, Enosh; 2 Qenan, Mahalalel, Jared; 3 Enoch, Methuselaḥ, La-
mech, 4 Noaḥ.

The Sons of Noaḥ

The sons of Noaḥ: Shem, Ḥam, and Japheth.

The Descendants of Japheth

5 The sons of Japheth: Gomer, Magog, Madai, Javan, Tubal, Meshech, and
Tiras. 6 And the sons of Gomer: Ashkenaz, Diphath, and Togarmah. 7 The sons of
Javan: Elishah and Tarshish, Kittim and Rodanim.

The Descendants of Ḥam

8 The sons of Ḥam: Cush, Mizraim, Puṭ, and Canaan. 9 The sons of Cush:
Seba, Ḥavilah, Sabta, Raama, and Sabteca. The sons of Raama: Sheba and
Dedan. 10 And Cush sired Nimrod; he was the first to become a warrior in the
land. [11 And Mizraim sired (the) Ludim, the Anamim, the Lehabim, the Naphtuḥim, 12 the Pathrusim, and the Casluḥim who went forth from there, (the) Philistines and the Caphtorim. 13 And Canaan sired Sidon, his firstborn, Ḥeth, 14 the
Jebusites, the Amorites, the Girgashites, 15 the Ḥivites, the Arqites, the Sinites,
16 the Arvadites, the Zemarites, and the Ḥamathites.]

The Descendants of Shem

17 The sons of Shem: Elam, Ashur, Arpachshad, Lud, and Aram. The sons of
Aram: Uz, Ḥul, Gether, and Meshech. 18 And Arpachshad sired Shelaḥ and Shelaḥ sired Eber. 19 Two sons were born to Eber. The name of the first was Peleg, because in his days the land was divided, and the name of his brother was Joqṭan.
20 And Joqṭan sired Almodad, Shaleph, Ḥazarmawet, Jaraḥ, 21 Hadoram, Uzal,
Diqlah, 22 Ebal, Abimael, Sheba, 23 Ophir, Ḥavilah, and Jobab. All these were

sons of Joqṭan. 24Shem, Arpachshad, Shelaḥ, 25Eber, Peleg, Reu, 26Serug, Naḥor, Taraḥ, 27Abram, that is, Abraham.

The Descendants of Abraham

28The sons of Abraham: Isaac and Ishmael.

The Descendants of Ishmael

29These are their lineages: the firstborn of Ishmael Nebaioth, Qedar, Adbeel, Mibsam, 30Mishma, Dumah, Massa, Ḥadad, Tema, 31Jeṭur, Naphish, and Qedemah. These were the sons of Ishmael.

The Descendants of Qeṭurah

32The sons of Qeṭurah the concubine of Abraham: she gave birth to Zimran, Joqshan, Medan, Midian, Ishbaq, and Shuaḥ. The sons of Joqshan: Sheba and Dedan. 33The sons of Midian: Ephah, Epher, Enoch, Abida, and Eldaah. All of these were descendants of Qeṭurah.

The Sons of Isaac

34And Abraham sired Isaac. The sons of Isaac: Esau and Israel.

The Descendants of Esau

35The sons of Esau: Eliphaz, Reuel, Jeush, Jalam, and Qoraḥ. 36The sons of Eliphaz: Teman, Omar, Zephi, Gatam, Qenaz, Timna, and Amaleq. 37The sons of Reuel: Naḥath, Zeraḥ, Shammah, and Mizzah.

The Descendants of Seir

38The sons of Seir: Loṭan, Shobal, Zibeon, Anah, Dishon, Ezer, and Dishan. 39The sons of Loṭan: Ḥori and Homam. And the sister of Loṭan (was) Timna. 40The sons of Shobal: Alian, Manaḥath, Ebal, Shephi, and Onam. The sons of Zibeon: Ayyah and Anah. 41The sons of Anah: Dishon. The sons of Dishon: Ḥamran, Eshban, Ithran, and Keran. 42The sons of Ezer: Bilhan, Zaavan, and Jaaqan. The sons of Dishan: Uz and Aran.

The Edomite Kings

43These are the kings who reigned in the land of Edom before a king reigned among the Israelites: Bela son of Beor and the name of his town was Dinhabah. 44When Bela died, Jobab son of Zeraḥ from Bozrah reigned in his stead. 45When Jobab died, Ḥusham from the land of the Temanites reigned in his stead. 46When Ḥusham died, Hadad son of Bedad reigned in his stead. He was the one who struck down Midian in the territory of Moab. The name of his town was Avith. 47When Hadad died, Samlah from Masreqah reigned in his stead. 48When Samlah died, Saul from Reḥoboth on the River reigned in his stead. 49When Saul died, Baal Ḥanan son of Achbor reigned in his stead. 50When Baal Ḥanan died, Hadad reigned in his stead. The name of his town was Pai.

The Edomite Chieftains

51When Hadad died, the chieftains of Edom were the chieftain of Timna, the chieftain of Alyah, the chieftain of Jetheth, 52the chieftain of Oholibamah, the chieftain of Elah, the chieftain of Pinon, 53the chieftain of Qenan, the chieftain of Teman, the chieftain of Mibzar, 54the chieftain of Magdiel, the chieftain of Iram; these were the chieftains of Edom.

The Sons of Israel

2:1These are the sons of Israel: Reuben, Simeon, Levi, Judah, Issachar, Zebulun, 2Dan, Joseph, Benjamin, Naphtali, Gad, and Asher.

Textual Notes

1:2. "Mahalalel" *(mhll'l)*. So MT. Cf. LXX Μαλελεήλ.

1:4. "Noaḥ. (And) the sons of Noaḥ" (נח ובני נח). So LXX^{AB} and cursive y. MT, followed by some witnesses to LXX^{L}, reads "Noaḥ, Shem, Ḥam, and Japhet." Osborne (1979: 160–61) and R. Braun (1986: 14) think that LXX is expansionistic, because in previous cases (vv. 1–3) only one son is listed per father, but MT may have lost the longer reading by haplography (*homoioteleuton*; Podechard 1916: 376). Moreover, the terminology of LXX^{AB} conforms to the pattern "PN_1: the sons of PN_1," found in vv. 5–9, 28. The author likely adapted the material for this verse from Gen 10:1 (instead of Gen 5:32).

1:5. "Javan" *(yāwān)*. Thus MT. LXX^{AB} *Iōyan*. LXX^{AB} adds *(H)elisa* (Elishah), one of Javan's sons (v. 7). Cursive y adds *Thoben*.

"Meshech." So MT *(mšk)*. LXX^{B} Gen 10:2 and LXX 1:5 *Mosoch*. Vg. follows suit. Cf. Tg. Gen 10:2 מושך.

1:6. "(and) Diphath." Thus MT (ודיפת). The readings of LXX^{B} c_2 *(kai Ereiphath)*, LXX^{L} *(Rheiphath)*, Vg. *(et Riphath)* and MT Gen 10:3 (ריפת) have suffered a *dālet/rêš* confusion. As Allen (1974b: 114) points out, the testimony of LXX 1 Chr 1:6 is more complex than *BHS* would have it. LXX's *Vorlage* may have read יריפת, a slight corruption of וריפת. On the name "Diphath," see the NOTE to 1:6.

1:7. "Tarshish." So the versions and Gen 10:4. MT's anomalous "Tarshishah" (cf. *trsyš*; 2 Chr 9:21; 20:36–37) results from a dittography of *hê* after Elishah.

"Rodanim." Thus MT 1:7 and SP Gen 10:4. LXX 1:7 and LXX Gen 10:4 *Rhodioi*. MT Gen 10:4 "Dodanim"—followed by many Heb. MSS as well as LXX^{L} Vg. and Syr. 1 Chr 1:7—reveals a *dālet/rêš* confusion. Some (e.g., Neimann 1973: 121) favor MT Genesis and speak of the Danuneans or Dodonoi, but the earliest textual witnesses to Chronicles have "Rodanim."

1:8. "Cush (and) Mizraim, Puṭ and Canaan." So MT 1:8 and SP Gen 10:6. MT Gen 10:6 "Cush and Mizraim and Puṭ and Canaan."

"Mizraim." Some (e.g., NRSV) trans. as "Egypt" (NOTE to vv. 8–9).

1:9. "Raama" *(rʿmʿ)*. So MT (twice). MT Gen 10:7 has "Raamah" *(rʿmh)* twice.

"and Dedan" (ודדן). So MT and LXX^{L} *(kai Dadan)*. LXX^{B} *kai Ioudadan* results from the *wāw* being construed as part of the PN.

1:10. "sired" (ילד). The usage is typical of the J source; see vv. 10, 11, 13, 20 (all of which stem from J in Gen 10).

"Nimrod" (נמרוד). So MT 1:10 and SP Gen 10:8. MT Gen 10:8 (נמרד) does not have the plene spelling.

"warrior" *(gibbôr)*. So MT. LXX^{A} *(gigas kunēgos)* follows MT Gen 10:9 *(gibbôr ṣayid)*, "a warrior, a hunter."

1:11–16. "and Mizraim . . . the Ḥamathites." These verses appear in brackets because it is uncertain whether they are original to Chronicles. The verses, lacking in LXX^{B} and ghc_2, are *sub ast.* in the Syro-Hexapla. In cursive i only vv. 13–16 are missing. All of vv. 11–23 are *sub ast.* in cursives cn, although the text-critical significance of these variations is disputed (Allen 1974a: 98–99; 1974b: 159).

Verses 11–16 appear in MT, LXX^{AN}, and Arm. LXX^{B} has the *lectio brevior* and there is no obvious mechanism for haplography. By the same token, the want of this material in LXX^{B} is puzzling, given the headings in v. 4 and the inclusion of Ḥam's other descendants (vv. 8–10). The deviation between MT and LXX may confirm what numerous text critics have claimed since the publication of variant biblical manuscripts from Qumran: there was some fluidity in the content, organization, and length of many biblical texts until the first century C.E.

1:11. "Ludim" *(lwdym)*. So Qere and MT Gen 10:13; cf. Kethib *lwdyym*.

1:12. "the Casluḥim . . . Philistines." So MT and LXX (maximum variation). Citing Amos 9:7, NAB transposes, "who came forth from there, the Philistines" *(ʾšr yṣʾw mšm plštym)* after "and the Caphtorim" *(wʾt-kptrym)*. But if a copyist's mistake was made, the corrupt reading was already in the Chronicler's *Vorlage*. See MT Gen 10:14.

1:13. "Sidon" (צידון). So MT 1:13 and SP Gen 10:15. MT Gen 10:15 (צידן) does not have the plene spelling.

1:14–16. "the Jebusites . . . Ḥamathites" (החמתי . . .). Whereas gentilics in pl. form characterize vv. 11–12, for example, "Ludim" (לודים), gentilics in sg. form characterize vv. 14–16, a fact many modern translations obscure. In each case, Chronicles punctiliously reproduces its sources: Gen 10:13–14 and Gen 10:16–18.

1:17b–24a. "Arpachshad, Lud . . . Shem, Arpachshad." So MT. These verses appear neither in LXX^{B} nor in cursives ghc$_2$ (they, like vv. 11–16, are *sub ast.* in the Syro-Hexapla). But they were probably lost through haplography *(homoioteleuton* from *ʾarpakšad* to *ʾarpakšad)*.

1:17. "Aram. The sons of Aram (וארם ובני ארם)." MT reads, "and Aram and Uz" *(wʾrm wʿwṣ)*, but both MT and LXX Gen 10:22–23 have "and Aram. And the sons of Aram were Uz" *(wʾrm wbny ʾrm ʿwṣ)*, a lemma one also finds in a Heb. MS and LXX^{AN} of Chronicles. As it stands, MT makes Aram, Uz, Ḥul, Gether, and Meshech all sons of Shem. It seems more likely that MT 1:17 has suffered a haplography *(homoioteleuton* from *ʾrm* to *ʾrm)*.

"Uz." Reading both with MT and LXX Gen 10:22–23. The prefatory *wāw* of MT 1:17 may be a later addition.

"and Meshech." Thus MT *(wmšk)* and LXX^{L} *(Mosoch)* 1:17; as well as LXX Gen 10:23 *(Mosoch)*. NAB "and Mash" *(wmš)*, following a few Heb. MSS, the Peshiṭta, MT Gen 10:17, SP *(wmšʾ)*, and 1QM 2.11.

1:18. "Arpachshad." Reading with MT 1:18 and MT Gen 10:24 *(lectio brevior)*. LXX^{AL} 1:18 and LXX Gen 10:24 reflect a later variant tradition, adding "Arpachshad sired Canaan and Canaan sired Shelaḥ." See also LXX Gen 11:10–13 and Luke 3:36.

1:19. "were born" (יֻלַּד). Reading with MT *(lectio difficilior)*. The sg. verb is used to precede a compound subj. (GKC, §§145o, 146d). Vg. and Tg. have the expected pl.

1:21. "Uzal" *(ʾwzl)*. So MT 1:21 and MT Gen 10:27. SP, LXX* 1:21 *Aizēl*, and Tg. Gen 10:27 *ʾyzl*.

1:22. "Ebal" (עיבל). So MT 1:22 and SP Gen 10:28 (cf. some witnesses to LXX

Gen 10:28 *Abimeēl*). A few Heb. MSS and Syr. 1 Chr 1:22 have "Obal" (עובל), as does MT Gen 10:28.

1:24. "Shem." Thus MT. LXX^{AN} "the sons of Shem were" assimilates toward the introduction in v. 17 (see also v. 28).

1:27. "Abram, that is Abraham." Reading with MT (אברם הוא אברהם) and LXX^{ALN}. LXX^{B} "Abram" is the *lectio brevior*, but LXX^{B} probably reflects a haplography (from אברם to אברהם). Note that v. 28 begins with "the sons of Abraham."

1:29. "Adbeel" (*'db'l*). So MT 1:29 and SP Gen 25:13 (cf. MT Gen 25:13 *'rb'l*). A form of the name appears in Akk., Gk., and OSA texts (Vattioni 1991a; last NOTE to v. 29). LXX^{AN} *Nabdeēl*; LXX^{B} and hc$_2$ *Nabdaiēl*. The texts of LXX^{L} *kai Abdiēl* and Josephus (*Ant.* 1.220) *Abdeēlos* have suffered metathesis. See also the related "Nodab" in 1 Chr 5:19 (Albright 1956: 13).

"Mibsam." So MT (*mibśām*). LXX *Massa*.

1:30. "Massa." So MT. MT Gen 25:14 "and Massa." LXX *Manassē*.

"Ḥadad." So MT. A few Heb. MSS have "Ḥadar."

1:31. "Qedemah" (*qdmh*). So MT and LXX (*Kedmah*). Cf. 1 Chr 5:19 "Nodab."

1:32. "Qeṭurah . . ." So MT (*lectio difficilior*), which literally reads, "and the sons of Qeṭurah, concubine of Abraham, she bore." The longer reading of LXX^{B}, "and she bore to him" (= וילדה לו), eases the syntactical difficulty, but this lemma may assimilate toward Gen 25:1. Arnold Ehrlich (1914) follows Syr., which lacks "she gave birth to" (ילדת-את), but the confusion may stem simply from the author's reworking of two different texts, Gen 25:1–2 and Gen 25:6 (Japhet 1993a: 61).

"Ishbaq" (*yišbāq*). So MT 1:32 and Gen 25:2. LXX^{B} and c$_2$ *Sobak*.

"Dedan." Thus MT. LXX^{AB} and y *Daidan*; *b*b'e$_2$ *Dardan*. Some witnesses to LXX continue with a list of Dedan's progeny, but this lemma assimilates toward the source text (Gen 25:3).

1:33. "Enoch" (חנוך). So MT 1:33 and SP Gen 25:4. MT Gen 25:4 (חנך) lacks the plene spelling.

1:34. "Esau and Israel." So MT (maximum variation). LXX^{B} "Esau and Jacob" (cf. LXX^{A} "Jacob and Esau") is preferred by Benzinger (1901) and Kittel (1902), but, excepting the poem of 1 Chr 16:13, Chronicles always renders Israel for Jacob (Williamson 1977b: 62).

1:35. "Jeush" (*y'wš*). So MT, Qere Gen 36:5; see also SP and LXX Gen 36:5 (*Ieous*), and 4QGen-Exod^{a} Gen 36:5. Kethib "Jeish" (*y'yš*) reflects a *wāw/yôd* confusion. LXX^{AB} 1:35 *Ieoul*.

1:36. "Zephi." Thus MT (צפי). Many Heb. MSS, Syr., and MT Gen 36:11 have "Zepho" (צפו). LXX^{AB} Gen 36:11 and 1 Chr 1:36 *Sōphar* (= צפר). Wevers (1993: 595) calls attention to Job's friend צפר (2:11; 11:1; 20:1; 42:9). The variants reflect a *wāw/yôd/rêš* confusion.

"(and) Timna and Amaleq" (*wĕtimnā' wa'ămālēq*). Thus MT. LXX^{B} *kai tēs Thamna Amalēk*, "and of Timna, Amaleq." LXX^{AN} follow MT (and 4QGen-Exod^{a}) Gen 36:12, "and Timna was the concubine for Eliphaz, the son of Esau, and she bore for Eliphaz Amaleq."

1:38. "Dishon (and) Ezer (and) Dishan." So MT. 4QGen-Exod^{a} וד[שון וא]צר. LXX^{B} *Dēsōn Ōnan* may reflect a haplography. LXX^{AN} is closer to MT, *Dēsōn kai Asar kai Rhisōn.* Cursives ny add "seven" after the last PN.

1:39. "Homam" (הומם). Thus MT. LXX^{B} *Haiman*; *b*b′ *Iman*; ye$_2$ *Eman* (= הימן). Vg. reflects הומן. MT Gen 36:24 הימם.

"the sister of Loṭan (was) Timna." Thus MT. LXX^{B} and c$_2$ "and Ailath and Namna" reflects, in part, an orthographic confusion between נו and ת (Allen 1974b: 123).

1:40. "Alian" (עלין). So MT. The variation with "Alvan" (some Heb. MSS; LXX^{L} *Halouan*; Gen 36:23 עלון) reflects a *wāw/yôd* confusion. The *wāw/yôd* confusion is also common in the textual witnesses to Samuel (S. Driver 1912: lxiv–lxvi). LXX^{N} *Gōlam* may reflect a transposition: עלון vs. עולן (Allen 1974b: 119; contra Gilbert 1896–97: 297).

"Shephi" (שפי). Thus MT. Some Heb. MSS and Gen 36:23 have "Shipho" (שפו). LXX^{B} and c$_2$ *Sōb*; LXX^{A} *Sophar.* The variants reflect a *wāw/yôd/rêš* confusion. Compare the variants to "Zephi" in v. 36.

1:41. "the sons of Anah: Dishon." So MT and the versions. Myers (1965a: 5) argues for the *Sebir* "son." Allen (1974a: 161) thinks that *Sonan* in LXX indicates that *huios* ("son") originally stood in the translator's *Vorlage*, causing a dittography of the "s," but *Sonan* also appears in v. 40. The use of "sons" *(bĕnê)* is purely formulaic. The writer selectively quotes from Gen 36:25 without completely reworking his source.

"Dishon" (דישון). Thus MT and SP Gen 36:25. MT Gen 36:25 "Dishan" (דישן) may assimilate toward Gen 36:21 (//1 Chr 1:38). LXX^{A} and *b*b′y assimilate toward Gen 36:25 by adding "and Elibama was the daughter of (H)ana."

"Ḥamran." So MT (maximum variation). Some (e.g., NAB) read "Ḥemdan," following several Heb. MSS, LXX^{A}, and MT Gen 36:26. The variants reflect a *dālet/rêš* confusion.

1:42. "Bilhan." LXX's *Balaam/n* substitutes a familar name for an unfamilar one.

"Zaavan" *(zʿwn).* So MT 1:42 and MT Gen 36:27. LXX^{B} 1:42 *Zoukam*; LXX^{A} 1:42 *Azoukan.* SP Gen 36:27 *zwʿn*; LXX^{L} 1:42 *Zauan.*

"and Jaaqan" (ויעקן). So MT. The lemma of MT Gen 36:27 "and Aqan" (ועקן) is followed by some LXX cursives of Chronicles. LXX^{B} *Ōnan.*

1:43. "and these are the kings . . . Israelites." So MT as well as MT and LXX Gen 36:31. It is difficult to believe that the *lectio brevior* of LXX^{A}, "and these (are) their kings," offers the most primitive reading, because there is no clear antecedent to "their kings." Part of a rubric has been lost from LXX^{A} (cf. vv. 28–29a). Some witnesses (e.g., LXX^{AN}) contain a long plus after "their kings" (βασιλεῖς αὐτῶν), enumerating the sons of Israel, but this plus is *sub ast.* in cursives i and n.

"Bela" *(belaʿ).* LXX *Balak*; Tg. *blʿm.*

1:45. "Ḥusham" (חושם). LXX *Hasom* reflects metathesis (חשום).

1:46. "Bedad." LXX^{AB} *Barad*; LXX^{L} *Badram.* Similarly, MT Gen 36:35 "Bedad;" LXX "Barad."

"Avith" עֲוִית). So Qere and MT Gen 36:35 (cf. Kethib עיות). LXX^{AB} *Geththaim* (= עתים?).

1:47–49. LXX has most of this material after v. 51, beginning with "and he reigned" (v. 47) and ending with "Saul" (v. 49). The material was probably lost by haplography *(homoioteleuton)*, but later reinserted after v. 51 (Rudolph 1955).

1:47. "Samlah." So MT. Some witnesses to LXX *(Samaa; Salma; Sabaa)* reflect an inner Gk. corruption (Podechard 1916: 384).

1:48. "Reḥoboth on the River." Some (e.g., NRSV) trans. "Rehoboth on the Euphrates," but such a usage is unlikely in this context (NOTE to v. 48).

1:50. "Baal Ḥanan." So MT and SP Gen 36:39 *(lectio brevior)*. LXX^{AB} add "son of Achbor," following MT Gen 36:39, but the occurrence of "son of Achbor" in Gen 36:39 may represent a dittography of "son of Achbor" in Gen 36:38.

"Hadad." Reading with MT and LXX *(Hadad)*. MT, SP, and Tg. Gen 36:39 "Hadar." The confusion is common (e.g., MT and LXX 1 Kgs 11:14, 25; Knoppers 1993c: 160–62).

"Pai." So MT. Some witnesses to both LXX (cf. LXX^{AB} and Eusebius. *Phogōr*; ce *Phoor*; *b Phaoua*) and LXX Gen 36:39 may reflect an original "Peor" (Num 23:28). Cursives dfjpqtz *(Phoou)*, Syr., Vg., and Tg. have "Pau" in conformity with MT Gen 36:39. MT continues with "and the name of his wife was Meheṭabel daughter of Maṭred daughter of Me-zahab," but this material does not appear in LXX^{B} *(lectio brevior potior est)*. MT assimiliates toward Gen 36:39.

1:51. "when Ḥadad died." Most translate "and Ḥadad died" (RSV, NJPS), but the structure and syntax are similar to that of previous verses.

"chieftains of Edom" *(ʾallûpê ʾĕdôm)*. So MT and LXX (maximum variation). MT and LXX Gen 36:40 "chieftains of Esau."

"chieftain" *(ʾallûp)*. Some (e.g., NRSV; NJPS; Orlinsky 1969: 116–18) contend that *ʾlwp* signifies "a clan," based upon two considerations: the meaning of *ʾlp* as "thousand," "group," or "contingent" (Mendenhall 1958) and the context of Gen 36:9–14 (the list of Esau's descendants through his three wives) in which each individual *(bn)* is thought to represent a clan or tribe. The etymology of *ʾlwp* is disputed, however. It may be related to *ʾlp*, "thousand," to Ug. *ʾulp*, "leader, ally," or to *ʾlp*, "cattle" (cf. Ug. *ʾalp*; Phoen. *ʾlp*; Akk. *alpu*). In the last case, the name of a male animal would be used for prominent leaders (P. Miller 1970; Cross 1973: 4–5). The Song of the Sea, for instance, parallels the *ʾallûpê ʾĕdôm* with the *ʾêlê môʾāb*, "rams of Moab" (Exod 15:15; Cross and Freedman 1975: 37, 44). As for the argument based on context, the analogy with Gen 36:9–14 and Gen 36:15–19 would seem just as easily to count against trans. *ʾallûp* as "clan" in Gen 36:40–43 and in its parallel, 1 Chr 1:51–54. The shift in vocabulary from "son" *(bn)* to *ʾlwp* may signify a different sense for each term. The writer may use *ʾallûp* to designate the leaders of Edom, as opposed to its descendants. Note also the usage of "sons" *(bny)* and "chieftains" *(ʾallûpê haḥōrî)* in speaking of the Seirites (Gen 36:20–30). In brief, the trans. of *ʾallûp* as "chieftain" should be retained.

"Timna" *(timnāʿ)*. LXX^{B} and c_2 *Thaiman*; LXX^{A} *Thamana*.

"Alvah" *(ʿlwh)*. So Qere, many Heb. MSS, LXX^{L} (Aloua); Vg.; Tg., Arm. (Alua); and MT Gen 36:40 (cf. Kethib "Alyah" [*ʿlyh*]). LXX^{AB} 1:51 and Gen 36:40 *Gōla* have suffered metathesis (= עולה).

1:52. "Oholibama" (אהליבמה). Syr. אהליבה.

1:54. "Iram" (*ʿîrām*). So MT (cf. LXX^{A} *Airam*; LXX^{L} *Heram*). LXX^{B} *Zaphōein*; c_2 *Zephōein*. Similar variants for Iram ("young male donkey"; *ʿîr* + *-ām* enclitic morpheme; Layton 1990a: 178–79) occur in MT and LXX Gen 36:43. Assuming an aggregate of twelve, some commentators add a chieftain "Zepho" after Iram. But there are no firm text-critical grounds to harmonize LXX with MT by restoring a chieftain to both. Nor is there any basis to derive *Zaphōein* from *Airam* (contra Torrey 1910: 94).

2:1–2. Contrary to the versification found in our Bibles in which 1 Chr 2:1–2 begins a new chapter, the material in 2:1–2 basically belongs with what precedes, rather than with what follows. The enumeration of Israel's seed concludes the section begun in v. 34, dealing with the descendants of Abraham and Isaac. Having furnished the names of the descendants of Isaac's eldest son Esau in vv. 35–54, the writer turns his attention to the offspring of Isaac's other son, Jacob (Israel), in 2:1–2. The material in 2:3 begins another major section: the genealogies dealing with the descendants of Israel's various sons (2:3–8:40).

2:1. "these are the sons." So MT, LXX^{L}, and Arm. LXX^{AB} "these are the names of the sons" assimilates toward Exod 1:1 (Allen 1974a: 186).

"Issachar" (יִשָּׂכָר). Reading with many Heb. MSS. MT יִשָּׂשכָר.

NOTES

1:1–4a. "Adam . . . Noaḥ." The list of ten names, representing ten generations, is a miracle of condensation. The substance in these verses has been extracted from the much longer and more detailed narrative lineage of Adam in Gen 5:1–32 ("these are the lineages [*tōlĕdôt*] of Adam . . ."), ascribed to the Priestly writer(s) (P). Unlike the Yahwist (J) and P, Chronicles makes no explicit reference to the flood. Nor does the Chronicler explain the relationships between the persons he includes in his genealogy. One has to know his source to recognize the force of his presentation. As genealogies occurring in list form, the lineages in vv. 1–4a and 24–27 (NOTE) resemble certain other unilineal genealogies from the ancient Near East, for example, the Sumerian and Assyrian king lists (R. Wilson 1977: 72–114). The unilineal lineages found in the Safaitic inscriptions, although achieving a depth of up to ten generations (#399; Winnett and Harding 1978: 107–8), are not as helpful as an analogy because these genealogies do not occur in list form.

"Adam." The beginning of the Chronicler's work has a universal focus. Such a global dimension is, of course, characteristic of the Yahwistic (Gen 2:4b–25) and Priestly (Gen 1:1–2:4a) creation stories. But it is also found in other late compositions such as the prayer of Neh 9, which begins with creation (v. 6), and one of the historical psalms (136: 1–9; Rendtorff 1992).

1:4. "sons of Noaḥ." The heading may be compared with that of Gen 10:1. By excising much of Gen 10:1 (P) and prefacing this material with a reference to Noaḥ (v. 4a), the Chronicler creates his own rubric. Each of Noaḥ's three sons can be associated with a relatively large area: Shem (peoples to the east; vv. 17–27),

Ḥam (peoples to the south and southwest; vv. 8–16), Japheth (peoples to the north and west; vv. 5–7). Ḥam also includes Canaan, perhaps because of its long political relationship with Egypt (Aharoni 1979: 6; cf. Curtis and Madsen 1910: 62–65). Modern scholars believe that Canaan was ethnically and linguistically Semitic.

1:5–23. These verses may be compared with Gen 10:1–29, the Table of Nations from which the author draws heavily. The Table of Nations enumerates approximately seventy descendants of Noaḥ's sons, which symbolize seventy peoples of the world, thereby creating a genealogical tree by which all the nations of the world are related to each other through a common forefather. Such biblical and early Jewish lists and longer narrative texts are exercises in "cognitive mapping," attempts "to impose order on the chaos of spatial perception" (Alexander 1992: 978). The resulting statement of relationships may at best only partially comport with external reality.

1:5–7. "sons of Japheth." Derived from Gen 10:2–4, these verses comprise a segmented genealogy with a depth of three generations. The sons of Japheth (most distant from the point of view of the biblical writers) encompass a wide variety of lands ranging from the east to the northwest: Iran (Madai), Anatolia (e.g., Togarmah, Tubal, Meshech), and Asia Minor, including Greek settlements (Javan), and islands in the Mediterranean Sea, such as Elishah (Cyprus), Kittim (Kition in southern Cyprus), and Rodanim (Rhodes). The distribution of these sites may have been influenced by a writer's perceptions of the process of Greek colonization of the eastern Mediterranean, which had already begun in the eighth century B.C.E. Alternatively, it has been argued that the configuration of the sons of Japheth (in P) has been made to correspond to the extent of the Persian empire (Vermeylen 1992).

1:5. "Madai" *(māday)*. The name often refers to the Medes (Isa 13:17) or to the land of the Medes (2 Kgs 17:6; 18:11; Isa 21:2; Jer 25:25; 51:11, 28), east of the Zagros mountains and south of the Caspian Sea.

"Javan" *(yāwān)* refers to the Ionian Greek settlements on the coast of Asia Minor (Isa 66:19; Ezek 27:13). Some texts reflect the later usage of Javan to refer more generally to Greece (Joel 3:6; Zech 9:13; Dan 8:21; 10:20; 11:2).

"Tubal, Meshech." Tubal *(tubāl)* and Meshech *(mešek*; Akk. *Mušku, Muškāya*; Hit. *Musakaia)* appear in Ezek 27:13 (along with Javan) as trading in slaves and bronze goods. Traditionally located in eastern Anatolia, the two appear together in Assyrian inscriptions and letters from the ninth and eighth centuries B.C.E. (*HALOT* 646). Note also *Móschoi . . . Tibarēnoi* in Herodotus (*Hist.* 3.94; cf. 7.78). "Meshech" reappears in v. 17 as a son of Aram.

1:6. "Gomer" (גמר) is considered to be the eponymous ancestor of the Cimmerians (cuneiform *Gimir*[*r*]*i*), whose entrance into Asia Minor through the Caucasus from the north is recounted by Herodotus (*Hist.* 1.15, 103; 4.11). "Gomer" is an ally of Togarmah in Ezek 38:6 (Lipiński 1990: 40–41).

"Ashkenaz" *(ʾaškĕnaz)* is associated in Jer 51:27 with Ararat (Assyr. *Urarṭu*) and Minni (Assyr. *Mannay*). Here, Ashkenaz represents the residents of an area between the Black and Caspian Seas. An Assyr. text, dating to the time of Esarhaddon, mentions a group, *ašguzay* (or *iškuzay*), who were allies of the Mannay in their revolt against Assyria. This group is to be identified with the Scythians mentioned by Herodotus (*Hist.* 1.103, 106; 4.1; Lipiński 1990: 48).

"Diphath" (דיפת). The name may be related to Persian *dahyu-pati*, signifying "chief of the people/region" (Lipiński 1990: 49–50). In Elamite texts from Persepolis the term is *da-a-ú-bat* (with an affix *ti-iš*) and *da-i-bat* (with an affix *ti-iš*).

1:7. "Tarshish." Given the association of the name with smelting (and a certain kind of ship), a number of sites may have borne this name (cf. Akk. *Tar-si-si* [Borger 1956, §57.10–11]; Gk. *Tartēssós* [Herodotus, *Hist.* 1.163; 4.152]; LXX *Tharsis*). The attempts at identification include: Carthage, Sardinia, and Tarsus in Cilicia (Lemaire 2000b).

1:8–16. "sons of Ḥam." A segmented genealogy derived from Gen 10:6–9, 13–18. The names of Ḥam's children are those of peoples and areas in the Egyptian political sphere: Cush to the south (Sudan, Nubia), Mizraim (Egypt), Puṭ to the west (Libya), and Canaan to the north (Lipiński 1992).

"Canaan," the eponymous ancestor of the pre-Israelite inhabitants of the land (Palestine and Phoenicia). The usage suggests geography, rather than ethnicity or linguistic relationships.

1:9. "The sons of Cush" feature some of the lands in southern Arabia thought to have connections with Africa: Seba, Ḥavilah, Raama, Sheba, and Dedan.

"Seba" *(sĕbāʾ)*. Cf. Assyr. *Sabʾaya* (Parpola 1970: 297) and OSA *sbʾ* "Sabaean" or, as a collective, "Sabaeans" (Biella 1982: 323). The name is linked to that of Sheba (NOTE below). Recent research points to the existence of a Sabaean state located either in Ethiopia or in southern Arabia in the eighth century B.C.E. (Ephʿal 1984: 86–88). The Sabaeans (*lúsa-ba-ʾ-a-a*), along with groups from northern Arabia and north Sinai, are mentioned in the Summary inscriptions of Tiglath-pileser III (4:27′; 7:r.3′; 13:9′; H. Tadmor 1994). Psalm 72:10 groups Seba together with Sheba, while other texts group Seba with Egypt and Cush (Isa 43:3; 45:14). On the name, see also Strabo (*Geogr.* 16.4.8, 10) and Ptolemy (*Geogr.* 4.7.8). The identification made by Josephus (*Ant.* 2.10.2) of "Seba" with *Meroē* is probably mistaken (Müller 1992: 1064).

"Ḥavilah" (OSA *Ḥwln)* refers to an area in southern Arabia, but available references do not allow greater precision (Gen 2:11; 25:18; Strabo, *Geogr.* 16.4.2; Pliny, *Nat.* 6.157). In v. 23 "Ḥavilah" reappears as a son of the Semite Joqṭan.

"Sabteca" *(sabtĕkāʾ)*, an unknown population group or toponym in southern Arabia. Some wish to identify the name with Shabataka (ca. 702–690 B.C.E.), the second member of the twenty-fifth (Ethiopian) dynasty of Egypt (Astour 1965: 422–25; Lipiński 1992: 146–47).

"Sheba" *(šĕbāʾ)* appears three times in the universal genealogy: the sons of Cush (v. 9; Gen 10:7); the sons of Joqṭan (v. 22; Gen 10:28); and the sons of Qeṭurah (v. 32; Gen 25:3). On the basis of Assyrian and biblical references (Isa 60:6; Jer 6:20; Ezek 27:22–23; 38:13; Job 1:15; 6:19; 2 Chr 9:1–12), some scholars (e.g., Ephʿal 1984: 227–29; *HALOT* 1381) posit two Shebas, one in northern Arabia (1 Chr 1:9, 32; Job 6:19) and the other in southern Arabia (1 Chr 1:22; Jer 6:20; Ps 72:10). Other scholars (e.g., Kitchen 1997) only admit to a Sheba in southern Arabia.

"Dedan." The Dedanites appear as a commercial people in the prophets, not infrequently with a note of condemnation (Isa 21:13; Jer 25:23; 49:8; Ezek 25:13; 27:15 [MT], 20; 38:13). The place is identified as modern *al-ʿUlā* in the Ḥeǧâz region of northern Arabia (Isa 21:13–14; Jer 25:23; Albright 1953). Cf. uru*Da-da-nu* in Neo-Babylonian sources (Ephʿal 1984: 180–85). Both Sheba and Dedan reappear in v. 32 as descendants of Qeṭurah.

1:10. "Cush sired Nimrod." Another segmented genealogy. The switch in formulas from "sons of PN_1, PN_2, PN_3" (vv. 8–9) to "PN_1 sired PN_2" in v. 10 reflects the change in the author's sources: from Gen 10:6–7 to Gen 10:8.

"warrior [*gibbôr*] in the land." In Gen 10:9 (usually ascribed to J), *gibbôr* is glossed by *ṣayid*, leading Westermann (1984) to speak of the legendary Nimrod as the first hunter. That Chronicles does not mention the Mesopotamian domains of Nimrod, such as Babylon, Erech, and Akkad (Gen 10:10–12) results in a geographically more consistent presentation, because it lessens the territorial overlap between the descendants of Shem and Ḥam in Mesopotamia (J vs. P).

1:11–16. The lists of the descendants of Mizraim and Canaan closely follow Gen 10:13–18. The exact provenance of a number of these peoples, with some exceptions (e.g., the Philistines), is unknown.

1:11. "Ludim." The Lydians in Asia Minor (Isa 66:19; Jer 46:9; Ezek 27:10; Herodotus, *Hist.* 1.80–81).

"Naphtuḥim." The location of these Egyptians is probably to be distinguished from *Nathō* mentioned by Herodotus (*Hist.* 2.165). Redford (1992: 406) favors reconstructing *Niʾw.t-ptḥ*, "the city of Ptaḥ," thus making the Naphtuḥim inhabitants of Memphis.

1:12. "Pathrusim" *(patrusîm)*. The prophets mention Pathros (*pathrôs*; cf. Akk. *Pa-tú-ri-si* and *Pa-tu-ru-si/su* [Parpola 1970: 276]) as a designation of Upper Egypt (Isa 11:11; cf. Jer 44:1, 15; Ezek 29:14; 30:14). The usage of Eg. *Pʾ-tʾ-rśy* to designate the name of a territory, "land of the south," begins in the New Kingdom and becomes common in demotic (Redford 1992: 405–6).

"Caphtorim." The location of Caphtor is disputed. Strange (1980) associates Caphtor with Cyprus, but most scholars (e.g., Rendsburg 1987: 89–91) argue that it refers to Crete (cf. Akk. *kaptaru*; Eg. *kftyw* or *kftiw*).

1:13–16. An extensive inventory of eleven Canaanite peoples. Standard MT Pentateuchal lists of autochthonous Canaanite peoples involve six or seven ethnic names. The composition of these lists admits to some variation (Ishida 1979: 461–90; P. Stern 1991: 89–113). Especially interesting is the testimony of LXX, which often (but not always) lists seven nations where MT lists six. But many of these variations may be explained on text-critical grounds (O'Connell 1984). The standard list in Exodus comprises six nations: the Hittites, Amorites, Canaanites, Perizzites, Ḥivites, and Jebusites (Exod 3:8, 17; 33:2; 34:11). In Deuteronomy and the Deuteronomistic History the list sometimes includes a seventh nation: the Girgashites (Deut 7:1; Josh 3:10; 24:11; Judg 3:5; cf. Deut 20:17). Five of the first six names mentioned in vv. 13–16—Ḥeth, the Jebusites, the Amorites, the Girgashites, and the Ḥivites—also appear in these stereotyped Pentateuchal litanies. There is a more expansive list in Gen 15:19–21: the ten peoples inhabiting the land that Abram and his descendants are to inherit. But only four of the eleven peoples mentioned in vv. 13–16—the Hittites (Ḥeth), the Amorites, the Girgashites, and the Jebusites—appear in the list of Gen 15:19–21; as for the Canaanites, they appear merely as one of many peoples in the land (Gen 15:21; cf. v. 8). The other five peoples—the Arqites, the Sinites, the Arvadites, the Zemarites, and the Ḥamathites—are all peculiar to Gen 10:13–18//1 Chr 1:13–16.

1:13. "Sidon" *(ṣîdôn)*. Probably meant here as a broader designation for Phoenicia (Deut 3:9; Judg 3:3; 10:6, 12; 18:7; 1 Kgs 5:6; 11:1, 5, 33; 16:31; 2 Kgs 23:13), rather than as a designation of the city itself.

"Ḥeth." The eponymous ancestor of the Hittites. The term can specify a certain people within central Anatolia or function as a broad designation for the entire area of Syria-Palestine (e.g., the land of Ḫatti in Neo-Assyrian and Neo-Babylonian inscriptions). For the latter usage, see also Josh 1:4.

1:14. "the Jebusites." The native inhabitants of Jerusalem.

"the Amorites" *(hāʾĕmōrî)*. The term can be used to designate a specific people within ancient Canaan, usually a Transjordanian kingdom (Num 21:13; Deut 3:8; Josh 2:10), or more broadly to designate the population of Palestine and the Transjordan (e.g., Gen 15:16; 48:22; Josh 24:15; 2 Sam 21:2; Ezek 16:3, 45). In Neo-Assyrian annals "Hittite" and "Amorite" can be practically synonymous (Lipiński 1992: 155).

1:16. "the Arvadites" *(hāʾarwādî)*. Arvad, modern Ruād, was located by the Mediterranean coast some 80 km north of Byblos. Cf. Ezek 27:8, 11; 1 Macc 15:23.

"the Zemarites" *(haṣṣĕmārî)*. Zamar is perhaps to be associated with *Ṣumur(u)* in the El Amarna letters (59:34; 60:23, 27; 61 rev. 4; 68:16) and Akk. *Ṣimirra* (cf. Eg. *Ḏu-mu-ra*). If so, the town was located about 19 km southeast of Arvad.

"the Ḥamathites" *(haḥămātî)*. Referring to the inhabitants of Ḥamath on the Orontes as opposed to their namesakes in eastern Babylonia (Zadok 1976: 117–18).

1:17–23. "sons of Shem." A segmented genealogy in narrative form following Gen 10:22–29 very closely. The shift in genealogical formulas from "sons of PN_1, PN_2, PN_3" to "PN_1 sired PN_2" in v. 18 reflects (again) a change in the author's sources: 1:17//Gen 10:22–23 (P) and 1:18–23//Gen 10:24–29 (J). Israelite and Judahite writers posited fundamental affinities with the Semitic peoples of the east, even though they lived in Canaan. Shem is the great-grandfather of Eber (*ʿēber*; v. 18), the eponymous ancestor of the Hebrews *(ʿibrî)*.

1:17. "Elam" was located in southwest Asia, east of ancient Babylon and north of the Persian Gulf (modern southwestern Iran). Elamite is not directly related either to Semitic or to Indo-European. The grouping with the descendants of Shem reflects geopolitical considerations.

"Ashur." Assyria.

"Arpachshad" *(ʾarpakšad)* is the grandfather of Eber (Gen 10:22, 24; 11:10–14; cf. *Jub.* 9:4; Jdt 1:1; Luke 3:35–36), but the derivation of the name, which is not Semitic, is unclear. Gunkel (1926) and Westermann (1984) think that the name stands for Babylon, but the serious problems with deriving *ʾarpakšad* from Babylonian *kašdu* (cf. Heb. *keśed*, "Chaldea") should not be skirted. Another proposal involves linking *ʾarpakšad* to cuneiform *ʾararpaḫa* or *ʾarapḫa*, interpreted as being either a province of Assyria abutting Armenia or as corresponding to modern Kirkūk in northeastern Iraq (Blenkinsopp 1992: 90).

"Lud." Lydia in Asia Minor.

"Aram" extended from northern Mesopotamia to middle Syria and north Transjordan.

"sons of Aram." Of the names mentioned only one, Meshech (3rd NOTE to v. 5), can be identified. The other locations, Uz, Ḥul, and Gether, are uncertain.

"Uz" *(ʿûṣ)* appears as a son of Naḥor in Gen 22:21, which would place Uz to the northeast of Palestine, perhaps in the Syrian desert southeast of Damascus. But the Uz of v. 42 (2nd NOTE) points in a southeasterly direction (Lipiński 1993: 200–201).

1:18. "Eber." See the NOTE to vv. 17–23.

1:19. "the land was divided." The Heb. (from Gen 10:25) puns on the root of Peleg's name *(plg)*, which means "to divide, split" (cf. Akk. *palgu*, "ditch," "canal"; *puluggu*, *pulungu*, "district").

"Joqṭan" *(yoqṭān)* as well as the names of some of his descendants, such as Sheba, Ḥavilah, and Ophir, are associated with regions of southern Arabia. Cf. Pun. *yqṭ*. Some would specifically associate Joqṭan with the area of Yemen (*HALOT* 430–31).

1:20. "Ḥazarmawet" *(ḥăṣarmāwet)* may be associated with modern *Ḥaḥramaut* in southern Arabia (Lipiński 1993: 207–9).

1:23. "Ophir" *(ʾôpîr)*, "the land of gold" (1 Kgs 10:11; Job 22:24; 28:16; 1 Chr 29:4; 2 Chr 8:18). An eighth-century ostracon from T. Qâsile reads: "gold of Ophir for Beth-ḥoron [. . .]: 30 shekels" (Davies, §11.002.1). The site is often located within southwestern Arabia (e.g., Kitchen 1997: 145), although Albright (1968a: 133–34) associates Ophir with the land of Punt in Egyptian sources, that is, the northeastern African coast.

"all these were sons of Joqṭan." A summary borrowed from Gen 10:29.

1:24–27. "Shem . . . Abram." This linear genealogy, like the linear genealogy of vv. 1–4a (NOTE), is composed of ten names, representing ten generations. The lineage of vv. 24–27 is extracted from the much longer narrative lineage of Shem in Gen 11:10–26: "These are the lineages (*tōlĕdôt*) of Shem" (P). Again, the author does not explain the relationships between the persons he includes in his genealogy. One has to follow the context and his source to grasp the sense of this highly condensed lineage. Unlike the Priestly writers, the author does not reproduce the full lineage of Teraḥ (Gen 11:26–32). His interest lies with Abraham.

1:27. "Abram." This notation is probably taken from Gen 11:26 (*pace* Bendavid 1972: 17). References to Abra(ha)m are infrequent in Chronicles. According to Japhet (1993a: 60), the pervasive references to Jacob as Israel, when compared to the sporadic references to Abraham in Chronicles, reflect "the superior significance of Israel, the actual father of the twelve tribes, over Abraham, their more distant ancestor." One can scarcely dispute the importance of Jacob/Israel in Chronicles, but Noaḥ and Abraham have priority in 1:1–2:2. Two major units in the Chronicler's genealogies are dominated by Noaḥ (1:4b–23) and Abraham

(1:24–34a), respectively. Even the importance accorded to the descendants of Isaac (1:34b–2:2) is directly related to Isaac's connection to Abraham (STRUCTURE).

"that is Abraham." An explanation from the Chronicler, based on his reading of Gen 17:1–8. The clarification bridges the end of v. 27 (Abram) and the beginning of v. 28 (Abraham).

1:28. "sons of Abraham." Comparison with the author's compositional technique in vv. 1–4 is relevant. As in v. 4 ("the sons of Noaḥ"), he creates his own heading to introduce the material borrowed from his *Vorlage*.

"Isaac and Ishmael." A very brief genealogy fashioned from narratives in Genesis (16:11; 17:18–19; 25:9). In listing Abraham's children in this format, the author momentarily passes over Abraham's children through Qeṭurah (vv. 32–33).

"Ishmael." In biblical traditions, Ishmael is associated with the northern part of the Sinaitic Peninsula and northwestern Arabia (Ephʿal 1984: 233–40). On the divine promises to Ishmael, see Gen 16:10–12 (J); 17:20 (P); 21:13 (E). Extrabiblical references suggest the rise of a North Arabian confederacy beginning in the eighth century B.C.E. Some form of this league may have lasted into the early Persian period (Knauf 1989: 88–91).

1:29–31. A segmented genealogy, which draws upon Gen 25:12–18: "These are the lineages (*tōlĕdôt)* of Ishmael" (P). Like Israel (2:1–2) and Aram (Gen 22:20–24), Ishmael has twelve descendants, representing a larger confederation.

1:29. "these are their lineages" *(tōlĕdôt)*. Abridging and slightly rewriting the introduction to the genealogy for Ishmael, "these are the lineages of Ishmael" (Gen 25:12), turns this heading into an introduction for the descendants of both Isaac and Ishmael. In what follows, the author has used the technique of inverted quotation (Seidel 1955–56; Beentjes 1982) to reposition narrative blocks found in his source.

Offspring of Qeṭurah:	Gen 25:1–3	1 Chr 1:32–33
Offspring of Ishmael:	Gen 25:12–16	1 Chr 1:29–31

As much as the author is indebted to the Priestly editors (and the Yahwist), his recontextualization of older material provides it with a new significance.

"firstborn of Ishmael." The enumeration of Ishmael's dozen sons in vv. 29–31 is drawn from Gen 25:13–15 (P). No geographical and chronological details are provided (cf. Gen 25:16–18). Most of Ishmael's progeny are unattested in extrabiblical sources until the eighth century B.C.E. Taken together, these Ishmaelites are associated with a far greater proportion of territory than Gen 25:18 might suggest, extending from northern Sinai and the land of Gilead to the end of the Wâdī Sirḥān and beyond (Ephʿal 1984: 236–37).

"Nebaioth" *(nĕbāyôt)*. The association between the Nebaioth and Qedar (Gen 25:13; 1 Chr 1:29; Isa 60:7) is also found in the Rassam Cylinder account of Ashurbanipal's campaigns against the Arabs (Ephʿal 1984: 221): kur*Qi-id-ri* and kur*Na-ba-a-a-ti*. According to Assyrian texts, the king of Nebaioth made an agreement with Ashurbanipal to pay annual tribute and swear allegiance (*adê sulummē epēš ardūti*; Ephʿal 1984: 150). Arabic inscriptions from Jebel Ghunaym, dating to the sixth century B.C.E. or significantly later (Roschinski 1980), speak of a war between the people of Tema and the people of Nebaioth (Winnett, Reed, et al. 1970: 99–101 [§§11, 13, 15]). Bartlett (1979: 62–66) wishes to see the Nebaioth *(nbywt)* as precursors to the Nabateans, *nbṭ(w)* (cf. Arab. *ʾanbaṭ*), but this connection is rejected by others on the basis of linguistic and geographic considerations (Ephʿal 1984: 222–23; Knauf 1989: 92–96; 1995a: 94). Genesis 28:9 and 36:3 suggest a relationship between Nebaioth and Edom. This, coupled with the evidence supplied by the Jebel Ghunaym inscriptions, points toward the northwestern part of the Arabian peninsula, south of the Wâdī Sirḥān, for the location of the Nebaioth. The Assyrian evidence portrays the Nebaioth as ranging farther afield, as far as the western border of Babylonia.

"Qedar." The eponym of an important tribe (or group of tribes) and state in northern Arabia (Isa 42:11; Jer 2:10; 49:28–29; Ps 120:5; Song 1:5). Qedar was the main North Arabian power from the eighth to the fourth century B.C.E. In biblical sources, the Qedarites are associated with sheep breeding (Isa 60:7), skilled archery (Isa 21:13–17), and trade in livestock (Ezek 27:21). In eighth to seventh-century Assyrian records, the location of the Qedarites ranges across the Syro-Arabian desert (H. Tadmor 1994: 106–9 [III.A:2]). The fifth-century Aramaic T. el-Maskhuṭeh inscription mentions Qaynū son of Gašmū (biblical Geshem; Neh 2:19; 6:1–2, 6) as the king of Qedar (Dumbrell 1971). Some (e.g., Knauf 1989: 103–8) think that this inscription testifies to an expanded Qedarite presence in the northern Sinai and along Egypt's eastern border during the Persian age, but others (e.g., Bartlett 1979: 59–62; Ephʿal 1984: 223–27) doubt whether the evidence can pinpoint Qedarites power at this time.

"Adbeel" *(ʾadbĕʾēl)*. Among the seminomadic groups in northern Arabia and the border regions of Palestine mentioned by Tiglath-pileser III in his Palestinian campaigns are ^{lú}*i-dì-ba-ʾi-il-a-a* or ^{lú}*i-dì-bi-ʾi-i-li/lu* (4:28′; 7:r.3′; 13:10′; H. Tadmor 1994). Most scholars identify "Adbeel" (1st TEXTUAL NOTE to v. 29) with the *idibaʾilu* (alt. *idibiʾilu*) in royal Assyr. records.

1:30. "Mishma" *(mišmāʿ)* later appears, along with Mibsam (v. 29), as a descendant of Simeon (4:25). Multiple associations within genealogies may reflect multiple claims about a group's ties and allegiances. Mibsam and Mishma may have been Arabian or Edomite groups living in the southern border region of Palestine during the Persian period (Knauf 1989: 68).

"Dumah" *(dûmâ)* is sometimes identified as Dūmat al-Jandal in the oasis of el-Jōf in northern Arabia (*HALOT* 216–17; cf. Nabatean *dwmt*). A site by the name of ^{uru}*adummatu/adumutu* was destroyed by Kings Sennacherib and Esarhaddon of Assyria (Borger 1956: 53; Ephʿal 1984: 118–21). Whether [*a*]*dummu* (Nabonidus Chronicle 1.17), conquered by Nabonidus in his expedition against Tema, refers to the same location is uncertain.

"Massa" *(maśśāʾ)*. The eponymous ancestor of a north Arabian tribe (Albright 1956). Tiglath-pileser III claims to have subjugated a people by the name of ^{kur}*Ma-sa-ʾ*, along with the residents of Tema, Sabaʾ (Sebaʾ in v. 9), the tribe of the Idibaʾileans (Adbeel in v. 29), and other peoples (2nd NOTE to v. 9).

"Tema" *(tēmāʾ)*, the eponym of Taymāʾ in northern Arabia (Parpola 1970: 350), an important oasis town located on a major trade route (Isa 21:14; Jer 25:23–24;

Job 6:19). Tema paid tribute to Tiglath-pileser in 734 B.C.E. (H. Tadmor 1994 [4:27′; 7:r.3′; 13:9′]) and for a decade it became the residence of the Neo-Babylonian monarch Nabonidus (553–543 B.C.E.). An Aramaic stela and a number of Aramaic inscriptions have been discovered at the site (Cross 1986).

1:31. "Jeṭur, Naphish, and Qedemah." First Chronicles 5:19 presents Jeṭur, Naphish, and Nodab (along with the Hagrites) as enemies of Reuben, Gad, and half-Manasseh (NOTE to 5:19).

"Jeṭur" *(yĕṭûr)*. Some associate this name with Nabatean *Iatouros* in Hauran (*HALOT* 409). Unlike the situation with respect to the descendants of Qeṭurah (Isa 60:6, 22; Ezek 27:20), biblical sources do not ascribe to most of the descendants of Ishmael trade in spices or trade in other luxury goods (Isa 60:7, 21; Jer 49:29; Ezek 27:20; 1 Chr 5:21). Assyrian records suggest, however, that these so-called Ishmaelite groups did engage in luxury trade. Biblical writers may not have known of such trade with these groups in the extended border area of Palestine (Ephʿal 1984: 234–38).

"these are the sons of Ishmael." A summary derived from Gen 25:16.

1:32–33. "sons of Qeṭurah." A segmented genealogy largely abridged and adapted from Gen 25:1–4. The heading is the author's own (cf. vv. 4, 28).

"concubine of Abraham." Again, this is the Chronicler's language. Qeṭurah appears in Genesis as Abraham's second wife, taken sometime after the death of Sarah (25:1–2). The reference to her as a concubine may be based on a reading of Gen 25:1–2 in light of Gen 25:5–6. The latter mentions that Abraham "gave all that he had to Isaac," but to his sons by his concubines "Abraham gave gifts . . . and sent them away from Isaac toward the east." In other words, v. 32 is an instance of *sĕmûkîn*, an exegetical technique made famous by the rabbis (Fishbane 1985), in which one text is read in the light of another in close proximity.

"she gave birth." Some scholars (e.g., Osborne 1979: 180–83) see a denigration of Qeṭurah and these descendants, because Qeṭurah is described as a concubine, a person of lower social status. The situation is more complex, genealogically speaking. By referring to Zimran, Joqshan, etc. as the offspring of Qeṭurah, the writer simultaneously recognizes their importance and distances them from Abraham's children through (unnamed) Sarah and Hagar (v. 28). The descendants of Qeṭurah range far afield, being associated with areas to the south and southeast of Israel.

"Midian" is consistently associated with peoples to the southeast of Israel such as the Ishmaelites (Judg 8:24), Medanites (Gen 37:28, 36), Moabites (Numbers 22–25), and Edomites. Some sources suggest early and important associations between the Midianites and the Israelites (Exod 2:15–16; 3:1; 4:19; 18:1; Num 10:29–32), but others suggest a history of mutual animosity (Num 31:1–12; Josh 13:21; Judg 6–8; 9:17).

"Ishbaq" *(yišbāq)* may appear as ^{kur}*ia-as-b-qa-a* in the Monolith Inscription of Shalmaneser III, dating to the ninth century B.C.E. (Albright 1953: 9; Oppenheim 1969: 277). If so, the term refers to a people in northern Syria.

"Shuaḥ." Whether this name should be associated in some way with a district in the middle Euphrates region by the name ^{kur}*šuḫi* or *Sūḫu* (Parpola 1970: 316) is unclear.

"Sheba." See the 2nd NOTE to v. 9.

1:33. "sons of Midian." Both the list of offspring and the summary conclusion, "all these were descendants of Qeṭurah," are taken from Gen 25:4. Sargon II speaks of the people of Ephah (lú*Ḫa-ia-pa-a*), along with others, as "the distant Arabs living in the desert, who knew neither overseers nor officials and had not brought their tribute to any king" (Ephʿal 1984: 105). The location of Ephah is thought to be in northern Arabia (cf. Isa 60:6).

1:34–37. This segmented genealogy, listing the children of Sarah and Abraham, draws upon Gen 25:19–26 and Gen 36:10–13 (Kegler and Augustin 1991).

1:34. "Abraham sired Isaac." A transition created by a slight rewrite of Gen 25:19 (P), "Abraham, the one who sired Isaac."

"the sons of Isaac: Esau and Israel." This heading is the Chronicler's own, differing somewhat from "these are the lineages of Isaac son of Abraham" (Gen 25:19). It introduces a long section marked by an enumeration of figures directly and indirectly associated with Esau (1:35–54), as well as an enumeration of the twelve descendants of Israel (2:1–2). In what follows, the author has again used the technique of inverted quotation (1st NOTE to v. 29) to reposition material from his sources.

Offspring of Esau/Seir/Edom:	Gen 36:2–43	1 Chr 1:35–54
Offspring of Jacob:	Gen 35:22b–26	1 Chr 2:1–2

The amount of attention accorded to Seir and Edom is extraordinary, but needs to be understood in the context of the author's geographic-historical situation. An Edomite presence in the eastern Negev is attested from at least the seventh century B.C.E. (Beit-Arieh 1995; 1996). With the publication of hundreds of Edomite ostraca (written in Aramaic) dating to the Persian period (Lemaire 1996a; Ephʿal and Naveh 1996), scholars have begun to acknowledge that the Edomites were more of a presence in southern Palestine than had earlier been recognized. Given his geopolitical situation, it is not surprising that the author displays an active interest in the peoples to the south and southeast and their connections with the southern tribes (COMMENT).

1:35–37. "sons of Esau." A segmented genealogy abridged and adapted from Gen 36:2–14. The heading is taken from either Gen 36:5 or 10. On the divine promises to Esau, see Gen 25:23; 27:39–40. The compositional history of the Edomite material in Gen 36 is complex and much-debated (R. Wilson 1977: 167–83; Knauf 1985a).

1:35. "Eliphaz . . . Qoraḥ." This bare list is derived from the more detailed Gen 36:4–5, which mentions other facts (e.g., the names of Esau's wives). The name Eliphaz *(ʾĕlîpaz)* is born by one of Job's comforters, called a Temanite (Job 2:11). Job himself hails from the land of Uz (1:1), also mentioned in 1 Chr 1:42 (cf. v. 17). Teman (see also v. 53) appears as one of Eliphaz's sons in v. 36. The name Qoraḥ reappears in the Judahite genealogy (2:43) as a son of Ḥebron and part of the family of Caleb.

1:36. "Qenaz." The eponymous ancestor of the Qenizzites, who inhabited the Negev (Num 32:12; Josh 14:6, 14). In some texts (Josh 15:17; Judg 1:13; 3:9, 11), Calebite and Othnielite groups, presented as descendants of Qenaz, become part of Judah (NOTES to 4:13–14).

"Timna" and "Amaleq" appear as sons of Eliphaz, but Gen 36:12 mentions Timna as Eliphaz's concubine and the mother of Amaleq. Curtis and Madsen (1910: 76) argue that the Chronicler's version of events results from a misreading of Gen 36:11–12, but the confusion (or variant text) was probably in the Chronicler's source (2nd TEXTUAL NOTE to v. 36). Amaleq was a traditional foe of the Israelites in southern Canaan, especially in the Negev (Gen 14:7; Exod 17:8–16; Num 13:29; 14:25; Deut 25:17–19; Judg 10:12; 12:15; 1 Sam 15:2; 30:1ff.; 2 Sam 1:8, 13). Such animosity also appears in Chronicles (1 Chr 4:43; 18:11).

1:37. "sons of Reuel." Gleaned from Gen 36:13.

1:38–42. "sons of Seir." A segmented genealogy abridged and adapted from Gen 36:20–28. In Noth's estimation (1981b: 18), all of Gen 36:15–43 stem from additions either to P or to the completed Pentateuch. Westermann (1985: 561) thinks that all of Gen 36:9–43 stems from a single source originating in the Jerusalem royal chancery, added either by P or by a later redactor. In Chronicles, this is the first time that Seir is mentioned. Neither the author nor his various biblical sources directly claim that Seir is part of Esau's genealogy. But the Chronicler, following his sources, makes indirect links between the two. The name of Seir *(śēʿîr)* is associated with hair *(śēʿār; HALOT* 1344–45), and the Genesis narratives repeatedly play on Esau's hairiness *(ʿēśāw;* Gen 25:25; 27:11, 23). The author associates Seir with Esau by listing the genealogy of Seir (Gen 36:20–29) in the context of the genealogies and lists of Edom (Gen 36:1–19, 31–43). The Seirites and Edomites are presented as coinhabitants of the land in Gen 36:20 (cf. Josh 24:4). Most scholars interpret the biblical references to Seir as designating a mountainous part of Edom or as a synonym for Edom itself (Knauf 1988: 50–60). It is entirely plausible that the designation of Seir changed over time, as the Chronicler's own narratives attest (Dicou 1994; 2 Chr 25:11–20; cf. 2 Kgs 14:7–14).

1:38. "Shobal" also appears among the Calebite families in Judah (2:50–52). It is possible that tribal movements from east to west sometime in the sixth century or later explains this overlap in names (Knauf 1995a: 103–6). In the following verses, there are a number of other connections between Seirites and Judahites (Zadok 1998).

1:39. "Ḥori" *(ḥōrî)* and the Ḥorites may originally refer to a Seirite group in the southern Transjordan (Knauf 1989: 10–11, 61–65). In this reconstruction, the connection with Calebite Ḥur *(ḥûr)*, who appears in the genealogy of Judah (2:19, 50; 4:1), reflects a later development.

"Timna" *(timnāʿ)*. There are a number of Timna(h)s in the Bible (see v. 36), but this one may be associated with the mining region of Timna on the western side of the Wâdī el-Arabah just north of Elath.

1:40. "Manaḥath," a descendant of Seir, is sometimes associated with the Menuḥoth *(mnwḥwt)* or the Manaḥathites *(mnḥwt)* in the Judahite genealogy (2nd TEXTUAL NOTE to 2:52). In spite of the animus toward Edom in some biblical texts (Glazier-McDonald 1995), the genealogies in Chronicles suggest a number of contacts and kinship relationships between Judean and Edomite groups.

"Onam" *(ʾônām)* reappears as a Jeraḥmeelite in Judah's genealogy (2:25–26).

1:41. "Anah." Referring to Anah the son of Seir (v. 38).

"Dishon." Consistent with the form and content of the segmented genealogy begun in v. 38, this refers to Dishon son of Seir (v. 38).

"Ithran" *(yitrān)* may be associated with Judahite Jether *(yeter)* in 1 Chr 2:32 and the Judahite Ithrites *(yitrî)* in 1 Chr 2:53 (Wellhausen 1870: 28–30).

1:42. "Dishan." Referring to the last son of Seir (v. 38).

"Uz" is linked to the Ḥorites in Gen 36:28. Uz appears as Job's homeland (Job 1:1). A land to the southeast is also suggested by Jer 25:20 (*pace* W. Holladay 1986: 674) and Lam 4:21, but the readings in these texts are not secure. See also the last NOTE to v. 17.

"Aran" *(ʾrn)* is perhaps to be connected with the Jeraḥmeelite "Oren" *(ʾrn)* in the Judahite genealogy (2:25).

1:43–51a. "These are the kings." Older attempts to date these monarchs are highly problematic for two reasons. First, the original list incorporated into the author's source may have pertained to Aramaean kings (Lemaire 1988). In this reconstruction, the transformation of "Aram" (ארם) to "Edom" (אדם) was already part of the Chronicler's *Vorlage.* Second, recent studies of the material remains from a variety of sites suggest that the rise of a modest Edomite state took place no earlier than the eighth or seventh centuries B.C.E. (Bartlett 1995; Knauf 1995a; Bienkowski 1995; LaBianca and Younker 1995). This makes the claims in Genesis and of Num 20:14–21, repeated by Chronicles, all the more striking, namely, that the rise of kingship among the Edomites preceded that of the Israelites (NOTE to v. 43). The lists of Edomite monarchs (1:43–51a) and Edomite chieftains (1:51b–54) are adapted and slightly abridged from Gen 36:31–39 and Gen 36:40–43, respectively. The author changes his sources' headings and transitions and makes some abbreviations. The structure of the list in Genesis differs from that of Chronicles. In Genesis the transition between Edomite monarchs is "RN died and RN_2 reigned," whereas in Chronicles the formula is better translated as "when RN died, RN_2 reigned." In his earlier editing the writer excised much anecdotal information from his sources, but in this instance he includes much of it.

1:43. "before a king reigned among the Israelites" (לפני מלך-מלך לבני ישׂראל). The writer presents Edom's past, derived from Genesis, in capsule form up to the time of the inception of the Israelite monarchy, the beginning of his own narrative history (10:1; Japhet 1993a).

1:44. "Bozrah" (בצרה), one of two sites in this list that can be located with some assurance, is situated southeast of the Dead Sea, some 45 km north of Petra.

"reigned in his stead." Given that the Edomite kings stemmed from different lines and were associated with different sites, a single dynastic kingship is not attributed to the Edomites. The nature and authority of these kings has been compared to those of Israelite chieftains (שׁפטים; Bartlett 1965; Myers 1965a).

1:46. "Avith" (Qere עוית; Kethib עיות). An unidentified town in Moab or Edom (cf. Gen 36:35; Bartlett 1965: 301–14; B. MacDonald 2000: 189).

1:48. "Reḥoboth on the River." "The River" *(hannāhār)* can designate the Euphrates (Gen 31:21; Exod 23:31; Num 22:5; Josh 24:2, 3, 14, 15), but such an identification seems highly unlikely in this context. Many scholars have sought to locate Reḥoboth by the Wâdī el-Ḥesā, but no nearby site has been found to justify the epithet (Bartlett 1989: 50–51).

1:51. "When Hadad died, the chieftains of Edom were." The transition between lists differs from that of Gen 36:40: "These are the names of the chieftains of Esau by their families (משפחתם), by their places according to their names." In Chronicles the list of Edomite chieftains is dated generally to the time of Hadad's death. The two lists, paratactically ordered in Genesis, are largely consecutive in Chronicles. The chieftain list itself (vv. 51–54) consists mostly of toponyms.

1:52. "Pinon" (Heb. *pînôn*; Arab. *Fênān*) is located east of the Arabah. Kartveit (1989: 115–17) discerns a "soft polemic" in the apparently limited geographic distribution of territory that the author ascribes to the Edomites (cf. Ps 137:7; Mal 1:2–5; Num 20:18–21). But the connections between the Seirites/Edomites and the Judahites (NOTES to vv. 38–42) must also be taken into account.

1:53. "Teman." Some (e.g., Aharoni 1979) wish to situate Teman approximately 70 km south of the Dead Sea, but Teman in most contexts refers to a region, rather than a site, the northern area of Edom (de Vaux 1969). The association of Teman with (southern) Edom is not unique to this text (Jer 49:7, 8, 20; Ezek 25:12–14; Amos 1:12; Hab 3:3; Obad 9). In this context, the reference to "Yhwh of Teman" in the recently discovered inscriptions from *Kuntillet ʿAjrûd* (Emerton 1982; Hadley 1987; Davies, §8.021.1) is also relevant.

2:1–2. "sons of Israel." The list of Jacob's descendants concludes the section begun in v. 34 (TEXTUAL NOTE). In the following section, the author presents a major genealogical introduction to the people of Israel: their identity, kinship relationships, and land (2:3–8:40). First Chronicles 9:1a concludes this next section by summarizing "So all Israel was genealogically registered" (וכל-ישׂראל התיחשׂו).

2:1. "Israel." The author, like the Priestly writers, posits a continuous line from Adam to Jacob. This confers on Israel a certain dignity and legitimacy, yet it is too much to say that the election of Israel begins with Adam (*pace* Japhet 1989: 116–24). Theological terms such as "election" (בחר) do not appear in 1:1–2:2. Nor does the Chronicler elsewhere refer to the election of Israel, even though he does speak of the election (בחר) of the Levites (2 Chr 29:11), Judah (1 Chr 28:4), Jerusalem (2 Chr 6:5–6 [//4Q1 Kgs 8:16]; 6:34 [//1 Kgs 8:44]; 6:38 [//1 Kgs 8:48]; 12:13), the temple (2 Chr 7:16), David (1 Chr 28:4; 2 Chr 6:6 [//1 Kgs 8:16]), and Solomon (1 Chr 28:5–6, 10; 29:1). To put the matter differently, if one were to speak of the election of Israel on the basis of the genealogy of nations, one would also have to speak of the election of other figures such as Esau for whom the author traces a direct line of descent from Adam (1:1, 4, 24–28, 34).

"Reuben." There are a number of tribal lists in the Bible, but the precise order of Israel's sons in vv. 1–2 is unique (Noth 1930: 3–86; R. Wilson 1977: 183–95, 224–30; Kallai 1997: 80–81). Most of the catalogue is implicitly organized by mother, but unlike some earlier authors (Gen 29:31–30:24; 35:16–20 [J]; 35:23–26 [P]) the writer omits any direct mention of the mothers and the one daughter (Dinah). The beginning of the genealogy is not surprising. It commences with the sons of Leah: Reuben, Simeon, Levi, Judah, Issachar, and Zebulun (Gen 29:32–35; 30:17–20 [J]; 35:23 [P]). In accordance with Priestly tradition, it ends with the sons of Zilpah: Gad and Asher (Gen 35:26; cf. 30:10–13 [J]). Unlike the Yahwist and the Priestly writers, the author does not mention the two sons of Bilhah, Dan and Naphtali, in sequence (Gen 30:5–8 [J]; 35:25 [P] [MT and 4QGen-Exod[a]]). That he lists the two sons of Rachel, Joseph and Benjamin, after the progeny of one female servant but before the progeny of the other female servant conforms to neither the pattern of J nor of P (Gen 30:22–24; 35:16–20 [J]; 35:24–26 [P]).

2:2. "Joseph." In mentioning both Joseph and Levi, the lineage of vv. 1–2 follows one traditional pattern of ordering and configuring the tribes. Both Joseph and Levi are registered, but not Joseph's offspring Manasseh and Ephraim (Gen 35:23–26; 49:3–27; Deut 27:12–14; Ezek 48:31–35). The other well-established custom in duodecimal biblical presentations of Jacob's sons is to list Manasseh and Ephraim, but not Joseph and Levi (Num 1:5–15; 2:3–31; 7:12–83; 10:14–28; 13:4–15; Josh 21:4–7; 21:9–39). The Chronicler shows familiarity with the former order by reproducing it in vv. 1–2, but this is not the order he himself follows in his genealogies. Consistent with his claim that the birthright among Jacob's sons went to Joseph and not to Reuben (5:1–2), the genealogies provide coverage of both of Joseph's sons, Manasseh (5:23–24; 7:14–19) and Ephraim (7:20–29). Chronicles also provides extensive lineges for Levi (5:27–6:66 [ET 6:1–81]). Unlike some earlier writers, the author is not completely fixated upon the number twelve as applied to Jacob's sons (Auld 1998: 115–16). There is no genealogy for Zebulun (NOTE to 7:6–11) and one can reconstruct only the briefest of genealogies for Dan (1st TEXTUAL NOTE to 7:12).

SOURCES, SELECTION, AND GENRE

With the exception of some headings and summaries, all of the material in 1:1–2:2 has been taken from Genesis. For the sake of convenience, the division of verses in Genesis according to the documentary hypothesis, Yahwist vs. Priestly (Noth 1981b), follows in parentheses. Readers should be aware, however, that this division by sources, especially as it has been applied to the Table of Nations, has come under heavy criticism in recent years (e.g., Rendtorff 1986: 132–34; Redford 1992: 400–8; Van Seters 1992: 174–87).

Chronicles	*Source*
1:1	Gen 5:1, 6 (P)
1:2	Gen 5:9, 12, 15, 18 (P)
1:3	Gen 4:17 (J); 5:21, 25 (P)
1:4	Gen 10:1 (P)
1:5–7	Gen 10:2–4 (P)
1:8–9	Gen 10:6–7 (P)
1:10	Gen 10:8 (J)
1:11–16	Gen 10:13–18a (J)
1:17	Gen 10:22–23 (P)
1:18	Gen 10:24 (P?)

1:19–23	Gen 10:25–29 (J)
1:24–27	Gen 11:10–26 (P)
1:28	Gen 16:11 (J); 17:18–19 (P); 25:19 (P)
1:29–31	Gen 25:12–16 (P)
1:32–33	Gen 25:1–4 (J)
1:34a	Gen 25:19 (P)
1:34b	Gen 25:21–26a (J)
1:35a	Gen 36:10 (P) or 36:5 (P)
1:35b	Gen 36:4–5 (P)
1:36–37	Gen 36:11–13a (P)
1:38–42	Gen 36:20–28
1:43–50	Gen 36:31–39
1:51–54	Gen 36:40–43a
2:1–2	Gen 35:22b–26, etc.

In some cases (e.g., vv. 1–4, 24–27), the author extracts names from long narratives. In other cases, the writer rearranges blocks of material from Genesis to suit his own purposes (e.g., 1:29–31, 32–33, 35–54; 2:1–2). The editing of sources also involves changing headings and creating new transitions. Since the author's major concern is with the names themselves, he sometimes omits the geographical, anecdotal, and chronological details found in his *Vorlage*.

The culling, selection, and reuse of materials from Genesis raises an additional issue. The writer's approach is fairly comprehensive; he draws from the main genealogical blocks in Genesis: ch. 5; 10–11; 25; 35–36 (Podechard 1916: 362–86). The inclusion of these disparate lines manifests broad literary and antiquarian interests, leading one scholar to assert that 1:1–2:1 "represents the book of Genesis, from which all of its material is taken" (Japhet 1993a: 52). In my judgment, the genealogy of nations may be compared to one of the genres developed in the classical and postclassical worlds: the epitome (ἐπιτομή), a short abridgment or compendium of an older work (Kaster 1996: 549). The first known writer to compose such an epitome was Theopompus of Chios, who lived at about the same time or slightly before the Chronicler (ca. 378–320 B.C.E.). Theopompus wrote an epitome of Herodotus in two books (*FGrH* T 1, frg. 1–4; 115; Shrimpton 1991: 183–95). In classical antiquity such epitomes generally tended to be schematic summaries, rather than stylish shorter histories (Hornblower 1994: 21). In the Roman era, when epitome writing became quite popular, authors sometimes used the epitome to introduce much longer accounts of contemporary events. Attention should be drawn, in this context, to the epitome contained in 2 Maccabees. It should be pointed out, however, that in condensing Genesis the Chronicler's interests are not all encompassing. He ignores some substantial genealogical materials in Genesis. The Cainite and Sethite lines are not given (Gen 4:17–26). The lineage of Teraḥ (Gen 11:27–32) is not included. Neither the lineage of Lot (Gen 19:30–38) nor that of Naḥor (Gen 22:20–24) appear in Chronicles. The descendants of Dedan and Midian are also passed over (Gen 25:3–4). Why does the author include many, but not all, of the genealogies from Genesis? Rather than seeing the writer's approach as completely encyclopedic, it might be more helpful to say that the Chronicler's epitome includes more and more genealogical material from Genesis as he nears his chief interest: the genealogies of Israel (2:3–9:1). The detailed attention given to the descendants of Ishmael and Esau (vv. 28–54) anticipates the very detailed treatment given to the descendants of Israel.

COMPOSITION

The genealogies of 1 Chr 1 raise a variety of interesting literary and thematic issues. In what follows, I will first summarize major arguments for disunity and then engage arguments for unity. Those scholars who contend for a complicated redaction history of 1 Chr 1 speak of duplications (e.g., vv. 9, 22–23, 32), inconsistencies (e.g., vv. 17–23, 24–27), discrepancies in style (vv. 11–12, 14–16), and digressions (e.g., vv. 10, 32–33, 51–54). How does one best explain these features? Some have also argued that 1 Chr 1 displays features that are not characteristic of the Chronicler's interests. Rudolph (1955: 6) contends that the list of Noaḥ's descendants (vv. 4b–23) interrupts the flow of the presentation (from vv. 1–4 to vv. 24–27) and is incongruent with the Chronicler's theology. For similar reasons, Podechard (1916: 372ff.), Rudolph (1955: 7), and Williamson (1982b: 43) excise the genealogy of Qeṭurah's descendants (vv. 32–34a). Finally, Rudolph (1955: 9) and Roddy Braun (1986: 21) view the material accorded to the Seirites and the Edomites (vv. 43b–54) as later additions. Considering that Rudolph (1955: 7) also excises vv. 35–42 as a later addition, this leaves him with only vv. 1–4a, 24–27, and 34b as original.

The force of the questions about composition should not be minimized. The thematic issues raised, for example, about the material relating to Edom are substantial. Why would the writer magnify the position of Edom at a time in which Yehud was struggling to establish itself in the late Persian period? If Israel is the focal point of the Chronicler's interests, why mention the descendants of Esau at all? The question may be sharpened. Verses 35–37 deal with the progeny of Esau, vv. 38–42 enumerate the progeny of Seir, vv. 43–51 list the kings of Edom, and vv. 51–54 register the chieftains of Edom. First Chronicles 1:35–54 provides, therefore, particulars on only a few subjects: Esau, Seir, and Edom. To argue that this whole chapter is nevertheless somehow about Israel (De Vries 1989: 33) skirts the issue.

Despite the weight of these arguments for disunity, the arguments for overall unity raised by scholars, especially by recent scholars such as Kartveit (1989: 19–23), Oeming (1990: 73–97), and Japhet (1993a: 55–56), are substantial. The question is not whether the text of 1:1–2:2 is composite. Enjoying the privilege of having access to the Chronicler's sources for this chapter, we know that it is. Nor is it a question of whether some scattered additions have been made to the text. Comparison between the textual witnesses indicates that there were such additions. The principal question is whether the chapter's composite character is best explained by positing a series of redactions or by positing one principal author, who draws upon, but does not completely rewrite, disparate sources. The question of redaction(s) may be addressed in two complementary ways: by analyzing the material in this chapter in relation to the source material in Genesis and by comparing the composition of this chapter in relation to the Chronicler's compositional technique elsewhere.

As demonstrated above, almost all of 1:1–2:2 is derived from various contexts in Genesis. While it is true that the author abridges much of the material he cites—omitting various formulas, territorial remarks, anecdotal references, and chronological notes—the material he does include is often followed punctiliously. This means that tensions in the text of Genesis are largely reproduced in Chronicles. Indeed, the Table of Nations itself has been called a "heterogeneous collection of material" (Redford 1992: 402). Names such as Meshech, Sheba, Dedan, Uz, and Ḥavilah appear two or even three times (NOTES). Such duplication (or triplication) cannot be explained by the documentary hypothesis, because there are variations in style and content within the sources (J and P) themselves. Gentilics in plural form appear, for instance, in vv. 11–12 in accordance with Gen 10:13–14 (J), while gentilics in singular form appear in vv. 14–16 in accordance with Gen 10:16–18 (J). Meshech appears both among the descendants of Japheth in v. 5 (P) and among the descendants of Shem in v. 17 (P). Sheba appears among the descendants of Ḥam in v. 9 (P), among the descendants of Shem in v. 22 (J), and among the descendants of Qeṭurah in v. 32 (J).

The author's light editing—his adherence to his sources—has its costs, inevitably resulting in repetition and inconsistency. But this situation is essentially no different from the situation in the Chronicler's treatment of the united and divided monarchies. A conservative reproduction of texts selected from his *Vorlagen* of Samuel and Kings is part, albeit not the whole, of the Chronicler's compositional technique (McKenzie 1985; Sugimoto 1992). In both cases, the replication of disparate sources unavoidably generates some uneveness in the Chronicler's own presentation.

But the genealogy of nations in 1:1–2:2 is more than a jumble of materials extracted from Genesis. The placement and organization of names reflect stylization. The chapter begins with a linear genealogy composed of ten members (vv. 1–4a). Having provided a heading for the next section, "the sons of Noaḥ: Shem, Ḥam, and Japheth" (v. 4b), the author sets out their descendants: approximately seventy nations (text-critical variants make it impossible to be precise about the exact number) in segmented genealogies (vv. 5–23). There are seven sons of Japheth, seven descendants of Cush, and seven descendants of Mizraim. Canaan together with his offspring number twelve. The enumeration of some seventy offspring from Noaḥ's sons is followed by another linear genealogy composed of ten members, beginning with Shem and culminating in Abram (vv. 24–27). Hence, what some scholars describe as an intrusive interpolation is not so to others. Whereas Rudolph views the pericope of vv. 5–23 as one of many disruptive interpolations, Japhet (1993a: 52–54) views the same verses as an integral part of the Chronicler's original composition. In her judgment, vv. 1–4 together with vv. 24–27 comprise an *inclusio* enveloping vv. 5–23. The first ten generations (vv.

1–4) are antediluvian, while the latter ten (vv. 24–27) are postdiluvian. In between lie the seventy nations that emerge in the postdiluvian world.

Consistent with earlier practice (v. 4b), another heading introduces the next major genealogical section: "the sons of Abraham: Isaac and Ishmael" (v. 28). The propensity to schematization continues in the genealogies and lists of 1:29–2:2, although it is not as pronounced as it is in 1:1–27. Both Seir and Eliphaz have seven sons. There are also twelve sons of Ishmael and twelve sons of Israel.

One can discern another regular pattern in 1:1–2:2. The text consistently provides information on subsidiary lines first (Ackroyd 1973a: 31). In this, the Chronicler's compositional technique is indebted to the work of the Priestly writers (Gen 10:1ff.). For example, 1:4 lists the sons of Noaḥ as Shem, Ḥam, and Japheth. In the following verses, the descendants of Noaḥ's sons appear beginning with Japheth (1:5–7), continuing with Ḥam (1:8–16), and concluding with Shem (1:17–23). Similarly, after introducing Abraham's children as Isaac and Ishmael (1:28), the text first lists the offspring of Ishmael (1:29–31). In somes cases, the order of the genealogies contained in Genesis (Jacob [Gen 35:23–26] then Esau [Genesis 36]) is reversed to comply with this preferred arrangement (Esau [1:35ff.] then Jacob/Israel [2:1–2]). Hence, the text consistently lists peoples whose independent histories will not be recounted prior to the listing of peoples whose development will be recounted (1:4, 17, 34; 2:1).

In speaking of regular patterns within the genealogies, I do not mean to suggest that the author simply imposed paradigms upon his sources. Quite the contrary, he found some patterns already present within his sources. I am suggesting, however, that the Chronicler continued and elaborated tendencies toward schematization already present within his sources ("Excursus: The Genealogies"). This he did by reworking and repositioning sources and by supplying new rubrics when they were needed. Schematization in genealogies and lists, including the use of favorite numbers, is paralleled in ancient Mesopotamia (Malamat 1968; R. Wilson 1977) and Greece (West 1985). Similarly, in early Christian tradition, Matthew's genealogy of Jesus is a highly structured work, consisting of three groups of fourteen generations (Matt 1:1–17; Mussies 1986). In the case of 1:1–2:2, headings, summaries, and numerical patterns serve a larger purpose: unifying collections of disparate names.

As for the arguments for disunity based on content, the exclusion of the Table of Nations and the lists of Edomite kings and chieftains from the Chronicler's record presumes that the Chronicler pursues narrow ideological interests. In other words, the decision to excise vv. 5–23, 32–33, 35–42, and 43–54, because they do not comport with the Chronicler's theology, is ironically predicated upon the premise that the Chronicler cares exclusively about Judah. Perhaps, however, this material about other cultures is not extraneous. Rather than removing entire sections of the text because they do not accord with one's understanding of an author's purpose, it might be better to reevaluate one's conception of the author. The Chronicler's ideological interests may not be as parochial as they are purported to be. One is drawn to the conclusion that apart from some scattered additions (TEXTUAL NOTES), 1 Chr 1:1–2:2 stem from the Chronicler's own hand.

STRUCTURE

Almost all of the material in 1:1–2:2 has been borrowed and adapted from Genesis. Yet the choice of certain genealogies (and not others), the editing and repositioning of those genealogies, and the Chronicler's own minor additions produce a distinctively new presentation. At the risk of oversimplification, the structure of 1:1–2:2 may be outlined as follows:

- Adam to Noaḥ (1:1–4a)
  - The Descendants of Noaḥ (1:4b)
    - Japhet (1:5–7)
    - Ḥam (1:8–16)
    - Shem (1:17–23)
  - Shem to Abram (1:24–27)
    - The Descendants of Abraham (1:28)
      - Ishmael (1:29–31)
    - The Descendants of Qeṭurah (1:32–33)
      - Isaac (1:34a)
        - The Descendants of Isaac (1:34b)
          - Esau (1:35–37)
            - Seir (1:38–42)
            - Edomite Kings (1:43–51a)
            - Edomite Chiefs (1:51b–54)
          - Israel (2:1–2)

The principle of genealogy is employed to organize and classify ethnic data. The various nations of the world are traced to a common progenitor. In spite of the concern with the classification of peoples, lands, and languages in Gen 10:5, 20, 31, there is little information provided to locate the nations on the earth's surface or to relate them to the reader's own position. Nor is there any information that might help readers orient themselves geographically. To make sense of the genealogical tree, readers have to know where at least some of the nations mentioned in the major family trees are placed vis-à-vis their own positions. If readers have such a requisite knowledge, they can locate, however approximately, a number of other nations by assuming that the closer the nations are genealogically, the closer they are geographically. Such an operation suggests a variety of links between different nations and locations even if readers are unable to pinpoint the exact location of each people. In this respect, the genealogical format has its limitations. The reader is hard-pressed to draw enough specific information from the lists to visualize the precise location of each nation. But the genealogical format also has its advantages. A genealogy may suggest, in a way that an actual map cannot, ethnic, political, and linguistic connections among various peoples.

The beginning and end of the section are of considerable import. The line the Chronicler traces begins with the first human and culminates in the eponymous ancestor of the twelve tribes (2:1–2). In tracing the origins of a panorama of nations to a common ancestor, the author devotes special attention to the descendants of one of Noaḥ's sons: Shem. Even among these descendants, there is a narrowing of focus. Among the descendants of Shem the writer privileges the descendants of Abraham and Isaac. In calling attention to Abraham's descendants, the Chronicler's supplementation of the Table of Nations provides it with a new significance (Kartveit 1989: 112; Willi 1991: 17–18). Whereas the Table of Nations actually gives very little attention to the ancestors of Israel, the Chronicler's genealogy of nations does. Inserting much of the Table of Nations (Gen 10:1–32//1 Chr 1:5–23) into the midst of other genealogies extending from the first person, Adam (1:1), to the progenitor of the twelve tribes, Israel (2:1), takes the earlier classification a number of steps further. The narrowing of focus from the seventy descendants of Noaḥ to the descendants of Isaac demonstrates that the writer's purpose was not to compile an exhaustive enumeration of all human cultures, but rather to create a certain picture of humanity, an *imago mundi* (image of the world), that reflects the circumstances of his own time. Employing the information available to him from Genesis, the Chronicler concentrates on those nations to whom he believed Judah was most closely related.

COMMENT

In his genealogy of humanity, the author posits a direct connection between the first person and the progenitor of the twelve Israelite tribes. But by the same token, this continuity occurs in the context of segmented genealogies that underscore the blood relations between various peoples of the world (Knoppers forthcoming [c]). Indeed, if a major purpose of genealogies is to configure or rewrite kinship ties (R. Wilson 1977; Osborne 1979: 318), 1 Chr 1:1–2:2 establishes such ties between Israel and a host of other nations, most notably Seir and Edom. The opening to the Chronicler's work may be best understood in the context of other relevant works from the ancient Mediterranean world. When one compares this opening chapter in the Chronicler's work with other historical writings from ancient Mesopotamia and Greece, one is struck by a number of features. First, the author does not confer any special dignity upon the first human. Adam is not described as "the image of God" (*ṣelem ʾĕlōhîm*; Gen 1:27). The origins of Adam go unexplained (Willi 1991: 47). Nor is Adam a liminal figure, like Adapa in second millennium B.C.E. Mesopotamian lore (Speiser 1969: 101–3), the figure who reappears transformed as Oannes in the *Babyloniaca* of Berossus (Verbrugghe and Wickersham 1996: 44–48). There is no indication that the primal human was of any special descent, bridged the divine and human spheres, functioned as either a royal priest or a prophet, enjoyed any special divine favors, or experienced any intimate relations with the gods (Neimann 1973: 124; Callendar 2000: 206–7). In fact, neither Yhwh nor any momentous theological term, such as "election," appear in 1:1–2:2. The first reference to Yhwh occurs appropriately in the context of the genealogy of Israel, specifically the lineage of Judah (2:3). In Chronicles, Adam is no more and no less than the first human in a series.

Second, with the exceptions of Nimrod and the Edomite kings and chieftains, the text does not ascribe any special offices to the figures listed. The Chronicler traces certain lines of descent among the figures he lists, but he neither establishes nor defends a hierarchy among individuals. Significant achievements or shortcomings are not listed. In exhibiting, or not exhibiting, certain features, the universal genealogy differs markedly from works such as the Sumerian King List (Jacobsen 1939) and the Assyrian King List (Oppenheim 1969: 564–66; R. Wilson 1977: 86–101), which mention titles, select military or political achievements, and chronological details.

Third, the genealogies evince a spatial dimension. Names found in the Table of Nations—for instance Cush (Sudan or Ethiopia), Mizraim (Egypt), and Canaan in Gen 10:6 (//1:8)—are inherently territorial. The overlap between eponyms, tribal names, and place-names is also known from other ancient lands, for instance, Babylon (Brinkman 1968: 270–71; Zadok 1976: 117–18). Although the geographical relevance of the list in Genesis has been stressed by many commentators (e.g., Aharoni 1979; Neimann 1973), some commentators on Chronicles are skeptical that these names have any geographical importance (e.g., Rudolph 1955: 7; Osborne 1979: 169–70; Lipiński 1990: 40–53; Japhet 1993a: 57–58). It is true that the Chronicler omits most of the geographic digressions and explanations in the Table of Nations from his own presentation (e.g., Gen 10:5, 10–12, 19–20, 30). But this pattern of exclusion is consistent with his compositional technique throughout much of 1:1–2:2. Concentrating on the lists themselves, the writer excises many of the headings, anecdotes, and conclusions found in his sources (e.g., Gen 5:2–5, 7–8, 10–11, 13–14, 16–17, 19–20; 10:1, 31–32). Exceptions are to be found, of course, in the lists of the Edomite kings and chieftains (1:43–54). In any case, the distinction between ethnicity and land suggests, if not promotes, a false dichotomy. Peoples are not free-floating Platonic entities unsullied by connections to the material world, but are inevitably tied to certain places and territories. For readers familiar with the various regions of the ancient world, names such as "Elishah and Tarshish, Kittim and Rodanim" (v. 7) have territorial referents. This is true not only of names gleaned from the Table of Nations but for other names as well (e.g., Teman, Qenaz, Timna, and Amaleq in v. 36).

To put the matter somewhat differently, no one contends that the genealogies of Israel in 2:3–8:40 lack any spatial dimensions. For the sake of consistency, it would be strange to contend that the genealogies of 1:1–2:2 do. Again, no one contends that the Chronicler's genealogy of nations lacks a chronological dimension, even though he systematically excises the chronological information from his sources (esp. in vv. 1–4, 24–27). For the sake of consistency, it would be odd to affirm a temporal dimension but deny a spatial dimension. One does not need to insist that all of the eponyms and ethnic names are somehow also place-names. This seems highly unlikely. Nevertheless, as a number of scholars (Curtis and Madsen 1910; Aharoni 1979; Kartveit 1989) have recognized, many of the names included from the author's sources do have geographical associations (NOTES). The spatial range of names found in the Chronicler's genealogy of nations far exceeds, in fact, that found in the Hesiodic *Catalogue of Women*, a work which has been compared with the Table of Nations (Hess 1990: 252; Van Seters 1992: 176–77). The *Catalogue of Women* contains a series of segmented genealogies that are largely limited to detailing the names of Greek-speaking peoples, groups, and places (West 1985: 36–124).

Fourth, the Chronicler admits, much like earlier biblical writers before him, that Israel was a relative latecomer to the stage of world history. Eber, the eponymous ancestor of the Hebrews, does not appear until well into the genealogy of nations (1:18). Israel (Jacob) appears many generations later (2:1). Unlike the authors of the Babylonian creation story *Enūma eliš*, who correlate the establishment of Babylon with the culmination of the divine creative process (Dalley 1989: 262ff.), the author does not view the rise of Israel as coterminous with cosmogony. Israel emerges as part of a longer historical process. If Israel is to have a privileged place among the nations, the author tacitly acknowledges that the other nations have some legitimacy as well. After all, in both preliterate and literate societies, having a history is itself a mark of status and authority (Sahlins 1985: 49).

Fifth, the author follows the Yahwist and Priestly writers in locating the eponymous ancestor of the Hebrews, Eber, among the descendants of Shem. This means that he does not see Israel as indigenous to its land (*pace* Japhet 1979). Canaan, the figure associated with the land that bears his name, is presented as one of the sons of Ḥam. If one of Shem's descendants were to occupy the land of Canaan at some later point, he would have to do so as an outsider. To this it may be objected that the Chronicler is merely reproducing older materials bequeathed to him. This he does. But if the Chronicler wished to depart from the script written by earlier authors (e.g., the Yahwist and the Priestly writers), he could have modified their presentations. Comparison with the presentation of *Jubilees* (second century B.C.E.) is apt. In his rewriting of the Genesis narrative, the author of *Jubilees* has Noaḥ explicitly promise the land of Palestine to Shem (*Jub.* 8:12–21). While Shem is awarded most of Asia, Ḥam is awarded Africa (*Jub.* 8:22–24; Alexander 1982; 1992; 1997). In this highly developed *imago mundi*, Zion becomes the omphalos of the earth, and the three Ionian continents, Europe, Asia, and Libya (Africa), are correlated with Noaḥ's three sons, Japheth, Shem, and Ḥam (*Jub.* 8:12–9:15). The author of *Jubilees* locates Israel in the middle of all peoples and in the middle of all lands. If Ḥam to the south is hot and Japheth to the north is cold, Shem is just right (*Jub.* 8:30; VanderKam 1994). As for Canaan, his lot falls very far to the west (*Jub.* 9:1). It is only Canaan's envy of the allotment given to Shem and his rebellion against his father's wishes that leads him to occupy a territory, "the land of Lebanon," that was not his to inherit (*Jub.* 10:27–34). When *Jubilees* finally describes this land as "Canaan" (e.g., *Jub.* 10:34), the term takes on a whole new meaning—the land that was stolen by Canaan.

The implications of *Jubilees* are clear. Should one of the descendants of Arpachshad (the son of Shem) come to occupy the land of Canaan, he would inherit what was originally and properly his (*Jub.* 9:4). By presenting Canaan as a usurper, the author of *Jubilees* completely revises the force of Gen 9–10 even as he faithfully reproduces many individual details. The Chronicler, by contrast, lets the force of the Table of Nations go uncontested. His summary (vv. 24–27) presents

Abram as the tenth generation after Shem, both chronologically and ethnically differentiated from the descendants of Japheth (vv. 5–7) and Ḥam (vv. 8–16). As in Genesis, Canaan's offspring are Ḥeth, the Jebusites, the Amorites, the Girgashites, the Ḥivites, and so forth (vv. 13–16). This is not to say that the Chronicler's reuse of Genesis lacks its own individual perspective. Rather, this distinctive perspective must be sought in how the Chronicler recontextualizes and extends the Table of Nations within his own presentation.

To do justice to the force of 1 Chr 1:1–2:2, one has to reckon with the continuity from Adam to Esau and Israel, the common humanity of all peoples, and the diversity of the various nations who inhabit the world. Two overlapping dimensions—the linear and the spatial—are present in the universal lineage. On one level, the presentation moves diachronically from Adam and the primeval age to the descendants of Noaḥ, Abraham, Isaac, Esau, and Israel in the postdiluvian age. Israel (Jacob) is the focus of the remaining genealogical material in 1 Chr 2–8. On this diachronic level, the lineages achieve greater elaboration and greater focus as they progress toward the descendants of Israel. Seen in this context, the presentation promotes an *imago mundi* in which the tribes of Israel emerge at the end of a long development. Israel may be the focus of the Chronicler's presentation, but his *imago mundi* also presents Israel as very much related to the other nations, which preceded Israel or developed alongside it. The descendants of Israel will be singled out for exclusive attention, but these descendants live within a community of nations of which they are but one part.

If on one level the presentation moves diachronically, situating the appearance of Israel against the background of other peoples, on a second level, the presentation moves laterally, situating Israel spatially within the world it inhabits. The segmented genealogies of Japheth, Ḥam, Shem, Esau, and Seir illustrate the author's acknowledgment that a great diversity of peoples in a great diversity of places inhabit his world. The nations may be linguistically, geographically, and ethnically dispersed, but they share a common humanity and a common progenitor. The ethnographic horizons of the Chronicler's genealogical outline generate a map of the world *(mappa mundi)* in verbal form. The descendants of Abraham and Isaac are situated within a larger international context. The Chronicler's ethnographic perspective displays a variety of contours, but it is basically centered on southern Canaan (cf. Ezek 5:5; 38:12; Kartveit 1989: 114–17; Oeming 1990: 89–91). Given the setting of the author in Yehud, it is important that the ethnographic ties to those nations traditionally situated to the south and southeast of Judah are particularly strong. The spatial interest, sustained beyond the material extracted from the Table of Nations, extends into the material about Ishmael, Qeṭurah, Esau, Seir, and the Edomite kings. In this respect, the Chronicler's vision is less grandiose than that of the author of *Jubilees*. The genealogies of Judah (2:3–4:23) and Simeon (4:24–43) develop many of the ties hinted at in 1:29–33, 35–54 between the southern tribes and their southern neighbors (2:25–26, 32, 50–53; 4:25, 39–43). His narratives about the United Monarchy (18:11–13; 27:30; 2 Chr 8:17; 9:1–12) and Judah (2 Chr 17:11; 20:1–23; 21:8–10, 16–17; 22:1; 25:11–12, 14, 20; 26:7–8; 28:17) continue and elaborate this interest.

By situating the emergence of Israel in the context of the emergence of other peoples in other lands, the Chronicler anticipates an important feature of early Jewish historiography. The *imago mundi* becomes a consistent feature of medieval Jewish and Christian literature (Alexander 1974; 1982: 201–3). Like earlier biblical authors, the Chronicler is most interested in stories about Israel, but he also recognizes that Israel did not emerge out of a vacuum. Indeed, one can only appreciate the experience of Israel within its land if one has some understanding of lands and peoples relevant to Israel and how they are related to Israel.

II. The Genealogy of Judah, Part I (2:3–55)

Introduction

[3]The sons of Judah: Er, Onan, and Shelah; three were born to him by Bathshua the Canaanite. Although Er was the firstborn of Judah, he did evil in the sight of Yhwh and he killed him. [4]And Tamar his daughter-in-law bore him Perez and Zeraḥ. The sons of Judah were five in all.

The Sons of Perez

[5]The sons of Perez: Ḥezron and Ḥamul.

The Descendants of Zeraḥ

[6]The sons of Zeraḥ: Zimri, Ethan, Heman, Calcol, and Darda; altogether five. [7]The sons of Zimri: Carmi. The sons of Carmi: Achar, the troubler of Israel, who violated the ban. [8]The sons of Ethan: Azariah.

The Descendants of Ḥezron

[9]The sons of Ḥezron, who were born to him: Jeraḥmeel, Ram, and Celubai.

The Descendants of Ram

[10]And Ram sired Amminadab, and Amminadab sired Naḥshon the chieftain of the sons of Judah. [11]And Naḥshon sired Salma and Salma sired Boaz. [12]And Boaz sired Obed and Obed sired Jesse. [13]And Jesse sired Eliab his firstborn, Abinadab the second, Shimea the third, [14]Nethanel the fourth, Raddai the fifth, [15]Ozem the sixth, David the seventh. [16]Their sisters were Zeruiah and Abigail. The sons of Zeruiah: Abshai, Joab, and Asah-el—three. [17]Abigail gave birth to Amasa. The father of Amasa was Jether the Ishmaelite.

The Descendants of Caleb

[18]Caleb son of Ḥezron sired (children through) Azubah [his] wife and Jerioth. These were her sons: Jesher, Shobab, and Ardon. [19]When Azubah died, Caleb took for himself Ephrath and she bore him Ḥur. [20]Ḥur sired Uri and Uri sired Bezalel.

Additional Descendants of Ḥezron

[21]After Ḥezron had sexual relations with the daughter of Machir, the father of Gilead (he married her when he was sixty years old), she bore him Segub. [22]And Segub sired Jair. He had twenty-three towns in the land of Gilead, [23]but Geshur and Aram took Ḥavvoth Jair from them along with Qenath and its dependencies:

sixty towns. All these were descendants of Machir the father of Gilead. 24 (After the
death of Ḥezron, Caleb had sexual relations with Ephrathah.) The wife of Ḥezron
was Abijah and she bore him Ashḥur the father of Teqoa.

The Descendants of Jeraḥmeel

25 These were the descendants of Jeraḥmeel the firstborn of Ḥezron: Ram the
firstborn, Bunah, Oren, Ozem, and Aḥijah. 26 Jeraḥmeel had another wife whose
name was Aṭarah; she was the mother of Onam. 27 The sons of Ram the firstborn
of Jeraḥmeel: Maaz, Jamin, and Eqer. 28 The sons of Onam: Shammai and Yada.
The sons of Shammai: Nadab and Abishur. 29 The name of the wife of Abishur
was Abiḥail. She bore him Aḥban and Molid. 30 The sons of Nadab: Seled and Appaim, but Seled died without sons. 31 The son of Appaim: Ishi. The son of Ishi:
Sheshan. The son of Sheshan: Aḥli. 32 The sons of Yada the brother of Shammai:
Jether and Jonathan, but Jether died without sons. 33 The sons of Jonathan: Peleth
and Zaza. These were the descendants of Jeraḥmeel.

The Descendants of Sheshan

34 Sheshan did not have any sons, only daughters, but Sheshan had an Egyptian
servant whose name was Jarḥa. 35 Sheshan gave his daughter to Jarḥa his servant as
[his] wife, and she bore him Attai. 36 Attai sired Nathan and Nathan sired Zabad
37 and Zabad sired Ephlal and Ephlal sired Obed 38 and Obed sired Jehu and Jehu
sired Azariah 39 and Azariah sired Ḥelez and Ḥelez sired Eleasah 40 and Eleasah
sired Sismai and Sismai sired Shallum 41 and Shallum sired Jeqamiah and Jeqamiah sired Elishama.

Additional Descendants of Caleb

42 The descendants of Caleb the brother of Jeraḥmeel: Mesha his firstborn, who
was the father of Ziph, and his second son Mareshah the father of Ḥebron. 43 The
sons of Ḥebron: Qoraḥ, Tappuaḥ, Reqem, and Shema. 44 Shema sired Raḥam the
father of Jorqeam and Reqem sired Shammai. 45 The son of Shammai: Maon.
Maon was the father of Beth-zur. 46 Ephah, a concubine of Caleb, bore Ḥaran,
Moza, and Gazez. And Ḥaran sired Gazez. 47 The sons of Jahdai: Regem, Jotham,
Geshan, Peleṭ, Ephah, and Shaaph. 48 A concubine of Caleb, Maacah, gave birth
to Sheber, Tirḥanah, 49 Shaaph the father of Madmannah, Sheva the father of
Machbenah, and the father of Gibea. The daughter of Caleb was Achsah.
50 These were the descendants of Caleb.

The Descendants of Ḥur

The sons of Ḥur the firstborn of Ephrathah: Shobal the father of Qiriath-jearim,
51 Salma the father of Bethleḥem, Ḥareph the father of Beth-gader. 52 Shobal
the father of Qiriath-jearim had sons: Haroeh [and] half of the Manaḥathites.
53 The families of Qiriath-jearim: the Ithrites, the Puthites, the Shumathites, and
the Mishraites. From these came the Zorathites and the Eshtaulites. 54 The sons of
Salma the father of Bethleḥem: the Neṭophathites, Aṭroth-beth-joab, half of the
Manaḥathites, (and) the Zorites. 55 The families of the scribes, inhabitants of
Jabez—the Tirathites, the Shimeathites, the Sucathites—they were Qenites who
came from Ḥammath the father of Beth-rechab.

TEXTUAL NOTES

2:3. "Shelah." So MT. The LXX lemmata (LXX^{BL} *Sēlōn;* LXX^{AN} *Sēlōm*; cf. Arm. *Selō*) resemble LXX Gen 46:12.

"were born" (נולד). One Heb. MS has the pl. (נולדו).

"Bath-shua" (בת־שׁוע). MT can also be translated "the daughter of Shua" (so some witnesses to LXX). See Gen 38:2. For "shua," LXX^{ABN} have *Sauas* (cf. Gen 38:2, 12). Both Gen 38:10 and Tg. 1 Chr 9:3 go on to mention the death of Onan. Rudolph (1955: 15) ingeniously reconstructs וגם אונן משנהו רע בעיני יהוה וימיתהו (cf. Tg.), assuming a haplography, but it is more likely that Tg. is assimilating toward the source text of Genesis.

2:5. "Ḥamul" (חמול). LXX^{ABN} *Hiemouēl;* LXX^{L} *Hamouēl* (= חמואל) and Syr. agree with SP Gen 46:12. Cf. 1 Chr 4:26.

2:6. "Zimri" (זמרי). LXX *Zambrei.* The contrast with MT Josh 7:1 "Zabdi" suggests both a *bêt/mêm* and a *dālet/rêš* confusion, which would not be impossible (McCarter 1986: 44–46). One of the northern kingdom's monarchs (1 Kgs 16:9–20; 2 Kgs 9:31) has similar variants: MT "Zimri;" LXX^{BL} *Zambr(e)i.* It is also possible that the author of Chronicles is punning on the root of the name Zimri (*zmr,* "to sing," "to prune"), because the lineage was cut off (Olyan 1985).

"Darda" *(drdʿ).* Following many Heb. MSS, some LXX cursives, Eusebius, Vg., Syr., some Tg. MSS, and MT 1 Kgs 5:11. MT's "Dara" *(drʿ),* a *hapax legomenon,* has suffered a haplography of *dālet* after *rêš.*

2:7. "sons of Zimri: Carmi. The sons of Carmi" (ובני זמרי כרמי ובני כרמי). It appears that MT and LXX^{AB} have suffered a haplography by *homoioteleuton,* "and the sons of Carmi" (ובני כרמי). The reconstruction follows Josh 7:1, 18.

"Achar" (עכר). So MT and LXX. A few Heb. MSS and MT Josh 7:1, 18, 20, 24 "Achan" (עכן). Since LXX^{B} and Syr. Josh 7:1 read *Achar,* it is possible that the Chronicler's *Vorlage* reads *Achar.*

2:8. "and the sons of Ethan: Azariah." So MT and LXX. There is no need to emend the text. The use of "sons" is formulaic (e.g., 1 Chr 2:7, 8, 31; 4:15).

2:9. "Ram." So MT, LXX*, and Peshiṭta (vv. 9ff.); MT Ruth 4:19; Matt 1:4. LXX^{L}, Arm. 2:9, and LXX^{A} Ruth 4:19 *Aram;* LXX^{B} Ruth 4:19 *Arran.* Similar variants occur in Job 32:2. Luke 3:33 *Arni,* but some MSS *Aram.*

"Celubai" (כלובי). So MT *(lectio difficilior);* cf. LXX^{L} *ho Chalōbi.* LXX^{AN} have the expected "Caleb" (LXX^{B} has suffered metathesis: *Chabel*) and add "and Aram." LXX^{AN} thus provide Ḥezron (v. 9) with a fourth son, but there is inner-Greek evidence that LXX^{AN} may be corrupt (Allen 1974a: 154). As for "Celubai," it seems that he and "Caleb" (כלב) are one and the same (vv. 18, 42). The former name may simply be a variant of the latter (Wellhausen 1870: 13). See also "Celub" (כלוב) in 1 Chr 4:11 and 27:26.

2:10. "Ram." LXX^{B} c_2 *Arran;* LXX^{ALN} *Aram.* See also the 4th TEXTUAL NOTE to v. 9. In these witnesses Arran or Aram is the father of Am(m)inadab.

"chieftain of the sons of Judah" (נשׂיא בני יהודה). LXX "chieftain of the house of Judah."

2:11. "Salma" (שׂלמא). So MT. LXX^{AB} *Salmō*. Ruth 4:20–21 has both "Salmah" (שׂלמה) and "Salmon" (שׂלמון). On the name, see also vv. 51, 54. Salma and Salmon represent the same PN with two different hypocoristic endings.

2:13. "Jesse." Only here (in MT; cf. LXX *Iessai*) is the name of Jesse spelled "Ishi" (אישי instead of ישי). I read with LXX and MT v. 12 (see GKC, §47b).

"Abinadab." So MT. LXX *Ameinadab*, perhaps reflecting a *bêt/mêm* confusion (Gilbert 1896–97: 292; cf. Rehm 1937: 43). But see LXX 1 Chr 8:33; 9:39; 10:2; 13:7.

"Shimea" (שמעא). So MT 1 Chr 20:7, and Qere 2 Sam 21:21. LXX^{BLN} 1 Chr 2:13 *Samaa*; MT 1 Sam 16:9; 17:13, "Shammah" (שמה; LXX^{B} *Sama*); 2 Sam 21:21 (Kethib) "Shimei" (שמעי).

2:15. "Ozem" (אצם). LXX^{AB} and Vg. *Asom*. LXX^{L} *Asam*.

"David the seventh." Thus MT and LXX (maximum variation). First Samuel 16:10, followed by Syr. and Arab. of this verse, lists seven sons followed by David as the eighth. To complicate matters further, MT 1 Chr 27:18 lists "Elihu" as a brother of David (LXX "Eliab;" cf. 1 Sam 16:6; 17:13). In accordance with Chronicles, Josephus (*Ant.* 6.156–65; 7:372) lists six brothers of David. On the early and medieval interpretation of these texts, see Kalimi (1995a: 308–10; 2001).

2:16. "Abigail" (אביגיל) appears here as Jesse's daughter. The situation is more complicated in the witnesses to 2 Sam 17:24–25. There she is the daughter of either "Naḥash" (MT; LXX^{AB}) or "Jesse" (LXX^{LMN}) and the sister of Joab's mother "Zeruiah." At least in the first instance, the texts of MT and LXX^{AB} are likely in error (McCarter 1984: 392).

"Abshai." MT 2:16 reads "Abshai" here and in 11:20; 18:12; 19:11, 15. MT 2 Sam 10:10, 14 also have "Abshai." MT 2 Sam 2:18; 23:18 and the lemmata of LXX^{B} *Abeisa*; LXX^{AN} *Abisa*; Tg., Vg. *Abisai* (in 1 Chr 2:16) all reflect "Abishai." The fuller readings of LXX Chronicles seem to be so consistent that one is lead to the conclusion that the *Vorlage* employed by the LXX translators was more orthographically developed than MT Chronicles is.

2:17. "Jether" (יתר). MT 2 Sam 17:25 "Ithra" (יתרא) provides a longer form of the same name.

"the Ishmaelite" *(hyšmʿly)*. So MT, LXX*, and Vg. *(lectio difficilior)*. One Heb. MS, a few LXX cursives, and MT 2 Sam 17:25 read "the Israelite" *(hyśrʾly)*. The expansion in Tg., which employs both terms, reveals that "the Ishmaelite" was in Tg.'s *Vorlage*. One Heb. MS and Syr. lack the term altogether.

2:18. "sired . . . sons." MT literally reads: "sired Azubah, (his) wife, and Jerioth and these are her sons" (הוליד את-עזובה אשה ואת-יריעות ואלה בניה). A few Heb. MSS lack "wife," perhaps due to haplography (אשה after עזובה; Freedman: personal communication), while another lacks the conjunction and direct object marker (ואת). The direct object marker together with "Jerioth" are lacking in one Heb. MS. Instead of MT's "sired," LXX^{AN} have "took" (= לקח), a verb, that in certain contexts, esp. with לאשה, denotes marriage (BDB 543). The evidence provided by LXX is diverse and complicated (Allen 1974a: 143; 1974b: 112). Vg.: Caleb "received a wife named Azubah who gave birth to Jerioth" *(accepit uxorem nomine Azuba de qua genuit Ierioth)*. Syr.: Caleb "sired Jerioth by Azubah his wife" (הוליד מן עזובה אשתו את-יריעות). NAB and REB follow suit by interpreting the first *ʾt* as a prep. and the second *ʾt* as the direct object marker, thus making Azubah the wife and Jerioth the daughter to whom the following expression, "these were her sons," refers. The course taken by KJV, RSV, NIV, NJPS is different: construing *ʾt* as a prep. "with" or "by," they offer the translation (MT) Caleb "had children by his wife Azubah and by Jerioth; these were her sons." This course is preferable to that of NAB and REB because the pattern in the following verses is to trace sons through the wife or concubine and not through the daughter.

"Jesher" (ישר). So MT. LXX^{ABN} *Iōasar*; bb′ *Sar*. Reconstructing an original יועזר on the basis of LXX *(BHK)* is unjustified (Allen 1974b: 45).

"Shobab." The reading of LXX^{B} *kai Iasoub* (cf. c_2 *kai Iassoub*; LXX^{L} *Soubab*) may have been influenced by *Iōasar* (previous TEXTUAL NOTE).

"Ardon" (ארדון). LXX^{B} *Orna*; LXX^{L} *Abdōm*.

2:19. "Ephrath" (אפרת). Thus MT, but the form Ephrathah (with the locative -*āh* ending) appears elsewhere (1 Chr 2:24, 50; 4:4; Gen 35:16; 48:7; Ruth 4:11; cf. אפרתים in Ruth 1:2).

2:21. "after Ḥezron had sexual relations with the daughter of Machir" (ואחר בא חצרון אל-בת-מכיר). The syntax of MT is difficult. The prep. אחר with the finite verb בא is used to structure a temporal transition in a subordinate clause (cf. Lev 14:43; Jer 41:16; Job 42:7; *HALOT* 35; Waltke and O'Connor, §11.2.1).

"he married her" (והוא לקחה). LXX^{L} expands to: "he, Gilead, took Achem."

"Segub." LXX^{B} *Serouch*.

2:23. This verse is not found in Syr.

"but Geshur . . . Gilead." The syntax is difficult. MT literally reads "took Ḥavvoth Jair from them, Qenath and its dependencies: sixty towns." I am construing *ʾt* as a prep. "along with," hence, "along with Qenath and its dependencies."

"sons" (בני). So MT. LXX^{B} has "sons" in the genitive *(huiōn)*, leading Begrich *(BHK)* to read לבני.

2:24. "Caleb had sexual relations with Ephrathah" (בא כלב אל אפרתה). This reconstruction is based on that of Wellhausen (1870: 14) in view of the evidence provided by LXX and Vg. Among other things, an *ʾālep* has been lost to MT "in Caleb Ephrathah" (בכלב אפרתה), and the prep. אל has been lost through haplography before (אפרתה). On the context, see v. 19.

"(and) the wife of Ḥezron was Abijah." So MT. Lacking in Syr. Some scholars omit the *wāw* so that they can construe Caleb as the subj. throughout this verse.

"Abijah" (אביה). Thus MT and LXX *(Abia)*. "Abijah" may be understood, in this instance, as a female name (e.g., 2 Chr 29:1; Williamson 1979). Another option (e.g., Wellhausen, Kittel, Rudolph, Michaeli) is to emend to "his father" (אביהו). In this line of interpretation, the following phrase, "she bore him Ashḥur" (ותלד לו את-אשחור), relates to Caleb and not to Ḥezron. But given that vv. 21–23 deal with Ḥezron and v. 19 has already depicted Caleb's relationship with Ephrathah, there is no compelling reason to emend the text.

2:25. "Ram." So MT and LXX^{ALN} *(Rham)*. LXX^{B} hc_2 *Rhan*; Syr. "Aram" (TEXTUAL NOTES to vv. 9, 10).

"Bunah" (בונה). Variants are בנה (a few Heb. MSS); LXX^{B} c_2 *Banaia* (= בניה; LXX^{L} *Amina*; LXX^{AN} *Baana* (= בענה).

"Oren, Ozem." LXX^{B} *Araia kai Ambram kai Asan* reflects a dittography.

"Aḥijah" (אחיה). LXX^{B} offers another interpretation of practically the same consonants, *ʾadelphos aʿutou* "his brother" (= אחיהו). Syr. "their brothers" (חתהון).

2:26. "Onam" (אונם). The variant in LXX^{B} *Ozom* (cf. LXX^{N} *Ounom*) reflects a *zayin/nûn* confusion.

2:27. "Ram." Thus MT and LXX^{ALN}. LXX^{B} "Aram" (TEXTUAL NOTES to vv. 9, 10).

"Jamin." So MT and LXX. Syr. "Jabin."

"Eqer." LXX^{AB} *Akor*. LXX^{L} *Iker* e_2 *Semei*; *b*b′ Semei; y *kac Iada kae Semei*.

2:28. "Shammai." So MT and LXX^{B} *(Samai)*. Cursives b and y *Semmei*.

"Yada" (ידע). So MT and LXX^{AB}. Lacking in cursives bhn. For "and Yada" (וידע), Syr. exhibits metathesis יוידע. Cf. 1 Chr 2:32.

2:29. "Abiḥail" (אביחיל). So many Heb. MSS and Syr. (cf. LXX^{AB} *Abeichaia*). MT and Tg. "Abihail" (אביהיל). The variants reflect a *hê*/*ḥêt* confusion.

"Molid" (מוליד). LXX^{B} ic_2 *Moēl*.

2:30. "Seled" (סלד). LXX^{B} *Salad*; LXX^{L} *Saled*.

"and Appaim" (ואפים). Thus MT *(lectio difficilior)*. Some follow LXX^{B} c_2 "and Ephraim" (both here and in v. 31), but LXX substitutes a familiar name for an unfamiliar one.

2:31. "sons of Appaim: Jesse." See the TEXTUAL NOTE to v. 8.

"Jesse" (ישעי). LXX^{B} c_2 *Isem(i)ēl* (cf. *Ho Ismaēlitēs* in v. 17); Syr. ישעיה.

"Sheshan." LXX^{AB} and Syr. reflect "Shoshan" (cf. vv. 34, 35).

"Aḥli" (אחלי). LXX^{B} *Achai*; *b*b′ *Oulai*; y *Alai*.

2:32. "Yada." LXX^{B} *Idouda*; c_2 *Idoula*.

2:34. "Jarḥa" (ירחע). LXX^{AB} *Iōchēl*.

2:35. "to Jarḥa his servant." Thus MT and LXX^{AB}. Syr. "to him."

2:37. "Ephlal" (אפלל). Variants include *Aphamēl* (LXX^{Bb} c_2), *Aphamēd* (LXX^{B*}), and *Elphael* (LXX^{L}; Allen 1974b: 16).

"Obed" (עובד). Syr. Jobab (יובב).

2:39. "Eleasah" (אלעשׂה). LXX^{B} *Emas*.

2:40. "Sismai" (ססמי). LXX^{B} *Sosomai*.

2:42. "Mesha" (מישע). LXX^{AB} *Marēisa*; c_2 *Marisa*; *b*b′e_2 *Mousa*; Arm. *Muš*. The lemma of LXX^{AB} likely reflects an original מרשה.

"Mesha his firstborn . . . and his second son Mareshah the father of Ḥebron" (מישע בכרו. . .ובנו משנה מרשה אבי חברון). The reconstruction follows Rudolph (1955: 18). MT, which problematically lists the sons of Mareshah as the father of Ḥebron, has suffered a haplography *(homoioarkton)* of "and his second son" (ובנו משנה) before "Mareshah." For different emendations, see Curtis and Madsen (1910: 95) and Noth (1932: 107).

2:44. "Jorqeam" (ירקעם). LXX^{B} *Ieklan*; LXX^{AN} *Ierkaan*; LXX^{L} *Ierekam*. *BHK*, followed by Roddy Braun (1986: 38), reconstructs an original *yqdʿm* (MT Josh 15:56). This assumes both a *dālet*/*rêš* confusion and metathesis. The lemma of LXX Josh 15:56 *(Iareikam)* agrees with Chronicles.

2:45. This verse does not appear in Syr.

"Beth-zur" (בית-צור). LXX^B *Gedsour.*

2:46. "Ḥaran." So MT. LXX^B *(Harran)* and cursive y (Haran). Cf. *b*b′e$_2$, *Hōrōn*; Arm. *Oroun.*

"Moza" (מוצא). LXX^B *Iōsan*; LXX^{AN} *Iōsa.*

"Gazez" (גזז). A few Heb. MSS *gzn*; LXX^{AB} *Gezoue* and y; *b*e$_2$ *Gaz(e)i*; b′ *Gazē.*

2:47–49. These verses do not appear in Syr.

2:47. "Jahdai." So MT and LXX^A *(Iadai).* Some Heb. MSS "Jahdi."

"Geshon" (גישון). So MT and LXX^{AL} *(Geisōn).* LXX^B *Sōgar.*

2:48. "(she) gave birth" (ילדה). So a few Heb. MSS (LXX^B and cursives *b*b′), some witnesses to LXX, Vg., and Tg. MT "he begot" (ילד). See further GKC, §145u.

"Tirḥanah." Reading with LXX^L *(lectio brevior).* MT and LXX^{ABN} add at the beginning of v. 49 "and she gave birth to" (ותלד), while Vg. has the expected "and he sired" (= ויולד).

2:49. "Achsah" (עכסה). The lemma of LXX^B and Vg. *Ascha* reflects metathesis (Gilbert 1896–97: 291).

2:50. "sons of Ḥur." Reading with the versions *(lectio facilior).* MT "son of Ḥur."

2:51. "Salma" (שלמא). So MT (cf. Tg. שלמא) and Vg. LXX^{AB} *Solōmōn* is a corruption of *Salmōn* (Allen 1974a: 186; cf. v. 11).

"Ḥareph" (חרף). In spite of LXX^{AB} *Hareim* and LXX^L *Harēm*, the reconstruction *חרם (*BHK*, citing LXX) is flawed.

"Beth-gader" (בת-גדר). LXX^B *Baithgaidōn*; LXX^A *Baithgedōr* (= בת-גדור).

2:52. "Haroeh." So MT (הָרֹאֶה). The name is an alternative form of "Reaiah" (ראיה) in 1 Chr 4:2 (Demsky 1986: 52). LXX^B *Haiō*; LXX^{AN} *Haraa.* LXX^L lacks *Haiō* through *Iaeir* (= "Jair") in v. 53.

"half of the Manaḥathites." MT חצי-המנחות is rendered by NJPS as "half of the Menuhoth." Many emend to חצי המנחת (see v. 54), but MT may simply reflect a pl. formation (Knauf 1995a: 103–4). LXX^B c$_2$ *Heseira* probably reflects חצר.

2:53. "the Ithrites, the Puthites . . ."(. . .היתרי והפותי). Cf. LXX^B *Haithaleim kai Meipheitheim*, etc.

"from these came the Zorathites and the Eshtaulites." LXX "from these came the Saratheans and the sons of Esthaam." Some, but not all, of these discrepancies can be explained as inner-Greek developments (Allen 1974a: 144, 165; 1974b: 16, 112, 116, 157).

2:54. "Salma the father of Bethleḥem." The reconstruction follows v. 51 and assumes that MT "Salma Bethleḥem" has suffered a haplography of אבי (שלמא אבי בית לחם to שלמא בית לחם).

2:55. "inhabitants" (ישבי). So Qere; Kethib "they inhabited" (ישבו). LXX^B *katoikountes* supports Qere.

"scribes" (ספרים). There is no need to repoint the text to read "Siphrites," purportedly the earlier inhabitants of Qiriath-seper (A. Ehrlich 1914). Within the context of Chronicles, the reference to scribes is intelligible (1st NOTE to v. 55). The text does not state that scribal practice was exclusive to these families or specific to these locations (*pace* Rudolph 1955: 25).

"who came from (הבאים מן) Ḥammath the father of Beth-rechab." The expression is better understood in a spatial sense than in a strictly genealogical sense (Knights 1993: 13–15).

NOTES

2:3. "Judah." That Judah commences the tribal genealogies breaks with two precedents: the precedent set in 1 Chr 1, in which subsidiary lines were dealt with first, and the precedent set by other tribal listings, in which Reuben appears first (2nd NOTE to 2:1). The choice to begin with Judah is deliberate. The reason involves more than an interest in David (Rothstein and Hänel 1927: 133; Rudolph 1955: 65–66; Myers 1965a: xxx–xl; Ackroyd 1973a: 28, 48), although the Davidic line stands at the center of the Judahite genealogy (1 Chr 3:1–24). For the Chronicler, Judah is not a subsidiary line, but the most dominant tribe in Israelite history. Hence, he allocates his longest lineage to Judah (1 Chr 2:3–4:23). Two major interests characterize this work. First, the author takes an active interest in the different subdivisions within the tribe and their relations to each other. Second, the author pursues Judah's connections to other tribes and its non-Israelite neighbors. The Chronicler's high estimate of Judah's significance is evident in his introduction to Reuben (1 Chr 5:1–2; Willi 1994b). The Chronicler acknowledges that Reuben was firstborn (1 Chr 2:1–2; 5:1), but in the Chronicler's way of thinking this status does not automatically entitle Reuben to a position of preeminence among the descendants of Jacob. The writer decouples birthright from firstborn status, tying the former to proper conduct (Knoppers 2000b). Because of Reuben's misconduct, the birthright was given to Joseph (5:2). As for Judah, he was not the firstborn (1 Chr 2:1–2), but he "grew mighty among his brothers" (5:2).

"Onan." Consistent with the Chronicler's selective treatment of his subject matter, he does not pursue the fate of all the people mentioned in his genealogies. He supplies no information about the demise of Onan, although he may have assumed that his readers were familiar with the story. The addition supplied by Tg., based on Gen 38:7–10, attempts to fill the gap (3rd TEXTUAL NOTE to v. 3).

"Shelah." In his long schematic treatment of Judah, the author does not resume his discussion of Shelah and his descendants until 1 Chr 4:21–23.

"Bath-shua the Canaanite." The writer does not moralize against the important roles that non-Israelites played in his people's past. Quite the contrary, he calls attention to them (Knoppers 2001c). The Targum avoids these implications by calling Bath-shua a "trader" *(prqmṭ(y)tʾ)* instead of a "Canaanite." The Targum thus plays on the meaning of "Canaanite" (*hknʿnyt*; Job 40:30 [ET 41:6]; Zeph 1:11; McIvor 1994: 46) and transforms the text to comply with the prohibitions against intermarriage with members of the autochthonous nations (Exod 34:16; Deut 7:3; Josh 23:15–16; Knoppers 1994d).

"Er was the firstborn of Judah." The author draws on and summarizes Gen 38:1–7 for the material in the second half of this verse.

"did evil." Er's wrongdoing, the details of which go unmentioned in Chronicles (cf. Gen 38:7–10; 46:12; Num 26:19), is only of interest to the author in demonstrating how the firstborn lost his life and his privileged place (Greenspahn 1994). In this respect, Er anticipates Reuben (1 Chr 5:1–2; Japhet 1993a: 74–75).

"in the sight of Yhwh." This is the first mention of Yhwh in Chronicles. It is consistent with the Chronicler's theology that this reference occurs in the context of his discussion of Judah's lineages. For the Chronicler, there is no gap between the Ancestral age and the revelation of the name of Yhwh (cf. Exod 3:13–22; 6:2–8). Yhwh is the God of Israel from Israel's very beginnings (Japhet 1989).

2:4. "his daughter-in-law bore him." An allusion to the sexual relationship between Judah and Tamar (Gen 38:12–26). Having earlier referred to the Canaanite status of Bath-shua, the Chronicler affirms another unusual feature of Judah's lineage. The reference to Judah's relationship with Canaanite Tamar is remarkable, especially when considered against the background of Priestly injunctions (Lev 18:15; 20:12; cf. *Jub.* 41:1–24; *T. Jud.* 10:1–6; 11:1–5; 12:1–10; *Gen. Rab.* 95.2). In the lineages which follow, Tamar's line dominates.

"Perez and Zeraḥ." In the genealogy the major figures are Tamar's twins: firstborn Perez and his brother Zeraḥ. "Zeraḥ" (זרח) also appears as a descendant of Esau through Reuel (1:37) and as the father of an Edomite monarch (1:44).

2:5. "the sons of Perez: Ḥezron and Ḥamul." The introduction to the lineage of Perez may be compared to the longer introduction in Ruth 4:18 ("these are the generations [תולדות] of Perez; Perez sired Ḥezron"). The reference to Ḥamul being a son of Perez is drawn from Gen 46:12 (cf. Num 26:21).

2:6–8. "sons of Zeraḥ." This creative segmented genealogy draws upon two principal biblical sources: Josh 7:1 //1 Chr 2:6a, 7 and 1 Kgs 5:11 (4:31 ET)//1 Chr 2:6b. The writer selects, rearranges, and supplements his sources. The result is a genealogy unique to Chronicles.

2:6. "Zimri" or "Zabdi" (see the 1st TEXTUAL NOTE to v. 6) is mentioned as a son of Zeraḥ in Josh 7:1.

"Ethan, Heman, Calcol, and Darda." First Kings 5:11 (4:31 ET) lists a series of preeminent sages to whom Solomon is compared: Ethan the Ezraḥite, Heman, Calcol, and Darda. All four seem to be Canaanite names (Albright 1968a: 127), and all four are mentioned in 1 Kgs 5:11 as the offspring of "Maḥol" (מחול). In 1 Chr 2:6 these four distinguished individuals are dissociated from Maḥol (and from Solomon) and join Zimri as the five sons of Judahite Zeraḥ. This transformation is carried a step further in Tg. 1 Chr 2:6, where all five are acclaimed as prophets. (See also the NOTES to 25:1–3.) Because of the association of Ethan and Heman with song and music in two Psalm headings (88:1; 89:1) and in Chronicles (1 Chr 15:17–19; 25:2–7; 2 Chr 5:12; cf. 2 Chr 29:30), some scholars (e.g., Albright 1966: 47–49; Osborne 1979: 213–15) contend for an association with Levi. This is quite feasible, but there is another possibility. Given that the patronymics and phratries assigned to Heman (6:18–23) and Ethan (6:29–32) in the Levitical genealogy differ from those in 1:6, it is possible that members of two different tribes claimed Heman and Ethan among their ancestors. The appearance of these well-known names in two different lineages may reflect competing ancestral claims. Such a phenomenon in the composition of genealogies is also attested in ancient Greece (Thomas 1989).

2:7. "Carmi" is also listed as a son of "Zabdi" (= "Zimri") in Josh 7:1 (1st TEX-

TUAL NOTE to v. 6). Joshua 7:1 also mentions that Achan (Achar) was Carmi's son (Hess 1994: 89–93).

"Achar (עָכָר), the troubler (עוֹכֵר) of Israel." A pun on Achar's dubious status as a "troubler" (*ʿkr*, "to trouble, ruin") of his people. A play on words is also found in the text of Josh 7:24–26 (cf. 1 Kgs 18:17–18), but it involves the death sentence imposed upon Achan and his family in the "Valley of Achor" (Hess 1994: 94–96).

"violated (*māʿal*) the ban (*ḥerem*)." The term *mʿl* is a favorite of the Chronicler (NOTE to 10:13), but in this case it was found already within his source (Josh 7:1). In the Chronicler's usage, the object of the rebellion is normally a person, not a thing (1 Chr 5:25; 10:13; 2 Chr 12:2; 26:16; 28:19, 22; 29:6; 30:7; 36:14).

2:8. "Azariah." The claim that Azariah is a son of Ethan is unique to Chronicles.

2:9. "sons of Ḥezron." The writer's introductions to the descendants of Perez (vv. 5–8) and Ḥezron (vv. 9–41) are similar. The lineages of the three sons born to Ḥezron—Jeraḥmeel, Ram, and Celubai (Caleb)—are the focus of vv. 10–41. The genealogy of Ḥezron may be compared with the linear genealogy found in Ruth 4:18–22. But the Chronicler's combination of linear and segmented genealogies provides a more comprehensive and complex presentation than that of Ruth.

"Ḥezron," listed as a son of Perez in Gen 46:12 and Num 26:21, also appears as Reuben's third son (Gen 46:9; Exod 6:14; Num 26:6) and is associated with the southern part of Canaan in Reuben's genealogies (Gen 46:9; 3rd NOTE to 1 Chr 5:3). In Josh 15:3, Ḥezron appears as a town on the southern border of Judah between Qadesh-barnea and Qarqa (cf. Num 34:4; Josh 15:25). In the Judahite genealogy, Ḥezron is an integral part of Judah (see also 4:1). Three phratries derive from Ḥezron: the Ramites (vv. 10–17), the Calebites (vv. 18–20, 42–50a), and the Jeraḥmeelites (vv. 25–33). In 4:1 Ḥezron has a brother named Carmi, just as Reubenite Ḥezron does (Gen 46:9). This is a sign of an ancient writer positing multiple relationships, rather than of confusion in the text (*pace* Myers 1965a: 14).

"Jeraḥmeel." The name is relatively infrequent outside of Chronicles (e.g., Jer 36:26). Apart from Chronicles, our main source for the Jeraḥmeelites is Samuel (the name does not occur in the linear genealogy of Ruth 4:19). The Jeraḥmeelites inhabit a particular district of the Negev and constitute an independent group (1 Sam 27:8–10; 30:26–30). Many scholars (e.g., Wellhausen 1870: 24–25; de Vaux 1978: 536–37) have presented the Jeraḥmeelites as nomadic in character with no established or permament affiliation with particular districts or towns. But the reference to the "towns of the Jeraḥmeelites" (1 Sam 30:29) suggests that they are better characterized as seminomadic. One of the functions of ancient genealogies is to incorporate marginal figures or clans into a central group (R. Wilson 1977: 183). In this case, the author incorporates the Jeraḥmeelites fully into Judah (vv. 25–33; cf. 1 Chr 24:29). Chronicles even makes Jeraḥmeel Ḥezron's "firstborn" (v. 25), thus enhancing his prestige within the overall lineage.

"Ram." The name appears in Job 32:2 as the phratry of Job's so-called comforter Elihu. Apart from Job 32:2, Ram is unique to the genealogies of Ruth and Chronicles.

"Celubai" (TEXTUAL NOTE) is probably not to be identified with the Caleb of the conquest stories (Num 13:30; 14:24; Josh 14:6–15; 15:13–17; Judg 1:12–15; 3:9; Ben Sira 46:9–10), because that Caleb is consistently said to be the son of Jephunneh (Num 13:6; 14:6, 30, 38; 26:65; 32:12; 34:19; Deut 1:36; 1 Chr 4:15; 6:41). Because Chronicles presents two Calebs—Caleb son of Ḥezron and Caleb son of Jephunneh—its presentation of the Calebites is more complex than that of the Pentateuchal sources and the Deuteronomistic History (NOTE to 4:15). In Chronicles, Caleb son of Ḥezron receives much more attention than Caleb son of Jephunneh does. There is, however, one major similarity between the Chronicler's depictions of Caleb son of Ḥezron and Caleb son of Jephunneh. He situates both of them, along with their families and residences, firmly within Judah (Zwickel 1993: 481–83).

2:10–17. "Ram . . . Amasa." Aside from the partial parallel in Ruth 4:19b–22, which is organized into a strictly linear genealogy, this lineage is unique. The genealogy in Chronicles exhibits both linear (vv. 10–12) and segmented (vv. 13–17) forms. The parallel figures in the lineages of Chronicles and Ruth are identical, allowing for divergent spellings of a few names (TEXTUAL NOTES). Most scholars (e.g., Noth 1957: 119–20; Rudolph 1955: 16; C. McCarthy 1985; Braun 1986: 33; Japhet 1993a: 71) believe that Chronicles was the source of the material in Ruth. In fashioning this lineage, the author may have drawn on variety of scattered passages dealing with the descendants of Judah: Gen 46:12; Num 1:7; 2:3; 26:19–21; 1 Sam 16:1–17:1–51.

2:10. "Amminadab" the father of Naḥshon (Num 2:3).

"Naḥshon" is presented as a contemporary of Moses and Aaron in Exod 6:23 and Num 2:3 (both P). Aaron's wife Elisheba was, in fact, a sister of Naḥshon (Exod 6:23).

"the chieftain (*nāśî'*) of the sons of Judah." So the census list in Num 2:3. On the meaning of *nāśî'* in Chronicles, see the 2nd NOTE to 4:38.

2:11. "Naḥshon sired Salma and Salma sired Boaz." Apart from the parallel in Ruth 4:20–21, this information is unique to Chronicles.

2:13–15. "And Jesse sired." The lineage of Jesse's sons, listed ordinally, has been drawn, in part, from the narratives of 1 Sam 16:1–23, which records Samuel's election and anointing of David, and 1 Sam 17:1–51 (MT), which portrays the battle of David and Goliath. In these stories David appears as the youngest of Jesse's eight (not seven) sons, three of whom are explicitly named—Eliab, Abinadab, and Shammah (TEXTUAL NOTES). The names of the fourth through sixth of Jesse's sons—Nethanel, Raddai, and Ozem—are unique to Chronicles.

2:16. "Zeruiah and Abigail." The lineage of Jesse's daughters is likely connected to 2 Sam 17:24–25, which deals with the lineage of Absalom's commander Amasa (cf. 1 Chr 2:17). The problem with positing a close link between the two texts is that the details of 2 Sam 17:24–25 do not comport with the details of 1 Chr 2:15–17. The author's *Vorlage* of 2 Sam 17:24–25 probably differed in some respects from MT 2 Sam 17:24–25 (TEXTUAL NOTES).

"sons of Zeruiah." Of all Jesse's daughters and sons, the Chronicler provides further genealogical information for only three: the two daughters, Zeruiah and Abigail, and the last son, David (1 Chr 3). The Chronicler's lineage of Zeruiah draws upon 2 Sam 2:18, which mentions that Zeruiah was the mother of Joab, Abishai, and Asahel. Whatever one makes of the discrepancies between the lists of Samuel and Chronicles, close study of each reveals the extent to which David relied upon relations to administer his state.

2:17. "Jether (יתר) the Ishmaelite." This is one of a number of affiliations between Judahites and neighboring peoples in the Judahite genealogy (1 Chr 2:3, 17, 34, 55; cf. 2 Sam 17:25; 1 Kgs 2:5, 32). In this case, the kinship ties relate to David's family (vv. 15–17).

2:18–20. "Caleb." The descendants of this Ḥezronite are a major focus in the Judahite genealogy, taking up a sizable portion of its lineages (1 Chr 2:18–20, 42–55; 4:1–7). Much of this material is unparalleled. Given the problems that bedevil portions of the genealogy, it may be a wise procedure to begin with what seems clear and then discuss major problems in sequence. According to vv. 18–20, Caleb has a succession of at least two paramours—Azubah and Ephrath—and descendants through each. Of the two paramours, the second one, along with her offspring, is of more sustained interest (NOTES to vv. 50b–55).

2:18. "her sons" (1st TEXTUAL NOTE to v. 18). The antecedent could be either Azubah or Jerioth. Given the content of v. 19, I am taking the antecedent to be Azubah.

"Jesher, Shobab, and Ardon." David had a son named Shobab (2 Sam 5:14; 1 Chr 3:5; 14:4), but these names are otherwise unique to Chronicles.

2:19. "Caleb took for himself" (ויקח-לו כלב). In certain contexts, the verb "to take" (לקח) can designate marriage (e.g., Gen 4:19; 24:4; 25:1; 34:16; 1 Chr 2:21). The author explains the different subdivisions within the Calebites and their relations by recourse to Caleb's relationship with different women (cf. 1 Chr 2:50; 4:4). This arrangement allows the writer to posit multiple connections between the Calebites and other peoples in the region. In this instance, the marriage indicates a peaceful integration of different families in the region between Bethleḥem in the north and Mareshah and Ḥebron in the southwest (vv. 42–43).

"Ephrath." See the 2nd NOTE to v. 24.

"Ḥur." The text identifies Ḥur as the grandfather of Bezalel (Exod 24:14; 31:1–5) with a son of Caleb. Caleb's progeny thus include some illustrious figures in Israelite history (NOTES to 4:1, 4), but the genealogy raises its own set of questions. Earlier sources present Caleb (*ben* Jephunneh) and Bezalel as basically belonging to the same Exodus generation. In vv. 19–20, Caleb (*ben* Ḥezron) appears as the great-grandfather of Bezalel. See, further, the 1st NOTE to 4:15.

2:20. "Uri." As a son of Ḥur, see Exod 31:1–2.

"Bezalel." In the Priestly source, Bezalel is singled out by Yhwh as an extraordinarily gifted individual and is commissioned, along with Oholiab, to make the ark, the Tent of Meeting, and all of its furnishings (Exod 31:1–5; 35:30; 38:22). In Chronicles, these furnishings of Bezalel are honored by Solomon (2 Chr 1:5).

2:21–23. "after Ḥezron had sexual relations with the daughter of Machir" (ואחר חזרון בא אל-בת-מכיר). The subject shifts back to Ḥezron, the father of Jeraḥmeel, Ram, and Caleb (Celubai; v. 9). Hence, the material in vv. 21–23 should not be subsumed under "descendants of Caleb" (so many commentators).

What follows is genealogical material pertaining directly to Ḥezron and not to his earlier three sons. Because of the chronological and contextual problems, many construe vv. 21–23 (or vv. 21–24) as: (1) part of a later redaction (Galling 1954: 24; Rudolph 1955: 13), (2) a quotation from a source (Japhet 1993a: 72), or (3) as a gloss (R. Braun 1986: 40). Each of these views is defensible. Note the repetitive resumption of "Machir, the father of Gilead" (מכיר אבי גלעד) near the beginning and at the end of the passage (vv. 21, 23). But one must also press beyond such matters to inquire as to why the material was added? Whether these verses were interpolated by an editor or a later glossator, what effect does their inclusion have on the Judahite genealogy? The major factor at work is the relationship between the progeny of Judah and those of Machir.

2:21. "Machir." An early Yahwistic poem (Judg 5:14) mentions Machir as one of the major groups in early Israel. Perhaps reflecting later tribal movements and developments, Machir is associated with Manasseh, most often as Manasseh's son (Gen 50:23; Num 32:39–40; Deut 3:14–15; Aharoni 1979: 243). A territorial connection with Gilead and Bashan is affirmed in the allotment of Josh 17:1. The genealogies of Chronicles affirm the traditional tie between Machir and Manasseh (NOTES to 1 Chr 7:14–17). Because the genealogical literary form, as a statement of relationships, can convey social, ethnic, and geographic connections among individuals, peoples, and places, it comes as no surprise that these lineages posit multiple ties among a variety of groups and regions.

"father of Gilead." In ancient genealogies the boundaries among personal names, ethnic names, and toponyms may be fluid. The claim that Machir was the "father" (i.e., founder) of Gilead is a case in point (so also Num 26:29; 27:1; 36:1). That Ḥezron married into Machir's family establishes early links between the tribes of Judah and Manasseh.

"Segub." Not otherwise attested.

2:22. "Jair" appears as a son of Manasseh in Num 32:39–42 and Deut 3:14, but here he appears as a Judahite, the grandson of Ḥezron. In this manner, the writer establishes an association between Jair and Judah.

"twenty-three towns." Within Israelite literature the land of Gilead is characteristically understood as the domain of Manasseh (Num 32:39–42; Deut 3:14–15; Josh 13:29–31; 17:1–2). The conquest and renaming of these towns by Jair (hence, Ḥavvoth Jair, "villages of Jair") is mentioned in Num 32:41. A second tradition (Deut 3:8–15) likewise reports the conquest of Amorite lands, but presents the territory of Bashan (the Argob district) as far as the boundary of the Geshurites and Maachites as a bequest to Jair (cf. Judg 10:8).

2:23. "Geshur and Aram took Ḥavvoth Jair from them." Geshur is presented as an active city-state during the early monarchy. First Samuel 27:8 mentions David's campaigns against the Geshurites, while 2 Sam 3:3 reports that Absalom was the offspring of the marriage between David and Maacah, the daughter of King Talmai of Geshur. It is not surprising, then, that Absalom later took refuge with the King of Geshur (2 Sam 13:37–38). In spite of these references to Geshur in connection with the early monarchy, the notice that Geshur and Aram (= Syria) took these towns is unparalleled in biblical literature. Since Ḥavvoth Jair belongs to the Ramoth-gilead district in 1 Kgs 4:13, this note must relate either to the late United Monarchy (1 Kgs 11:23–25) or, as is more likely, to the dual monarchies, when Israel's relations with its northeastern neighbors were often turbulent (1 Kgs 20:1–34; 2 Kgs 6:8–7:20; 16:5; Isa 7:1–17; Pitard 1987: 88, 99–189). The territorial struggles among Israel, Judah, and Aram are very much in evidence in the recently published Tel Dan inscription (Biran and Naveh 1993; 1995).

"Qenath and its dependencies" (קנת ואת-בנתיה). These were said to be captured by Nobah of Manasseh in Num 32:42. Their location is uncertain.

"all these were descendants of Machir the father of Gilead." An unexpected summary for a list of people who stem from the union between Ḥezron and Machir's daughter (v. 21). The notice forms part of a literary device used to interpolate vv. 21–23 within the larger Judahite genealogy (NOTE to vv. 21–23). It has the effect of underscoring the Transjordanian character of these people (and sites), even though they are said to belong to Judah. Given the reaffirmation of the connection with Machir, it seems unlikely that the author wished to stake a claim about Jair that is diametrically opposed to those found in the Pentateuch (*pace* Japhet 1993a: 80–81). It is more likely that the author qualifies the exclusive association of these individuals and their territories with Machir. By mentioning intermarriage between members of the tribes of Judah and Manasseh in the distant past, the writer posits a relationship between them. In this respect, Judah and Manasseh share interests in Gilead.

2:24. "(and) after the death of Ḥezron" (ואחר מות-חזרון). This note qualifies the assertion about the timing of Caleb's relationship with Ephrathah (v. 19). Noth (1932: 107) contends that it should be placed between 1 Chr 4:4 and 4:5.

"Ephrathah" appears as a geographical location associated with Bethleḥem in a number of different contexts (Gen 35:19; 48:7; LXX Josh 15:59a; Mic 5:1; Ps 132:6; Ruth 4:11). Ephrathah's importance to the lineages of Judah is underlined not only by the repeated references to her (2:19, 24, 50; 4:4) but also by the fact that she appears as the matronymic for Ḥur's descendants (vv. 50b–55).

"Abijah . . . bore him." The subject returns again to the paramour(s) of Ḥezron. Williamson (1979b: 355) contends that this note is a misplaced comment on v. 21 in which Machir's daughter is unnamed, but that union brought forth different children (vv. 21–22). In the present form of the Judahite genealogy, Ḥezron has three distinct sets of offspring: (1) Jeraḥmeel, Ram, and Celubai through an unnamed paramour (v. 9), (2) Segub through Machir's daughter (v. 21), and (3) Ashḥur through Abijah (v. 24).

"Ashḥur" (אשחור) reappears in 1 Chr 4:5, where his line continues. This note supplies vital information about Ashḥur's precise ancestry, which is missing there. It is possible, of course, that Ḥur (חור) is short for Ashḥur (Curtis and Madsen 1910: 92), but there is no hint to this effect in 4:4–5.

"father of Teqoa." Another case of the clear overlap between the ethnic and geographical dimensions of certain names, signaling an expansion of the Ḥezronites into northern Judah. Both Teqoa and Ephrathah are listed as part of the Judahite tribal inheritance (LXX Josh 15:59a; Kallai 1986a: 392). The association between Ashḥur and Teqoa (*Khirbet Tequʿ*), south of Bethleḥem (= Ephrathah; LXX Josh

15:59a), is consistent with the allusions to the ethnographic and geographic relationship between Ḥezron, Caleb, and Ephrathah (2:19, 24, 50; 4:4). Like Ziph, Mareshah, and Beth-zur, Teqoa appears in the list of Reḥoboam's fortresses (2 Chr 11:5–12).

2:25–41. "Jeraḥmeel." Having pursued the subsidiary lines of Ram (vv. 9, 10–17) and Caleb (vv. 9, 18–19), the writer returns to the progeny of Ḥezron's firstborn (3rd NOTE to v. 9). The genealogies of vv. 25–33 and 34–41 have no biblical parallels; they are unique to Chronicles.

2:25. "(and) these were the descendants of Jeraḥmeel" (ויהיו בני-ירחמאל). Together with the virtually identical formula in v. 33, "these were the descendants of Jeraḥmeel" (היו בני ירחמאל), this phrase forms an *inclusio* around the segmented genealogy of vv. 25–33.

"Ram the firstborn." The nephew of Ram (v. 9), a case of neponymy (naming someone after an uncle). See also 2:46; 4:21.

"Bunah, Oren, Ozem, and Aḥijah." The descendants of Jeraḥmeel's offspring by an unnamed mother are not pursued in the verses that follow.

2:26. "Aṭarah; she was the mother of Onam." For her offspring, see vv. 28–33.

2:27. "Maaz, Jamin, and Eqer." No larger ethnographic or geographic affiliations are known for these sons of Ram.

2:28–33. "sons of Onam." Introducing two consecutive segmented lineages: five generations of Shammai's descendants (vv. 28b–31) and three generations of Yada's descendants (vv. 32–33).

2:28. "sons of Onam: Shammai and Yada." The similarities between these and other names in the Jeraḥmeelite genealogies and those in the Seirite and Edomite genealogies (1:35–54) has led to various speculations about the early relations between Judah and Edom (e.g., Noth 1932: 112–24; Aharoni 1979: 255). The early history of Edom is a legitimate and interesting issue, especially given recent archaeological research (NOTE to 1:43–51a), but one should also inquire about the meaning of the overlap between Judean and Edomite names in the context of the Persian period, the time in which the Chronicler wrote. The Edomite presence in parts of southern Judah, begun in the late monarchy, is attested by literary (Jer 40:11; Ezek 35:3–15; Obad 19; Joel 3:19; Ps 137:7; Lam 4:21–22), epigraphic (Davies, §§2.024.20; 040.9, 15; Lemaire 1977), and material sources (Bartlett 1989; 1992; Beit Arieh 1995). To be sure, the traffic was probably not one-way. Elements of a Judean presence within Idumea are also possible (MT Neh 11:25–30;Ephʿal 1984: 197–201), and the Edomites may have themselves been one of several loosely affiliated groups in the northern Sinai and the Transjordan. Nevertheless, the recent publication of hundreds of Edomite inscriptions written in Aramaic from the fifth and fourth centuries B.C.E. suggests that the Edomite presence in southern Palestine during this era has been underestimated (Lemaire 1996a; Ephʿal and Naveh 1996). In the fourth and third centuries B.C.E., the territory south of Beth Zur becomes known as Idoumea (Diodorus Siculus, *Bibl.* 19.95.2; 19.98.1). In this respect, the prophetic denunciations of Edom may have misled modern scholars into thinking that Edom underwent a precipitous decline in southern Judah during the Persian period (Jer 49:7–22; Ezek 25:12–14; Obad

1, 7; Mal 1:2–5; Glazier-McDonald 1995). The new Aramaic inscriptions, most of which are ostraca, have been found not only in Idoumea but also in other regions of Palestine, such as Ashdod and Samaria. The author's genealogies and lists may function as a tacit acknowledgment and affirmation of numerous ties between Judean and Edomite (Idoumean) circles.

2:32–33. "Yada." A segmented lineage of Onam's second son (v. 28).

2:34–41. "Sheshan." This linear genealogy is remarkable for two reasons. First, beginning with Sheshan/Jarḥa and ending with Elishama (v. 41), the lineage achieves an extraordinary depth—some thirteen generations. Most ancient genealogies are just a few generations in length. Only a few, such as the Davidic (3:1–24), priestly (5:27–41), and Saulide (8:29–40//9:35–44) genealogies, are longer than this Sheshanide lineage. Second, the claim that "Sheshan did not have any sons" (v. 34) contrasts with the earlier statement that Aḥli was Sheshan's son (v. 31). Hence, most scholars distance this lineage from the preceding one. Such a procedure is also warranted because Aḥli does not appear anywhere in the lineage of vv. 34–41. The counterproposal (Japhet 1993a: 85) that vv. 25–33 relate to family relationships, while vv. 34–41 demarcate precise genealogical pedigrees is interesting but not altogether helpful, because it is unclear what the upshot of such a distinction might be. Construing Aḥli as a daughter and not as a son of Sheshan (Curtis and Madsen 1910: 94) leads to a false harmonization of the two texts. In short, it may be the better part of wisdom to accept that the text presents us with two different lineages for Sheshan.

2:34. "daughters." References to daughters are common in this part of the Judahite genealogy (e.g., vv. 4, 21, 34, 35, 49), but are not systematically pursued. In some cases, the interest involves extenuating circumstances (vv. 4, 34, 35), which allow the writer to explain from a patriarchal vantage point unusual aspects of Judah's lineage and kinship relations.

"Egyptian servant." The story recalls tales of the ancestors in Genesis, particularly the stories about Abram's relationship with Hagar (Gen 16). The difference between the two centers on the unqualified success of the arrangement in Chronicles (vv. 35–41; cf. Gen 21:9–21). Japhet (1992: 79–91) argues that this tale embodies an application of the law concerning slaves found in Exod 21:4.

2:36. "Attai sired Nathan." The identification of this Nathan with the prophet Nathan by some commentators is speculative. In Samuel-Kings, Nathan has no patronymic (2 Sam 7:1–17; 1 Kgs 1:10–14, 38; cf. 1 Kgs 4:5).

2:41. "Elishama." Although there are many distinguished individuals by this name, some can be ruled out for identification by virtue of their pedigree (Num 2:18; 7:48; 10:22; 1 Chr 7:26; 2 Chr 17:8). In other cases, the picture is less clear (Jer 36:12, 20; 41:1; 2 Kgs 25:25). Within extrabiblical inscriptions, *'lšmʿ* is a fairly common name (Davies, §§100.059.2; 072.1; 100.1; 224.2; 244.2; 423.2; 504.1; 566.2; 658.2; 659.2; 660.2; 729.1; 755.1; 807.1; 810.1; 835.2).

2:42–50a. "descendants of Caleb." This is the second of a series of segmented genealogies for Caleb (cf. vv. 18–20). With the possible exception of v. 49b, which may engage Josh 15:16–19 or Judg 1:11–15, this lineage is unparalleled. Its limits are clearly set by the *inclusio* framing its introduction, "The descendants of Caleb, brother of Jeraḥmeel" (v. 42), and conclusion, "these were the descendants of Caleb" (v. 50a). Four distinctive traits characterize this presentation. First, unlike the previous verses devoted to the descendants of Jeraḥmeel (vv. 34–41), these verses abound in toponyms. Second, many of the sites listed also occur in the Judahite town list of Josh 15, but some do not. Third, the lineages within the larger genealogy are not directly connected to each other. Two are organized according to Caleb's concubines (vv. 46, 48–49a) and one is organized by Caleb's daughter (v. 49b), but the others appear seriatim. Fourth, none of the names in this list are found in the other genealogies attributed to Caleb (2:18–20, 50b–55).

2:42–45. "Mesha his firstborn." This lineage, in segmented form, traces the offspring of Caleb and an unnamed woman to a maximum depth of seven generations. The statement of a kinship relationship of Caleb with Jeraḥmeel (cf. v. 9) forms part of the introductory rubric and there is no sound reason to excise it as a later addition (contra Noth 1932: 104). It may be no accident, genealogically speaking, that the PN Mesha is borne by Moabites (*KAI* 181; 2 Kgs 3:4) and by Judahites and Benjaminites (1 Chr 8:8–9), who live near the land of Moab.

2:42. "Mesha . . . was the father of." As with other genealogies (e.g., 1 Chr 2:24; cf. 4:16–19; M. Johnson 1988), a locality, city, or town can be the child of its fathers, the father of its inhabitants, or the father of its dependencies. According to some scholars, this phenomenon can be pinpointed more exactly. In the view of Noth (1932: 100; cf. Zöckler 1877: 44), the formula "PN_1 the father of PN_2"—as opposed to "PN_1 sired PN_2" or "son of PN_1, PN_2, PN_3"—constitutes a specific genealogical code, signifying geographic appellations. There is some merit to the theory. The "PN_1 the father of PN_2" formula can designate "GN_1 the founder of GN_2." Although this is often the case, as in vv. 42–50a, there are exceptions (e.g., 1 Chr 2:17). Moreover, the so-called father formula should not be construed as the only genealogical formula with geopolitical overtones. Other genealogical formulas (e.g., 1 Chr 4:12, 14) can bear geographic and ethnographic designations.

"Ziph," T. Zîf, is located in the Judean hills approximately 7 km south-southeast of Ḥebron. This site is mentioned in both the Judahite tribal inheritance (Josh 15:55) and the list of Reḥoboam's fortresses (2 Chr 11:8). Boling (1982: 389) speaks of an additional Ziph in the Negev (MT Josh 15:24; NOTE to 1 Chr 4:16).

"Mareshah," part of the Judahite tribal allotment (Josh 15:44), is identified as T. Ṣandaḥanna, about 6 km east northeast of Lachish in the Shephelah (2 Chr 11:8; 14:9–14; 20:37). Excavations reveal that this was an Edomite site in the sixth and fifth centuries. In the fourth century Mareshah manifests a Phoenician and (later) a Greek presence (Kloner 1997: 24–35, 67).

"Ḥebron," el-Khalîl, has a number of related associations—the Calebites (Josh 14:15; 15:13–19), Judah (Judg 1:10–11), Caleb and Qenaz (Judg 1:12–15)—signaling its importance to a number of Judean phratries. Both David and his son Absalom were crowned at Ḥebron. In its other name, Qiriath-arba (Judg 1:10), Ḥebron appears in the stylized catalogue of MT Neh 11:25 as a site in which some Judeans lived.

2:43–45. "sons of Ḥebron." Many, but not all, of the names listed in these verses are to be associated with settlements. The exact locations of some sites are unknown.

2:43. "Qoraḥ" (קרח) appears as an Edomite clan (a son of Esau) in the universal genealogy (1 Chr 1:35//Gen 36:5). There seems to be a connection between this Qoraḥ, who hails from Ḥebron, and the Levitical Qoraḥites, who serve at the Jerusalem Temple during the monarchy and the Persian period (Num 26:57–58; Pss 42–44; 49; 84–85; 87–88; 1 Chr 9:17–32; 26:1–19; 2 Chr 20:19; Meyer 1906: 352; J. Miller 1970: 64–67). On Qoraḥ and the Qoraḥites, see, further, the 1st NOTE to 9:19.

"Tappuaḥ," also called Beth-tappuaḥ (Josh 15:53), may be identified with Taffûḥ, a few km west northwest of Ḥebron.

"Reqem." Whether this refers to a clan name or a toponym is uncertain (Knauf 1988: 89). There is also a Benjaminite Reqem (Josh 18:27).

"Shema" (שמע). Knauf (1992b: 665) associates this town with ʿas-Samûʿ (Eshtemoa), south-southwest of Ḥebron. This is possible, but given the distinction made in the Judahite territorial allotment between "Shema" (שמע) in the Negev district (Josh 15:26) and "Eshtemoa(h)" (אשתמה/ע) in the hill country (Josh 15:50), the location for "Shema" should be sought elsewhere, perhaps T. es-Saʿwi northeast of Beer-sheba (Boling 1982: 382). Shema's southern associations are also evident by its appearance in the Simeonite territorial allotment (LXX Josh 19:2; cf. MT "Sheba").

2:44. "Jorqeam" *(yrqʿm)* should probably be identified with "Joqdeam" *(yqdʿm)* in MT Josh 15:56 (TEXTUAL NOTE to v. 44; Boling 1982: 389). Jorqeam is often associated with Khirbet er-Raqaʿh just a few km southwest of Ziph (Kallai 1986a: 390).

2:45. "Maon," Khirbet Maʿîn, is located about 6 km east-northeast of Eshtemoa. Mentioned in the tribal inheritance of Judah (Josh 15:55), Maon was frequented by David in his flight from Saul (1 Sam 23:24–25; 25:2). One of the Arad ostraca, dating to the late monarchy, mentions a shipment of taxes to Arad from Maon (Davies, §2.025.4). See also Ezra 2:50(//Neh 7:52) and the NOTES to 1 Chr 4:41.

"Beth-zur," associated with Khirbet eṭ-Ṭubeiqeh, is approximately 6 km north of Ḥebron. Beth-zur is part of the Judahite tribal inheritance (Josh 15:58). Residents from Beth-zur as well as from Teqoa participated in rebuilding Jerusalem's walls under Nehemiah (Neh 3:5, 16). Aharoni (1979: 418) argues that Teqoa and Beth-zur served as regional administrative centers within the province of Yehud for the southern hill region, but it does not seem likely that Yehud controlled the region south of Beth-zur (Carter 1999).

2:46. "Ephah" (עיפה). This segmented genealogy achieves a depth of two generations. By organizing portions of the Calebite lineages by concubine (vv. 46, 48–49) and presumably spouse (vv. 42–45), the writer explains social differentiation within the larger group. The author may be signaling a second-order Calebite connection to the southern Transjordan. The name "Ephah" is usually Midianite (Gen 25:4; Isa 60:6; 1 Chr 1:33; cf. 2:47).

"Gazez." Another example of neponymy (2nd NOTE to v. 25).

2:47. "the sons of Jahdai." Two related issues arise with this lineage. First, there has been no previous reference to Jahdai. Nor is there a subsequent statement about Jahdai's origins. Second, the relationship, if any, between the Ephah of v. 46 and the Ephah of v. 47 is obscure. Some scholars regard the Ephah of v. 47 as the Ephah of v. 46, but the introductory rubric, "the sons of Jahdai," signals male offspring. Other scholars emend the last name in v. 46 so that Ḥaran sires "Jahdai" instead of "Gazez." This approach brings coherence to the text, but it is essentially harmonistic in nature and lacks any text-critical support. It seems best to admit that there is a gap in the text. Based on ancient Greek precedent, it is possible to suggest another explanation. The authors of the Hesiodic *Catalogue of Women* do not establish clear links among all of the families they list, even though they may intimate larger affiliations by placing families or individuals within a certain genealogical context (West 1985: 29–30). The same may be true here. The writer associates "the sons of Jahdai" with the Calebites by placing them within a clearly demarcated Calebite context (vv. 42, 50). This loose association, rather than the determination of a precise bloodline, may be sufficient to achieve the writer's purpose.

2:48–49a. "Maacah." See the 1st NOTE to v. 46.

2:49. "Madmannah," part of the Judahite tribal inheritance in the Negev (Josh 15:31), is associated with Khirbet Tatrît (Aharoni 1979: 383, 439). The name is preserved in nearby Khirbet Umm ed-Dēimineh (Kallai 1986a: 358).

"Sheva." On the PN (שוא), see also *AP* 40.1; *BMAP* 13.1, 9 (Grelot 1972: 492); and שוה in a fourth-century B.C.E. fiscal document from Ketef Yeriḥo (A:9, 10; B.II.5; Eshel and Misgav 1988: 170).

"Gibea" (גבעא). There is more than one Gibea(h) or "Geba" (גבע). The precise location of Gibea(h) (גבעה) of Judah (Josh 15:57) is uncertain (2nd NOTE to 8:6).

"the daughter of Caleb was Achsah." In Joshua and Judges this information is applied to Caleb son of Jephunneh (Josh 15:16–19; Judg 1:11–15). But the nearest antecedent is Caleb son of Ḥezron (1 Chr 2:9, 18–20, 42). There are four ways of dealing with this problem. First, one can assert with the majority of scholars that this passage actually refers to the Caleb of conquest fame, Caleb son of Jephunneh (Num 13:6; 14:6, 30, 38; Deut 1:36; Josh 15:16–17; Judg 1:12–13). But given that Caleb son of Jephunneh is only introduced in 1 Chr 4:15, it seems artificial to introduce him proleptically here. Second, one can omit the reference to Achsah as a gloss, but this is too facile a solution (contra Rudolph 1955: 22). A third option is to argue that Caleb is a fluid personality who can be referred to in different ways (Wellhausen 1870; Demsky 1986). If this were true, one would not expect the text to be so specific in referring to this Caleb as the brother of Jeraḥmeel (2:42; cf. 2:9, 25). Fourth, consistent with the author's earlier presentation (2:9, 18), but not with Josh 15:16–17 and Judg 1:12–13, he understands this Caleb to refer to Caleb son of Ḥezron (Japhet 1993a: 87). This last interpretation has the merit of being most consistent with the earlier references to Caleb (Celubai) in 1 Chr 2.

2:50b–55. "sons of Ḥur." Ḥur is to be associated with the Ḥorites and Seirites, rather than with the Hurrians of the second millennium B.C.E. (1st NOTE to 1:39). Largely without parallel, this segmented genealogy of Ephrathites reverts to the line of Ḥur, who is mentioned in v. 19 as a son of Caleb and in v. 20 as the father of Uri and the grandfather of Bezalel. Names of persons, groups, and towns all appear. The genealogy exhibits internal variety, introducing Ḥur's three sons, their lineages, the towns they founded, and the families associated with them. The sites involved range from Qiriath-jearim, Eshtaol, Manaḥath, and Zorah to the west of Jerusalem to Bethleḥem and Neṭophah to the south. Further genealogies for the descendants of Ḥur occur after the genealogies of David (4:2–4).

2:50b–51. "Shobal" appears earlier as a Seirite (NOTES to 1:38; 2:52) and as the "father" of Manaḥath (Gen 36:20, 23//1 Chr 1:40). Each of Ḥur's three sons is depicted as a founder (literally "father") of a town: Shobal of "Qiriath-jearim" (v. 50), Salma of "Bethleḥem" (v. 51; cf. v. 54), and Ḥareph of "Beth-gader" (v. 51). Bethleḥem belongs to Judah's allotment (Josh 15:59). "Qiriath-jearim," associated with Deir el-ʿÂzar, was located on the border of Judah (Josh 15:60; 18:14) and Benjamin (Josh 18:14), at least 10 km west-northwest of Jerusalem (Kallai 1986a: 133–35). In the Achaemenid period, Qiriath-jearim is mentioned as one of the homes from which people "who came up out of the captivity" stemmed (Ezra 2:25; Neh 7:29). "Beth-gader" is a *hapax legomenon* (cf. Josh 12:13 "Geder"). The site is unknown, although it is regarded by some (e.g., Demsky 1986: 51) as a variant of "Gedor" (4:4).

2:52–54. "Haroeh." The segmented genealogy of the Ephrathites continues with additional "sons" of Shobal and Salma. In these verses the term "sons" can refer to towns, parts of towns, or groups.

2:52. "Haroeh [and] half of the Manaḥathites." On this reading, see the TEXTUAL NOTES to v. 52. Although some commentators construe "Haroeh, half of Manaḥath" as one entity, it is more likely that these two terms refer to two different entities (2:54; 4:2). "Manaḥath" is thought by some to be el-Mâlḥah, located some 4–5 km west-southwest of Jerusalem (Aharoni 1979: 248), but others disagree with this identification (4th NOTE to 8:6). Manaḥath *(Manachō)* is also mentioned in the so-called Bethleḥem district of Josh 15:59a (LXX). That 1 Chr 1:40 mentions Manaḥath as a descendant of Seir raises the possibility of another connection between the Seirites and the Judeans (Knauf 1992b: 493–94; NOTE to v. 28). On the geographic expansion implied by these verses, see Demsky (1986: 51–53). According to 1 Chr 8:6, Benjaminites were later exiled to Manaḥath. This reinforces the notion that Manaḥath had a mixed population.

2:53. "families of Qiriath-jearim." Having traced the founding of the town to Shobal the son of Ḥur (v. 50), the author lists its leading families (משפחות). Growth in these families, in turn, introduces further differentiation into the lineage ("the Zorathites and the Eshtaulites") and, by implication, further geographical expansion.

"Ithrites" (היתרי). See the NOTE to 1 Chr 11:40.

"the Zorathites and the Eshtaulites." Zorah (T. Ṣarʿa), in the northern Shephelah and Eshtaul, (either Išwaʿ [Niemann 1999: 26–28]) or Khirbet Dēr eš-

Šūbēb [Kallai 1986a: 368]), are linked elsewhere: occasionally as part of Judah (Josh 15:33) and more often as part of Dan (Josh 19:41; Judg 13:25; 16:31; 18:2, 8, 11; Na'aman 1986a: 108, 116). Zorah appears as one of Reḥoboam's fortresses (2 Chr 11:10) and as a place of residence for Persian period Judeans (MT Neh 11:29).

2:54. "The sons of Salma" comprise one town, Aṭroth-bet-joab, and three groups, the Neṭophathites, the Manaḥathites, and the Zorites. Neṭophah (נטפה) may be associated with Khirbet Bedd Fālûḥ, located about 5 km south-southeast of Bethleḥem. Both Bethleḥem and Neṭophah contain Levitical settlements in the Persian period (Ezra 2:22//Neh 7:26; 1 Chr 9:16; Neh 12:27–28). The references to the Manaḥathites and the Zorites are less clear. The former could simply designate the other "half of the Manaḥathites" (NOTE to v. 52). The gentilic "Zorites" (הצרעי) seems to designate, however, the same entity as that of v. 53, "the Zorathites" (הצרעתי). Cf. 1 Chr 4:2.

2:55. "families (משפחות) of the scribes." The writer does not provide any genealogical connection with the preceding lineages of Caleb. The scribal profession was one which could be handed down, by proper training, through the generations. Scribes appear regularly in the Chronicler's work (1 Chr 18:16; 24:6; 27:32; 2 Chr 24:11; 34:13, 15, 18, 20; cf. 1 Chr 21:2; 2 Chr 2:2, 16; 26:11; 32:17; 34:15, 30), as well as in Ezra (2:55; 7:6, 11) and Nehemiah (7:57; 8:1, 4, 9, 13; 12:26, 36; 13:13; Zadok 1980: 114; Schams 1998: 44–71). Note also the appearance of [ה]ספר, "[the] scribe," on various Hebrew, Moabite, Ammonite, and Aramaic (ספרא) seals (Aufrecht 1989: no. 139; Avigad and Sass 1997: 467; Deutsch and Heltzer 1997: no. 106). One does not have to hold to any dramatic increase in literacy in the Persian period to acknowledge that writing was becoming a more common fixture of elite life (Millard 1995; Whitt 1995: 2389; Avigad and Sass 1997: 21–22, 33; P. Davies 1998; Coogan 1999). Because the author wrote during the Persian period, a time in which the Chronicler had access to a variety of earlier biblical writings, it comes as no great surprise that he ascribes scribal activity to an earlier age (contra A. Ehrlich 1914: 327). Particularly interesting in this context is the claim that these scribes were inhabitants of the town of Jabez. Most ancient Near Eastern scribes were employed in state and Temple administration (Pearce 1995: 2272–73). Traditionally, the Temple and palace were the mainstays in the support and training of scribes. During the Neo-Babylonian and Achaemenid periods (626–331 B.C.E.), one has to add, however, a third sector in the economies of major ancient Near Eastern societies—households, both large and small scale (Dandamaev 1979; 1987; 1990; 1996). In addition to royal palaces and temples, such households became sources of employment for skilled workers. The economic situation in Greece was also becoming more complicated during this period (Burford 1972). There is not a great deal of information available about the economy of Yehud, but recent studies have made progress in understanding the importance of households and larger kinship groups in economic matters, especially in matters of land tenure and land ownership (e.g., Weinberg 1976; 1992; Blenkinsopp 1988; Dion 1991; Levine 1996; Watts 2001). The assemblage of specialists within a particular town or within a certain geographical area is attested elsewhere in the ancient Mediterranean world (cf. 4:14, 21, 23 [NOTES]). It is tempting, therefore, to associate the remark about the scribes of Jabez as reflecting, to some extent, conditions that existed in the author's own time. But whether the reference indicates that the authors of Chronicles should themselves be associated with the scribal circles associated with Jabez (Weinberg 1996: 278–81) rather than with scribes who worked and resided in Jerusalem seems doubtful. There are too many links between the coverage of the book and Jerusalem (note especially the lavish attention given to Davidic rule in Jerusalem and the copious references to the Temple and its cultus) to discard the common assumption that the author was a Jerusalemite. On Jerusalem's importance in the Chronicler's work, see, for example, the recent work of Dennerlin (1999).

"inhabitants of Jabez" (יעבץ). There is no previous mention of Jabez in the genealogy of Judah (cf. 1 Chr 4:9–10). The precise location of this town is unknown.

"the Tirathites, the Shimeathites, and the Sucathites." Since all of these groups are described as "Qenites" (הקינים), they should probably be associated with the ancient Qenites (קיני; Gen 15:19; Num 24:21–22; 1 Sam 27:10; 30:29[MT]), whose fierce and seminomadic ways find precedent in the life of their eponymous ancestor Cain (קין; Gen 4:1–25). The name קין is also common in Nabatean, Safaitic, Thamudic, and Aramaic inscriptions (Kalimi 1988: 391–92). In some texts, the Qenites are depicted as a non-Israelite group, one of the indigenous peoples in the land (Gen 15:19; Kalimi 1988: 389–90). Other texts, while also clearly distinguishing between Israelites and Qenites, speak of friendly relations between the two (Judg 4:17–21; 5:24–27; 1 Sam 15:6). In one tradition (Judg 1:16; 4:11) the Qenites are distant relations to the Israelites by virtue of their descent from Hobab, the father-in-law of Moses. (To complicate matters, Num 10:29–32 depicts Hobab as the brother-in-law of Moses, while Exod 2:15–22 depicts Reuel as a father-in-law of Moses.) In any case, the Qenites, along with the Judahites, are said to have settled in the Negev of Arad (Judg 1:16). In the tribal inheritances, Qayin, which is probably Khirbet Yaqîm, 3 km northeast of Ziph (Noth 1953: 98), is assigned to Judah (Josh 15:57). Here, "the Tirathites, the Shimeathites, and the Sucathites" in particular and the Qenites in general are absorbed into Judah. Depicted as non-Israelites or as only loosely associated with the Israelites in other contexts, the Qenites are one of the constituent elements of Judah in Chronicles.

"Ḥammath the father of Beth-rechab." The precise referent for each of these terms is obscure. The only other "Ḥammath" in the Scriptures is located in Naphtali (Josh 19:35), but "Ḥammath" may not be a toponym (Knights 1993: 16–17). Talmon (1960b) proposes deriving "Ḥammath" (חַמַּת) from חם, "father-in-law," and חמות, "mother-in-law" (cf. Akk. *ḫammu*, *ḫammatu*), thus associating the term with a "family-in-law," rather than with a person or site. But given the common usage of the "PN_1 the father of PN_2" formula to designate the founding of a town (1st NOTE to v. 42), a personal name or toponym cannot be ruled out. The equation that many scholars have made of "Beth-rechab" (literally, "house of Rechab") with the "house of the Rechabites" (Jer 35:1–11) has been questioned (Knights 1993: 17). The Rechabites were a nonsedentary, nonagriculturally based group active in the late Judahite monarchy, although their precise configuration and history are debated (Jer 35; cf. 2 Kgs 10:15–17, 23–24; Levin 1994; Knights 1996). Some (e.g., Frick 1971) think that the Rechabites were a guild of metallurgical craftsmen. Samuel Klein (1926: 414) proposes associating "Beth-rechab" (בית רחב) with a site, "Beth-markaboth" (בית המרכבות; Josh 19:5; 1 Chr 4:31). See also the last TEXTUAL NOTE to 4:12.

SOURCES AND COMPOSITION

The lineages found in 2:3–55 are part of a larger group of genealogies relating to the descendants of David (3:1–24) and the rest of the tribe of Judah (4:1–23). A discussion of the sources and composition of this material (2:3–55; 4:1–23) appears following the NOTES to 4:1–23, while a discussion of the sources and composition of the Davidic lineages appears following the NOTES to 3:1–24.

III. The Davidic Genealogy (3:1–24)

The Children of David

1 These are the sons of David who were born to him at Ḥebron. The firstborn
was Amnon by Aḥinoam the Jezreelite, the second Daniel by Abigail the Carmelite, 2 the third Absalom son of Maacah daughter of Talmai king of Geshur, the
fourth Adonijah son of Ḥaggith, 3 the fifth Shephaṭiah by Abiṭal, the sixth Ithream
by Eglah his wife. 4 Six were born to him in Ḥebron. He reigned there for seven
years and six months and he reigned in Jerusalem for thirty-three years. 5 These
were born to him in Jerusalem: Shimea, Shobab, Nathan, and Solomon—four by
Bath-shua daughter of Ammiel. 6 Ibḥar, Elishua, Eliphelet, 7 Nogah, Nepheg, Japhia, 8 Elishama, Beeliada, Eliphelet—nine. 9 All were sons of David in addition
to the sons of (his) concubines. Tamar was their sister.

The Descendants of Solomon

10 The son of Solomon: Reḥoboam, his son Abijah, his son Asa, his son Jehoshaphaṭ, his son 11 Joram, his son Aḥaziah, his son Joash, his son 12 Amaziah, his son
Azariah, his son Jotham, his son 13 Aḥaz, his son Ḥezeqiah, his son Manasseh, his
son 14 Amon, (and) his son Josiah.

The Sons of Josiah, Jehoiaqim, Jeconiah, and Pedaiah

15 The sons of Josiah: the firstborn Joḥanan, the second Jehoiaqim, the third
Zedeqiah, the fourth Shallum. 16 The sons of Jehoiaqim: his son Jeconiah, his son
Zedeqiah. 17 The sons of Jeconiah the prisoner: Shealtiel, 18 Malchiram, Pedaiah,
Shenazzar, Jeqamiah, Shama, and Nedabiah. 19 The sons of Pedaiah: Zerubbabel
and Shimei.

The Descendants of Zerubbabel

The sons of Zerubbabel: Meshullam and Ḥananiah. Shelomith was their sister.

20The sons of Meshullam: Ḥashubah, Ohel, Berechiah, Ḥasadiah, Jushab-ḥesed—five. 21The son of Ḥananiah: Pelaṭiah, his son Jeshaiah, his son Rephaiah, his son Arnon, his son Obadiah, his son Shecaniah. 22The sons of Shecaniah: Shemaiah. The sons of Shemaiah: Ḥaṭṭush, Igal, Bariaḥ, Neariah, and Shephaṭ—six. 23The sons of Neariah: Elioenai, Ḥizqiah, and Azriqam—three. 24The sons of Elioenai: Hodaviah, Eliashib, Pelaiah, Aqqub, Joḥanan, Delaiah, and Anani—seven.

TEXTUAL NOTES

3:1. "the second" *(hšny)*. LXX, Syr., and Tg. have the expected article before the ordinal. See "the firstborn" *(hbkwr)* earlier in the verse and "the third" *(hšlšy)*, etc. in v. 2. The reading of MT *(šny)* may reflect a haplography.

"Daniel." The witnesses to 2 Sam 3:3 and 1 Chr 3:1 provide different names for David's second son. Instead of "Daniel" (MT), *Damniēl* (LXX^{B}), or *Daniēlos* (Josephus, *Ant* 7.21), MT Sam 3:3 has *kl'b* (followed by Syr. 1 Chr 3:1 *klb*), which, given the initial *l'b* in the following word, is probably corrupt. McCarter (1984: 101) cites 4QSam^{a} d̊l[ ]., LXX 2 Sam 3:3, and LXX^{ALN} 1 Chr 3:1 *Dalouia* to argue for an original "Daluiah." The spelling *Damniēl* (LXX^{B} c$_2$) may reflect contamination from *Amnōn* (Allen 1974b: 34).

"the Carmelite." Reading with MT, LXX, 4QSam^{a}, and LXX 2 Sam 3:3. MT 2 Sam 3:3 explicates: *'št nbl*.

3:2. "Absalom" *('bšlwm)*. So many Heb. MSS, Syr., and Tg. The reading of MT *l'bšlwm* assimilates to *l'bygyl* earlier in the verse. LXX presents the same lemma *(Abessalōm)* as it presents for "Absalom" *('bšlwm)* in 2 Chr 11:20 (2nd TEXTUAL NOTE to 2:16). Cf. *'byšlwm* ("Abishalom") in 1 Kgs 15:2, 10.

"Adonijah." Reading with MT, LXX^{AB}, MT 2 Sam 3:4, and 4QSam^{a}. The readings of LXX^{B} 2 Sam 3:4 and e$_2$ 1 Chr 3:2 *Orneia*, as well as LXX^{L} 1 Chr 3:2 *Ornias*, reflect inner Greek corruptions.

3:3. "by Abiṭal" *(l'byṭl)*. So MT, LXX, LXX 2 Sam 3:4, and 4QSam^{a}. MT and Syr. 2 Sam 3:4 "son of Abiṭal" *(bn 'byṭl)* reflects a shift in formularization for the third and fourth sons.

"Ithream" *(ytr'm)*. So MT and 2 Sam 3:5. Syr. *'yṭwrm*.

"his wife." So MT and LXX. Syr. follows MT 2 Sam 3:5 "wife of David."

3:4. "six were born to him in Ḥebron." So MT and LXX. MT 2 Sam 3:5 "these were born to him in Ḥebron." The lemma is consistent with the numerical summary notations found elsewhere in the genealogy (vv. 5, 20, 22, 23, 24). The change from Samuel likely reflects the Chronicler's reworking of his source.

"he reigned there for seven years and six months." So MT and LXX^{ALN}. Absent from LXX^{B} and hc$_2$ (*sub ast.* in cursive i). The missing words may have been lost due to haplography.

3:5. "were born." Reading with a few Heb. MSS נוֹלְדוּ. MT נוּלְדוּ (cf. 1 Chr 20:8); MT 2 Sam 5:13 וַיִּוָּלְדוּ. See GKC, §69t.

"Shimea" *(šimʿāʾ)*. Thus MT. The variants are many: LXX^{B} c$_2$ *Saman*; LXX^{ALN},

Theodoret *Samaa*; Syr., MT 2 Sam 5:14, and 1 Chr 14:4 *šammûʿa*; 1 Sam 16:9 *šammâ*.

"four by Bath-shua daughter of Ammiel." So MT and LXX. The absence of this phrase in Syr. may reflect an assimilation to 2 Sam 5:14//1 Chr 14:4.

"Bath-shua." So MT. LXX *Bērsabee* (be$_2$, Theodoret *Bērsabeai*), like LXX 2 Sam 11:3, associates the name of Uriah's wife with the name of a town (Allen 1974a: 135–36). Vg. reads Bathsheba in conformity with 2 Sam 11 and 1 Kgs 1.

"Ammiel." For MT's *ʿammîʾēl* (LXX^B *Amiēl*), LXX^L and Theodoret have *Hēla*.

3:6. "Elishua" (*ʾĕlîšûăʿ*). So a few Heb. MSS, MT 2 Sam 5:15, 1 Chr 14:5, and perhaps LXX^B c$_2$ 1 Chr 3:6 (*Eleisa*). Cf. Syr. MT 1 Chr 3:6 "Elishama" (*ʾelîšāmāʿ*), followed by Tg. and LXX^{ALN} (*Elisama*), assimilates toward "Elishama" in v. 8.

3:6–7. "Elipheleṭ, Nogah." So MT, both here and in 1 Chr 14:5–6. Although these names are also attested in LXX^{BL} and apparently in 4QSam^a, they are not found in MT 2 Sam 5:15. Given the repetition of Elipheleṭ later in the list, Wellhausen (1871: 165) argues that MT 2 Sam 5:15 is the most primitive reading. But given the numerical summary of nine sons (v. 8; cf. 2 Sam 5:14–16), these names were undoubtedly in the Chronicler's *Vorlage* (contra Curtis and Madsen 1910: 100; Begrich in *BHK*).

3:7. "Nepheg." So MT. LXX^B *Naphath*; LXX^L and Arm. *Neeg*. Josephus (*Ant*.7.70) *Naphēn* reflects an inner Greek corruption (McCarter 1984: 148).

"Japhia." The difference between MT (*ypyʿ*) and LXX^B c$_2$ *Ianoue* (cf. Josephus, *Ant*.7.70 *Ienae*) reflects a *nûn*/*pê* confusion (Rehm 1937: 58). Cf. Arm. *Akʿikam*; LXX^L *Achikam* (= אחיקם).

3:8. "Beeliada" (*bʿlydʿ*). Reading with LXX cursive n (*Baeliada*) and MT 1 Chr 14:7 (*bʿlydʿ*). Cf. LXX^L 2 Sam 5:16 *Baaleidath*. MT, LXX^B, and MT 2 Sam 5:16 "Eliada" (*ʾlydʿ*). "Beeliada" (*bʿlydʿ*) is probably the earliest reading. Because of the common association of the theophorous element *bʿl* with the Canaanite deity Baal/Haddu, *bʿl* was eschewed in favor of Yhwh or El in some texts.

3:10. "son of Solomon." So MT. A few Heb. MSS, LXX^B, and Syr. "sons of Solomon."

"Abijah" (*ʾăbîyāh*). This form of the king's name "my (divine) father is Yah(weh)" is consistent with 2 Chr 13:1–14:1. In contrast, 1 Kgs 15:1–8 has "Abijam" (*ʾăbîyām*), which may reflect either "my (divine) father is Yam" or "my (divine) father" with the ending *-ām* (Noth 1928: 234). The change in spelling from Kings to Chronicles could have been deliberate (so most commentators), or it could have been inadvertent, triggered by by a *hê*/*mêm* confusion.

3:12. "Azariah." The variants to this name in other books are also reflected here: *ʿzryh(w)* (many Heb. MSS; 2 Kgs 14:21; 15:1, 6, 8, 17, 23, 27; Jer 43:2; Dan 1:6, 11, 19); *ʿzyh* "Uzziah" (LXX^L *Ozias*; Syr.). Cf. 2 Chr 26:1–23 *ʿzyhw*. Tg. clarifies by identifying Azariah as Uzziah.

3:15. "Joḥanan." So MT and LXX^{AB}. LXX^{LN} (*Iōachas*; y *Iōachaz*) and Arm. have the expected Jehoaḥaz (2 Kgs 23:31). 1 Esd 1:32 has (erroneously) *Iechonian*. Kittel (1902: 22–23) argues for Jehoaḥaz, but MT and LXX^{AB} have the *lectio difficilior*.

3:16. "sons of Jehoiaqim: his son Jeconiah, his son Zedeqiah." Verses 15–16 present two different Zedeqiahs and, therefore, two versions of Zedeqiah's relationship to Jeconiah. The first version of the relationship, enumerated in v. 15 is that Zedeqiah is a son of Josiah. This claim comports with LXX 2 Chr 36:10 and 2 Kgs 24:17 (MT and LXX[L]), which depict the Zedeqiah who succeeds Jeconiah (Jehoiachin) as Jeconiah's uncle (contra M. Johnson 1988: 47). The second version of the relationship, enumerated in v. 16, is that Zedeqiah is a son of Jeconiah. This view is shared by LXX[B] 2 Kgs 24:17, namely, that *Iōacheim* was replaced by *Maththan huion autou*. Similarly, 1 Esd 1:44 has Zedeqiah replace Jehoiachin (the second *Iōakeim*), although this text does not mention any kinship relationship. The two variants in vv. 15–16 are not reconciled in the genealogy of Judah; they may constitute what Talmon (1960a) terms a double reading. Alternatively, one could argue that there were two Zedeqiahs. But neither of these Zedeqiahs qualifies as the brother of Jeconiah (MT 2 Chr 36:10). Nor does the writer explain why he does not pursue Zedeqiah, the son of Jeconiah (v. 16). Hence, Chronicles does not present readers with an internally consistent position on Zedeqiah's relationship to Jeconiah. The text provides readers with a complex, not altogether congruent, presentation of relationships. See also the NOTES to vv. 15–19.

"Jeconiah." So MT and LXX. Matt 1:11 speaks of Josiah being succeeded by "Jeconiah and his brothers" (Ἰεχονίαν καὶ τοὺς ἀδελφοὺς αὐτοῦ), but no such brothers are attested either here or in 2 Kgs 24:6–16; 25:27–30. Scholars have long puzzled over Matthew's source. It may be MT 2 Chr 36:10, which speaks of Zedeqiah as Jehoiachin's "brother" (for other variants, see the previous TEXTUAL NOTE). If not the result of a simple textual error by haplography (*homoioteleuton* from אחי אביו to אחיו), this reading may be based on an interpretation of 1 Chr 3:15–17. The issue may not be so much that the "PN_1, his son PN_2" sequence in v. 16 (*pace* Johnson 1988: 46) was interpreteted fraternally, but rather that the beginning of v. 17, which reads "The sons of Jeconiah," was interpreted as signaling a fraternal relationship (Johnson 1988: 47). Since v. 16b is a linear genealogy ("Jeconiah his son, Zedeqiah his son"), one would normally expect the following lineage to begin with the last name in the previous sequence (Zedeqiah).

"Zedeqiah" *(ṣdqyh)*. Thus MT and LXX *(Sedekias)*. A ninth- or tenth-century C.E. fragment (TS NS 172: 11) with Palestinian vocalization reads *ṣdqyhw* (Revell 1969: 60).

3:17. "sons." Reading with MT and LXX[B] *(lectio difficilior)*. Syr. "son," but see the TEXTUAL NOTE to 2:8.

"the prisoner"—*h's(y)r*—a conjecture. That MT's *'assir* is understood by most of the versions (LXX, Tg., Vg.) as a PN is understandable, given the context and the other instances of Assir as a PN (Exod 6:24; 1 Chr 6:7, 8, 22). Syr. *'sr š'yl* construes *'sr* as part of the following name (Shealtiel). As many have suggested, the most likely understanding of *'assir* is as *'assîr* or *'āsîr*, "captive" (cf. 2 Kgs 24:12–16; 2 Chr 36:10). It may be best to restore the article (lost by haplography after *yknyh*).

"Shealtiel." Following some LXX cursives and Vg. *(lectio brevior)*. MT and LXX[ABL] add "his son" *(bnw)*. Some (e.g., Rudolph 1955; Williamson 1982b) suggest emending MT to "his firstborn" *(bkrw)*.

3:18. "(and) Malchiram." Both the context and the appearance of the copula before Malchiram indicate that the influential suggestion of Qimḥi is unlikely, namely, that Malchiram, Pedaiah, etc. are actually sons of Shealtiel. Qimḥi's interpretation harmonizes 3:18–19 with Hag 1:1, 12, 14 and Ezra 3:2. Following Malchiram and each of the following names in v. 18, Syr. adds "his son." In other words, vv. 17–18 form a linear genealogy in Syr.

"Shenazzar, Jeqamiah, Shama, and Nedabiah." So MT *(lectio difficilior)*. Arm. *Osama et Nadabias et Sanasar et Iechonias.*

"Shenazzar" *(šen'aṣṣar)*. Thus MT. LXX^B *Sanesar*; LXX^L *Sanassar*; e_2 *Sanasar*; Vg. and Arm. *Sennaser.*

"(and) Shama." A conjecture. Cf. LXX^L kai Ōsama; Syr. "and Shammua" *(wšmwʿ)*; Vg. *Sama.*The form of MT is anomalous, "Hoshama" *(hwšmʿ)*. LXX^B and c_2 *Hōsamōth*. Noth (1928: 107) queries whether the text has lost an initial element, *yw* or *y.*In reconstructing *wšmʿ*, I assume a dittography of *hê* after Jeqamiah. On the name, see both the Judahite seals listed in Davies (§§100.016.1; 068.1; 071.1; 167.1; 245.2; 346.1; 416.2; 548.2) and 1 Chr 11:44.

"Nedabiah." So MT and LXX^L. LXX^B and c_2 *Denethei*; LXX^A *Nabadias*; cem *Danabias* reflect inner Greek corruptions (Allen 1974a: 155).

3:19. "Pedaiah" *(pdyh)*. Reading with MT, LXX^L *(Phadaia)*, and Vg. *(lectio difficilior)*. LXX^{AB} *Salathiēl* (= Shealtiel), a reading that is consistent with Ezra 3:2; Neh 12:1; Hag 1:1, 12, 14; 2:2, 23; Matt 1:12; Luke 3:27. Syr. "Nedabiah."

"Shimei. (And) the son[s] of Zerubbabel." So MT, LXX^{ALN}, and Arm. Lacking in LXX^B and dpc_2 due to haplography (*homoioteleuton* from Zerubbabel to Zerubbabel).

"sons of Zerubbabel." So LXX^{ALN}, Arm., and Syr. MT "son of Zerubbabel."

3:20. "(and) the sons of Meshullam" (ובני משלם). A restoration. The list of five individuals in MT and LXX v. 20 has no direct link to what precedes. Benzinger (1901: 12–13) wonders whether the names in v. 20 are original, but another solution seems preferable. It seems best to restore a rubric at the beginning of this verse (cf. vv. 19, 20, 21, 22, 23, 24). Since the continuing genealogy in v. 21 resumes with "the son[s] of Ḥananiah," referring to the Ḥananiah mentioned in v. 19, the genealogy of v. 20 is likely listing the progeny of Zerubbabel's other son (v. 19). In this context, the pattern of the genealogy of David's descendants in vv. 5–9 is relevant. Unlike the children of David introduced in v. 5 with a numerical summary ("four") and an identification of their mother ("Bath-shua"), the children mentioned in vv. 6–8 receive only a numerical summary ("nine"). The mother is not identified, but the rubric in v. 9, "all were sons of David," alerts the reader to the children's general identity. The situation is somewhat similar, albeit more fragmentary, in the case of Zerubbabel's lineage. After introducing Zerubbabel's sons, Meshullam and Ḥananiah, in v. 19b, the author mentions their sister, Shelomith. As in vv. 6–8, another list of sons follows. As in v. 8, the numerical summary in v. 20 covers only the second list of sons. Unlike the situation in v. 9, there is no rubric linking the second list with a certain father. Hence, it seems appropriate to restore "sons of Meshullam."

"Ḥashubah" (חשבה). So MT. The variants are many: LXX^B *Asoube*; LXX^{AN}, Arm. *Aseba*; LXX^L *Lasabath*; f *Asoue*; Syr. *yhw'l*. Begrich *(BHK)* proposes either Ḥashabiah or Ḥushabiah, while Noth (1928: 189) proposes Ḥashabah.

"Ohel." So MT. The lemma of LXX^{B} *Osa* reflects inner Greek corruption (Allen 1974b: 18). Cf. LXX^{A} *Oul*; LXX^{N} *Ool*. On the name, "Ohel" (אהל), compare אוהל (a PN) found on a seventh- or sixth-century bulla from the City of David (Davies, §100.829.2) and אהל on a recently discovered Phoen. inscription from Tel Dor (Naveh 1998; cf. Benz 1972: 262).

"Jushab-ḥesed" *(yûšab ḥesed)*. Reading tentatively with some Heb. MSS and the versions (c_2 *Asobasok*; LXX^{N} and Arm. *Asobaesed*; Vg. *Iosabesed*), which construe this as one name. Comparison between MT (יושב חסד) and LXX^{B} *Arobasok* reveals a *wāw/rêš* confusion (Allen 1974b: 121). The variants of y *Iōsabee* and e_2 *Iōsabeai* suggest *y(h)wšbʿ*, "Je(h)osheba."

"five." So MT and LXX^{ABL}. Some read the expected *ḥmšh*, rather than MT's *ḥmš*. Some of the variants—cursive f *pemptos* and Arm. "eight"—attempt to rectify the perceived discrepancy in numbers (vv. 19–20).

3:21. "son of Ḥananiah." So MT (ובן-חנניה). A few Heb. MSS, LXX, Syr., and Tg. "sons."

"Pelaṭiah, his son Jeshaiah . . . his son Shecaniah." Following LXX and Vg., which have "his son" in all five instances in the verse. LXX and Vg. present a linear genealogy: LXX^{B} *Phalleti kai Isaba huios autou Rhaphal huios autou Orna huios autou Abdeia huios autou Sechenia huios autou.* Vg. is similar *Phaltias pater Ieseiae cuius filius Raphaia; huius quoque filius Arnan, de quo natus est Obdia cuius filius fuit Sechenias.* MT, followed by Tg., reads "Pelaṭiah and Jeshaiah, the sons of Rephaiah, the sons of Arnon, the sons of Obadiah, the sons of Shecaniah" (פלטיה וישעיה בני רפיה בני ארנן בני עבדיה בני שכניה). If one follows LXX and Vg., Zerubbabel's descendants extend an additional four generations beyond the total presumed by one interpretation of MT (the meaning of MT is disputed). Since the discrepancy between MT and LXX is of considerable importance, it bears discussing at some length. Some older scholars favor LXX (e.g., Benzinger, Kuenen). Other commentators, especially recent ones (e.g., Osborne, Williamson, R. Braun, De Vries, Willi) favor MT, but differ as to its meaning. Roddy Braun (1986: 52) thinks that "the sons of Rephaiah, the sons of Arnon," etc. refer to families of Davidides. Pomykala (1995: 83) thinks, with some justification, that MT signals a break in the Davidic genealogy. There is no continuity between the son(s) of Ḥananiah (v. 21) and the sons of Shecaniah (v. 22). De Vries (1989: 42) contends that "the sons of Rephaiah, the sons of Arnon," etc. are regular introductions to an absent name list. NJPS also assumes ellipsis, "the sons of [Jeshaiah]: Rephaiah; the sons of [Rephaiah]: Arnon," etc. There is a third position. Kittel (1902), Begrich *(BHK)*, and Rudolph (1955: 28–31) omit reference to all four occurrences of "sons"/"his son" and replace each with conjunctive *wāw*. This emendation is puzzling, because LXX and Vg. are not textually problematic. With respect to MT, the proposed emendation produces a smooth text, but it fails to fulfill the primary text-critical task of explaining the readings provided by the major textual witnesses. Given that the major textual discrepancy between LXX and MT is actually small (בני vs. בנו), it is impossible to be dogmatic about which reading is earlier. Graphically, the *yôd* and *wāw* are easily confused in certain manuscript traditions, for example in the different textual witnesses to Samuel (S. Driver

1912: lxv–lxvi), in MT Isaiah and 1QIsa[a] (Kutscher 1974), and elsewhere in Chronicles (Allen 1974b: 116–17). The presence of *huios autou* at the end of v. 21 (= בנו) could have been lost to MT by haplography (before ובני שכניה at the beginning of v. 22). Of the two remaining options ("sons" vs. "his son") the arguments for the originality of "his son" would seem to be the strongest. First, one sees the "PN_1, his son PN_2, his son PN_3" pattern regularly elsewhere in the genealogy with respect to Solomon (vv. 10–14), Jehoiaqim (v. 16), and Jeconiah (v. 17). The introduction to the lineage of Solomon, "the sons of Solomon: Reḥoboam, his son Abijah, his son Asa," etc. (v. 10) is akin to LXX v. 21. Moreover, the pattern "PN_1, his son PN_2, his son PN_3" is one regular way of constructing linear genealogies elsewhere in 1 Chr 1–9. Conversely, construing "the sons of PN_1, the sons of PN_2" as families or phratries is problematic (*pace* Japhet 1993a: 101–2). There are no other such cases of this pattern in the genealogy of David. Elsewhere families or groups are usually expressed through gentilics, whether in sg. (1:11–12, 53, 54) or in pl. form (1:14–16), or by the straightforward designation, "the families of" (e.g., 2:53, 55). One would think that if the author wished to digress by listing clans of Davidides, he would have done so using one of these standard formulae. Second, reading "his son" fits contextually in vv. 21–22. The lineage of Shecaniah (v. 22) picks up the last figure (Shecaniah) mentioned in the genealogy of v. 21, which begins with "The son of Ḥananiah: Pelaṭiah." To be sure, one could make a case for MT as the *lectio difficilior* (Barthélemy 1982: 434). But this text-critical principle cannot be allowed to overrule all other considerations in the effort to recover the earliest text. As Albrektson (1981) has observed, the most difficult reading may also be the most corrupt. The point is that the introductory rubric in v. 22, found in all witnesses to the text, fits well with v. 21 being a linear genealogy.

"Jeshaiah" *(yšʿyh)*. So MT; LXX^B *Isaba*; LXX^{AN} *Ieseia*; b′ *Iesaie*; *b Ieseai*; ie_2 *Iessaia*; y *lessai*.

"Rephaiah" *(rpyh)*. So MT, LXX^{AN}, Arm. LXX^B, c_2 *Rhaphal* reflects *rpʾl*.

"Arnan" *(ʾrnn)*. Thus MT (maximum differentiation). LXX^L *Arnōn*; LXX^B *Orna*. Cf. MT 1 Chr 21:15–30. *ʾornān*; LXX *Orna*.

3:22. "sons of Shecaniah." So MT, LXX^L, Arm., and Tg. LXX^{AB} "son."

"(and) Ḥaṭṭush." So miniscules b′ei *(lectio brevior)*. MT's reading, "and the sons of Shemaiah: Ḥaṭṭush," is followed by LXX^N, c_2, and Arm. LXX^{AB}, Syr., and Vg. "and (the) son of Shemaiah: Ḥaṭṭush." The phrase "son(s) of Shemaiah" was added due to dittography (from שמעיה to שמעיה). The summary later in the verse is "six," but MT only contains five names.

"Igal" *(yigʾāl)*. So MT and LXX^L. LXX^{AB} *Iōēl* may substitute a familiar name for an unfamiliar one (Allen 1974b: 151).

3:23. "sons of Neariah." So a few Heb. MSS, LXX, and Tg. MT and Vg. "son."

"Neariah" *(nĕʿaryāh)*. Thus MT and LXX^L. The difference between these sources and LXX^{AB} *Nōadeia* reflects a *dālet/rêš* confusion.

3:24. "Elioenai" *(ʾlywʿyny*; MT). The name has various forms in MT and LXX 1 Chr 4:36; 7:8; 8:20; 26:3; Ezra 8:4; Neh 12:41 (cf. Josephus, *Ant.*19.342 *Eliōnaion ton tou Kanthēra*). See further the TEXTUAL NOTE to 8:20.

"Hodaviah." Kethib *hdywhw*; Qere *hôddavyāhû*. LXX^{B}, c_2 *Hodalia*; LXX^{AN}, Vg. *Oduia*; LXX^{L}, g *Hōdia* (= הוֹדִיָּה ?); Arm. *Udiay*. LXX supports the Qere and points to a metathesis in the Kethib. Biblical and extrabiblical forms of the name also lend credence to the Qere: *hwdwyh* (1 Chr 5:24; 9:7; *TAD*, §B5.1:9; 2.9:18; 3.1:22; 7.3:2); *hwdyh* (Davies, §100.155.2), *hwdwyhw* (Davies, §§1.003.17; 100.555.2; 100.617.2); *hwdyhw* (Davies, §4.101.8; 100.359.3; 100.367.1).

NOTES

3:1–3. Drawn from the author's version of 2 Sam 3:2–5.

3:1. "sons of David." David's lineage follows naturally 1 Chr 2:9–17, which enumerates the descendants of Ram, including David and the sons of David's two sisters Zeruiah and Abigail.

"firstborn was Amnon by Aḥinoam the Jezreelite." Actually, all of these sons are firstborn (by David's various wives), not just Amnon. Presumably, Amnon is the firstborn of the firstborn. The author selectively uses 2 Sam 5:5 as a rubric to organize his summary of David's children. The list that he creates is, therefore, not an exhaustive tabulation. Some of the progeny may not have actually been born in Ḥebron (1 Sam 25:43–44; 27:3; 30:5; 2 Sam 2:2).

"Daniel." No other information is provided about him. The same can be said for all of David's sons, save chosen Solomon. In contrast, the so-called Succession Narrative or Court History (2 Sam 9–20*; 1 Kgs 1–2*) details the struggles among David's sons for their father's throne. In Chronicles the only other time Solomon's siblings appear is when they endorse Solomon's enthronement unanimously (1 Chr 29:24).

"Abigail the Carmelite." On Abigail, see 1 Sam 25:2–42; 27:3; 30:5, 18; 2 Sam 2:2. Carmel (Khirbet el-Kirmil), 12 km south of Ḥebron, is one of the towns allotted to Judah (Josh 15:55).

3:2. "Absalom son of Maacah daughter of Talmai king of Geshur." A strategic diplomatic marriage on David's part, given that Ishbaal the son of Saul laid claim to this area (2 Sam 2:9; Levenson and Halpern 1980: 507–18).

3:4. "reigned there for seven years and six months." This verse draws upon and reworks 2 Sam 5:5. In so doing, the writer creates a chiastic structure that carefully marks the transition from Ḥebron to Jerusalem (vv. 4–5a; cf. Kalimi 1995a: 222).

a six were born to him in Ḥebron
  b he reigned there
    c for seven years and six months
    c′ for thirty-three years
  b′ he reigned in Jerusalem
a′ these were born to him in Jerusalem

Second Samuel 5:5 speaks of David's reign over Judah and his reign over Israel, but the author of this verse, consistent with the pan-Israel tenor of David's tenure in 1 Chr 11–29, avoids such a distinction. The very summary differentiating David's rule in Ḥebron from his rule in Jerusalem (cf. 1 Chr 29:27) shows, however, that the Chronicler was aware of and did not completely suppress information that conflicted with his own presentation of history. The mention of David's rule in Ḥebron resonates with the links drawn between Ḥebron and the tribe of Judah (2:43–44). The allusion to David's rule in Jerusalem (the first mention of Jerusalem in Chronicles) anticipates the close links the author draws between the Davidides and this royal city in his narrative history (Beentjes 1996).

3:5–8. These verses are largely dependent upon 2 Sam 5:14–16. A very similar summary can be found in 1 Chr 14:4–7.

3:5 "Nathan." Luke's genealogy of the Davidides traces Jesus' ancestry through Nathan (Luke 3:31), not Solomon (Matt 1:6). Explanations for Luke's giving pride of place to Nathan vary (M. Johnson 1988: 229–52; R. Brown 1977: 85).

"four by Bath-shua." This statement is not found in Samuel. Based on 2 Sam 11:1–12:25, it comes as a surprise to see Solomon mentioned as the fourth son in David's relationship with Bath-shua (Bathsheba). It is unclear why the author makes this claim, but its importance should not be underestimated. The appeal to a hypothetical source (e.g., Rudolph 1955: 26) lessens but does not dispose of the problem, because one has to ask why an author or editor included a source that conflicted with Samuel. Another possible explanation is that the list, "Shimea, Shobab, Nathan, and Solomon," does not reflect order of birth. If so, this list would be exceptional.

"daughter of Ammiel." Bath-shua's patronymic, "my (divine) kinsman is ʾĒl," is a variant of the patronymic "Eliam" that appears in Samuel (e.g., 2 Sam 11:3; 23:24).

3:8. "nine." This numerical summary is consistent with the other numerical tallies in the genealogy of Judah and likely stems from the Chronicler's own hand.

3:9. "All were sons of David in addition to the sons of (his) concubines." A summation based upon 2 Sam 5:13.

"Tamar was their sister." A statement likely drawn from 2 Sam 13:1. A Bath-shua and a Tamar are also mentioned in Judah's biography (1 Chr 2:3–4; Japhet 1993a: 96).

3:10–14. "son of Solomon." A fifteen-generation linear genealogy extending from Solomon to Josiah. The writer selectively demarcates a line of consecutive generations, rather than creates a segmented lineage of all members of the royal Davidic line. Other passages demonstrate that the Chronicler knew of and took an interest in a variety of royal princes (e.g., 2 Chr 11:18–23; 21:1–3) as well as other major royalty such as Athaliah, whose reign he, like the Deuteronomist, treats as an interregnum (2 Chr 22:2–23:15). As with a number of earlier linear genealogies—1 Chr 1:1–4 (Adam to Noaḥ) and 1:24–27 (Shem to Abram)—the author examines a substantial amount of material (1 Kgs 11–2 Kgs 22), culls data of interest to him, and presents it in highly condensed form.

3:15–19a. "sons of Josiah." A segmented genealogy from Josiah to Pedaiah. Although the author had access to earlier biblical sources, this statement of ancestry is unparalleled. Like the segmented genealogy of Jesse's sons (2:13–15) and the segmented genealogy of David's sons born in Ḥebron (3:1–3), the segmented genealogy of Josiah's sons (v. 15) is marked by ordinals. The switch from linear to segmented genealogies is especially appropriate in this context, because regular succession ceased in the last decades of the Judahite monarchy. The textual witnesses to Chronicles and Kings do not agree, however, about the relationships among Judah's final monarchs. The order of their rule is not in dispute: Josiah (2 Kgs 22:1; 2 Chr 34:1), Jehoaḥaz (2 Kgs 23:30; 2 Chr 36:1), Eliaqim/Jehoiaqim (2 Kgs 23:34; 2 Chr 36:4), Jehoiachin (2 Kgs 24:1; 2 Chr 36:9), and Mattaniah/Zedeqiah (2 Kgs 24:17; 2 Chr 36:10). Since Jer 22:11 states that Josiah's son Shallum succeeded him, scholars assume that Jehoaḥaz and Shallum are two different names for the same person (2 Kgs 23:30; 2 Chr 36:1). The problems begin when one attempts to correlate the succession of Josiah's sons in v. 15, Joḥanan, Jehoiaqim, Zedeqiah, and Shallum, with the regnal notes in Kings and Chronicles that provide the age of a king at his accession:

Jehoaḥaz,* age 23	(2 Kgs 23:31; 2 Chr 36:2)
Jehoiaqim, age 25	(2 Kgs 23:36; 2 Chr 36:5)
Jehoiachin, age 18	(2 Kgs 24:8; age 8 in 2 Chr 36:9)
Zedeqiah,* age 21	(2 Kgs 24:18; 2 Chr 36:11).

The text of Chronicles does not provide information about the queen mother for the post-Ḥezeqian kings of Judah (Macy 1975), but 2 Kgs 23:31, 24:18, and Jer 52:1 list Jehoaḥaz and Zedeqiah (the kings starred above) as having the same mother: "Ḥamuṭal daughter of Jeremiah of Libnah." If Shallum and Jehoaḥaz are two different names for the same person (Jer 22:11), how could Shallum, the youngest son of Josiah, take office at age 23 in 609 B.C.E. and his older brother Zedeqiah take office in 597 B.C.E. at age 21? It may be that the figure of twenty-five in 2 Kgs 23:36 is corrupt (Tadmor and Cogan 1988: 305). A closely related issue is who Zedeqiah's mother is. Williamson (1982b: 56) thinks that 2 Kgs 24:18 (Ḥamuṭal) is in error. Whatever the case, I would argue that 1 Chr 3:15–17 are ambiguous, perhaps deliberately so, the very ambiguity allowing for multiple interpretations.

3:15. "the firstborn Joḥanan." Not otherwise attested. Many commentators think that he died prematurely. It is not impossible that Joḥanan represents the expected Jehoaḥaz (2 Kgs 23:31; 2 Chr 36:1; Wellhausen 1885: 216) because fluidity in names and positions of names is characteristic of genealogical transmission (R. Wilson 1977; Flanagan 1983). But Shallum is a more likely candidate than Joḥanan (see further below).

"Jehoiaqim." The second successor to Josiah after Jehoaḥaz (2 Kgs 23:36; 2 Chr 36:4–8).

"Zedeqiah" came to power after the exile of Jeconiah, also called Coniah (Jer 22:24; 37:1) and Jehoiachin (2 Kgs 24:8–15; 25:27–30; 2 Chr 36:8–10). But is this Zedeqiah the Zedeqiah who succeeded Jeconiah? Or is Zedeqiah the son of Jeconiah (v. 16), the successor to Jeconiah? The former is more likely than the latter, considering Jeconiah's age at succession, but the presence of two Zedeqiahs in this genealogy may not be accidental. The appearance of each may have been occasioned by what the writer found in earlier traditions. In other words, the genealogy of Josiah's descendants results, at least in part, from inner-biblical exegesis. Faced with conflicting evidence in his sources, the writer composed a genealogy that would take account of the possibilities. The text of v. 15, in conformity with the tradition represented by LXX 2 Chr 36:10 and 2 Kgs 24:17 (MT and LXX[L]) presents Zedeqiah as a son of Josiah and, therefore, as Jeconiah's uncle. The text of 1 Chr 3:16, in conformity with the tradition represented in LXX[B] 2 Kgs 24:17, presents Zedeqiah as a son of Jeconiah. The one possibility not explicitly accounted for is the claim of MT 2 Chr 36:10 that Zedeqiah is a brother of Jeconiah. But the text of 2 Chr 36:10 is in dispute (MT אחיו; LXX *adelphon tou patros autou*).

"Shallum" is not mentioned (by this name) again in Chronicles. According to Jer 22:11, Shallum succeeded Josiah and so many think that Shallum and Jehoaḥaz are two different names for the same person (W. Holladay 1986: 590). Verses 15–16 do not refer explictly to Jehoaḥaz, but the final chapter of Chronicles does (2 Chr 36:1–3). The Targum identifies Shallum with Zedeqiah and, playing on the root *šlm*, speaks of David's kingdom coming to an end *(dšlymt)* in Shallum's days (cf. *b. Ker.* 5b; *b. Hor.* 11b).

3:16. "Jeconiah" (יכניה). Also called Jehoiachin (יהויכן; 2 Chr 36:8–10) and Coniah (e.g., Jer 22:24). Elsewhere the name "Jeconiah" occurs in Jer 24:1; 28:4; 29:2; and Esth 2:6, but this is its only appearance in Chronicles.

3:17. "sons of Jeconiah." The author follows the offspring of David through Jeconiah and not through Zedeqiah as one might expect, given the linear genealogy of v. 16. That the lineage of v. 17 begins with Jeconiah may suggest (again) that the writer is attempting to accommodate two discrete traditions within his own presentation. To complicate matters, there is a historical consideration to bear in mind. All of Zedeqiah's sons were executed before he was brought to Babylon (2 Kgs 25:7). Hence, either the author may not have known the names of Zedeqiah's sons or he chose not to mention them because the issue of Zedeqiah's offspring was a moot point.

"the prisoner." Albright (1942: 50) intimates that this epithet was added to identify Jeconiah's exilic status. In any case, this writer shows some of the same interest in Jeconiah as that evinced in the final passage of Kings, the notice of Jehoiachin's release (2 Kgs 25:27–30). Administrative documents from Babylon, dating approximately from 595 to 570 B.C.E., mention rations for Jehoiachin and at least five sons (Oppenheim 1969: 308).

3:18. "Malchiram" *(mlkyrm)*. The name, meaning "my (divine) king is exalted," is unique within the HB. But *mlkrm* is well known in Phoenician and Punic inscriptions (Benz 1972: 140), and the related name *mlkyrm*, "may my [divine] king be exalted," is attested on a Canaanite-Phoenician arrowhead (Deutsch and Heltzer 1995: 17).

"Shenazzar." His precise identity is in dispute. The theory that Shenazzar is the Babylonian name of Pedaiah (Rothstein 1902: 27–31) is unlikely because it fails to account for the differentiation between the two in this lineage. Hoonacker's influential thesis, defended by Albright (1963: 86–87), Cross (1998: 179–80), and Sacchi (2000: 60), that Shenazzar *(šnʾṣr)* and Sheshbazzar *(ššbṣr)*, the prince *(nāśîʾ*;

Ezra 1:8, 11) or governor (*peḥâ*; Ezra 5:14–17) of Judah and leader of the first returnees in 538 B.C.E., refer to the same person has also been contested. In this theory, the two Heb. names reflect different transliterations (and corruptions) of an original Babylonian name, such as *Šîn-ab-uṣur*, the medial *'b* having been lost by haplography. One also notes that the placement of "Shenazzar" and "Zerubabbel" (v. 19) in this genealogy comports with the sequence of Sheshbazzar and Zerubbabel in Ezra. But Berger (1971) argues on the basis of Akkadian evidence that Sheshbazzar and Shenazzar represent two distinct names: *Šamaš/Šaššu-aba-uṣur* (dUTU-AD-URÙ/PAB) and *Šîn-uṣur*. Cross (1998) counters that the element *Šamaš* as a vocative (or frozen form) would not appear in assimilated form *(Šaššu)* in a name of this type and lists examples of corruptions of other Babylonian names. The evidence provided by the Greek versions and Josephus of Sheshbazzar (*Sanabassaros* [1 Esd 2:11, 14; 6:17, 19]; Josephus *Abasaros* [*Ant.* 11.11]; *Sanabasaros* [*Ant.* 11.93]; *Sanabassarēs* [*Ant.*11.100]; 2 Esd (B) *Sabanasar* [metathesis of *beta* and *nu*]) is inconclusive.

3:19a. "sons of Pedaiah: Zerubbabel and Shimei." Other than here, Zerubbabel is always described as the son of Shealtiel (Ezra 3:2; 5:2; Neh 12:1; Hag 1:1, 12, 14; 2:2, 23; Matt 1:12; Luke 3:27). If, as seems likely, Pedaiah is the original reading (TEXTUAL NOTE), there is no easy means to reconcile the discrepancy. Theories abound. Rothstein and Hänel (1927: 41) think that Shealtiel was the Babylonian name of Pedaiah. Keil (1873: 81–82), followed by Rudolph (1955: 29) with some modifications, posits a levirate marriage, while Albright (1921: 108–9) thinks that the two are cousins referred to by the same name. Goettsberger (1939: 47–48) revives the view that Pedaiah took over the family after Shealtiel's premature death. Curtis and Madsen (1910: 101) contend that Zerubbabel succeeded Shealtiel and was considered his son. While each of these harmonizations is possible, it is equally possible that the lineage preserves a variant tradition about Zerubbabel's parentage.

19b–24. The list of Davidic descendants from Zerubbabel to the sons of Elioenai is unique to Chronicles.

3:19b. "Zerubbabel," a governor in Yehud, is associated, along with Jeshua the high priest, with the rebuilding of the Temple in 520–515 B.C.E. (Ezra 3:2; 5:2; Neh 12:1; Hag 1:1, 14; 2:2; Josephus, *Ant.* 11.32). Herodotus (*Hist.*3.89) describes the organization of Achaemenid satrapies and the use of native governors within the provinces. The use of the term פחה ("governor") in epigraphic sources from Samaria and Yehud confirms this impression (Ephʿal 1998: 117–18). But given the evidence supplied by a recently published Babylonian document (Stolper 1998), the administrative division of "Babylonia and Beyond the River" must have postdated the death of Darius I (486 B.C.E.). There is another issue in the scholarly criticism affecting Zerubbabel, as well as Jeconiah and Shenazzar (often thought to be the same person as Sheshbazzar; 2nd NOTE to v. 18) before him: Were these Davidic descendants viewed as veritable monarchs? Some scholars (Sacchi 1989; 2000: 46–62; Bianchi 1991; 1994; Niehr 1999; cf. Lemaire 1996b) think so, contending that Jehoiachin, Sheshbazzar, and Zerubbabel served as royal vassals to the Babylonian and Achaemenid kings. That Jehoiachin was given a client treaty by the Babylonians seems doubtful (*pace* Janssen 1956: 79). It is unlikely that the Babylonian emperor would ratify a vassal treaty with a state prisoner even if he decided to provide him with some blandishments (2 Kgs 25:27–30). With respect to the Persian period, the issue is difficult to resolve definitively because we do not know in sufficient detail how various Judeans within Yehud perceived the status of these Davidides nor all of what they read into the title פחה. The problem is not defining the use of a local to govern a (sub)province, but determining how both Persian authorities and local populations conceived of his title(s) and position (the two perspectives need not have been identical). In this respect, the Davidic genealogy does not throw much light on the question. Unlike many other genealogies ("Excursus: The Genealogies"), it neither offers numerous explanatory digressions nor comments on the status of individual descendants (SOURCES AND COMPOSITION).

"Meshullam." At this point, the genealogies of Matt 1:12–16 (Salathiel, Zerubbabel, Abiud, Eliaaim, Azor, etc.) and Luke 3:26–27 (Salathiel, Zerubbabel, Rhesa, Joanan, Joda, etc.) diverge (again) from the list of Zerubbabel's descendants presented here (M. Johnson 1988: 139–45). Even though the genealogies of Chronicles, Matthew, and Luke all trace the latter portion of the Davidic lineage through Zerubbabel, there is precious little overlap among them.

"Ḥananiah" (*ḥănanyāh*) is not referred to elsewhere in the Scriptures. A storage jar at Ramat Raḥel with the stamp "Yehud: Ḥananah" (*yhwd/ḥnnh*) may refer to a governor's officer in charge of fiscal matters (Avigad 1976: 4–5 [#3, pl. 5]). Given that Ḥananiah is not an uncommon name in the Persian period (e.g., Neh 1:2; 7:2; *TAD* A4.1:1, 10; 4.3:7), an identification between *ḥnnh* and "Ḥananiah" is not assured.

"Shelomith was their sister." Shelomith may appear as the owner of a seal, dating to the late sixth century B.C.E., "belonging to Shelomith the maidservant of Elnathan [the] governor" (*lšlmyt/ʾmt ʾln/tn pḥ[wʾ]*; Avigad 1976: 11–13 [#14, pl. 15]; Davies, §106.018.1). This same Elnathan appears on a bulla, which is also dated to the late sixth century, "belonging to Elnathan [the] governor" (*lʾlntn/pḥwʾ*; Avigad 1976: 5–7 [#5, pl. 6]; Davies, §106.017.1). The evidence from Chronicles' genealogy and this recently discovered seal indicates Shelomith's prominence in Yehud. Since Elnathan was a successor to Zerubbabel, the mention of Zerubbabel's daughter Shelomith in connection with Elnathan suggests a continuing association between the Davidic line and the governor of Yehud (E. Meyers 1985). But Shelomith's precise role as *ʾmh* is disputed (Davies, §4.401; Avigad 1976; Williamson 1988a; Lemaire 1996b; Bordreuil, Israel, and Pardee 1996: 74–75).

3:21. "Jeshaiah, his son Rephaiah." Some have cited the genealogy in vv. 21–24 (following the LXX; 2nd TEXTUAL NOTE to v. 21) to argue that Zerubbabel's generations extend into the third century B.C.E. This raises larger questions about the date of composition for vv. 19b–24, if not for the book of Chronicles itself ("Introduction"). Nevertheless, one should mention a particular consideration based on comparative anthropology, a point emphasized by Freedman (personal communication). Anthropologists typically assume an average twenty-year gap between generations given the contrary effects in the ancient world of early childbearing and high rates of infant mortality. In contrast, many biblical scholars have worked with figures of twenty-five, thirty, or even forty years per generation. What concerns us, in this context, is the actual passage of years between generations, not the typological use of numbers, such as forty, by certain ancient writers.

If one works with the twenty-year figure and applies it to the period from the projected time of Solomon (ca. 950 B.C.E.) to that of the second Babylonian exile (586 B.C.E.), one arrives at the year 590 for the latter event (18 generations x 20 years). This calculation would seem to verify the fundamental accuracy of the twenty-year figure, even though there were undoubtedly many exceptions to the mean. If one basically uses LXX (TEXTUAL NOTES) and applies the twenty-year figure to the rest of the genealogy, beginning with King Jeconiah and the time of the second Babylonian exile (586 B.C.E.), one arrives at the approximate date of 346 B.C.E. (12 generations x 20 years = 240 years). Alternatively, if one basically uses MT (TEXTUAL NOTES) and applies the twenty-year figure to the rest of the genealogy, one arrives at the approximate date of 426 B.C.E. (8 generations x 20 years = 160 years). The end of the genealogy need not be the time in which the author (or editor) wrote. The author of the priestly genealogy (5:27–41) ends his work with the exile even though he lived sometime in the Persian or the Hellenistic era. Nevertheless, the larger point remains the same. Only by employing figures of twenty-five or more years per generation in calculations, a procedure that does not follow the averages provided by most anthropologists, does one arrive at the fourth—(MT) and third-century (LXX) averages provided by many biblical commentators. Retaining the figures of thirty or forty years per generation forces one to revise downward the dates provided in traditional calculations.

3:22. "Ḥaṭṭush" *(ḥṭwš)*. Ezra 8:2 mentions a Davidide named Ḥaṭṭush, who returned with Ezra from Babylon. The case has been made that Ḥaṭṭush is associated with "the sons of Shecaniah" (Ezra 8:3), but the text there is not altogether clear (cf. 1 Esd 8:29; Batten 1913: 319; Rudolph 1949: 78; Williamson 1985: 107–8). A name may well be missing from Ezra 8:3 ("PN from the sons of Shecaniah"). There are other occurrences of Ḥaṭṭush as a PN in the Late Monarchy and Persian period (e.g., Neh 3:10; 10:5; 12:2; Davies, §100.556.1). See also the 2nd TEXTUAL NOTE to v. 22.

3:23. "Azriqam" *(ʿzryqm)*. Within the Bible the name appears only in Chronicles (1 Chr 8:38; 9:14, 44; 2 Chr 28:7) and Nehemiah (11:15), but *ʿzrqm* occurs in late preexilic bullae (Avigad 1986: 91–93 [#138, #139]).

3:24. "Aqqub" *(ʿaqqûb)*. An Aqabiah *(ʿqbyh)* son of Elioenai *(br ʾlywʿyny)* is attested in an early Ptolemaic Jewish inscription from the El-Ibrahimiya necropolis in Alexandria, dating to the third or second century B.C.E. (Lidzbarski 1902–15: 49; Horbury and Noy, §3). The inscription is Aram., but the names are Heb. Legitimate doubts have been raised whether Aqqub can be identified with Aqibiah in spite of the similar patronymic (Kalimi 1998b). Obviously, such a determination also depends on how many generations one reconstructs in vv. 19–23 (NOTES).

"Anani" *(ʿănānî)*. The name also appears in the Aramaic papyri from Elephantine, referring to an important person in Jerusalem (AP 30.19; cf. 26.23). The case has been made that the two are identical (Kraeling 1953: 108–9; Bianchi 1994: 163), but Anani's brother Ostanes (*'wstn*; AP 30.18) does not appear among Anani's siblings here.

SOURCES AND COMPOSITION

Large portions of the Davidic genealogy show an indebtedness to earlier biblical sources. Much of the material is drawn from narrative sources, but the author also shows some familiarity with parts of Jeremiah. In evaluating the following sources, readers should be aware that the texts available to and used by the Chronicler were, in all likelihood, not identical to MT (TEXTUAL NOTES).

1 Chr 3	*Source Material*
1–3	2 Sam 3:3–5
4	2 Sam 5:5
5–8	2 Sam 5:14–16
9	2 Sam 5:13; 13:1
10–14	1 Kgs 11–2 Kgs 22
15–19	2 Kgs 23–25; Jer 22:11

The genealogy in vv. 10–16 was probably composed by the writer himself, employing Kings and Jeremiah. The genealogical material in vv. 17–24 is unique to Chronicles. If the writer had access to some version of Ezra-Nehemiah, the Persian period prophets, or the sources used by the authors of these works, he apparently chose to go his own way in spite of them (NOTES to v. 19).

The genealogy as a whole manifests both linear and segmented forms. The depth of the lineage is truly extraordinary. Whether one counts David's generations as twenty-six (MT) or thirty (LXX), the genealogy is the longest in the Scriptures. The genealogy of Ḥezron (2:9–17), which culminates in David and his sisters, adds another eight generations to the total. The author shows a fondness for numerical summaries, usually as a conclusion, rather than as an introduction, to segmented portions of the genealogy (3:4, 5, 8, 20, 22, 24).

Substantial doubts have been raised as to whether the Davidic genealogy, in whole or in part, stems from the Chronicler. Many think that all of Ch. 3 is a later interpolation, presumably written by a writer in the Chronistic tradition (e.g., Benzinger 1901: 6; Ackroyd 1973a: 34–35; Galling 1954: 24; Myers 1965a: 19; Osborne 1979: 228; Kartveit 1989: 48–49). Some of the arguments for disunity are weaker than others. The argument that the Chronicler would only cover the period up to the time of David (Rudolph 1955: viii, 22) confuses the presumed subject matter with the totality of authorial interests in the Persian period and is belied by other evidence within the genealogies themselves (4:34–43; 5:18–22, 27–41; 8:29–40//9:35–44; Im 1985: 31). Similarly, the claim that the duplication between the list in 3:5–8, dealing with David's progeny born in Jerusalem, and the parallel list in 1 Chr 14:3–7(//2 Sam 5:13–16) signals the secondary status of 3:5–8 is unconvincing because it fails to acknowledge the possibility that the same writer might wish to use basically the same material in two different places for different purposes (e.g., Herodotus, *Hist.* 7.204; 8.131). Im (1985: 28–31) and Japhet (1993a: 92–94) contend that the writer of 3:1–9 combines two separate lists, one of David's children at Ḥebron and another of his children at Jerusalem, to provide readers with a complete picture of David's offspring. The list in 14:3–7 functions somewhat differently, confirming David's kingdom and underscoring the theme of divine blessing on his house.

More substantive reasons for viewing the genealogy, or at least the latter portions of it (vv. 15–24), as stemming from a list or as comprising a later addition can be made at the level of composition. Two factors come into play. First, there is a disparity in names between this text and the narration of the monarchy in Chronicles (e.g., Azariah vs. Uzziah; Shallum vs. Jehoaḥaz; Jeconiah vs. Jehoiachin). It is odd that such names appear here and never again in the book. Second, as we have seen, the writer shows some familiarity with competing versions of the post-Josianic succession in Judah. The genealogy accommodates different possibilities of Zedeqiah's relationship to Jeconiah found in other biblical sources (NOTES to vv. 15–16). Using Samuel, Kings, Jeremiah, and perhaps other texts, the author attempts to reconcile the variant evidence they furnish about royal succession to reconstruct a continuous Davidic genealogy for the final decades of Judah's independent existence (1st TEXTUAL NOTE to v. 16). This is where things become more complicated, because of the difficult state of the text. If the distinctive reading of MT 2 Chr 36:10 is based on an interpretation of 1 Chr 3:15–17 and is not the result of a text-critical error (2nd TEXTUAL NOTE to v. 16), one is drawn to the conclusion that the material in vv. 15ff. stems from a source in the Chronicler's employ. If MT 2 Chr 36:10 results from a text-critical error, it becomes more likely that vv. 15ff. are a later addition. The author of this material would not be the Chronicler himself but a later writer in the Chronistic tradition. Either this same genealogist or a later writer completed the genealogy up to a time in the fourth century B.C.E. (NOTES to vv. 19b–24; esp. NOTE to v. 21).

COMMENT

Detailed comments about Judah's genealogy (2:1–55; 4:1–23) follow the discussion of 1 Chr 4:1–23. The focus of these remarks is the Davidic lineage itself, a lineage that had elicited a variety of interpretations already within antiquity. For a longer review of interpretation, see Knoppers (2001b). A messianic interest is evident in the Targum (Le Déaut and Robert 1971a: 32; 1971b: 18; McIvor 1994: 57), which plays on the name of the very last figure in the genealogy, Anani (*ʿnny*), to depict the one who would come with "the clouds (*ʿnny*) of heaven" (Dan 7:13; Rev 1:7). In associating Anani with the Messiah, the writers of the Targum may have been influenced by Talmudic discussions (*b. Sanh.* 98a; Levey 1974: 162). One also sees a messianic application of the Davidic lineage in the New Testament genealogies (Matt 1:1–17; Luke 3:23–38; M. Johnson 1988). The messianic line of interpretation still has its major advocates (e.g., Rothstein 1902: 121–62; Noordtzij 1940; Botterweck 1956; Brunet 1959; Kaufmann 1961: 5–6; Stinespring 1961; Willi 1972: 43; Im 1985: 33–34; Selman 1994a: 99–101; cf. B. Kelly 1995).

Other scholars oppose a messianic interpretation because they see no clear evidence for it in the text (e.g., König 1923: 283–85; Rudolph 1954: 408–9; Caquot 1966; Mosis 1973: 93–94; Pomykala 1995: 77–111). Marshall Johnson (1988: 79–80) even speaks of 3:10–24 as an "anti-climax" to the genealogical treatment of David. In this context, it is important to ask what precisely constitutes a "messianic" viewpoint or expectation, because messianism can exhibit different forms and meanings (Coppens 1968: 17–36; Saebø 1980: 85–97). There is no mention of the term "anointed" *(māšîaḥ)* in 1 Chr 3. Indeed, the verb "to anoint" occurs only five times in the book (1 Chr 11:3; 14:8; 29:22; 2 Chr 22:7; 23:11). The adjective "anointed" only appears twice and in both cases it is derived from a source (1 Chr 16:22//Ps 105:15; 2 Chr 6:42//Ps 132:10). Nor is there any explicit statement about a Davidic restoration in 1 Chr 3, although von Rad (1930: 128–32, 135) may be close to the mark in intimating that the whole point of the abiding interest in David is to keep the Davidic tradition alive in hope of such a restoration at a later time.

Some scholars construe the Davidic lineage differently. Ackroyd (1973a: 35) speaks of continuing Davidic importance in the postexilic period. Similarly, Pomykala (1995: 106–7) suggests that the genealogy recognizes the size and leadership of Davidic families in the restoration community. For some, the Davidic line reveals an interest in the past. According to Coggins (1976: 26), the final names in the list reveal an interest in pedigree. Roddy Braun (1986: 54–55) likewise contends that the Davidides in vv. 20–24 are included because of their distinguished predecessor. My purpose in what follows is not to refute all of these particular views. Quite the contrary, each contains a measure of truth. The following discussion will develop some of the aforementioned insights while pursuing new directions.

My interpretation is based upon both the structure and the composition of the lineage. It may be appropriate to begin with some general observations. First, apart from listing the order of progeny and tracing succession from one generation to the next, there are few indications of status. The process of leveling one sees in the genealogies of Adam, Noah, and Abraham (1:1–2:2) is also evident here. The terms "king," "kingship," or "reign" never appear. One effect of this leveling is that the genealogy does not elevate Davidides who became monarchs above those later Davidides who did not. Comparison can also be made with the earlier and later genealogies of Judah in which anecdotes, epithets, and digressions identify a range of characters (e.g., 2:3, 7, 55; 4:9–10, 21, 23). It is, therefore, no slight against the figures who appear near the end of the list that they receive no extraordinary attention (contra M. Johnson 1988). Indeed, because there are no titles or special signs of status accorded to most figures, exilic and postexilic figures share the same relative position as preexilic figures who appear earlier.

Second, the structure of the genealogy belies a preoccupation with the crises identified by historians as the most important in Jerusalem's history: the division (ca. 931 B.C.E.), the invasion of Sennacherib (701 B.C.E.), the Babylonian invasion (598 B.C.E.), the Babylonian exile (586 B.C.E.), and the return (538 B.C.E.). In many commentaries on Chronicles (e.g., Rudolph 1955: 26–29; Myers 1965a: 17–18; R. Braun 1986: 47–48), one finds this chapter organized along the following lines: David's sons (vv. 1–9), the Judahite kings (vv. 10–16), the exilic and postexilic periods (vv. 17–24). In conceiving of the material in this way, scholars accommodate the genealogy to major events in Israelite history: the introduction of the monarchy, the independent state of Judah, the Babylonian exile, and Achaemenid rule. But this approach lacks literary sensitivity to the organization of the genealogy itself. If there are discrete sections within this continuous genealogy, they are associated with the figures of David (vv. 1–9), Solomon (vv. 10–14), Josiah and his successors (vv. 15–19a), and Zerubbabel (vv. 19b–24). With the exception of the allusion to Jeconiah as "the prisoner" (v. 17), none of these major events is even hinted at. A contrast may be drawn with another, later genealogy of David. The schematic periodization in the lineage, consisting of the groups of fourteen generations, found in the Gospel of Matthew calls attention to certain eras: Abraham (Matt 1:1, 17), the kingdom of David (Matt 1:6, 7, 17), the deportation under Jeconiah (Matt 1:11, 12, 17), and the time of the messiah (Matt 1:1, 17). The lineage in Chronicles does not exhibit such a schematization of history. Instead, it underscores an unbroken succession in spite of the vicissitudes of history.

Third, examination of the genealogy reveals some relevant details about its selection of coverage. Given David's prominence (1 Chronicles 11–29), it is not surprising that the most concentrated attention is given to David's sons (vv. 1–9). Nor is it astonishing that Josiah receives some attention (vv. 14–15), given his stature as a consumate reformer (2 Chronicles 34–35; Knoppers 1989). What is surprising is that three other very prominent monarchs, all favorites of the Chronicler—Solomon (2 Chronicles 1–9), Jehoshaphaṭ (2 Chronicles 17–20) and Ḥezeqiah (2 Chronicles 29–32)—receive no special attention. The whole period of the Judahite monarchy is, for the most part, dealt with in great brevity, a linear genealogy extending from Solomon to Josiah (vv. 10–14). An attempt to coordinate this section of the genealogy with the Chronicler's history of Jerusalem, like attempting to organize the genealogy according to international crises, misapprehends the character and structure of this history of generations.

Fourth, whether the genealogy delineates either twenty-six generations (one interpretation of MT) or thirty generations (LXX), it plots six to seven hundred years of continuous Davidic succession. The progression from generation to generation in 3:1–24 contrasts with the situation in 2:1–55 and 4:1–23, both of which have the lineages of some of Judah's descendants either coordinated or interrupted to introduce lineages of other Judahites. In ch. 3 there are complications—for example, with the descendants of Josiah—but no anecdotes, digressions, or wholesale breaks. The chapter documents an unbroken succession from David to the sons of Elioenai.

One does not have to look far to see what the impetus might have been to compose (and update) such a genealogy. The development of daybooks, annals, and priestly genealogies began in Thebes in Egypt in the early first millennium B.C.E. to reinforce priestly pedigree and status in the wake of the capital's move away from Thebes (Redford 1970; 1986). With the governmental apparatus no longer there to support the priesthood directly, the priests found it necessary to bolster their position by other means. An analogy may be made to the situation of the Davidides in Yehud. Following the first few decades of the return, the Davidides apparently did not serve as governors of Yehud. The impetus to compose and maintain a royal genealogy may have been the absence of substantial political authority rather than the possession of it. In this context, the emphasis on continuous succession is especially noteworthy because, following the rule of Zerubbabel as governor in the late sixth century B.C.E., such a preoccupation with internal order could be viewed as unnecessary. Rather than view the purpose of the genealogy as simply a demonstration of endurance—David's family "became *in extenso*"(De Vries 1989: 43–44)—one must also come to terms with the fact that the authors of the genealogy argue for a particular succession within the Davidic line up to the point of the final generation. The last section of the genealogy (vv. 19b–24), even though it exhibits both breadth and depth, is hardly a neutral accounting of the progress of David's seed. It argues for a particular line of succession within the Davidic house (from Zerubbabel to Elioenai).

It would seem, then, that the writer's purpose was not simply to condense the history of the United Kingdom, the Judahite monarchy, the Exile, and the Persian period, but to trace a continuous line through them. In this sense, the genealogy transcends, even defies history. In the annals of Judahite history, 586 B.C.E. marked one disaster for the Davidic monarchy (2 Kgs 25:1–21; 2 Chr 36:13–21). The royal capital was conquered, the Temple was burnt, and members of the royal dynasty were humiliated, exiled, or executed. History seemed to refute the notion of an eternal Davidic kingdom (2 Sam 7:5–16; Ps 89:38–52).

The breath of our nostrils, Yhwh's anointed,
was caught in their traps;
he in whose shade we had thought
we could live among the nations. (Lam 4:20)

The appointment of a series of non-Davidic governors—Elnathan, Jehoʿezer, Aḥzai, Neḥemiah—may have marked another major disappointment to the Davidic dynasty (Avigad 1976; Lemaire 1996b). The authors of the Davidic genealogy address neither these past setbacks nor the earlier hopes for a restoration under Zerubbabel (cf. Hag 2:20–23). Nevertheless, by carefully documenting an unbroken succession of Davidides for approximately seven centuries, the genealogy of David rebuts the notion that the Davidic dynasty had been dealt a death blow by any major disappointment (cf. *m. Taʿan.* 4:5). Quite the contrary, a centuries-long pedigree would suggest that the Davidic house survived and maintained itself with assistance from above. As long as a once prominent line survives the ravages of history, the members of that line and their supporters are always free to hope for a restoration to power. In this respect, the written documentation of a genealogy contributes to the legacy of the family itself. The careful demarcation of continuity among the descendants of David throughout periods of tremendous change demonstrates the dynasty's resiliency and importance. The lineage of royal descendants forms the centerpiece of the lineage of the eponymous ancestor, who "grew mighty among his brothers" (5:2). In this respect, one does not have to argue that the history of generations serves a larger purpose. The vitality evinced by the Davidic genealogy speaks for itself.

IV. The Genealogy of Judah, Part II (4:1–23)

Introduction: The Descendants of Judah

1 The descendants of Judah: Perez, Ḥezron, Caleb, Ḥur, and Shobal.

The Descendants of Reaiah

2 Reaiah son of Shobal sired Jaḥath and Jaḥath sired Aḥimai and Lahad. These
were the families of the Zorathites.

The Children of Eṭam

3 These are the sons of Eṭam: Jezreel, Ishma, and Idbash. And the name of their
sister was Hazlel.

The Descendants of Ḥur

4 Penuel was the father of Gedor and Ezer was the father of Ḥushah. These were
the sons of Ḥur, the firstborn of Ephrathah the father of Bethleḥem.

The Descendants of Ashḥur, Ḥelah, and Naarah

5 Ashḥur father of Teqoa had two wives: Ḥelah and Naarah. 6 Naarah bore him
Aḥuzzam, Ḥepher, Temeni, and the Aḥashtarite. These were the sons of Naarah.
7 The sons of Ḥelah were Zereth, Zoḥar, and Ethnan.

The Descendants of Qoz

8 Qoz sired Annub, Zobebah, the families of the brother of Rechab, and the
sons of Harim.

Jabez

9 Now Jabez was more honored than his brothers. His mother named him
Jabez, saying "indeed I have given birth in affliction." 10 And Jabez invoked the
God of Israel, saying "Oh, that you would truly bless me, enlarge my territory, and
that your hand might stay with me and refrain from evil so as not to afflict me."
And God granted what he requested.

The Men of Recah

11 Celub brother of Shuḥah sired Meḥir. He was the father of Eshton. 12 And
Eshton sired Beth-rapha, Paseaḥ, and Teḥinnah the father of the city of Naḥash.
These were the men of Recah.

The Descendants of Qenaz

13 The sons of Qenaz: Othniel and Seraiah. The sons of Othniel: Ḥathath and
the Maonathites. 14 The Maonathites sired Ophrah and Seraiah sired Joab the father of Ge-Ḥarashim, [named as such] because they were craftsmen.

The Descendants of Caleb

15 The sons of Caleb son of Jephunneh: Ir, Elah, and Naam. The sons of Elah: Qenaz.

The Descendants of Jehallelel

16 The sons of Jehallelel: Ziph and Ziphah, Tiria and Asarel.

The Descendants of Ezrah and His Egyptian and Judahite Wives

17 The sons of Ezrah: Jether, Mered, Epher, and Jalon. Jether sired Miriam,
Shammai, and Ishbah father of Eshtemoa. 18 These are the sons of Bithiah the
daughter of Pharaoh, whom Mered wed. She gave birth to Jered the father of
Gedor, Ḥeber the father of Soco, and Jequthiel the father of Zanoaḥ. 19 The sons
of his Judahite wife, the sister of Naḥam, were the father of Qeilah the Garmite
and Eshtemoa the Maacathite.

The Sons of Shimon

20 The sons of Shimon: Amnon, Rinnah the son of Ḥanan, and Tilon.

The Descendants of Ishi

The sons of Ishi: Zoḥeth and the son of Zoḥeth.

The Descendants of Shelah

21 The sons of Shelah the son of Judah: Er the father of Lecah, Laadah the father
of Mareshah, and the families of the house of linen work at Beth-ashbea, 22 Joqim,
the men of Cozeba, Joash, and Saraph, who married into Moab. And they resided
in Bethleḥem. (The records are ancient.) 23 They were the potters and residents of
Netaim and Gederah. With the king in his service they resided there.

TEXTUAL NOTES

4:1. "the descendants." So MT and LXX *(lectio brevior)*. Syr. "these are the descendants."

"Caleb." MT and the versions read "Carmi." As Wellhausen (1870: 20) and others have pointed out, Carmi (cf. 2:7) is a mistake for either Caleb (2:18, 42, 50) or Celubai (2:9). It is possible that MT reflects confusion with the sequence of Reuben's sons Ḥezron and Carmi in Gen 46:9 and 1 Chr 5:3 (Williamson 1982b: 59).

4:2. "Aḥimai." See LXX^{B} c_2 (followed by Syr.) *Acheimei*; LXX^{N} *Amichai*; LXX^{L} and Arm. *Achiman*; other cursives *Achimai*. MT's "Aḥumai" *(ʾḥwmy)* reflects a *wāw/yôd* confusion.

4:3. "these." Syr. "and these are the sons of Amminadab and these are" indicates that some words may have dropped out of the text. The *Vorlage* of LXX v. 3 may have been corrupt (Allen 1974b: 151), but this is also the case with MT.

"sons of Eṭam." Thus LXX^{AB}. Cf. Vg. *stirps*, "stock"; Tg. *rbny* "leaders." The reading of MT (and *b*ye$_2$), "the father of Eṭam," assimilates to the use of *ʾby* in v. 4. The reconstruction favored by Benzinger, Kittel, and Curtis and Madsen, "[and these are] the sons of Ḥur the father of Eṭam," blends elements of MT with LXX and conforms the material to the end of v. 4, while the emendation favored by

Rothstein, Noth, Rudolph, and Japhet, "and these are the sons of Ḥareph the father of Beth-gader," harmonizes this verse with 2:51 and 4:4. Neither proposal has sufficient text-critical support.

"and the name of their sister was Hazlel." MT "Hazlelponi;" LXX[B] c_2 *Esēlebbōn*. The entire clause is missing from Syr. The name *hṣllpwny*, whether transcribed as "Hazlelponi" or "the Hazlelponite," is suspect. Begrich (*BHK*), following a suggestion of Noth (1932: 105), proposes two sisters: *yhll'l* (see v. 16) and *ṣpwny*. Rudolph (1955: 30) reconstructs, "[her name] is placed before the name of her sister" (*hṣb lpny šm 'ḥwth*), a marginal gloss he thinks was added concerning vv. 6–7, to explain the order of v. 5b. I prefer the simpler solution of Curtis and Madsen (1910: 108), that *pwny* is based on a dittography of the following *pnw'l* (v. 4).

4:4. "the father of Gedor, and Ezer was the father of Ḥushah." So MT and LXX. Missing from Syr.

"Ḥushah." See the 3rd TEXTUAL NOTE to v. 11.

"father of Bethleḥem" (*'by byt lḥm*). To avoid a conflict with the claim of 1 Chr 2:51 that Salma was the father of Bethleḥem, Rothstein and Hänel posit a haplography of *hê* (after Ephrathah) and a dittography of *by*, reconstructing "that is, Bethleḥem" (*hy' byt lḥm*; cf. Gen 35:19).

4:5. "Ashḥur" (*'šḥwr*). So MT, LXX[AN], Arm. LXX[B] c_2 *Sara* may reflect an inner-Greek corruption (Allen 1974b: 76, 115).

"Ḥelah (*ḥl'h*) and Naarah (*n'rh*)." So MT. LXX[B] c_2 *Haōda kai Thoada*. The clause is absent from Syr. For Ḥelah, compare bye_2 *Helda*; LXX[AN] *Halaa*. The PN ("Jewelry" or "Adornment") may fall under the category of PNs having to do with jewelry and cosmetics (Stamm 1980: 123). For "Naarah," compare c_2 *Aodda*; LXX[L] *Noera*; LXX[AN] *Noora*; Arm. *Nooba*.

4:6. "Aḥuzzam" (*'ḥzm*). So MT and Tg. The lemmata of LXX[B] *Ōchaia*; c_2 *Achaia*; LXX[AN] *Ōchazam*; and Vg. *Oozam* presuppose a different *Vorlage*.

"Temeni" (*tymny*). So MT. LXX* (*Thaiman* = *tymn*).

"the Aḥashtarite" (האחשתרי). Reading the final *yôd* as a gentilic.

4:7–8. These verses are not found in Syr.

4:7. "Zoḥar" (*ṣḥr*). So Qere and a few LXX cursives. Kethib, Tg., and Vg. "Izḥor" (*yṣḥr*). LXX[B] *Saar*; LXX[N] *Sara*; Arm. *Asaar*.

"Ethnan." So MT and LXX. The addition of some witnesses to Tg., "and Qoz," is followed by Kittel (1902: 29), Rudolph (1955: 30), Williamson (1982b: 59), and Japhet (1993a: 108), who suppose a haplography (v. 8). But the textual support for a haplography is weak and late.

4:8. "Zobeba" (*hṣbbh*). Some (e.g., Begrich in *BHK*) insert "Jabez" after Zobeba to make better sense of v. 9. The evidence for "Zobeba" (*ṣbbh*) being another name for or a corruption of Jabez (*y'bṣ*; Curtis and Madsen 1910: 108) is nonexistent.

"(and) the families of the brother of Rechab" (ומשפחות אחי רחב). This reconstruction is based partially on LXX[B] (*kai gennēseis adelphou Rhēchab*) and partially on MT "and the families of Aḥarḥel" (*'ḥrḥl*), which is corrupt (*pace* Allen 1974b: 29). Examining the form of "Aḥarḥel" (*'ḥ rḥl*) reveals that the difference between MT and LXX[B] (= *'ḥy rḥb*) is actually slight. The longer reading of LXX[L] seems to combine elements of both traditions: "these are the fathers of Noera of Araiēl [y Areēl] brother(s) of Rhēchab."

"and the sons of Harim" *(hrym)*. The text is "unquestionably in disarray" (Rudolph 1955: 30). My reconstruction is largely based on LXX. The contrast between LXX[B] *huiou Hiareim* (= **bny hrym*?) and MT "son of Harum" *(bn hrwm)* reflects, among other things, a *wāw/yôd* confusion (Allen 1974a: 161; 1974b: 117). LXX[L] lacks the expression altogether. In MT an offspring is referred to by the standard formula "PN_1 son of PN_2" without identifying precisely who PN_1 is ("the brother of Rechab").

4:9. "Jabez was more honored (נכבד) than his brothers." It is also possible to translate "Jabez was heavier than his brothers." If one follows the latter interpretation, the introduction to the tale explains why the birth of Jabez caused his mother so much suffering.

"in affliction" *(bʿṣb)*. So MT. LXX also plays on the name of Jabez *(Igabēs)* "sorrow" *(hōs gabēs)*, but *hōs gabēs* may presume *kʿbṣ* (Allen 1974b: 111).

4:10. "oh, that you would." The particle *ʾm* expresses the optative (GKC, §151e; Williams, §458). It is also possible to construe *ʾm* as signaling a condition with an implicit conclusion (GKC, §167a).

"enlarge" *(hrbyt)*. The emendation proposed by Begrich *(BHK)*, *hrḥbt* ("expand"), is unnecessary.

"territory" (גבול). Some translate "border," but גבול can mean land or territory, esp. in late texts (Josh 13:23, 25; 15:12, 47; Ezek 43:12; Mal 1:4).

"refrain from evil" *(ʿśyt mrʿh)*. A *dālet/rêš* confusion explains LXX[AN] *poiēses gnōsin* (= *ʿśyt mdʿh*). Some scholars assume that MT is corrupt. Begrich *(BHK)* suggests a number of emendations, including *marpeh* or *merḥāb lî* (cf. Arm. *misericordiam*). Rudolph (1955: 30) contends that MT reflects a haplography and inserts "victory" *(yšwʿty)* after *ʿśh*, hence "win victory" (cf. Isa 26:18). But MT may be idiomatic.

"from evil." Many Heb. MSS (מְרָעָה); MT מֵרָעָה.

"to afflict me" (עָצְבִּי). On the use of the nominal suf. with the inf., see Joüon §65a.

4:11. "Celub" *(klwb)*. So MT. LXX[AB], Syr., Vg. "Caleb" *(klb)*. The *Vorlage* of *Paraleipomenon* evidently was shorter (had fewer *matres lectionis*) than MT (Allen 1974b: 75–80). Compare, for instance, MT *byt rpʾ* with LXX *Bathrepha* (v. 12) and MT *mʿwnty* with LXX *Manathei* (v. 14).

"brother" *(ʾḥy)*. Reading with MT (maximum variation). The reading of a few Heb. MSS and LXX[AB], "father" *(ʾby)*, assimilates to "father" *(ʾby)* later in the verse.

"Shuḥah" *(šwḥh)*. Reading with MT *(lectio difficilior)*. The lemma of LXX[AB] *Ascha(s)* and Arm. *Eschas* corrects to 1 Chr 2:49 (LXX *Ascha*; MT *ʿksh*). Cf. Syr. *(d)ʾḥyʾ* (= *ʾḥyh*). It is possible, as some scholars assert, that metathesis has occurred: "Ḥushah" (*ḥwšh*; cf. v. 4). If so, "Shuḥah" could be the original reading (Jer 2:6; 18:20, 22; Prov 22:14; 23:27).

4:12. "Eshton sired" *(hwlyd)*. So MT and LXX. The impulse to emend the text to read "father" (Noth 1932: 106) results from a wooden understanding of what each genealogical formula conveys (1st NOTE to 2:42).

"Beth-rapha" *(byt rp')*. So MT. LXX[AN] *Bathrepha* (cf. LXX[B] c_2 *Bathraian*); Syr. *rwp'*. See the 1st TEXTUAL NOTE to v. 11.

"Paseaḥ." So MT. LXX[B] *Bessēe*; LXX[AN] *Phessē*.

"Teḥinnah." So MT (maximum variation). LXX[B] *Thaiman* (cf. LXX[A] Arm. *Thana*) replicates "Temen" in v. 6 (LXX* *Thaiman*).

"Naḥash." Thus MT *(lectio brevior)*. LXX adds "brother of Eselom [LXX[A] *Eselōm*; LXX[L] *Aththōm*] of the Qenizzites (= *'ḥy 'š/śl wn hqnzy*)."

"men of Recah" *('nšy rkh)*. So MT *(lectio difficilior)*. LXX[BL] "men of Rhechab" (LXX[A] *Rhēpha*), followed by Tg. (Knights 1987), assimilates to "brother of Rechab" in v. 8. See also Allen (1974b: 34).

4:13. "and the Maonathites." Thus LXX[L] *kai Maōnathei* (= *wmʿwnty*). Miniscule a *kai Manathei*. MT and LXX[AB] lack the phrase. A haplography has taken place at the end of v. 13 (see *wmʿwnty* at the beginning of v. 14).

4:14. "(and) the Maonathites." Reading with MT and LXX[L]. LXX[AB] *Manathei* (previous TEXTUAL NOTE).

4:15. "Ir . . . Qenaz." Syr.[A] expands to "the sons of Caleb son of Jephunneh. The name of his firstborn was Elah, and the name of his second was Naam, and the name of his third was *qʿz*, and the name of the fourth was *'syp*, and the name of his fifth was Joel, and the name of his sixth was *yrhwb*."

"Ir and Elah" *(ʿyr w'lh)*. MT and Tg. "Iru, Elah" *(ʿyrw 'lh)*. The evidence provided by LXX[B] c_2 *Ēr Adai*, Arm. *Erala*, and Vg. *Hir et Hela* point to a misdivision of the text (the connective *wāw* was mistakenly attached to the preceding PN). The PN "Ir" also appears in MT 1 Chr 7:12 (cf. "Iri" in 1 Chr 7:7). The alternative suggested by Curtis and Madsen (1910: 109) to reconstruct the "city of Elath" *(ʿyr 'ylt)*, is not compelling in light of the succeeding genealogy.

"the sons of Elah." Some would emend to "son," but this is not necessary (TEXTUAL NOTE to 2:8). For MT "Elah," compare LXX[B] c_2 *Ada*; LXX[AN] *Ala*, and see the 1st TEXTUAL NOTE to 9:8.

"Qenaz." Reading with a few Heb. MSS, LXX, and Tg. *(lectio brevior)*. MT and Vg. "and Qenaz" *(wqnz)*. Curtis and Madsen (1910: 104), followed by Japhet (1993a: 111), suggest a transposition: "these were the sons of Qenaz" *('lh bny qnz)*, referring to vv. 13–14. It is possible that a PN before Qenaz dropped out (Kittel 1902: 31).

4:16. "the sons of Jehallelel." So MT. LXX[B] *kai huios autou Geseēl, Amēachei*; LXX[A] *kai huios Iallelēm, Ziphli*. There is no compelling warrant to replace "Jehallelel" with "Jeraḥmeel" (contra Curtis and Madsen 1910: 104, with reference to 1 Chr 2:42).

"Tiria" (תיריא). Thus MT. One Palestinian ninth/tenth century C.E. fragment has terminal *hê*, תיריה (Revell 1969: 60).

"Asarel" *('śr'l)*. Reading with MT. LXX[B] *Iseraēl*; LXX[AN] *Eseraēl*; Arm. *Esrael*. The argument that the text is disturbed and should be emended to "Israel" is unlikely in view of the appearance of similar names elsewhere: "Asriel" *('śry'l*; Num 26:31; Josh 17:2; 1 Chr 7:14 [TEXTUAL NOTE]), "Asarelah" *('śrylh*; 1 Chr 25:2), and the collective "the Asrielites" (*h'śry'ly*; Num 26:31).

4:17. "sons of Ezrah." Reading with many Heb. MSS, LXX, and Vg. MT has "son."

"and Jalon." MT and LXX^AN. Allen (1974b: 149) suggests that LXX^B c_2 *Amōn* reflects a haplography after *kai*.

"(and) Jether sired." So LXX *kai egennēsen Iether* (= ויולד יתר). The verb was evidently lost by parablepsis after *wylwn* (Begrich in *BHK*; Rudolph 1955: 32), and *ytr* was corrupted to *wthr* (Allen 1974b: 137). The reading of MT, "and she became pregnant" *(wthr)*, contains both a non sequitur and an unususal construction (cf. 1 Chr 7:23; Allen 1974a: 117). NJPS masks the difficulty by translating *wthr* with a double verb, "she conceived and bore." Given the reconstruction proposed here, the emendation adopted by many commentators (e.g., Benzinger, Zöckler) of transposing the final summary clauses of v. 18 "These are [or 'were'] the sons of Bithiah . . ." to preface "she conceived Miriam" in v. 17 is unnecessary. Nevertheless, their insight that a transposition has taken place in the Heb. text is valid (see below).

"Miriam, Shammai, and Ishbah." So MT. Inner-Greek corruptions explain some, but not all, of the variants supplied by LXX^B *ton Maiōn kai ton Semen kai ton Mareth* and LXX^L *ton Meōr* (c_2 *Meōn*) *kai Iamein kai Narea* (c_2 *Mereth*; Allen 1974a: 104, 140; 1974b: 109). Some (e.g., Galling, Rudolph) believe that a loss of material has occurred at the end of v. 17.

4:18–19. "these are the sons of Bithiah." The initial reading of MT v. 18 is puzzling, "and his wife the Judahite" *(w'štw hyhdyh)*. LXX^B *kai hē gynē autou hautē Hadeia* (cf. dfjpqtz *Haidia*; LXX^AN *Hidia*). LXX may presume *hy' hdyh* (Allen 1974b: 105, 155). Begrich *(BHK)* thinks that a few words are missing from the beginning of v. 18. Certainly, the summary at the end of v. 18, "these are [or 'were'] the sons of Bithiah daughter of Pharaoh, whom Mered wed," conflicts with the statements made at the beginning of the verse. To complicate matters further, MT v. 19 begins with the rubric "the sons of the wife of Hodiah" *('št hwdyh*; cf. LXX^B *gynaikos tēs Hidouias*). Solutions to these problems vary. Rudolph (1955: 34), for instance, reconstructs "and Mered had two wives, one Egyptian and one Judahite" *wlmrd šty nšym 'šh mṣryh w'šh yhwdyh)*. I would suggest an alternative reconstruction that also addresses the difficulties at the beginning of v. 19. A dittography (*w'štw hyhdyh* [MT] in v. 18 from **'štw hyhwdyh* [*'št hwdyh* MT] in v. 19) triggered a displacement in the sequence of v. 18, which originally read "These are the sons of Bithiah the daughter of Pharaoh, whom Mered wed. She gave birth to Jered . . . father of Zanoaḥ." The text continued (v. 19) "The sons of his Judahite wife." There are three advantages to this reconstruction. First, it addresses the repetition in vv. 18–19. Second, it involves rearranging the text without resorting to large-scale text-critical surgery. Third, it does justice to the claims in vv. 18–19 that two different wives were responsible for the two different sets of children.

"Ḥeber" (חבר). Thus MT. LXX^B *Habeisa*; LXX^ALN *Haber*.

"Jequthiel." LXX^B *Chetiēl*; b'e_2 *Iephthiēl*; b *Iephthēēl*. The PN *(yĕqûtî'ēl)* may be understood as "God is my protection" (Layton 1990b: 137–38) or as "God will nourish" (Noth 1928: 36, 203; Fowler 1988: 99, 359).

"Bithiah." So MT. LXX^B *Gelia*; LXX^L *Phaththouia*; LXX^AN *Beththia*.

"Mered." So MT. LXX^B *Nōrōēl* may be influenced by *Chetiēl* in v. 18 (Allen 1974b: 23). Cf. LXX^AN *Mōrēd*; LXX^L *Marō*; Arm. *Marou*. Again, Begrich *(BHK)* thinks that a few words are missing at the end of v. 18.

4:19. "his Judahite wife" *(ʾštw hyhwdyh)*. So the proposal of Rothstein and Hänel (1927), based on LXX^{AN} *(Hioudaias)* and the context (v. 18). The lemma of MT "the wife of Hodiah" *(ʾšt hwdyh*; cf. LXX^{B} *gynaikos tēs Hidouias)* has suffered haplography.

"sister of Naḥam." LXX^{B} continues "and Daleila was the father of Qeila and Semegon was the father of Joman and Manaem the father of Qeila" *(kai Daleila patēr Keeila kai Semegōn patēr Iōman kai Manaēm patros Keeila)*. Instead of *Manaēm*, LXX^{AN} have "the sons of Naem" *(huioi Naēm = bny nḥm)*. Some scholars think that the addition may be original. In this view, MT has suffered a haplography by *homoioteleuton* (Rudolph 1955: 34–36; cf. Allen 1974b: 82, 138–39). I am more inclined to view the plus as an addition interpolated through repetitive resumption from *dlyh ʾby qʿylh* to *ʾby qʿylh*. As a result of this insertion both Daleila and Menaḥem (or the sons of Naḥam) become the father of Qeilah.

"the Garmite" (הגרמי). So MT and LXX^{L}. LXX^{B} *Hatamei*; LXX^{AN} *ho Tarmi*.

"Eshtemoa" (אשתמע). Rudolph (1955: 36) emends to "Ishi," but this simply harmonizes v. 19 with v. 20.

4:20. "Shimon" *(šymwn)*. So MT. The difference with LXX *Semiōn* (= *šmywn*) reflects a transposition.

"Tilon." I read with Qere, LXX^{A} (cf. c*e *Thēlōn*), Vg., Tg., and Arm. Kethib "Tolon." LXX^{B} c_2 *Inōn;* LXX^{L} *huios Thōleim (b -lēm)*.

"son of Zoḥeth." Thus MT. LXX "sons." Some (e.g., Kittel, Williamson) think that a few words have dropped out at the end of this verse. Syr. for this verse bears expected affinities with vv. 20–21, but also unexpected affinities with v. 19, "and the sons of Shimon, Amon, Rumiah, and Rinnah, and Shelah" (= *wbny šmywn ʾmwn wrwmyh wrnh wšlh*). The continuation of the verse, "these were the sons of Judah brother of Naḥum father of Qeilah" (= *ʾlh bny yhwdyh ʾḥy nḥwm ʾby qʿylh*), both depends on and diverges from v. 19.

4:21. "Shelah" (שלה). The rendering of this name as *Sēlōm* (LXX^{AB} *Sēlōm*; LXX^{L} ac_2 *Sēlōn*; cf. Arm. *Selaunay*) is fairly consistent (Gen 38:5, 11, 14, 26; 46:12; Num 26:20; cf. 1 Chr 2:3).

"Laadah father of Mareshah." Thus MT, LXX^{A}, LXX^{L} (*Lada* [bb'e_2 *Ladēi*] *patēr Marēsa* [e_2 *Madisa*]), and Arm. LXX^{B} c_2 *Madath patēr Maicha*.

"the house of linen work" *(byt-ʿbdt hbwṣ)*. Reading with MT. As Allen (1974a: 62; 1974b: 124) points out, the Greek translator transliterated part of this phrase (e.g., LXX^{B} c_2 *oikiōn ephrath habak*), perhaps because his *Vorlage* was defective.

4:22. "(and) Joqim" (ויוקים). LXX *kai Iōakeim*. Rudolph (1955: 36) argues that the text evinces a haplography by *homoioteleuton*, hence "the house of dye-workers and weavers" *(ʾt-byt ṣbʿ wrqm)*.

"Cozeba" *(kzbʾ)*. Thus MT, LXX^{AN} (cf. Arm. *Chuzeba*). LXX^{B} *Sōchētha*; c_2 *Sōchēth*.

"Joash" *(ywʾš)*. So MT, LXX^{AN}, Arm. LXX^{B} *Iōada*.

"Saraph" *(śrp)*. So MT, LXX^{AN}, Arm. LXX^{B} *Saia*; c_2 *Sōa*.

"who married into Moab" *(ʾšr bʿlw lmwʾb)*. Thus MT. LXX^{AB} "who resided in Moab" *(hoi katōkēsan en Mōab)*. My translation follows NJPS. Because some commentators (Rothstein; Rudolph; R. Braun) assume that *bʿl* indicates rule over Moab, they deem the text corrupt. Dijkstra (1975) thinks that *bʿlw* may be a dialectal variant of *pʿlw*, "they worked for." But the most common meaning of the verb *bʿl* is "to marry" (Gen 20:3; Deut 21:13; 22:22; 24:1; Isa 54:1, 5; 62:4, 5; Mal 2:11; Prov 30:23). This is also how Tg. understands *bʿl*.

"and they resided in Bethleḥem." MT's *wyšby lḥm* is defective. LXX^{B} *kai apestrepsen autous* (= *wyšb lhm*?). It is possible to construe MT's *wyšby lḥm* as "the dwellers of Leḥem" (Williamson 1982b: 61). Cf. "dwellers of Netaim" *yšby nṭʿym* in v. 23. A *wāw*/*yôd* confusion is also possible, "and they returned to Bethleḥem" (*wyšbw byt lḥm*; Kittel; Begrich [*BHK*]; Rudolph). I prefer to read, "and they resided in Bethleḥem" (*wyšbw byt lḥm*) or "they resided in Leḥem" (*wyšbw lḥm*), assuming that *byt* was dropped, as it sometimes was in compound names (Aharoni 1979: 121). Cf. "they resided there," *yšbw šm* in v. 23.

"the records are ancient" (*hdbrym ʿtyqym*). The translator of LXX evidently found his *Vorlage* corrupt and transliterated *habedērein athoukiein* (= *hbdryn ʿtqyn*). LXX^{L} *hoi de logoi palaioi eisi kai Debeir* (*b Dabēr*; b′y *Dab*[*e*]*ir*) *kai Nathoukeim*.

4:23. "they." So MT (*hmh*). LXX (*houtoi* = *ʾlh*).

"and residents." So MT. LXX, Tg., and Vg. lack the *wāw*.

"with the king" (*ʿm hmlk*). Construing the prep. *ʿm* as denoting assistance (Williams, §336).

"in his service" (*bmlʾktw*). So MT and LXX^{L}. LXX^{AB} "in his kingdom" (= *bmmlktw*) may reflect influence from *hmlk*. LXX adds "they grew strong" (*enischysan*).

Notes

4:1. "descendants of Judah." The introduction to the third section of the genealogy of Judah (בני יהודה) replicates the introduction to the first section of the genealogy (2:3). After the intervening royal Davidic genealogy, the writers return the reader's attention to the major phratries of Judah.

"Perez, Ḥezron, Caleb, Ḥur, and Shobal." At first glance, one might think that these were brothers. Indeed, this is the normal significance of the pattern "the sons of PN_1: PN_2, PN_3, and PN_4" in the genealogies. But here the pattern indicates, broadly speaking, a line of descent (see 2:4–5, 9, 19, 21–24, 50–52). One may compare it with the linear genealogies of 1:1–4, 24–27, but those genealogies are not prefaced with "the sons of PN_1" introduction. What the writer offers is a capsule summary of the Perizzite phratry of the Judahite tribe. Having done so, he sets the stage for the lineage of Reaiah (son of Shobal), which follows (v. 2).

"Perez." One of Judah's two sons by Tamar (2:4).

"Ḥezron." One of the two sons of Perez (2:5).

"Caleb." A son of Ḥezron (2:9), Caleb is a major figure in the first set of Judahite lineages (2:18–20, 42–50).

"Ḥur" was a son of Caleb (2:19, 24).

"Shobal." A son of Ḥur (2:50–52).

4:2–23. "Reaiah son of Shobal." One of the unusual features of the genealogies of these verses is their order. In the lines that follow the introduction of v. 1, the writer follows a broadly ascending order. He begins with one of the youngest descendants of Judah mentioned in 2:3–55; Reaiah son of Shobal (v. 2; cf. 2:52), continues with the next youngest Ḥur (v. 4), and later provides a genealogy for Ashḥur son of Ḥezron (vv. 5–7). Genealogies for two different Calebs follow later (vv. 11, 15). The author concludes with Shelah son of Judah (vv. 21–23). With the clear exception of Shelah (vv. 21–23), most of the lineages in vv. 2–23 evidently pertain to descendants of Perez (2:4–5). This suggests, however, more of a tightly knit order to these lineages than there is. In contrast to the pattern of the Davidic genealogy in which a continuous line of descent is sketched over many centuries, there are hardly any connecting links among these Judahite lineages. The lines are mostly coordinate. In brief, 4:2–23 is basically a collection of miscellaneous genealogies. Some explicitly develop parts of the opening rubric (v. 1), while others do not. Some resonate with lineages in 2:3–55, while others do not. The significance of this mode of presentation is best addressed in the section on SOURCES AND COMPOSITION.

4:2. "son of Shobal." Reaiah is referred to as "Haroeh" in 2:52. This segmented genealogy picks up the thread of 2:52–53, which detail Shobal's lineage.

"families of the Zorathites" *(hṣrʿty)*. The writer of 2:53 claims that the Zorathites *(hṣrʿty)* were one of two families that stemmed from other families, who populated Qiriath-jearim. That the authors of Chronicles acknowledge multiple claims about Zorathite origins may reflect a series of different historical migrations (Niemann 1999).

4:3. "sons of Eṭam" (עיטם). There is no stated connection with the preceding genealogy of Reaiah. Even if the emendation proposed by some scholars making Eṭam a son of Ḥur (2nd TEXTUAL NOTE to v. 3) were adopted, the sons listed (Jezreel, Ishma, etc.) do not match any of the sons listed in 2:20, 50. "Eṭam" *(Aitam)* is mentioned as part of Judah's allotment in the so-called Bethleḥem district (LXX Josh 15:59a). Boling (1982: 391) identifies Eṭam as *ʿAin ʿAṭān*, which preserves its ancient name, but the actual site is more likely to be Khirbet el-Ḫōḥ, a few km southwest of Bethleḥem. Eṭam also appears in the genealogy of Simeon (4:32) and in the list of Reḥoboam's fortresses (2 Chr 11:6).

"Jezreel." Not the famous Jezreel southeast of Megiddo, but evidently an unidentified village in southern Judah (Josh 15:56; 1 Sam 25:43; Kallai 1986a: 390).

4:4. "Penuel was the father of Gedor." There is no introductory formula to this ascending segmented genealogy. Most of the names in this lineage are toponyms. Penuel and Ezer (עֵזֶר), as well as their father Ḥur, are all founders of towns. Penuel ("face of God") served for some time as the capital of the northern kingdom under Jeroboam I (1 Kgs 12:25). See also Gen 32:32 and Judg 8:4–17. Penuel is occasionally associated with Tulūl ed-Dhahab eš-Šerqîyeh in Gilead, but more recently with T. Dēir ʿAllā (e.g., B. MacDonald 2000: 148–49). In Chronicles, the name Penuel also appears as a family of Benjamin (8:25 [Qere]).

"Gedor," identified as Khirbet Jedûr, is situated about 5 km north of Beth-zur.

Gedor is listed in the Judahite inheritance (Josh 15:58). Given the mention of Penuel, the author is positing some long-range migrations and contacts between the Transjordan and Judah. See also 1 Chr 2:21–24 and 4:18 (MT).

"Ḥushah." Two of David's warriors were Ḥush(ath)ites (2 Sam 21:18; 23:27; 1 Chr 11:29; 20:4; 27:11). "Ḥushah" (חושה), associated with modern *Ḥūsān*, was located a few km southwest of Bethleḥem.

"sons of Ḥur." In the author's pattern of ascending lineages, Ḥur is mentioned after Reaiah his grandson (NOTE to vv. 2–23). The claim that Ḥur was the firstborn of Ephrathah is consistent with 1 Chr 2:50.

"father of Bethleḥem." In 1 Chr 2:51 Salma son of Ḥur bears this distinction.

4:5. "Ashḥur father of Teqoa." The segmented lineage of vv. 5–7 with no opening or closing formulas nicely continues the Ḥezronite lineage of 2:21–24, which ends by mentioning that Abijah, wife of Ḥezron, "bore him Ashḥur father of Teqoa." Since Ashḥur is a son of Caleb (2:24), the authors of the Judahite genealogy are moving in an inverse order from the descending order they pursued in the first section of the Judahite genealogy (2:3–55). Like the figures in the previous genealogical list, Ashḥur is the founder ("father") of a town. "Teqoa" (Θεκὼ) is part of the so-called Bethleḥem district of Judah (LXX Josh 15:60).

"two wives: Ḥelah and Naarah." The segmented genealogies of vv. 6–7 detail the offspring of these two women. Unfortunately, many of the names are obscure.

4:6. "Ḥepher" (חפר). The precise referent is unclear. Ḥepher, which appears as a PN in the list of David's warriors (11:36), is usually associated with the land of Manasseh. Ḥepher appears as a son of Gilead (Num 26:32–33; 27:1) and is part of Manasseh's allotment (Josh 17:2–3). In one reconstruction, Ḥepher is associated with el-Ifshâr (Aharoni 1979: 310, 436) on the Sharon near the Mediterranean coast. In another reconstruction, Ḥepher refers to T. el-Muḥaffar, on the northwestern side of the Plain of Dothan (Zertal 1992; Na'aman 1986a: 182). Kallai (1986a: 53–54) thinks that Ḥepher refers to an entire region (cf. 1 Kgs 4:10).

"Aḥashtarite" (אחשתרי). Apparently, a Persian loan word (Esth 8:10, 14).

4:7. "Zoḥar" (צחר) appears in two other contexts: as a family name for Ephron of Ḥebron (Gen 23:8; 25:9) and as a son (clan) of Simeon (Gen 46:10).

4:8. "Qoz sired Annub." The beginning of another brief genealogy, apparently unconnected to the preceding (see the TEXTUAL NOTES to v. 8). Like the previous genealogies, the genealogy of Qoz contains at least one toponym. There are also connections between socioethnic and geographic circumstances. "Annub" (*ʿnwb*) may well be equivalent to Anab (*ʿnb*), Khirbet ʿInâb eṣ-Ṣeġîrah, located in the southern hill country some 22 km south of Ḥebron (Josh 15:50).

"Rechab" perhaps refers to the father of Jonadab, the founding father of the Rechabites (last NOTE to 2:55). If so, the author is positing an indirect link between the Rechabites and a particular branch of Judahites—the descendants of Qoz.

"Harim." The son(s) of Harim are mentioned in two other postexilic contexts: the list of those who agreed to divorce their wives (Ezra 10:31) and the narrative portraying the rebuilding of Jerusalem's wall (Neh 3:11).

4:9. "more honored than his brothers." This carefully written anecdote introduces a new section in 4:1–23 connected directly neither with what follows nor with what precedes (Japhet 1993a: 108–11). In 2:55 "Jabez" *(yʿbṣ)* is mentioned as a town in which various families of scribes reside. The story evinces a chiastic design:

a Introduction: Jabez's distinguished status
  b Explanation of name: Mother's affliction in childbirth
  b′ Request for relief: Jabez's connection with affliction
a′ Conclusion: Jabez's success

"in affliction" *(bʿṣb)*. The Heb. plays on the name of Jabez *(yʿbṣ)*. In the ancient Semitic world, names often characterized a person's identity (e.g., *Enūma eliš* I.1–18 [Dalley 1989: 233]; Gen 2:19–20; 17:5, 15–16; 32:28–29). The story treats the circumstances of Jabez's birth as an omen; his mother gave birth to him "in affliction" *(bʿṣb)*; cf. Gen 3:16). Jabez asks the God of Israel to free him from an association between his name and his fate, "so that I might not suffer affliction" *(bʿṣby)*.

4:10. "invoked the God of Israel." As Williamson (1982b: 59–60) points out, this vignette anticipates an important theme in the Chronicler's narration of the monarchy: the importance of prayer. Because the text speaks of his calling out to "the God of Israel," some scholars (e.g., De Vries 1989: 46) doubt whether Jabez is an Israelite. The context suggests that he is.

"granted what he requested." This illustrates another one of the Chronicler's favorite themes: the coherence between actions and effects.

4:11. "Celub . . . sired." This introduces a three-generation genealogy that is both linear (v. 11) and segmented (v. 12) in form. Given his identification ("brother of Shuḥah"), this Caleb is to be distinguished from Caleb (a.k.a. Celubai) son of Ḥezron (2:18) and brother of Jeraḥmeel (2:9, 18) and from Caleb the son of Jephunneh (4:15).

4:12. "Beth-rapha" (בית רפא) is most probably a place-name, but its precise location is not known. Given the context, it would seem to lie in the region between Bethleḥem and Ḥebron.

"Paseaḥ" (פסח) is mentioned only in postexilic sources. It appears both as a family name of Temple servants (*ntnym*; Ezra 2:49//Neh 7:51; Noth 1928: 227) and as the patronymic of Joiada, who worked on the walls of Jerusalem (Neh 3:6).

"Teḥinnah." The PN also appears in a fourth-century B.C.E. fiscal document found at Ketef Jeriḥo (Eshel and Misgav 1988: 169).

"Ir-Naḥash" (עיר נחש), meaning "town of bronze," may refer to Dēr Naḫḫās, 9 km north of Lydda (*HALOT* 691), or to Khirbet en-Naḥâs at the northern end of the Arabah (Aharoni 1979: 436). In this context, a location so far to the southeast would be surprising, unless most of the place-names associated with the Qenizzites (see below) actually pertain to sites in the Arabah, on the slopes of Edom (Kallai 1986a: 117–18).

4:13–14. "sons of Qenaz" *(qnz)*. In this segmented lineage, both individuals and families are presented as founders of towns. As we have seen (1st NOTE to 1:36), Qenaz has strong links to southern Canaan. One Qenaz appears as the son of Eliphaz in the line of Esau (1 Chr 1:36//Gen 36:11), while another appears as an Edomite chieftain (1 Chr 1:53//Gen 36:42). In the vision of Abram (Gen

15:13–21), the Qenizzites are one of many indigenous peoples who inhabit Canaan (Gen 15:19). Caleb son of Jephunneh (1 Chr 4:15) appears as a Qenizzite in Num 32:12 and Josh 14:6, 14 (1st NOTE to 4:15). First Samuel 27:10 and 30:29 portray David and his band as launching raids against the Qenizzites (so LXX^{B}; 4QSam^{a}; cf. MT "Qenites"). In Chronicles, however, the Qenizzites become Judahite.

"Othniel" is sometimes mentioned as a son of Qenaz (Josh 15:17; Judg 1:13; 3:9, 11), but here Othniel may be a clan name. In Josh 15:17 and Judg 1:13, Othniel is described as a kinsman of Caleb.

"Maonathites" *(mʿwnty)*. The text of 1 Chr 2:45 (1st NOTE) lists Maon *(mʿwn)* as the son of Shammai, one of the descendants of Caleb of Ḥezron.

4:14. "sired Ophrah." In 1 Chr 2:45 Maon appears as the founder of Beth-zur. In this case, the Maonathites establish Ophrah. A town by this name is identified with eṭ-Ṭayyĭbeh, northeast of Bethel. That Ophrah is sometimes associated with Benjamin (Josh 18:23; 1 Sam 13:17), while at other times with Manasseh (Judg 6:11) may reflect shifting borders in the course of Israelite and Judahite history. Aharoni (1979: 323) contends that Ophrah *(ʿprh)* is one of the dependencies of Bethel—"Ephrayin" (*ʿpryn*; Qere) or "Ephron" (*ʿprwn*; Kethib)—taken from the northern kingdom by Abijah of Judah (2 Chr 13:19).

"Seraiah (*śĕrāyâ*) sired Joab." This is probably the source of the comment by Josephus (*Ant.* 7.11) that the father of Joab (the commander-in-chief of David) was named *Souri* (cf. LXX^{B} 4:14 *Saraia*; bc$_{2}$ *Sarai*; LXX^{A} *Saria*). Biblical sources consistently list Joab's mother as Zeruiah, identified as the sister of David in 1 Chr 2:16, but do not mention Joab's father (1 Sam 26:6; 2 Sam 2:13; 3:39; 8:16; 14:1; 16:9; 17:25; 18:2; 19:22; 21:17; 23:18, 37; 1 Kgs 1:7; 2:5, 22; 1 Chr 11:6, 39; 18:12, 15; 26:28; 27:24).

"Ge-Ḥarashim" *(gyʾ ḥršym)* means "Valley of Craftsmen." The obtuse comment may suggest that Joab from the family of Seraiah was credited with founding a colony of artisans in this particular valley. In Sirach the high value of scribes and rulers is contrasted with that of artisans, potters, and smiths, whose skills are essential to urban life but who are neither sought out for advice nor "attain eminence in the public assembly" (Sir 38:27–34). There is some truth to Ben Sira's judgment. The work of scribes was prized in both ancient Egypt (Wente 1995: 2218–20) and ancient Mesopotamia (Pearce 1995). Nevertheless, Ben Sira's verdict is too severe. Assyrian kings sometimes had themselves portrayed as workmen carrying tools in foundation rituals (Matthews 1995: 459). Such displays suggest a certain respect for the work of craftsmen and would be most surprising if society held artisans in low esteem. The congregation of craftsmen within a particular section of a town or within a certain geographical area finds precedent elsewhere in the ancient Mediterranean world (Matthews 1995: 460–61; 1st NOTE to 2:55). The location of "Ge-Ḥarashim" is unknown. Some scholars (e.g., Aharoni 1979: 245) favor a site southeast of the Dead Sea, but "Ge-Ḥarashim" is mentioned in the idealized list of MT Neh 11:35 as a residence of Persian period Benjaminites.

4:15. "Caleb son of Jephunneh." Because this new reference to Caleb is surprising, some scholars (e.g., Benzinger, Kittel, Curtis and Madsen) view the entire verse as a later interpolation. Three considerations tell against such a maneuver. First, there is no text-critical evidence for seeing this verse as secondary. Second, there is no great conflict with surrounding lineages. In 4:1–23 one finds a collection of genealogies listed seriatim, rather than a uniform and continuous lineage. Third, the reasons given for excising v. 15 have to do with a perceived tension with earlier claims (2:9, 18–20, 42–50), specifically that Caleb son of Ḥezron is somehow equivalent to Caleb son of Jephunneh. If so, this lineage would either contradict the material in 1 Chronicles 2 or be redundant. But the genealogies of Judah, including the Calebite lineages, have to be understood in their own right—related to but also independent of earlier biblical traditions. The distinctiveness of the approach taken in Chronicles can be seen by comparing it with earlier biblical statements about Caleb. Caleb son of Jephunneh is prominent in the traditions of Israel's conquest as one out of only two of the original twelve spies to make it into the land of Canaan (Num 13:6; 14:6, 30, 38; 26:65; 32:12; 34:19; Deut 1:36; 1 Chr 6:41). His loyal conduct won him the gift of Ḥebron (Josh 14:13–14). As for his provenance, both Caleb son of Jephunneh and the Calebites are associated with southern parts of Canaan (Josh 14:6–15; 15:13–17; Judg 1:20; 1 Sam 25:2–3). In fact, there is doubt as to whether either the Calebites or the Qenizzites were originally Israelites (Gen 36:9–11, 15, 42; 1 Sam 30:14; Mendenhall 1973: 162; R. Braun 1986: 33; 1st NOTE to vv. 13–14). Caleb is sometimes called a Qenizzite (Num 32:12; Josh 14:6, 14) and sometimes a brother of Qenaz (Josh 15:17; Judg 1:13; 3:9). Only the Priestly writers, it seems, regard Caleb as fully Judahite (Num 13:6; 34:19). The Priestly view of Caleb's pedigree undoubtedly had some influence on the Chronicler, but the earlier sources did as well.

The portrayals of Caleb in Pentateuchal and Deuteronomistic sources shed some light on the Chronicler's presentation of multiple Calebs: Caleb son of Jephunneh, Caleb son of Ḥezron (2:9, 18) and brother of Jeraḥmeel (2:42), and Caleb brother of Shuḥah (4:11). The very manner in which they are identified suggests that they represent different figures. As Japhet (1993a: 113) points out, the Chronicler differentiates among various Calebite elements within the tribe of Judah. Japhet regards the Chronicler's complex stance as mainly independent of and more historically accurate than that found in the Hexateuch. In my judgment, the Chronistic presentation of Caleb son of Jephunneh is both indebted to and different from earlier presentations. A main section of the tribe appears as descendants of Ḥezron. This branch, fully integrated into Judah and central to its collective identity (2:9, 18–20, 42–50), attracts some of the features associated with Caleb son of Jephunneh in Pentateuchal traditions and the Deuteronomistic History. Although the bulk of coverage is devoted to the descendants of Caleb son of Ḥezron, this coverage is complemented by two minor sections devoted to Caleb brother of Shuḥah (4:11–12) and Caleb son of Jephunneh (4:15). Ironically, the Caleb who receives the most attention elsewhere in biblical sources receives the least attention here. Moreover, neither of the minor Calebite branches is completely integrated into the tribe through clear genealogical links. In the case of Caleb brother of Shuḥah, little more can be said, because his roots are obscure. In the case of Caleb *ben* Jephunneh, there is more to go on. The lack of complete integration into Judah may be explained, in part, by the author's exegesis of earlier biblical materials. Like some biblical writers, he acknowledges an association between the Calebites and the Qenizzites. He situates the lineage of Jephunnite Caleb immediately after the lineage of Qenaz (vv. 13–14). Indeed, one of the descendants of Caleb is Qenaz (v. 15). Like the Priestly writers, this writer renders Caleb son of Jephunneh as a Judahite. Hence, both the Qenizzites and the Calebites (from Jephunneh) are Judahite, but neither is fully integrated into one of Judah's main phratries. Not fully affiliating Caleb with the other Judahite lineages creates some distance between them. In this way, the Chronicler negotiates the positions contained within his sources and pursues his own distinctive direction.

"Ir, Elah, and Naam." These descendants differ from those mentioned in the other Calebite lineages (2:18–20, 42–50; 4:11). Save for the occurrence of Elah in the "Valley of Elah," the names are not common. Wellhausen (1870: 39) associates the PN Ir with Iram (Ir with an *-ām* ending), one of the chieftains of Edom (1:54). Granting the possibility of an Edomite connection, it is relevant that the writer places these entities within the compass of Judah's heritage (COMMENT).

"the sons of Elah: Qenaz." The relationship between this Qenaz and the Qenaz of v. 13 is not stated. Given their disparate contexts, the two could be treated as different entities. But given that the genealogies of 4:1–23 generally follow an ascending order, beginning with Reaiah (v. 2) and ending with Shelah (v. 21), there may be a link between them. Following an inverse order, the sons of Qenaz (v. 13) should appear before Qenaz himself (v. 15). If this supposition is correct, the Chronicler's stance on the relationship between Caleb son of Jephunneh and Qenaz varies somewhat from earlier biblical positions in that he makes Caleb neither a Qenizzite (Num 32:12; Josh 14:6, 14) nor a brother of Qenaz (Josh 15:17; Judg 1:13; 3:9). By presenting Qenaz as a grandson of Caleb, the writer may turn Qenaz into a Calebite. In any case, he affirms a relationship between them (1st NOTE to v. 15).

4:16. "Jehallelel." This name is only mentioned twice in the Heb. Scriptures. The other Jehallelel is a Levite belonging to the sons of Merari (2 Chr 29:12).

"Ziph and Ziphah." Ziph is mentioned as the firstborn of Mesha the son of Caleb in 2:42 (2nd NOTE). Japhet (1993a: 114) would identify Ziphah as the other Ziph in the Judahite inheritance (Josh 15:24), associated with a site southwest of Kurnub by Boling (1982: 382).

"Tiria (תיריא) and Asarel (אשׂראל)." The locations are unknown. The former is a *hapax legomenon.* Asriel (אשׂריאל) appears in some texts as a Manassite clan with connections to Gilead (Num 26:31; Josh 17:2; 1 Chr 7:14 [1st TEXTUAL NOTE]; cf. 1 Chr 25:2 אשׂראלה). The name *šr'l* appears in the Samaria ostraca (#42, 48) as the name of a district (Davies, §§3.042.1; 048.1; Lemaire 1973a: 239–43; Na'aman 1986a: 159–60). The connection, if any, between Manassite Asriel and Judahite Asarel is unclear.

4:17–19. "sons of Ezrah." This segmented genealogy comprises a distinct unit, tracing Ezrah's descendants through two of his sons: Jether and Mered. Each of these two sons functions as the founder of towns. The organization of Mered's offspring reflects the bigamous and endogamous relationships of their father (vv. 18–19). On the formidable textual problems that these verses present, see the relevant TEXTUAL NOTES.

4:17. "Epher" (עפר) is also the name of a son of Midian in 1 Chr 1:33(//Gen 25:4). Another Epher appears as a chieftain within Manasseh (5:24).

"Jether sired Miriam." The only other Miriam in biblical tradition is Moses' sister, one of the leaders of early Israel (Exod 15:20; Num 12:1–15; 20:1; 26:59; Deut 24:9; Mic 6:4; 1 Chr 5:29).

"Eshtemoa" *(ʾštmʿ)* or "Eshtemoah" *(ʾštmh), es-Samûʿa,* was located in the hill country of Judah south of Ḥebron (Josh 15:50; 21:14; 1 Sam 30:28). In 1 Chr 6:42 (//Josh 21:14) Eshtemoa is a town of refuge for the sons of Aaron.

4:18. "Bithiah the daughter of Pharaoh, whom Mered wed (לקח)." A most unusual case in which a Judahite (Mered) marries one of the daughters of the Egyptian king. The question that must be considered here is not whether Egyptian royal daughters were given in marriage more often than most scholars have realized, a matter of considerable debate (Kitchen 1986), but what the stated effect of such a purported marriage is on Judah. The author connects three sites (literally grandchildren) with this connubium: Gedor, Soco, and Zanoaḥ. In this respect, the genealogy documents a Judean writer's admission of traditional Egyptian interests in southern Judah.

"Gedor." On the location, see the 2nd NOTE to v. 4. The authors acknowledge multiple claims about Gedor's origins and affiliations.

"Soco" (שׂוכו). This probably refers to the Soco located southwest of Ḥebron and west of Eshtemoa (Josh 15:48). Another Soco is situated in the Shephelah (Josh 15:35; 1 Sam 17:1; 2 Chr 11:7; 28:18).

"Zanoaḥ" (זנוח). There are two possibilities for the location of Zanoaḥ: one near Beth-shemesh in northern Judah (Josh 15:34; Neh 3:13; 11:30) and the other an unidentified site in southern Judah (Josh 15:56; Kallai 1986a: 390). Given the context, the latter possibility is more probable.

4:19. "Naḥam" (נחם). Not otherwise attested.

"Qeilah (קעילה) the Garmite." The only context in which a Garmite is mentioned. "Qeilah" (Khirbet Qîlā) is located 13.5 km northwest of Ḥebron. Although Qeilah is mentioned as a Judahite possession in Josh 15:44, the narrative of 1 Sam 23:1–13 presupposes that it lies deep within Philistine territory. During the monarchy it may have been an independent town that, because of its location, was important to both Israelite and Philistine interests. In one Persian period text, Qeilah appears as a district *(plk)* under Judean control (Neh 3:17–18).

"Eshtemoa the Maacathite." The Maacathites appear in a variety of contexts: as a non-Israelite group within the territory assigned to Manasseh (Deut 3:14; Josh 13:11); as the inhabitants of an Aramaean land (Josh 12:5) or kingdom (2 Sam 10:6); and as the residents of Beth-maacah near Dan (2 Sam 20:14–15; McCarter 1984: 429–30). The possibilities are not mutually exclusive (last NOTE to 9:35). Given the admission that the Maacathites lived alongside the Israelites (Josh 13:13), it would not be surprising that some Maacathite elements became part of

Israel and Judah (2 Sam 23:34; 2 Kgs 25:23//Jer 40:8). We have already seen Maacah referred to as Caleb's wife (2:48). In this case, the connection may run in the opposite direction. A Maacathite appears as genealogically related to a Judahite clan living in southern Judah.

4:20. "sons of Shimon." Like most of the lineages in 4:1–23, this terse genealogy is not directly connected to what precedes or follows.

"Ishi." There is no patronymic given for this Ishi and it appears doubtful that he is related to Jeraḥmeelite Ishi (2:31; see the previous NOTE).

4:21. "sons of Shelah." This rubric introduces the final section of the genealogy of Judah (vv. 21–23). In referring to Shelah, the text reverts to the very beginning—the third son of Judah (2:3–4). This branch of the Judahite tribe—the Shelanites (*hšlny*)—is not well-attested in the Persian period (Neh 11:5//1 Chr 9:5 [1st TEXTUAL NOTE]).

"Er." Another instance of neponymy (2nd NOTE to 2:25).

"Lecah" (לכה) has occasionally been associated with Lachish, but this identification is uncertain.

"Mareshah." In 1 Chr 2:42 the sons of Mareshah are depicted as descendants of Caleb "the father" (= founder) of Ḥebron, suggesting affiliations between the Shelanites and the Calebites. On the location, see the 3rd NOTE to 2:42.

"families (משפחות) of the house of linen work." The reference to a lineage's devotion to a specialized craft is fascinating. In the ancient Mediterranean world such skills normally would be passed down through the generations, and professional lineages could endure for centuries. In certain cases, professions could even be used as family names (Weisberg 1967: 77–85; Matthews 1995: 463). Examination of studies on crafts in ancient Israel (e.g., Macalister 1905; Mendelsohn 1940a; de Vaux 1965: 76–78; Demsky 1966: 212–15) reveals that a good deal of the evidence cited stems from Chronicles (2:55; 4:14, 21, 23) and another postexilic text (Neh 3:8, 31–32; 11:35). Rather than focus exclusively on the monarchy, it seems prudent to recognize that the Persian period witnessed a growing interest in the organization and development of certain professions. Indeed, this was a period in which markets and international trade flourished. Although craftsmen could be organized in groups and families, there is no clear evidence for the rise of professional guilds with their own constitutions and officials before the fifth century B.C.E. (Matthews 1995: 463; *pace* Weisberg 1967: 101–5). The rise of such professional associations may be linked to developments in the West.

"linen work" (הבץ). This term for linen בֻּץ or בוץ (cf. Akk. *bûṣu*; Phoen. *bṣ*), technically byssus, is almost exclusively found in late sources (except 2 Sam 6:14). Earlier sources refer to שֵׁשׁ (e.g., Gen 41:42; Exod 25:4; 26:1, 31, 36; 28:5; 39:27). According to Ezek 27:16, fine linen was a commodity prized by Tyre and traded by Edom (so many Heb. MSS; MT "Aram"). In Esther fine linen is a feature of the Achaemenid royal court (1:6; 8:15), while in Chronicles fine linen characterizes the attire of both kings and priests during the United Monarchy (1 Chr 15:27; 2 Chr 2:13 [ET 2:14]; 3:14; 5:12). In the ancient Near East specialized workshops are attested (Weisberg 1967: 98–99), but spinning, weaving, and other textile work could be done in the house.

"Beth-ashbea" (בית אשבע). The location is unknown. A site in the Judahite Shephelah is suggested by the context.

4:22. "Cozeba, Joash, and Saraph." Not all of these sites have been securely identified. Many would associate "Cozeba" (כזבא) with Achzib (אכזיב; Josh 15:44; Mic 1:14) or Chezib (כזיב) in Gen 38:5 (SP כזבה; LXX *Chasbi*). There is no consensus about the location. Chezib/Achzib is most often associated with T. el-Beiḍā in the Judahite Shephelah (Rainey 1983: 5; Kallai 1986a: 385), but a location north of Akko on the Mediterranean coast has also been proposed (Na'aman 1986a: 57–60). The latter may involve, however, a different settlement with the same name (Josh 19:29; Judg 1:31).

"who married into Moab. And they resided in Bethleḥem." Chronicles again posits some close links between Judah and its neighbors in the past (COMMENT). Intermarriage with Moabites in the Persian period is both attested and denounced in Ezra (9:15.) and Nehemiah (13:23). The association with Moab and Bethleḥem greatly interested the authors of Tg., who developed a number of parallels between this brief narrative and the story of Ruth.

"the records are ancient." An intriguing aside, the significance of which is not altogether clear. The statement could refer to the veracity, antiquity, or opacity of the claims made in the previous lines. The statement could be a marginal gloss that somehow made its way into the text.

4:23. "the potters" (היוצרים). Presumably these potters, laboring in workshops near their supplies of clay, water, and fuel, would seek to meet the demand from larger urban markets (Matson 1995). On the roles and affiliations of craftsmen, see also the 3rd NOTE to v. 14.

"Netaim and Gederah." The identification of these sites is uncertain. "Gederah" is mentioned in the Judahite inheritance (Josh 15:36). By context (Josh 15:33–36), locations in the Judahite Shephelah are suggested.

"with [the assistance of] the king in his service they resided there" (*yšbw šm*). On the syntax, see the 3rd TEXTUAL NOTE to v. 23. One of the main ways to support the work of artisans in the ancient Near East was through state patronage. Such craftsmen would not necessarily have to work at the royal palace in a state workshop, although such centralized work areas are attested (Matthews 1995: 462). State-sponsored workshops could also be located in nearby villages. In some cases, craftsmen and artisans would travel to work for the court. The reference to such state sponsorship here is rather general in form. Hence, it is unclear how much light this verse can shed on the specific question of the production and distribution of *lmlk* Judahite stamped jars in the late eighth and seventh centuries (Welten 1969: 127–30; contra de Vaux 1965: 77–78).

Composition and Structure

In his universal genealogy (1:1–2:2) the Chronicler draws heavily upon genealogies and lists in Genesis to construct a long lineage extending from the primal human—Adam—to his main interest—Israel. Even a cursory study of the Judahite genealogy reveals the extent to which this work represents a different situation. The lineages show an indebtedness to a range of earlier biblical texts, especially at the beginning, but these texts are not extensively quoted. The scope and extent of the Judahite lineages are unprecedented in earlier biblical literature. But the genealogy of Judah (2:3–4:23) differs from the universal genealogy for another reason. Whereas the universal genealogy is relatively easy to follow, the genealogy of Judah is not. Adjectives, such as *confused, disorderly, corrupt,* and *incoherent,* are often used to describe the presentation. In some cases lineages are interrupted to introduce other lineages (e.g., 2:18–20, 21–24). In other cases, one confronts a series of genealogies that apparently have no relation to each other (e.g., 4:16, 17–19, 20). There are also inconsistencies and tensions within the lineages themselves. This raises a paradox. One might think that because the writer had to create a genealogy of Judah with relatively few biblical sources, the product would be fairly polished. Instead, the product is highly complex.

Scholars differ widely on how to account for this heterogeneity. Although space constraints do not permit a complete source-critical analysis, it is possible to provide an overview of three trends that can be observed during the past century and a half. (For a more thorough review of scholarship and an in-depth treatment of the text, see Knoppers 2000a; 2001c). In speaking of three different approaches to the complexity of the material in 2:3–4:23, one has to be careful not to imply that these approaches are exclusive. The three trends clearly overlap and one finds scholars employing two or even three approaches simultaneously. First, there is a longstanding tradition of scholars who, having deemed the Judahite genealogy to be corrupt, propose all manner and sorts of emendations (e.g., Wellhausen 1870; Curtis and Madsen 1910). The emendations extend to more than names and toponyms. Because some of the lineages have no ties to each other, scholars propose reconstructions to link them together (TEXTUAL NOTES). Second, many scholars have focused their attention on recovering the disparate sources that the Chronicler may have used to compose the genealogy. Having identified these materials, commentators employ them to recover the early history of Judah (e.g., Wellhausen 1870; 1885; Noth 1932; 1934) or to trace the Chronicler's use of these materials in composing the larger genealogy (e.g., Williamson 1979b; Japhet 1993a). Third, some scholars have focused their attention on tracing the genealogy's redaction history. These scholars (e.g., Noth 1943; Rudolph 1955; Kartveit 1989), who envision the Chronicler as employing far less in the way of sources than the second group does, contend that the genealogy of Judah evinces many different layers of composition and numerous additions.

In what follows, I will not be arguing that the genealogy is the seamless work of one writer. As the TEXTUAL NOTES and NOTES indicate, the Judahite lineages show the work of more than one hand. This seems especially true in the first section of the genealogy (2:3–55). Nor is it my contention that the Judahite genealogy is completely unified. To be sure, the work exhibits more marks of unity than many scholars have recognized. But the disunity in the genealogy is also important. The gaps and incongruities in the lineages should be neither ignored nor denied. One wonders whether the questions have been framed in the best possible way. The search for complete coherence in the text presumes that the text was authored and edited with complete coherence in mind. Even those scholars who contend that the bulk of the genealogy as we now have it is the product of numerous redactions, interpolations, and rearrangements have to acknowledge that the editors who were responsible for this long process of composition brought greater disunity to the text, not greater unity.

My proposal is not to deny the disunity, but to argue that some have misapprehended it. Scholars have long noticed, for example, that many of the lineages in 4:1–23 are neither integrated with each other nor linked to the previous lineages in 2:3–55. When composing a highly segmented genealogy, there are advantages to establishing connections between certain rammages and failing to do so for others. It may well be that the Chronicler and later editors differentiate between elements within Judah who comprise the main body of the tribe, such as the descendants of Caleb son of Ḥezron (2:9, 18–20), and those elements who were not completely integrated into the tribe, such as the descendants of Qoz (4:8). There are advantages to be had in refraining from artificially rationalizing all of the elements within Judah's genealogy. Both Caleb and Qoz belong to Judah, but the former is fully integrated, while the latter retains some independence. A certain amount of disorder in 2:3–4:23 may be precisely the point. Both determinacy and indeterminacy, the links between units and the lack thereof are significant.

Consistent with the schematized outline of the nations (1:1–2:2), the treatment of Judah reflects patternization. As in the genealogies from ancient Greece and elsewhere in the Mediterranean world (M. Johnson 1988; West 1985), this schematization includes the use of typical numbers. There are three children of Bath-shua (2:3), Ḥezron (2:9), Ram (2:27), Neariah (3:23), Ḥelah (4:7), Eshton (4:12), Caleb son of Jephunneh (4:15), Jether (4:17), and Bithiah (4:18). There are seven sons of Jesse (2:13–15) and of Elioenai (3:24). There are ten generations in the genealogy of Ram (2:9–17). Sheshan and his long line of descendants total fourteen (2:34–41). Numerical sums punctuate parts of the work (e.g., 2:3, 4, 6, 16). But more important than these minor patterns is the division of the genealogy into three major sections. The first (2:3–55) and the third (4:1–23) are set apart from the second (3:1–24) through the use of opening and closing formulas. Both the first and the third sections begin with similar rubrics: "The sons [descendants] of Judah" (2:3; 4:1). Both end with similar appendices: lists of professionals (2:55; 4:22–23). There is also a correspondance between the introduction to the genealogy of Judah and its close. The prologue to Judah's sons in 2:3–4 forms an *inclusio* with the enumeration of the descendants of one of these sons: Shelah (4:21–23; Williamson 1979b).

Each of the three parts within the genealogy (2:3–55; 3:1–24; 4:1–23) bears its own distinctive character. In the first section of the genealogy, the lineages are listed in generally descending order. But the authors artificially apportion lineages of certain figures (e.g., Ḥezron, Caleb) throughout this section. In other words, the writers interrupt their own genealogies so that they will conform to a larger literary design.

The Sons of Judah (3–4)
The Sons of Perez (5)
The Descendants of Zeraḥ (6–8)
The Descendants of Ḥezron, I (9)
The Descendants of Ram (10–17)
The Descendants of Caleb, I (18–20)
The Descendants of Ḥezron, II (21–24)
The Descendants of Jeraḥmeel (25–33)
The Descendants of Sheshan (34–41)
The Descendants of Caleb, II (42–50a)
The Descendants of Ḥur (50b–55)

Subdividing the lineages of Ḥezron and Caleb creates some short-term discontinuity in the overall progression of the genealogy, but it also has some long-term structural benefits. First, it allows for the placement of the Davidic genealogy in roughly the center of the other genealogies. If one were to insist on a linear descent, the list of David's descendants (3:1–24) would have to follow the list of his ancestors (2:10–17). Second, as Japhet (1993a: 73) observes, the positioning of the genealogy of David after the descendants of Ḥur (2:50b–55) connects David to Ephrathah and "Salma the father of Bethleḥem" (2:50, 54). Third, postponing the conclusions to certain genealogies from 1 Chr 2 to 1 Chr 4 creates ties between the two sections surrounding the Davidic genealogy.

If the lines in the first part of the genealogy generally progress in a descending order, a number of those in the third part progress in an ascending order. The sequence of at least some units in chapter 4 bears an inverse relationship to corresponding units within chapter 2. There is a descending order within individual lineages, but an ascending order in the genealogy as a whole. The lineage of 2:52 mentions the sons of Shobal, including Haroeh (= Reaiah), whereas the lineage of 4:2 begins with Reaiah son of Shobal. The lineage of 2:50 introduces "the sons of Ḥur, the firstborn of Ephrathah," while the lineage in 4:4 concludes with virtually the same rubric: "these were the sons of Ḥur the firstborn of Ephrathah." The second lineage of Ḥezron (2:21–24) concludes with the notice that Abijah, Ḥezron's wife gave birth to "Ashḥur the father of Teqoa" (2:24). The lineage of 4:5–7 begins where the second lineage of Ḥezron ended: "Ashḥur father of Teqoa had two wives" (4:5). Finally, the first Judahite lineage in 2:3 commences with an enumeration of Judah's sons: Er, Onan, and Shelah, whereas the last lineage in 4:1–23 ends with the sons of Shelah (4:21).

1. Sons of Judah (2:3–4)	4. Reaiah (4:2)
2. Ashḥur (2:24)	3. Sons of Ḥur (4:4)
3. Sons of Ḥur (2:50–55)	2. Ashḥur (4:5)
4. Haroeh (= Reaiah) (2:52)	1. Shelah (4:21–23)

One caveat must be offered. It is difficult to discern whether the inverse principle obtains anywhere else in chapter 4. The section of 4:1–23 contains a series of mostly unrelated genealogies, listed paratactically. It is unclear whether these miscellaneous genealogies follow an inverse chronological order. There is, however, one hint that the inverse principle is operative. The lineage of 4:13–14 lists the sons of Qenaz, but the following lineage of Caleb son of Jephunneh (v. 15) ends with Qenaz. Normally, one would expect the order to be reversed. Upon presenting Qenaz as the only son of Elah (v. 15), the genealogy would continue with the sons of Qenaz (vv. 13–14). That the opposite holds true suggests that the inverse principle may operate elsewhere in 4:2–23.

Having sketched some of the literary devices that are operative in the Judahite genealogy, it may be useful to address how these function. An obvious reason for this pattern of arrangement is the elaborate system of relationships it creates within the genealogy. It also allows the authors to include a variety of unrelated materials within the context of a larger structure. Ambiguity has its place. From the perspective of the writers, it is sufficient to situate the descendants of Qenaz (4:13–14) and Jehallelel (4:16) within the larger Judahite genealogy without abandoning the structure of the whole. As for the correspondence between the descending order of 2:1–55 and the ascending order of 4:1–23, it calls attention to the intervening genealogy—the descendants of David. David is firmly related to one of Judah's major families and his descendants occupy a privileged place within the tribe as a whole.

a The Descendants of Judah
  b The Descendants of David
a′ The Descendants of Judah

The genealogy of Judah (2:3–55; 4:1–23) frames, therefore, perhaps the most famous facet of Judah's enduring legacy: the house of David (3:1–24). The clans of Judah call attention to David, even as the impressive list of his descendants calls attention to David's indebtedness to his forebears. The chiastic arrangement of genealogies is no accident. In the Chronicler's conception, Yhwh chose David to govern Israel against the background of Judah's privileged place among the other tribes (1 Chr 5:1–2; 28:4–8; 2 Chr 13:4–8; Knoppers 1993a; 2000b). Both the extensive coverage given to Judah and the detailed coverage given to David's progeny are, therefore, in keeping with the interests exhibited by the book at large.

COMMENT

At first glance, the lineage of 1 Chr 2:3–4:23 manifests a simple and consistent theme—the growth of the tribe whose eponymous ancestor "grew mighty among his brothers" (5:2). As time passes, these "sons" of Judah become associated with certain towns within the larger context of the other tribal territories. But upon closer scrutiny, the situation is not so straightforward. The genealogies of Judah manifest substantial social, ethnic, and geographic complexity. Rather than presenting a facile picture of intergenerational descent, the Chronicler's linear and segmented lineages indicate a history of multiple ethnic affiliations and manifold social circumstances. Links with the Canaanites, Ishmaelites, Edomites, Moabites, and Egyptians are all attested. What seem to be non-Israelites or distant relations of the Israelites in other biblical contexts—the Jerahmeelites, Maacathites,

Qenizzites, and Qenites—appear as constituent elements of the tribe of Judah. Some of the lineages that are incorporated, such as the Jeraḥmeelites, are fully affiliated with other clans in Judah, but others, such as the Qenizzites, are not. While part of Judah, these latter families have an indeterminate status. There are intimations of inner-Israelite tribal connections with Manasseh, Benjamin, Levi, and Simeon. Geographically, there is occasional contraction, but mostly gradual expansion. The stress on internal development, the one reference to military defeat notwithstanding (2:23), is consistent with the pattern found in the Chronicler's other genealogies (Japhet 1979: 205–18). Given the complex picture of Judah's development—its origins, its socioethnic composition, its ties to other peoples, and the migrations of its individual units—one can also see why this genealogy appeals to scholars, who have advocated peaceful-immigration and internal-development models of early Judahite history.

Beyond observing the complex ethnic and demographic processes that characterized Judah's development, one should address the consequences of that development. What is the net result, geographically speaking, of the tribe's enlargement from the time of its eponymous ancestor? Examination of the sites listed in the genealogy reveals that the Chronicler ascribes large areas to the tribe. The settlements associated with Judah's clans overlap with a number of the sites listed in the Judahite tribal inheritance (Josh 15:20–63), in particular, those mentioned in the Negev (Josh 15:21–32), the Shephelah (Josh 15:33–47), the hill country (Josh 15:48–60), and the so-called Bethleḥem district (LXX Josh 15:59a). The genealogy lacks any direct mention, however, of the wilderness sites *(mdbr)* mentioned in Josh 15:61–62. The authors assume Davidic sovereignty over Jerusalem (1 Chr 3:5–9; cf. Josh 15:63). The genealogists accredit, moreover, settlements to Judah that are ascribed to or shared by other tribes, such as Benjamin (Josh 18:22), Manasseh (Josh 13:29–31; 17:1–3), and Dan (Josh 19:41).

The comparison can be extended to Yehud itself. Scholars disagree about the exact dimensions of Yehud's borders in the Persian period (e.g., E. Stern 2001: 428–43; Ofer 1993a; Carter 1994; 1999; Kallai 1998: 63–91; Lipschits 1999; 2001), but most agree that Yehud was geographically more circumscribed than Judah was during much of the monarchy. Many scholars see the southern border of Yehud as extending no farther than Beth Zur (NOTE to 2:28). Significant sites, such as Ekron in the west, Lachish and Mareshah in the southwest, and Ḥebron in the south may have been situated outside of Yehud's borders. But the phratries and families in Chronicles extend beyond the borders of Yehud to the south and to the west. Kartveit (1989: 166) claims, in fact, that the Chronicler furnishes Judah with the greatest possible territory based on the traditions available to him. Whatever the case, one should ask, What were the striking territorial dimensions of this genealogy designed to achieve in a postexilic context? How did the authors intend the genealogy of Judah to function at a time in which their people enjoyed only limited autonomy and limited territory? The writers, it seems, do not accept Yehud's circumscribed boundaries as normative for their people. Like the works of previous authors on the subject of tribal allotments (Kallai 1997; 1998; 1999; Na'aman 1986a), there is an idealistic aspect to the presentation in Chronicles.

Extending the genealogy back to the time of the Ancestors, the authors stake a claim in the present. Current restrictions are not determinative in ascertaining Judah's legacy.

Aside from ascribing many clans, families, and sites to Judah, the authors portray Judah as ethnically diverse. The genealogy of Israel's most dominant tribe is also its most socially heterogeneous. The figures who appear in Judah's lineages are not a list of eminent and distinguished heroes, the kind of ancient Israelite hall of fame that would later conclude the work of Ben Sira (Sir 44:1–50:24). The genealogy includes some prominent people—the leader of Judah at the time of Moses (Naḥshon), the builder of Israel's sacred realia (Bezalel), and the founder of a royal dynasty (David). But it also includes an executed wrongdoer and a stoned "troubler of Israel." The point is clearly not to idealize all of the individual figures depicted within the tribe's development. Nor is it to present a simplistic and romantic picture of past accomplishments. The many and varied relationships that allow the authors to depict primary, secondary, and tertiary kinship relations also hint at different levels of social stratification within the larger group. Wives (2:18, 24, 26, 29, 35; 3:3; 4:5, 7, 19), concubines (2:46, 48; 3:9; cf. 2:21, 24), sisters (2:16–17; 3:9, 19; 4:3, 19), daughters (2:4, 21, 34, 35, 49; 3:2, 5; 4:18), and mothers (2:26; 4:9) all play recognized roles. One of Judah's major clans is matriarchal in nature (2:50b–55; 4:4). The attribution of significant roles to a variety of women in Judah's past resonates with anthropological reconstructions of rural life in ancient Mediterranean agricultural societies (C. Meyers 1999). To be sure, the Chronicler's historiography is male-dominated and patriarchal in character (Laffey 1992: 112–13). But the genealogy does affirm that a range of humans—male and female, ancestor and slave, Israelite, Canaanite, Edomite, Moabite, Ishmaelite, and Egyptian—had a role to play in Judah's development.

In the context of the late Persian period, the social and ethnic diversity the authors impute to Judah contrasts with the exclusiveness promoted by Ezra and Nehemiah. By reserving the term "Israel" for the returned exiles and speaking generally of "the peoples of the land," the authors of Ezra and Nehemiah promote a very restricted notion of what constitutes Israel. The preservation of the "holy seed" (זרע הקדש) is deemed necessary to secure the future of Israel (Ezra 9:2). To be sure, the argument has been made that the list of the returnees in Ezra 2:43–55(//Neh 7:46–57) also evinces some diversity (Zadok 1980: 110–16). But the strictures of Ezra (9:1–10:44) and Nehemiah (13:23–28) should not be underestimated in their scope and application. The attempt by Ezra and Nehemiah to preserve a distinct Israelite identity involves a number of steps. Having identified Israel with the diaspora group, the leaders mandate the divorce of the wives and children of those exiles who intermarried with native peoples. The repertoire of autochthonous nations in Ezra 9:1 is drawn only in part from the standard Pentateuchal lists (Fishbane 1985: 125–26). It is extended to apply to nations not originally covered by the injunctions of Exod 34:11–16 and Deut 7:1–4. The expansion of the list to include Egyptians, Ammonites, Moabites, and Edomites (LXX) in Ezra 9:1 is critical to mandating the divorce and expulsion of people not included in the earlier prohibitions (Knoppers 1994d).

The genealogy of Judah undercuts a critical premise of Ezra and Nehemiah's position in its very presentation of Judah's origins. Like the authors of Ezra and Nehemiah, the authors of Chronicles selectively draw on Pentateuchal traditions (NOTES), but they do so to a very different effect. Judah's complex network of primary, secondary, and tertiary lineages, which involve links with different peoples, resists any attempt at easy categorization. The multilayered depiction of Judah's development underscores its ethnic diversity. Some groups are well-integrated into the tribe, while others are only loosely affiliated. The intimations of links not only with the Canaanites but also with a variety of other peoples stand in sharp contrast with the strictures of Ezra. In fact, two out of the four peoples added to the list of autochthonous nations in Ezra—the Egyptians and the Moabites—appear within Judah's genealogy. Judah at its core represents an amalgamation of various groups and families. The authors of the genealogy show no signs of being defensive about Judah's inclusiveness. Quite the contrary, the incorporation of different individuals, families, groups, and towns facilitates the growth and expansion of the larger tribe.

V. The Descendants of Simeon (4:24–43)

Introduction

24 The descendants of Simeon: Nemuel, Jamin, Jarib, Zeraḥ, and Saul, 25 Shallum his son, Mibsam his son, Mishma his son. 26 The sons of Mishma: Ḥammuel his son, Zakkur his son, Shimei his son. 27 Shimei had sixteen sons and six daughters. But his kin did not have many descendants. All of their families did not proliferate as much as the Judahites did.

The Simeonite Settlements

28 They resided in Beer-sheba, Shema, Moladah, Ḥazar-shual, 29 Bilhah, Ezem, Tolad, 30 Bethuel, Ḥormah, Ziqlag, 31 Beth-markabot, Ḥazer-susim, Beth-biri, and Shaaraim. These were their towns and their villages until David became king. 32 Eṭam, Ayin, Rimmon, Tochen, and Ashan—five towns 33 and all their villages which surrounded these towns as far as Baal. Such were their residences.

Genealogical Registration

Their genealogical enrollment: 34 Meshobab, Jamlech, Joshah son of Amaziah, 35 Joel, Jehu son of Joshibiah, son of Seraiah, son of Asiel, 36 Elioenai, Jaaqobah, Jeshoḥaiah, Asaiah, Adiel, Jesimiel, Banaiah, 37 and Ziza son of Shiphi, son of Allon, son of Jedaiah, son of Shimri, son of Shemaiah. 38 These were the ones entered by names—chieftains according to their families and their ancestral houses.

Simeonite Expansion to the West

They increased in abundance 39 and went to the approaches of Gerar up to the eastern side of the valley to seek pasture for their flocks. 40 They found rich and fine pasture. The land was spacious on every side—quiet and at ease—although those from Ḥam were residing there before (them). 41 These, the ones written by names, came in the days of Ḥezeqiah king of Judah and attacked the clans of Ḥam, along with the Meunites that were found there, and annihilated them to this day. They resided there in their place, because there was pasture there for their flocks.

Simeonite Expansion to Seir

42 From them, that is, from the men of Simeon, five hundred men went to the hill country of Seir with Pelaṭiah, Neariah, Rephaiah, and Uzziel—the sons of Ishi at their head. 43 They struck down the surviving remnant of Amaleq and have resided there to this day.

TEXTUAL NOTES

4:24. "descendants of Simeon." So MT and LXX. In Syr. these words appear as the introduction to v. 25.

"Nemuel" *(nmwʾl)*. So MT, LXX, and MT Num 26:12. The lemma of Gen 46:10 and Exod 6:15 *ymwʾl* may be older, assuming a *yôd* (or *wāw*) and *nûn* confusion.

"Jamin." Syr. reads with Gen 46:10 and Exod 6:15 in adding *ʾōhad*. But the source text (Num 26:12), like MT and LXX 1 Chr 4:24, lacks this name.

"Jarib" *(yryb)*. So MT and LXX^{AN} (maximum variation). LXX^{B} *Iarein*. Syr. *ykyn* (adopted by NAB) assimilates toward Gen 46:10; Exod 6:15; Num 26:12.

"Zeraḥ" *(zrḥ)*. So MT and Num 26:13. LXX^{B}, c_2 *Zares*; LXX^{L} *Zara*. Syr. *ṣḥr* follows Gen 46:10 and Exod 6:15.

"Saul." So MT, LXX, and Num 26:13. Syr. adds *ʾlh bny šlh bn-yhwdh*. Syr.^{A} adds a few other words. Hence, in Syr. the Judahite genealogy ends here. Because 1 Chr 4:24 draws on Num 26:14, it lacks "the son of a Canaanite woman" found in both Gen 46:10 and Exod 6:15.

4:25. "Shallum his son." So MT (cf. LXX *Saleim*). Syr. "and the sons of Simeon" begins the Simeonite genealogy here, not in v. 24.

4:26. "sons of Mishma." So MT, LXX^{L} *(huioi Masma)*, and Arm. *filii Mašmei*. Lacking in LXX^{AB}, probably because of haplography (from *mšmʿ* in v. 25 to *mšmʿ* in v. 26).

"Ḥammuel." On the PN, "the [divine] father-in-law is God," see Layton (1990b: 62–63). The lemmata of LXX^{ALN} *Amouēl* and Arm. *Amuel* do not reflect the gemination of *mêm*.

4:27. "Shimei" (לשמעי). So LXX^{B} c_2 *(lectio brevior)*. MT prefaces *wāw*.

"six." So MT and LXX^{L}. Many Heb. MSS and LXX^{AB} "three."

"their families." Reading with two Heb. MSS and LXX. MT "their family."

"proliferate" *(hrbw)*. Syr. *ʿdmʾ dʾtw lwt*. Begrich *(BHK)* proposes inserting *lbwʾ* after *hrbw* (cf. 2 Sam 23:19).

4:28. "Shema." Lacking in MT, but present in LXX^{B} *kai Sama(a)* (= *wšmʿ*). See also MT and LXX Josh 15:26 *wšmʿ*, and LXX^{B} and OL Josh 19:2 *wšmʿ* (MT *wšbʿ*). Rudolph (1955: 38) hypothesizes that the readings of Josh 15:26 and 19:2 result from dittography: **bʾr-šbʿ (w)šbʿ*, but I am inclined to the opposite conclusion, that a haplography *(homoioteleuton)* has occurred from *bʾr-šbʿ* to *(w)šmʿ*.

"Moladah." LXX[A] and LXX[L] add *Sama(a)* (see previous TEXTUAL NOTE). Josh 15:27 mentions additional sites.

4:29. "Bilhah" *(blhh)*. LXX[B] *Abella*. LXX[AN] *kai en Balaa*; LXX[L] (and Arm.) *kai en Balaad*; Josh 15:29 *bʿlh wʿyym* (cf. *bʿlh* in MT and 4QSam[a] 2 Sam 6:2); 19:3 *blh*.

"(in) Ezem" *(bʿṣm)*. LXX[B] *kai Boosal* likely results from an inner-Greek corruption (Allen 1974b: 16).

"(in) Tolad" *(btwld)*. So MT and LXX[L] *(en Thōulath)*. The reading of LXX[B] *(kai Thoulaem)* evinces an inner-Greek corruption (Allen 1974a: 144). Syr. reads *ʾltwld* by attraction to Josh 15:30; 19:4.

4:30. "(in) Bethuel" *(bbtwʾl)*. LXX[B] *kai Bathoun*; LXX[L] *kai en Bathouēl*. MT Josh 19:4 *btwl*. The derivation of the name is much-debated (Layton 1990b: 55–56). Syr. "and in Nesel" *(nsl)* may assimilate toward *ksyl* of Josh 15:30. Note also the appearance of *Baithēl* in LXX[B] Josh 15:30 and "Bethel" *(byt-ʾl)* in the list of MT 1 Sam 30:27. But LXX[B] 1 Sam 30:27 has *Baithsour*.

"Ziqlag" *(ṣyqlg)*. On LXX[B] *Okla*, see Allen (1974b: 117). Syr. adds *wbhṣr gdh wbḥšmwn wbbyt plṭ wbṣqlg wbmdmnh wsmslh*; cf. Josh 15:27, 31.

4:31. "Beth-markabot" (בית-מרכבות). So MT 1 Chr 4:31 and MT Josh 19:5. Josh 15:31 "Madmannah" (מדמנה).

"Ḥazer-susim" (חצר סםים). Thus MT. The reading of LXX[B*] *Huisusesoram* may reflect *ḥṣy srsm* in the *Vorlage* of LXX (Allen 1974b: 76, 121). Josh 19:5 "Susah;" cf. Josh 15:31 "Sansannah."

"Beth-biri, and Shaaraim" *(byt brʾy wbšʿrym)*. LXX[B] misreads as one unit *oikon Braoumseōreim*. MT Josh 15:32 *wlbʾwt*; 19:6 *byt lbʾwt*. For MT *(brʾy)*, compare LXX[L] *-bareim*.

"Shaaraim" *(šʿrym)*. Josh 15:36 and 1 Sam 17:52 *šʿrym*. Cf. Josh 15:32 "Shilḥem" *(šlḥym)* and 19:6 "Sharuḥen" *(šrwḥn)*. The reconstruction of Rudolph (1955: 38), *wbšrwḥn šlš ʿśrh ʿrym*, harmonizes 1 Chr 4:31 with Josh 19:6, *wšrwḥn ʿrym šlš ʿśrh*. Others (e.g., Boling 1982: 384) view "Shaaraim" as a corruption of "Sharuḥen" (or vice versa).

"these were their towns and their villages until David became king." Verses 31b–32a literally read "these were their towns until David became king and their villages." Many understand the phrase "and their villages" as introducing the following list ("Eṭam, Ayin," etc.). But in the Chronicler's *Vorlage* the two lists of locations (Josh 19:2–6; cf. 1 Chr 4:28–32a; Josh 19:7–8; cf. 1 Chr 4:32–33) are both concluded with enumerative summaries referring to towns and villages. The writer complicates this pattern by introducing the temporal reference to David's reign (v. 31), but he does not sever the connection altogether. Hence, I take "and all their villages" *(wḥṣryhm)* in v. 32a as applying to the list of vv. 28–31. If the author wished to redefine "Eṭam, Ayin, Rimmon, Tochen, and Ashan" (v. 32) as villages, it is unlikely that he would have left standing their designation as "towns" (v. 33; cf. Josh 19:7). The second list in Chronicles, like the list in his *Vorlage* (Josh 19:7–8), distinguishes between five or four (Joshua) towns "and all their villages which surrounded these towns" (1 Chr 4:32–33).

"became king" *(mĕlōk)*. Reading with MT (cf. 1 Chr 1:43). Many Heb. MSS, LXX, Vg. have the noun *melek*.

4:32. "Eṭam" *(ʿyṭm)*. So MT and cursives *bb*′. LXX^{ABN} *Aitan*; ye$_2$ *Aitam*; Syr. *ʿqym*. Cf. the toponyms in Josh 15:42 (*ʿtr*; LXX^{B119} *Ithak*; LXX^{L} *Athak* [= *ʿtk*]); 19:7 *(ʿtr)*; and 1 Sam 30:30 *(ʿtk)*.

"Ayin, Rimmon" *(ʿyn rmwn)*. So MT and Josh 19:7: *ʿyn rmwn*. LXX^{B}, bc$_2$ *kai Rimmon* may reflect a haplography after *kai* (cf. LXX^{L} *kai Hēnremmōn*). MT could more easily be translated as "Ayin-rimmon" (cf. *ʿēn rimmôn* Neh 11:29), but in referring to two different sites I follow some witnesses to LXX, Syr., MT Josh 15:32 *(ʿyn wrmwn)*, and the numerical summary "five towns" at the end of the verse. In this case, one has to distinguish between textual criticism (discerning the oldest witnesses to Joshua and Chronicles) and historical reconstruction (2nd NOTE to v. 32).

"Tochen" *(tkn)*. LXX^{B} *Thokka*. Rudolph (1955: 40) et al. compare "Tochen" with *ʿtr* in Josh 15:42 and 19:7, and *ʿtk* in 1 Sam 30:30. But LXX^{B} Josh 19:7 includes both "Ether" and *Thalcha* (< *Thachan*?).

"Ashan." LXX^{B} and c$_2$ *Aisar*. LXX^{L} adds *kai Iech(th)em*.

"five towns." See the 5th TEXTUAL NOTE to v. 31 and Josh 19:7.

4:33. "Baal." So MT, LXX^{AN}, and Arm. *(lectio difficilior)*. LXX^{B} reads expected "Baalath" (Josh 19:8; 1 Kgs 9:18). LXX^{L} and Arm. *Balaad*.

"such *(zʾt)* were their residences." An exception to the rule that a predicate conforms in gender and number to its subject (GKC, §145a). The Chronicler's wording results from his selective rewriting of his source (Josh 19:8; Japhet 1993a). On the use of the predicate as a substantive, see Kropat (§8).

"(and) their genealogical enrollment" *(whtyḥśm lhm)*. Thus MT and LXX^{L} *(lectio difficilior)*. The prep. phrase *lhm* intensifies the foregoing pronominal suf. (cf. 1 Chr 7:2, 4). LXX^{AB} *kai ho katalochismos autōn*, "and their enrollment."

4:34–37. These verses are lacking in Syr.

4:34. "Meshobab, (and) Jamlech" *(mšwbb wymlk)*. LXX^{L}, "and returning, he ruled" *(kai epistrephōn ebasileusen)*, construes the initial terms in v. 34 as a ptc. *(poʿlel* of *šwb)* and a verbal form, rather than as PNs.

"Joshah" *(ywšh)*. LXX^{AB} *Iōs(e)ia(s)*; LXX^{L} *Iōas*.

4:35. "Jehu" *(yhwʾ)*. Reading with MT and LXX$^{B(2)ALN}$. LXX^{B*} and c$_2$ "and he" (= *whwʾ*) reflects a *wāw/yôd* confusion.

4:36. "Jeshoḥaiah" (ישוחיה). A *hapax legomenon*. LXX^{B} *Iasouia*; LXX^{L} *Iesouia*.

4:36b–37. "Adiel, Jesimiel, Banaiah, and Ziza son of Shiphi, son of Allon, son of Jedaiah, son of Shimri, son of Shemaiah." So MT. LXX^{B} differs in a number of readings *huioi Aōsal huiou Saphal huiou Amōn huiou Idia huiou Samar huiou Symeōn*. "Adiel and Jesimiel" were probably lacking in the *Vorlage* of LXX, perhaps due to haplography. Comments on certain details follow.

4:36. "Jesimiel" *(yśymʾl)*. So MT. A few Heb. MSS, LXX^{ALN}, and Arm. *yśmʾl*. The PN means "(my) God will establish."

4:37. "Shiphi." LXX^{B} *Saphal* assimilates toward *Aōsal* (Allen 1974b: 4).

"Ziza." LXX^{A} "Zuza."

"Shimri." So MT. LXX^{B} c$_2$ *Samar* (= *šmr*); LXX^{L} *Samarei*.

"Shemaiah" *(šmʿyh)*. So MT and LXX^{L} (maximum variation). LXX^{B} "Simeon" (= *šmʿwn*; cf. vv. 24, 42).

4:38. "these were the ones entered by names" *(ʾlh hbʾym bšmwt)*. LXX^{B} *hoi dielontes* evinces a haplography of *th (hoi dielthontes*; Allen 1974b: 56). The same verb is used, but with a different meaning in v. 41 *(wybʾw ʾlh hktwbym bšmwt)*. Thinking that the text is corrupt, Begrich *(BHK)* proposes *hyw bʾym bšmwt*. Rudolph (1955: 40) favors either *hrʾym bšmwt* or *hʾwym*. The wording is unusual, but it does not require emendation (NOTES).

"They increased in abundance" (פרצו לרוב). Literally, "they broke out in abundance." On this idiomatic use of *prṣ*, compare Gen 28:14; Exod 1:12; 1 Chr 13:2 (2nd TEXTUAL NOTE); 2 Chr 11:23; 31:5.

4:39. "to the approaches" *(lmbwʾ)*. LXX^{B} *heōs tou elthein*; LXX^{L} *tou elthein*. Begrich *(BHK)* proposes a transposition *mlbwʾ*.

"Gerar." So LXX^{ABL} *grr(h)*. The reading of MT "Gedor" *(gdr)* reflects a *dālet/rêš* confusion.

"up to the eastern side of the valley" *(ʿd mzrḥ hgyʾ)*. The lemma of LXX^{B} "up to the east of Gai" *(heōs tōn anatolōn tēs Gai)* construes *gyʾ* as a toponym.

4:40. "the land was spacious on every side." Literally, "the land was spacious of both hands" *(hʾrṣ rḥbt ydym)*. LXX^{B} "the land before them was spacious" *(hē gē plateîa enantion autōn)* replicates the more common form of this expression: *hʾrṣ(hnh) rḥbt ydym (lpnyhm)* (Gen 34:21; cf. Judg 18:10; Isa 22:18; 33:21).

"although those from Ḥam were residing there before (them)." On the concessive use of *ky* (LXX^{B} *hoti*), see Williams, §448. *BHK*, followed by NAB, transposes this clause after v. 41a.

"from Ḥam." Thus MT *(lectio brevior)*. LXX, Vg., and Tg. explicate, "from the sons of Ḥam."

4:41. "the clans of Ḥam" *(ʾhly ḥm)*. The readings of both MT and LXX are problematic: MT (and LXX^{L}) "their tents" *(ʾhlyhm)*; LXX^{B} "their houses" *(tous oikous autōn)*. Arnold Ehrlich (1914: 329), *BHK*, and Rudolph (1955: 42) propose reading *ʾhly ḥm*, but differ as to what this means: "tents of Ḥam" (cf. Gen 9:27 *ʾhly-šm*; 2 Chr 14:14 [ET 14:15] *ʾhly mqnh*; Begrich [*BHK*]) or "clans of Ḥam" (Ehrlich; Rudolph). In defense of the last suggestion, one can cite LXX^{AN} (and Arm.) *oikētoras*, as well as comparative philological evidence: Phoen. *ʾhl*, "family" (Krahmalkov 2000: 38); Arab. *ahl*, "clan"; OSA *ʾhl* "people," "family," or "clan;" Liḥyanite *ʾl* "people" (Biella 1982: 7). See also *ʾhly ʾdwm*, "clans of Edom" (Ps 83:7 [ET 83:6]).

"the Meunites." So Qere הַמְּעוּנִים. Given the appearance of "the Meunites" elsewhere in Chronicles (2 Chr 20:1 [LXX^{AB}]; 26:7 [MT], 8 [LXX]; Rehm 1954: 18), this reading need not be viewed as surprising (Williamson 1982b: 62). The other variants are: Kethib הַמְּעִינִים and LXX *tous Minaious*, "the Mineans"; Syr. *mbwʿʾ* (= *hmʿynym*), "the springs"; and Vg. *habitores*, "inhabitants." Given the possibility of a *wāw/yôd* confusion, it is impossible to be dogmatic about which reading is earlier. Rudolph (1955: 42) pursues a third option, citing Arab. *maʿān*, "dwelling," to reconstruct "their dwelling places" *(mʿwnyhm)*. In this regard, see also the variant readings of some Tg. MSS *mdwryʾ* (= *hmʿwnym*), "their dwellings" (McIvor 1994: 63). But given the context, it is more likely that the text is referring to an ethnic group than it is to a type of residence (Lemaire 1997: 134–37).

4:42. "from them." The *mêm* in *mēhem* is partitive (GKC, §119w; Williams, §324). Only one section of the Simeonite tribe is involved.

"Neariah." LXX^{AB} *Nōad(e)ia*; Syr. *mttyh.*

"sons of Ishi" *(bny yšʿy)*. The reading of LXX^{B} *(huioi Iesthen)* evinces an inner-Greek corruption (Allen 1974a: 155). Syr. adds *ʾlh ʾrbʿt ʾnšym bny yšʿy hlkw.*

4:43. "surviving remnant" *(šʾryt hplṭh)*. On the expression, compare *šʾryt wplyṭh* in Ezra 9:14 and 2 Kgs 19:31.

"resided there." So MT and LXX^{AN}. Lacking in LXX^{B}. Vg. adds "in their stead" (= *tḥtyhm*) by attraction to v. 41.

NOTES

4:24–27. "descendants of Simeon." The genealogy contains both segmented and linear (vv. 25–26) forms. Simeon's line is traced through what appears to be his youngest son Saul. The names in v. 24 (Nemuel, Jamin, Jarib, Zeraḥ, and Saul) are derived, with some variations, from Gen 46:10 (P), Exod 6:15 (P), and Num 26:12–14. Of these three Pentateuchal texts, Num 26:12–14 is closest to the formulation of v. 25 (TEXTUAL NOTES to vv. 24–25). The rest of the genealogy (vv. 26–27) is unique to Chronicles.

4:25. "Mibsam (מִבְשָׂם) his son, Mishma (מִשְׁמָע) his son." That "Mibsam" and "Mishma" also occur as names for Ishmael's sons (1 Chr 1:30; Gen 25:14) suggests some sort of relationship. "Mishma" is associated by Knauf (1989: 9) with Išammeʾ (Arab. **Yus*$_1$*āmiʿ*), a north Arabian tribe attested in the seventh-century B.C.E. Assyrian inscriptions of Ashurbanipal. During the sixth and fifth centuries B.C.E. Arabian tribes became more of a visible presence in the areas of Ammon, Moab, Edom, and southern Palestine. The genealogy may provide indirect testimony to this process. By postulating the emergence of such (Arabian) elements in Simeon, the author connects them to an Israelite context.

4:27. "proliferate as much as the Judahites did." On the strength and success of Judah, see the COMMENT on 1 Chr 4:1–23 and the NOTES to 1 Chr 5:1–2.

4:28–33. This list of Simeonite settlements is taken, with some changes, from Josh 19:2–8. The list of Judahite towns near the Edomite border (Josh 15:20–32, esp. vv. 26–32) also merits close study (Rudolph 1955: 39), but the closest parallels are with the list of Simeonite towns and villages in Josh 19:2–8 (TEXTUAL NOTES). The limits of this pericope are set by the introduction "They resided (וישבו) in Beer-sheba" (v. 28) and the conclusion "Such were their residences" (מושבתם; v. 33).

4:28. "Beer-sheba" (Josh 19:2) is associated by most scholars with T. es-Sebaʿ, although Naʾaman (1980a: 150–51) makes a case for the nearby site bearing Beer-sheba's ancient name: Bîr es-Sebaʿ. In the expressions "from Beer-sheba to Dan" and "from Beer-sheba to the hill country of Ephraim" (1 Chr 21:2; 2 Chr 19:4; 30:5) Beer-sheba appears as the southern outpost of Israel. During the Iron Age (II) the town was rebuilt and destroyed four times. The excavator (Herzog 1993) believes that Beer-sheba functioned as a royal administrative center, housing military commanders, officials involved in trade, and priests, who served at its sanctuary. Following a gap of nearly three centuries, the site was reoccupied in the fourth century B.C.E. The Persian period fortress was built in this period. Some forty Aramaic ostraca found at the site, dating to 358–329 B.C.E., contain the names of Judeans, Edomites, and Arabs and refer to quantities of wheat and barley. In the Hellenistic period a large fortress and a temple (similar in design to the solar shrine at Lachish) were constructed.

"Shema." Another site that seems to be claimed for both Judah (Josh 15:26; 4th NOTE to 1 Chr 2:43) and Simeon (so LXX^B and OL Josh 19:2; cf. MT *wšbʿ*).

"Moladah." Part of both the Simeonite inheritance (Josh 19:3) and the Judahite inheritance (Josh 15:26). Possibly Khirbet el-Waṭan some 12 km east-northeast of Beer-sheba (Aharoni 1979: 261, 439). The site is also mentioned in the idealized settlement list of Neh 11:26.

"Ḥazar-shual." The location is unknown. It is listed both as part of Simeon (Josh 19:3) and as part of the Judahite Negev district (Josh 15:28). See also Neh 11:27.

4:29. "Bilhah." See the 1st TEXTUAL NOTE to v. 29.

"Ezem" (עצם) may be associated with Umm al-ʿAẓām, 25 km south of Beer-sheba. While some think that "Ezem" is the same site as Ether (עתר; Josh 19:7; cf. 1 Sam 30:30 [1st TEXTUAL NOTE to v. 32]), the names are orthographically distinct. Moreover, both Ezem (Josh 15:29; 19:3) and Ether (Josh 15:42; 19:7) occur in the allotments for Judah and Simeon. "Ezem" appears on an eighth to seventh-century B.C.E. ostracon from T. eš Šārîʿa (Oren and Netzer 1974: 265; Davies, §12.001.1).

"Tolad" is mentioned *(tld)* on an eighth-century B.C.E. ostracon (# 1) from Beer-sheba (Aharoni 1973: 71–73; Davies, §5.001.2). The precise location of "Tolad" or "Eltolad" (*ʾltwld*; Josh 15:30; 19:4) is unknown.

4:30. "Bethuel" (TEXTUAL NOTE) also appears in the Simeonite inheritance of Josh 19:4, but the site is unknown. T. Umm Bētīn, 4 km northeast of Beer-sheba, has been suggested as one possibility (Naʾaman 1980a: 147). Given the context, the place may be distinct from the much-debated "Bethulia" (LXX^B *Baitouloua*; Vg. *Bethulia*) in Jdt 4:6; 6:11ff.; 7:3, 13; 8:3 (Moore 1985: 150–51).

"Ḥormah," a site assigned to Simeon (Josh 19:4), also appears in the Negev district of Judah (Josh 15:30). Ḥormah figures prominently in the conquest accounts of early Israel (Num 14:45; 21:3; Deut 1:44; Josh 12:14; cf. 1 Sam 30:30), but the location is unclear (Kartveit 1989: 130–31). Among the possibilities are Khirbet el-Mešâš (or T. Māśōs), 12 km east of Beer-sheba (e.g., Soggin 1981: 28; Boling 1982: 327; Nelson 1997: 287); T. el-Milḥ 11 km northeast of Beer-sheba (e.g., B. Mazar 1965: 297–99); and T. el—Ḫŭwēlfe (Naʾaman 1980a: 142–43). See also the 2nd NOTE to v. 32.

"Ziqlag." A site assigned to both Simeon (Josh 19:5) and Judah (Josh 15:31), which most scholars believe is T. eš-Šhārīʿa, between Beer-sheba and Gaza. According to 1 Sam 27:6, Ziqlag was a Philistine town given to David by Achish king of Gath. Remains from the Persian period consist of houses, grain silos, various imported Greek vessels, Greek terra-cottas, and some Aramaic ostraca (Oren 1993: 1334). Ziqlag is mentioned as a place of Judahite residence in Neh 11:28.

4:31. "Beth-markabot." Another site that appears in the Simeonite allotment (Josh 19:5). See also the 4th NOTE to 1 Chr 2:55.

"Ḥazer-susim," or "Ḥazer-susah" (Josh 19:5), is mentioned on a seventh-century ostracon from Arad [*ḥṣr*]*swsh* (#32; Aharoni 1975: 60–62; Davies, §2.032.1). See also the 2nd TEXTUAL NOTE to v. 31.

"Beth-biri" (בית בראי) may appear in the list of Simeonite towns as "Beth-lebaoth" (בית לבאות; Josh 19:6) and as "Lebaoth" in the Judahite Negev district of Josh 15:32 (לבאות).

"Shaaraim." There is no consensus as to the location of this site, nor its relationship, if any, to "Sharuḥen" (Josh 19:6; 4th TEXTUAL NOTE to v. 31). The latter has been associated with T. el-Fârʿah, west of Beer-sheba (Albright 1929: 7), although Kempinski (1974: 145–52) proposes a minority view: T. el-ʿAğûl. Contextual considerations (Josh 15:36; 1 Sam 17:52) would place Shaaraim to the west of Socoh and Azeqah.

"their towns . . . until David became king." There is no urgent reason (*pace* Noth 1953: 113; Rudolph 1955: 39) to view this comment as a gloss, although it does not appear in Josh 19:6. In Chronicles the monarchy in general (1 Chr 1:43) and David's reign in particular mark a major turning point in Israelite history. The precise significance of the statement is, however, another matter. Some (e.g., Kallai 1986a) interpret the phrase as an allusion to David's census (1 Chr 21//2 Sam 24). Others argue that it refers to David's sovereignty over these towns (1 Sam 30:27; Benzinger 1901: 17; Cross and Wright 1956: 214; Williamson 1982b: 62; R. Braun 1986: 67). While the latter suggestion is more plausible than the former, it is also clear from what follows that the author views Simeon as retaining a measure of tribal integrity and independence in the post-Davidic era (1 Chr 4:41; 2 Chr 34:6).

4:32. "Eṭam." On its location, see the 1st NOTE to 4:3.

"Ayin, Rimmon." The presentation of Josh 15:32 and Chronicles notwithstanding (TEXTUAL NOTE), most scholars think that this refers to one site (cf. Josh 19:7 *ʿyn rmwn*). The location is disputed. Many (e.g., Noth 1953: 113) favor Khirbet Umm er-Ramāmîn, 18 km northeast of Beer-sheba, as the site of "Ayin-rimmon" or "En-rimmon," but Aharoni (1979: 262, 434) favors Khirbet Ḫŭwēlfe, about 10 km southeast of T. Bēt Mirṣim (Debir). Neh 11:29 mentions "En-rimmon" as a residence of returning exiles.

"Tochen" (תכן) is included in the Simeon allotment of Josh 19:7 (3rd TEXTUAL NOTE to v. 32), but its location is unknown.

"Ashan" (עשן) appears in both the Shephelah district of Judah (Josh 15:42; cf. LXX* 21:16; 1 Chr 6:44) and the Simeonite allotment (Josh 19:7). Whether both refer to the same place is unclear. Aharoni (1979: 354) thinks that Judahite "Ashan" refers to T, Bēt Mirṣim, but Simeonite "Ashan" may refer to Khirbet

ʿAsan, 3.2 km north of Beer-sheba. The same site is referred to as *bôr ʿāšān* ("the spring of Ashan") in 1 Sam 30:30.

4:33. "as far as Baal." The parallel of Josh 19:8 is both more expansive—"Baalath-beer, Ramath-negeb"—and textually problematic (Kallai 1986a: 359). Aharoni (1979: 261) thinks that the site is Khirbet (Ġ)azzah (Ḥurba(t̠) ʿŪzah) southeast of Arad, but a location to the southeast of Beer-sheba would be more likely.

4:33b–38a. "Their genealogical enrollment" (והתיחשׂם להם). The introduction and conclusion to the list of Simeonite chieftains form an *inclusio* marked by references to the Simeonite registrations. In other words, "their genealogical enrollment" is best understood as introducing the proper names listed in vv. 34–37. It is also possible to construe the clause as a concluding notice to vv. 32–33a (R. Braun 1986: 63), but these verses already have a summary notation: "such were their residences" (v. 32). Moreover, vv. 32–33a pertain to geographical sites, not to genealogical registration.

Some observations may be made about the use of the verb (יחשׂ) relating to genealogical registrations in Chronicles. Of the twenty occurrences of this verb in the HB (always in the *hitpaʿel*), fifteen occur in this particular book (ten in the genealogies of 1 Chr 1–9; Beentjes 1999). The other five occurrences are all in Ezra and Nehemiah. Insofar as genealogical registration involves including certain individuals or groups within a larger membership, it confers status (rights, honors, privileges) upon the registrees. The verb, which pertains more to the result of genealogical enrollment than it does to the actual process of genealogical registration (Mosis 1990), is not applied to any of the three central tribes of the Chronicler's own day—Judah, Levi, and Benjamin ("Introduction"). That the verb is used with respect to a number of the other tribes (Simeon, Reuben, Gad, Issachar, Asher) may signify an attempt to "save all these 'forgotten tribes' from oblivion" (Beentjes 1999: 237).

4:36. "Asaiah" *(ʿśyh)*. The longer form of the PN *(ʿśyhw)*, "Yhwh has acted," appears often in Heb. epigraphs (Davies, §§1.022.7; 100.027.2; 038.1; 062.3; 109.2; 365.1; 532.2; 534.2).

4:37. "Ziza (זיזא) son of Shiphi . . . son of Shemaiah." Like the previous lineages in vv. 34–35, the lineage of vv. 36–37 becomes an ascending lineage at its conclusion. In each case, this has the effect of calling attention to the importance of certain figures ("Joshah" in v. 34; "Jehu" in v. 35; "Ziza" in v. 37).

4:38b–43. "they increased in abundance." The third section of the Simeonite genealogy deals with the expansion of the tribe demographically and geographically. Two anecdotes chart this violent expansion. An increase in Simeon's population leads the Simeonites to enlarge their territory (vv. 39–40) to the west (v. 41) and to the southeast (vv. 42–43) by overcoming some of the native inhabitants of these regions. There are parallels between this tale and the story of Laish's conquest by the tribe of Dan (Judg 18; Curtis and Madsen 1910: 116; Japhet 1993a: 120).

4:38. "entered by names." Living in an age in which literacy was somewhat more prevalent than in earlier times, the Chronicler envisions the genealogical registration as taking written form (1st NOTE to 1 Chr 2:55). That the Chronicler posits a written, not an oral, enrollment is clear from the later assertion that those who campaigned against Simeon's enemies to the west were "the ones written by names" (*ʾlh hktwbym bšmwt*; v. 41). The emphasis on written registration in vv. 38 and 41 contrasts with the more general locutions for registration elsewhere in Chronicles, for example, "to be designated by name" (*nqb bšm*; 1 Chr 12:32; 16:41[MT]; 2 Chr 28:15; 31:19; cf. Num 1:17; Ezra 8:20).

"chieftains" *(nśyʾym)*. The term *nāśîʾ* can be translated "chieftain" or "prince" depending on context. In the Book of the Covenant (Exod 22:27) the *nśyʾ* appears as a tribal representative (Noth 1930: 151–62). The term bears similar connotations in the Priestly writings. There the *nśyʾ* functions as a leader, group representative, and tribal head (e.g., Exod 16:22; 22:27; 34:31; 35:27; Num 1:2–16, 20–46; 2:3–29; Josh 9:15, 18–21; 13:21; 22:32). In 1 Kgs 11:34 (MT) and Ezekiel the *nśyʾ* appears as a lesser monarch or prince (Ezek 7:27; 12:10, 12; 21:17; 26:16; cf. 17:12; Zimmerli 1979: 209, 273). In the latter portions of Ezekiel, especially in the reconstruction program, one encounters another designation of *nśyʾ*, that of a future Davidic prince or ruler (Ezek 34:24; 37:25; 44:3–48:22; Levenson 1976: 55–107; Zimmerli 1983: 438–543). In somewhat similar fashion, the term *nśyʾ* is applied to Sheshbazzar, the head of the early Jewish community in the Persian period (Ezra 1:8). The conception of the *nśyʾ* in Chronicles has much in common with earlier sources, especially the Priestly source, and virtually nothing to do with the use of *nśyʾ* in Ezekiel and Ezra (1:8). In Chronicles the monarch in Jerusalem is referred to as a *melek*, as are foreign emperors. The term *nāśîʾ* is never applied to Davidic or non-Davidic kings. The *nśyʾym* play an important leadership role within a tribal context (1 Chr 2:10; 4:38; 5:6; 7:40). They are also active during the United Monarchy, again as local or tribal representatives (2 Chr 1:2; 5:2). Thereafter they disappear completely from view. They are never mentioned in the Chronicler's depiction of the Judahite monarchy.

"according to their families and their ancestral houses" (במשפחותם ובית אבותיהם). The reference to "ancestral houses" pertains to one categorization of registration for Simeon's leadership. Next to the tribe, the ancestral house *(byt ʾbwt)* is the largest unit of kinship in Chronicles, Ezra, and Nehemiah (1st NOTE to 1 Chr 15:12).

4:39. "Gerar" (TEXTUAL NOTE), associated with T. Abu Ḥurēra northwest of Beer-sheba, is not mentioned in either the Judahite or the Simeonite town lists of Joshua (cf. 2 Chr 14:12–14).

"valley." The location may be Naḥal Gerar (Wâdī eš-Šharîʿa) in the western Negev (Gen 26:17). Given the association with Gerar (previous NOTE), it is unlikely that the reference is to Wâdī Mûsâ at the entrance of Petra (*pace* Knauf 1992b: 802). Note also that the Philistines (associated with Gerar in Gen 26:1, 6, 26) are regarded as descendants of Ḥam (1 Chr 1:12).

4:40. "rich and fine pasture" *(mrʿh šmn wṭwb)*. On the expression, compare: "is the land rich or is it poor?" (*hʾrṣ hšmnh hwʾ ʾm rzh*; Num 13:20); "rich pasture" (*mrʿh šmn*; Ezek 34:14); "rich soil" (*ʾdmh šmnh*; Neh 9:25); and "spacious and rich land" (*ʾrṣ hrḥbh wšmnh*; Neh 9:35).

"those from Ḥam were residing there before [them]." By qualifying the claim that the land was tranquil, the author hints at the clash which is to come (v. 41).

"Ḥam." See the NOTE to 1 Chr 1:4.

4:41. "these, the ones written by names" (אלה הכתובים בשמות). Alluding to the genealogical registration of vv. 34–37, those "entered by names" (אלה הבאים בשמות; v. 38).

"days of Ḥezeqiah." Many scholars view this anecdote as supplying additional historical evidence for Judahite expansion during the late eighth or early seventh century. According to 2 Kgs 18:8, Ḥezeqiah invaded Philistia as far as Gaza. It should be noted, however, that Chronicles depicts the campaigns of vv. 41–43 as essentially a tribal affair.

"Meunites." A group of disputed origin, mentioned in late biblical texts: 2 Chr 20:1 (LXX^{AB}); 26:7 (MT), 7–8 (LXX); Ezra 2:50 (Qere); Neh 7:52. According to one theory, the Meunites are a Transjordanian or Arabian group who are attested in the eighth century B.C.E. (Ephʿal 1984: 77–80, 219–20; Borger and Tadmor 1982: 250–51). The proponents of this position argue that the Meunites appear as the "Muʾnaeans" (^{kur}*Mu-uʾu-na-a-a*) in a summary inscription (ND 400) of Tiglath-pileser III (8.22–23; H. Tadmor 1994: 178–79). In the inscription, the Munaeans are active in the frontier area between Egypt and Palestine. According to a second theory, the Meunites hail from one of the sites called *māʿôn* or *maʿān*: Maon in the hill country of Judah (1st NOTE to 1 Chr 2:45); Maon (Khirbet el-Maʿîn) about 20 km south of Gaza; or the *Maʿān* region of southeastern Edom. Given the mention of both "Gerar" (v. 39) and the "clans of Ḥam" (v. 40), the first of these options can be safely ruled out. Note with respect to the last option, the association between the Meunites and the hill country of Seir in the Chronicler's narration of Jehoshaphaṭ's reign (2 Chr 20:10, 22–23; 2nd TEXTUAL NOTE to v. 41). According to a third theory, the Meunites, or more accurately the Mineans (LXX *hoi Minaioi*; 2nd TEXTUAL NOTE to v. 41), were associated with an Arabian city-state called *mʿn* (Knauf 1985b: 117–22; 1992b: 801–2). The Mineans, active in the incense trade during the fourth century, established a variety of trading posts in Egypt, western Arabia, and Mediterranean ports (Diodorus Siculus, *Bibl.* 3.42.5; Knauf 1985b: 116–17). Whatever the merits of the third theory, it is interesting that the LXX translators construed the disputed term as the Mineans in each and every instance (TEXTUAL NOTE). This indicates that the Mineans were well-known to the translators of LXX during the third and second centuries.

"and annihilated them" *(wyḥrymm)*. The use of the "ban" *(ḥerem)* in a martial context is a hallmark of Deuteronomic (Deut 20:15–18) and Deuteronomistic definitions of Israel's conduct in sacral war (Josh 2:10; 6:18–19, 21; 7:1, 7–15; 8:26; 10:1, 28–40; 11:12–21). Even though the Chronicler embraces the notion of sacral war, his understanding of this institution differs significantly from that espoused by the authors of Deuteronomy and the Deuteronomistic History (Ruffing 1992; Knoppers 1999c). The ban, understood as the total annihilation of an opponent and the complete devotion of that opponent's goods to Yhwh, is not a necessary component of sacral wars in Chronicles (e.g., 2 Chr 13:2–20; 14:8–14). This does not mean, however, that a religious sense of the verb "to ban" or "to annihilate" *(ḥrm)* no longer existed in the time of the Chronicler, as some assert. The Chronicler's own presentation suggests otherwise (1 Chr 2:7; 2 Chr 20:23; 32:14). Whether the account amounts to a full-fledged polemic against Edom (Kartveit 1989: 134–35) is not entirely clear, but it does seem evident that the author has a continuing interest in the areas to the south and southwest of Yehud (COMMENT).

"there was pasture there for their flocks." This statement forms an *inclusio* with the introduction of v. 39, "to seek pasture for their flocks" (v. 39). In fact, the vignette (vv. 39–41) evinces a broadly chiastic design.

a Pasture for flocks sought after and discovered (39)
  b Pasture occupied by Ḥam (40)
    c Extermination of Ḥam (41)
  b′ Pasture occupied by Simeonites (41)
a′ Pasture for flocks attained (41)

4:42–43. "men of Simeon." Unlike the previous campaign, this campaign is not justified by the need to search for new grazing land. The long-standing enmity between Israel and Amaleq lies in the background of the story of this conflict (Exod 17:8–16; Num 24:20; Deut 25:17–19; 1 Chr 18:11).

4:42. "hill country of Seir" *(hr śʿyr)*. Compare "the hill country of Ephraim" (*hr ʾprym*; Josh 17:15; 19:50; 20:7; 1 Chr 6:52; 2 Chr 13:4; 19:4), "the hill country of Israel" (*hr yśrʾl*; Josh 11:16, 21; Ezek 17:23; 20:40), and "the hill country of Judah" (*hr yhwdh*; Josh 11:21; 20:7; 21:11). In earlier texts "Seir" is associated with the highlands of Edom (Judg 5:4; Deut 33:2; Cross 1973: 100–101; Knauf 1988: 50ff.). See also the NOTES to 1 Chr 1:38–42.

4:43. "surviving remnant of Amaleq." Quite possibly an allusion to the effects of the battles fought during the time of Saul and David (1 Sam 14:48; 30:1; 2 Sam 8:12; *pace* 1 Sam 15:2–21). See also the 2nd NOTE to 1 Chr 1:36.

"resided there to this day." The precise significance of this statement is debated. According to a majority of scholars (most recently, Japhet 1993a: 126–27), the statement is not the Chronicler's own but stems from a preexilic source that is incorporated without alteration or commentary by the author into his narrative. In this view, the truth claim only reflects the preexilic time in which the source was written. This position is defensible. Japhet (1993a: 126) points out that almost all of the "to this day" pronouncements in Chronicles derive from earlier (biblical) sources, the implication being that the same holds true here. According to a minority of scholars (e.g., Aharoni 1979; R. Braun 1986), the statement "to this day," whatever its origins, carries more permanent connotations. In Aharoni's view the areas populated by these Simeonites had become dissociated from Judah already in the years 597–586 B.C.E. Hence, many, if not most, of their residents were not exiled. Similarly, in Braun's view, the Chronicler presents certain Simeonites as surviving the Babylonian destructions and continuing to live in these territories. I am inclined to support the minority view for three additional reasons. First, if the Chronicler strenuously disagreed with the locution "to this day," he could have qualified it. In this respect, many of the other "to this day" assertions drawn from earlier biblical texts imply ongoing states of affairs (1 Chr 5:26; cf. 2 Kgs 17:23;

1 Chr 13:11[//2 Sam 6:8]; cf. 1 Chr 17:5[//2 Sam 7:6]; 2 Chr 5:9[//1 Kgs 8:8]; 2 Chr 10:19[//1 Kgs 12:19]). Second, a limited exile is consistent with the Chronicler's presentation of the final decades of the Judahite monarchy (Japhet 1989). Third, archaeological evidence supports the view that the Babylonian deportations were not entirely exhaustive, but limited to certain areas (A. Mazar 1990; Ofer 1993; 1997; Zorn 1997; 2003; Lipschits 1998; 1999; 2003). The notion of an empty land (Barstad 1988; 1997: 77–87; 2003; Carroll 1992) has much to do with how certain Judahite authors wished to construe the devastation of Judah and the force of divine judgment against their people. But Chronicles, Lamentations, and the material evidence suggest some continuity in the occupation of the land.

SOURCES AND COMPOSITION

The most elaborate case for the disunity of the genealogy comes from Rudolph (1955: 38–42), who argues for four levels of composition: (1) vv. 24–27, (2) vv. 28–33*, (3) vv. 34–43*, and (4) later additions. Rudolph's reconstruction calls attention to the different sections within the genealogy along with their different foci, but his arguments are not compelling. Kartveit (1989: 61–65), who rightly criticizes Rudolph for disregarding the importance of geography in the Chronicler's genealogies, makes a strong case for the literary unity of most of the passage. To his detailed arguments, comparative evidence can be added from ancient Greece. Classical genealogies contain many anecdotes of both a geographical and historical nature. Because ancient lineages were composed of names that were deemed to be significant and designed to support an author's speculations, they were often interlaced with digressions and narrative comments explaining what particular groups did, what battles they fought, or where their descendants settled ("Excursus: The Genealogies"). This is precisely the kind of material one finds both in the genealogy of Simeon and in the other genealogies within Chronicles.

Two major source-critical issues have occupied scholars' attention in dealing with the Simeonite genealogy. First, there is the matter of the author's biblical sources. No one contests that Num 26:12–14 was a source for the Simeonite genealogy, but commentators debate the connection between 1 Chr 4:28–32; Josh 15:26–32, 42; and Josh 19:2–8. Some think that the Judahite allotment of Josh 15:26–32, 42 is a source for 1 Chr 4:28–32, while others derive both Josh 19:2–8 and 1 Chr 4:28–32 from the base text of Josh 15 (Alt 1953: 285; Noth 1953: 113; Rudolph 1955: 38). The relationship between Josh 15:26–32, 42 and Josh 19:2–8 is a legitimate issue (e.g., Albright 1924), but one that need not be settled here. There are, as we have seen (TEXTUAL NOTES), many parallels between Josh 19:2–8 and the Simeon town list in Chronicles. Conversely, there are no parallels between Josh 15:26–32, 42 and 1 Chr 4:28–32 that are not also found in Josh 19:2–8. There is, moreover, material in Josh 15:26–32, 42 that does not appear in either Josh 19:2–8 or 1 Chr 4:28–32. This evidence strongly suggests that 1 Chr 4:28–32 is connected in some fashion to Josh 19:2–8. To be sure, it is theoretically possible that the authors of Chronicles and Joshua each drew upon an administrative document or that the list in Chronicles precedes that of either Josh 15 or Josh 19 (e.g., Kallai 1958). But there is no convincing evidence that the list in Chronicles is independent of or precedes that of Josh 19 (TEXTUAL NOTES). The most economical way to explain the relationship between 1 Chr 4:28–32 and Josh 19:2–8 is to say that 1 Chr 4:28–32 is indebted to a version of Josh 19:2–8.

Many scholars (most recently, Japhet 1993a: 119–20) have thought that the author also incorporated some authentic extra-biblical sources into his composition. But given the Chronistic stylistic and theological tendencies reflected in nonparallel material within 1 Chr 4:24–43 (NOTES), one has to be skeptical that such sources can be isolated with any significant degree of confidence. In its present form, the genealogy of Simeon exhibits sufficient unity to be marked as the Chronicler's own composition.

COMMENT

Various texts in the Hebrew Scriptures point to a close connection between geographically contiguous Judah and Simeon. The ties between the tribes are evident in Judg 1:3, 17, which portray the two as leagued together in a single effort to remove the Canaanites from their territories. Of the two, Judah was by far the more dominant. The pattern of Judahite domination over and even absorption of Simeon is strongly suggested by the Deuteronomistic work. In the tribal allotments of Joshua, the places one might associate with Simeon (Josh 15:26–32, 42) are mentioned within the context of Judah's inheritance (Josh 15:1–63). Similarly, the list of Simeon's towns falls within Judah's limits (Josh 19:1–9). At first glance, the Chronicler's presentation seems to resonate with these earlier texts. The genealogy of Simeon follows that of Judah. Both occupy a large variety of towns (Augustin 1994: 301). The comparison between the prolific offspring of Judah and the not-so-prolific offspring of Simeon (v. 27) points to Judah's prominence. Simeon's wars and conquests recall the descriptions of individual tribal campaigns at the beginning of Judges (1:1–36; Boling 1975: 50–67; Soggin 1981: 15–33). In this respect, whatever historical reconstruction of early Israel one adopts, it seems apparent that the author was influenced by previous literary (biblical) presentations.

But the Chronicler's portrayal of Simeon does not simply follow earlier patterns. First, unlike the author(s) of the tribal allotments in Joshua, he does not discuss Simeon (4:24–43) within the confines of his discussion of Judah (2:3–4:23). Simeon appears as an independent tribe within a larger framework. Second, even though the Chronicler draws heavily from Joshua to depict Simeon's settlements, he does not speak of tribal allotments (Kartveit 1989: 128–29; Japhet 1993a: 122–23). Simeon occupies (ישב) various towns and territories; Simeon does not receive and later settle an inheritance (נחלה). Third, the geographical areas covered in the violent series of Simeonite expansions (4:38–43) lead Simeon to occupy a larger territory than Josh 19:2–8 allocate. Fourth, Simeon does not vanish from view with the advent of the monarchy. Taking a cue from the Blessing of Jacob (Gen 49:5–7; Gevirtz 1981) and Samuel-Kings, many modern scholars have interpreted Joshua's incorporating Simeon within the larger context of Judah as evidence for Simeon's disappearance by the time of the dual monarchies. But the Chronicler's presentation of Simeon, both here and in the narration of the monarchy, contends for the tribe's resiliency (1 Chr 12:25; 27:16; 2 Chr 15:9; 34:6). Not only does Simeon remain a viable entity alongside the other tribes, but Simeon is perfectly capable of launching its own military campaigns against local foes. One of these offensives occurs during the reign of an eighth- to seventh-century monarch.

What should one make of the Chronicler's distinctive presentation? It is difficult to assess the extent to which his portrayal of Simeon engages preexilic realities. According to many scholars (e.g., Myers 1965a: 25–31), the genealogy reflects a time—the early monarchy—in which Simeon had not yet been consolidated into Judah. But given the reference to Ḥezeqiah (v. 41), a longer time span has to be in view. At the very least, one can say that the Chronicler's presentation functions as a useful counterbalance to the typological concentration on the northern and southern kingdoms found in Kings (Knoppers 1993c; 1994e). How significant a role individual groups and ethnic factions played in Israel and Judah is obscured by a schematic presentation of events. From the Deuteronomistic work one gains the impression that Israel progressed from a tribal confederacy (Joshua-Judges) to a monarchy (Samuel-Kings). In the Deuteronomistic treatment of the monarchy little is heard about the fate of individual tribes and clans. But the internal histories of Israel and Judah were undoubtedly much more complicated than the Deuteronomists acknowledge. The Samaria ostraca, for example, attest to the continuing importance of local elements during the eighth-century Israelite monarchy (Davies, §3.001–107; Stager 1985; Vanderhooft 1999b). In Chronicles clans and tribes do not disappear with the advent of the monarchy. Instead, they coexist. Whatever one makes of the details of the Chronicler's presentation, the insistence that local leaders and regional politics continued to play significant roles during the monarchy is undoubtedly correct.

The degree to which a fairly autonomous tribe of Simeon endured in spite of the ravages of history is, however, unclear (2nd NOTE to v. 43). That some Yahwists existed in the author's own time south of Yehud, whom the author associated with Simeonites, is not impossible. One could also think of southern Judahites surviving from the Babylonian invasions up to the time in which the author lived (R. Braun 1986: 68). The very fact that the authors of Neh 11:26–29 (MT) can speak of Judeans as settling in Beer-sheba, Moladah, Ḥazar-shual, Ziqlag, and En-rimmon, despite these towns being situated outside the borders of Yehud, may point to connections between Judeans and certain inhabitants within these towns. In this respect, there may be an analogy between the idealized list in Neh 11 and the Simeonite genealogy. Both reflect aspirations to areas once controlled by the kingdom of Judah. But the claim that a distinct social and geopolitical entity named Simeon retained its independence throughout the monarchy is greeted by historians with great skepticism. To begin with, there are archaeological problems in positing such a continuity of identity (Augustin 1994). There is also a problem with the other literature from the Persian era. The treatments (Ezra 1:1–8:36) and lists of the postexilic residents found in Chronicles (1 Chr 9:2–34), Ezra, and Nehemiah (7:6–69; 11:3–36; 12:1–29) mention neither a tribe of Simeon nor any Simeonites.

Historiographically speaking, the author's presentation should be understood in the time in which it was written—the late Persian period. The attention it lavishes on various Israelite tribes may be compared with that given to the tribes in other (relatively) late biblical works such as the Priestly source and Ezekiel. These works also speak of a distinct entity called Simeon (e.g., Exod 1:2; 6:15; Num 1:6, 22–23; 2:12; 7:36; 13:5; 25:14; 26:14; Ezek 48:24, 25, 33). In this respect, the common argument (most recently, Dombrowski 1997: 67) that the Persian period writings reveal a concern with national coherence rather than with tribal divisions and bonds needs to be critically reexamined. Whether looking back or looking forward, the Priestly writing, Ezekiel, and Chronicles conserve, even promote, the notion of a tribal Israel. The Chronicler's treatment of Simeon may also be compared with Simeon's appearance in later Jewish Hellenistic and Roman writings such as *Jubilees* (28:13; 34:20; 44:13), the *Testament of Simeon, Joseph and Aseneth* (23:2–27; 27:6), and Theodotus (*Praep. Evan.* 9.22.8–9), although these works are more interested in the activities and traits of the eponymous ancestor than in the tribe named after him. In certain instances, the tribe of Simeon is mentioned as a point of origin (Jdt 6:15; 9:2; 4 Macc 2:19; *Liv. Pro.* 12:1; 13:1).

The Chronicler's coverage of Simeon is an act of literary conservation and redefinition. Living centuries after the Assyrian campaigns, the Babylonian deportations, and the rise of the Achaemenids, the author revives the ideal of a larger tribal federation. In this respect, the coverage may be compared with prophetic hopes for the restoration of Israel (Jer 16:14–15; 23:7–8; 31:5–6; Hos 2:16–23; Zeph 2:7–9). It should be observed that some prophetic writers do not simply call for a reinstatement of an older status quo. The very hopes for renewal entail transformation. This is, of course, evident in the oracles calling for both a restoration of Israel and a rearrangement of the Israelite tribes in Ezekiel (34:13–16; 36:8–12, 22–38; 37:21–25; 48:1–29). But it is also evident in other contexts, such as Obadiah's prophecy (Obad 19; Raabe 1996: 255–61):

the Negev shall possess the hill country of Esau,
the Shephelah (shall possess) the Philistines,
they shall possess the territory of Ephraim,
(they shall possess) the land of Samaria,
and Benjamin (shall possess) Gilead.

In Chronicles, the reconstitution of Simeon on a literary level—its lineages, settlements, genealogical registration, and campaigns—effects a portrait of the tribe as separate from its northern neighbor Judah. In Judah's genealogy personal names and toponyms are constantly in flux, but in Simeon's genealogy lineages, settlements, genealogical registrations, and campaigns are all distinguished. Judah grows through peaceful migration, intermingling with other peoples and tribes, and gradual expansion. Simeon has connections to other peoples (vv. 25–26) and experiences internal growth (v. 27), but it expands through warfare and conquest (vv. 41–43). The ruthlessness displayed by the Simeonites recalls the intemperate behavior of their eponymous ancestor (Gen 34:25–29; 49:5–7). In this manner, the author fashions a distinctive presentation of each one of the tribes that collectively constitute Israel. His act of writing preserves the memory of Simeon. But it also does more than that: By creating a unique Simeonite genealogy, the Chronicler makes his own contribution to Simeon's legacy.

VI. The Transjordanian Tribes (5:1–26)

Reuben, Judah, and Joseph

[1]The descendants of Reuben, firstborn of Israel. Indeed, he was the firstborn, but when he defiled the bed of his father his birthright was given to Joseph, the son of Israel, and he could not be registered as having the birthright. [2]Although Judah grew mighty among his brothers and a leader came from him, the birthright belonged to Joseph.

The Sons of Reuben

[3]The descendants of Reuben the firstborn of Israel: Enoch, Pallu, Ḥezron, and Carmi. [4]The sons of Joel: Shemaiah his son, Gog his son, Shimei his son, [5]Micah his son, Reaiah his son, Baal his son, [6]Beerah his son—whom Tilgat-pilneser the king of Assyria exiled—he was a chieftain among the Reubenites. [7]His kin, by their families, according to their registration by generations: the head, Jeiel, and Zechariah [8]and Bela son of Azaz, son of Shema, son of Joel. He began to reside in Aroer and as far as Nebo and Baal-meon. [9]To the east he resided as far as the approaches to the wilderness, on this side of the river Euphrates, because their herds had become numerous in the land of Gilead. [10]In the days of Saul they made war with the Hagrites, who fell by their hand, and they resided in their tents throughout the region east of Gilead.

The Sons of Gad

[11]The descendants of Gad resided opposite them in the land of Bashan as far as Salchah. [12]Joel was the head and Shapham the second. And Janai was the officer in Bashan. [13]Their kin according to their ancestral houses: Michael, Meshullam, Sheba, Jorai, Jakan, Zia, and Eber—seven. [14]These are the sons of Abiḥayil, son of Ḥuri, son of Jaroaḥ, son of Gilead, son of Michael, son of Jeshishai, son of Jaḥdo, son of Buz, [15]son of Abdiel, son of Guni, head of the house of their fathers. [16]They resided in Gilead, in Jabesh and its dependencies, and among all of the open spaces of Sharon to their boundaries. [17]All of them were registered in the days of Jotham king of Judah and in the days of Jeroboam king of Israel.

Reuben, Gad, and East Manasseh at War

[18]The sons of Reuben, Gad, and the half-tribe of Manasseh had warriors, men who carried the shield and sword, drew the bow, and were well-versed in war—44,760 ready for military service. [19]They made war with the Hagrites, along with Jeṭur, Naphish, and Nodab, [20]and they prevailed over them. The Hagrites and everything with them were delivered into their hands, for they cried out to God in battle and their entreaty was granted, because they trusted in him. [21]They took into (their) possession their livestock—50,000 camels, 250,000 small cattle, 2,000 asses, and 100,000 living persons. [22]Indeed, there were many who fell slain because the battle was from God. They resided (there) in their stead until the exile.

The Half-Tribe of East Manasseh

[23]As for the descendants of the half-tribe of Manasseh, they resided in the land from Bashan as far as Baal Ḥermon, Senir, and Mount Ḥermon. And in the Lebanon they became numerous. [24]These are the heads of their ancestral houses: Epher, Ishi, Eliel, Azriel, Jeremiah, Hodaviah, and Jaḥdiel—men (who were) valiant warriors, men of repute, heads of their ancestral houses.

Assyrian Exile

[25]But they transgressed against the God of their fathers and prostituted themselves to the gods of the peoples of the land whom God had destroyed before them. [26]The God of Israel stirred up the spirit of Pul the king of Assyria, to wit Tilgat-pilneser the king of Assyria, and he exiled them—the Reubenites, the Gadites, and the half-tribe of Manasseh—and he brought them to Ḥelaḥ, Ḥabor, and the river of Gozan (where they are) to this day.

Textual Notes

5:1. "when he defiled" *(ûbĕḥallĕlô)*. The prep. *b-* is used with the inf. in a temporal clause (Williams, §§241; 504).

"the bed" *(yṣwʿy)*. On the pl. formation, see also Pss 63:7 [ET 63:6]; 132:3; Job 17:13 (cf. *miškĕbê ʾābîkā*; Gen 49:4); GKC, §124a.

"his birthright" *(bkrw)*. So MT. LXX^{B} "his blessing" *(eulogian autou = brktw)*. Although LXX^{B} offers basically the same variant in v. 2, the context shows that birthright, and not blessing, is at stake (Benzinger 1901: 18; Wlliamson 1977a: 89–95; contra von Rad 1930: 72–74; Rudolph 1955: 43). As Rothstein and Hänel (1927) and P. J. Williams (1998) point out, the LXX lemma may have been influenced by Gen 48:15 *(wybrk)*. Alternatively, the *Vorlage* of LXX may have suffered metathesis.

"to Joseph." Reading with several Heb. MSS *(lywsp)*. *Lectio brevior praeferenda est.* Both LXX^{AB} "to his son Joseph" *(tō huiō autou Iōsēp = lbnw ywsp)* and MT "to the sons of Joseph" *(lbny ywsp)* reflect confusion, perhaps caused by dittography (*bn*: *lbny ywsp* [MT] or *lbnw ywsp* [LXX]). Syr. retains part of the original reading: "to Joseph his brother" (= *lywsp ʾḥyw*).

"and he could not be registered" *(wĕlōʾ lĕhityaḥēś)*. The negative *lōʾ* is used in an absolute sense with the inf. construct (Joüon, §160j; Waltke and O'Connor, §36.2.1g). The antecedent to "he" is unclear. Some versions (LXX, Vg.) and modern translations (e.g., NRSV) present Reuben as the antecedent, because Reuben is the subj. introduced at the beginning of v. 1. Qimḥi and a number of rabbinic commentators make a case for Joseph, introduced in v. 1b, as being the intended antecedent. Contextually, however, the subj. should be Reuben, because the next verse concludes that "the birthright belonged to Joseph."

5:2. "grew mighty" *(gābar)*. Thus MT. The reading of LXX^{ABL} *dynatos ischyi (kai)*, "mighty of power (and)," interprets the Heb. consonantal text as signfying a noun *(gibbōr)*.

"among his brothers" *(bʾḥyw)*. Begrich *(BHK)* proposes emending to *min*, "more than his brothers" (*mʾḥyw*; cf. NJPS, "more powerful than his brothers").

"and a leader came from him" *(wlngyd mmnw)*. Two Heb. MSS simply read "and a leader" *(wngyd)*. LXX^{BL} *kai eis hēgoumenon ex autou*, "and for the leading was from him." I am reading the *lāmed* as emphatic (Kropat, §I.2), introducing a subj. (cf. 2 Chr 11:22). Others prefer to see the subj. of the noun clause as the pron. in *mmnw*, "and of him one became a prince" (GKC, §141a).

"the birthright" *(hbkrh)*. So MT. LXX^{B}, which has *kai hē eulogia* ("and the blessing"), may reflect metathesis *(hbrkh)*. The emendation proposed by Rudolph (1955: 42) and largely adopted by REB to insert *lô lōʾ* (cf. Ps 78:67, 68a) is unnecessary and conflicts with the force of v. 1 (Williamson 1977b: 89–95).

5:4. "sons of Joel" *(bny ywʾl)*. So MT and LXX^{AB} *(lectio difficilior)*. LXX^{L} *Iōēl huios autou*, "his son [= *bnw*] Joel," establishes a link with v. 3. The same impulse may be present in Syr. and Arab., which have *krmy*.

"Shemaiah" *(šmʿyh)*. So MT *(lectio brevior)*. LXX^{B} adds *kai Banaia* (= *wbnyh*), while LXX^{L} adds *Danaia* (b′e_2) or *Daneas (b)*. LXX's addition may have been triggered by reading בנו as a PN (Zöckler 1877: 63).

"Gog" *(gwg)*. Thus MT, LXX^{B} *Goug*, and LXX^{L} *Gō*. Syr. *dwʾg*.

5:5. "Micah" *(mykh)*. So MT and LXX^{AN} *Micha(a)*. LXX^{B} c_2 *Ēcha*.

"Reaiah" *(rʾyh)*. So MT and LXX^{L} *(Rhaeia)*. LXX^{BN} *Rhēcha*; Syr. *ʾwryh*.

"Baal" *(bʿl)*. Reading with MT and LXX^{AN} (maximum variation). LXX^{BL} read *Iōēl* by attraction to *Iōēl* in v. 4. Syr. *(blʿ)* has suffered metathesis.

5:6. "Beerah" *(bʾrh)*. Reading with MT and LXX^{L} *(Bara)*. LXX^{B} *Beēl*.

"Tilgat-pilneser" *(tlgt-plnʾsr)*. So MT, LXX^{B}, and c_2 *(lectio difficilior)*, which read the standard form of this name in Chronicles (1 Chr 5:26; 2 Chr 28:20). The readings of many Heb. MSS, LXX^{L} *Theglathphalasar* (b′ *Theglaphalasar*; e_2 *Thelathphalsar*), Tg., and Syr. *tglt-plnʾsr*, assimilate toward the more common *tglt-plʾsr* (e.g., 2 Kgs 15:29; 16:10; cf. 2 Kgs 16:17). The metathesis attested here is not unprecedented (cp. *ʾalmuggîm* in 1 Kgs 10:11; *ʾalgûmmîm* in 2 Chr 9:10; Willi 1972: 87). In Akk., the name is *tukultī-apil-ešarra*, "my help is the son of Esharra (the temple of the god Ashur in the city of Ashur)."

5:7. "his kin" *(ʾḥyw)*. Because *ʾāḥ* can refer to both a brother and a kinsman, there is no need to emend to *ʾaḥar* (contra Rudolph 1955: 44–45).

"by their families." So LXX^{L}, Arm., Syr., Tg., Vg., which have the 3 pl. suff. (= *lmšpḥtm*). MT "by his families," *lmšpḥtyw* (cf. LXX^{B} *tē patridi autou*) assimilates toward *ʾḥyw*.

"Jeiel" *(yʿyʾl)*. Thus MT. The lemma of LXX^BL *Iōēl* assimilates toward the name appearing in vv. 4 and 8.

5:8. "Azaz" *(ʿzz)*. So MT. LXX^B *Ozouz*; LXX^L *Iō(a)zaz* (= *ywʿzz*); Syr. *ʿwzy*, "Uzzi."

"Shema" *(šmʿ)*. So MT. LXX^B *Sama*; LXX^L *Sem(e)ei* (= *šmʿy*). See also the 1st NOTE to v. 7.

"he began to reside in Aroer" *(hwʾ ywšb bʿrʿr)*. So MT. LXX^B *houtos katōkēsen en Aroēr* (= *hwʾ yšb bʿrʿr*). The use of a ptc. as a predicate is common in Chronicles, Ezra, and Nehemiah (Kropat, §8). On the periphrastic use of the ptc., especially in LBH, see Joüon (§121g).

5:9. "as far as the approaches to the wilderness" *(ʿd lbwʾ mdbrh)*. Usually this infinitival phrase includes "Lebo Ḥamath" (e.g., Josh 13:5; Judg 3:3; Ezek 47:20; Amos 6:14; 1 Chr 13:5). But there are exceptions (Ezek 47:15; 2 Chr 26:8; Waltke and O'Connor, §36.2.3d).

"on this side of the river Euphrates" *(lmn-hnhr prt)*. The prep. *min* is used to express a spatial relationship (Williams, §323).

"the river Euphrates" *(hnhr prt)*. As in some other cases in LBH, the proper noun is used in apposition to the thing named (Ezra 8:21; 9:1; Esth 8:15; Joüon, §131h).

"because their herds" *(ky mqnyhm)*. Reading with MT and LXX^AN *(lectio difficilior)*. LXX^B and c_2 *hoti ktēnē autō*, "because his cattle." The lemma of Syr., "because they and their herds" (= *ky hmh wmqnyhm*), is expansionary.

"had become numerous" *(rābû)*. Thus MT (cf. ye_2 *eplēthynthē*; bb′ *eplēthynthēsan*). LXX^B *polla* (= *rb*).

5:10. "the Hagrites" *(hhgrʾym)*. LXX^AB *tous paroikous*, "the aliens" (= *hgrym*); LXX^L *tōn agarēnōn*.

"they resided in their tents" *(wyšbw bʾhlym)*. So MT. LXX^B *katoikountes en skēnais* (= *ywšbym bʾhlym*). It is also possible to translate *ʾhl* as "clan" (1st TEXTUAL NOTE to 4:41).

"throughout the region east of Gilead" *(ʿal-kol-pĕnê mizrāḥ laggilʿād)*. LXX^B *heōs pantes* (= *ʿd-kl* or *ʿd-lkl*; Allen 1974b: 86) *katʾ anatolas tēs Galaad*, "as far as all the region east of Gilead." Whether one opts for MT or LXX, the expression is quite unusual. In geographical descriptions, the prep. phrase *ʿal-pĕnê* usually means "opposite" or "facing" (Gen 23:19; 25:18; Num 21:11; Josh 15:8; *HALOT* 944).

5:11. "opposite them" *(lngdm)*. Literally, "before them."

"in the land" *(bʾrṣ)*. Thinking that a haplography *(homoioarkton)* has occurred, Rudolph (1955: 44, 46) reconstructs *bʾrṣ hglʿd w*, "in the land of Gilead and."

"Salchah" *(slkh)*. So MT and LXX^LN. LXX^AB *Elcha* has suffered haplography after *heōs* (Allen 1974b: 43). Arm. *Melche*. Syr.^L expands to *sybh wslkh*.

5:12. "the head . . . the second." The construction *hrʾš* followed by an ordinal *(hmšnh)* is common in Chronicles (1 Chr 12:19; 23:17, 19, 20; Kropat, §17). Syr. and Tg. interpret *hmšnh* as "study" (cf. Syr. and Tg. 2 Chr 34:22; Tg. 2 Kgs 22:14).

"Shapham" *(špm)*. LXX^B and c_2 *kai Sabat*; cf. Tg.^AS *špṭ*; LXX^L *kai Saphan*; Vg. *et Saphan* (= *wšpn*).

"Janai" *(yʿny)*. LXX^{B} *Iōani* (= *ywʿny*).

"the officer" *(hšṭr)*. Thus LXX* *ho grammateus*; Tg. *dyyn*ʾ (= *haššōṭēr* or, less likely, *haššōpēṭ*). In Chronicles *grammateus* translates *sōpēr* (e.g., 1 Chr 2:55; 18:16; 24:6; 27:32) and *šōṭēr* (1 Chr 23:4; 27:1; 2 Chr 19:11), but never *šōpēṭ* (contra Rudolph 1955: 46). MT's "Shaphaṭ" *(šāpāṭ)* assimilates toward Shapham *(šāpām)* earlier in v. 12.

5:13. "Jorai" *(ywry)*. So MT and LXX^{B} *(Iōree)*. LXX^{L} *Iō(a)reim*.

"Jakan" *(yʿkn)*. LXX^{B} *Chima*; ye$_2$ *Iacha*; bb′ *Iōacha*.

"Zia" *(zyʿ)*. So MT (cf. LXX^{L} *Zeia*). LXX^{B} *Zoue* (= *zwʿ*).

"Eber" *(ʿēber)*. So MT and LXX^{L} *(Heber)*. A few Heb. MSS *ʿōbēd*; cf. LXX^{B} *Ōbēd*; LXX^{AN} *Iōbēd*. The difference reflects a *dālet/rêš* confusion.

5:14. "Abiḥayil" *(ʾbyḥyl)*. So MT. LXX^{ABN} *Abeichaia*; LXX^{L} *Abiēl*.

"Jaroaḥ" *(yrwḥ)*. One Heb. MS *yrwʿ*; LXX^{B} *Idai*; LXX^{A} *Adai*; LXX^{L} *Aroue*; Syr. *zrḥ*; Vg. *Iaro*.

"Michael" *(mykʾl)*. Reading with MT and LXX *(Meichaēl)*. Syr. *mākîr*.

"Jeshishai" *(yšyšy)*. So MT. LXX^{B} *Isai*, LXX^{A} *Iessai*, and LXX^{L} *Sousei* have suffered haplography (Allen 1974b: 63). Cf. Vg. *Iesesi*.

"Jaḥdo" *(yḥdw)*. The textual variants reflect graphic confusion *(dālet/rêš; wāw/yôd)* and the transposition of consonants: LXX^{B} *Iourei*; LXX^{A} *Ieddai*; LXX^{L} *Ieddō* (Allen 1974b: 96).

"Buz" *(bwz)*. Reading tentatively with MT, LXX^{L}, and Arm. LXX^{B} and c$_2$ *Zaboucham*. Given the lemma of LXX^{AN} *Achibouz* (= *ʾḥybwz*), one may say that either MT (as witnessed by the beginning of v. 15, *ʾḥy*) or LXX^{AN} reflect metathesis.

5:15. "son of Abdiel." Reading with LXX^{L} and Syr. *(lectio brevior)*. LXX^{AB} *huiou Abdeēl* (but see the previous TEXTUAL NOTE). MT *ʾḥy bn-ʿbdyʾl* is problematic: "brother of the son of Abdiel." Rudolph (1955: 46) thinks that *ʾaḥay* is a PN (short for Aḥiyah or Aḥyo). Similarly, Allen (1974b: 14) believes that LXX* reflects *Achai*. But *ʾḥy* is very rarely attested as a PN.

"Guni" *(gwny)*. Reading with MT and LXX *(Gounei)*. Syr. *ʿly*.

5:16. "in Gilead." Not in Syr. LXX^{L} and Arm. expand to "in the land of Gilead" (cf. v. 9).

"in Jabesh." Reconstructing *bybš*. MT "in Bashan" *(bbšn)* is followed by LXX^{AL} *(Basan)* and Arm. LXX^{B} *Basam*. But note the following phrase, "and in its dependencies" *(wbbntyh)*. MT may have been influenced by the repeated appearance of Bashan in vv. 11–12. Begrich *(BHK)* proposes *bgwln*, "in Golan" (cf. Deut 4:43; Josh 20:8; 21:27; 1 Chr 6:56). In this case, however, one could posit a simple haplography of *bgwln* before *bbšn*.

"and in . . . their limits." The entire expression is lacking in Syr.

"and among all" *(wbkl)*. So MT and LXX^{L}. LXX^{BL} and Arm. read "and all" (= *wkl*).

"the open spaces of Sharon" *(mgršy šrwn)*. Chronicles, in distinction from most earlier biblical texts, always employs the term *migrāš* in the pl. (Barr 1984). This is true whether there is a named town or not.

"Sharon" *(šrwn)*. Instead of MT's "Sharon," LXX^{B} has *Geriam*. Benzinger (1901: 20) and Kittel (1902: 37), followed by Begrich *(BHK)* reconstruct *śiryôn* (cf. Deut 3:9; Ps 29:6), but Rudolph (1955: 48) wisely argues for retaining MT (last NOTE to v. 16).

"to their boundaries" *(ʿd-twṣʾwtm)*. So LXX[AB] *heos*, Vg. *ad* (A. Ehrlich 1914: 329). MT *ʿl-twṣʾwtm*. The term *twṣʾwt* is mostly found in P and late sources (BDB 426).

5:17. "Jotham." Reading with MT, LXX[AB] *(Iōatham)*, and c_2 *(Iōtham)*. Cf. LXX[L] *Iōas*; e_2 *Iōab*.

"Jeroboam." So MT and LXX[ABN]. LXX[L] c_2 add *tou Iōas* (c_2 *Iōatham*; *Iōab*).

5:18. "Gad" *(gd)*. So LXX[BL], Vg., Tg. MT *gdy* should have the article (A. Ehrlich 1914: 329).

"had warriors" *(mn-bny-ḥyl)*. Thus MT and LXX[AB] *ex huiōn dynameōs*. Lacking in Syr.

"men." So MT and LXX[AB]. LXX[L] prefaces *kl*.

"well-versed in war" *(lĕmûdê milḥāmâ)*. Although *lmd* "to learn" takes the form of a passive ptc., Joüon (§50e) lists a number of cases in which the *qāṭûl* formation has virtually an active sense. There is, therefore, no need to revocalize MT as *limmûdê* (contra Begrich in *BHK*).

"ready for military service" *(yṣʾy ṣbʾ)*. The ptc. in construct is often used with a following genitive, especially with the verbs *yṣʾ* and *bwʾ* (Joüon, §121n). Hence, it is not necessary to follow Begrich *(BHK)* in emending to *yṣʾw*.

5:19. "Jeṭur, Naphish, and Nodab." Lacking in Syr.

"Nodab" *(nwdb)*. So MT. LXX[AB] *kai Nadabaiōn*; LXX[L] *kai Nēdabaiōn* (y *Nabataiōn) kai Nadibaiōn (b Nalimaiōn)*. Begrich *(BHK)* calls attention to Gen 25:15 *wqdmh* ("and Qedmah"), which follows "Jeṭur, Naphish." Along with Albright (1956: 13–14), Knauf (1989: 67), and Vattioni (1991a: 481–82), it is possible to connect Nodab with Adbeel *(ʾdbʾl)* in 1 Chr 1:29(//Gen 25:13). The LXX variants to Adbeel in 1:29 and Nodab in 5:19 differ. According to Eupolemus (Eusebius, *Praep. ev.* 9.30.3), the "Nabdeans" *(Nabdaious)* were among the peoples David conquered. See further the NOTE to v. 19.

5:20. "and they prevailed over them" *(wyʿzrw ʿlyhm)*. Lacking in Syr. For the verb, LXX[AB] has *katischysan* (= *wygbrw*), LXX[L] *eboēsan* (= *wyʿzqw*), Vg. *praebuerunt* (= *wyʿzrw*). Rudolph (1955: 48) thinks that LXX[L] is a corruption of *eboēthēthēsan* (= MT).

"the Hagrites and everything with them" *(hhgryʾym wkl šʿmhm)*. So MT and LXX[L]. The entire phrase is lacking in Syr. Instead of "and everything with them," LXX[B] has *kai panta ta skēnōmata autōn*, "and all of their tents."

"and their entreaty was granted" *(wnʿtwr)*. The use of *ʿtr* with the prep. *l-* is consistent with late usage (Gen 25:21; 2 Chr 33:13, 19; Ezra 8:23), but the use of the inf. absolute to qualify a following pron. is rare (Waltke and O'Connor, §35.5.2d). The inf. absolute of *ʿtr* (in the *nipʿal*) conveys the sense "to be entreated by" or "to grant the entreaty of" and continues the preceding verbal form (Joüon, §123x).

5:21. "took into (their) possession" *(wayyišbû)*. Thus MT and LXX *kai ēchmalōteusan*, "took captive." Rothstein and Hänel (1927) emend to *wayyāšōlû*, "plundered," but MT is not corrupt (BDB 985). Alternatively, one could repoint MT (as the *hipʿil* of the root *šwb*; BDB 998) to *wayyāšîbû*, "brought back."

"50,000." So MT. LXX^{AB} 5,000, perhaps reflecting confusion between *hê* and *mêm* (Allen 1974b: 121). In Chronicles the larger number is more likely to be original.

5:23. "descendants of the half-tribe of Manasseh." So MT. LXX^{ABL} *hoi hemiseis (tēs) phylēs Manassē*, "the half-tribe of Manasseh."

"resided in the land." So MT, LXX^{LN}, and Arm. LXX^{B} and c_2 lack "in the land" *(bāʾāreṣ)*.

"from Bashan." Thus MT and LXX* *(apo Basan)*. As the NOTES to vv. 23–24 make clear, there is no need to view the text as corrupt (*pace* Begrich in *BHK*).

"Baal Ḥermon" *(bʿl ḥrmwn)*. LXX^{B} and c_2 *Ba(a)leim*.

"Mount Ḥermon" *(hr ḥrmwn)*. So MT and LXX^{ABL} *(oros Haermōn)*. Rudolph (1955: 50) would emend *hr* to *hwʾ*, "that is."

"and in the Lebanon." So LXX* *kai en tō Libanō* (= *ûballĕbānôn*), which precedes "they became numerous" *(hmh rbw)*. The phrase has been lost from MT due to haplography *(homoioteleuton)* from *whr ḥrmwn* to *wblbnwn*. For a different view, which sees LXX as reflecting the influence of Judg 3:3, see Allen (1974b: 142).

5:24. "Epher." Reading with LXX^{AB} *(Opher)*, LXX^{L} *(Apher)*, Vg., and Tg. *(lectio brevior)*. MT adds the conjunction, although it is possible that a name has dropped out (A. Ehrlich 1914: 329; Goettsberger 1939: 62). Syr. has *ʿph*.

"Ishi" *(yšʿy)*. So MT, LXX^{L} *(Iessei)*, and Arm. LXX^{B} *Seei*; Syr.^{W} *wšwb*; Syr.^{A} *wywšb*.

"Eliel" *(ʾlyʾl)*. LXX^{B} *Eleiēl*; LXX^{A} *Eliēl*; cf. bb′ *Ediēl*; ye_2 *Iediēl*; Syr. *ʾldʿh*.

"Hodaviah" *(hwdwyh)*. LXX^{B} *Hōdouia*; LXX^{L} *Iōdouia*. See the 2nd TEXTUAL NOTE to 3:24.

"Jaḥdiel" *(yḥdyʾl)*. LXX^{B} *Ieleiēl*; Syr. *ḥzʾl*.

"men of repute" *(ʾnšy šmwt)*. The pl. of a genitival group, in which both nouns are in the pl., occurs quite often in Chronicles (Kropat, §2; Joüon, §136o).

5:26. "the God of Israel." Syr. explicates by inserting the tetragrammaton before and *ʿlyhm* after this locution.

"the spirit of Pul the king of Assyria." Syr. lacks this phrase through haplography *(homoioarkton)* from *ʾt-rwḥ* to *ʾt-rwḥ*.

"Pul" *(pûl)*. LXX^{B} *Phalōch(ōs)*; LXX^{A} *Phalōs*; LXX^{L} *Phoul*.

"to wit." Understanding *wāw* in "Pul the king of Assyria, (and) Tilgat-pilneser king of Assyria" *(pwl mlk-ʾšwr wʾt-rwḥ tlgt plnsr mlk ʾšwr)* as explicatory. It is also possible that the author thought that Pul (2 Kgs 15:19) and Tiglath-pileser III (2 Kgs 15:29) referred to two different people.

"Tilgat-pilneser." See the 2nd TEXTUAL NOTE to v. 6.

"and he exiled them" *(wayyaglēm)*. So MT *(lectio difficilior)*. LXX* and Vg. lack the suf., but determining the *Vorlage* for LXX is, in this instance, difficult. The use of the verbal suf. (with a noun in apposition) is anticipatory (Joüon, §146e; Muraoka 1985: 65ff.). The author is citing 2 Kgs 15:29 *wayyaglēm (ʾaššûrāh)*.

"to Ḥelaḥ" *(lḥlḥ)*. So MT. Cf. LXX^{AN} *Chala*. LXX^{B} and c_2 *(Chaach)* have suffered a haplography of *lāmed*.

"Ḥabor." Following LXX[AB] and Syr. *(lectio brevior)*. MT (cf. LXX[L] *kai Harran*) adds "Hara" *(hrʾ)*, which is also lacking in 2 Kgs 17:6 and 18:11. It is possible that the MT lemma is a remnant of *hārê mādāy*, "mountains of Media" (LXX 2 Kgs 17:6) or of *ʿārê mādāy*, "cities of Media" (MT 2 Kgs 17:6). See further below.

"and the river." So MT and LXX[L]. LXX[AB] *kai epi potamon*, "and by the river" (= *wʿl-nhr*). Syr. and 2 Kgs 17:6 and 18:11 lack the conjunction. In MT Kings "the river Gozan" explicates "Ḥabor," but in Chronicles Ḥabor appears as a site distinct from "the river of Gozan."

"Gozan" *(gwzn)*. So MT. LXX[B] *Chōzar*. Syr. adds *ʿry mdy*, perhaps by attraction to 2 Kgs 17:6 *(ʿry mdy)* and 18:11 *(ʿry mdy)*. Alternatively, as Freedman points out (personal communication), MT could have suffered a haplography *(homoioarkton)* from *ʿry mdy* to *ʿd*.

NOTES

5:1. "descendants of Reuben." The anecdote (vv. 1–2), set in context through the literary technique of repetitive resumption (from בני ראובן בכור-ישׂראל in v. 1 to בני ראובן בכור-ישׂראל at the beginning of v. 3), is necessary because Chronicles does not place Reuben first in the sequence of Israel's tribes (2:3–9:1). The author acknowledges that Reuben was firstborn (2:1–2), but in the Chronicler's way of thinking this status does not automatically entitle Reuben to a position of preeminence among Jacob's offspring.

"firstborn of Israel." In making this claim, the text is following the pattern of older genealogies, narratives, and lists about Jacob's sons (Gen 29:31–30:24; 35:23–26; 46:8–9; Exod 1:2; 6:14; Num 26:5; Ezek 48:31–35). See also 1 Chr 27:16.

"defiled (*ḥll*) the bed of his father." According to Gen 35:22, Reuben had sexual relations with Jacob's concubine (פילגשׁ)—Bilhah. Reuben's action is condemned in the Blessing of Jacob (*ḥllt yṣwʿy*; Gen 49:4; Augustin 1994: 302), which is the source of the present statement. It is interesting to observe that in the explication of this verse, Tg. assumes that the birthright, kingship, and priesthood all could have been Reuben's. The birthright went to Joseph because of Reuben's sin with Bilhah; the kingship went to Judah because he became a mighty man *(gbyrʾ)* and kingship came from him; and the high priesthood went to Levi because he was a godly man and did not behave sinfully in the golden-calf affair (Le Déaut and Robert 1971b: 21; McIvor 1994: 64). On this line of interpretation, see also *Tg. Onq.* Gen 49:3–4. In contrast with the brief comment in Chronicles, the circumstances and consequences of the relationship with Bilhah receive a great deal of attention from other early interpreters (*Jub.* 33:1–6; *T. Reu.* 1:6–10; 3:10–15; *b. Šabb.* 55b; Kugel 1995).

"birthright was given to Joseph." This action is not directly attested elsewhere in the Hebrew Scriptures. It is likely, however, that the author did not draw this comment out of thin air. His claim about Joseph was likely influenced by an intriguing sequence of incidents near the close of Jacob's life (Gen 47:25–48:22). Genesis 48:5 depicts an elderly Jacob assuring Joseph that his two sons born in Egypt, Ephraim and Manasseh, "will be mine, no less than Reuben and Simeon." At stake in this family decision is the addition of two tribes to Jacob's family, which represents the larger Israelite federation (Westermann 1986: 185). Jacob's bequest means that two of his grandsons will share in his estate. In this manner, Joseph, by virtue of his two Egyptian sons, gains two shares of his father's inheritance. Also suggestive is Jacob's later comment to Joseph that he is assigning Joseph *šekem*, perhaps a "shoulder" (a mountain ridge) or "Shechem" itself, "one more than to your brothers" (*'ḥd 'l-'ḥyk*; Gen 48:22). Whatever one's interpretation of elusive *šekem*, Jacob is clearly bestowing upon Joseph a special privilege not accorded to his other sons (de Vaux 1978: 637–40; Westermann 1986: 192–93). From this statement, it is not a gigantic interpretive leap to understand Joseph as receiving one more share than his brothers do. Indeed, many of the early interpreters came to precisely this conclusion on the basis of their reading of Gen 35:22, 48:22, and 49:3–4 (*Gen. Rab.* 97; *Tg. Onq.*; *Tg. Ps.-J.*; *Tg. Neof.* I). Finally, the Blessing of Jacob (and that of Moses in Deut 33:13–17) accords to Joseph sustained attention (Gen 49:22–26) and unique praise: "May they [the blessings of your father] be upon the head of Joseph, upon the crown of the elect (*nāzîr*) of his brothers" (Gen 49:26). Conversely, Jacob's final treatment of Reuben bestows no special provisions. In short, if there is a candidate for chief heir among Jacob's twelve sons in the texts depicting Jacob's dotage, it is Joseph and not Reuben. See further, Knoppers (2000b).

"he could not be registered" (*wĕlōʾ lĕhityaḥēś*). The claim is not merely that Reuben was not genealogically recorded as having the birthright (de facto), but that he could not be (de jure) registered as such (TEXTUAL NOTES to v. 1). The Chronicler seems to couple the lack of evidence for Reuben's receiving a preferential share of his father's estate with the special treatment of Joseph and to read Jacob's scolding of Reuben (Gen 49:4) in light of this earlier material. In other words, he argues from the latter to the former. Reuben's sexual affair with Bilhah, explicitly condemned by Jacob, explains why Reuben could not attain right of birth. To be sure, the author does not claim that Joseph displaced Reuben from having primary (firstborn) status. The Chronicler's own genealogy of Israel lists Reuben first (2:1). But being the firstborn is not a failsafe predictor of achievement. Of Jacob's sons, Judah gained preeminence and Joseph gained the birthright.

5:2. "grew mighty among his brothers." Judah's preeminence is also apparent in the Priestly source. There Reuben is recognized as firstborn (Num 1:5–15), but Judah enjoys a primary position in the encampment of the Israelite tribes (Num 2:3–31) and in the order of presenting daily offerings (Num 7:12–83; Halpern 1983: 113–17). In Chronicles, Judah is the first tribe for whom Chronicles provides a genealogy (Willi 1994b: 152–55). Judah's status is further enhanced by the extensive coverage given to its lineages (2:4–4:23).

"a leader came from him" (*wlngyd mmnw*). Alluding to David's kingship, which eventually encompassed all twelve tribes (1 Chr 28:4; 1 Sam 13:14; 25:30;

Mic 5:1). The Blessing of Jacob speaks of the scepter *(šebeṭ)* as not departing from Judah (Gen 49:10). Psalm 78 puts Judah's rise to prominence in blunter terms. On the one hand it speaks of Yhwh's nonchoice *(lō bāḥār)* of Ephraim and his rejection *(m's)* of Joseph. On the other hand it speaks of his choice *(bḥr)* of Judah, which is associated with building a sanctuary, and Yhwh's choice *(bḥr)* of David, which is associated with David's tending "Jacob his people and Israel his possession" (Ps 78:67–71).

"the birthright belonged to Joseph." The Chronicler dissociates firstborn status (*bĕkōr;* Gen 25:13; Exod 11:5; 13:13, 15; Num 3:41; Jer 31:9; Neh 10:37 [ET 10:36]) from birthright (*bĕkōrâ;* Gen 25:31–34; 27:36; 43:33). In some earlier works the two go together. In adjudicating a case of bigamy in which a husband wishes to favor the firstborn of his favorite wife over his biological firstborn from a less favored wife, the author of Deut 21:15–17 protects patri-primogeniture. The father must accord the birthright to his firstborn, "the first fruit of his vigor," whether or not that son is the firstborn of his favorite wife (Deut 21:17). Hence, the husband must give a preferential share of the estate (Gen 48:22; Tigay 1996: 196, 382) to the biological firstborn of his wives (Deut 21:17). But in the ancient Near East, the linkage between being the firstborn and preferential status is not a necessary one (Tigay 1996: 195). The Chronicler, in fact, decouples firstborn status from birthright. Reuben is firstborn, but Joseph attains the birthright. Judah was not the firstborn of Israel, but he gained preeminence among his brothers. In this respect, the point made in 5:1–2 is not unique in the Chronicler's work (1 Chr 26:10; 28:1–5; 2 Chr 11:22; Knoppers 2000b).

5:3. "descendants of Reuben." The list is drawn from Exod 6:14 (Japhet 1993a: 130) or Num 26:5–6. If the latter text is in view, the author takes longer material and reduces it to a bare list (cf. 1:1–4, 24–27).

"Pallu." One source text (Num 26:8–11), not cited here, has a lineage for Pallu extending three generations.

"Ḥezron" *(ḥeṣrôn)*. There are a number of genealogical links between Judah and the other Israelite tribes (NOTES to 2:1–55; 4:1–23), including Reuben. The clans of Judah and Reuben share two names: Ḥezron (1 Chr 2:5, 9–55; 4:1, 5–7) and Carmi (see next NOTE). Of import to the ties between Reuben and Judah is the possibility of Reubenite inhabitation of (Josh 15:5–7, 16; 18:17) some land on the west bank of the Jordan River (Cross 1988b: 49).

"Carmi" *(karmî)* represents the other Reubenite clan with possible ties to Judah (Gen 46:9; Exod 6:14; Num 26:6; Josh 7:1, 18, 24, 26; 1 Chr 2:7; 4:1). The proper name, "the one of the vineyard," is attested both in epigraphic Hebrew (Davies, §§100.477.1; 568.2) and in Ug. (*kar-mu-nu, krmn;* Layton 1990a: 209).

5:4. "Joel." This linear genealogy is not connected with the preceding genealogy, nor is it attested elsewhere. The lineage itself is telescopic in nature; the seven generations are not enough to extend from the sons of Reuben (v. 3) to the Assyrian exile (v. 6). A fondness for certain numbers is evident here.

5:5. "Baal." As one element, Baal *(baʿal)* is not uncommon in early biblical proper names (PNs). Hebrew epigraphic sources are, however, another matter. Some examples of PNs with the element *bʿl* have been discovered, mostly in the

Samaria ostraca (Tigay 1986; Davies, §§3.001.7; 3.003.3; 3.027.3; 3.028.3; 3.031.3). Interestingly enough, the only attestations of Baal as a PN in the HB occur in Chronicles (1 Chr 5:5; 8:30; 9:36). There may be one case of *bʿl* as a PN in the Samaria ostraca (#12), but the reading is unclear (Davies, §3.012.2).

5:6. "Beerah *(bĕʾērâ)* . . . whom Tilgat-pilneser exiled." Over against the Deuteronomistic work, which largely loses its concentration upon individual tribes in its coverage of the dual monarchies, Chronicles maintains a continuous interest in the fate of individual tribes (Japhet 1989: 278–85). Particularly remarkable is the claim that the Assyrian king Tiglath-pileser III exiled one of Reuben's chieftains (see also the NOTES to vv. 25–26).

"chieftain *(nāśîʾ)* among the Reubenites." The use of *nāśîʾ* to refer to a tribal leader, usually Israelite, is common in Priestly lore. There it appears some eighty times (Noth 1930: 156–62; 2nd NOTE to 4:38).

5:7. "His kin" *(ʾḥyw)*. That is, Beerah's kin (v. 6). It is unlikely that Reuben (vv. 1, 3; R. Braun 1986: 70–71) is the antecedent if Shema *(šemaʿ)* son of Joel (v. 8) is the hypocoristicon of Joel's son Shemaiah *(šĕmaʿyāh)* in v. 4. See also the 2nd TEXTUAL NOTE to v. 4.

"by their families." One should not think of "families" *(mišpāḥôt)* exclusively as kinship groups. Rather, the *mišpāḥâ* may be an expanded family whose unity is based on both territory and lineage (Halpern 1983: 242–44). In this respect, a *mišpāḥâ* may be as much a neighborhood as it is a literal family (Gottwald 1979: 316–17; Vanderhooft 1999b).

"their registration by generations" *(bhtyḥś ltldwtm)*. The registration proceeds by families *(lmšpḥtm)* according to the principle of genealogy. In Joshua the allotment of territories to individual tribes regularly mentions the subdivisions *(mišpāḥôt)* of each tribe (e.g., Josh 13:15, 24, 29), but the text does not explicate the identity of the individual families. The Chronicler's treatment of these tribes informs the reader about at least some tribal subdivisions. The primary concern lies with documenting authority and genealogical relationships rather than with obtaining a census count (cf. Num 2; 1 Chr 21:5; 23:3–5). The verb *yḥś*, "to register (oneself)" (always in the *hitpaʿel*) only occurs in Chronicles (1 Chr 4:33; 5:1, 7, 17; 7:5, 9, 40; 9:1, 22; 2 Chr 31:16–19), Ezra (2:62; 8:1, 3), and Nehemiah (7:5, 64). Ironically, the text stipulates how the registration was conducted, but not when it occurred. Guesses as to the date depicted range from the time of Saul (Keil, Zöckler) to the Assyrian period (Benzinger, Curtis and Madsen).

5:8b–10. "He began to reside." The antecedent to "he" is not entirely clear. Is it Bela or Reuben? Augustin (1994: 303–4) makes a case for Bela, but Reuben seems to be the most likely possibility, as vv. 8b–10 relate to the entire tribe (represented by their eponymous ancestor) and not to just one family within the tribe. In what follows, the author does not seem to have made any systematic use of the Reubenite allotment found in Josh 13:15–23 (Mittmann 1995).

5:8. "son of Joel." The three-generation ascending genealogy of v. 8 culminates in Joel, the figure first introduced in v. 4 (with a descending genealogy).

"Aroer" *(ʿărōʿēr)*, Khirbet ʿArāʿir, was a strategically positioned fortress on the north bank of the Arnon (Wâdī al-Mūjib; Num 32:34; Deut 2:36; 3:12; 4:48; Josh 12:2; 13:9; Judg 11:26). Aroer was a contested site, occupied in sequence by the Israelites, the Moabites (*KAI* 181.26), the Syrians (2 Kgs 10:32–33), the Assyrians, and the Babylonians (Josephus, *Ant.* 10.181). In later centuries, the site was partially abandoned as the region came under the control of the Qedarites and Liḥyanites. The site was repopulated during the Hellenistic period (Olávarri-Goicoechea 1993: 93).

"Nebo" *(nĕbô)* refers to a place, rather than to a mountain (Num 33:47; Deut 32:49; 34:1; 1 Macc 9:37; *KAI* 181.14–18), 7 km west of Madaba. Most commentators situate Nebo around the southwestern slopes of Mount Nebo at Khirbet el-Muḥayyiṭ, but the case has been made that Nebo should be located north of the ridge of Mount Nebo in the well-watered valley of ʿAyûn Mûsā, the valley over against Bêt Pĕʾōr (Num 32:3, 38; 33:47; Isa 15:2; Jer 48:1, 22; Cross 1988b: 51–52; B. MacDonald 2000: 86–87). There are Iron Age remains at both sites.

"Baal-meon" *(baʿal mĕʿôn)*, also called Bet-meon (*bêt mĕʿôn;* Jer 48:23) and (*bêt baʿal mĕʿôn*; Josh 13:17), was a town lying between Nebo and Aroer, some 7 km south of Medeba (Num 32:3, 38; Ezek 25:9). Nebo and Baal-meon are mentioned in earlier lists of Reubenite settlements (Num 32:38; Josh 13:15–17). All three sites—Aroer, Nebo, and Baal-meon—appear on the late-ninth-century Moabite Stone. King Mesha claims to have (re)built Baal-meon (*KAI* 181.9), captured Nebo (*KAI* 181.14–18), and (re)built Aroer (*KAI* 181.26).

5:9. "the approaches to the wilderness, on this side of the Euphrates River" *(lĕbōʾ midbārâ lĕmin-hannāhār pĕrāt)*. The eastern boundary of the Reubenite settlement appears as the wilderness extending east of Moab and Gilead to the Euphrates. Less likely is the proposition that the Reubenites inhabited the wilderness extending to the Euphrates (2nd TEXTUAL NOTE to v. 9).

"their herds (*miqnêhem*) had become numerous." This area was already known in earlier sources as favorable to the raising of livestock (Num 32:1, 3–5).

"land of Gilead." Gilead has multiple connotations. It can designate the area north of the Jabbok or the area south of the Jabbok, hence the two halves of Gilead (Num 32:39; Josh 12:2; 13:25, 31). In some cases, Gilead refers more generally to the whole (Israelite) zone east of the Jordan (Aharoni 1979: 38–39). In one instance (v. 14), Gilead becomes a descendant of Gad. In this case, Gilead seems to refer to the territory east of the Jordan, which is south of the Jabbok and north of the Arnon. At least some of this land is alloted to Gad in Josh 13:24–25.

5:10. "The Hagrites" were a seminomadic people living in the Transjordan. The Hagrites appear allied together with Edom, Ishmael, and Moab in Ps 83:7 [ET 83:6]. A connection between the Hagrites (*hagrîʾîm* or *hagrîm*; Ps 83:7 [ET 83:6]) and Hagar *(hāgār)*, Sarah's servant (Gen 16:1–16; 21:9–21; 25:12), was alleged already within antiquity (Bar 3:23) and commonly appears in modern sources (e.g., Rehm 1954: 19). But the connection is still unproven (Knauf 1989: 16–35, 49–53). The narratives in Genesis consistently link Hagar to her son, Ishmael (Gen 16:1–16; 21:8–21; 25:12). Hagar is, therefore, the ancestress of the Ishmaelites. Some scholars connect the Hagrites with the *agraioi* or *agraei* mentioned by Greek and Latin geographers (Pliny the Elder, *Nat.* 6.159–61;

Strabo, *Geogr.* 16.4.2 [767C]; Ptolemy, *Geog.* 5.19.2) and situated by them in northern Arabia. See further the NOTE to v. 19.

"east of Gilead." From the Jordan rift eastward, Gilead is only about 40 km wide before one begins to encounter desert. Hence, it is not surprising that the author portrays the Reubenites as pursuing a seminomadic lifestyle in this area.

5:11. "descendants." The text lists some of Gad's posterity, but does not provide an actual genealogy of Gad's offspring. The reason for the omission is not known. Gadite genealogies are mentioned in the Chronicler's sources (e.g., Gen 46:16; Num 26:15–17). In referring to his conquests, King Mesha admits that the people of Gad had lived in the land of Aṭaroth for ages (*mʿlm*; *KAI* 181:10).

"opposite them" *(lĕnegdām)*. That is, facing the Reubenites. In the presentation of Chronicles, which has been influenced by Joshua (13:8–12, 24–28), Gad occupies the region of Bashan up to Salchah.

"Salchah" *(salkâ)* is often associated with Nab. *ṣlḥd* (Arab. *ṣalḥad*) of the Jebel Druze, on a spur of the Hauran (*HALOT* 757). In Deut 3:10 Salchah is one of the easternmost towns of Gilead and Bashan conquered by the Israelites under Moses (cf. Josh 12:5). In Josh 13:11 Salchah marks the eastern border of Bashan assigned to the Reubenites, the Gadites, and East Manasseh.

5:12. "Janai was the officer" (3rd and 4th TEXTUAL NOTES to v. 12). Given the Gadite occupation of Bashan (v. 11), there is no need to discard this statement as a gloss (contra Benzinger 1901).

5:14. "the sons of Abiḥayil." The language is formulaic. No sons of Abiḥayil follow. Instead, one finds a nine-generation ascending genealogy culminating with Guni (v. 15). The genealogy of Reuben also contains an ascending genealogy (v. 8). The long ascending genealogy found here may be compared with the many multigenerational ascending genealogies found among the Safaitic inscriptions (e.g., §§53; 167; 399; 463; Winnett and Harding 1978). Consistent with the *seriatim* treatment of Reuben (vv. 3–5), the authors place this lineage after the preceding material (vv. 12–13) without drawing a genetic connection between them.

5:16. "Gilead." Numbers 32 and Josh 13 demarcate certain geographical areas and towns for the various tribal possessions, but the possessions ascribed to the Transjordanian tribes are not always consistent. In Num 32:34 some of the sites rebuilt by Gad, specifically Dibon and Aroer (cf. v. 7), are located south of Reuben, whose sites are mostly clustered around Ḥeshbon (Num 32:37). Ataroth, however, is located north of Reuben (Num 32:34). In the territorial allotments of Josh 13, Reuben is clearly the furthest south of the Transjordanian tribes (Josh 13:15–23) with Gad occupying Jaazer, all of the Gilead towns, half of the land of Ammon, and Maḥanaim in the north (Josh 13:24–26). Gad's holdings also include most if not all of the eastern Jordan Valley (Josh 13:27). There is only a partial resonance between the description of Gad's territorial holdings in Chronicles and that of Joshua. Like Josh 13, Chronicles locates Gad to the north of Reuben. But Gad occupies not only Gilead (3rd NOTE to v. 9) and Jabesh (see the next NOTE) but also Sharon (presumably toward the south) and Bashan (v. 11) in the north. In Josh 13:29–30 Bashan is awarded to Half-Manasseh. Hence, there is no exact match between the areas that Chronicles assigns to Reuben and Gad and earlier biblical descriptions.

"Jabesh," or Jabesh-gilead, was located in the Transjordan (Judg 21:8–14; 1 Sam 11:1–10 [4QSam[a]]; 31:11–13; 2 Sam 2:4–7; 21:12; 1 Chr 10:11–12), but its exact location is disputed. Noth (1960: 167) and Aharoni (1979: 437) identify it as T. el-Maqlûb on the upper course of the Wâdī Yābis, but many others (e.g., McCarter 1980b: 202) identify the site as T. Abū Ḫaraz, about 32 km south of the Sea of Kinnereth just east of the Jordan River.

"open spaces." A *migrāš* designates the belt of land or open space outside a town or a sanctuary (Barr 1984; Borowski 1987: 30) that could be used for livestock, cattle, and other animals (Josh 14:4). This type of village commons is to be distinguished from residential land and farmland used for the raising of crops. The use of such terminology is necessary in the case of the Levites, because mention of their residences does not point to larger territories inhabited by this group. The other Israelite tribes occupied lands, of which towns were one part, but the Levites were in the unique position of living in towns situated within the holdings of the other tribes. According to the schema for Levitic towns found in Num 35:1–8, a *migrāš* was to extend one thousand cubits from the outer wall of the town and two thousand cubits in any direction. This puzzling description may mean that the open land's measurements form a square of two thousand cubits per side and that the perimeter of the open land is one thousand cubits in every direction from the town wall (Milgrom 1982). According to this schema, the *migrāš* would increase in size along with any expansion of the Levitical town itself.

"Sharon." That Sharon in this context does not refer to the coastal Sharon plain, the common designation of Sharon (Aharoni 1979: 24–25), is evident from the use of the expression "open spaces of Sharon" (*mgršy šrwn*; previous NOTE). This same Sharon is mentioned in the Mesha inscription (*KAI* 181.13).

5:17. "Jotham . . . Jeroboam." The chronology of the divided monarchy, as reconstructed from the textual witnesses to Kings and certain dates in Assyrian records, allows only a narrow overlap between the tenures of these two monarchs. Since Jotham king of Judah reigned approximately from 750–735 B.C.E. (perhaps from 750–742 B.C.E. as a coregent) and Jeroboam (II) king of Israel reigned approximately from 786–746 B.C.E. (J. Miller 1976: 80–82), the registration of Gad would have to have taken place between 750 and 746 B.C.E. The reference to Jotham may not be accidental. According to 2 Chr 27:5, Jotham fought and won a war against the Ammonites and their king, which resulted in Ammonite tribute payments for three consecutive years.

5:18. "Reuben." As in a number of earlier traditions (Num 32:1–42; Deut 3:12–16; 29:7–8; Josh 13:8–31) and once elsewhere in Chronicles (1 Chr 12:38), Reuben, Gad, and East Manasseh are treated as a larger entity. This unity is underscored as these tribes join forces, share a common muster, partake in the spoils of war, and experience a common fate (5:25–26).

"44,760." The number is notable for its specificity, not for its large size (NOTE to 12:38). In the pan-Israel muster at Ḥebron, the two and a half Transjordanian tribes send 120,000 armed troops to support David (12:38).

5:19. "Jeṭur, Naphish, and Nodab." In conformity with Gen 25:15, 1 Chr 1:30–31 presents Jeṭur, Naphish, and Qedemah as the sons of Ishmael. As such, these names have clear connections with the desert regions between Palestine and Egypt. Some scholars associate Jeṭur *(yĕṭûr)* with Nab. *Iatouros* (Roman Iturea; *Itouraia* Lk 3:1) in Hauran (*HALOT* 409). As attested by Eupolemos (Eusebius, *Praep. ev.* 9.30.3), the Ituraeans were still living in the northern Transjordan in the second century B.C.E. Nodab *(nôdāb)* is a *hapax legomenon* that may have a connection to Ishmaelite Adbeel *(ʾadbĕʾēl)* in 1 Chr 1:29(//Gen 25:13), while Naphish *(nāpîš)* only appears in Gen 25:15 (P), 1 Chr 1:31, and here. The list of Ezra 2:50 mentions the sons of "Nephusim" (*npwsym*; Qere) or "Nephisim" (*npysym*; Kethib), a group some scholars (Zadok 1982: 296; Blenkinsopp 1988: 90) wish to see as descendants of Ishmaelite Naphish. In dealing with the Hagrites, Jeṭur, Naphish, and Nodab, one is confronted with a paradox. These groups are depicted as active during the early monarchy, if not much before then, but virtually all of the sources that speak of them are relatively late (Gen 25:13, 15; 1 Chr 1:29–30; 5:10, 19–20; 11:38; cf. LXX^{LMN} 2 Sam 23:36). Psalm 83, like most psalms, is difficult to date. In speaking of the Hagrites, Jeṭur, Naphish, and Nodab, the Chronicler (Ephʿal 1984: 100–101, 234–39) or a later redactor (Knauf 1989: 49–52) may well have been presuming an ethnogeographical situation in the Transjordan that existed in his own time.

5:20. "delivered into their hands" *(wyntnw bydm)*. The so-called *Übereignungsformel*, "Yhwh/God gave them into the hand of," is adapted from the Deuteronomic and Deuteronomistic literature in which it appears some 87 times (Richter 1963: 22). Similar formulas appear in writings from Mari and other sites in the ancient Near East (Kang 1989).

"cried out (*zāʿăqû*) to God in battle." The Chronicler, like a number of earlier biblical authors (Judg 6:6–7; 10:10; 1 Sam 7:8–9), employs the verb *zʿq* to signify a plaintive appeal in war narratives (2 Chr 18:31; 20:9; 32:20). More regularly than in the Deuteronomistic work, the Chronicler's major characters call out to God or pray to God in the context of war (Pratt 1987; Selman 1994a: 106).

"their entreaty was granted" *(naʿtôr)*. God also answers prayer in the sacral wars of the Judahite monarchy (2 Chr 13:14; 14:10 [ET 14:11]; 20:5–12; 32:20), but the language here is somewhat different. With *ʿtr*, the closest parallels are the divine responses to Manasseh's prayer in Babylon (2 Chr 33:12–13, 19) and to Ezra's prayer by the Ahava River (Ezra 8:23).

"they trusted (*bṭḥ*) in him." The verb *bṭḥ*, rare in Chronicles, is frequently used to depict the proper human response to Yhwh in a time of crisis (Gonçalves 1986: 409–12). In 2 Kgs 18–20 the term functions as a catchword (cf. 2 Chr 32:10) to extol Ḥezeqiah's response to Sennacherib's invasion: "In Yhwh the God of Israel he trusted, and after him there was no one like him among all the kings of Judah, nor among those before him" (2 Kgs 18:5; Knoppers 1992b: 418–25).

5:21. "livestock." The booty associated with this victory is consistent (in kind) with other depictions of the seminomadic Ishmaelites and their assorted allies (Ephʿal 1984: 234–40). Biblical sources do not ascribe to the descendants of Ishmael trade in luxury goods (Isa 60:7; Jer 49:29; Ezek 27:20–21). But the highly exaggerated and rounded numbers—"50,000 camels, 250,000 small cattle, 2,000 asses, and 100,000 living people"—are typical of Chronicles (NOTE to 12:38).

5:22. "the battle was from God." For similar sentiments, see 2 Chr 20:15; 25:8; 32:8. The incredible losses suffered by the enemy are consistent with those in other battles depicted in which Yhwh acts directly against Judah's foes (2 Chr 13:17; 14:12 [ET 14:13]; 20:24; 32:21; Ruffing 1992).

"until the exile." That is, the Assyrian exile of the Transjordanian tribes in 733–732 B.C.E. (v. 26). The migration mentioned in v. 22 may have been influenced by settlements in the northern Transjordan during the Persian period (Knauf 1985a: 51–52).

5:23. "descendants." As with the Gadites (vv. 11–17), the author does not provide an actual genealogy of Manasseh's progeny. Instead, he discusses areas of residence (v. 23) and tribal leadership (v. 24).

"half-tribe of Manasseh." In biblical traditions, the Manassites live on both sides of the Jordan. The western half of the tribe settled in the central hill country (Josh 17; 1 Chr 7:14–19).

"Bashan" is part of the heritage of East Manasseh in Josh 13:29–31. Since Gad also occupies Bashan (1 Chr 5:11–12), there is some overlap between the lands that Gad and Half-Manasseh (East Manasseh) inhabit.

"Baal Ḥermon" is elsewhere mentioned only in Judg 3:3 as part of the hill country of the Lebanon *(har hallĕbānôn)*. If Baal Ḥermon is part of the Lebanon range, the tribes of East Manasseh, Reuben, and Gad occupy more territory than is alloted to the Transjordanian tribes in Numbers (32:33–42), Deuteronomy (3:13–15), and Joshua (13:29–31). East Manasseh, in particular, occupies a great deal of land stretching from Bashan in the south to Baal Ḥermon and Mount Ḥermon in the northwest.

"Senir" *(śĕnîr)*. According to Deut 3:8–10, the Sidonians called Mount Ḥermon Sirion (שׂרין), while the Amorites called it Senir (שׂניר). Senir was probably part of the Ḥermon range (Ezek 27:5; Song 4:8).

"Mount Ḥermon," located in the southern part of the Anti-Lebanon range, is presented in a number of texts (Deut 3:8; Josh 11:3, 17; 12:1, 5; 13:5, 11) as the northwestern limit to the land (beyond the Jordan) allocated to the Israelites. Traditions differ as to whether this territory was taken (Deut 3:8) or not (Josh 12:5–6; cf. Judg 3:3).

"became numerous." As in the Priestly source (Gen 1:22, 28; 8:17; 9:7), this is a mark of divine blessing (1 Chr 4:27; 5:9, 23; 7:4; 8:40; 23:17; 28:5; 2 Chr 11:21).

5:25. "transgressed" (מעל). The context clarifies that the subject is "the Reubenites, the Gadites, and the half-tribe of Manasseh" (v. 26). In describing the Assyrian exile of 733–732 B.C.E., the Deuteronomist mentions that Peqaḥ did not desist from following in the ways of his predecessor Jeroboam I (2 Kgs 15:28; Knoppers 1994e: 13–44), but he does not depict any large scale rebellion by the masses against the deity. This account of the fall of the Transjordanian tribes should be ascribed to the Chronicler's own hand. The verb *mʿl* is one of the Chronicler's favorites for describing transgression and insurrection against the deity (1st NOTE to 10:13). The scenario portrayed is, in most respects, the exact opposite of that depicted in the earlier sacral war (vv. 18–22).

"prostituted themselves to." NJPS's "went astray after" is too weak to convey the sense of *znh*, "to fornicate," "to be a harlot." The language is adapted from earlier injunctions against, warnings about, or descriptions of Israelite intercourse with other gods (Exod 34:15–16; Lev 17:7; 20:5–6; Deut 31:16; Judg 2:17; 8:33). Such actions lead to divine rejection and abandonment (Lev 20:5–6; Deut 31:17–18).

"gods of the peoples." The author acknowledges that other peoples have their own deities (2 Chr 25:14, 20; 28:23; 32:13, 14, 15, 19; 35:21; Japhet 1989: 41–53), but these deities have no ontological reality. They are "the work of people's hands" (2 Chr 32:19).

"whom God had destroyed before them" *(ʾăšer-hišmîd ʾĕlōhîm mippĕnêhem)*. References to an Israelite conquest are not nearly as ubiquitous in Chronicles as they are in Deuteronomy (e.g., 2:12–13, 21–24; 7:23–24; 9:1–3; 12:29–30) and the Deuteronomistic History (e.g., Josh 9:24; 11:14–15, 20–23; 12:1–24; 21:43–45; 23:1–5, 9–10; 24:8–13; 2 Sam 7:23; 2 Kgs 21:9). Nor does Chronicles reproduce the invasion stories from Numbers, Deuteronomy, and Joshua. Nevertheless, the Chronicler knows of the conquest tradition and occasionally affirms it. In the universal genealogy, Israel is not autochthonous to its land (COMMENT on 1:1–2:2). In some instances, the Chronicler reproduces references to the conquest from his *Vorlagen* (e.g., 1 Chr 16:18–22; 17:21–22; 2 Chr 33:9), and in a few other instances, he introduces his own references (1 Chr 5:25; 2 Chr 20:7–8, 10–11). In this case, he alludes to Israelite victories in the Transjordan, which provided Reuben, Gad, and East Manasseh with their land (Num 21:10–35; Deut 2:24–3:17; 29:6–7 [ET 29:7–8]; Josh 12:1–6).

5:26. "stirred up *(wayyāʿar)* the spirit." The same verb (again in the *hipʿil*) is used to describe how Israel's God rouses other groups of enemies to punish his people. In one case, Yhwh stirs up the Philistines and Arabs to rebel against Jehoram (2 Chr 21:16). Here, the verb is used with respect to the Persians, led by King Cyrus, who allowed the people of Judah to return home (2 Chr 36:22–23). The language is reminiscent of Deutero-Isaiah (Isa 41:2, 25; 45:13). In yet another case, that of Neco of Egypt, a foreign monarch actually claims that Josiah is interfering with God's will by coming up against Neco, while Neco was on his way to Carchemish (2 Chr 35:20–21; cf. 36:22//Ezra 1:1; Ben Zvi 1999). The issue goes beyond the Chronicler's monotheism, which does not allow for the existence of other deities. In Chronicles the God of Israel is sovereign over the nations and their leaders, whether they acknowledge him or not. The relationship between Yhwh and his people is of primary authorial concern, and insofar as other peoples and their leaders participate in this picture, they are subject to Yhwh's bidding.

"Pul the king of Assyria." Pul (2 Kgs 15:19; cf. Assyr. ^{m}*Pu-u-lu*) is a caritative by which Tiglath-pileser III is referred to in some late cuneiform sources and in the Hellenistic Ptolemaic canon (Tadmor and Cogan 1988: 172; H. Tadmor 1994: 280).

"exiled them." Referring to Tiglath-pileser's campaigns of 733–732 B.C.E., which were primarily directed against Rezin of Damascus (Younger 1998: 206).

According to 2 Kgs 15:29, Tiglath-pileser captured the regions of Gilead and Galilee—"all the land of Naphtali"—and deported their populations to Assyria. The fragmentary annals and summary inscriptions of Tiglath-pileser III provide information about additional sites overrun by the Assyrians during his campaigns to the west (Tadmor and Cogan 1988: 174–75; H. Tadmor 1994: 81–83, 188–89, 281 [Ann. 18:1′–6′; 24:1′–10; Summ. 9:9–12; Summ. 13:17′–18′]). The early deportations may have been unidirectional as opposed to the bidirectional deportations of 722 B.C.E. (Younger 1998). Site surveys of Galilee indicate a significant depopulation of this area, especially the lower Galilee from the late eighth century through the sixth century B.C.E. (Gal 1992: 109).

"Ḥelaḥ" (Akk. *ḫalaḫḫa*) is both a city and a province northeast of Nineveh in northern Mesopotamia. The destination of the captives is not mentioned in 2 Kgs 15:29. The list of sites in this verse is borrowed from 2 Kgs 17:6 (repeated in 18:11), which details the destinations of the Samarian deportees in the Assyrian exile of 722 B.C.E. In other words, the writer has coupled features of the Assyrian exile in 733–732 B.C.E. with the list of destinations for the Israelite deportees in the Assyrian exile of 722 B.C.E.

"Ḥabor." Akk. *ḫābūru* designates a district northwest of Assyria as well as an eastern tributary of the Euphrates.

"Gozan" *(gôzān)* Akk. *guzāna*, modern T. Ḥalāf, was located on the upper Ḥabor. Gozan served as the capital of the Assyrian province of Bīt Baḫian from the second half of the ninth century onward.

"to this day" *(ʿad hayyôm hazzeh)*. The prep. *ʿad* has a pregnant sense (Joüon, §103m). From the perspective of the writer, living centuries after the events depicted, the two and a half Transjordanian tribes are still exiled (COMMENT).

Sources and Composition

In spite of intensive study, there is no consensus about the composition of 1 Chr 5:1–26. Some commentators (e.g., Curtis and Madsen 1910: 118–21; Japhet 1993a: 129–32; Selman 1994a: 104–8) believe that all of the material stems from the Chronicler, whose inclusion of fragmentary traditions causes some breaks in his text. Others (e.g., Noth 1957: 120; Rudolph 1955: 43–51; R. Braun 1986: 72–75; Kartveit 1989: 65–69, 135–45; Schorn 1997: 272–73) believe that the work was composed in a series of editions that date to different times and circumstances. But there is no agreement about the definition, nature, and extent of these redactions. Schorn (1997: 268ff.) provides a useful overview of recent discussions. There is some consensus that the battle narrative in v. 10 has been reworked and expanded into a longer midrash in vv. 18–22 (e.g., Benzinger 1901: 20; Curtis and Madsen 1910: 121). If so, the latter has all the marks of being a Chronistic composition. The narrative reflects the style and content of other martial narratives in Chronicles (NOTES to vv. 18–21; Oeming 1990: 135–41; Wright 1997).

In what follows, I am assuming that more than one author has been at work in composing vv. 1–26. The literary diversity in the chapter cannot all be attributed to sources purportedly in the Chronicler's employ. Nevertheless, my comments will concentrate on the present form of the text. One question that needs to be pursued involves the use or nonuse, as the case may be, of earlier biblical materials. Surprisingly, this important issue has not received the detailed attention it deserves. The material in the following verses shows some indebtedness to, if not outright borrowing from, earlier biblical texts.

1 Chronicles 5	*Source*
1–2	Gen 35:22; 47:25–48:22; 49:4
3	Exod 6:14 or Num 26:5–6
25–26	2 Kgs 15:29; 17:6 (18:11)

What is truly amazing is not the exegesis and reuse of earlier sources found in vv. 1–2 and 25–26, as these are common features in the composition of Chronicles, but the amount of biblical material that the authors did not employ in their own work. The following table summarizes the sources which have been largely neglected in the Transjordanian genealogies. The table focuses on texts dealing with the lineages and settlements of Reuben, Gad, and East Manasseh.

Sources Not Cited	
Num 26:8–11	Descendants of Pallu
Gen 46:16; Num 26:15–18	Descendants of Gad
Num 21:10–20	Travels through the Transjordan
Num 21:21–31	Victory against Amorite Sihon
Num 21:33–22:1	Victory against Og of Bashan
Num 32	Grants to Gad, Reuben, and Manasseh
Num 33:41–49	Itinerary through the Transjordan
Deut 2:24–37; 29:6 [ET 29:7]	Victory against Sihon
Deut 3:1–7	Victory against Og
Deut 3:8–17	Lands Seized
Deut 29:6–7	Victories over Sihon and Og
Josh 12:1–6	Defeated Kings East of the Jordan
Josh 13:5–6	The Remaining Land in the North
Josh 13:8–13	Conquests East of the Jordan
Josh 13:15–23	Allotment for Reuben
Josh 13:24–28	Allotment for Gad
Josh 13:29–31	Allotment for East Manasseh
Ezek 47:13–23	New Boundaries of the Land
Ezek 48:1–29	Tribal Reallotments

Not included in this list are stories that could have been used by the authors (e.g., Josh 22; Judg 11:1–12:7). This is a legitimate issue because even though the writers are composing genealogies (broadly construed), the figures mentioned in older tales do not reappear anywhere within the genealogies. In contrast to the integration of Joshua, for example, into the genealogy of Ephraim (1 Chr 7:27), the authors have not integrated figures such as Jephthah of Gilead into the lineages. That the authors also ignore most of the genealogical materials available in older books is particularly interesting, given that such materials are cited for a number of the other tribes. In this context, it is relevant to observe that the authors neither cite nor rehearse the oft-mentioned victories against Sihon and Og found in Numbers, Deuteronomy, and Joshua. Instead, they have supplied their own sketchy anecdotes about regional territorial struggles (vv. 10, 18–22).

One of the consistent interests displayed by other genealogies in Chronicles is the relationship between individual tribes (or subsections thereof) and certain lands and towns. This is also the case in 5:1–26, but some of the sites in Jazer and Gilead awarded to Gad and Reuben (Num 32) go unmentioned here. Similarly, most of the sites mentioned in the Transjordanian itinerary (Num 33:41–49) do not appear among the domains of the two and a half tribes. It is entirely possible that the writers knew of the lists of lands seized in the Transjordan and selectively drew information from the initial summaries in Deut 3:8–10 (or those of Josh 12:1–6; 13:8–13). Nevertheless, the descriptions of the occupied lands are at variance with the descriptions provided in Deut 3:12–17 and Josh 13:15–31 (NOTES). It seems that the authors have eschewed quoting the detailed tribal allotments in Joshua in lieu of providing their much more sweeping, idealized territorial summaries. The authors also seem not to have made any use of the territorial (re)allotments in Ezekiel (47:13–23; 48:1–29). There the tribes of Reuben, Gad, and Manasseh are endowed with access to land, but not to land in the Transjordan. In the territorial rhetoric of Ezekiel there is no Transjordanian tribal land. In short, the authors had access to a variety of biblical sources, but chose to use only a fraction of them in composing their work. The result is an account unique to Chronicles.

FORM AND STRUCTURE

The treatment of each of the Transjordanian groups contains a number of standard components: a stereotypical introduction, comments about the territory occupied by the tribe, a list of ancestral heads, and anecdotes about population growth or new tribal residences. In this respect, the presentation of Reuben, Gad, and East Manasseh is similar to that of Simeon (4:24–43). Each section devoted to the two and a half tribes is introduced in the same way: "the descendants of PN" (vv. 1, 11, 23). The standard components within each of the major sections appear, however, in different orders. Actual genealogies make up only a small portion of the coverage given to these two and a half tribes. In fact, the coverage devoted to East Manasseh does not contain any genealogical material at all. It is common in the genealogical works attested from ancient Greece to include many anecdotes and tales within a larger genealogical framework, but it is quite unusual in Chronicles to eschew genealogies entirely.

In treating East Manasseh (vv. 23–24) as a separate entity from the rest of Manasseh (7:14–19) and grouping this half-tribe with Reuben and Gad, the authors emphasize its solidarity with the other Transjordanian tribes. Further binding these groups together are accounts of common warfare (vv. 18–22), overlapping settlements (NOTES to v. 18), and a common exilic destination (vv. 25–26).

COMMENT

Geographically set apart from the other Israelite tribes, the Transjordanian tribes are regarded with suspicion by some biblical authors (Hackett 1987; Schorn 1997: 224–81). The suspicions not only involve the physical separation of Reuben, Gad, and East Manasseh from the other tribes, but also involve larger questions of polity, dialect, and religious practice (Num 32; Josh 22; Judg 8:4–7; 11:29–40; 12:1–6; Halpern 1983: 166–70). Indeed, there is disagreement among biblical writers as to whether Gilead even belongs to "the land of Canaan" (de Vaux 1978: 128–32). In the Priestly writing (as reconstructed by some scholars), the promised land does not include the Transjordan (Num 34:1–12; Weinfeld 1993: 52–75).

To be sure, there are other sources that portray the Transjordan more positively. Reuben's privileged status as firstborn is affirmed in the Blessing of Jacob:

Reuben, my firstborn,
You are my strength,
The prime of my might,
Preeminent in power. (Gen 49:3; Cross and Freedman 1975: 49)

Gad is adept in battle (Gen 49:19; Deut 33:20–21) and productive (Gen 46:16; Num 26:15–18). As the eldest of Jacob's sons, Reuben's status is at play in the Joseph story (Gen 37:21–22, 29–30; 42:22, 37).

But even some of these same sources contain more equivocal commentary. The Blessing of Jacob ominously predicts that Reuben's days of preeminence are numbered (Gen 49:4). The depiction of Reuben in the Song of Deborah is at best ambivalent. Reuben contains a number of divisions (פלגות), but the Reubenites respond to the tribal muster with debates rather than with action (Judg 5:15b–16). Moreover, the Song of Deborah lists Reuben fourth, not first. Of Gilead the poet simply says that he "camps beyond the Jordan" (Judg 5:17). The Blessing of Moses, places the very future of Reuben in doubt:

Let Reuben live,
Let him not die,
Although his men be few. (Deut 33:6)

Narrative accounts also hint at a complicated, if not embattled, history of the Transjordan. One tale, depicting Israelite resurgence in the era of Judges, presumes that the Moabites had overrun the old territory of Reuben between the Arnon and Ḥeshbon (Judg 3:12–30). In another, the story of Jephthah, the author mentions Ammonite pressure on the Israelites in the region of Gilead (Judg 11). In 1 Sam 11, as preserved in 4QSam[a] (10.6–9; Cross 1983a; McCarter 1980b: 198–203) and partially in Josephus (*Ant.* 6.68–71), the Ammonites decimate the Reubenites and Gadites, leaving only a remnant of seven thousand, who flee to Jabesh-gilead. Due to the typological concentration upon the monarchy in

Samuel-Kings, references to individual tribes are hard to come by. The very nomenclature modern writers use—the united and divided monarchies—witnesses to the influence of the Deuteronomistic writers on modern scholarly conventions. To be sure, mention is made of certain Transjordanian areas (1 Sam 31:11–13; 2 Sam 2:8–9), groups (2 Sam 17:24–29; 23:36), and towns (1 Kgs 12:25), but only rarely to individual hamulas and tribes.

There are numerous indications in archaeology, epigraphy, and the Latter Prophets that regional polities developed in the Transjordan during the Iron Age II. Archaeological evidence suggests that Ammon became an extended city-state beginning some time in the Iron IIB period (LaBianca and Younker 1995; Herr 1997: 148–50). The Iron IIC period may have been a particularly prosperous time for the Ammonites (Herr 1997: 168–72). The Tel Siran inscription (*CAI* 78; Thompson and Zayadine 1973ab; Jackson 1983), dating to ca. 600 B.C.E., mentions three kings of Ammon. Continuity in the material remains exists well into the Persian period. Ammon is mentioned as the name of a Persian province on three Persian period seals (Herr 1992: 163–66).

The Iron Age II also saw a growth in the number and size of sites in the lands east of the Dead Sea (Dearman 1997). The ninth-century Mesha inscription, which details the achievements of the Moabite king in reconquering territory taken by Omri of Israel, speaks of the land of Aṭaroth as long inhabited by Gadites (*KAI* 181.10–11). King Mesha claims to have dealt with his opponents harshly. With respect to Aṭaroth, he asserts, "I killed all of the people" (*w'hrg.'t.kl.hʿm*; *KAI* 181.11). Whether Mesha controlled much, if anything, south of the Arnon is in doubt (J. Miller 1992). In any case, towns ascribed to Reuben in Pentateuchal sources are captured and rebuilt by Mesha (4th NOTE to v. 8). In predicting the doom of Moab, the authors of Isa 15–16 and Jer 48 presume that many towns east of the Dead Sea have been in Moabite hands for quite some time.

If the ascent of regional Moabite and Ammonite polities represented one important development in the region, the growing power of Aram Damascus represented another (Pitard 1987). The recently published Tel Dan inscription celebrates the triumph of one Aramaean king, probably Ḥazael, against the kings of both Israel and the house of David (Biran and Naveh 1993; 1995). According to 2 Kgs 10:32–33, Yhwh began to cut off *(lĕqaṣṣôt)* Israel through the aegis of a series of foreign conquerors, including Ḥazael of Damascus, who defeated the Israelites from the Jordan eastward, "all the land of Gilead—the Gadites, Reubenites, and Manassites." The reach of Aram from Mount Lebanon down to the towns of Gilead and Abel . . . seems to be conceded in the inscriptions of Tiglath-pileser III (H. Tadmor 1994: 281 [Summ. 4:6′; Summ. 9:r.3–4]). In this context, it is appropriate to mention another major development: successive Assyrian campaigns to the west. Moab is mentioned some twelve times in texts from the reigns of Adad-nirari III, Tiglath-pileser III, Sargon II, Sennacherib, Esarhaddon, and Ashurbanipal (Parpola 1970). Moab is regarded either as a tributary state or as a land belonging to Assyria in the royal inscriptions of Tiglath-pileser III, Sennacherib, Esarhaddon, and Ashurbanipal. Similarly, in the neo-Assyrian Geography of Sargon (lines 45–50), dating to Sargon II or Sennacherib, Moab and Edom belong to the southwestern tier of the Assyrian empire (Horowitz 1993; 1998: 89–90). From a Deuteronomistic perspective, the final blow to the Israelite inhabitants of the Transjordan came with Tiglath-pileser's campaigns of 733–732 B.C.E., which involved the deportation of native populations to Assyria (2 Kgs 15:29; NOTES to v. 26). In Kings the campaigns of Tiglath-pileser III mark the definitive end of a meaningful Israelite presence in the Transjordan. Given this situation, it is not surprising to find some later prophetic writers yearning for the return of the exiles back to Gilead and Bashan (Jer 50:19; Obad 19; Zech 10:10).

Citing epigraphic evidence and anthropological theory, some scholars (e.g., Augustin 1994; Schorn 1997; 2000) even doubt that entities such as Reuben ever existed in the Iron Age (I and II). But one should not dismiss too quickly the proposition that segmentary societies persisted both east and west of the Jordan in spite of the rise of small regional states (Younker 1997a). The very Mesha inscription that celebrates Mesha's victories against Israel also concedes that Israel controlled a number of sites, including areas north of Moab, before Mesha's ascent to power (*KAI* 181.4–6, 7–8, 11, 14, 18–19). King Mesha claims, for example, to have decimated Israelite inhabitants of Nebo and to have captured "th[e ves]sels of Yhwh and carried them before the face of Kemosh" (*KAI* 181.14–18). In brief, it may be safer to say that the Transjordan became a contested area, the target of a number of different indigenous and foreign claims and campaigns during the Iron Age (II and III). Whatever the case, to understand the handling of the Transjordan in Chronicles, one has to deal with the testimony provided by earlier biblical books, because the authors of Chronicles had access to versions of most of these works. In this respect, reconstructing the history of the Transjordan is distinct from, albeit related to, addressing the relations between Israelite and Judean literary texts dealing with the Transjordan.

In contrast to the gradual demise of the Transjordan in the Former Prophets, Chronicles presents a strikingly variant tradition. The authors do not explain precisely when the Transjordanian tribes came to inhabit their lands, but they posit continuous occupation by discrete groups named Reuben, Gad, and East Manasseh until the campaigns of Tiglath-pileser III. The anecdotes do not include references to Moabite, Ammonite, or Syrian pressures during the united and dual monarchies. Scattered references to individual kings appear in the coverage devoted to the two and a half tribes (vv. 10, 17). This means that the Israel of Chronicles, unlike the Israel of Samuel-Kings, continues to be organized on the basis of a tribal system throughout the monarchy. The contrast in the coverage of Reuben is especially acute. In the Deuteronomistic historical work Reuben largely disappears during the United Monarchy. The demise of Reuben as a segmentary society with a fixed territory is suggested by David's census, which mentions only Gad (and not Reuben) north of the Arnon (2 Sam 24:5; de Vaux 1978: 577–78; Cross 1988b). Similarly, the system of Solomon's districts includes Gilead (MT 1 Kgs 4:19) or Gad (LXX), Maḥanaim (1 Kgs 4:14), and Ramoth-gilead (1 Kgs 4:13), but not Reuben. In Chronicles Reuben not only survives intact into the eighth century but even expands by dint of population increase and war (5:9–10). In examining the testimony of 1 Chr 5:1–26, one has to confront, therefore, a fundamental contrast between the assumptions, methods, and claims of the Deuteronomists and those of the authors of Chronicles.

In Chronicles individual tribes retain a significant degree of independence. During the reign of Saul, the Reubenites conduct their own military campaign against the Hagrites (v. 10). Together with the tribes of Gad and East Manasseh, the Reubenites share a muster, raise their own army, and fight their own war against a common enemy (vv. 18–22). Campaigns by individual tribes are also mentioned in Judg 1, but all campaigns are premonarchical by definition and many are unsuccessful. In contrast, each of the campaigns mentioned in the genealogies (4:41–43; 5:10, 18–22; 8:13) is successful. No losses are recorded until the Assyrian exile.

Genealogical registrations occur during the monarchy (5:17), but proceed in accordance with the internal structure of tribes: intergenerationally within individual families (v. 7). Members of the tribes appear as valiant and important figures: chieftains (v. 6), officers (v. 12), warriors (v. 24), heads of ancestral houses (vv. 7, 12, 15, 24), and men of repute (v. 24). The authors seem to be, in fact, more interested in registrations, geography, settlements, and battles than they are in actual genealogies. In any case, not only do individual tribes survive the advent of the monarchy, but these tribes themselves reflect internal hierarchies of leadership and service. If there is a trend in the tribal histories, it is one of gradual expansion rather than one of retraction or steady decline. Territorial expansions follow the course of wars (vv. 10, 18–22) and population increase, whether of livestock (v. 9) or of humans (v. 23). The text presents a romantic notion of tribal holdings. Taken together, the two and a half tribes come to occupy a most impressive utopian range of territories, at least as many as depicted in any older biblical source.

In this context, one is inclined to adopt a more positive view of the image Chronicles presents of Reuben (and the other Transjordanian tribes) than that held by some scholars. Chronicles does mention the Transjordanian exile and attributes the deportation to transgression *(mʿl)*, but the Judahite exile is similarly attributed to widespread transgression (*mʿl*; 2 Chr 36:12–16). Similarly, the notice of deportation in the summary concluding the genealogies (NOTES to 9:1) declares that "they were exiled to Babylon on account of their transgression" *(mʿl)*. Few would argue that the authors of Chronicles promote a negative view of Judah. There are, moreover, features of the text that belie a one-dimensional portrait of Reuben, Gad, and East Manssseh. The authors present an idealized and stylized picture of Transjordanian tribal holdings, leaders, and developments. The Transjordanian tribes, East Manasseh in particular, inhabit lands that go unconquered elsewhere (Josh 13:5–6). It is also significant that the text devotes more coverage to the Transjordanian tribes than to Dan, Naphtali, Ephraim, and (West) Manasseh put together (7:12–29).

In assessing the divergent pictures provided by Samuel-Kings and Chronicles, two related issues arise. The first concerns the nature of the past the authors depict, while the second involves the function of the presentation in the Persian period. There are some scholars who take the testimony of Chronicles as reflecting authentic conditions in the preexilic era (e.g., Japhet 1989: 306–8; cf. Rudolph 1955: 48–49). In this scenario, the two and a half tribes survive, retain a fair degree of autonomy, and even conduct miltary campaigns, which are not controlled or directed by a central monarchical authority. But given the extrabiblical (epigraphic) evidence for Moabite, Ammonite, Aramaean, and Assyrian activities in the Transjordan during the Iron Age, it is difficult to believe that groups such as Reuben and East Manasseh maintained themselves as integrated tribal entities with fixed territories for such long periods of time. It is possible, of course, that some elements east of the Jordan survived and maintained contacts with affiliated units east and west of the Jordan. It is also possible that the lists of exiles "who returned to Jerusalem and Judah" (Ezra 2:1) contained Israelite families from the other side of the Jordan (Cogan 1979). But such possibilities do not require the survival of independent and territorially distinct Transjordanian tribes. The use of 1 Chr 5:1–26 to reconstruct a detailed history of preexilic Israel encounters another problem. Some of the peoples mentioned in the genealogies of Reuben, Gad, and East Manasseh are only attested during the late monarchy, the Persian period, or later (NOTES to vv. 10, 19).

Given that the authors of Chronicles wrote during the Achaemenid era, and not during the monarchy, it is appropriate to return to the second issue raised above: the function of the text in the postexilic age. In writing about the two and a half tribes, the authors were undoubtedly influenced by skirmishes and migrations of their own times (Knauf 1989), but their stated subjects are the titles and activities of the descendants of eponymous ancestors and not such contemporary peregrinations. In contributing to a topic that had been addressed by a variety of previous writers, the authors extend Israel's tribal legacy. Although they believed that the deportation of the Transjordanian tribes occurred centuries before their writing, their account continues to tie the groups to the lands east of the Dead Sea and the Jordan River. This attachment to the land is accentuated by references to genealogical registrations (5:1, 7, 17), internal positions of authority (5:1–2, 6, 12, 13, 15, 24), and kinship relations *(passim)*. Preexilic Transjordanian tribes win victories against what appear to be postexilic enemies. In this manner, the authors sustain the notion of a pan-Israelite ideal during the late Persian period. Reuben, Gad, and East Mansseh are integral to Israel. The nation's various tribes outlast the very monarchy that, in Samuel-Kings, seems to supplant them.

By the same token, even this hopeful construction of the past concedes that the pan-Israelite ideal no longer has a corresponding reality. By the Persian period, Reuben, Gad, and East Manasseh had been exiled for centuries. The tribes remain banished "to this day" (v. 26). It would have been easy, if exile was unimportant, to ignore it or downplay its effects, but the writers portray its effects as definitive. There is not even a hint of a return. Yet even in the assertion of a continuing exile, one can discern traces of an optimistic vision of history. Because the Transjordanian tribes still exist, albeit as émigrés in other lands, Israel as a larger reality remains. A segmentary Israel, distinguished and conserved in the act of writing, now exists as an international phenomenon. The authors of Chronicles do not share the sentiment of earlier biblical writers, who distance the Transjordanian tribes from the rest of the Israelite tribes by reference to dialect, polity, and religious practice. Quite the contrary, the two and a half tribes exhibit polities similar to those described for other tribes. Nevertheless, the text distances these tribes through another means—exile. In this respect, the writers of Chronicles recognize a disjunction between the past they depict and the present they maintain.

VII. From Levi to Jehozadaq: A Priestly Heritage (5:27–41)

[27]The sons of Levi: Gershon, Qohath, and Merari. [28]The sons of Qohath: Amram, Izhar, Ḥebron, and Uzziel. [29]The children of Amram: Aaron, Moses, and Miriam. The sons of Aaron: Nadab, Abihu, Eleazar, and Ithamar. [30]Eleazar sired Phineḥas, Phineḥas sired Abishua, [31]Abishua sired Buqqi, Buqqi sired Uzzi, [32]Uzzi sired Zeraḥiah, Zeraḥiah sired Meraioth, [33]Meraioth sired Amariah, Amariah sired Aḥiṭub, [34]Aḥiṭub sired Zadoq, Zadoq sired Aḥimaaz, [35]and Aḥimaaz sired Azariah. It was he who officiated as priest in the temple that Solomon built in Jerusalem. And Azariah sired Joḥanan, [36]Joḥanan sired Azariah, [37]Azariah sired Amariah, Amariah sired Aḥiṭub, [38]Aḥiṭub sired Zadoq, Zadoq sired Shallum, [39]Shallum sired Ḥilqiah, Ḥilqiah sired Azariah, [40]Azariah sired Seraiah, and Seraiah sired Jehozadaq. [41]And Jehozadaq went into exile when Yhwh exiled Judah and Jerusalem at the hand of Nebuchadnezzar.

TEXTUAL NOTES

5:27–41. In many English translations, these verses appear as 6:1–15.

5:27. "Gershon" *(gēršôn)* is the normal designation for this son of Levi (Gen 46:11; Exod 6:16; Num 3:17). MT also uses *gēršōm* in 1 Chr 6 (see the TEXTUAL NOTE to 6:1).

"Gershon, Qohath, and Merari." So MT 5:27 and SP Exod 6:16. MT Exod 6:16 "Gershon and Qohath and Merari."

5:28. "Amram." So MT. Construing *ʿamrām* as a verbal-sentence name, meaning "the (divine) kinsman is exalted." LXX^{B} *Ambram.* Cf. LXX^{B} 5:29 *Ambran;* LXX^{L} *Ambra(a)m.*

5:29. "Miriam" *(miryām).* Reading with MT and LXX. Rudolph (1955: 52) thinks that "Miriam" is an addition, but *bĕnê* is used as a convention (TEXTUAL NOTE to 2:8).

"Abihu" *(ʾăbîhûʾ).* LXX *Abioud* (= *ʾăbîhûd*?).

5:30. "Abishua" *(ʾăbîšûaʿ).* LXX* *Abeisou.* LXX^{L} and Arm. *Abioud* assimilates to the previous lemma.

5:31. "Buqqi." So MT, along with Ezra 7:4 and 1 Esd 8:2. LXX[B] 1 Chr 5:31 *Bōe*; Syr. *(l)'byq(w)r*; 2 Esd 1:2 *Borith*.

"Uzzi" *(ʿuzzî)*. So MT. LXX *Ozei*. Syr. *(l)ʿzry*; 1 Esd 8:2 *Saouia* (B* *Ozeiou*).

5:32. "Zeraḥiah." Thus 1 Chr 5:32 and Ezra 7:4, cf. *(Zariou)*. Lacking in 1 Chr 9:10–11(// Neh 11:10–11). 2 Esd 1:2 *Arna*.

"Meraioth" *(mrywt)*. So MT and LXX[AN]. LXX[L] *Mariōth*; LXX[B] c_2 *Mareiēl*. Syr. *(l)mrw*. In 1 Chr 9:10–11(//Neh 11:10–11) "Meraioth" is the father of Zadoq, while in Ezra 7:3 and 2 Esd 1:2 "Meraioth" (2 Esd 1:2 *Marimoth*) is the father of Azariah (2 Esd 1:2 *Aziei*).

5:33. "Amariah." 2 Esd 1:1–2 adds Heli, Phineḥas, and Aḥijah before continuing with Aḥiṭub and Zadoq. The three extra names are not found in any other list (Ezra 7:1–5; 1 Chr 5:29–41; 9:10–11[//Neh 11:10–11]; 1 Esd 8:1–2; Josephus, *Ant.* 10.152–53). Cf. 1 Sam 14:3; 22:20.

"Aḥiṭub." LXX reads *Achitōb* here and elsewhere in vv. 34–38.

5:35. "Aḥimaaz sired Azariah." So MT, LXX, and Josephus (*Ant.* 10.152). In 1 Kgs 4:2 Azariah is the son, rather than the grandson, of Zadoq.

"Azariah." Following Bertheau (1873) and others, I am transposing the anecdote of v. 36 here: "it was he who officiated as a priest in the Temple that Solomon built in Jerusalem" (1 Kgs 4:2). The Azariah of v. 35 became confused with the Azariah of v. 36. Josephus (*Ant.* 10.152) and the other lists provide other variants. Josephus speaks of Zadoq as the first high priest *(archiereus)* of the Temple that Solomon built, while 1 Chr 9:11(//Neh 11:11) depicts Aḥiṭub as "the leader *(nāgîd)* of the house of God." Ezra 7:5 mentions Aaron as the "chief priest" (הכהן הראש), while 1 Esd 8:2 describes Aaron as the "first priest" *(prōtou hiereōs)*. 2 Esd 1:1–3 lack any reference to a particular priest or leader of the Temple.

"it was he" *(hûʾ)*. One Heb. MS specifies the antecedent by adding "Azariah." Supposing a haplography *(homoioarkton* from *hāriʾšôn* to *hûʾ)*, many preface (or add) *hāriʾšôn*, "the first."

"officiated as a priest" *(kihēn)*. So MT and LXX[AB] *(hierateusen)*. Cf. Exod 40:13; Lev 16:32. LXX[L] *ho hierateusas*.

"Joḥanan." So MT and LXX. At this point, the high priestly list of Josephus (*Ant.* 10.152) diverges *(Iōramos)* from MT and LXX.

5:36. "Azariah." See the 2nd TEXTUAL NOTE to v. 35.

5:37–38. "Amariah . . . Aḥiṭub . . . Zadoq." So 1 Chr 5:37–38, Ezra 7:2–3, and 1 Esd 8:1–2. In 1 Chr 9:10–11(//Neh 11:10–11) an alternate sequence occurs (Aḥiṭub . . . Meraioth . . . Zadoq). That the sequence in vv. 37–38 duplicates the sequence found in vv. 33–34 is suspicious. The question involves not simply the repetition of certain names (the practice of papponymy was common in Achaemenid and Hellenistic times; NOTE to v. 36) but the repetition of a sequence of names and the paucity of names in the total list (contra Curtis and Madsen 1910: 129). From the time of the United Monarchy (Zadoq) onward, the genealogist posits only twelve generations of priests (vv. 36–41). This meager total may be compared with the tally of seventeen generations of kings from Solomon to Zedeqiah (3:10–16) and the tally by Josephus of either seventeen (*Ant.* 10.152–53) or eighteen (*Ant.* 20.224–31) high priests for the same period. The list of priests in

vv. 27–41 seems to be too short. Given the patterns evident in the genealogy (SOURCES AND COMPOSITION), the compressed nature of the list may represent deliberate artifice. Even briefer priestly lineages may be found in Ezra 7:1–5, 1 Chr 9:10–11(//Neh 11:10–11), 1 Esd 8:1–2, and 2 Esd 1:1–3.

5:38. "Zadoq." So MT. Josephus (*Ant.* 10.153) *Soudaias*. Josephus adds a number of names not found in either MT or LXX (*Iouēlos, Iōthamos, Ourias, Nērias, Ōdaias*). Some of these names show a Heb. *Vorlage* (e.g., *ʾûrîyāh, nērîyāh, hôdawyāh*) and cannot be dismissed for text-critical purposes.

"Shallum." So MT. LXX^{B} *Salōm*; LXX^{ALN} *Selloum*; y* *Salloum*; Arm *Selum*; 1 Esd 8:1 *Salēmos*; Josephus (*Ant.* 10.153) *Salloumos*. At this point, the list of Josephus rejoins that of MT and LXX.

5:40. "Seraiah" (*śĕrāyāh*). So MT (and LXX) 5:40, Ezra 7:1, and 1 Esd 8:1. Lacking in both Josephus (*Ant.* 10.153) and 1 Chr 9:10–11, but not in Neh 11:11.

"Jehozadaq." So MT. LXX^{B} c_2 *Iōsadak*. LXX^{ALN} *Iōsedek* (= "Jehozedeq"). Josephus (*Ant.* 10.153) *Iōsadakos*. Syr. *(l)ṣdwq* assimilates toward the more common Zadoq (vv. 34, 38). "Jehozadaq" is absent from all of the Ezra lists (Ezra 7:1–5; 1 Esd 8:1–2; 2 Esd 1:1–3) and 1 Chr 9:10–11 (//Neh 11:10–11).

5:41. "and Jehozadaq." So MT and LXX^{AB}. Cursive c_2 adds "sired Azariah."

"went (*hālak*) into exile (*baggālût*)." So LXX^{L} *tō apoikizein* (= *baggālût*). Cf. Jer 40:1. MT: "went" (*hālak*). LXX^{AB} *eporeythē en tē metoikiao meta Iouda*, "went into the resettlement with Judah." Citing the evidence of LXX^{L}, as well as Tg. *bglwtʾ* (cf. Syr. and Arab.), some scholars read (*baggôlâ*; see Jer 48:11; 49:3; Amos 1:15). While it is possible that the versions assimilate toward the readings offered by Jeremiah and Amos, it is more likely that *baggālût* was lost by haplography (*homoioarkton*) before "when Yhwh exiled (*bĕhaglôt*) Judah." In any case, there is no text-critical warrant (contra Rothstein and Hänel 1927; Michaeli 1967) to add a reference to Jeshua (cf. Ezra 3:2; Hag 1:1). Both in MT (followed by LXX) and in Josephus (*Ant.* 10.153), the passage ends with exile.

NOTES

5:27–6:66. The tribe of Levi takes center stage in the genealogies of Israel (2:3–9:1). If Judah (2:3–4:23) and Benjamin (8:1–40) anchor the lineages, Israel's priestly tribe occupies the central position. After Judah, Levi receives the most extensive coverage of any tribe. As with the other sodalities, considerable attention is paid to issues of identity and location: who the Levites are (5:27–6:38) and where they live (6:39–66). There is yet another parallel among the lineages of Judah, Levi, and Benjamin. Each contains at least one long descending lineage: David (3:1–24), Levi (5:27–41), and Jeiel (8:29–40//9:35–44). The depth of these genealogies, the shortest being some thirteen generations, is truly extraordinary. Most genealogies achieve a depth of only a few generations.

5:27. "sons of Levi." Some commentators sever vv. 27–28 from the lineage dealing with Aaron (vv. 29–41), but this artificial separation ignores the consistent literary pattern displayed by the other major genealogies. In Chronicles the Ancestral period, and not the Sinaitic period, is of paramount importance for tracing the origins of each of Israel's tribes. Within the tribal genealogies, the lineages of the priests (5:27–41), the Levites (6:1–15), and the Davidides (2:10–17; 3:1–24) all begin with the Ancestral epoch, the time of the patriarch Israel (2:1–2). By using the same starting point as that used for the tribes, the author underscores how important the Levites, priests, and Davidides are to the very constitution of his nation.

"Gershon." The material in 5:27 is paralleled in 6:1. The writer is indebted to earlier texts (e.g., Gen 46:11; Exod 6:16–25; Num 3:2, 17–20) for his presentation of this segmentation (vv. 27–30). Many of the remaining relationships in vv. 31ff. are unique to Chronicles.

5:28. "Qohath." Of Levi's three male offspring (Gershon, Qohath, and Merari), the author begins by tracing the lineage of the second son Qohath, whose descendants include Amram, Aaron, Eleazar, and Phineḥas. The lineage of 6:1–2 presents a more normal course by pursuing the offspring of the firstborn Gershon. In listing the Qohathites first the author replicates the precedent of the Priestly writer in Num 4:1–15. There the Qohathites receive special attention, presumably because they have responsibility for transporting the most sacred *sancta* of the tabernacle (Milgrom 1990: 24). References to the Qohathites may be found only in P (Gen 46:11; Exod 6:16–18; Num 3:17–30; 4:2–15; 7:9; 10:21; 16:1; 26:57–58), Chronicles, and (the Priestly influenced text of) Josh 21 (21:4–5, 10, 20, 26). Within Chronicles the Qohathites appear both in the genealogies (5:27–41; 6:1–7, 18, 23, 39, 46, 51, 55; 9:32) and in the narratives about the monarchy (15:5; 23:6–12; 2 Chr 20:19; 29:12; 34:12). Whereas the Priestly writers acknowledge Aaron's Qohathite ancestry (e.g., Num 26:58–60), they usually distinguish between the status and work of Aaron (and his sons) and the status and work of the Qohathite Levites (e.g., Num 3:1–4:49). There is also a contrast between the coverage of Qohath and the Qohathites in Chronicles and in Ezra-Nehemiah, which does not refer to Qohath and the Qohathites. See also the 1st NOTE to 15:5.

"Izhar." See Exod 6:18–21 and the NOTES to 23:18 and 24:22.

5:29–34. "sons of Aaron." The precise content (sequence and names), but not form, of this descending genealogy is paralleled in 6:35–38.

5:29. "Aaron" (*ʾahărōn*). The fact that the author of this genealogy contextualizes Aaron within the larger Levitical lineage is highly significant (cf. Gen 46:11; Exod 6:18, 20, 23, 25). Many scholars have argued that Aaron's family did not originally belong to the tribe of Levi (e.g., Cross 1973: 195–215; Friedman 1987: 40–42, 72–79). The debates about Aaron's original status are based on varying coverage of him in the narrative and poetic sources of the HB (Haran 1971). The J and E source(s) of the Pentateuch depicts the elder brother of Moses as his spokesman and partner in leading the Israelites out of Egypt (Exod 4:10, 27–31; 10:3–6; 11:10). But the Pentateuch also contains stories of conflict among different priestly factions and some of these (e.g., Exod 32*) do not reflect well on Aaron. These tales may reflect rivalries among different priestly houses in the history of ancient Israel (Cross 1973: 198–206). The Deuteronomic authors hardly ever mention Aaron and then only to condemn and bury him (Deut 9:16, 20; 10:6; 32:51). References to Aaron and the Aaronides are also scarce in Samuel and Kings (1 Sam 12:6, 8). It is in the Priestly writing that Aaron occupies a position of greatest prestige and prominence (Exod 28:1–3, 41–43; 29:44; 40:13–15; Lev 8:1–3; Num 6:23–27; 18:1–7). There his name occurs some 296 times. In P, Aaron appears as the priest and the progenitor of a priestly family (Rivkin 1976; Grabbe 1996). Certain psalms extol Aaron and his priesthood (77:21 [ET 77:20]; 99:6; 105:26; 106:16; 115:10, 12; 118:3; 133:2). The Chronicler is heir to these traditions, but his references to Aaron are most indebted to the Priestly source. Like the Priestly writers, the authors of Chronicles derive Aaron from Levi and identify the specific task of the sons of Aaron as officiating at the central sanctuary (6:34; 23:13). Yet the presentation of Aaron also bears some distinctive marks. The Chronicler contends for a close relationship between the Aaronides and the Levites (COMMENT on 6:1–38).

"Eleazar." The Chronicler follows the lineage of Aaron through Eleazar (Num 20:28; Josh 14:1). Many scholars believe that Zadoqites (here traced to the sons of Eleazar) dominated the priesthood in the Persian period. The descendants of Ithamar are also attested and given legitimacy (1 Chr 24:1–6; cf. Ezra 8:2; Cody 1965: 170–72), but they neither exhibit the same numbers nor wield comparable power.

5:30. "sired" *(hôlîd)*. In his reconstruction of ancient Israelite history, Wellhausen (1885: 127–31) spoke of an early period in which there was no hereditary priesthood. Similarly, Bartlett (1968) makes the case that most, if not all, of the major Jerusalem Temple priests were royal appointments (1 Kgs 1:7; 2:27–35; Amos 7:10–17; cf. Judg 18:19). The king's choice for the office rested upon the person's ability, and the priest served only as long as the king wished (Bartlett 1968: 13–15). Only in a few cases is priestly succession documented in the Deuteronomistic History. Royal prerogative is a valid consideration, but one should distinguish between priestly succession within a given family and the occupation of the highest priestly post. There is evidence from various lands in the ancient Mediterranean world of heredity in cultic affairs. A stela from Carthage, for example, mentions three generations of priests from one family (*KAI* 81). Some priestly offices were handed down through the generations in ancient Egypt (te Velde 1995: 1733–35). Continuity in the holding of a prebend was a mark of status. Nevertheless, a specific bloodline did not automatically entitle one to the occupation of a specific post or overrule all other considerations. In ancient Egypt, priestly offices were always subject to royal ratification. Central and local officials might also seek Temple positions for friends and relatives (O'Connor 1995: 321). The development of the priesthood(s) within ancient Israel and Judah witnesses an increasing concern with heredity (Olyan 1997). To put things somewhat differently, if there ever was an era in Israelite history in which there was no hereditary priestly succession, the authors of Chronicles do not acknowledge it. In this respect, Chronicles may reflect influence from the Priestly source (e.g., Lev 16:32; Num 25:11–13). From the Chronicler's point of view, the members of sacerdotal families might serve in a variety of cultic posts, but it was their bloodline that made them eligible to fulfill such vocations.

"Phineḥas" *(pînḥas)*, the son and successor to Eleazar, is attested in a variety of earlier contexts (e.g., Exod 6:25; Josh 24:33; Judg 20:28). In Num 25:11–13 (P) Phineḥas' loyalty wins him a divine pledge of a perpetual covenant of priesthood (Num 25:13). Ben Sira (Sir 45:23; 50:24; Skehan and Di Lella 1987: 550) and Josephus (*Ant.* 8.1.3) construe this promise as confirming that Phineḥas was the legitimate successor to the high priesthood. Milgrom (1990: 216–17) presents a different view, contending that the promise guarantees Phineḥas that his line will be the exclusive officiants at the sanctuary. The pact with Phineḥas is, however, not mentioned in Chronicles. In 1 Chr 9:20 Phineḥas appears as the "officer" *(nāgîd)* of the Qohathites in their work of service *(mĕleʾket hāʿabôdâ)* as guards of the threshold of the Tent.

"Abishua." The name appears elsewhere in Chronicles (8:4) and Ezra (7:5), but this particular descendant of Phineḥas is not otherwise attested.

5:33. "Aḥiṭub" is called "ruler of the house of God" in the priestly genealogy of 1 Chr 9:11//Neh 11:11 (cf. Jer 20:1; 2 Chr 31:13; 35:8). The use of *nāgîd* to denote a high priest is only attested in later sources (משיח נגיד; Dan 9:25–26; 11:22; Collins 1993: 355, 382).

5:34. "Zadoq." Situating Zadoq within a much larger Qohathite lineage is unique to Chronicles. There is no agreement as to whether this contextualization has any historical merit. In the view of Wellhausen (1885: 126), followed by many scholars, Zadoq appears as a *homo novus*, without precedent and without genealogy. In 2 Sam 8:17(//1 Chr 18:16) Zadoq is simply listed as the son of Aḥiṭub. Even the author of Ezek 44:9–16, who distinguishes between the Levites and the Levitical priests descended from Zadoq, does not list Zadoq's ancestors. Some scholars (e.g., Bentzen 1933; Rowley 1939; Welch 1939; Judge 1956; Hauer 1963) view Zadoq as a priest of the old Canaanite sanctuary in Jerusalem (Jebus). In this popular reconstruction, David's appointment of Zadoq was a political move designed to placate an important non-Israelite priestly(-royal) figure. But the Jebusite hypothesis has come under severe criticism by other scholars (e.g., Cross 1973: 207–15; Olyan 1982; Laato 1994a: 96–97) on both philological and historical grounds. These scholars tie Zadoq to Aaronide circles in Ḥebron (Num 26:58; Josh 21:10, 13; 1 Chr 6:42). In this alternative theory, David's highly unusual move of appointing both Zadoq and Abiathar represented a compromise on his part, designed to win support from two rival priestly houses. The Mushite clans were associated with Shiloh and Dan, while the Aaronides were associated with Bethel and Ḥebron. There is a third theory. The Aaronides and the Zadoqites represent two different priestly factions in preexilic Israel and Judah (Kennett 1904–1905; Judge 1956; Meeks 1929; Allan 1982; Blenkinsopp 1998). In this hypothesis, the Zadoqites were supplanted, probably only temporarily, by the Aaronides during the exilic period. It is relevant to observe, in this regard, that Ben Sira bestows lavish and extensive praise on Aaron and the Aaronic priesthood (Sir 45:6–22). His coverage of Aaron is, in fact, almost triple that of his coverage of Moses (44:23–45:5). Yet Ben Sira's treatment of Israel's great ancestors (44:1–49:16) makes no mention whatsoever of Zadoq. Nor does Zadoq figure in the lengthy panegyric to the high priest Simeon II (Sir 50:1–24). Only in the concluding litany of praise (Sir 51:12i–xvi), often considered to be a later addition on text-critical grounds (Skehan and Di Lella 1987: 568–71), do the sons of Zadoq make a brief appearance (51:12ix). The work of Ben Sira postdates Chronicles, but his position reveals that debates about the priesthood did not disappear in the Persian and Hellenistic periods. The Chronicler's work is sometimes said to reflect Zadoqite dominance in postexilic Judah, but the situation is more complicated. The stance cannot be construed as a passive aquiescence to the emergence of a new status quo, because as the evidence provided by Malachi (O'Brien 1990) suggests, it is unlikely that any one stand on the priesthood won unanimous acceptance in the Persian period. It is more likely that the authors of Chronicles attempt to mediate among a variety of positions. The sons of Zadoq are related to Aaron (5:29) and appear within the context of a larger Qohathite genealogy (5:27–41; 6:34–45). See further the COMMENT.

"Aḥimaaz." As the son of Zadoq, see 2 Sam 15:27, 36; 17:17, 20; 18:19–29 (cf. 1 Kgs 4:15).

5:35. "officiated as priest" *(kihēn)*. The usage of this denominative verb (1 Chr 24:2; 2 Chr 11:14; cf. Sir 45:15) is familiar from the Priestly source (Exod 28:1, 3, 41; 29:1, 44; 30:30; 31:10; 40:13, 15; Lev 7:35; 16:32), although the verb is also occasionally found in other sources (Deut 10:6; Ezek 44:13; Hos 4:6).

5:36. "Azariah." A case of papponymy (naming someone after his grandfather). The practice of papponymy is well-attested in the Persian, Hellenistic, and Classical Jewish periods among not only biblical texts, such as Chronicles, but also extrabiblical inscriptions, such as the Samaria papyri, the Ammonite inscription from Tel Sīrān, the Elephantine papyri (Porten 1968: 235–37), and the Aramaic inscription from Taymā' indicate (Cross 1974: 5–6; 1986; 1998: 157, 193).

5:37. "Amariah" (II) likely refers to the high priest who served under Jehoshaphaṭ (2 Chr 19:11).

5:38 "Shallum" (שלום). On the name, compare the Qohathite Meshullam (משלם), who helps supervise the Temple reconstruction project in the time of Josiah (2 Chr 34:12). The list of priests in 1 Chr 9:10–11(//Neh 11:10–11) mentions a Meshullam (משלם) *ben* Zadoq. The two—Shallum *(ben* Zadoq) and Meshullam *(ben* Zadoq)—may be variants of the same name.

5:39 "Ḥilqiah" appears as a high priest in the reign of Josiah (2 Kgs 22:8–12; 2 Chr 34:9, 14–22; 35:8).

"Azariah." At first glance, it might be tempting to correlate this Azariah (III) and the previous Azariah (II; v. 37) with the two Azariahs appearing during the reigns of Uzziah (2 Chr 26:17) and Ḥezeqiah (2 Chr 31:10; Laato 1994a: 93), but the placement of these two figures frustrates such an attempt. Azariah III, for example, appears after the time of Ḥilqiah (and Josiah). Confirmation of this may come from epigraphic evidence. The name appears on a late seventh- to early-sixth-century Jerusalem bulla, לעזריהו בן חלקיהו, "belonging to Azaryahu son of Ḥilqiyahu" (Davies, §100.827; Schneider 1988) and on a seal dating to the same time, לעזריהו חלקיהו, "belonging to Azaryahu [son of] Ḥilqiyahu" (Avigad and Sass 1997: 139 [§307]).

5:40. "Seraiah" was "chief priest" at the time of the second Babylonian exile of 586 B.C.E. (2 Kgs 25:18, 21; Jer 52:24, 27). Ezra's lineage is traced through Seraiah (Ezra 7:1; 1 Esd 8:2 [ET 8:1]; 2 Esd 1:1).

"Jehozadaq" is mentioned quite often as the father of Jeshua, the high priest, in the early postexilic period (Hag 1:1, 12, 14; 2:2, 4; Zech 6:11; Jozadaq in Ezra 3:2, 8; 5:2; 10:18). The connection to Aaron legitimates Jehozadaq's priesthood and, by implication, that of his Persian period successors.

5:41. "exiled." Whereas Seraiah was captured and executed in 586 B.C.E. at Riblah (2 Kgs 25:18–21), Jehozadaq was exiled to Babylon. If Seraiah was the father, as opposed to the grandfather, of Jehozadaq, Jehozadaq would have been truly durable.

"Judah and Jerusalem." Referring to the exile of 586 B.C.E. (2 Chr 36:11–21; 2 Kgs 25:1–21). In speaking of the deportation of both "Judah and Jerusalem," the author depicts a major displacement affecting both urban and rural areas. The Assyrian and Babylonian exiles do not carry the force in Chronicles that they do in Kings, but they are still highly important events in the history of Israel and Judah (NOTES to 5:6, 22, 25–26; 9:1).

SOURCES AND COMPOSITION

The commentary on the Levitical genealogies is divided into different sections (5:27–41; 6:1–38, 39–66), so it is appropriate to make some remarks about the composition of the whole (5:27–6:66). Most scholars agree that the Levitical genealogies were not written in one piece. Divergent orders of presentation (Qohath, Gershon, Merari vs. Gershon, Qohath, Merari), different genealogical forms, the priority of Heman over Asaph, the placement of Ethan instead of Jeduthun at the head of Merari (6:16–33; cf. 15:17–19; 16:41–42), and discrepancies among the genealogies (esp. those for Merari in 6:14–15 and 6:29–32) are the reasons most often cited for multiple authorship. But, given the evidence for substantial textual corruption, especially in the lists (TEXTUAL NOTES), it is not always easy to discern where authorial (or editorial) activity ends and scribal activity begins. In any case, the Levitical genealogies seem to have had a complicated texual history.

Many scholars (e.g., Willi 1972: 214; R. Braun 1986: 81–82; Kartveit 1989: 77–87) view 6:1–38, as the core of the unit and 5:27–41 as a later addition. In this reconstruction, the elaborate lineage of 5:27–41 is based on the parallel and more limited list of Aaronide priests in 6:35–38 (Aaron to Aḥimaaz). Some of these same scholars (e.g., Kartveit 1989: 154) think that the list of Levitical towns (6:39–66) is the latest addition to the Levitical genealogy. The relationship of the Levitical town list to the rest of the Levitical genealogy and to Josh 21 is a special subject that is best postponed to the commentary on this section of chapter 6 (chapter IX, "The Levitical Settlements"). To return to the makeup of the priestly genealogy in 5:27–41 and its relationship to other genealogies, there is much to be said for the minority view (e.g., Möhlenbrink 1934: 203–5; Williamson 1982b: 74) that the list of the "descendants of Aaron" in 6:35–38 is a later addition, based on the parallel and more extensive list of priests in 5:27–41. To begin with, the genealogy of 5:27–41 fits better contextually. Beginning the genealogy with the Qohathites (5:27–28) conforms to the interest in the Qohathites displayed elsewhere in the Levitical genealogy (6:3, 7–12, 18–23, 39–41, 46, 51–55). By contrast, the reference to "the descendants of Aaron" in 6:35 is a non sequitur, genealogically speaking. The partial repetition of the genealogy from 5:27–41 could have been created when an editor wished to insert a priestly complement to the genealogies of the Levitical singers (6:1–32) centered in the United Monarchy.

There is, however, another common argument for the priority of 6:35–38 over 5:27–41 that needs to be addressed at some length, an argument that involves the other priestly lists in biblical and postbiblical writings (1 Chr 9:10–11[// Neh 11:10–11]; Ezra 7:1–5; 1 Esd 8:1–2; 2 Esd 1:1–3), including the oft-neglected high-priestly genealogy of Josephus (*Ant.* 10.152–53). Bartlett (1968), Marshall Johnson (1988: 38–41), Roddy Braun (1986: 83), and others think that the longest list (5:27–41) is the latest of the various lists found in Chronicles, Ezra, Nehemiah, 1 Esdras, and 2 Esdras. In this way of thinking, the briefest of all the lineages (1 Chr 9:10–11//Neh 11:10–11) is also the oldest (or based on the oldest source). This prevalent way of dealing with the differences among the lists legitimately calls attention to the possibility of expansion. One wonders, for example, whether the unparalleled appearance of Eli, Phineḥas, and Aḥijah before Aḥiṭub and Zadoq in the late genealogy of 2 Esd 1:1–3 (second century C.E.) attempts to harmonize the lineage of the Elides (1 Sam 14:3; 22:20; 1 Kgs 2:27, 35) with that of the Aaronides. But this way of thinking also exhibits a number of flaws, requiring critical scrutiny.

First, there is the issue of length. The twenty-five-generation genealogy of 5:27–41 is in all likelihood too short for the extensive period covered. When identical or similar names are repeated within a single lineage, one has to allow for the possibility that both horizontal and vertical haplographies may have occurred during the course of textual transmission (TEXTUAL NOTE to vv. 37–38). By way of contrast to the lineage of 5:27–41, Josephus presents seventeen or eighteen generations of priests following Zadoq (*Ant.* 10.152–53; 20.231). A brief list that mentions seven names to cover the tenth century to the sixth century is inherently problematic. If one contends that the genealogy of (1 Chr 9:10–11//Neh 11:10–11) is original, one has to concede, as Osborne (1979) does, that the genealogy is purely telescopic in nature. But this position needs to be argued and not presumed.

Second, the theory neglects the possibility that some of the lists (e.g., Josephus) represent abridgments of a longer list either directly or indirectly related to 5:27–41. The variations in length do not seem to have resulted from a process of amorphous growth. Both the beginnings and the endings of the genealogies reflect conscious choices on the part of authors. The point about endings should be quite obvious. The editor of Ezra incorporates Ezra into a traditional priestly genealogy (7:1–5). The editor of Neh 11:10–11(//1 Chr 9:10–11) ties Jachin, Jedaiah, and Jehoiarib to an older priestly lineage. The author of 6:35–38 ends his lineage with Aḥimaaz of the united monarchy, which is appropriate to the context (6:16–18, 24, 29). Similarly, the different starting points of the genealogies do not seem to be accidental. That one of the genealogies of Josephus (*Ant.* 10.152–53) begins with Zadoq and that of Neh 11:10–11(//1 Chr 9:10–11) with the grandfather of Zadoq privileges the Zadoqites. In these lineages, the genealogy of priests becomes a genealogy of Zadoqites. By contrast, the lineages of 1 Chr 6, Ezra 7 (1 Esd 8; 2 Esd 1), and Josephus (in another context—*Ant.* 20.224–31) privilege Aaron. In these lineages, the genealogy of priests becomes a genealogy of Aaronides. That the genealogy of 5:27–41 begins with Qohath *ben* Levi privileges the Qohathites, who figure prominently elsewhere in the genealogy of Levi. Since the names appearing at the beginning and end of ancient genealogies were most relevant in establishing the author's point, the variant beginnings and endings of these genealogies should not occasion too much surprise. The point is that at least some of the writers may have had access to longer versions of the priestly genealogy than the genealogy that they actually chose to include within their works.

Third, the theory approaches the differences among the lists from primarily a literary (redaction-history) point of view. A series of editors supposedly add a name or a cluster of names to an older and much briefer text. But before proceeding to literary criticism, one should begin with textual criticism. Most text-critical variants arise from inadvertent editorial and scribal errors. By focusing on text-critical issues, one can begin to make some progress in understanding the internal relations among the major lists. (See table, p. 410)

Examination of these lineages reveals clear signs of textual confusion, some of which were caused by haplography (TEXTUAL NOTES). In Ezra 7:1–5 (and 1 Esd 8:1–2) a major haplography *(homoioteleuton)* has occurred from "Amariah" (I) to "Azariah" (Amariah II). The considerable gap in the ascending list of priests in 1 Chr 9:10–11(//Neh 11:10–11) may have also been triggered by haplography. The other possibility is that the Aḥiṭub who appears as the grandfather of Zadoq in 1 Chr 9:10–11(//Neh 11:10–11) is in fact Aḥiṭub II (Bartlett 1968). In this case, fifteen of the first twenty-five names in 5:27–41 are lacking in 9:10–11(//Neh 11:10–11). The problem is, however, Meraioth, who appears as the son of Zeraḥiah in 1 Chr 5:32–33, 1 Chr 6:36–37, Ezra 7:3, and 1 Esd 8:2 *(Marēroth tou Zaraiou)*. There is only one Zeraḥiah attested, Zeraḥiah *ben* Uzzi of 1 Chr 5:32, 1 Chr 6:36, and Ezra 7:4 (1 Esd 8:2 *Zaraiou tou Saouia*). This evidence makes it more likely that 9:10–11(//Neh 11:10–11) has suffered a major haplography from Meshullam to Zadoq (I) caused by the repetition of Zadoq in the list (from Zadoq II to Zadoq I). To be sure, my theory does not explain why Aḥiṭub is the father of Meraioth (1 Chr 9:10–11//Neh 11:10–11) instead of his grandson (5:33; 6:37), but this is a problem for any reconstruction. Given the evidence for telescoping and haplography in the shorter lists, one cannot dismiss the value of the longer lists for scholarly reconstruction. In any case, it seems best not to begin with the lineages of 9:10–11(//Neh 11:10–11) and Ezra 7:1–5. On text-critical grounds, these may be the most problematic and corrupt of all the priestly lineages. On these and other related matters, see further Knoppers (2003).

5:27–41	*6:35–38*	*Ezra 7:1–5*	*Josephus*	*9:10–11*
Levi				
Qohath				
Amram				
Aaron	Aaron	Aaron		
Eleazar	Eleazar	Eleazar		
Phineḥas	Phineḥas	Phineḥas		
Abishua	Abishua	Abishua		
Buqqi	Buqqi	Buqqi		
Uzzi	Uzzi	Uzzi		
Zeraḥiah	Zeraḥiah	Zeraḥiah		
Meraioth	Meraioth	Meraioth		
Amariah	Amariah			
Aḥiṭub	Aḥiṭub			Aḥiṭub
				Meraioth
Zadoq	Zadoq		Sadōkos	Zadoq
Aḥimaaz	Aḥimaaz		Achimas	
Azariah			Azarias	
Joḥanan			Iōramos	
Azariah		Azariah	Iōs	
Amariah		Amariah	Axiōramos	
Aḥiṭub		Aḥiṭub	Phideas	
Zadoq		Zadoq	Soudaias	
			Iouēlos	
			Iōthamos	
			Ourias	
			Nērias	
			Ōdaias	
Shallum		Shallum	Salloumos	Meshullam
Ḥilqiah		Ḥilqiah	Elkias	Ḥilqiah
Azariah		Azariah	Azaros	Azariah
Seraiah		Seraiah		
Jehozadaq			Iōsadakos	
		Ezra		Jachin, etc.

Structure

The Levitical genealogies evince signs of a unified editorial design. In their present form, the genealogies exhibit an eightfold structure. There are two genealogies of priests (5:27–41; 6:35–38), two genealogies of Gershonites and Gershonite singers (6:5–6, 24–28), two genealogies of Qohathites and Qohathite singers (6:7–12, 18–23), and two genealogies of Merarites and Merarite singers (6:14–15, 29–32). Within this eightfold structure, the attention given to the priests forms an *inclusio* around the coverage given to the Levites. Two genealogies of priests (5:27–41; 6:35–38) frame six genealogies of Levites (6:1–33). The genealogies consistently feature three Levitical phratries: the Qohathites, the Gershonites, and the Merarites. This tripartite focus is maintained even in discussing the Levitical places of residence (6:39–66). Within this setting, the Qohathites occupy a privileged position. The Levitical genealogies open with a lineage of Qohathite priests (5:27–41). Similarly, the section on Levitical towns opens with Qohathite settlements in Judah and Benjamin (6:39b–45).

Both the first priestly genealogy and the Levitical genealogies begin with the Ancestral era: "the sons of Levi" (5:27; 6:1). Both passages begin with segmented genealogies (5:27–29; 6:1–4a) before giving way to linear genealogies. Each of the three major Levitical phratries (6:1–15), as well as those Qohathites who were specially designated as priests (5:27–41), can claim an ancient pedigree. The Deuteronomists consistently emphasize the importance of the Exodus as a foundational event in Israelite history, but these genealogies emphasize the age of Matriarchs and Patriarchs as pivotal to the development of Israel's priestly tribe (5:27–28; 6:1–4a, 23, 28, 32).

The genealogies of the priests and Levitical singers also focus attention on the United Monarchy. The Levitical singers receive their charge and their employment in the time of David and Solomon (6:16–17, 18, 24, 29). The first priestly genealogy mentions that Azariah served as priest in the Temple that Solomon built (5:35). This priestly genealogy is structured to call attention to Zadoq at its center. There are twenty-five descendants from Qohath to Jehozadaq. If Qohath is the first pertinent scion of Levi and Jehozadaq the last, the midpoint is Zadoq. Commentators have called attention to a possible connection to MT 1 Kgs 6:1, which dates the building of the Temple to 480 years after the Exodus (Knoppers 1993c: 95–96). The calculation of a typological figure of forty years per generation is suggestive (12 x 40 = 480), but the Exodus is not in view. Rather, the time of Zadoq marks the halfway point between the Ancestral era and the Babylonian exile. Twelve generations of priests (12 x 40 = 480 years) precede him (Qohath to Aḥiṭub) and twelve generations of priests (12 x 40 = 480 years) succeed him (Aḥimaaz to Jehozadaq). The beginning and end of the genealogy call attention to Levi and Jehozadaq, and the chiastic order of 5:27–41 accents the critical place of Zadoq.

The second priestly genealogy calls attention to the time of David and Solomon in a different way, beginning with the Sinaitic era (Aaron) and ending with the United Monarchy (6:35–38). If the Sinaitic era is the definitive age for the establishment of the priesthood, the United Monarchy is the definitive age for the establishment of the Levitical singers. But the latter does not replace or render obsolete the former. As the Levitical singers were stationed by David and Solomon during this time of national consolidation (6:16–17, 18, 24, 29), the Aaronide priests (6:35–38) continued to carry out their traditional duties. In this respect, the list of Aaronides (6:35–38) complements the lists of the Levites (Qohathites, Asaphites, and Merarites in 6:18–33). Given the stated connection with the United Monarchy, it is appropriate that the list stops with Aḥimaaz the son of Zadoq, rather than continue to the Babylonian exile (cf. 5:41). In short, one can discern a logic in the partial repetition of the list from 5:27–41.

COMMENT

Over the course of the centuries it has become a commonplace to refer to 1 Chr 5:27–41 as a high-priestly genealogy. The Chronicler or a later editor traced a postexilic institution all the way back to the time of Israel's origins. In this calculation, Aaron is but the first of a long line of high priests. The list ends with Jehozadaq, but by implication the pattern of high-priestly succession extends into the Persian period. A variation of this line of interpretation calls special attention to the position of Zadoq. The Chronicler or a later editor attempts to document Zadoqite claims to the high priesthood in Persian period Yehud by providing Zadoq with an Aaronide priestly ancestry. In spite of the immense popularity of both of these views, one needs to be questioned and the other needs to be qualified (Knoppers 2003).

One may begin by questioning whether the lineage of 5:27–41 is indeed a list of high priests in genealogical dress. The text makes no such assertion. The genealogy simply begins with the rubric "the sons of Levi." Were either Levi or Qohath high priests? When the genealogy switches from segmented to linear form, it does so with a view to Eleazar's progeny (v. 30). Unlike the author of Ezra 7:5, who refers to Aaron as "the chief priest" *(hakkōhēn hārōʾš)*, this author does not label any of the figures in these verses as "the chief priest" (*hakkōhēn hārōʾš*; 2 Kgs 25:18//Jer 52:24; 2 Chr 19:11; 24:6, 11; 26:20) or "the high priest" (*hakkōhēn haggādôl*; Lev 21:10; Num 35:25, 28; Josh 20:6; 2 Kgs 12:11 [ET 12:10]; 22:4, 8; 23:4; Zech 3:1, 8; 6:11; Hag 1:1, 12, 14; 2:2, 4; Neh 3:1, 20; 2 Chr 34:9). Some are listed in narrative sources as having one of these titles, but most are not. A comparison with the Davidic genealogy may be apt. Even though the Davidic lineage begins with David (3:1) and plots a continuous succession to the generation of Elioenai (3:24), no one contends that all of these figures actually held kingly office.

If 5:27–41 were, strictly speaking, a lineage of high priests, its content would be rather odd. Some of the most prominent priests who figure in the Deuteronomistic and Chronistic accounts of the Judahite monarchy—most notably Jehoiada (2 Chr 22:11–24:16), Uriah (2 Kgs 16:10–16), and Azariah (in the reign of Uzziah; 2 Chr 26:20)—do not appear in this account. To sharpen the question, the narrative portions of Chronicles mention a number of priests and Levites who, while not having the titles "chief priest" or "high priest," are depicted as heavily involved in the supervision of the Temple (Bartlett 1968: 6–13). These include "Jehoiada the leader (*nāgîd*) of Aaron" (12:28), "Azariah, ruler of the house of God" (2 Chr 31:13), and perhaps "Zechariah son of the priest Jehoiada" (2 Chr

24:20–22). Zechariah ([ז]כריהו) appears in a recently discovered Hebrew ostracon (line 3), yet to undergo critical scrutiny, as the addressee in a widow's petition (Bordreuil, Israel, and Pardee 1996). But with the possible exception of Azariah, none of the figures appear in the genealogy. In one case, the text refers to three different "rulers of the house of God"—Ḥilqiah, Zechariah, and Jeḥiel—(2 Chr 35:8), but only one (Ḥilqiah) appears in this genealogy. In other words, the problem is not terminology. Whether one chooses the title *hakkōhēn hārōʾš, hakkōhēn haggādôl,* or *nĕgîd bêt hāʾĕlōhîm,* there is at best only a partial correlation among the figures who bear these titles in narrative sources and the figures who appear in this lineage. One could argue, of course, that these absentee priests dropped out of 5:27–41 through some sort of textual accident (e.g., haplography), but it seems unlikely that all of these figures did so.

Given the universal understanding of the genealogy as a high-priestly list, it is not surprising that scholars have expressed consternation that Azariah would be singled out as officiating at Solomon's Temple (TEXTUAL NOTE to v. 35). Why mention Azariah (1 Kgs 4:2), as opposed to Zadoq (2 Sam 20:25; 1 Kgs 2:35; 4:4–5; Josephus, *Ant.* 10.152), Jehoiada, or Ḥilqiah? The question may presume too much. Not all, or perhaps even most, of the figures listed in 1 Chr 5:29–41 were regarded by the author as high priests. Given this understanding, it should not occasion great surprise that one figure would be singled out as serving at the first Temple. The anecdote about Azariah may serve as a clue about the function of the genealogy. Rather than being a lineage of high priests, the text of vv. 27–41 may simply be one version of a Qohathite Aaronide lineage. In the genealogist's reckoning, some of the priests, such as Azariah (v. 35), served as major figures within the Jerusalem Temple administration, but others may not have. The point of such a genealogy is to legitimize a line of priests in Persian period Yehud rather than to provide a continuous list of chief priests.

The question of heredity was especially acute in the Persian period, the era in which the Chronicler lived ("Excursus: The Genealogies"). Given the paucity of thorough genealogical information (e.g., in earlier biblical books), some of the priests who considered themselves to be of excellent pedigree may have had difficulty substantiating their claims. This deficiency the authors of Chronicles seek to rectify. In spite of the disruptions caused by the Babylonian deportations, the plundering of Jerusalem, and the destruction of the Temple, Jehozadaq and his successors command continuity in succession from the time of the Ancestors (Levi) onward. Such a continuity through the generations suggests divine favor. In this respect, the function of the priestly genealogy is similar to the functions of other genealogies in Chronicles. Persian period customs, families, institutions, and memories are validated by recourse to ancient times. From the perspective of the genealogist, the pedigree of Yehud's Qohathite priests stretches back over a millennium.

Some confirmation of this alternative line of interpretation comes from the excerpt of the priestly genealogy in 6:35–38. There the genealogy, stretching from Aaron to Aḥimaaz, is accompanied by a job description (6:34). It is true that 6:35 (or 6:34–38) may be the work of a later editor (see SOURCES AND COMPOSITION), but, even if this is so, the passage still provides vital clues about how an early interpreter understood the list of priests in 5:29–41. Even as an addition, 6:35–38 is still the earliest exposition of the priestly list available to us. Its work profile for "Aaron and his sons" revolves around their "sacrificing upon the altar of burnt offering and upon the incense altar for every work of the Holy of Holies to atone for Israel according to all that Moses the servant of God had commanded" (6:34). The passage connects the priests to sacrifice just as the Levitical singers (6:33) are tied to song. There is nothing said about high priests, chief priests, commanders of the house of God, or leaders of the priests (*śārê hakkōhănîm*; 2 Chr 36:14; Ezra 8:24). There is no discussion of the supervision of other priests or of the administration of the sanctuary. In speaking of the high priest, the Priestly authors refer to his being anointed with oil (Lev 21:10; Num 35:25) and to his "consecration to wear the vestments" (Lev 21:10), but no such references appear here.

Given the consolidation (if not establishment) of the high-priestly office in the Persian period and the appearance of some figures, identified in narrative contexts as high priests or chief priests, it is not too surprising that later interpreters construed the entire list as a high-priestly inventory. Josephus (*Ant.* 10.152–53; 20.224–31) repeatedly refers to an unbroken succession of high priests. The point about succession is inherent to the passage, but the point about the genealogy being a high-priestly list is a later extrapolation. In this context, it is appropriate to return to the other issue raised above—the claim that the lineage of 5:27–41 constitutes a charter for Zadoqite control over the postexilic priesthood. This assertion needs to be qualified. To be sure, situating Zadoq within a long Qohathite lineage validates Zadoqite claims to an excellent pedigree (Blenkinsopp 1998: 40–41). To underscore the point, Zadoq appears at the very center of the lineage. The genealogist does not furnish a lineage for the other relevant son of Aaron, Ithamar. This has the effect of favoring the line from Qohath, Amram, Aaron, and Eleazar to Zadoq. Zadoq also plays a significant role during David's reign (1 Chr 12:28; 15:11; 16:39; 18:16; 24:3, 6, 31; 27:17; 29:22). Nevertheless, the presentation cannot be construed as exclusively pro-Zadoqite. Chronicles characteristically speaks of the priests as the sons of Aaron (12:27; 15:4; 23:13, 32; 24:1, 19, 31; 2 Chr 13:9, 10; 26:18; 29:21; 31:19; 35:14) and never as the sons of Zadoq. In only one instance does the book refer to a house (dynasty) of Zadoq (2 Chr 31:10). In the case of this priestly genealogy, the author pushes things back further. There are other priestly lines within the Qohathite lineage. The broad formulation recognizes the existence of other offshoots of the Qohathite line and allows for the possibility that non-Zadoqites could officiate as priests. Aside from the sons of Eleazar (1 Chr 5:30–40; 9:20; 11:12; 23:21, 22; 24:1–6, 28), the other surviving priestly phratry within the broad Qohathite designation is the sons of Ithamar (5:29; 24:1–6). In 1 Chr 24:5 both the sons of Eleazar and the sons of Ithamar are described as "officers of the sanctuary and officers of God."

The presentation thus provides a broader purview than Ezekiel's Temple vision, which grants sole legitimacy to the Zadoqites (48:11). In Ezekiel the Zadoqites are traced to Levi, but only the Zadoqites may approach Yhwh to minister to him (40:46; 43:19–21; 44:15–16). The concern with whether Chronicles supports a pro-Zadoqite monopoly on the postexilic (high) priesthood ironically obscures one of the distinctive features of its presentation. By situating the descendants of Zadoq within a broader genealogical context, the author avoids developing antitheses between priests and Levites, Aaronides and Zadoqites, Eleazarides and Ithamarides. The writer negotiates among established positions and synthesizes disparate traditions. In Chronicles the Aaronides are, broadly speaking, Levites (1 Chr 5:27). To some extent, the Levitical genealogies relativize the distinction between priests and Levites by speaking of Qohathites, Merarites, and Gershonites. Within these large phratries there can be specializations. Some Qohathites are priests (5:27–41), while other Qohathites are singers (6:7–13, 18–23). The Qohathite priests clearly have a privileged position. But the Merarites, Qohathites, and Gershonites who function as singers (6:5–33) can lay claim to the same impeccable roots (6:1–4) as the Qohathite priests (5:27–29). All are Levites, who share a common genealogy. Some biblical and postbiblical authors draw clear contrasts among sacerdotal groups, but in Chronicles they all are ultimately part of the same organization.

VIII. The Levitical Genealogies (6:1–38)

The Gershonites, Qohathites, and Merarites

1 The sons of Levi: Gershon, Qohath, and Merari. 2 These are the names of the
sons of Gershon: Libni and Shimei. 3 The sons of Qohath: Amram, Izhar, Ḥebron,
and Uzziel. 4 The sons of Merari: Maḥli and Mushi. These are the families of the
Levites according to their ancestors: 5 belonging to Gershon—Libni his son, Jaḥath his son, Zimmah his son, 6 Joaḥ his son, Iddo his son, Zeraḥ his son, Jeatherai his son; 7 the descendants of Qohath—Amminadab his son, Qoraḥ his son,
Assir, 8 Elqanah, and Abiasaph his sons, Assir his son, 9 Taḥath his son, Uriel his
son, Uzziah his son, Shaul his son, 10 Elqanah his son, Amasai his son, Maḥath his
son, 11 Elqanah his son, Zuphai his son, Naḥath his son, 12 Eliab his son, Jeroḥam
his son, Elqanah his son, Samuel his son; 13 the sons of Samuel: Joel the firstborn
and Abijah the second; 14 the descendants of Merari—Maḥli, Libni his son,
Shimei his son, Uzzah his son, 15 Shimea his son, Ḥaggiah his son, Asaiah his son.

David's Commission for Choral Music

16 It was these whom David appointed to be in charge of song at the House of
Yhwh when the Ark came to rest. 17 They were serving before the Tabernacle of
the Tent of Meeting with song until Solomon built the Temple of Yhwh in Jerusalem and they stood according to their prescription with respect to their service.

The Qohathite, Gershonite, and Merarite Singers

18 These were the ones who stood, along with their sons: from the descendants
of Qohath—Heman the singer, son of Joel, son of Samuel, 19 son of Elqanah, son
of Jeroḥam, son of Eliel, son of Toaḥ, 20 son of Zuph, son of Elqanah, son of Maḥath, son of Amasai, 21 son of Elqanah, son of Joel, son of Azariah, son of Zepha-

niah, [22]son of Taḥath, son of Assir, son of Abiasaph, son of Qoraḥ, [23]son of Izhar, son of Qohath, son of Levi, son of Israel; [24]his kinsman Asaph—the one stationed at his right—Asaph the son of Berechiah, son of Shimea, [25]son of Michael, son of Maaseiah, son of Malchijah, [26]son of Ethni, son of Zeraḥ, son of Adaiah, [27]son of Ethan, son of Zimmah, son of Shimei, [28]son of Jaḥath, son of Shimei, son of Gershon, son of Levi; [29]the descendants of Merari—their kinsmen on the left—Ethan son of Qishi, son of Abdi, son of Malluch, [30]son of Ḥashabiah, son of Amaziah, son of Ḥilqiah, [31]son of Amzi, son of Bani, son of Shemer, [32]son of Maḥli, son of Mushi, son of Merari, son of Levi. [33]And their kinsmen according to their ancestral houses—the Levites, they were assigned to all the service of the Tabernacle of the House of God.

The Aaronide Priests

[34]As for Aaron and his sons, they were sacrificing upon the altar of burnt offering and upon the incense altar for every work of the Holy of Holies to atone for Israel according to all that Moses the servant of God had commanded. [35]These are the descendants of Aaron: Eleazar his son, Phineḥas his son, Abishua his son, [36]Buqqi his son, Uzzi his son, Zeraḥiah his son, [37]Meraioth his son, Amariah his son, Aḥiṭub his son, [38]Zadoq his son, Aḥimaaz his son.

TEXTUAL NOTES

6:1–38. In many English trans., these verses appear as 6:16–53.

6:1. "Gershon." Reading after LXX *(Gedsōn)* and Syr., which consistently manifest *gršwn* for this son of Levi (Gen 46:11; Exod 6:16; Num 3:17). MT has anomalous "Gershom" throughout this ch. (6:1, 2, 5, 28, 47, 56). In earlier tradition (Exod 2:22; 18:3; Judg 18:30) and elsewhere in Chronicles (1 Chr 23:15, 16; 26:24; cf. Ezra 8:2), Gershom is a son of Moses. Conversely, the name Gershon identifies a son of Levi (1 Chr 5:27; 23:6). The gentilic "Gershonite(s)" appears in 1 Chr 23:7; 26:21; 29:8; 2 Chr 29:12. In Canaanite PNs, the terminations *-m* and *-n* sometimes interchange (Layton 1990b: 181). Since the name Gershom *ben* Levi only appears in 1 Chr 6 and the form is textually disputed, one may be dealing simply with a problem in MT textual transmission that has been leveled through one particular section of the text.

6:4. "these are the families" *(w'lh mšpḥwt)*. So MT. LXX^{AB} *kai hautai hai patriai*. Cf. LXX^{L} *kai hautai hai syngeneiai*, "and these are the kin."

"according to their ancestors" *(l'bwtyhm)*. So MT. LXX *kata patrias autōn*.

6:6. "Joaḥ." Thus MT. LXX "Joab."

"Jeatherai" *(y'try)* is a *hapax legomenon*. LXX *Iethrei*. Cf. v. 26 "Ethni" *('etnî*; LXX^{AB} *Athanei)*.

6:7. "Amminadab" *('ammînādāb)*. So MT and LXX^{B} *(lectio difficilior)*. LXX^{AN} *Issaar* reflects *yiṣhār* of v. 23, while LXX^{L} combines the two readings, prefacing *Is(s)aar huios autou*. LXX^{L} reads *huiou Aminadab huiou Issaar* in vv. 22–23.

"Amminadab his son." So MT and LXX. Rudolph (1955: 54) deletes "his son," thus making both Amminadab and Qoraḥ sons of Qohath (cf. v. 23). Möhlenbrink (1934: 201) thinks that Amminadab was added to substitute for Amram. The lineages of Gershon and Merari pass through their firstborn sons, and it might be expected that the same would hold true for Qohath. Osborne (1979: 272) argues that Amminadab was added to connect David to the tribe of Levi (Exod 6; Ruth 4:18–22).

6:7–8. "Qoraḥ his son, Assir, Elqanah, and Abiasaph his sons, and Assir his son" *(qrḥ bnw ʾsyr ʾlqnh wʾbyʾsp bnyw ʾsyr bnw)*. MT reads "Qoraḥ his son, Assir his son, Elqanah his son, and Ebiasaph his son, and Assir his son" *(qrḥ bnw ʾsyr bnw ʾlqnh bnw wʾbysp bnw wʾsyr bnw)*. The presence of *wāw* before both Abiasaph and Assir is surprising. According to Exod 6:24, Assir, Elqanah, and Abiasaph were the sons of Qoraḥ. Similarly, 1 Chr 6:22 has "son of Assir, son of Abiasaph [MT Ebiasaph], son of Qoraḥ." LXX^{B} reads *Haresei huios autou Elkana kai Abiathar huios autou*, "Assir his son, Elqanah and Abiathar his son." This evidence raises the distinct possibility that the tradition underlying MT (and partially LXX) has been made to conform to the "PN^{1} his son, PN^{2} his son" pattern of surrounding verses. As Curtis and Madsen (1910: 132) observe, the lemma בניו (before אסיר) was misread as בנו ו.

6:8. "Abiasaph." So some Heb. MSS *(ʾăbîʾāsāp)* and LXX^{A} *(Abiasaph*; cf. LXX^{N} *Abisaph)*. On MT's "Ebiasaph" *(ʾebyāsāp*; cf. SP Exod 6:24 *ʾbysp)*, see the 4th TEXTUAL NOTE to 26:1.

6:10. "Elqanah his son, Amasai his son, Aḥimoth his son." MT is corrupt: "the sons of Elqanah: Amasai and Aḥimoth." The reconstruction is partially based on LXX^{L} *Amassai* (y *Amasi*; bb′ *Amasa*) *huios autou Amiōth huios autou*. Cf. vv. 20–21.

"Maḥath." A reconstruction based on v. 20. MT and LXX$^{Aa?N}$ "Aḥimoth" *(ʾḥymwt)*. LXX^{B} and c_2 *Aleimōth* (cf. 1 Chr 6:45: MT *ʿalemet*; LXX^{L} *Alamōth*). Some favor reconstructing *ʾaḥîw maḥat*. A more likely possibility is metathesis *(*mḥt > ḥmt)* followed by the addition of prothetic *ʾālep (ʾḥmt)*. The name Aḥimoth, "my (divine) kinsman is Mot," is a *hapax legomenon*.

6:11. "his son." So Kethib, LXX*, Tg.; cf. Qere *bĕnê*. MT adds "Elqanah" (by dittography). I read with LXX and Syr. *(lectio brevior)*.

"Zuphai." So LXX^{B} *Souphei* (= *ṣûphai*). MT *ṣôphai*; LXX^{A} *Souphi* (= Ṣuphi). Syr. has Zuph in accordance with Qere v. 20 and MT 1 Sam 1:1 (cf. 1 Sam 9:5). Zuph and Zuphai are variants of the same name.

"Naḥath." So MT, LXX^{L} dp *(Naath)*, and Arm. LXX$^{Aa?BN}$ *Kainath*. The parallel in v. 19 has *tôaḥ*. Some read *tōḥû* with MT 1 Sam 1:1, but the variants there (LXX^{B} *Thoke*; LXX^{L} *Thōe*) point toward *tôaḥ*.

"his son." Syr. adds a few words.

6:12. "Eliab" *(ʾĕlîʾāb)*. V. 19 *ʾĕlîʾēl*; MT 1 Sam 1:1 *ʾĕlîhûʾ*.

"Jeroḥam" *(yrḥm)*. So also v. 19. LXX^{B} *Idaer*; LXX^{Amin} *Ieroboam*. The lemma of LXX^{L} *Ieremaēl*; y *Ieremeēl* replicates 1 Sam 1:1 (LXX *Ieremeēl*; MT *yrḥmʾl*). The variants *yrḥm* and *yrḥmʾl* represent shorter and longer forms of the same name.

"Samuel his son." Reading *Samouēl huios autou* with LXX^{L}. MT and LXX^{AB} are lacking. The restoration is based on five considerations: the testimony of

LXX^L, the pattern of v. 13 ("the sons of Samuel"), the content of vv. 18–19 ("Joel son of Samuel, son of Elqanah"), the testimony of 1 Sam 1:1, 20, and the probability of haplography *(homoioteleuton)* from בנו to בנו.

6:13. "Joel." So LXX^L, Syr., and Arab. See also 1 Sam 8:2. The name *yôʾēl* was lost by haplography *(homoioteleuton)* after *šĕmûʾēl*.

"Abijah the second [*haššēnî*]." Thus LXX^L *(ho deuteros)*, Syr., and Arab., and LXX 1 Sam 8:2. MT 1 Chr 6:13 *vašnî*; MT 1 Sam 8:2 *mišnēhû*.

6:14. "the descendants of Merari." Thus MT. Lost in LXX*.

"Maḥli." So MT. Lacking in LXX*. Syr. "his son Maḥli."

"Libni his son." LXX* "the sons of Libni his son."

6:15. "Ḥaggiah." So MT. LXX^B and c_2 *Hama*; LXX^L *Hanaia*; y *Hanani*; Syr.^{A} *ḥnyʾ*.

6:16. "in charge of song" *(ʿl-ydy-šyr)*. So MT and LXX^{AB} *(epi cheiras adontōn)*; cf. LXX^L *echomena hōdēs*.

6:17. "with song" *(baššîr)*. Thus MT and LXX^L. LXX^{AB} *en organois*, "with instruments."

"Tabernacle of the Tent of Meeting" *(miškan ʾōhel-môʿēd)*. LXX^{AB} *skēnēs oikou martyriou* ("Tent of the House of Testimony") may combine elements of two readings: *miškan bêt ʾĕlōhîm* (1 Chr 6:33) and *miškan hāʿēdût* (Num 1:50, 53; 10:11).

6:18. "from the descendants of Qohath." So LXX* and Tg. *(lectio brevior)*. MT "from the descendants of the Qohathites."

6:19. "Jeroḥam." Thus MT. LXX^B *Eaal*; LXX^L *Ieremaēl*. See the 2nd TEXTUAL NOTE to v. 12.

"Toaḥ" *(tôaḥ)*. LXX^B and c_2 *Theie*; LXX^L *Naath*. LXX^{AN} *Thoou(e)*, Vg. *Thou*, and Syr. may reflect *tōḥû* of MT 1 Sam 1:1. See also the 3rd TEXTUAL NOTE to v. 11.

6:20. "Zuph." So Qere, many Heb. MSS, and most of the versions. Cf. Kethib "Ziph" and the 2nd TEXTUAL NOTE to v. 11.

"Amasai" *(ʿmśy)*. So MT. LXX^B *Amatheiou*; Syr.^{A} *mʿšy*; Syr.^{W} *mwšy*.

6:22. "Abiasaph." So LXX^{ALN} *Abiasaph* (cf. g *Abēasaph*). On MT's "Ebiasaph," see the 4th TEXTUAL NOTE to 26:1.

6:25. "Maaseiah." So a few Heb. MSS, LXX^B *(Maasai*; cf. y *Masēl)*, and Syr. MT "Baaseiah" reflects a *bêt/mêm* confusion.

6:28. "son of Jaḥath, son of Shimei" On the basis of v. 2, one can posit a haplography *(homoioarkton)* and add "son of Shimei" to MT "son of Jaḥath" (Rudolph 1955: 56). See also 1 Chr 23:10 (Jaḥath *ben* Shimei).

6:29. "the descendants *(wbny)* of Merari." Arnold Ehrlich (1914) emends to *wmbny* (cf. v. 18 *mbny hqhty*).

"their kinsmen." So MT and LXX^L (maximum variation). LXX^{AB}, Syr., and Arab. have the sg., "their kinsman."

"Qishi." Thus MT and LXX^B, c_2 *(Keisai)*. Many Heb. MSS, LXX^L *Kousei* (cf. ye_2 *Chous(e)i*), and Vg. "Qushi." See also the TEXTUAL NOTE to 15:17 and the 3rd NOTE to v. 29.

"Abdi." So MT and LXX*. Syr.^{A} *ʿmry*; Syr.^{W} *ʿmrw*.

6:32. "son of Maḥli, son of Mushi." Thus MT, LXX^{AN}, and $bgnyc_2e_2$ *(lectio dif-*

ficilior). The formulation of Maḥli as Mushi's offspring is most unusual (cf. v. 4). LXX[B] "son of Maḥli, Mushi." Syr. "sons of Maḥli, Mushi."

"son of Mushi, son of Merari." Thus MT and LXX[ABN]; cf. c_2 "sons of Merari."

6:33. "And their kinsmen *(w'ḥyhm)* according to their ancestral houses" *(l'bwtyhm).* Thus LXX[B]. MT has the *lectio brevior,* but it is likely that the lemma found in LXX[B] (cf. v. 4) was lost to MT by haplography *(homoioteleuton).* The alternative, that LXX[B] was somehow influenced by Num 3:20, *lbyt 'bwtm,* seems unlikely (*pace* Allen 1974a: 187).

6:34. "to atone" *(ûlĕkappēr).* The inf. with *l-* preceded by *w-* continues the preceding verb, *maqṭîrîm* (Joüon, §124q).

6:37. "Meraioth." So MT and LXX[L] *(Mariōth).* LXX[B] c_2 *Mareiēl;* Syr. *mrw,* but see 1 Chr 5:32.

Notes

6:1 "sons of Levi." This verse repeats material from 1 Chr 5:27–28. There the introduction to Levi's offspring led to a genealogy of the Qohathites extending to the time of the Babylonian exile (5:41). In 6:1–38 the focus is not so narrow. After providing the introduction to Levi's offspring (v. 1), the writer traces one generation of male offspring for each of Levi's three sons: Gershon (vv. 2, 4b–6), Qohath (vv. 3, 7–13), and Merari (vv. 4a, 14–15). Further lineages of Qohath (vv. 18–23), Gershon (vv. 24–28), and Merari (vv. 29–32) follow with a view to the participation of their offspring as singers in national worship.

"Gershon." This son of Levi (Gen 46:11; 1 Chr 5:27; 6:1, 5, 28, 47, 56; 15:7) is to be distinguished from Gershom the son of Moses (Exod 2:22; 1 Chr 26:24; cf. Judg 18:30; TEXTUAL NOTE to v. 1). The Gershonites figure prominently in P and Priestly-style texts (Gen 46:11; Exod 6:16–17; Num 3:17–25; 4:22, 24, 27, 38, 41; 10:17; 26:57; Josh 21:6, 27, 33), where their duties are to transport the furnishings of the Tabernacle (Num 4:24–28), but they are the least mentioned of Levi's three sons in Chronicles (1 Chr 5:27; 15:7; 23:6, 7; 26:21; 29:8; 2 Chr 29:12). Like the Qohathites, the Gershonites go unmentioned in Ezra and Nehemiah.

"Merari." This son of Levi (Gen 46:11; Exod 6:16, 19; Num 3:17, 20; 4:29; 7:8; 10:17; 26:57) represents the third branch of the Levites. The duties of the Merarites in transporting Tabernacle furnishings are outlined in Num 4:29–33 (Milgrom 1970: 8–12). Attention is sometimes drawn to the size and prominence of the Qohathite branch of the Levites, as opposed to the Merarites, in the Second Commonwealth. There is certainly merit to this observation (e.g., 5:27–41). But the Merarites, in spite of the incomplete and discordant genealogies of 6:14–15 and 6:29–32, consistently receive coverage during the monarchy (1 Chr 15:6, 17; 23:6, 21; 24:26–30; 26:10, 19; 2 Chr 29:12; 34:12) and the return (1 Chr 9:14). Unlike the Qohathites and the Gershonites, the Merarites are mentioned in Ezra (8:19). Either the Merarites were a more significant force in Yehud than scholars have imagined, or the writer wished to draw attention to their cause.

6:3. "Amram, Izhar, Ḥebron, and Uzziel." These four are consistently listed as sons of Qohath (Exod 6:18; Num 3:19, 27), but see NOTE to v. 7.

"Ḥebron." Perhaps originally a place-name (cf. 1 Chr 2:42; 1 Macc 5:65) or the name of a prominent family. As a son of Qohath, see Exod 6:18; Num 3:19; 1 Chr 5:28; 6:3; 23:12. The gentilic occurs in Num 3:27; 26:58; 1 Chr 26:23, 30–31. In the Levitical town list, Qohathites inhabit Ḥebron (Josh 21:11–13// 1 Chr 6:40–41). A link between the Aaronides and Ḥebron is suggested by Josh 21:10(//1 Chr 6:42).

"Uzziel." Like Ḥebron, Uzziel appears as a son of Qohath in Exod 6:18; Num 3:19; 1 Chr 5:28; 6:3; 23:12.

6:4. "Maḥli and Mushi." In standard genealogies, they appear as sons of Merari (Exod 6:19; Num 3:20; Ezra 8:18–19; 1 Chr 6:4; 23:21; 24:26). Similarly, in Num 3:20, 33, the Maḥlites and Mushites are listed as clans of Merari. Not a few scholars (e.g., Wellhausen 1885: 126–61; Cross 1973: 196–98) connect Mushi *(mûšî)* to Moses *(mōšeh)*, assuming that the Mushites derived their name from Israel's lawgiver (Exod 17:2–7; 33:7–11; Num 11:16–30; 14:13; Deut 31:1, 14; Judg 18:30 [LXX]). According to Wellhausen (1885: 126), the priesthoods at both Shiloh and Dan are associated with the ancient Mushite house. In the view of Cross (1973: 208), David's unusual choice of both Abiathar and Zadoq to be his priests reflects a strategic compromise between the two rival priestly houses of his time: Abiathar, scion of the Mushite Elide house of Shiloh and Zadoq, scion of the Aaronide house of Ḥebron.

"according to their ancestors" *(la'ăbôtêhem)*. See also v. 33. The principle of lineage is used to organize the major sections of Israel's cultic officiants (3rd NOTE to 5:7).

"by their service." On Levitical service *('ăbōdâ)* in Chronicles, see the 3rd NOTE to v. 33.

6:5–6. "belonging to Gershon." The names in these verses reappear, allowing for the vagaries of textual transmission and other factors, as part of an ascending genealogy in vv. 24–28.

6:5. "Libni." Tracing Gershon's lineage through Libni rather than through Shimei (vv. 2, 28 [TEXTUAL NOTE]). Jaḥath's lineage is also traced through Shimei in 1 Chr 23:10.

6:7–13. "descendants of Qohath." This material is paralleled to a large extent in the ascending genealogy of vv. 18–23. A similar alternation between descending and ascending genealogies obtains for the Gershonites (vv. 5–6, 24–28) and the Merarites (vv. 14, 29–32).

6:7–8. "Qoraḥ . . . Assir his son." Drawn from Exod 6:24.

6:7. "Amminadab." This is the only case in which Amminadab ("my [divine] kinsman is generous") appears as a son of Qohath. Normally, Amram, Izhar, Ḥebron, and Uzziel appear as Qothath's offspring (as in v. 3). In the later lineage (vv. 18–23), which corresponds to the lineage of vv. 7–13, Izhar appears. A Levite named Amminadab serves David (1 Chr 15:10–11), but he is a son of Uzziel (cf. v. 3). The reason for the discrepancy is unclear. See the TEXTUAL NOTES to v. 7.

6:8. "Elqanah." Otherwise unattested: The name reappears in other Levitical contexts (1 Chr 6:11[!]; 9:16; 15:23).

6:9. "Uriel." Another Uriel appears as the "leader" *(śr)* of the Qohathite Levites during the reign of David (1 Chr 15:5).

6:10. "Elqanah." In v. 21 Elqanah, the father of Amasai (vv. 10, 20–21), is the son of Joel.

"Maḥath." A Maḥath son of Amasai (so also v. 20) is attested in the reign of Ḥezeqiah (2 Chr 29:12). In both cases, Maḥath is a Qohathite.

6:12–13. "Samuel." This lineage is drawn from 1 Sam 8:1–2 (TEXTUAL NOTES to vv. 12–13).

6:12. "Eliab." Another name that reappears elsewhere in Levitical contexts, specifically among the Levitical appointments in David's reign (1 Chr 15:18, 20; 16:5).

"Samuel his son." Samuel and his father are both integrated into a Qohathite genealogy. No such correlation is made in Samuel. In fact, the evidence indicates that Samuel's father, Elqanah, belonged to the tribe of Ephraim (1 Sam 1:1).

6:13. "Joel the firstborn and Abijah the second." Taken from 1 Sam 8:2.

6:14–15. "descendants of Merari." The text follows Merari's descent through his son Maḥli (vv. 1, 4a). The ascending Merarite lineage of vv. 29–32 bears hardly any resemblance, apart from a few common names (Merari, Maḥli, Mushi), to this descending genealogy. Both genealogies in their present form seem to be defective, characterized by confusion and various kinds of textual corruption (TEXTUAL NOTES). To be sure, the two Merarite genealogies need not be strictly parallel, because the first genealogy is a general Merarite genealogy while the latter is a genealogy of Merarite singers. But there are detailed correspondences between the two sets of Qohathite and Gershonite genealogies and some of the sequences supplied in the Merarite genealogies are suspect when compared to those found in other biblical writings.

6:14. "Libni . . . Shimei." Shimei is usually paired with Libni (Exod 6:17; Num 3:18; 1 Chr 6:2; cf. 6:5, 14; 23:7; 26:21) as Gershon's progeny. Here, Libni and Shimei appear anomalously as the son and grandson, respectively, of Maḥli.

6:15. "Asaiah." Possibly this is the same figure who appears as the leader of the Merarites in the time of David (15:6, 11).

6:16. "these." It is quite common in Chronicles for the authors to interrupt or conclude lists and genealogies with anecdotes and explanations ("Excursus: The Genealogies"). In this case (vv. 16–17), the writer alludes to the duties of the Gershonites, Qohathites, and Merarites during the United Monarchy, the time in which the Temple was built. Three specific descendants from the three Levitical phratries outlined in vv. 1–15—Asaph from Gershon (vv. 24–28), Heman from Qohath (vv. 18–23), and Ethan from Merari (vv. 29–32)—took on official roles in the national cultus. From the perspective of the writer living during the Persian period, it is more important to establish a continuity from the Ancestral age (Levi) to the classical age (David and Solomon) than it is to trace these lineages to his own time. In the ancient Mediterranean world, it was common for genealogists to ignore or skip over the intermediate past, in distinction from the recent past and the distant past. What is unusual in this context is that no attention is paid directly to the recent past at all. But see also the 1st NOTE to v. 18.

"song." Levitical choirs are an intrinsic component of the Chronicler's worship, appearing some thirty times in his work (e.g., 1 Chr 13:8; 15:19–21; 16:4–42; 25:7; 2 Chr 5:11–13; 7:6; 23:13, 18; 29:28). Some scholars have suggested that in presenting singers as full Levites, Chronicles represents a different (and later) perspective from that of Ezra (2:41, 65) and Nehemiah (7:44; 12:46–47; cf. 12:27–30; Gese 1974: 147–58; Blenkinsopp 1988: 89). There the singers (and musicians) are said to be in a category apart from the Levites. For a different view, see Torrey (1896: 22) and Laato (1994a). In highlighting singing, the text may be compared with sentiments expressed in the Psalms (e.g., 28:7; 69:31 [ET 69:30]; 137:4).

"House of Yhwh." Either the tent shrine David established for the Ark in Jerusalem (1 Chr 15:1–16:1; cf. 2 Sam 6:1–17) or the Tabernacle (1 Chr 6:17).

"when the Ark came to rest" *(mimmĕnôaḥ hāʾārôn)*. Alluding to the ascent of the ancient palladium into the City of David from the house of Obed-edom (2 Sam 6:1–17; 1 Chr 13:13–14; 15:1–16:1). The formulation is indebted to the "rest" theology of the Deuteronomist (Knoppers 1995c). By (re-)presenting the roving Ark as needing a fixed home, the Deuteronomist implies that this sacred artifact served only a penultimate role until a "place" *(māqôm)* for it could be built (1 Kgs 8:21). The Ark is thus suitably honored and preserved for posterity, but it plays no continuing role except as part of a larger permanent structure. Conversely, by presenting the Temple as enduring, the Deuteronomist and the Chronicler portray its cultus as definitive for succeeding generations. When the Ark journeys to Jerusalem in the time of David (1 Chr 13:1–14; 15:1–16:1) and is subsequently placed in the Temple during Solomon's reign (2 Chr 5:1–14), it has fulfilled its purpose.

6:17. "Tabernacle." In Chronicles, the arrival of the Ark in Jerusalem leads to a temporary bifurcation in national worship. While certain Levites tend to the ancient palladium in Jerusalem (16:1–6, 36–37), others tend to the Tent of Meeting in Gibeon (16:39–42). Although both arrangements are legitimate, they are only temporary. With Solomon's construction of the Temple, both the Ark and the Tent find their way into Israel's permanent national shrine (2 Chr 5:1–14).

"according to their prescription" (כמשפטם). Referring to a prevailing or traditional custom among the Levitical singers (cf. 1 Kgs 18:28; 2 Kgs 11:14). The author does not directly state that the Levitical singers stood according to a prescription(s) of Yhwh (משפט יהוה; Exod 21:1; Lev 18:4; Ps 19:10 [ET 19:9]). Rather, he claims that the Levitical singers took their positions in accordance with their own regulations or customs.

6:18–23. "descendants of Qohath." In this ascending genealogy, Heman's ancestry is traced along the lines of the genealogies found in vv. 1, 3, 7–13, except that the genealogy of vv. 18–23 extends the Qohathite lineage one generation at the beginning to Israel (v. 23) and one generation at the end to Heman (v. 18).

6:18. "stood, along with their sons." Heman, Asaph (v. 24), and Ethan (v. 29) represent three classes or guilds of singers who receive new appointments during the time of David, the definitive age for the Levitical singers. Hence, the patronyms Asaph, Heman, and Ethan serve as organizing principles for the Levitical singers (2 Chr 5:12; 29:14; 35:15). Whether presented in descending or ascending style, the genealogies of 6:1–33 highlight two different epochs in Israelite history: the time of origins (the eponymous ancestors Levi, Gershon, Qohath, and

Merari) and the time of the United Monarchy. But the genealogies also point forward to the work of future generations of singers. The text speaks, after all, not only of the singers being stationed but also of "their sons." In this respect, the lineages point toward the author's own time in which the singers had become a constituent feature of Temple worship.

"Heman the singer" plays a prominent role in David's reign, being one of the singers whom David appoints to accompany the Tabernacle at Gibeon (15:17, 19; 16:41–42). In 1 Chr 25:1–6, the singing of Heman, Asaph, and Jeduthun is described as a kind of prophecy.

6:19. "Eliel." The name is common in Levitical settings (1 Chr 15:9, 11; 2 Chr 31:13), but it also appears in a variety of non-Levitical contexts (1 Chr 5:24; 8:20, 22; 11:46; 12:12). Within the HB, the name is only found in Chronicles.

6:20. "Maḥath." The name (cf. Arab. *maḥt*; Noth 1928: 225) appears elsewhere in Chronicles (2 Chr 29:12; 31:13) and in Eg. Aram. (AP 22.82).

6:21. "Joel, son of Azariah." Another Joel *ben* Azariah appears in the reign of Ḥezeqiah, helping to sanctify the Temple (2 Chr 29:12). Both are Qohathites.

6:24–28. "Asaph." In this ascending genealogy, Asaph's pedigree is traced back to Gershon. The lineage bears similarities, as well as some differences, to the descending genealogy of vv. 5–6. One of the biggest differences is that this genealogy is six generations longer (Asaph through Malchijah) than the earlier linear genealogy. Consistent with the pattern of the earlier Qohathite genealogy (vv. 18–23) and the later Merarite genealogy (vv. 29–32), this Gershonite genealogy takes the reign of David as its starting point.

6:24. "his kinsman Asaph." That is, kinsman to Heman, introduced in v. 18.

"stationed at his right." The three phratries are each assigned a position in the cult. The guild of Heman occupies a central position (vv. 18–23), the guild of Asaph stands to the right of Heman, and Ethan to the left (v. 29). Much fuller consideration is given to the singers—their selection and courses—in 1 Chr 25. In Chronicles the positions taken by the three groups, much like their ministry of song, predate the Temple.

6:27–28. "Shimei son of Jaḥath." As opposed to the sequence depicted in the earlier Gershonite genealogy (Jaḥath *ben* Libni *ben* Gershon; v. 5), Shimei appears as the son of Jaḥath and the grandson of Gershon. On the sons of Shimei, see the NOTES to 23:10.

6:29–32. "the descendants of Merari." In contrast with the seven-generation lineage of vv. 14–15, this ascending lineage extends to thirteen generations. See further the NOTE to vv. 14–15.

6:29. "their kinsmen." That is, to the Qohathites (vv. 18–23) and the Gershonites (vv. 24–28).

"Ethan." If Asaph and Heman represent the Gershonites and Qohathites respectively, Ethan represents the Merarites (6:18, 29; 15:17). In a number of other instances, Jeduthun serves in this role (1 Chr 16:41; 25:1, 3, 6; 2 Chr 5:12; 29:14; 35:15). Hence, Chronicles does not speak with one voice on this issue (NOTE to 15:17).

"Qishi." The information concerning Maḥli's offspring is unique to Chronicles. Qishi is a hypocoristicon of a longer PN, probably *qyšyhw* (TEXTUAL NOTE to 15:17). A Qish appears in 1 Chr 23:21–22 and 24:29 (as the son of Maḥli). A Merarite named Qish, also the son of Abdi, is mentioned in the reforms of Ḥezeqiah (2 Chr 29:12). See also the TEXTUAL NOTE to 15:17.

6:32. "Maḥli son of Mushi." This formulation is unique. The closest parallel (if the problem has not been caused by textual corruption [TEXTUAL NOTES to v. 32] is Num 26:58. There the clans of the Levites are the Libnites, the Ḥebronites, the Mushites, the Maḥlites, and the Qoraḥlites. In this text, the antiquity of which is maintained by Möhlenbrink (1934: 191–97), names appear in parallel that normally appear as the second (Libni, Ḥebron, Maḥli, Mushi) and third (Qoraḥ) generation after Levi. Maḥli is, however, absent from LXX Num 26:58. See further the 1st NOTE to v. 4.

6:33. "their kinsmen according to their ancestral houses—the Levites." The author construes the Levites as a broad category, encompassing more than simply singers. Other Levites, also drawn from the Gershonites, Qohathites, and Merarites (vv. 1–15), have other roles to play on behalf of the Israelite tribes. Whether derived from Gershon, Qohath, or Merari, the Levites are all "kinsmen," sharing a common ancestry.

"they were assigned" *(nĕtûnîm)*. The use of the passive ptc. of *ntn* with this meaning (Phoen. *ytn*, "dedicate;" Knoppers 1992a: 106; cf. Akk. *širku*, "devoted, presented, devotee"; Speiser 1963) is reminiscent of P (Num 3:9; 8:15–16; 18:6; Milgrom 1990: 17). There the Levites are dedicated *(ntn)* to Yhwh (Num 8:5–22), whereas the priests are sanctified *(qdš)* to Yhwh. In some late texts (e.g., Ezra 2:43, 58, 70; 7:7; 8:17, 20; Neh 3:26, 31; 7:46, 60, 72 [ET 7:73]; 10:29 [ET 10:28]; 11:3, 21), a special class of Temple servants is referred to as *nĕtînîm*, but this term is only used once in Chronicles in an undisputed context (1 Chr 9:2//Neh 11:3). In this case, the Levites have a formal assignment *(nĕtûnîm)* in connection with the Tabernacle, but no rigid Priestly demarcation between priests and Levites is observed (see the following NOTES).

"service of the Tabernacle of the House of God" *(ʿăbōdat miškan bêt hāʾĕlōhîm)*. The term *ʿăbōdâ* in P usually designates "work" (e.g., Num 3:7, 8; 8:15; 16:9), the physical labor associated with assembling, maintaining, guarding, dismantling, and moving the Tent of Meeting (Milgrom 1970: 60–82). In P (Num 3:5–10; 18:1–7) and Ezekiel (44), such a work profile is part of a larger arrangement in which the Levites function as assistants to the priests. There is some demarcation of duties in Chronicles as well, but complementarity, not hierarchy, is stressed (Knoppers 1999a). The Levitical *ʿăbōdâ* in Chronicles bears broader connotations and is best translated as (cultic) service (1 Chr 9:19, 28; 23:24, 26, 28, 32; 25:1, 6; 26:8; 28:14, 21; 29:7; 2 Chr 29:35; 31:21; 34:13; 35:10). Indeed, the principle of coordination extends not only to the relationship between priests and Levites but also to the relationships among the various Levitical branches (2 Chr 5:11–14; 29:3–18; 30:13–21; 35:10–19). It should also be pointed out that in contradistinction to the custom of P, Chronicles does not use this expression with exclusive reference to the Levites. In 1 Chr 9:13 the priests are numbered for "the work of the service of the House of God." One of Josiah's reforms is to reappoint the priests to their offices and to encourage them in the "service of the House of Yhwh" (2 Chr 35:2). In 1 Chr 28:13 both the priests and the Levites are mentioned in reference to "every work of the service of the House of Yhwh."

6:34. "sacrificing upon the altar of burnt offering." The Aaronic priests officiate within the sanctuary and make offerings (1 Chr 23:13, 30–32). Outside of Chronicles, this mandate to the Aaronides is detailed in a number of Priestly contexts (e.g., Exod 29:38–42; 30:1–10; Lev 8:1–9:24; Ezek 44:15). For the Tabernacle altar itself, see Exod 27:1–8.

"incense altar" *(mizbaḥ haqqĕṭōret)*. According to Exod 30:1–8 (P), Aaron was to burn aromatic incense every morning and every evening at dusk. The incense altar, overlaid with gold, belonged to the category of "most holy things." As such, it could only be directly handled by Aaron and his descendants.

"Holy of Holies" *(qōdeš haqqŏdāšîm)*. In P and Ezekiel, the most holy place is the exclusive domain of the priests (Exod 26:33–34; Num 18:1–5; Ezek 44:15–16; 2 Chr 5:11; 29:7). Other members of the Levite tribe may serve as Temple staff, but the priests alone may officiate at the inner sanctuary. Tabernacle oversight is also an obligation of the priests (Num 4:16; 18:1–2).

"to atone (*lĕkappēr*) for Israel." The formulation is directly indebted to the Priestly work in which the Aaronic priests are singled out to effect atonement in divine-human relations (Lev 4:20, 31; 8:34; 10:17; 16:34). Of the fifty-three instances of the verb *kpr* in the *piʿel* in P, the subject is most often the priest (Maass 1997: 626). Hence, in Lev 16:32–34 the priest, appointed to succeed his father, makes expiation both for the priests and for the entire congregation. This is "an everlasting law: to atone *(lĕkappēr)* for the Israelites and their sins once a year" (Lev 16:34). Similarly, in the covenant of Phineḥas (Num 25:11–13), Yhwh charges Phineḥas and his seed "to atone *(lĕkappēr)* for the children of Israel" (Num 25:13). In Chronicles the beneficiary of priestly atonement is also Israel. One of Ḥezeqiah's reforms, following the major decline ushered in by Aḥaz, involves purification of the Temple and a sacrifice of atonement led by the priests (2 Chr 29:20–24). But such atonement does not operate mechanically. In the ensuing celebration of Passover, the failure of some of the participants to purify themselves leads Ḥezeqiah to pray on their behalf (2 Chr 30:15–20). In response to Ḥezeqiah's petition, Yhwh grants atonement.

6:35–38. "descendants of Aaron." The lineage is partially parallel to the list of Qohathite priests in 1 Chr 5:27–41 (esp. 5:29–35). The editors have positioned this second priestly lineage, which ends the Levitical genealogies, to complement the position of the first priestly lineage, which introduces the Levitical genealogies. But the introduction of Aaron is a non sequitur given the segmented genealogical introduction of 6:1–4 (see further SOURCES AND COMPOSITION for 5:27–41). Consistent with the stress placed on the United Monarchy in 6:1–38, the list stops with Aḥimaaz the son of Zadoq. The earlier list continues to the Babylonian exile (Jehozadaq; 1 Chr 5:41).

6:38. "Zadoq." By situating the Aaronide genealogy (vv. 35–38) immediately after the list of Aaronide responsibilities at the Tabernacle (v. 34), the author intimates that these Aaronide duties were continued by Zadoq and his descendants during the monarchic period. On the question of Zadoq's pedigree, see the 1st NOTE to 5:34.

SOURCES, COMPOSITION, AND STRUCTURE

Some of the material in this section of the Levitical genealogies is drawn from earlier biblical sources. The borrowing may be summarized as follows:

Chronicles 6	*Source*
1–4	Gen 46:11; Exod 6:16–19; Num 17–20
7–8	Exod 6:24
12	1 Sam 1:1
13	1 Sam 8:2
18	1 Sam 8:2
19–20	1 Sam 1:1

Apart from this modest indebtedness to earlier biblical sources, most of the material in vv. 1–38 is unique to Chronicles. The following observations will concentrate on the Levitical genealogies in 6:1–34. On the composition of 6:35–38, see the section on SOURCES AND COMPOSITION for 5:27–41. In vv. 1–15 the text provides descending lineages for all three of Levi's progeny: Gershon (vv. 5–6), Qohath (vv. 7–13), and Merari (vv. 14–15). The short digression that follows (vv. 16–17) is highly important, as it explains that these phratries were appointed by David and installed by Solomon as managing the ministry of song at the House of Yhwh. Complementing the three sets of descending lineages in vv. 1–15 are three sets of ascending lineages in vv. 18–32: Qohath (vv. 18–23), Gershon (vv. 24–28), and Merari (vv. 29–32). The latter section of vv. 18–32, consistent with the force of the commission of vv. 16–17, takes the reign of David as their starting point. The section ends with another explanation (v. 33).

a Gershonites, Qohathites, and Merarites (vv. 1–15)
b Commission and Installation of Choristers (vv. 16–17)
a′ Gershonite, Qohathite, and Merarite Choristers (vv. 18–32)
b′ Levitical Responsibilities at the Tabernacle (v. 33)

This outline suggests, however, more congruence among the individual subsections than there actually is. To begin with, there are some incongruities between the introductory lineages in vv. 2–4 and those that appear in vv. 5–14. The genealogies of vv. 18–32 vary from and are longer than their counterparts in vv. 1–15, even though each corresponding set of descending and ascending genealogies shares at least a few common names. The ascending Gershonite lineage (vv. 24–28) exhibits both similarities to and differences from the descending lineage (vv. 5–6). The ascending genealogy is also much longer than the earlier linear genealogy. The line of Qohath (vv. 18–23) extends the earlier Qohathite lineage (vv. 7–13) one generation at the beginning to Israel (v. 23) and one generation at the end to Heman (v. 18). There are also discrepancies between some of the individual names (NOTES). In the case of the Merarites (vv. 29–32), there are many more incongruities with the lineage of vv. 14–15 than there are congruities. The ascending genealogy (vv. 29–32) is also significantly longer than the descending genealogy (vv. 14–15). Both the similarities and the differences may be sketched as follows:

Gershonites		
(1 Levi)	Levi	
5 Gershon	Gershon	
Libni	Shimei	
Jaḥath	28 Jaḥath	
	Shimei	
Zimmah	Zimmah	
6 Joaḥ	27 Ethan	
Iddo	Adaiah	
Zeraḥ	Zeraḥ	
Jeatherai	26 Ethni	
	Malchijah	
	Maaseiah	
	25 Michael	
	Shimea	
	Berechiah	
	24 Asaph	
Qohathites		*1 Sam 1:1; 8:2*
	Israel	
(1 Levi)	Levi	
7 Qohath	Qohath	
Amminadab	23 Izhar	
Qoraḥ	Qoraḥ	
Assir, 8 Elqanah, and Abiasaph	Abiasaph	
Assir	Assir	
9 Taḥath	22 Taḥath	
Uriel	Zephaniah	
Uzziah	Azariah	
Shaul	Joel	
10 Elqanah	21 Elqanah	
Amasai	Amasai	
Maḥath	Maḥath	
11 Elqanah	Elqanah	
Zuphai	20 Zuph	Zuph (1:1)
Naḥath	Toaḥ	Toaḥ (1:1)
12 Eliab	Eliel	Elihu (1:1)
Jeroḥam	Jeroḥam	Jeraḥmeel (1:1)
Elqanah	19 Elqanah	Elqanah (1:1)
Samuel	Samuel	Samuel (8:1)
13 Joel and Abijah	Joel	Joel and Abijah (8:1)
	18 Heman	

Merarites	
([1] Levi)	Levi
[14] Merari	Merari
Mushi and Maḥli	[32] Mushi
	Maḥli
Libni	Shemer
Shimei	Bani
Uzzah	[31] Amzi
[15] Shimea	Ḥilqiah
Ḥaggiah	Amaziah
Asaiah	[30] Ḥashabiah
	Malluch
	Abdi
	Qishi
	[29] Ethan

It should be pointed out that there is no necessary reason to believe that the descending lineages should correspond exactly to the ascending lineages. The former are genealogies of the three Levitical phratries, while the latter comprise genealogies of singers drawn from each of these three phratries. Some overlap is to be expected, but not a one-to-one correspondence. Nevertheless, in their present form, the lineages seem to be defective (TEXTUAL NOTES). Various kinds of textual corruption may explain some incongruities. Nevertheless, the descending and ascending genealogies may stem from different hands. Assuming composite authorship, the following COMMENT addresses the entire text.

COMMENT

By repeating the material pertaining to the derivation of the Gershonites, Qohathites, and Merarites from Levi (5:27–28) at the beginning of his genealogies of the Temple singers (6:1), the writers tie the priests and singers together. Both groups ultimately share the same Levitical pedigree. Whether they be priests (5:27–41), Levites and Levitical singers (6:1–32), or those "assigned to all the service of the Tabernacle of the House of God" (v. 33), all descend from one progenitor: Levi. In this manner, a basic kinship is maintained between the Levites who serve as priests and the Levites who serve as singers. But the authors also distinguish between priests and Levites. One of the differences involves status. The sons of Aaron—"officers of the sanctuary and officers of God" (24:5)—officiate at the House of Yhwh. The distinct position of the Qohathite priests within the tribe of Levi is secured by birth and succession (5:27–41). The priests also have a distinct function: to sacrifice "upon the altar of burnt offering and upon the incense altar for every work of the Holy of Holies to atone for Israel" (6:34). The purpose of the singers, by contrast, is to perform "at the House of Yhwh" (6:16). The mandate is more fully detailed later in David's reign: "to stand every morning to give thanks and to praise Yhwh, and likewise in the evening, and whenever burnt offerings are offered to Yhwh for the sabbaths, new moons, and festivals" (23:30–31).

Another difference between the priests and the choristers is history. For the singers, unlike the priests (5:27–41), the United Monarchy is definitive. The genealogists acknowledge that the system of Levitical singers was not a Sinaitic development. In contrast, the authority for the Aaronic appointment lies in "all that Moses the servant of God had commanded" (6:34; Dörrfuß 1994: 126–29). Because the implementation of a system of national sacrifice is associated with the Sinaitic era, the transition to the United Monarchy entails more of a change in venue for the priests than a change in practice. For the singers the United Monarchy is formative because David makes the Levites responsible for the musical liturgy (6:16).

This is clearly a case in which Chronicles goes beyond Deuteronomic and Priestly precedent. Recourse to the model of the author being simply an exegete of older sources will not suffice to explain the portrayal of the Levitical singers. There are stipulations governing priests, prophets, judges, and kings in Deuteronomy (16:18–18:22), but none governing singers and musicians. Singers and musicians, as a class, do not even appear in Deuteronomy. The Priestly code addresses a great variety of issues and covers many topics not found in earlier biblical law, but the roles to be played by cultic singers and musicians are not among them. With some justification Kaufmann (1960: 3–4) refers to the Priestly Tent of Meeting as a sanctuary of silence. Similarly, Knohl (1996: 20) contends that within the priestly realm of the Temple, "there is room neither for petitional prayer nor for hymns of thanksgiving." Levine (1993: 176) observes that the Priestly source hardly ever refers to ritual recitations.

The authors of Chronicles do not directly address the origins, nature, and configuration of the Tabernacle cultus. In this respect, they do not attempt to rewrite the Priestly version of the Sinaitic narrative. They do take advantage of the temporal limitations imposed by the coverage of the Priestly work by positing the transformation of older institutions in the time of the monarchy. Singers and musicians play an integral role in the administration established by David (6:16–17; 16:4, 7–38; 23:5). To this end, the ascending genealogies highlight the role played by Heman (v. 18), Asaph (v. 24), and Ethan (v. 29). For the genealogist, eager to ensconce the singers firmly within Israel's classical heritage, the connection with David is paramount. The dual movement in the descending and ascending lineages converges on David's reign. The Levitical genealogies do not even directly address the post-Davidic and the post-Solomonic eras of Israelite and Judean history. It is enough, for the authors' purposes, to transform the Tabernacle from being a sanctuary of sacrifice and silence to being a sanctuary of sacrifice and song. The occasion for this metamorphosis is the divinely authorized incorporation of the Tabernacle in the Temple. By invoking an ancient precedent antedating the very beginning of Jerusalem Temple worship, the authors simultaneously acknowledge Priestly custom and subvert it by recourse to a divinely blessed monarchical innovation.

But the claims made for the Levitical singers' descent are even stronger than the appeal to Davidic precedent might suggest. The genealogists' link between the three guilds of singers and the Ancestral era are no less striking than the ancestral link established for the Qohathite priests. Living in an age in which one could only serve as a member of the Temple staff with a demonstrable pedigree (Ezra 2:61–63//Neh 7:61–65), the authors postulate such a pedigree for the Levitical singers. Recourse to an archaic era elevates the status of newer institutions. The lineages of the Temple singers include a wide panorama of figures: Amram, Izhar, Ḥebron, Samuel, and Heman for Qohath; Libni, Shimei, and Asaph for Gershon; and Maḥli, Mushi, and Ethan for Merari. Links to known figures buttress the positions of unknown figures. Endurance through the generations suggests divine approval and support. In this respect, the segmented genealogies of vv. 1–4 and the descending genealogies of vv. 5–15 anticipate the ascending genealogies of vv. 18–32. Finally, the text identifies each of the Qohathite, Gershonite, and Merarite classes of Temple singers as Levitic, thereby underscoring a basic kinship between them and the Qohathite priests. I have argued elsewhere that the Chronicler posits a complementary relationship between the priests and the Levites in his narratives about the monarchy (Knoppers 1999a). As the links between the lineages of the priests and the singers demonstrate, this coordination is already anticipated in the genealogical prologue.

IX. The Levitical Settlements (6:39–66)

39 These are their places of residence according to their settlements within their territories.

Aaronide Qohathite Settlements in Judah and Benjamin

Belonging to the descendants of Aaron who were of the family of the Qohathites, for they received the (first) lot:
40 they gave Ḥebron to them in the land of Judah along with its surrounding open lands,
41 but they gave the territory of the town and its villages to Caleb son of Jephunneh.
42 To the descendants of Aaron they gave the [following] towns of refuge: Ḥebron along with its open land, Libnah along with its open land, Jattir along with its open land, Eshtemoa along with its open land,
43 Ḥilen along with its open land, Debir along with its open land,
44 Ashan along with its open land, Juṭṭah along with its open land, and Beth-Shemesh along with its open land;
45 from the tribe of Benjamin: Gibeon along with its open land, Geba along with its open land, Alemeth along with its open land, and Anathoth along with its open land. All of their towns, with their families, were thirteen.

Tallies of Settlements for the Qohathites, Gershonites, and Merarites

46 Belonging to the remaining descendants of Qohath: from the families of the tribe of Ephraim, from the tribe of Dan, and from the half-tribe of Manasseh—ten towns by lot.
47 Belonging to the descendants of Gershon, by their families: from the tribe of Issachar, from the tribe of Asher, from the tribe of Naphtali, and from

the tribe of Manasseh in Bashan—thirteen towns. 48 Belonging to the descendants of Merari, by their families: from the tribe of Reuben, from the tribe of Gad, and from the tribe of Zebulun—twelve towns by lot. 49 And the descendants of Israel assigned to the Levites the towns along with their open lands. 50 They assigned these towns, which they designated by name, by lot from the tribe of the descendants of Judah, from the tribe of the descendants of Simeon, and from the tribe of the descendants of Benjamin.

Qohathite Settlements in Ephraim, Dan, and East Manasseh

51 Some of the families of the descendants of Qohath, the Levites remaining from the descendants of Qohath, [also] had towns of their territory from the tribe of Ephraim. 52 They gave to them towns of refuge: Shechem along with its open land in the hill country of Ephraim, Gezer along with its open land, 53 Joqmeam along with its open land, Beth-ḥoron along with its open land; 54 from the tribe of Dan: Elteqe along with its open land, Gibbethon along with its open land, Ayyalon along with its open land, and Gath-Rimmon along with its open land; 55 from the half-tribe of Manasseh: Taanach along with its open land, Ibleam along with its open land—for the families of the remaining descendants of the Qohathites.

Gershonite Settlements in East Manasseh, Issachar, Asher, and Naphtali

56 Belonging to the sons of Gershon, from the families of the half-tribe of Manasseh: Golan in Bashan along with its open land, and Ashtaroth along with its open land; 57 from the tribe of Issachar: Qishon along with its open land, Dobrath along with its open land, 58 Ramoth along with its open land, and Anem along with its open land; 59 from the tribe of Asher: Mashal along with its open land, Abdon along with its open land, 60 Ḥuqoq along with its open land, and Reḥob along with its open land; 61 from the tribe of Naphtali: Qedesh in Galil along with its open land, Ḥammath along with its open land, and Qiriathaim along with its open land.

Merarite Settlements in Zebulun, Reuben, and Gad

62 Belonging to the remaining descendants of Merari, from the tribe of Zebulun: Joqneam along with its open land, Rimmon along with its open land, Tabor along with its open land, 63 from across the Jordan, Jericho; to the east of the Jordan, from the tribe of Reuben: Bezer in the wilderness along with its open land, Jahzah along with its open land, 64 Qedemoth along with its open land, and Mephaath along with its open land; 65 from the tribe of Gad, Ramoth in Gilead along with its open land, Maḥanaim along with its open land, 66 Ḥeshbon along with its open land, and Jaazer along with its open land.

Textual Notes

6:39–66. In some English translations, these verses appear as 6:54–81.

6:39. "according to their settlements" *(lĕṭîrôtām)*. Thus MT. LXX* *en tais kōmais autōn*, "in their villages."

"within their territories" *(bigbûlām)*. Referring to the precincts of the Levitical towns (last TEXTUAL NOTE to v. 51; cf. Num 35:27; Josh 13:33).

"the family." So MT and LXX[AN]. LXX[B] *tē patria autōn*, "to their lineage."

"the Qohathites." So MT and LXX. MT and LXX Josh 21:10 add "from the sons of Levi."

"the (first) lot." MT (and LXX) are elliptical. Some commentators (e.g., Rudolph 1955: 58) insert *r'šnh* on the basis of Syr. and Arab., but these versions may correct toward MT Josh 21:10 *(hgwrl r'šnh)*. The adjective *r'šnh* is lacking in LXX* Josh 21:10.

6:40. "Ḥebron." Thus MT and LXX. MT and LXX Josh 21:11 preface an explanation, based on Josh 15:13, which may be a later addition.

"the land of Judah." So MT and LXX[B]. LXX[ALN] assimilates toward MT and LXX Josh 21:11, "the hill country of Judah."

"open land." On the translation of *migrāš*, see the 3rd NOTE to 5:16.

6:41. "Jephunneh." MT and LXX Josh 21:12 add "into [MT his] possession."

6:42. "Aaron." MT Josh 21:13 adds "the priest," but this term is lacking in LXX* Josh 21:13. It is possible that the term has been lost by haplography, from *'hrn hkhn* to *'hrn* (Freedman, personal communication).

"towns of refuge" *('ārê hammiqlāṭ)*. There is no need to read *'îr (ham)miqlāṭ* on the basis of Josh 21:13 (contra Rudolph 1955: 58). Chronicles (v. 52) consistently reads the pl. The form *'ārê hammiqlāṭ* also repeatedly occurs in the Babylonian Talmud (e.g., *b. Soṭah* 48b).

"Ḥebron along with its open land." Reading with MT and LXX Josh 21:13. MT and LXX 6:42 lack *w't-mgršh* due to haplography. The formulaic repetition of phrases beginning with *(w)'t* in this section of the text, for example, "Judah along with its surrounding open lands" in v. 40 *(yhwdh w't-mgršyh sbybtyh)*, has triggered some haplographies in the transmission of the Chronicler's text.

"Jattir along with its open land." Again, reading with MT and LXX Josh 21:14. 1 Chr 6:42 lacks "along with its open land" *(w't-mgršh)* due to haplography *(homoioarkton)*. Instead of registering Jattir (MT Josh 21:14 and MT 1 Chr 6:42 *yattir*), major witnesses to LXX Josh 21:14 and LXX 1 Chr 6:42 have variants for Ḥilen (TEXTUAL NOTE to v. 43). The converse also holds: some LXX witnesses in v. 43 have variants for Jattir (transposition). In v. 43, LXX[B] *Ta Hieththar*; c_2 *Hiesthar*; LXX[AN] *Hiether* (cf. LXX* Josh 21:15 *Hiethar*).

6:43. "Ḥilen." So many Heb. MSS, some LXX cursives, and Arm. *Hēlon* (v. 42). Cf. v. 42 LXX[A] *Nēlōn* (< **Hēlōn*?). MT "Ḥilez" reflects a *zayin/nûn* confusion. LXX[B] *Selna* reflects both transposition and assimilation (Albright 1945: 66). Cf. LXX[L] *Alōm* (v. 42). The difference with *ḥōlon* (MT Josh 15:51; 21:15 [LXX[B] *Ailōm*; OL *Ailōn*]; Jer 48:21) reflects a *wāw/yôd* confusion.

6:44. "Ashan" *('āšān)*. So MT and LXX *(Asan)*, as well as MT Josh 15:42, 19:7, and LXX* Josh 21:16 *(Asa)*. MT Josh 21:16 "Ain" (cf. 1 Chr 4:32 and Josh 15:32 *'ayin rimmôn*).

"Juṭṭah along with its open land." Reading with LXX[B] *kai tēn Attan kai ta perisporia autēs*, Syr., and Josh 21:16. LXX[B] *Attan* may reflect an original **Iatta* (Albright 1945: 61, 66; cf. LXX Josh 21:16). MT 6:44 lacks the phrase due to haplography *(homoioteleuton)*.

Beth-shemesh "along with its open land." Thus MT, LXX^{L}, and Josh 21:16. Lacking in LXX^{B} *(Basamys)*. MT and LXX Josh 21:16 add a numerical summary.

6:45. "Gibeon *(ʾt-gbʿwn)* along with its open land." Restored on the basis of MT and LXX Josh 21:17. This phrase has been lost due to haplography *(homoioarkton)* before Geba *(ʾt-gbʿ)*.

"Alemeth" *(ʿālemet)*. So MT (cf. LXX^{L} *Alamōth*). LXX^{B} hc$_2$ *Galemeth*. MT Josh 21:18 *ʿalmôn*; LXX^{B} Josh 21:18 *Gamala*; OL *Galamath*; LXX^{A} *Almōn*. The name is derived from the root *ǵlm* and has the form of a common noun meaning "young girl, lass" (Layton 1990b).

"along with its open land." Josh 21:19 adds a numerical summary.

"All of their towns." So MT. MT and LXX Josh 21:19 "all of the towns of the Aaronide priests."

"with their families" *(bĕmišpĕḥôtêhem)*. So MT. LXX *kata patrias autōn*, "according to their lineages" (cf. *mimmišpĕḥōt* in v. 46). MT Josh 21:19 "and their open lands" *(ûmigrĕšêhen)*, but the phrase is lacking in LXX Josh 21:19.

6:46. "from the families of the tribe of Ephraim, from the tribe of Dan, and" *(mimmišpĕḥōt maṭṭēh ʾeprayim ûmimmaṭṭēh dān û-)*. This reconstruction is based on vv. 51–56 and MT Josh 21:5. MT 1 Chr 6:46 is fragmentary, *mimmišpaḥat hammaṭṭeh*, due to haplography (Allen 1974b: 187; *pace* Kallai 1986a: 465–68). LXX is similar to MT, but cursives bi preserve part of the earlier reading, *tois kataleleimmenois apō tēs syngeneias* (i *ek*) *tēs phylēs Ephraim*, "those left behind (from) the family of the tribe of Ephraim." Cf. LXX Josh 21:5 *tois kataleleimmenois ek tēs phylēs Ephraim*.

"from the half-tribe of Manasseh." So the versions *(lectio brevior)*. The addition of superfluous *ḥāṣî* in MT may have been influenced by the use of *ḥāṣî* in MT Josh 21:5.

6:47. "Issachar." See the 2nd TEXTUAL NOTE to 2:1.

"and from the tribe of Manasseh" (וממטה מנשה). Both because of the context (v. 46) and because MT and LXX add a geographical qualifier ("in Bashan"), it is not necessary to follow MT and LXX Josh 21:6 and read, "and from the half-tribe of Manasseh" (וממחצית מטה מנשה; *pace* Rudolph 1955: 60). It is possible, however, that מחצית was lost by haplography (Freedman, personal communication).

"in Bashan." So MT and LXX. MT Josh 21:6 adds "by lot" *(bgwrl)*, but this is lacking in LXX* Josh 21:6.

6:48. "Gad." So MT, LXX^{AN}, and Josh 21:7 (MT and LXX). LXX^{B} c$_2$ "Dan." Cursive h combines both readings: *Gad ek phylēs Dan*.

"by lot" *(bgwrl)*. Thus MT and LXX. Lacking in MT Josh 21:7, but present in LXX* 21:7.

6:49. "towns." Thus MT and LXX. Josh 21:8 along with Syr. and Arab. add the demonstrative pron. "these" (lacking in LXX Josh 21:8).

"along with their open lands." MT and LXX Josh 21:8 add: "as Yhwh commanded [MT: through the hand of] Moses by lot."

6:50. "They assigned . . . by lot." So MT and LXX. MT and LXX Josh 21:9 lack "by lot."

"these towns." MT adds the direct object marker *ʾēt*.

"from the tribe of the descendants of Benjamin." Thus MT and LXX^{L}. The phrase is missing from LXX[AB] due to haplography *(homoioarkton).* Mention of Benjamin is lacking in MT Josh 21:9, but present both in LXX* and in the introductory material of Josh 21:4.

6:51. "(And) some of the families" *(ûmimmišpĕḥôt).* Based on the parallels in vv. 46–50, there is no need to adopt LXX[L] and Vg. in following Josh 21:20, *ûlĕmišpĕḥôt* (*pace* Rudolph 1955: 60). Chronicles and Joshua contain both collocations in earlier verses.

"the descendants of Qohath, the Levites remaining from the descendants of Qohath" *(bny-qht hlwym hnwtrym mbny qht).* So MT and LXX Josh 21:20. See also v. 55. MT and LXX 1 Chr 6:51 have suffered whole-phrase haplography *(homoioteleuton)* from *bny qht* to *bny qht* (Rudolph 1955: 60).

"their territory" *(gbwlm).* So MT and LXX (cf. LXX Josh 21:20 *tōn horiōn autōn*). MT Josh 21:20 "their lot" *(gwrlm).* The term *gĕbûl* can denote "territory," especially in later sources (Num 34:6; 35:27; Ezek 43:12; Mal 1:4; 2 Chr 11:13; *HALOT* 171).

6:52. "towns of refuge." See the 2nd TEXTUAL NOTE to v. 42. MT (and LXX) Josh 21:21 adds "of manslayer(s)" *(hārōṣēaḥ).*

"in the hill country of Ephraim" (בהר אפרים). So 1 Chr 6:52 and MT Josh 21:21. LXX Josh 21:21 differs, "and its open land."

6:53. "Joqmeam" *(yoqmĕʿām).* So MT (cf. LXX[B] *Ikaam*; LXX[A] *Iekmaan*). MT Josh 21:22 *qibṣayim* (lacking in LXX[B]) may represent the earlier reading. The case for graphic confusion is made by Rudolph (1955: 62) and Nelson (1997: 235).

"along with its open land." MT and LXX Josh 21:22 add a numerical summary.

6:54. "and from the tribe of Dan: Elteqe . . . Gibbethon along with its open land." So Josh 21:23. The expression is missing from Chronicles due to whole-phrase haplography *(homoioteleuton* from *ʾet-migrāšêhā* at the end of v. 53 to *ʾet-migrāšêhā).* It is possible that the Chronicler deliberately omitted this material from his genealogies, but the place-names that follow (Ayyalon and Gath-Rimmon) are regarded as part of the Danite inheritance (Josh 19:40–45; 21:23–24). See the 1st TEXTUAL NOTE to v. 46 and 1 Chr 7:12.

"Elteqe" *(ʾelteqēʾ).* Also spelled "Elteqeh" (*ʾelteqēh*; Josh 19:44).

"along with its open land." MT and LXX Josh 21:24 add a numerical summary.

6:55. "Taanach." Thus MT *tʿnk* and LXX[B] *Tanach* Josh 21:25 (cf. LXX[A] *Thaanach*). MT (and LXX[L]) 1 Chr 6:55 "Aner" *(ʿnr);* LXX[B] c_2 *Amar.* Attempts to derive Aner *(ʾt-ʿnr)* from Taanach *(tʿnk)* are predicated on a sequence of scribal errors (haplography and a *kāp/rêš* confusion; Albright 1945: 68–69; Noth 1953: 126).

"Ibleam" *(yblʿm).* Reading with two Heb. MSS, LXX[AN] *(Ieblaam*; cf. *b*b′ *lebaam*; cei *Iablaam),* Syr., Tg., Arm. and Arab. MT presents anomalous "Bileam" *(blʿm*; cf. Jdt 8:3 *Balamōn),* reflecting a haplography of the initial *yôd.* The expression "Ibleam along with its open land" is missing from LXX[B] c_2. MT Josh 21:25 "Gath-Rimmon" is corrupt (cf. Josh 21:24). LXX[B] Josh 21:25 *Iebatha* (< *Ieblea*; Margolis 1992: 410).

"along with its open land." MT and LXX Josh 21:25 add a numerical summary.

"for the families of the remaining descendants of the Qohathites" *(lĕmišpĕḥôt bĕnê qĕhāt hannôtārîm)*. Following Tg. 6:55 and MT Josh 21:26. MT 6:55 *lĕmišpaḥat libnê qĕhāt hannôtārîm*. MT and LXX Josh 21:26 also contain an earlier numerical summary: "(in) all ten towns and their open lands."

6:56. "from the families of the half-tribe." A reconstruction based on LXX *apo patriōn hēmisous phylēs (Manassē)*. Cf. MT *mimmišpaḥat ḥăṣî*. MT Josh 21:27 "from the families (*mimmišpĕḥôt*) of the Levites from the half-tribe." See also the 1st TEXTUAL NOTE to v. 46.

"Manasseh." MT and LXX Josh 21:27 add "the town of refuge for manslayer(s)."

"Ashtaroth." So MT and LXX^{L} *Astarōth* (cf. LXX^{B} *Asērōth*). MT Josh 21:27 has (erroneously) "Beshterah" (LXX^{B} *Bosoran*; LXX^{A} *Beethara*).

"along with its open land." MT and LXX Josh 21:27 add a numerical summary.

6:57. "Issachar." See the 2nd TEXTUAL NOTE to 2:1.

"Qishon" *(qîšôn)*. Thus MT and LXX *(Keisōn)* Josh 21:28. MT (and LXX) "Qadesh" assimilates toward v. 61(//Josh 21:32).

"Dobrath." So MT 6:57 and MT Josh 21:28. LXX^{B} *Deberei*; LXX^{B} Josh 21:28 *Debba*.

6:58. "Ramoth" *(rāʾmôt)*. So MT and LXX^{L}. LXX^{B} *Dabōr*; LXX^{AN} *Anōs*. MT Josh 21:29 *yarmût* (LXX^{B} *Rhemmath*).

"Anem" *(ʿānēm)*. So MT and LXX^{AN}. The expression "Anem along with its open land," is lacking in LXX^{B}. Kallai (1986a: 425) thinks that "Anem" may be an abbreviation of *ʿên gannîm* (//MT Josh 21:29). Some major witnesses to LXX Josh 21:29 are corrupt: *pēgēn grammatōn*, "fount of scribes" (cf. *Pēgēn Ganneim*; Margolis 1992: 413). Albright (1945: 70–71) reconstructs an original עין ענם.

"along with its open land." MT and LXX Josh 21:29 add a numerical summary.

6:59. "Mashal" *(māšāl)*. LXX *Maasa*. MT Josh 19:26; 21:30 *mišʾāl*; LXX Josh 19:26 *Maasa*; LXX^{B} 21:30 *Basellan* (LXX^{A} *Masaal*).

"Abdon" *(ʿabdôn)*. So MT and MT Josh 21:30. The discrepancy with Josh 19:28 *ʿebrōn* reflects a *dālet/rêš* confusion.

6:60. "Ḥuqoq." LXX^{B} nc_2 *Hikak*; LXX^{L} *Hakōk*. Josh 21:31 "Ḥelqath" (LXX* *Chelkat*) may be the earlier reading (cf. Josh 19:25). Josh 19:34 Ḥuqoqah; LXX^{A} *I(a)kōk*; LXX^{B} *Iakana*.

"along with its open land." MT and LXX Josh 21:31 add a numerical summary.

6:61. "Ḥammath." A reconstruction based on MT Josh 19:35 "Ḥammath" and LXX* 6:61 *Chamōth*. MT (and LXX^{AN}) 6:61 "Ḥammon" reflects a ון/ת error (Allen 1974a: 188). MT Josh 21:32 *ḥammōt dōʾr* (LXX^{B} *Nemmath*). Albright (1945: 71–72) thinks that the list of LXX Josh 19:35 is original and that one name fell out of both MT Josh 21:32 and 1 Chr 6:61, but as Rudolph (1955: 62) points out, the numerical summaries of Josh 21:6 and 1 Chr 6:62 do not support this view.

"Qiriathaim." So MT and LXX*. MT Josh 19:35 *raqqath*; 21:32 *qartān*.

"along with its open land." MT and LXX Josh 21:32–33 add a numerical summary for Naphtali and another summary for the Gershonites as a whole.

6:62. "descendants of Merari." MT and LXX Josh 21:34 add "the Levites."

"Joqneam along with its open land." Reading with LXX[AN] *(Iekoman)*, cursives cehin, Arm. 1 Chr 6:62, and MT Josh 21:34 (cf. LXX[B] *Maan*; LXX[A] *Eknam*). MT and LXX[B] 1 Chr 6:62 lack the phrase due to haplography *(homoioteleuton)*. Alternately, one could treat the lemma of LXX[AN] as a correction toward MT Joshua, but these LXX witnesses contain relatively few such corrections.

"open land." Thus MT and LXX*. The addition of "Qartah along with its open land" in Josh 21:34 is suspect (cf. Josh 21:32).

"Rimmon" *(rimmôn)*. So LXX *(Rhemmōn*; cf. Josephus *Eremmôn)* and MT Josh 19:13 *rimmôn*. MT 6:62 "Rimmono"; cf. LXX[B] Josh 19:13 *Rhemmōna*. MT Josh 21:35 "Dimnah" reflects a *dālet/rêš* confusion.

"Tabor." Thus MT. LXX[B] *Thachcheia*; LXX[L] *Thabōr*. Josh 21:35 differs: *Nahălāl* (LXX[B] *Sella*; LXX[A] *Naalōl*) and adds a numerical summary.

6:63–64. These verses are not attested in MT Joshua, although some Heb. MSS contain them. LXX* Josh 21:36–37 (or 21:35a-b, 36–37; Margolis 1992: 417–20) and arithmetic (Josh 21:1–8, 40–41) bear witness to their originality. This is another instance in which the testimony of Chronicles can be used to reconstruct an older form of Joshua.

6:63. "to the east." Cf. LXX[B] *kata dysmas*, "toward the setting (of the sun)." Lacking in LXX Joshua.

"Bezer (*bṣr)* in the wilderness." So MT and LXX. Some witnesses to LXX Josh 21:36 add *tē Meisōr* (transliterating Heb. *mîšōr*).

"along with its open land." So MT and LXX Chronicles, as well as LXX Joshua. Syr. inserts v. 64b here.

"Jahzah" (יהצה). LXX *Iasa*. See also "Jahaz" (Josh 15:4; Jer 48:34). LXX Josh 13:18 *Iassa* (MT *yhṣh*); 21:36 *Iazēr*. Cf. *Jahzah* (יהצה) in Num 21:23; Deut 2:32; Judg 11:20.

6:64. "Mephaath" *(mêpaʿath)*. So MT. LXX[B] *Maephla*; LXX[LN] *Mōphaath* (cf. Kethib [and LXX] Jer 48:21 *môpāʿath*); LXX[B] Josh 21:37 *Mapha*. MT Josh 13:18 *mēpaʿath* (pausal form).

"along with its open land." LXX Josh 21:37 adds a numerical summary.

6:65. "from the tribe of Gad." So MT and LXX Chronicles, MT and LXX Josh 21:38; lacking in Syr. Josh 21:38 adds "town of refuge of manslayer(s)."

"Ramoth" *(rāʾmôt)*. So MT and LXX[ALN]. LXX[B] *Rhammōn*. MT Josh 21:38 *rāmōt* (LXX *Rhamôth*).

"Maḥanaim." So MT 6:65 and MT Josh 21:38. LXX[B] c_2 1 Chr 6:65 *Maanaith*; LXX[B] Josh 21:38 *Kamein*.

6:66. "Jaazer" *(yaʿzêr)*. So MT. LXX[B] *Gazer*. MT Josh 21:39 *yaʿzēr* (LXX* *Iazēr*).

"along with its open land." The account continues in MT and LXX Josh 21. Josh 21:40 adds a numerical summary for the Merarites, while Josh 21:41 adds a numerical summary for all of the Levitical towns. Josh 21:40 follows with another summary for the Levitical town assignments. A general promise-fulfillment notice pertaining to the conquest concludes the account in MT (Josh 21:43–45). But LXX Josh 21:42a-d adds yet another set of statements, detailing the award of an inheritance to Joshua (a town on Mount Ephraim) and commenting on the fate of Joshua's circumcision knives.

NOTES

6:39–66. These verses are drawn from the author's version of Josh 21:3–42. As the TEXTUAL NOTES indicate, the source differed from both MT and LXX Joshua in a number of ways. It is likely that the writer drew on a typologically earlier form of Josh 21 than is represented in MT Joshua (SOURCES, COMPOSITION, AND STRUCTURE).

6:39. "These are their places . . . within their territories." This is the Chronicler's own introduction to the material he culls from Joshua. In the context of Joshua, the assignment of Levitical towns arises from a request to Joshua from the priest Eleazar (Josh 21:1–3) after the other Israelite tribes were given their territorial allotments (Josh 13:1–19:51) and certain towns were set aside as places for asylum (Josh 20:1–9). Such allotments for the Levites were promised while the Israelites were still encamped on the plains of Moab (Num 35:1–8). The towns specially set aside as Levitical towns derive from the inheritances of the other tribes. The means by which the three Levitical phratries receive their estates is the casting of lots (Josh 21:4–8). Chronicles does not contain any of the material in Numbers and Joshua that sets the stage for the assignment of Levitical towns. Since the exodus and conquest are not prominent themes in Chronicles (Noth 1943: 175; Brunet 1954: 368–69; Rudolph 1955: ix; Japhet 1989: 374–86), it is not surprising that they do not figure prominently here. Nevertheless, by repeatedly alluding to the lottery (6:39, 46, 48, 50) and by making statements such as "they gave Ḥebron to them in the land of Judah" (v. 40), the author presumes that his readers know something of the context in which the Levites were (to be) assigned certain towns in Numbers and Joshua. In the setting of the Chronicler's own presentation, however, the introduction to the Levitical settlements acquires its own integrity and purpose. Having provided readers with lineages for the tribe of Levi (5:27–41; 6:1–38), the author supplies information about their places of residence. In this respect, the treatment of Levi is similar to that of other tribes. Information about identity and descent is coupled with information about settlements and history.

"descendants of Aaron." In the Chronicler's presentation of the Levitical settlements, pride of place is given to the Aaronides (1 Chr 6:39b–45//Josh 21:10–19). The concern is not so much distinguishing the Qohathites from the Gershonites (*pace* Auld 1990) as it is with maintaining a distinction between the Qohathite Aaronides and the rest of the Levitical lines. For this reason, it comes as no surprise that the other Qohathite settlements are not also moved forward, but appear later (1 Chr 6:46, 51–55//Josh 21:20–26). Although moving the Aaronide settlements forward rearranges the order presented in Josh 21 and introduces some confusion into the text of Chronicles (SOURCES, COMPOSITION, AND STRUCTURE), the procedure is broadly consistent with that followed in the genealogies themselves. The line of priests (from Levi through Aaron to Jehozadaq; 5:27–41) is presented first, followed by lineages for the Gershonites, the other Qohathites, and the Merarites (6:1–33). In the present text of Chronicles, another, shorter, Aaronide genealogy concludes the list (6:35–38), anticipating to some extent the coverage given to the Aaronide settlements that immediately follows (6:39–45).

6:40. "Ḥebron" and the other sites mentioned in vv. 40–66 did not become the domain of the Levites to the exclusion of other Israelites. Rather, the Levitic towns were sites in which the Levites had the prerogative to dwell and perhaps exercise certain rights (Lev 25:32–34). In Joshua, the lack of a territorial inheritance for the Levites stems from the fact that Yhwh (Josh 13:14, 33) or the priesthood of Yhwh (Josh 18:7) is their inheritance.

"land of Judah." The location of Aaronide settlements is rather interesting, because the geographical range of these sites is quite limited. Unlike the other Levitical settlements, which are dispersed over a range of geographical areas, the Aaronide settlements are clustered within the traditional domains of three tribes: Judah, Simeon, and Benjamin (see also vv. 49–50). According to the list, there were no Aaronide towns north of Benjamin. This reinforces the notion that the Aaronides were originally a southern group.

6:41. "the territory (*śdh*) of the town." On the usage, compare Gen 41:48; Obad 19; Neh 11:30; 12:29. Because the members of the Levitical tribe were to receive no inheritance, Ḥebron's fields and villages were granted to Caleb son of Jephunneh.

6:42. "towns of refuge" (*ʿārê hammiqlāṭ*). The reference to places of asylum here and in v. 52 presupposes the establishment of such towns in another context (Josh 20:1–3). The creation of such sanctuaries of refuge for unintentional killers conforms to Deuteronomic (Deut 4:41–43; 19:1–13) and Priestly law (Num 35:6–15, 25–28, 32). Most, if not all, of the towns designated for asylum (Josh 20:7–8) doubled as Levitical settlements. The language used in Chronicles, as opposed to Joshua—*ʿîr (ham)miqlāṭ hārōṣēaḥ*—is telling. Whereas Joshua designates specific sites as towns of asylum (Josh 21:13, 21, 27, 32, 38), Chronicles employs the pl. in two introductory rubrics (vv. 42, 52). It may be that the author designates all of the Levitical towns as asylum towns (Auld 1978; Svensson 1994), but it is also possible that he designates only those specific towns introduced by these rubrics: the Aaronide towns in Judah and Benjamin (vv. 42–45) and the Qohathite towns in Ephraim (vv. 51–54).

"Libnah" is usually identified as T. Bornâṭ, some 25 km northwest of Ḥebron (Josh 10:29; 12:15; 15:42; 2 Kgs 8:22; 19:8; 23:31; 24:18; 2 Chr 21:10).

"Eshtemoa." See the 3rd NOTE to 4:17.

6:43. "Ḥilen" or "Ḥolon" (Josh 15:51; 21:15) refers to a (priestly) town in the hill country of Judah. The "Ḥolon" of Jer 48:21 may refer to a different site.

6:44. "Ashan" (*ʿāšān*). See the 4th NOTE to 4:32.

"Beth-shemesh" in Judah is associated with T. er-Rumēle, 24 km west of Jerusalem (Josh 15:10; 21:16; 1 Sam 6:9; 1 Kgs 4:9; 2 Kgs 14:11, 13; 2 Chr 25:21, 23; 28:18).

6:45. "Gibeon." On this Benjaminite site, see the 2nd NOTE to 8:29.

"Geba." On the site, see the 2nd NOTE to 8:6.

"Anathoth." See the 2nd NOTE to 11:28.

"all of their towns . . . were thirteen." When these thirteen towns are considered together with the ten Qohathite towns in Ephraim, Dan, and Manasseh (vv. 46, 51–55), the Qohathites easily comprise the largest phratry in Levi (1st NOTE to 5:28).

6:46–50. Whereas 1 Chr 6:39–45 parallel Josh 21:10–19, 1 Chr 6:46–50 pick up the introductory material of Josh 21:5–9.

6:46. "belonging to the remaining descendants of Qohath" (ולבני קהת הנותרים). In the context of the presentation in Joshua, this declaration (Josh 21:5) follows the introductory summary of thirteen Levitical towns awarded to the Qohathite Aaronides from the tribes of Judah, Benjamin, and Simeon (Josh 21:4). The remaining descendants of the Qohathite Aaronides receive ten towns from the tribes of Ephraim, Dan, and East Manasseh (21:5). In the context of Chronicles the declaration receives new meaning because the summary of Josh 21:4 does not appear. In the setting of Chronicles, the reference to "the remaining descendants of Qohath" refers to those non-Aaronide Qohathites, who were not covered by the list of Qohathite towns in 6:39–45. As such, the text anticipates the list of vv. 51–55, which mentions ten Qohathite settlements in Ephraim, Dan, and East Manasseh. The summary of v. 55 again draws attention to the fact that the list of vv. 51–55 pertains to "the remaining descendants of the Qohathites" (לבני־קהת הנותרים).

"half-tribe of Manasseh." That is, East Manasseh (NOTE to 5:23). See also vv. 47, 55, 56.

6:47. "descendants of Gershon." In traditional lists of Levi's sons, Gershon occupies the primary position (Gen 46:11; Exod 6:16; Num 3:17; 26:57; 1 Chr 6:1; 23:6; cf. 1 Chr 5:28), but in this list the Qohathites come first and the Gershonites occupy a total of thirteen towns compared to the Qohathites' twenty-three.

"Manasseh in Bashan." On the territorial allotment of East Manasseh, see the NOTE to 5:23.

"thirteen towns." The overview anticipates the listing of Gershonite settlements in East Manasseh, Issachar, Asher, and Naphtali (vv. 56–61).

6:48. "twelve towns by lot." This heading anticipates the list of Merarite sites in Reuben, Gad, and Zebulun (vv. 62–66).

6:49. "assigned to the Levites." A summary that parallels Josh 21:8.

6:50. "designated by name." In the following verses, the towns go unmentioned, but recourse to the Chronicler's source (Josh 21:9) reveals that the towns spoken of are those that have already appeared in vv. 39–45(//Josh 21:10–19). The text of 1 Chr 6:51–66 returns to the material covered by Josh 21:20–40.

"Simeon" is referred to in the introductory material of Josh 21:4, 9, but not explicitly in the list of Aaronide settlements (Josh 21:10–19). Similarly, the presentation of Aaronide settlements in Chronicles explicitly mentions Judah (v. 40) and Benjamin (v. 45), but not Simeon.

6:51–66. These verses are largely paralleled by Josh 21:20–38.

6:51. "Levites remaining." Alluding to non-Aaronide Qohathites (cf. vv. 39–45).

6:52. "towns of refuge." See the 1st NOTE to v. 42.

"Shechem" (T. Balâṭah), located in the hill country of Ephraim between Ebal and Gerizim, was an important and historic town in ancient Israel (Josh 8:30–35; 17:7; 20:7; 21:21; 24:1–28; 1 Kgs 12:1–17; 1 Chr 6:52; 7:28; 2 Chr 10:1).

"Gezer," approximately 25 km northwest of Jerusalem, seems to be accorded to the tribes of Joseph in Josh 16:3. Gezer is associated with the specific territory of Ephraim in a variety of contexts (Josh 16:10; 1 Chr 7:28; 21:21; Judg 1:29; cf. 2 Sam 5:25; 1 Kgs 9:15–17; 1 Chr 14:16; 20:4).

6:53. "Joqmeam" *(yoqmĕʿām)*. The location is unknown. Two possibilities are Qūṣēn, west of Nablus (*HALOT* 431), and T. el-Mazâr, near the Ephraim-Manasseh border (Josh 12:22; 19:11; 21:34; B. Mazar 1960: 198). Some scholars think that Joqmeam is either a mistake for or an alternative spelling of Joqneam (v. 62; *HALOT* 431). In the discussion of Levites associated with the time of David, "Jeqameam" *(yĕqamʿām)* appears as a son of Ḥebron (1 Chr 23:19). Benjamin Mazar (1960: 193) suggests that the change of name (cf. Qibṣaim in Josh 21:22) indicates settlement by and connections with this Ḥebronite lineage (cf. 1 Chr 24:23).

6:54. "Elteqe" *(ʾelteqēʾ)*, or Elteqeh *(ʾelteqēh)*, was part of Dan's inheritance (Josh 19:44). The town is associated with T. eš-Šallâf (Aharoni 1979: 434).

"Gibbethon," another town in the Danite inheritance (Josh 19:44), is usually identified as T. Mēlât, 4.8 km west of Gezer. It appears as a Philistine site in 1 Kgs 15:27; 16:15, 17.

"Ayyalon" *(ʾayyālôn)*, 20 km west-northwest of Jerusalem, is listed as part of the Danite heritage in Josh 19:42 (cf. 1 Chr 8:13) and deemed to be the responsibility of the house of Joseph in Judg 1:35. See also 2 Chr 11:10 and 28:18.

6:55. "Ibleam." Known within biblical tradition as a (former) royal Canaanite city, Ibleam is associated with Khirbet Belʿame, 2 km southwest of Jenin (Josh 17:11; Judg 1:27; 2 Kgs 9:27; Jdt 8:3).

6:56–61. The itemization of Gershonite settlements in East Manasseh, Issachar, Asher, and Naphtali(//Josh 21:27–32) corresponds to the introductory tally of thirteen towns mentioned in v. 47(//Josh 21:6). The inventory of vv. 56–61 lacks the summary total provided in Josh 21:33.

6:56. "Ashtaroth" (probably modern T. Aštara, 4 km south of Šēḫ Saʿad) functions as a residence of King Og of Bashan in Joshua (9:10; 12:4; 13:12, 31). As is the case here, Ashtaroth falls within Manasseh (Josh 13:31; cf. *Jub.* 29:10).

6:57. "Qishon" *(qišôn)*, part of the inheritance of Issachar (Josh 19:20; 2nd TEXTUAL NOTE to v. 57), is identified as Khirbet Qēsun at the southern foot of Mount Tabor.

"Dobrath," or Daberath, is mentioned in the context of Zebulun's borders (Josh 19:12) and in the territorial allotment of Issachar (Josh 21:28). Dobrath (modern Debūriyeh) is located at the northwest end of Mount Tabor.

6:58. "Ramoth," or Remeth, in Issachar (Josh 19:21) is sometimes associated with Kôkab el-Hawā.

6:59. "Abdon," part of Asher (Josh 19:28; 21:30; 2nd TEXTUAL NOTE to v. 59), is associated with Khirbet ʿAbdeh, some 19 km northeast of Akko. The site may be mentioned on an eleventh-century B.C.E. arrowhead (עבדן; Cross 1995), but this reading is disputed (עבדי, "Abday;" Deutsch and Heltzer 1997a).

6:60. "Ḥuqoq." Based on Josh 19:25 and 21:31, one might have expected Ḥelqath (1st TEXTUAL NOTE to v. 60). Located near Tabor, Ḥuqoq is associated with the border area of Naphtali (Josh 19:34). As such, it cannot be automatically dissociated from Asher.

"Reḥob," part of Asher (Josh 19:28, 30; Judg 1:31), is associated with T. el-Bîr el-Gharbi, 11.2 km east-southeast of Akko (Aharoni 1979: 441; Boling 1982: 454). It should be distinguished from another site by the same biblical name (Reḥob),

T. eṣ-Ṣarim, one of the largest sites in Israel located at the juncture of the Jezreel and Jordan Valleys (Num 13:21; 2 Sam 10:8).

6:61. "Ḥammath" (TEXTUAL NOTE) is sometimes identified with Ḫammām south of Tiberias (Noth 1953: 120).

"Qiriathaim" *(qiryātayim)*, mentioned in connection with Reuben (Num 32:37; Josh 13:19), may signify *qrytn* on the Mesha stela (*KAI* 181.10). Many identify the site as Khirbet el-Qurēye, 9.6 km northwest of Dibon, but Kallai (1986a: 442) disagrees.

6:62–66. The list of Merarite towns in Zebulun, Reuben, and Gad(//Josh 21:34–39) corresponds to the introductory tally of twelve settlements mentioned in v. 48(//Josh 21:7). The account in Chronicles lacks the summary of Josh 21:40.

6:62. "to the remaining." The terminology is surprising in this context (cf. Josh 21:34). In v. 46 the expression marked those Qohathites who were not descendants of Aaron. But in this instance, the pericope of vv. 62–66 comprises the only listing of Merarite settlements (v. 48).

"Joqneam" (2nd TEXTUAL NOTE to v. 62), T. Yoqneʿam (Qēmûn) at the foot of Mount Carmel, was one of the three largest towns in the western Jezreel Valley (along with Megiddo and Shimron). Most of the archaeological remains date to the Iron Age, but both local and imported wares were found at the site dating to the fifth and fourth centuries B.C.E. An ostracon containing both Heb. and Phoen. names has also been recovered (Ben-Tor 1993).

"Rimmon," located in Zebulun (Josh 19:13), is usually identified with Rummâne on the southern fringe of the Sahl-el-Baṭṭof, west of Nazareth (*HALOT* 1242).

"Tabor." As a sacred site, see Hos 5:1.

6:63–64. "Reuben." The sites Bezer, Jahzah, Qedemoth, and Mephaath seem to be situated in the area north and northeast of Dibon. This means that the third Levitical family (the Merarites) are assigned towns in two widely separated districts: Zebulun (v. 62) and the Transjordan (vv. 63–66), with the latter area dominating (9 sites).

6:63. "Bezer in the wilderness." Also attested *(bṣr)* in the Mesha inscription (*KAI* 181:27–28), the site is unknown. Three suggested possibilities are Umm el-ʿAmad, a few km southeast of Ḥeshbon; Qaṣr Sāliyye, some 11 km east-southeast of Aroer; and Jalūl, a few km northeast of Madaba.

"Jahzah" *(yahṣāh)* is probably the same site as Jahaz (TEXTUAL NOTE; cf. Num 21:23; Deut 2:32; Josh 13:18; Judg 11:20; Jer 48:21, 34; W. Holladay 1989: 359). The site *yhṣ* mentioned in the Mesha inscription as (re)built and temporarily occupied by an Israelite king (*KAI* 181:18–20) is located somewhere near Dibon. James Miller (1989), Kartveit (1989), and Smelik (1992) propose Khirbet Libb directly to the north of Dibon, while Dearman (1997) favors Khirbet al-Mudayna to the northeast of Dibon. For other possibilities, see Burton MacDonald (2000: 103–6).

6:64. "Mephaath" is sometimes identified as T. Aj-jāwa, a site with important Iron Age II remains (Daviau 1997: 156–71), situated 10 km south of Amman, but this identification is disputed by Younker (1997b). Some favor Umm er-Raṣaṣ, some 13 km east of Dibon.

6:65–66. "Gad" is accorded a wide range of sites from Ramoth-gilead and Maḥanaim in the north to Ḥeshbon (cf. Num 32:37; Josh 13:17) in the south. In this respect, there is some consonance between the pattern of Levitical allotments for the Transjordanian tribes and the territories ascribed to the Transjordanian tribes in the Chronicler's genealogies (1 Chr 5:1–26; Kallai 1986a: 321–22).

6:65. "Ramoth" *(rā'môt)*. To be distinguished from both southern Ramah (*r'mt ngb* Josh 19:8; *rmtngb* Davies, §2.024.13, 16; cf. *rāmōt negeb* 1 Sam 30:27) in southern Judah and from Ramoth in Issachar (v. 58). Ramoth in Gilead, or Ramoth-gilead (1 Kgs 4:13), is usually identified as T. er-Rāmîth in the Transjordan, approximately 12.5 km east-northeast of 'el-Ḥuṣn.

"Maḥanaim" is located in the Transjordan on the Jabboq River (Wâdī Zerqā), but its precise location is unclear. The most commonly suggested ancient site is Tulūl 'eḏ-Ḏahab on the south bank of the Jabboq (Aharoni 1979: 439). Maḥanaim figures prominently in the narratives about the struggles of the United Monarchy (2 Sam 2:8, 12; 17:24, 27; 19:33 [ET 19:32]; 1 Kgs 2:8; 4:14).

6:66. "Ḥeshbon." According to most, T. Ḥisbân, but a few think Jalūl, a few km northeast of Madaba. See further Knauf (1990a).

"Jaazer." The identification with Khirbet eṣ-Ṣâr, about 11 km west of Rabbath-ammon, is uncertain (3rd NOTE to 26:31).

"open land." The parallel account in Josh 21:41–42 goes on to provide a summary, mentioning a total of forty-eight towns for the Levites as well as other material (2nd TEXTUAL NOTE to v. 66).

SOURCES, COMPOSITION, AND STRUCTURE

Dates for the composition of the Levitical town list in Josh 21 vary widely. Wellhausen (1885), followed by Noth (1953), places the material, which he considers to be of a utopian Priestly nature, in the postexilic age. Viewing this late date as implausible, Albright (1945), Benjamin Mazar (1960), Aharoni (1979), Hauer (1982), Roddy Braun (1986), and Kallai (1986a) redate the list to the time of the United Monarchy, the time (ostensibly) in which Israel controlled this far-flung assortment of sites. Some wish to push the date of the original list back farther. Following Kaufmann, Milgrom (1982) associates the concept of the Levitical towns, along with their common lands, with the era of the Israelite settlement. Other dates proposed for the account include the eighth century (Boling 1982: 492–97; 1985) and the age of Josiah (Alt 1953; Svensson 1994). Some scholars (Auld 1979; Haran 1961b; Na'aman 1986a) posit multiple stages of composition. Haran distinguishes between a historical core and a utopian Priestly expansion. Schmitt (1995) argues, with considerable justification, that the list cannot be aligned with any one particular period in the development of ancient Israel and Judah. Auld (1979; 1990) thinks that the text of Chronicles has experienced "disordered growth" and that the (later) text of Joshua attempts to correct its uneven results. Na'aman (1986a: 209–12) faults scholars who accept the historicity of the list for not first having come to terms with literary issues, such as the possible dependence of portions of Josh 21 on earlier narratives (e.g., Josh 13; 19; 20). A succession of recent scholars date the list in the Persian period (e.g., Auld 1979; Ben Zvi 1992; Spencer 1992), viewing the compilation of sites as reflective of a late ideal rather than of an early reality. Hence, the discussion has come full circle. Many scholars have returned to the date, albeit not the entire rationale, proposed by Wellhausen. A convenient summary of the discussion is available in Schmitt (1995).

Space limits do not permit a full discussion of the dates proposed for the original list or its earliest compositional history. What does merit our considered attention is the relationship between the material in MT and LXX^B Josh 21 and the material in 1 Chr 6. Until recently it was a commonplace to see the presentation of Levitical towns in Chronicles as either derived from the comparable list in Joshua (e.g., Curtis and Madsen 1910; R. Braun 1986) or to see both lists as derived from a common source (e.g., B. Mazar 1960). Within the past two decades a third view has come to the fore: the (original) presentation of Chronicles is antecedent to Joshua (Auld 1978; 1979; 1990; 1998). If Joshua is dependent on Chronicles, arguments for an early date for the Levitical town list are moot. This third view, argued in detail and with attention to textual variants, is not without merit. Chronicles offers a briefer text, free of some of the anecdotes, explanations, comments, and numerical summaries found in Joshua. References to the cities of refuge (Josh 21:13, 21, 27, 32, 38), the account of which (Josh 20:1–9) does not appear in Chronicles, occur only twice in Chronicles (6:42, 52). Some eight towns in MT Joshua do not appear in Chronicles.

Nevertheless, the textual evidence is more complex than any of the three theories allow. To begin with, there are five towns mentioned in Chronicles (6:63–64) that appear in LXX* Josh 21:36–37, but not in MT Joshua. One must also distinguish between MT Joshua and LXX^B Joshua. Assertions have been made that LXX^B Josh 21 represents either a parent text for both MT and LXX Chronicles (Spencer 1992) or a text lying between Chronicles and MT Joshua (Albright 1945; Auld 1979). There is some justification for such proposals (TEXTUAL NOTES), but the similarities between LXX^B Joshua and Chronicles should not be overplayed. Some of Albright's arguments for the distinctiveness of LXX^B Joshua are predicated not on actual readings of this witness, but on his reconstruction of LXX*. His judgments about which readings reflect the original LXX are informed, as they should be, by his analysis of LXX^B, LXX^A, and the various cursives, but such a reconstructed *Urtext* should not be confused with one of its witnesses (LXX^B). It should also be pointed out that the readings shared by MT and LXX^B Joshua far outnumber the readings shared by LXX^B Joshua and Chronicles. There are also cases in which MT Joshua and MT Chronicles share important readings over against LXX Joshua (TEXTUAL NOTES). This and other evidence suggest a certain fluidity in the development of biblical texts before the rise of the Common Era. But it also complicates any effort to posit a linear development from an original text of Chronicles to LXX^B Joshua and then to MT Joshua.

In spite of the good objections raised by Auld and Spencer, there is still something to be said for the text of Chronicles being derived from an earlier form of

Joshua (so also De Vries 1989: 64–68; Kartveit 1989: 69–77; Schmitt 1995: 37–40). But this earlier form of Joshua should be seen as significantly briefer than either MT or LXX Joshua (Knoppers forthcoming [d]). First, while it is true that Chronicles offers a less elaborate text than Joshua, this cannot be, in and of itself, a sure indication that Joshua is derivative. The Chronicler elsewhere shows himself perfectly capable of abridging his sources. His universal genealogy (1:1–2:2), for example, is culled from texts in Genesis. Precious little of the narrative material found in Genesis appears in Chronicles. Moreover, 1 Chr 1:1–2:2 includes only some of the anecdotes included in the lineages of Genesis. This comparative analysis does not prove, however, that the writers of Genesis derived their material from Chronicles. Quite the contrary, the comparative evidence strongly suggests that the author of 1 Chr 1 selectively reused certain materials from Genesis.

Second, there are expressions that occur in 1 Chr 6:39–66 that are not characteristic of Chronistic style or theology. These, as Ben Zvi (1992: 77–78) points out, include *gwrl*, "lot, allocation," which appears in vv. 39, 46, 48, and 50, but nowhere else in Chronicles; *ntn(w) ʿrym*, "he/they assigned towns," which appears in vv. 40, 42, 49, 50, 52, but nowhere else in 1 Chr 1–9; *mṭh bny PN*, "tribe of the descendants of PN" (v. 50), which occurs nowhere else in Chronicles, but appears elsewhere in Joshua (13:29; 15:20; 16:8; 18:11) and in P (Num 10:15, 16, 19); *mṭh PN*, "tribe of PN," which appears often in this list (vv. 45, 46, 47, 48, 51, 56, 57, 59, 61, 62, 63, 65), as well as in Joshua and P (Josh 7:1; Num 1:39; 13:12, etc.), but appears elsewhere only once in Chronicles (1 Chr 12:32); *yrdn yrḥw*, "the Jordan (near) Jericho" (v. 63 and nowhere else in Chronicles, but see Num 22:1; 26:3, 63; 31:12; 33:48, 50; 34:15; 35:1; 36:13; Josh 13:32; 16:1; 20:8; Smick 1973). Such expressions are important in two respects. First, they point toward an original context outside of Chronicles. Second, the appearance of material with affinities to that authored either by the Priestly writers or by writers who were influenced by the Priestly school militates against the notion that 6:39–66 has not undergone editing by a "Priestly" writer (*pace* Auld 1990: 152).

Third, certain expressions that appear to be quite awkward in 1 Chr 6:39–66 are best explained by their recontextualization in a new literary setting (Kartveit 1989: 76). In 6:50, the text speaks of certain towns being "designated by name," but the towns go unspecified in the following verses. Reference to Josh 21:9 shows that the towns spoken of are those which appeared earlier in vv. 39–45 (//Josh 21:10–19). Another example: v. 62 speaks of an allotment of towns "to the remaining descendants of Merari." The choice of such terminology is quite surprising in this context, because this verse introduces the only listing of Merarite settlements (vv. 62–66). The discrepancy reflects the fact that the writer's rearrangement of material from his *Vorlage* (Josh 21:34) has resulted in a few ungraceful transitions.

Finally, analysis of the structure of the two texts augurs against viewing Joshua as derivative from Chronicles. The point requires some explication. Joshua and Chronicles share similar content, but offer different sequences of presentation. Joshua first presents a historical context for the assignment of Levitical towns (21:1–3) and summarizes the number and tribal sources of the towns to be assigned to each of the four Levitical groups: the Aaronide Qohathites (21:4), the rest

	Joshua	*Chronicles*
Introduction	21:1–3	6:39a
Overview for Qohathite Aaronides	21:4	—
Overview for (Other) Qohathites, Gershonites, and Merarites	21:5–7	6:46–48
Summary	21:8	6:49
Introduction to Settlements in Judah, Simeon, and Benjamin	21:9	6:50
Qohathite Aaronide Towns in Judah, Simeon, and Benjamin	21:10–18	6:39b–45a
Summary for Qohathite Aaronides	21:19	6:45b
Qohathite Towns in Ephraim, Dan, and East Manasseh	21:20–25	6:51–55
Summary for Other Qohathites	21:26	—
Gershonite Towns in East Manasseh, Issachar, Asher, and Naphtali	21:27–32	6:56–61
Summary for Gershonites	21:33	—
Merarite Towns in Zebulun, Reuben, and Gad	21:34–39	6:62–66
Summary for Merarites	21:40	—
Summary Total of Levitical Towns	21:41–42	—
Fulfillment of Divine Promises	21:43–45	—
Joshua's Inheritance (LXX)	21:42a–d	—

of the Qohathites (21:5), the Gershonites (21:6), and the Merarites (21:7). Following a concluding summary (21:8), the text details these towns by name (21:9–40), according to both the order and the categorization provided in the earlier introduction: the Aaronide Qohathites (21:9–19), the rest of the Qohathites (21:20–26), the Gershonites (21:27–33), and the Merarites (21:34–40). Hence, in both major sections (vv. 1–8 and vv. 9–40) the Aaronide priests are listed first, followed by the remaining Qohathites, the Gershonites, and the Merarites. The account concludes with numerical summaries (21:41–42) and promise-fulfillment notices (21:43–45). LXX Josh 21:42a-d presents an additional commentary, centering on the figure of Joshua himself. Taking the presentation in Joshua as a reference point, the contrast with Chronicles may be summarized in the table above.

Comparison between the two texts sheds light on the distinctive features of the Chronicler's compositional technique. Chronicles lacks the extensive introduction of Joshua and contains only a brief introduction of its own ("these are their places of residence according to their settlements within their territories"; v. 39a). Chronicles also lacks many (but not all) of the summaries found in Joshua (21:4, 26, 33, 40, 41–42, 43–45). What the author includes and excludes from his *Vorlage* is revealing. Having provided his alternative, though terse introduction to the introduction found in Joshua, the author of Chronicles skips the introductory enumeration of Levitical towns awarded to the Qohathite Aaronides (Josh 21:4). He also skips, at least for the moment, the introductory tallies of Levitical towns awarded to the other Qohathites (21:5), the Gershonites (21:6), and the Merarites

(21:7), as well as the summary (21:8) and the introduction to the Levitical towns in Judah, Simeon, and Benjamin (21:9). Instead, the author immediately quotes the list of towns set apart for the Qohathite Aaronides (1 Chr 6:39b–45a//Josh 21:10–18). It is important to note that contrary to his pattern elsewhere, he also includes the numerical summary of thirteen Qohathite Aaronide towns found in his source (1 Chr 6:45b//Josh 21:19). This explains why he later omits the introductory overview of the Qohathite Aaronide settlements (Josh 21:4), when he returns to the earlier material in his source (Josh 21:4–8). This overview was unnecessary to the Chronicler's purposes because it duplicates the content of the summary (1 Chr 6:45b//Josh 21:19).

Having pushed the detailed listing of the Qohathite Aaronide settlements to the foreground of his own presentation (1 Chr 6:39b–45), he returns to the earlier sections of his source. He proceeds with the introductory tallies and summary for the remaining three groups to be covered: the other Qohathites, the Gershonites, and the Merarites (Josh 21:5–8//1 Chr 6:46–49). Because he includes the introductory tallies for the remaining Qohathites (v. 46), the Gershonites (v. 47), and the Merarites (v. 48), he can omit the summary tallies for them occurring after the actual town lists: the Qohathites (Josh 21:26), the Gershonites (21:33), and the Merarites (21:40). In this respect, the Chronicler is absolutely consistent. He has provided only one summary tally for each of the four groups in the Levitical towns account. But the makeup and placement of those summaries vary and his procedure can only be explained by recourse to the organization of his source (an older and shorter version of Josh 21). One could conceivably argue a related position, namely, that the one particular numerical summary, appearing in connection with the detailed listing of the Qohathite Aaronide towns (1 Chr 6:45b), and the three other numerical summaries, appearing as part of the introductory overview of the inheritances of the remaining Qohathites, the Gershonites, and the Merarites (1 Chr 6:46–48), were the only relevant summaries found in Joshua's Chronicles-like *Vorlage*. In this scenario, the other summaries were all later added by the authors of Joshua. If this were true, the author's *Vorlage* of Joshua was significantly briefer than either MT or LXX Joshua.

The summary introduction to the towns held by each of the three remaining Levitical groups (1 Chr 6:46–49//Josh 21:5–8) forms a natural bridge to the actual lists of the Levitical towns for the remaining Qohathites, the Gershonites, and the Merarites (1 Chr 6:51–66). In this context, the Chronicler can follow the pattern set by his source, omitting some summaries in the process (see above). But there is one problem: his source text also features an introduction to the Qohathite settlements in Judah, Simeon, and Benjamin (Josh 21:9). The writer includes this introduction within the context of his own presentation (1 Chr 6:50), but its position is odd because the enumeration of these settlements has already occurred (6:39b–45). One can argue that the notice of 1 Chr 6:50(//Josh 21:9) takes on a new meaning, functioning more as a summary than as part of a larger preamble to the list of the Levitical towns in Judah, Simeon, and Benjamin (Josh 21:10–19). Nevertheless, the rearrangement of source material has resulted in some awkwardness. In conformity with its source (Josh 21:9), 1 Chr 6:50 speaks of specifying certain towns by name, but the relevant towns appear earlier. As the text stands, the towns go unspecified in the following verses (1 Chr 6:51–66). Instead, the subject switches to the remaining allotments for the three Levitical phratries.

The question of whether this incongruity resulted from the Chronicler's own "infelicitous" editing (Curtis and Madsen 1910: 137) or from the work of a later editor (Benzinger 1901; Rudolph 1955: 61, 63; R. Braun 1986: 99–100) is debated. If one elects the latter option, one could still contend that an author of Josh 21 employed an earlier account of 1 Chr 6 for his own presentation. But such a position implicitly concedes a number of problems with the presentation in 6:39–66. The larger point remains that Chronicles exhibits a text that is typologically inferior to Joshua in its sequence of pericopes. It is improbable that the somewhat disjointed presentation of Chronicles is historically antecedent to the well-ordered sequence of Joshua.

We have seen that the rearrangement of material in Chronicles places the Aaronide inheritance in the foreground of the Chronicler's presentation. This raises the larger question of why he reworks his source. If the writer's *Vorlage* followed a logical order, why did he rearrange his source? In my judgment, the new sequence highlights the assignments given to the sons of Aaron, contextualized within the Qohathite phratry, and honors the distinction that the Chronicler observes between the tribe of Levi and those specific members (Aaronides) of this tribe who serve as priests. Such a reordering brings the Chronicler's text into line with his presentation of the Levitical genealogies. There he lists one particular priestly succession—the sons of Qohath through Amram and Aaron (5:27–41)—before discussing the other descendants of Levi, including the other Qohathites (6:7–33).

Given the comparative evidence *vis-à-vis* Josh 21 as well as the larger dynamic of the Chronicler's literary presentation of the Levitical genealogies, one is led to offer a fourth view of the relationship between Joshua and Chronicles, in many respects a combination of the first and second views mentioned above. The author was dependent upon an earlier form of Joshua. It is unlikely that the Chronicler and the author(s) of Josh 21 were simply drawing from a common source (view 2), because the Chronicler's text bears a number of traits that show the influence of the formulation and structure of Joshua. Nevertheless, the Chronicler's source was not identical to either MT or LXX Joshua. There are too many incidental discrepancies to warrant such a conclusion. Many of these variants do not constitute tendentious alterations of a standard and fixed text, but form genuine witnesses in their own right to the development of different text types extant in the history of the biblical writings. In this respect, Auld, Rofé (1982), Ulrich (1994; 1996), and others are justified in positing multiple stages in the growth of the text of Joshua.

Even though Chronicles is indebted to an earlier and shorter form of Joshua, each book has developed the list of Levitical towns in its own way. All three major witnesses (MT Joshua, LXX* Joshua, and MT and LXX Chronicles) exhibit textual corruption in the form of haplography, dittography, and graphic confusion (especially in place-names). In some cases, the witnesses to Chronicles offer a more primitive reading than can be found among the witnesses to Joshua. In these instances, Chronicles can be used to reconstruct an earlier form of Joshua. But the converse is also true. In some cases, the witnesses to Joshua offer a more primitive reading than can be found in Chronicles. In these instances, material in MT or LXX Joshua may be used to recover an older form of Chronicles. In short, comparison between the elaborately developed Josh 21 and the shorter 1 Chr 6 sheds light on the development of both texts.

COMMENT

Explaining how the Levites fit into the political and social structure of ancient Israel (Spencer 1992: 311) may be part of the reason the writer selected and rearranged the material of Joshua 21 into his larger presentation. But one should ask further questions: What functions did this material, whatever its origins might be, play in the time in which the author wrote? How important are the Levitical towns to his larger discussion? Is this an isolated interest or one germane to the presentation of the monarchy? It is important to begin by observing that the author ties the Levites to the land, just as he does with the other tribes. As with the other Israelite tribes, information about kinship relationships is coupled with information about settlement history. This in itself tells us something about the author's conception of the Levites. The wide geographical dispersion of this group suggests that its mission encompasses more than sacrifice. Indeed, most of the towns in the list are not "shrine cities" (Haran 1961b: 51–53). Traditional cult centers, such as Bethel, Bethleḥem, Dan, Gilgal, Mizpah, Shiloh, and Jerusalem, do not appear. Nor does the Chronicler add them. In this respect, the Levitical town list coheres with the other dimensions of the presentation in Chronicles. Elsewhere the Levites are more than cultic officiants. The author endorses the mandate for centralization of scarifice, in conformity with the legislation of Deut 12, but he does not interpret this legislation as entailing the centralization of Israel's priestly tribe. The Levites have administrative, judicial, and political responsibilities (e.g., 1 Chr 26:29–32; 2 Chr 17:7–9; 19:4–9). Ezekiel speaks of establishing a holy district for the sanctuary, the priests, and the Levites (45:1–5; 48:8–22), but Chronicles does not limit the priests and Levites to such a sacred preserve.

The association between the Levites and a variety of settlements is not unique to the genealogical section of the Chronicler's work. When David, early in his reign, takes counsel with the commanders of the thousands and hundreds to retrieve the Ark, he beckons "the entire assembly of Israel" to send out far and wide to their kin, including "the priests and the Levites in the towns of their open lands," that they might all gather themselves to Jerusalem (1 Chr 13:1–3). What is interesting in this passage is not only the reference to Levites living within their towns and open lands, exactly as the Levitical town list suggests, but also the more specific conception of the Levites as residing "in all the regions of Israel" (1 Chr 13:2). The topic of Levitical settlements reemerges in the presentation of the division of the kingdom following Solomon's death. In describing the consequences of the northern secession, the writer observes that priests and Levites throughout Israel, having abandoned their open lands and estates because Jeroboam and his sons excluded them from serving as priests to Yhwh, presented themselves to Reḥoboam from all of their territories (2 Chr 11:13–14). These northern refugees who migrated south are said to have strengthened the kingdom of Judah and Reḥoboam (2 Chr 11:17). One encounters a traditional picture of Levites inhabiting a variety of settlements throughout the north and south, then being disrupted by political upheaval. A final reference to the Levitical towns occurs in Ḥezeqiah's reforms. Following the neglect of the Jerusalem Yahwistic cult by Aḥaz, the new allocation of gifts and tithes to the Levites and priests involves distributing such portions to "each and every one of their towns with open lands" (2 Chr 31:19).

The language used in Chronicles to describe the Levitical communities is interesting. Their territories *(gbwlm)* are described in terms of both open land *(migrāš*; 1 Chr 6:40; 13:2; 2 Chr 11:14; 31:19) and property (*ʾăḥuzzâ*; 1 Chr 9:2; 2 Chr 11:14). The former term is, of course, reminiscent of the Levitical town list, but the latter may be compared with other writings. The authors of Deut 18:1–2 forbid Levitical priests from having any allotted portion *(ḥeleq)* or inheritance *(naḥălâ)*, because Yhwh is their inheritance *(naḥălâ)*. Similarly, Num 18:20 prohibits Aaron from having any landed inheritance *(bĕʾarṣām lōʾ tinḥāl)* and from having any allotted portion *(ḥēleq)*, because Yhwh is his inheritance *(naḥălâ)* and portion *(ḥēleq)*. The (Priestly) writer of Josh 14:4 speaks of the Levites not being given any portion *(ḥēleq)* except the towns for them to inhabit, along with their open lands *(migrĕšêhem)*. Joshua 21 employs the term *ʾăḥuzzâ* to describe the estates of Caleb and of Israel as a whole (vv. 12, 41), but not to describe what is granted to the three Levitical phratries (see also Josh 22:4, 9, 19).

As might be expected, the book of Ezekiel puts matters somewhat differently. Ezekiel 44:28 forbids the priests both from having any inheritance *(naḥălâ)*, because Yhwh is their inheritance *(naḥălâ)*, and from having any estate *(ʾăḥuzzâ)*, because Yhwh is their estate (*ʾăḥuzzâ*; cf. Ezek 45:6; 48:12, 18). Here, a distinction is made between priests and Levites. The strip of land given to the Levites within the holy district is explicitly called an "estate" (*ʾăḥuzzâ*; Ezek 45:5) and the "estate of the Levites" *(ʾăḥuzzat hallĕwiyyim)*. The text seems to assume that this possession will contribute to Levitical sustenance in the same way that the produce of the "estate of the city" *(ʾăḥuzzat hāʿîr)* will sustain the inhabitants of this holy city (Ezek 45:6–7; 48:18; Haran 1961b: 162).

The Jubilee legislation of Lev 25 also addresses the ancestral rights of the Levites, employing the term *ʾăḥuzzâ* to describe Levitical houses. (Ezekiel 45:4 also allows priests to have houses, but it does not speak of such domiciles as their property.) The Jubilee laws speak of Levitical dwellings within Levitical towns as an estate (*ʾăḥuzzâ*; perhaps to be understood as a "surrogate possession" [Levine 1989: 177]) that can be released and redeemed in a Jubilee Year (Lev 25:32–33). But although this legislation enables Levites to redeem houses in the towns of their possession *(ʾăḥuzzâ)*, it forbids the sale of their open lands *(migrāš)*, because such territories are their "estate forever" (*ʾăḥuzzat ʿôlām*; Lev 25:34). In other words, because the Jubilee measures treat Levitical houses, but not open lands, as a type of estate (*ʾăḥuzzâ*), these houses fall under *ʾăḥuzzâ* legislation. The Levites' landlessness cannot be used to deprive them of what holdings they might have. No property of theirs within their towns can be permanently alienated.

One could claim that the Chronicler's presentation, insofar as it speaks of Levitical towns, open lands, and possessions, merely reflects the time in which he lived. Certainly, his stance is echoed in Nehemiah (11:3//1 Chr 9:2), which depicts the Israelites, priests, Levites, temple servants, and sons of Solomon's servants living in various towns, "each in his own estate" (*ʾăḥuzzâ*). Nehemiah 12:29 speaks of Levitical villages (*ḥăṣērîm*) in Geba and Azmaveth outside Jerusalem. The book of Malachi also presupposes the existence of rural Levites (2:1–9). But if Levites had property (*ʾăḥuzzâ*) in the Persian period, whether conceived broadly as agricultural land or more narrowly as houses within Levitical towns, it is certainly relevant that the Chronicler defends this practice, perhaps with a view to the visions of Ezekiel, by recourse to preexilic precedent. Even in the case of Israel's sacerdotal orders, there are clear ties to the land, which extend far beyond the hallowed precincts of the Jerusalem Temple. In this respect, the debate about whether the original list of Levitical towns is utopian or realistic is largely beside the point. In a Persian period context most of the Levitical towns lie outside of Yehud. Indeed, even some of the Levitical towns allotted to Judah and Simeon lie outside Yehud's borders.

But it is precisely the disjunction between the array of Levitical towns and Achaemenid era realities that may be critical to appreciating the inclusion of this list within Chronicles. The writer's (re-)presentation of the Levitical towns reaffirms the ancestral rights of the three major Levitical phratries to inhabit these towns and villages. From his perspective, "these are their places of residence." Dissociating these sites from an entry into the land, Chronicles depicts the sundry towns as an intrinsic part of the Levitic heritage. In this manner, the author makes his own contribution to the Levitic legacy. He renews in writing what at best only partially exists in reality.

X. Issachar, Benjamin, Dan, Naphtali, Manasseh, Ephraim, and Asher (7:1–40)

Genealogy of Issachar

1 Belonging to the descendants of Issachar: Tola, Puah, Jashub, and Shimron—
four. 2 The sons of Tola: Uzzi, Rephaiah, Jeriel, Jaḥmai, Ibsam, Shemuel—heads
of their ancestral houses. Belonging to Tola were valiant warriors, according to
their lineages; their muster in David's days was 22,600. 3 The sons of Uzzi: Izraḥiah. The sons of Izraḥiah: Michael, Obadiah, Joel, and Isshiah—five. All of
them were heads. 4 Together with them, by their lineages according to their ances-

tral houses, were the detachments of the military campaign: 36,000, for they had many wives and children. [5]And their kinsmen, according to all of the families of Issachar: 87,000 valiant warriors enrolled by their genealogy.

A Genealogy of Benjamin

[6]The descendants of Benjamin: Bela, Becher, and Jediael—three. [7]The sons of Bela: Ezbon, Uzzi, Uzziel, Jerimoth, and Iri—five, heads of ancestral houses, valiant warriors. And their enrollment by their genealogy was 22,034. [8]The sons of Becher: Zemariah, Joash, Eliezer, Elioenai, Omri, Jeremoth, Abijah, Anathoth, and Alameth. All these were the sons of Becher [9]and they were enrolled by their genealogy according to their lineages—heads of their ancestral houses, valiant warriors—20,200. [10]The sons of Jediael: Bilhan. The sons of Bilhan: Jeush, Benjamin, Ehud, Chenaanah, Zethan, Tarshish, and Aḥishaḥar. [11]All these were sons of Jediael, heads of their ancestral houses, valiant warriors—17,200, going out on the military campaign.

Genealogies of Dan and Naphtali

[12]The descendants of Dan: Ḥushim his son—one. [13]The descendants of Naphtali: Jaḥziel, Guni, Jezer, and Shallum, the descendants of Bilhah.

A Genealogy of Manasseh

[14]The descendants of Manasseh: Asriel to whom his Aramaean concubine gave birth; she [also] gave birth to Machir the father of Gilead. The name of his sister was Hammolecheth. [15]And Machir took a wife. The name of the firstborn was Gilead and the name of the second was Zelopheḥad. And Zelopheḥad had daughters. [16]Maacah the wife of Gilead gave birth to a son and she named him Peresh. The name of his brother was Sheresh and his sons were Ulam and Reqem. [17]The sons of Ulam: Bedan. These were the sons of Gilead son of Machir son of Manasseh. [18]And his sister Hammolecheth gave birth to Ishhod, Abiezer, Maḥlah, and Shemida. [19]And the sons of Shemida were Aḥian, Shechem, Ḥeleq, and Aniam.

A Genealogy of Ephraim

[20]The descendants of Ephraim: Shuthelaḥ, his son Bered, his son Taḥath, his son Eleadah, his son Taḥath, [21]his son Zabad, his son Shuthelaḥ. As for Ezer and Elead, the men of Gath (those born in the land) killed them, because they had gone down to take their cattle. [22]Ephraim their father grieved many days and his brothers came to comfort him. [23]Then he had sexual relations with his wife, who conceived and gave birth to a son. She named him Beriah, because a calamity had occurred in his house. [24]His daughter was Sheerah. She built Lower and Upper Beth-ḥoron and Uzzen-sheerah. [25]His son Rephah, his son Resheph, his son Telaḥ, his son Taḥan, [26]his son Ladan, his son Ammihud, his son Elishama, [27]his son Non, his son Joshua.

The Settlements of Manasseh and Ephraim

[28]Their estates and settlements were Bethel and its dependencies, and on the east Naaran, and on the west Gezer and its dependencies, Shechem and its dependencies as far as Ayyah and its dependencies. [29]And under the control of the descendants of Manasseh: Beth-shean and its dependencies, Taanach and its dependencies, Megiddo and its dependencies, Dor and its dependencies. In these resided the descendants of Joseph, son of Israel.

A Genealogy of Asher

30 The descendants of Asher: Imnah, Ishvah, Ishvi, Beriah—four, and their sister Seraḥ. 31 The sons of Beriah: Ḥeber and Malchiel, who was the father of Birzaith. 32 Ḥeber sired Japhleṭ, Shomer, Ḥotham, and their sister Shua. 33 The sons of Japhleṭ: Pasach, Bimhal, and Ashvath. These were the sons of Japhleṭ. 34 The sons of Shomer his brother: Rohgah, Ḥubbah, and Aram. 35 The sons of Ḥotham his brother: Zophaḥ, Imna, Shelesh, and Amal. 36 The sons of Zophaḥ: Suaḥ, Ḥarnepher, and Shual. The sons of Imna: 37 Bezer, Hod, and Shamma. The sons of Shelesh: Ithran and Beera. 38 The sons of Jether: Jephunneh, Pispa, and Ara. 39 The sons of Amal: Araḥ, Ḥanniel, and Rizia. 40 All of these sons of Asher were heads of their ancestral houses, select men, valiant warriors, heads of the chieftains. They were enrolled by their genealogy as [fit] for the military campaign. Their muster was 26,000 men.

Textual Notes

7:1. "Belonging to the descendants of" *(wlbny)*. So MT and LXX^{BL} (maximum differentiation). On the *l-* of introduction, used in LBH, see GKC, §143e. LXX^{AN} *(kai houtoi huioi)*, Syr., Vg., and Arab. read *w'lh bny*.

"Issachar." See the 2nd TEXTUAL NOTE to 2:1.

"Tola (and) Puah, Jashub and Shimron." So MT and SP Gen 46:13. MT Gen 46:13 "Tola and Puah and Jashub and Shimron."

"Puah" (פוּאָה). So MT 7:1, SP Gen 46:13, SP Num 26:23, and MT Judg 10:1 (פוּאָה). MT Gen 46:13 פֻּוָּה; Num 26:23 פֻּוָּה.

"Jashub" *(yāšûb)*. So Qere, LXX, Vg., SP Gen 46:13, and MT Num 26:24. Kethib *yāšîb*; MT Gen 46:13 *yôb* (erroneous).

"Shimron." So also Gen 46:13 and Num 26:24. Judg 10:1 speaks of Tola as a son of Puah, living *(yšb)* in Shamir.

7:2. "Jaḥmai." So MT. LXX^{AN} *Iemou*; LXX^{B} *Eiikan*; LXX^{L} (and Arm.) *Iamin*; Syr. *lḥmy*.

"belonging to Tola" (לתולע). So MT and LXX. Omitted by NJPS.

7:3. "sons." See the TEXTUAL NOTE to 2:8.

"Uzzi." So MT and LXX^{L}. LXX^{B} and c$_{2}$ *Zeirrei*; Syr.^{A} *'wzr.*

"the sons of Izraḥiah" *(yzrḥyh)*. The suggestion that *yzrḥyh* is a dittography influenced by *ḥmšh* (Rudolph 1955: 64) has little to commend it.

"Michael" *(myk'l)*. So MT and LXX *M(e)ichaēl*. Syr. *mlk'yl.*

"five" *(ḥmšh)*. So MT and LXX. Syr. and Arab. have the expected "four."

7:4. "according to their lineages." Rudolph (1955: 64) deletes as a gloss from vv. 4 and 9.

"detachments" *(gĕdûdê)*. So MT *(lectio difficilior)*. Some of the versions read the more common "warriors" *(gibbôrê)*.

"military campaign" (צבא מלחמה). So MT. LXX παρατάξασθαι εἰς πόλεμον, "to be arrayed for battle;" Vg. *accincti ad proelium.* See also the 2nd TEXTUAL NOTE to v. 40.

7:5. "and their kinsmen." Reading with MT *(wʾḥyhm).* Some emend to *mʾḥyhm,* hence "[4]for they had more wives and children [5]than their kinsmen." But such an emendation renders the beginning of v. 5 *(lkl)* most awkward.

"Issachar." See the 2nd TEXTUAL NOTE to 2:1.

"valiant warriors" *(gbwry ḥylym).* On the late construction, see also v. 40 and GKC, §124q.

"enrolled by their genealogy" *(htyḥśm).* Omitting MT's concluding *lkl* (dittography from earlier in v. 5). LXX[B] *ho arithmos autōn tōn pantōn,* "(this was) their number of them all;" LXX[L] *hē genealogia autōn pantōn,* "their entire genealogy."

7:6. "descendants of Benjamin" *(bny bnymn).* So LXX[L] *(huioi de Beniamin),* Syr., Tg., Vg., and Arab. MT *bnymn* has suffered haplography *(homoioarkton).* On the question of whether this verse originally introduced the tribe of Zebulun, see the NOTE to vv. 6–11.

"Bela." So MT. Lacking in LXX*.

"Becher." LXX[B] *Abeira;* LXX[AN] *Bochor;* c *Bōchor.* Cf. Gen 46:21; Num 26:38; 1 Chr 8:1 "Ashbel" *(ʾašbēl).* LXX Gen 46:21 *Chobor* (metathesis).

"and Jediael—three." So MT, followed by LXX *(Adeiēl).* Gen 46:21 *(gērāʾ),* Num 26:38 *(ʾăḥîrām),* and 1 Chr 8:1 *(ʾaḥrāḥ)* read differently. The lists of Gen 46:21, Num 26:38–39, and 1 Chr 8:1–3 mention additional persons, although the names in these lists do not all comport with each other.

7:7. "Iri." So MT. LXX *Ouria.*

7:8. "Zemariah" *(zĕmaryâ).* So LXX[L] *(Zamaria)* and cursives ag (*Zamarias;* Noth 1928: 242). Cf. LXX[B] and c_2 *Amarias.* MT "Zemirah" *(Zĕmîrâ)* has suffered metathesis.

"Elioenai" (אליועיני). See the TEXTUAL NOTE to 8:20.

"Abijah" *(ʾbyh).* Thus MT. LXX[B] *Abioud.*

"Alameth" *(ʿālāmet).* LXX[B] *Gemeeth;* LXX[A] *Elmethem;* LXX[L] (cf. Syr.) *(A)lamōth.* On the name, see the 2nd TEXTUAL NOTE to 6:45.

7:9. "and they were enrolled by their genealogy." LXX[B] *kai ho arithmos autōn,* "and their number"; LXX[L] *kai hē genealogia autōn,* "and their genealogy." See the 4th TEXTUAL NOTE to v. 5.

"20,200." So MT and LXX[AB]. Cursives *b*b′y, Syr. 22,200. Presuming a haplography in MT, from *ʿśrym (w)šynym* to *ʿśrym,* Freedman (personal communication) would read with LXX[L] and Syr.

7:10. "sons." See the TEXTUAL NOTE to 2:8.

"Jeush" *(yĕʿûš).* So Qere, many of the versions, and 1 Chr 1:35. Kethib *yĕʿîš.*

"Tarshish." Thus MT and LXX[AN]. LXX[B] *Ramessai.*

7:11. "heads." So LXX *archontes* (= *rʾšy*) and Vg. *principes.* MT *lrʾšy* evinces dittography after *ydyʿʾl.*

7:12. "the descendants of Dan." The restoration is conjectural. MT "Shuppim and Ḥuppim" (cf. MT Num 26:39 "Shuppam" and "Ḥuppam;" LXX[B] *Sapphein kai Happhein*). MT continues "the sons of Ir" *(ʿîr;* cf. LXX[A] *Ōra;* LXX[L] *Ierimouth).* The emendation is based on several considerations. First, the segmented genealogy of vv. 6–11 is a self-contained whole (*pace* Williamson 1973: 375–79). By contrast, the genealogy of v. 12 is fragmentary and corrupt. Second, the brief genealogy which follows (v. 13) deals with Naphtali and concludes "the sons of Bilhah." The two sons of Bilhah are, of course, Dan and Naphtali (Gen 46:23–25). Third, Ḥushim (see next TEXTUAL NOTE) is listed as the son of Dan in Gen 46:23. Hence, the emendation to "the descendants of Dan" *(bny dn)* has much to commend it. See also Rudolph (1955: 66) and Japhet (1993a: 174).

"Ḥushim" *(ḥušim)*. So MT. Cf. MT Gen 46:23 *(ḥušîm)*. Perhaps lacking in LXX^{B}, but Rudolph (1955: 68) contends that LXX^{B} *(huioi) Rhaōm* is a corruption of *ir Asōm* (= *ʿyr hšwm*). LXX^{A} *Hōra Asob*; LXX^{L} *Ierimouth Iessoud*; cursive a and LXX Gen 46:23 *Hasom* (= *ḥāšōm*?). The discrepancy between Gen 46:23 *ḥušîm* and Num 26:42 *šûḥām* reflects a metathesis of *šîn* and *ḥêt*.

"his son" (= *bnw*). So LXX. MT "sons" *(bny)*. The *wāw/yôd* confusion is common, especially in this chapter (vv. 7, 17, 20, 23, 25, 26, 27, 29, 33, 36). One might think of restoring *šwḥm* before *bnw*, but the text on which the emendation is based (MT Num 26:42 "Shuḥam;" LXX *Sami*) may have undergone metathesis (see previous TEXTUAL NOTE).

"one" *(ʾḥd)*. MT "Aḥer" *(ʾḥr)*, evidently a PN, but a *hapax legomenon*. LXX^{B} *Aer*; LXX^{AN} *Aor*. Lacking in LXX^{L}. Given that Gen 46:23 ends with Ḥushim, it may be best to read "one" *(ʾḥd)*, hence "his son—one" (a *dālet/rêš* confusion). For other numerical summaries in this ch. see vv. 1, 6, and 7. Williamson (1973; 1982b: 78) prefers to reconstruct Benjaminite "Addar" *(ʾdr)*, a slip for "Ard" *(ʾrd*; Gen 46:21; Num 26:40).

7:13. "Jaḥziel" *(yḥṣyʾl)*. Many MSS and Tg. lack the second *yôd*. So also Gen 46:24; Num 26:48 *(yḥṣʾl)*. LXX^{B} *Ieisiēl*.

"Shallum." So MT 7:13, SP Gen 46:24, and SP Num 26:49. MT Gen 46:24 and Num 26:49 "Shillem."

"Bilhah." Thus MT. LXX^{B} *Balam*; LXX^{A} *Balla*; LXX^{L} *Balaam huios autou*.

7:14–19. "descendants of Manasseh." This segmented genealogy is not found in earlier biblical writings, even though some of the names are familiar from other Manassite contexts (Gen 50:23; Num 26:28–34; 27:1–7; 36:2–12; Josh 17:1–6). As Rothstein and Hänel (1927: 139–44) have observed in most detail, this genealogy evinces many signs of corruption. First, the syntax of the beginning of the genealogy is rough. "Asriel" (אשׂריאל) appears as the only offspring of Manasseh, but he does not appear again. In Num 26:30–31 "Asriel" is a son of Gilead. Second, there is a tension between the introduction (v. 14b) and the summary (v. 17b), on the one hand, and the content of the genealogy in vv. 15–17a, on the other hand. The two do not mesh. Both the introduction and the summary mention Gilead, but the genealogy itself seems to trace the offspring of Machir through his son Sheresh (v. 16), his grandson Ulam (v. 17), and his great-grandson Bedan (v. 17). Hence, the conclusion that "these were the sons of Gilead" (v. 17) is odd. Third, there are problems within the genealogy itself. Maacah is listed as both the sister (v. 15) and the wife of Machir (v. 16). Zelopheḥad appears as "the second" (v. 15), but there is no first. Finally, the sons of Shemida (v. 19) do not have any relation to the lineages that precede them (vv. 14–18). In brief, the text is confused in both

MT and LXX and needs to be reconstructed. The following TEXTUAL NOTES attempt to resolve some problems, but others remain.

7:14. "Asriel to whom" *(ʾśryʾl ʾšr)*. So MT. It is possible to construe "Asriel" as a dittography before *ʾšr yldh* (Kittel 1895: 61), although the similarity between the forms is not perfect. Cf. Num 26:31; Josh 17:2; 1 Chr 4:16.

"she (also) gave birth" (ילדת). Cursive y and Tg. supply the expected *wāw* (וילידת).

"the name of his sister was Hammolecheth." Following Japhet (1993a: 176), I am transposing this phrase from v. 15 (according to sense).

"his sister." So MT. One Heb. MS reads "his wife." Some propose "their sister," based on LXX^{L} and Tg.

"Hammolecheth" *(hmlkt)*. Along with many commentators, I emend based on the testimony of v. 18. MT "Maacah" *(mʿkh)*; LXX* *Moōcha*. Others insert "and the sons of Ḥepher the firstborn" (Num 26:33; Josh 17:3), but according to these earlier texts Ḥepher was the father of Zelopheḥad. Hence, referring to Ḥepher as the firstborn does not make sense.

7:15. "and Machir." Based on v. 17 ("these were the sons of Gilead"), some (e.g., *BHK*; Japhet 1993a: 176) emend to "and Gilead." But Machir appears again in MT 1 Chr 7:16, and it seems unlikely that MT is in error both times.

"took a wife." MT adds "for Ḥuppim and for Shuppim," a gloss (cf. v. 12). It is possible that a phrase such as "and her name was PN" (*wšmh* PN) has dropped out of the text, but it is unlikely that the name was "Maacah" (*mʿkh*; *pace* NAB). See below and vv. 16 and 18 (cf. Num 26:30–32; Josh 17:2).

"the name of the firstborn was Gilead" *(wšm hbkwr glʿd)*. My restoration is based on three factors: the existence of "the second" later in the verse, indicating that something has dropped out of the text, the double mention of Gilead being the son of Machir (vv. 14, 17), and the probability of a haplography *(homoioarkton* from to *wšm* to *wšm)*.

"the second" *(hšny)*. So MT. Some Heb. MSS (cf. LXX^{B}) read *hšnyt*. Others (e.g., Curtis and Madsen 1910: 152–53) emend to "and the name of his brother" *(wšm ʾḥyw)*.

"Zelopheḥad had daughters." Thus MT and LXX^{AN}. Lacking in LXX^{B}, perhaps due to haplography (Allen 1974b: 135).

7:16. "Gilead." The emendation is based on v. 17. MT and LXX *(Macheir)* both read "Machir."

"and she named him Peresh." So MT and LXX^{L}. Lacking in LXX^{B} due to haplography *(homoioteleuton* from *prš* to *šrš)*.

7:16–17. "and his sons were Ulam and Reqem. (And) the sons of Ulam." So MT. LXX^{B} ("his son Ulam") has suffered haplography (*homoioteleuton* from Ulam to Ulam). On the PN *ʾûlām* ("first one, leader"), see Noth (1928: 231).

7:17. "sons." See the TEXTUAL NOTE to 2:8.

7:18. "Hammolecheth." So MT. LXX^{ABN} *Malecheth*; LXX^{L} *Melchath*; Vg. *Regina*.

"Abiezer" *(ʾbʿzr)*. So also MT Josh 17:2. MT Num 26:30 "Iezer" *(ʾyʿzr)*; SP *ʾḥyʿzr*.

"(and) Maḥlah" *(w't mḥlh)*. LXX^B *kai ton Maela*; LXX^L *kai ton Maalath*. Lacking in Syr.

"and Shemida" *(w't šmydʿ)*. Restored on the basis of a haplography *(homoioarkton)* at the end of v. 18 "(and) Maḥlah" *(w't mḥlh)*, and before the beginning of v. 19, "and these were the sons of Shemida" *(wyhyw bny šmydʿ)*.

7:19. "Shemida" *(šmydʿ)*. The difference with LXX *Semeira* (= *šmyrʿ*) reflects a *dālet/rêš* confusion. Cf. MT Num 26:36 *šmydʿ*; LXX *Sumaer* (Wevers 1998: 443).

"Ḥeleq." So MT Num 26:30 (cf. LXX 26:34 *Cheleg*) and Josh 17:2. MT "Liqḥi" (LXX^B and c_2 *Lakeeim*) has undergone metathesis.

"Aniam" *('ănîʿām)*. LXX^B *Alialeim*; c_2 *Eliamein*.

7:20. "Bered" *(brd)*. Lacking in LXX^B. LXX^L *Rhaam*. Syr. and Arab. follow MT Num 26:35 *bkr*.

"his son Taḥath." Thus MT. The phrase is missing from a few Heb. MSS and from LXX^B. LXX^L *Thaath*. MT Num 26:35 *taḥan* (cf. SP *tḥm*; LXX *Tanach*; Wevers 1998: 445–46); LXX Gen 46:20 *Taam*.

"his son Eleadah" *('lʿdh bnw)*. So MT. LXX^B *huioi Laada*. Syr. *'ldʿ' bnw*.

"Taḥath." Thus MT. LXX^B *Noome*; LXX^{Aal} *Nomee*; LXX^L *Thaath*.

7:21. "Zabad" *(zābād)*. So MT and LXX^B *(Zabed)*. Na'aman (1991b: 107) emends to *bkr* (see the 1st TEXTUAL NOTE to v. 20) to create a symmetrical succession of names, but *zbd* and *bkr* share only one consonant and that consonant does not fall in the same position in both names.

"his son Shuthelaḥ." Thus MT. Lacking in LXX^{B*} due to haplography *(bnw* to *bnw)*. LXX^{AN} *Sōthele*.

"as for Ezer and Elead" *(wʿzr w'lʿd)*. Thus MT. LXX* lacks the initial *wāw*. Contrary to modern translations, the phrase should be interpreted as a *casus pendens* construction (Waltke and O'Connor, §4.7). First, the linear genealogical pattern "PN_1, his son PN_2, his son PN_3" ceases before Ezer and Elead. Second, the context (v. 22) dictates that Ezer and Elead must be either actual sons or grandsons (through Shuthelaḥ) of Ephraim and not several generations removed from him. Third, it seems more likely that the men of Gath killed two of Ephraim's sons (or grandsons) than that they killed all of Ephraim's male descendants (vv. 20–21a). These observations hold even if one follows NAB and transposes "those born in the land" (from later in the verse) to follow "Ezer and Elead."

"killed them." Thus MT and LXX^{AN}. LXX^B zc_2 "killed him."

7:23. "(and) she named him." Reading *wtqr'* with a few Heb. MSS, some Tg. MSS, Syr., and Arab. *(lectio difficilior)*. MT and LXX "he named" *(wyqr')*.

"in his house." Thus MT. LXX "in my house."

7:24. "She built Lower and Upper Beth-ḥoron." Thus MT. In this and in what follows, Syr. differs with MT and LXX* (Hogg 1901: 150–53). Syr. may represent a creative reinterpretation and expansion of an older tradition. It has "and his daughter was left [= שארה] at Lower and Upper Beth-ḥoron." Syr. also has this daughter curing (cf. MT רפה) both individuals and towns.

"and Uzzen-sheerah." So MT. LXX^B "and the sons of Ozan (were) Sheera" *(kai huioi Ozan Seēra)*.

7:25. "his son Resheph." So several Heb. MSS and LXX^{L}. MT "Resheph and Telaḥ" *(ršp wtlḥ).*

"his son Telaḥ." So MT. LXX* "Resheph and Telaḥ his sons." For "Telaḥ," LXX^{B} has *Thalees,* while LXX^{L} has *Thala.* With previous Resheph, Hogg (1901) restores an original "Shuthelaḥ" *(šwtlḥ > ršp wtlḥ).* Hogg and Rudolph posit an original reduplication of names in v. 25 from v. 20-(Shu)thelaḥ, Taḥath/n, Eleadah *(ʾlʿdh)*/Ladan *(lʿdn)*—but the parallels are not as close as one would like and certain names, such as Bered and Rephah, do not fit the pattern.

7:26. "Ladan" *(lʿdn).* Cf. MT Num 26:36 *lʿrn,* "belonging to Eran."

"his son Ammihud." LXX *huioi Amioueid,* "sons of Ammihud."

7:27. "Non" *(nôn).* LXX* *Nomu;* LXX^{L} *Noun.* The lemma of Vg. *(Nun)* assimilates toward the standard *nûn* (Exod 33:11 [LXX Ναυή]; Num 11:28; 13:8, 16; Judg 2:8; Neh 8:17).

7:28. "Naaran" *(naʿărān).* LXX *Naarnan.* LXX *Noaran;* MT Josh 16:7 *naʿărtâ.*

"Ayyah" (עַיָּה). So MT *(lectio difficilior).* Cf. LXX^{B} c_2 *Gaian.* The reading עַזָּה is reflected in many Heb. MSS, LXX^{AN} *(Gazēs),* some Tg. MSS, and Vg. *(Aza).* The discrepancy reveals a *zayin/yôd* confusion.

7:29. "and under the control." MT *wĕʿal-yĕdê* is often translated "also along the borders" (e.g., NJPS) in conformity with LXX *kai heōs horiōn,* "and until the borders." But *ʿl-yd* normally communicates subordination in Chronicles (e.g., 1 Chr 25:2, 3, 6; 26:28; 29:8; 2 Chr 12:10; 17:5, 16; 26:11, 13; 31:15; 34:10, 17). Hence, it is better to view MT as indicating possession (so also REB).

"Taanach and its dependencies." So MT. LXX^{B} adds *kai Bal(a)ad kai hai kōmai autēs.* It is possible that MT has suffered haplography (from *wbntyh* to *wbntyh*). MT Josh 17:11 has additional sites *(yiblĕʿām* and *ʿên-dōr),* but none corresponds to LXX's *Balaad.*

7:30. "Ishvah, Ishvi." Given that "Ishvah" does not appear in Num 26:44, dittography is likely. But if so, the error was already in the Chronicler's source (Gen 46:17).

"Beriah—four." MT simply reads "Beriah." The restoration is based on parallelism (vv. 1, 6, 7, 12) and the supposition of a haplography *(wbryʿh ʾrbʿh).*

31. "Birzaith" *(birzayit).* So Qere. Kethib *birzôt.* Some read *bĕrāzôt* or *bērĕzayit* (cf. LXX^{B} *Bēzayit;* Vg. *Barsaith;* Josephus *Bērzēthō* or *Bēthzēthō* [*Ant.* 12.397] and [*Bar*]*zētho* [*Ant.* 12.422]).

7:32. "Shomer." So MT and LXX^{ALN}. LXX^{B} *Samēr;* MT v. 34 *Šāmer;* Syr. *šmyr.* Noth (1928: 259) favors **šemer.*

7:33. "Bimhal" *(bimhāl).* LXX^{B} *Imabaēl;* LXX^{AN} *Bamaēl;* LXX^{L} *Baamath.*

"Ashvath" *(ʾašwāt).* Reading tentatively with MT (cf. LXX^{L} *Asouath*). Two Heb. MSS *ʾaśwāt;* LXX^{AB} *Aseith* (אשית<אשות*?) Vg. *Asoth**.

7:34–39a. These verses are missing from Syr.

7:34. "Shomer." So one Heb. MS, LXX^{ALN} *(Sōmēr),* e *Somēr,* Vg., and v. 32. MT *šāmer;* LXX^{B} *Semmēr.*

"his brother" *(ʾḥyw).* Reading *ʾḥy* with the following *wāw (wrwhgh).* MT "Aḥi" *(ʾḥy);* cf. LXX^{B} *Achiouia.*

"Rohgah." So Qere (and LXX*). Kethib *rôhăgâ.*

"(and) Ḥubbah" *(wĕḥubbâ)*. So Qere, a few Heb. MSS, LXX, and Vg. Kethib *yaḥbâ*.

7:35. "the sons of." So a few Heb. MSS, LXX^L, and Vg. MT "son."

"Ḥotham." Reading according to sense. On the name, see also 1 Chr 11:44. MT "Helem;" LXX^B *Balaam*; LXX^L *Iasoul*; Vg. *filii autem*. The two names "Ḥotham" and "Helem" likely refer to the same person (v. 32), but the precise cause of the textual confusion is difficult to determine.

7:36. "The sons of Imna" *(wbny ymnʿ)*. The reconstruction is based on the appearance of "Imna" (*ymnʿ*; v. 35). MT "and Beri and Imrah" *(wbry wymrh)*. LXX^B c_2 *Sabrei kai Imarē*.

7:37. "Hod" *(hôd)*. LXX^L *Iēoud* (= *ʾēhûd*).

"the sons of Shelesh" *(bĕnê šēleš)*. The reconstruction follows the segmentation pattern begun in v. 35 ("Zophaḥ, Imna, Shelesh, and Amal"). MT "Shilshah" *(šilšâ)*. LXX^B *Saleisa* (= *šalîšâ*?; cf. 1 Sam 9:4); Vg. *Salusa*. The term *bĕnê* has fallen out of MT by haplography after *šmʾ* and before *šlš* (Na'aman 1991b: 101).

"Ithran" *(ytrn)*. So MT. Some read "Jether" *(ytr)* with a few Heb. MSS (cf. 1 Chr 2:17, 32; 4:17), LXX (*Iether*; cf. v. 38), but both "Ithran" and "Jether" are probably variants of a longer PN with a divine element (e.g., "DN is preeminent").

7:39. "[and] the sons of Amal" (*ûbĕnê ʿāmāl*)." The reconstruction is based in part on the pattern of segmentation stemming from v. 35 ("Zophaḥ, Imna, Shelesh, and Amal"). MT "(and) the sons of Ulla" *(ûbĕnê ʿullāʾ)*. Cf. LXX^B *huioi ôla*; LXX^L *(I)ethran*. Lacking in Syr. "Ulla" is a *hapax legomenon*. Some emend to "Shua" (*šûʿā*; cf. v. 32) or "Shual" (*šûʿāl*; cf. v. 36), but "Amal" is more likely (Noth 1928: 253).

"Ḥanniel" *(ḥannîʾēl)*. Some editions *ḥănîʾēl*.

"and Rizia." So MT and LXX. Lacking in Syr.

7:40. "enrolled by their genealogy" *(htyḥśm)*. So MT. LXX *(ho) arithmos autōn* "their number." See the 4th TEXTUAL NOTE to v. 5.

"for the military campaign" *(bṣbʾ bmlḥmh)*. Thus MT. LXX εἰς παράταξιν τοῦ πολεμεῖν, "for the arranging (of soldiers) to do battle." See also the 2nd TEXTUAL NOTE to v. 4.

NOTES

7:1–5. The segmented genealogies of Issachar trace his descendants through his son Tola, his grandson Uzzi (v. 3), and his great-grandson Izraḥiah (v. 3). The descendants of collateral lines are not pursued (cf. Num 26:23–25; Judg 10:1). In the Song of Deborah, Issachar is loyal during a national crisis (Judg 5:15). In Chronicles the descendants of Issachar are distinguished individuals: "heads" of their ancestral houses and "valiant warriors" (vv. 2–3, 5). The tribe itself is strong and prolific. Its ranks of warriors numbered some 22,600 in the time of David (v. 2). The total of its military detachments, associated with the time of Izraḥiah, comes to an incredible 36,000 (v. 4). The tribe's census totals 87,000 (v. 5). On the piling up of huge numbers, see the NOTE to 12:38. The fantastic quantities exceed those for this tribe in the Priestly source: 54,400 (Num 1:29); 64,300 (Num 26:25).

7:1. "the descendants of Issachar." This list is drawn from the author's version of Gen 46:13 (cf. Num 26:23–24).

"Jashub" *(yāšûb)* also appears as a place-name in the Samaria ostraca (*yšb*; Davies, §3.048.3).

"four." A numerical summary the author adds to his source (Gen 46:13).

7:2–3. "The sons of Tola." This genealogy provided for Issachar's eldest son is unique to Chronicles.

7:2. "according to their lineages." The muster is conducted according to the principle of genealogy. Other censuses, also following the principle of lineage, are more specific about the mode of registration: "by the clans of their ancestral houses . . . head by head" (**לגלגלתם**; Num 1:18) or "you will muster by name" (**בשמות תפקד**; Num 4:32; Scolnic 1995: 39–58).

"in David's days." The United Monarchy, in particular the reign of David, is the context for a number of the tribal musters in the genealogies (2:15; 4:31; 6:16; 7:2; 9:22; cf. 21:1–3; 27:24). In this respect, the genealogies, like the narrative portions of the Chronicler's work, privilege the United Monarchy as a formative age in the history of Israel. The genealogies privilege the Ancestral epoch as the formative time of Israel's origins.

7:3. "all of them were heads." That is, of their ancestral houses (see v. 4).

7:4. "detachments of the military campaign" *(gĕdûdê ṣĕbāʾ milḥāmâ)*. Martial imagery appears repeatedly in this chapter, especially with respect to the tribes of Issachar, Benjamin, and Asher (vv. 2, 5, 7, 9, 11, 40). On the expression, compare **הבאים מצבא המלחמה**, "the ones coming from the military campaign" (Num 31:14); **יהוה צבאות מפקד צבא מלחמה**, "Yhwh of hosts is mustering a military campaign" (Isa 13:4); **בכל כלי צבא מלחמה**, "with all kinds of military weapons" (1 Chr 12:38); **גדוד צבא**, "army detachment" (Sir 36:31). See also the COMMENT.

7:6–11. "The descendants of Benjamin." Given the appearance of a more extensive genealogy of Benjamin in 1 Chr 8:1–40 and a more focused Benjaminite genealogy in 1 Chr 9:35–44, commentators, most extensively Curtis and Madsen (1910: 145–50), have made a plausible case for a disturbance in the text. One expects Zebulun (Gen 46:14; Num 26:26–27; 1 Chr 2:1) or Dan (1 Chr 2:2) to appear, but not Benjamin, who appears twice later. To this it can be added that Zebulun repeatedly appears elsewhere in the book as one of Israel's tribes (1 Chr 2:1; 6:48, 62; 12:34, 41; 2 Chr 30:10, 11, 18). Nevertheless, if a Zebulunite genealogy was originally part of 1 Chr 1–9, it is now lost to us. Attempts to rewrite vv. 6–12 as Zebulunite on the basis of Gen 46:14 have been executed more on the basis of literary-critical considerations than on the basis of text-critical evidence. None of Zebulun's three sons known from Gen 46:14 and Num 26:26 occurs in 1 Chr 7:6–12 and only with severe emendation can their names be made to appear in the text. Conversely, some of Benjamin's sons do occur (Gen 46:21; Num 26:38–39). To be sure, there are also features of the genealogy of vv. 6–11, that are unparalleled or problematic (TEXTUAL NOTES), but such features do not constitute a positive argument for a Zebulunite identity.

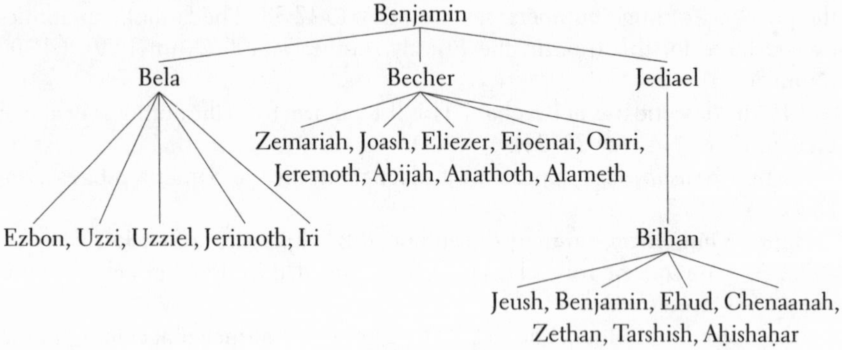

A GENEALOGY OF BENJAMIN

"Bela, Becher, and Jediael—three." The first two names also appear in the list of Gen 46:21, which goes on to mention a total of ten sons. Like Num 26:38–39, 1 Chr 8:1–2 mentions five sons, only one of which (Bela) appears here. "Jediael" does not appear in any of the three other Benjaminite lists (Gen 46:21; Num 26:38–41; 1 Chr 8:1–40).

7:7. "The sons of Bela." Again, the list (Ezbon, Uzzi, Uzziel, Jerimoth, Ir:) does not match those of Num 26:40 (Ard, Naaman) and 1 Chr 8:3–5 (Addar, Gera, Ehud, Abishua, Naaman, Aḥiaḥ, Gera, Shephuphan, Ḥuram).

"22,034." A number notable not for its magnitude, but for its specificity. Most of the musters in Chronicles, whether in the genealogies or in the narratives, involve high rounded numbers (NOTE to 12:38).

7:8. "The sons of Becher." In his segmented genealogy of Benjamin, the author systematically pursues the descendants of each of Benjamin's three sons: Bela (v. 7), Becher (vv. 8–9), and Jediael (vv. 10–11). For the first two sons the lineages are pursued for only one generation, but in the case of Jediael the lineage is pursued for two generations (see diagram above). The offspring of all three sons are described in valiant terms.

"Anathoth" was a Levitical Benjaminite town (Josh 21:18//1 Chr 6:45), the ancestral home of Jeremiah (1:1; 29:27; 32:7–9), and an oft-mentioned site in Persian period literature (Ezra 2:23; Neh 7:27; 1 Chr 6:45; 11:28; 12:3; 27:12; cf. Neh 10:19; 1 Chr 7:8). Anathoth was located about 5 km northeast of Jerusalem (Langston 1998: 158).

7:11. "17,200." In the Benjaminite genealogy (vv. 7, 9, 11), the census totals relate to particular subdivisions within the tribe. Unlike the situation with Issachar (v. 5) and Asher (v. 40), no total is given for the whole.

"going out on the military campaign." The descendants of Issachar, Benjamin, and Asher are all portrayed in military terms, but the heaviest concentration of such imagery is associated with Benjamin (vv. 7, 9, 11). This is in keeping with other biblical portrayals of the Benjaminites as adept, if not fierce, warriors (Gen 49:27; Judg 3:15, 21; 20:15–16, 20–21, 25; 1 Chr 7:11; 8:40; 12:2; Halpern 1988: 40–43).

7:12–13. "The descendants of Dan . . . The descendants of Naphtali." These two terse genealogies are taken from Gen 46:23–25 (cf. Num 26:42–43, 48–50). See the relevant TEXTUAL NOTES.

7:13. "The descendants of Bilhah" (בני בלהה). In Gen 46:23–25, both Dan and Naphtali are sons of Bilhah, the concubine of Jacob. It appears that the author has partially quoted Gen 46:25 (אלה בני בלהה), but omitted other details about Laban and Rachel. A partially published Qumran fragment (4QTNaph) relating to the *Testament of Naphtali* discusses the genealogy, birth, and naming of Bilhah (Stone 1996).

7:14–29. The author distinguishes between Manasseh (vv. 14–19) and Ephraim (vv. 20–27) as two separate entities, but he also considers the two tribes together (vv. 28–29). Genealogies of Manasseh (vv. 14–19) and Ephraim (vv. 20–27) are followed by a list of their towns and territories: Ephraim (v. 28) and Manasseh (v. 29).

a Descendants of Manasseh (vv. 14–19)
 b Descendants of Ephraim (vv. 20–27)
 b′ Towns of Ephraim (v. 28)
a′ Towns of Manasseh (v. 29)

The chiastic mode of presentation, a common literary device employed by the authors of Chronicles (Graham 1993; Kalimi 1995a), effectively ties the two tribes together. In his introduction to Reuben, the Chronicler comments that Jacob's birthright passed to Joseph, and not to Reuben (5:1–2). The importance of Joseph is reaffirmed in 7:29. On the Chronicler's particular presentation of Jacob's sons, see the NOTES to 2:1–2 and 5:1–2.

7:14–19. "The descendants of Manasseh." Given the distinction between the half-tribe of Manasseh, that is East Manasseh (1 Chr 5:23–24) in the Transjordan, and Manasseh proper, one might think that these lineages would focus on the latter. But the presentation of Manasseh in Chronicles is more complicated than such a traditional distinction allows (see following NOTES).

7:14. "Asriel" (אשׂריאל). According to Num 26:30–31, Asriel was a son of Gilead. In Josh 17:1–2 Machir, the father of Gilead, is the firstborn of Manasseh, but Asriel appears along with Abiezer, Ḥeleq, Shechem, Ḥepher, and Shemida, as the remaining (הנותרים) descendants of Manasseh. The name שׂראל occurs in the eighth-century Samaria ostraca (Davies, §§3.042.1; 3.048.1). See further the 2nd NOTE to v. 18.

"Aramaean concubine." According to LXX Gen 46:20, Manasseh's (unnamed) Syrian concubine gave birth to Machir *(Machir)*, who, in turn, sired Gilead *(Galaad)*. This tradition has been omitted in MT Gen 46:20 (Wevers 1993: 782–83), but it was evidently part of the Chronicler's *Vorlage* of Genesis (cf. Gen 50:23). The Aramaean associations of the patriarch Manasseh cannot be used either positively or negatively vis-à-vis the Exodus (*pace* Japhet 1993a: 178) because Manasseh's connection to his Syrian concubine and hence to his son Machir and to his grandson Gilead already appears in Genesis. In ancient genealogies the boundaries among personal names, ethnic names, and toponyms may be fluid. As a statement of relationships, the genealogical form can suggest social, ethnic, historical, and geographic connections among a variety of individuals, peoples, and places. The lack of explicit historical references, such as those to the Exodus, does not entail that the author denied that such events ever occurred. Absence of evidence is not necessarily evidence of absence. Similarly, the Manassite-Aramaean connections are suggestive (see next NOTE and 1st NOTE to v. 16), but the use of such genealogical conventions to suggest social and ethnic ties among groups does not constitute positive proof of continuous Manassite occupation of the land.

"Machir." There are different biblical traditions relating to this figure. In the Song of Deborah, Machir (and not Manasseh) appears as a willing ally of Deborah (Judg 5:14). But in LXX Gen 46:20 (see previous NOTE), Josh 17:1, Num 26:29, and Num 36:1, Machir appears, as he does in this verse, as Manasseh's eldest son and the father of Gilead. Given the geographical proximity of parts of Manasseh to the Aramaean states, it is not surprising that the author posits a number of links between them. Chronicles also posits connections between Machir and the tribe of Judah (1 Chr 2:21–23).

7:15. "Machir took a wife." This narrative genealogy manifests a different organization and geographic orientation of the Manassites from what one finds in other biblical contexts. In Josh 17:2–3 the majority of the descendants of Machir (and Gilead) settle west of the Jordan River: (Ab)iezer, Ḥeleq, Asriel, Shechem, Ḥepher, and Shemida. Indeed, these groups, along with Zelopheḥad's daughters, represent the entire tribe in the census of Num 26:29–33. To be sure, Josh 17:1 also notes that Gilead and Bashan were assigned to Machir, but he does not mention specific clans settling there. This deficiency is rectified by Chronicles, which provides genealogical information relating to the Manassite settlement of the Transjordan. The primary line, unattested elsewhere, is traced in the east from Manasseh through Machir (v. 14), Gilead, Peresh (v. 16), Ulam, and Bedan (v. 17). Some of the western affiliations of the tribe, expressed through the names of Zelopheḥad's daughters in other sources (Maḥlah, Noah, Ḥoglah, Milchah, and Tirzah), are not similarly stressed. Many of the names known from Joshua and Numbers are associated with Machir's sister Hammolecheth (Abiezer, Maḥlah, Ḥeleq [2nd TEXTUAL NOTE to v. 19], Shemida, and Shechem) and appear in new genealogical configurations. Hence, in Chronicles the tribe's western affiliations are linked to Hammolecheth and her offspring (vv. 18–19). To be sure, the genealogy documents that the tribe straddled both sides of the Jordan. But Manasseh's primary line is tied to the east and his subsidiary line is tied to the west. On the importance ascribed to the Manassite presence in the Transjordan, see also the NOTES on East Manasseh (5:23–24).

"Zelopheḥad." The Chronicler presents a variant to earlier tradition. According to Num 26:28–34, Zelopheḥad was fourth in line from Manasseh through Machir, Gilead, and Ḥepher (cf. Num 27:1–11; 36:1–12; Josh 17:3).

"Zelopheḥad had daughters." The segmented genealogy of Manasseh features three lines: Gilead, Hammolecheth, and Zelopheḥad. Of these, Zelopheḥad's is the only lineage that is not explicated by the writer (cf. Num 26:33; 27:1–11; 36:1–12; Josh 17:3–6).

7:16. "Maacah" (*maʿăkâ*). The name has Transjordanian associations. Maacah most often represents an Aramaean people or kingdom east of the Sea of Kinnereth in the Golan, south of Mount Ḥermon (Deut 3:14; Josh 12:5; 2 Sam 10:6), either abutting the territory of Manasseh or situated within it (Josh 13:11; Pitard 1987: 88). An Aramaean connection is also apparent in Gen 22:24 (J). There the union between Reumah (a concubine) and Naḥor, Abraham's brother, yields four offspring, the last of whom is Maacah. See also the last NOTE to 4:19.

"Ulam and Reqem" elsewhere appear in Benjaminite contexts (1 Chr 8:39–40; Josh 18:27).

7:17. "Bedan." His inclusion may be based in part on Samuel's farewell speech (MT 1 Sam 12:11). There his appearance after Jerubaal (Judg 6:11) and before Jephthah (Judg 11:1) intimates Gileadite connections.

7:18. "Hammolecheth" *(hmlkt)*. The writer traces the lineage of a collateral line in the Manassite genealogy. Machir's sister Hammolecheth ("she who reigns" or "Queenie" [Freedman, personal communication]) gives birth to four children. Of these offspring, the author traces the lineage of only one: Shemida.

"Abiezer" *(ʾbʿzr)*. The name appears in the eighth-century Samaria ostraca (Davies, §§3.013.1; 3.028.1). Some seven names from the Manassite tribal genealogies appear in these extrabiblical texts (Num 26:30–33; Josh 17:2–3; 1 Chr 7:14–19). From the genealogical references and the many inscriptions dealing with the dispatch of wine and oil, it is apparent that names such as Asriel, Abiezer, Ḥeleq, and Shemida (v. 19) have both genealogical and territorial connotations. "Abiezer," for example, likely represents both a clan (Aharoni 1979: 356–68) and an agricultural district (Vanderhooft 1999b).

"Maḥlah." Probably referring to a woman (Layton 1990b: 216). The PN elsewhere refers to one of Zelopheḥad's daughters (Num 26:33; 27:1; 36:11; Josh 17:3).

7:19. "the sons of Shemida." Of the sons listed, two—Shechem and Ḥeleq (TEXTUAL NOTE)—appear elsewhere as sons of Gilead (Num 26:29–31) and as sons/clans of Manasseh (Josh 17:2). A connection has also been posited between Noah *(nʿh*; Num 26:33; Josh 17:3; Davies, §§3.050.1; 3.052.1; 3.064.1) and Aniam *(ʾnyʿm)*, but this argument is philologically uncertain.

"Shemida," "Ḥeleq," and "Shechem" are also connected to Manasseh in Josh 17:2 (as sons and clans). As sons of Gilead, see Num 26:30–32. "Shemida" *(šmydʿ)* appears some eighteen times in the Samaria ostraca (Davies, §§3.003.2; 3.029.1; 3.030.1; 3.032.1, etc.), Ḥeleq appears six times (Davies, §§3.022.1; 3.023.1; 3.024.1; 3.025.1; 3.026.1; 3.027.1), and "Shechem" appears once (Davies, §3.044.1).

7:20–27. "The descendants of Ephraim." The genealogy bears little resemblance to the earlier Ephraimite lineages (LXX Gen 46:20; Num 26:35–37). To be sure, both list Shuthelaḥ first and there is some possibility for textual confusion (TEXTUAL NOTES), but the presentations diverge. In Num 26:35–37 one finds a segmented genealogy with a depth of two generations (from Ephraim to Shuthelaḥ, Becher, and Taḥan; and from Shuthelaḥ to Eran [*ʿērān*]). In LXX Gen 46:20 one finds two sons of Ephraim: *Southalaam* (Shuthelaḥ) and *Taam* (Taḥan) and one grandson of Ephraim: *Edem* (Eran). All of these are unattested in MT Gen

46:20, but with the exception of the missing Becher, the lineage is similar to that found in Num 26:35–37. In 1 Chr 7:20–27 one finds, however, a mixture of materials: a long linear genealogy (Ephraim, Shuthelaḥ, Bered, etc.), an anecdote that assumes that Shuthelaḥ, Ezer, and Elead are brothers (vv. 21b–24), and another linear genealogy ending with Joshua. Linear genealogies of the type "PN_1, his son PN_2, his son PN_3" are known elsewhere in the Chronicler's work (3:10–14; 6:5–12, 14–15). What remains unclear, however, is the relationship between the linear genealogy of vv. 20–21a and the linear genealogy of vv. 25–27 (see the following NOTES).

7:20. "Taḥath, his son Eleadah, his son Taḥath." A case of papponymy (NOTE to 5:36).

7:21b–24. "men of Gath." This anecdote interrupts the genealogy that continues in v. 25. The story is intrusive, because it breaks the pattern of linear genealogy in vv. 20–21a and vv. 25–27. Nevertheless, its function is partly genealogical, explaining the birth of Ephraim's son Beriah and the construction activities of his daughter Sheerah. Anecdotes and narrative digressions are a common phenomenon not only in the Chronicler's genealogies but also in the genealogies from ancient Mesopotamia and Greece ("Excursus: The Genealogies"). In its present context, the digression may be misplaced, however. It evidently pertains to the time of the first Shuthelaḥ (v. 20) and not to the second Shuthelaḥ (v. 21a; TEXTUAL NOTES to vv. 21–24).

7:21. "gone down" *(yrdw)*. The anecdote presupposes that Ephraim, his wife, and his sons and daughter were all residing in the land, more specifically in the hill country. In making this claim, my assumptions are (1) that Ephraim in v. 22 may refer to the patriarch Ephraim, not to some otherwise unattested descendant of Ephraim (but see Mazor 1988; Galil 1991), and (2) that Ezer and Elead are Ephraim's sons or grandsons (v. 21b) and not his distant descendants (3rd TEXTUAL NOTE to v. 21). If these assumptions are well-founded, the content of the anecdote conflicts with the presentation of Genesis and Exodus in which Ephraim is born in Egypt and never enters the promised land (Japhet 1979; 1993a: 182). To be sure, the story does not presuppose that Ephraim and his sons were all native to the land they inhabit because it distinguishes Ezer and Elead from the men of Gath, "those born in the land" (v. 21). Indeed, given the description of the men of Gath as indigenous to the land, the implication would seem to be that Ezer and Elead were not "born in the land." Nevertheless, because the story depicts Ephraim and his family as living in the land, it cannot be reconciled with an Israelite sojourn in Egypt of 400 (Gen 15:13) or 430 years (Exod 12:40). If one wishes to reconcile the story with the Exodus, the stay in Egypt would have had to last less than a generation. The case has been made, already in antiquity (*b. Sanh.* 92.2; *Tg. Song* 2:7; *Gen. Rab.* 44:18; *Exod. Rab.* 20:11; Tg. 1 Chr 7:21; Mulder 1975), that the text alludes to a premature and ill-fated exodus of Ephraimites (cf. Albright 1929: 6). But aside from the untimely demise of Ezer and Elead, there is no ill fate to bedevil the Ephraimites. In fact, one of Ephraim's offspring, Sheerah, is a successful builder. A more likely explanation for the story is that Chronicles preserves an alternative tradition in which Ephraim and his family came to reside in the land early as opposed to the one in which they endured a four-hundred-year stay in Egypt. Whether this position is the Chronicler's own, set in direct opposition to earlier biblical traditions (Japhet 1979; 1989), is less clear. As mentioned above, the digression of vv. 21b–24 is intrusive. The lineage of vv. 25–27 concludes with Joshua, the hero of the Conquest.

7:22. "grieved many days." The story of Ephraim's loss and how his kinsmen came to console him is reminiscent of the story of Job and his so-called comforters (Job 2:11–13; Rudolph 1955: 73; 1981; cf. Hoffmann 1980).

7:23. "Beriah" *(bĕrîʿâ)*. The narrator puns on the name, associating it with *(bĕ)râʿâ*, a "calamity" in Ephraim's house. See also the 1st NOTE to 8:13.

7:24. "Sheerah" is the only woman in the Heb. Scriptures credited with founding towns: Lower and Upper Beth-ḥoron and Uzzen-sheerah. According to 1 Kgs 9:17, Solomon fortified Lower Beth-ḥoron.

7:25. "his son Rephah." The antecedent is unclear. One possibility is Shuthelaḥ in v. 21 (NOTE to vv. 21b–24). But in the present form of the text Ephraim, mentioned in v. 22, and Beriah, introduced in v. 23, are also possibilities. Unlike the genealogies for Issachar, Benjamin, Naphtali, and Manasseh, which are segmented in form, the genealogy of Ephraim follows a linear pattern. The only segmentation occurs in the anecdote of vv. 21b–24.

7:26. "Ammihud, his son Elishama." This father-son combination appears in the wilderness census of Num 1. Elishama, head of his ancestral house, represents the tribe of Ephraim (Num 1:10; 2:18; 7:48). Similarly, the genealogy of David establishes a link between him and Naḥshon son of Amminadab (Num 1:7), the head of his ancestral house, who represents Judah.

7:27. "Joshua." The only genealogy attested for Joshua, son of "Non" *(nôn*; elsewhere always *nûn)*. According to many commentators, the genealogy from Ephraim (v. 20) to Joshua is too long and needs to be pared. The lineage may reflect a process of duplication (note the appearance of Shuthelaḥ in vv. 20, 21, and Telaḥ in v. 25; Taḥath in v. 20 [twice] and Taḥan in v. 25), but Chronicles contains other instances of long linear genealogies (NOTE to vv. 20–27). Aside from its extraordinary depth, two other facets of the Ephraimite lineage are remarkable. First, it features a person who is otherwise neglected in Chronicles (Joshua). Second, the genealogy has an interesting end point. The author makes no attempt to link a pivotal figure in the period of the Israelite settlement (Joshua) to more recent figures in the tribe of Ephraim, even though he obviously took pains to compose the lineage itself. Assuming a calculation of twenty years per generation, the Ephraimite lineage of vv. 20–21a, 25–27 is too short to be fully reconciled with the chronologies reflected in Hexateuchal traditions.

7:28–29. "their estates and settlements." The antecedent refers to both Manasseh and Ephraim. The interest in tribal inhabitations is by no means unique to the genealogies (e.g., 4:28–32; 5:8–11; 6:39–66), but the configuration of the Manassite and Ephraimite settlements warrants special consideration. The towns mentioned in vv. 28–29 may be compared with the Ephraimite and Manassite allotments in Josh 16:1–10 and 17:1–18. The Chronicler, like the author of Joshua, groups Manasseh and Ephraim together as sons of Joseph (Josh 16:1–4;

17:14–18). But the presentations of the two books also differ. Rather than providing a full list of boundaries for Ephraim (Josh 16:5–10), the author cites (and supplements) Josh 16 to list some towns on its borders: southern (Bethel), eastern (Naaran), western (Gezer), and evidently northern (Shechem). The precise location of Ayyah (cf. Isa 10:28 *ʿayyat*; Neh 11:31 *ʿayyâ*) is uncertain (Kallai 1986a: 157), although some would situate it to the east of Bethel. Preferring to read "Azzah" (עַזָּה; TEXTUAL NOTE) instead of "Ayyah," Demsky (2000) associates Azzah with modern *ʿAzzun* in the western foothills of Samaria. One of the sites mentioned in Josh 16:6, Michmethath (location uncertain; Boling 1982: 403), does not appear in Chronicles. Similarly, the writer cites Josh 17:11 to list four principal sites for Manasseh: Beth-shean, Taanach, Megiddo, and Dor (v. 29). Ibleam and En Dor (Josh 17:11) go unmentioned. All of these sites (Beth-shean, Taanach, Megiddo, and Dor) are situated along the northern reaches of Manasseh's territory. In other words, the close association between Manasseh and Ephraim evidently leads the author to omit any listing of southern sites and southern borders for Manasseh.

In contrast, the author of Josh 17:1–18 provides both a list of detailed borders and a list of towns. There is another difference between the lists. Whereas Joshua situates Manassite towns in Asher and Issachar (17:11) or abutting Asher and Issachar (Kallai 1986a: 173), Chronicles presents each of these sites as being "under the control of the descendants of Manasseh" (על-ידי בני-מנשה). According to Josh 16:10, the Ephraimites could not dispossess the Canaanites in Gezer and, according to Josh 17:11–13 (cf. Judg 1:27–28), the Manassites could not dispossess (להוריש) the Canaanite inhabitants of Beth-shean, Ibleam, Dor, En-Dor, Taanach, and Megiddo, even though they were able, when they became stronger, to impose corvée on them. It may be that the account in Chronicles has been influenced by two passages in Kings: 1 Kgs 4:11–12, which places Beth-shean, Taanach, Megiddo, and Naphath-dor under Israel's control, and 1 Kgs 9:15–17, which has the pharaoh ceding Gezer to Solomon. The picture presented is largely consonant with the Levitical town list, positing Levitical occupation of Shechem, Gezer (6:52), Beth-ḥoron (6:53), and Taanach (6:55).

7:29. "The descendants of Joseph." The coverage comports with the earlier claim that the birthright among Jacob's sons went to Joseph, and not to Reuben (5:1–2). Accordingly, the genealogies provide coverage of Joseph's two sons: Manasseh (5:23–24; 7:14–19, 29) and Ephraim (7:20–28). The Chronicler is indebted to earlier writers in listing Jacob's sons in this manner (Num 2:3–31; 26:5–51; Josh 21:4–7, 9–40). The other tradition in duodecimal presentations of Jacob's sons is to register both Joseph and Levi and not to register Joseph's offspring Manasseh and Ephraim (Gen 35:23–26; 49:3–27; Exod 1:2–4; Deut 27:12–14; Ezek 48:31–35).

7:30–40. "The descendants of Asher." The information contained in vv. 30–31 has been gleaned from Gen 46:17 (cf. Num 26:44–47). Much of the rest of the genealogy of Asher is unique to Chronicles. Like the genealogies of Issachar and Benjamin, the genealogy of Asher is highly segmented. The author traces the descent of Asher through his fourth offspring Beriah (vv. 30–31), Beriah's firstborn

Ḥeber (v. 32), and Ḥeber's firstborn Japhleṭ (v. 33). The offspring of Japhleṭ's brothers Shomer (v. 32) and Ḥotham (TEXTUAL NOTE) are the next focus of the author's interest. Only the three sons of Shomer are mentioned (v. 34), but the offspring of each of Ḥotham's four sons receive coverage: Zophaḥ, Imna, Shelesh, and Amal (v. 35). The Chronicler traces the offspring of Ḥotham through his sons Zophaḥ (v. 36) and Imna for one generation (vv. 36–37), and the descendants of Shelesh for two generations (vv. 37–38). The genealogy ends with the three offspring of Amal (v. 39). Hence, Asher's genealogy focuses on the various lineages descending from Ḥeber (vv. 32–39). As with the earlier genealogies dealing with Issachar and Benjamin, the author emphasizes the stature and valiantry of the tribe's leadership (v. 40).

7:30. "Beriah" *(bĕrîʿâ)*. As a son of Asher, see also Gen 46:17 and Num 26:44–45 (cf. 1 Chr 7:23). As an Ephraimite name, see 1 Chr 7:23, and as a Benjaminite, see 1 Chr 8:13, 15–16.

7:31. "Ḥeber" is a grandson of Asher (Gen 46:17; Num 26:45). Ḥeber also appears as a Qenite (Judg 4:11, 17, 21), a Judahite (1 Chr 4:18), and as one of the families of Benjamin (1 Chr 8:17). Japhet (1993a: 185) interprets Ḥeber as a toponym and situates it on the western outskirts of the Ephraimite hill country, but no such site has yet been attested.

"father of Birzaith." A detail missing from Gen 46:17 and Num 26:44–47. If Birzaith *(birzayit)* is to be associated with the site mentioned in 1 Macc 7:19 (cf. Josephus, (*Ant.* 12.397, 422), it probably refers to Khirbet Bīr eṣ-Zēt, 7 km north of Ramallah. If so, this would point to further connections between this clan of Asher and the tribe of Ephraim (Aharoni 1979: 244). The territorial allotment of Asher (Josh 19:24–31) situates Asher in the northwest portion of Israel (Frankel 1998), but the Asherite genealogy of 1 Chr 7:30–40, especially with respect to those Asherites connected to Ḥeber, evokes associations with southern and western Ephraim (Edelman 1988; Na'aman 1991b).

7:33. "Japhleṭ," like Birzaith (v. 31), has connections to the southern hill country of Ephraim (Josh 16:3).

7:35. "Amal" *(ʿāmāl)*. The name also appears on a late-seventh to early-sixth-century seal from the T. Beit Mirṣim area (Davies, §100.695).

7:36. "Ḥarnepher" is an Egyptian name. The Asherite lineages are noteworthy for the high number of non-Yahwistic names they contain. According to Weinberg (1981), the names better correspond to the onomastica of the preexilic period than they do to the onomastica of the Persian period.

"Shual" (cf. 1 Sam 13:17) and Shalishah *(šālîšâ* [1 Sam 9:4; 2 Kgs 4:42; cf. "Shelesh" in 1 Chr 7:35]) are associated with the districts of Benjamin and Ephraim (McCarter 1980b: 174).

7:38. "Ara" *(ʾr). The PN* ʾrʾ is quite rare, but appears on a few late-monarchic-era seals (Avigad and Sass 1997: §§95; 201; Deutsch and Heltzer 1999: 39).

7:39. "Araḥ" also appears in the list of the returnees in Ezra 2:5(//Neh 7:10). Whether the two refer to the same person is uncertain (Na'aman 1991b: 105; cf. Edelman 1988: 16).

40. "26,000." The census total is less than the censuses of Num 1:41 (41,500) and Num 26:47 (53,400), but this is no reason to restrict the tally solely to Ḥeber's clan (*pace* Curtis and Madsen 1910: 156).

Sources and Composition

In discussing the composition of the genealogies in this chapter, commentators often speak of extrabiblical sources in the Chronicler's employ. Given the distinctive nature of the presentation over against older biblical materials, one can readily understand this impulse. But what were the nature and extent of such putative sources? According to some scholars (e.g., Edelman, Myers, Naaman), major portions of the chapter were based on monarchic, exilic, and postexilic materials. Some are more specific, wishing to identify the source(s) as a military census list (Liver, R. Braun, Japhet, M. Johnson, Rudolph, Williamson). The argument has also been made that the genealogy of Asher (in vv. 31b–39) originally stemmed from an Ephraimite source that the Chronicler misread as Asherite, because of the mention of "Ḥeber" (Na'aman 1991b). While not denying the possibility of extrabiblical sources, one need not suppose that such sources derived from military census records. The language, high numbers, and heroic presentation of certain individuals comport well with features one finds in other sections of Chronicles. Indeed, it is quite possible that the martial terminology stems from the Chronicler himself (Na'aman 1991b). One also has to reckon with the possibility that the story within vv. 21b–24 is a later interpolation and that the Benjaminite genealogy (vv. 6–11) is a later addition, given that it conflicts so much with the Benjaminite genealogy of 1 Chr 8:1–40.

A related question involves the Chronicler's use or nonuse, as the case may be, of earlier biblical materials. Surprisingly, this important matter has not received the attention it deserves. The material in the verses in the table below shows at least some indebtedness to earlier biblical texts.

1 Chronicles 7	*Source*
1	Gen 46:13
6	Gen 46:21; Num 26:38–41
12	Gen 46:23
13	Gen 46:24–25
14	Gen 46:20 (LXX)
17	1 Sam 12:11 (MT)
19	Num 26:30–32
20	Num 26:35
26	Num 1:10; 2:18; 7:48
27	Exod 33:11 (or Num 11:28; 13:8, 16; Judg 2:8)
28	Josh 16:1, 3, 7
29	Josh 17:11
30–31	Gen 46:17

It appears that the authors of Chronicles have employed biblical sources to incorporate some introductory material, to list the names of certain individuals, and to provide certain other details, such as boundaries and settlements. In spite of using this basic information, the authors go their own way with the remaining material. What is truly amazing is the amount of biblical material that the writers did not employ in composing their genealogies. The sources in the table below have been neglected or at best only partially utilized in the composition of the genealogies. The table does not represent all of the possible texts that could have been considered. It is simply an attempt to record some of the major texts dealing with the lineages and settlements of these tribes.

Sources	*Not Cited*
Num 26:28–37	Descendants of Joseph
Num 26:38–41	Descendants of Benjamin
Num 26:48–50	Descendants of Naphtali
Num 27:1–11; 36:1–12	Daughters of Zelophehad
Josh 16:2, 4	Southern boundaries for the sons of Joseph
Josh 16:5–6, 8–10	Ephraimite allotment
Josh 17:1–6	Manassite allotment
Josh 17:7–10, 12–13	Boundaries for Manasseh
Josh 17:14–18	Josephite territory in the hill country
Josh 18:11–20	Boundaries for Benjamin
Josh 18:21–28	Benjaminite allotment
Josh 19:17–23	Allotment for Issachar
Josh 19:24, 30–31	Allotment for Asher
Josh 19:25–29	Boundaries for Asher
Josh 19:32–34	Boundaries for Naphtali
Josh 19:35–39	Allotment for Naphtali
Josh 19:40–48	Allotment for Dan

The table suggests that the authors chose to use only a fraction of the biblical sources in composing their own work. The list also highlights the degree to which the Chronicler and later editors created their own distinctive genealogies. The creation of genealogies for Issachar, Dan, Naphtali, Manasseh, Ephraim, and Asher was not an attempt at full comprehensiveness. The writers selectively employ Joshua to provide some settlement information for the sons of Joseph, but they do not do the same for Dan, Issachar, Naphtali, and Asher. The attention given to Dan and Naphtali is, in fact, minimal. One could argue that this information from Joshua and other biblical writings was somehow unavailable to the writers, but given that the writers employ their *Vorlagen* of Joshua and other biblical writings elsewhere in the genealogies, this line of argumentation fails to carry much force. One is drawn to the conclusion that the limited, albeit distinctive, attention afforded to Issachar, Dan, Naphtali, Manasseh, Ephraim, and Asher represents deliberate authorial choice.

COMMENT

In covering the divided monarchy, Chronicles focuses on three tribes: Judah, Benjamin, and Levi. It is no coincidence that the same three groups were the dominant players in the Persian period (1 Chr 9:2, 3, 7, 10–34; Ezra 2:40; 8:15, 18–20, 30–34; 9:1; 10:15; Neh 3:17; 7:1; 9:5; 10:1, 10, 29 [ET 9:38, 10:9, 28]; 11:4, 7, 15, 16, 31; 12:8, 23, 24; 13:5, 10; Mal 2:8). In keeping with their influential roles in Yehud, Judah, Benjamin, and Levi dominate the Chronicler's genealogies. By contrast, the six tribes of Issachar, Dan, Naphtali, Manasseh, Ephraim, and Asher receive a total of thirty-three verses (7:1–5, 12–40). For a couple of tribes (Dan and Naphtali), the text does no more than provide the barest of genealogical material from Genesis.

One question may be asked in light of the discussion of sources and composition: Why do the authors provide only limited coverage to these tribes? A second question is even more basic: Why does Chronicles devote coverage to the northern tribes at all? If Judah, Levi, and Benjamin dominated the scene in Yehud, why expend the energy and interest to develop lineages for the other groups traditionally associated with Israel? One is reminded of Wellhausen's observation (1885: 212) that in Chronicles "these extinct tribes again come to life." The influential answer given in recent years is that the Chronicler steadfastly maintains a pan-Israel ideal (Japhet 1972; 1989; Williamson 1977a; Willi 1995). Indeed, the very scope of the Chronicler's genealogical system underscores the indivisibility of Israel. However insightful this emphasis on the solidarity of Yhwh's people is, one should press the matter further. What are the contours and upshot of the pan-Israel presentation? What does the allocation of coverage say about the author's priorities? At a time in which the slight territory and population of Yehud formed a stark contrast with the territory and population ascribed to the United Monarchy in Samuel-Kings, what are the authors of Chronicles up to?

According to one recent scholar (Thompson 1997), the Chronicler speaks, as do all biblical writers for that matter, about a larger Israel in the past to create a group identity (if only within the text) in the present. But the Israel spoken of in these texts does not actually correspond in any meaningful way to past realities. Instead, it is purportedly a reflection of a transcendental or eschatological ideal. The Israel of biblical texts is not an old Israel, but a "new Israel" projected into the past (Thompson 1997: 182). The points about the forging of a group identity and a future dimension to the Chronicler's work are well-taken. Yet there is a need to take issue with the other elements in the proposed explanation. To begin with, writers—whether ancient, medieval, or modern—do not work within a historical vacuum or begin with a *tabula rasa*. They are always influenced by past and present circumstances. It is also unclear why writers living in the Persian period would create a range of closely related tribes out of whole cloth only to render them virtually defunct before their own time. Instead of appealing simply to an imaginary future, the Chronicler's notion of Israel should be understood in his contemporary context and the contexts provided by older traditions. Not all biblical writers can be understood as reflecting the same period or as saying the same thing (Deist 1995; Knoppers 1997b; 1999b). As we have repeatedly seen, the authors of Chronicles are heir to a number of older writings. There is a diachronic dimension to the development of biblical literature that one ignores to one's peril. In addition to being an act of self-definition formulated in light of a future ideal, the Chronicler's portrait of a larger Israel is also an act of national redefinition in light of his perceptions and evaluation of the past. The effect of this redefinition has implications for both the present and future, but its force can only be appreciated by recognizing that the author engages, contests, and revises older concepts of Israelite identity.

The tribal portrait in Chronicles may fruitfully be compared with those found in Genesis, Numbers, and the Deuteronomistic History. These works share a pan-Israelite ideal, but devote much more attention to the northern tribes than Chronicles does. They also present a much more complicated portrait of these tribes than the stylized genealogies do. Although they give due attention to Levi, Benjamin, and Judah, the authors of Gen 48–49 devote most of their attention to Reuben, Gad, Asher, Naphtali, Issachar, Zebulun, Dan, Simeon, and especially to Joseph and his two Egyptian sons, Ephraim and Manasseh. The contrast with Judges is even more stark. Judah does not even appear in the Song of Deborah (Judg 5:1–31). Judah is, in fact, conspicuously absent from most of Judges. Apart from the remarks concerning the incomplete nature of Judah's conquest (Judg 1:3–20), Judah does not appear elsewhere in the book.

Levi, Judah, and Benjamin fare better in the so-called Priestly portions of Joshua dealing with tribal patrimonies (Josh 13–21). There the other tribes receive about 45 percent of the coverage compared with 55 percent for Levi, Judah, and Benjamin. Judah also receives a privileged position in the all-Israelite censuses of Num 1 and 26. But even in these Priestly materials, the northern tribes dominate (73 percent). By contrast, the opposite holds true in Chronicles. Judah, Levi, and Benjamin receive both the vast majority of coverage (74 percent) and the critical positions in the genealogical prologue (2:3–9:1). As befitting their importance in the Persian period, Judah occupies the first position (2:3–4:23) and Levi, as Israel's priestly tribe, occupies the central position (5:27–6:66). A long genealogy of Benjamin concludes the Chronistic introduction to Israel (8:1–40; cf. 7:6–11; 9:35–44). In contrast, the tribes of Issachar, Dan, and Naphtali receive only limited genealogical coverage and no attention to territorial claims (cf. Josh 19:17–23, 32–48). Hence, the lineages effectively reverse the dominance of the northern tribes found in most of the Chronicler's sources. Ostensibly, the tribal lineages are all about the past, but their very structure and length say much about the present.

It is interesting that the characteristics ascribed to the northern tribes vary from their decidedly mixed characteristics in earlier materials. The genealogical presentation of Issachar, Ephraim, Manasseh, Dan, Naphtali, and Asher is positive, if not heroic. Here again the author shows himself fully capable of giving an independent presentation even as he draws on older materials. In this and other respects, his genealogies should be compared with those from ancient Greece. Like his western counterparts, the Chronicler fashions noble lineages for many of his chosen subjects. The men of Issachar are heads of their ancestral houses (vv. 2, 3), valiant warriors (vv. 2, 5), and prolific (vv. 2, 4, 5). Each of the sons (or grandsons) of Bela, Becher, and Jediael is a head of his ancestral house and a mighty warrior (vv. 7, 9, 11). Since there are not any descendants of Benjamin who do not have a high profile, the author's selectivity has the effect of accentuating Benjamin's status. Similarly, the author of 1 Chr 7:30–40 opines that "all of these sons of Asher were heads of their ancestral houses, select men, valiant warriors, heads of the chieftains" (v. 40). As with Issachar and Benjamin, there are associations of status with lineage and military service. The heads of Asher "were enrolled by their genealogy as (fit) for the military campaign" (v. 40). As in ancient Greece, the genealogies focus on society's elite.

The lineages hint at a variety of links among the Israelite tribes and their neighbors. In spite of the occasional conflict (v. 21b), geographic and kinship relationships exist among members of different tribes and other groups. The union between Manasseh and his Aramaean concubine, for example, is absolutely pivotal to the growth and geographic dispersion of his tribe (vv. 14–19). The Manassite and Ephraimite genealogies do not contain the martial language and references to ancestral houses found in the lineages of Issachar, Benjamin, and Asher, but they contribute to a positive picture of these tribes. Sheerah, Ephraim's daughter, is a builder of towns (v. 24). The tribes of Manasseh and Ephraim occupy a significant amount of territory, including towns that they did not conquer in Joshua (vv. 28–29).

The structure of the genealogies reflects the author's circumstances in the Persian period. In this context, one must take issue with the blanket assessment of Wellhausen (1885) about the Chronicler's resurrection of extinct tribes. In speaking of defunct tribes, Wellhausen was probably too influenced by the (typological) declarations about the nature and extent of the northern deportations at the hands of the Assyrians (2 Kgs 17:6–41). The Deuteronomists postulate an Israelite exile to Assyria (2 Kgs 17:6) and the introduction of foreign peoples into former Israelite territory (2 Kgs 17:24–41). Both occurred, but the epigraphic and archaeological evidence indicates that the northern exile only affected a part of the population (Knoppers forthcoming [f]). A majority of the surviving Israelite population remained in the land.

There were probably members of the Chronicler's audience who knew of or identified with certain phratries of Israel's "lost tribes." Even the authors of Kings, who deplore the record of the northern kingdom and sermonize on its exile, acknowledge that those immigrants who settled in the former northern kingdom worshiped Yhwh as well as other gods (2 Kgs 17:24–33, 41; cf. 2 Kgs 17:34!). As for the authors of Chronicles, they admit that the northern deportations were not comprehensive. Those northern Israelites who remained in the land (Asher, Ephraim, Manasseh, Dan, and Zebulun are mentioned by name) were appealed to by the Chronicler's Ḥezeqiah to attend a national Passover in Jerusalem (2 Chr 30:1–11). Some responded positively, made the journey, and celebrated the Passover. When the Jews at Elephantine wished to rebuild their temple in the late fifth century, they appealed for assistance to the authorities in both Jerusalem *and* Samaria (*TAD* 4.5, 6, 7, 8, 9, 10; Porten 1968: 284–98). The material remains from the southern Levant suggest that the Persian province of Samaria was more populous and wealthy than its southern neighbor (Zertal 1990; 1999). Of the many PNs (sellers, buyers, slaves) found within the fourth-century Samaria papyri, the "vast majority" are Yahwistic (Gropp 1992: 932). In short, one should not assume that when the Chronicler wrote, the areas traditionally inhabited by the northern tribes in Samaria were either bereft of Yahwists or bereft of people who identified with certain Israelite sodalities. The genealogies for Issachar, Dan, Naphtali, Manasseh, Ephraim, and Asher are testimony to the fact that the authors of Chronicles, writing during the Persian occupation, embrace a comprehensive, rather than a restrictive, definition of Israel.

To be sure, it would be hazardous to maintain that the northern genealogies all directly relate to or are carried through to the author's own day. It would be reductive to see every feature of this coverage as mirroring the author's own time. The genealogy of Ephraim is, to a certain extent, an intellectual exercise, tying one figure in the Ancestral period (Ephraim) to another prominent figure in a later period (Joshua). No attempt is made to trace the genealogy of Ephraim beyond Joshua. Chronicles includes genealogies of Asher, Issachar, Dan, and Naphtali, but the genealogy of the return (9:2–34) only mentions repatriates from Judah, Benjamin, Ephraim, Manasseh, and Levi. It seems likely that the writer wishes to accomplish at least two things with his genealogies of Issachar, Dan, Naphtali, Manasseh, Ephraim, and Asher. In one respect, the Chronicler's work reestablishes and contributes to the legacy of the northern tribes. The lineages honor the positive accomplishments and stature of the elite within these sodalities. If there is a "true Israel" in the genealogies, it is all of the tribes together and not a single part of them. In another respect, the author transforms the Israelite legacy even as he maintains it. The northern genealogies, limited and contextualized as they are, validate the importance the Chronicler ascribes to Judah, Levi, and Benjamin. He puts the various tribes of Israel in their place, much as he put the nations in their place within his universal genealogy (1:1–2:2). His work presents a broad understanding of Israel's identity in coordination with the prominent influence of Judah, Benjamin, and Levi in his own time. The minor genealogies draw attention to the major genealogies. The differences between the group identities posited in his sources and the group identity the author posits through his lineages reveal the passage of centuries. Indeed, the very fact that the Chronicler finds it necessary to contest, restructure, and supplement past traditions indicates that those traditions no longer met the needs of his contemporary situation.

XI. Last but Not Least: Benjamin (8:1–9:1)

Benjamin, Bela, and Ehud

1 Benjamin sired Bela, his firstborn, Ashbel the second, Aḥraḥ the third,
2 Noḥah the fourth, and Rapha the fifth. 3 And Bela had sons: Addar and Gera the
father of Ehud. 4 These were the sons of Ehud: Abishua, Naaman, Aḥiah, 5 Gera,
Shephuphan, and Ḥuram. 6 These were the ancestral heads of Geba's inhabitants,
and they exiled them to Manaḥath. 7 As for Naaman, Aḥiah, and Gera, he was the
one who exiled them. Then he sired Uzza and Aḥiḥud.

Shaḥaraim's Wives and Descendants

8 Shaḥaraim sired (children) in the country of Moab after he had sent them
away, his wives Ḥushim and Baara. 9 He sired (children) from Ḥodesh his wife:
Jobab, Zibia, Mesha, Malcam, 10 Jeuz, Sachiah, and Mirmah—these were ancestral heads. 11 He sired from Ḥushim: Abiṭub and Elpaal. 12 These were the sons of
Elpaal: Eber, Misham, and Shemer. He built Ono and Lud, along with its dependencies.

Beriah, Shema, Elpaal, and Jeremoth

13 As for Beriah and Shema, they were the ancestral heads of Ayyalon's inhabitants. They put Gath's inhabitants to flight. 14 Their kinsmen were Shashaq and
Jeremoth. 15 Zebadiah, Arad, Ader, 16 Michael, Ishpah, and Joḥa were the sons of
Beriah. 17 Zebadiah, Meshullam, Ḥizqi, Ḥeber, 18 Ishmerai, Izliah, and Jobab
were the sons of Elpaal. 19 Jachim, Zichri, Zabdi, 20 Elioenai, Zillethai, Eliel,
21 Adaiah, Beraiah, and Shimrath were the sons of Shimei. 22 Ishpan, Eber, Eliel,
23 Abdon, Zichri, Ḥanan, 24 Ḥananiah, Elam, Anthothiah, 25 Iphdeiah, and Penuel were the sons of Shashaq. 26 Shamsherai, Sheḥariah, Athaliah, 27 Jaarshiah,
Elijah, and Zichri were the sons of Jeroḥam. 28 These were the ancestral heads by
their lineages. These heads resided in Jerusalem.

The Jeielite Genealogy

29 The father of Gibeon, Jeiel, resided in Gibeon and the name of his wife was
Maacah. 30 Her firstborn son: Abdon, Zur, Qish, Baal, Ner, Nadab, 31 Gedor,
Aḥio, Zecher, and Miqloth. 32 Miqloth sired Shimeah, and they also resided op-
posite their kinsmen in Jerusalem. 33 Ner sired Qish, and Qish sired Saul, and
Saul sired Jonathan, Malchi-shua, Abinadab, and Eshbaal. 34 The son of Jonathan
was Merib-baal, and Merib-baal sired Micah. 35 The sons of Micah were Pithon,
Melech, Taarea, and Aḥaz. 36 Aḥaz sired Jehoadah, and Jehoadah sired Alemeth,
Azmaveth, and Zimri. Zimri sired Moza, 37 and Moza sired Binea; Raphaiah his
son, Eleasah his son, Azel his son. 38 Azel had six sons and these were their names:
Azriqam his firstborn, Ishmael, Sheariah, Azariah, Obadiah, and Ḥanan. All of
these were sons of Azel. 39 The sons of Esheq his brother: Ulam, Jeush the second,
Elipheleṭ the third. 40 The sons of Ulam were valiant warriors, archers, producers
of many children and grandchildren—150. All these were from the descendants
of Benjamin.

Genealogical Summary and Notice of Judah's Deportation

9:1 So all Israel was genealogically registered and their (records) were written in the book of the kings of Israel and Judah. And as for Judah, they were exiled to Babylon on account of their transgression.

TEXTUAL NOTES

8:1–2. "the second . . . the fifth." Gen 46:21 lacks the ordinals.

8:1. "his firstborn" *(bkrw)*. So MT and LXX. MT Gen 46:21 and 1 Chr 7:6 have "Becher" (*bkr*; cf. LXX Gen 46:21 *Chobor* [metathesis]), but this name does not occur in Num 26:38.

"Aḥraḥ." LXX^{B} c_2 *Iaphaēl*; LXX^{AN} *Aara*; LXX^{L} *Aēira*; y *Diera*; b′ *Diēra*; *b Dēira*. MT Num 26:38 "Aḥiram." One of Benjamin's sons in MT Gen 46:21 is "Eḥi." Cf. LXX Gen 46:21 *Agchis* (Wevers 1993: 784).

8:2. "Noḥah . . . Rapha." These names are not found in MT Gen 46:21, Num 26:39, and 1 Chr 7:6. MT Gen 46:21 "Muppim" and "Ḥuppim;" MT Num 26:39 "Shephupham" and "Ḥupham." But see 1 Chr 8:5.

8:3. "Addar." So MT and LXX^{L}. LXX Num 26:40 *Adar*. LXX^{B} 1 Chr 8:3 *Alei*. A few Heb. MSS and LXX^{AN} follow Gen 46:21 and MT Num 26:40 in reading "Ard." LXX* Gen 46:21 also lists a son of Gera, but names him *Arad*.

"father of Ehud." Reading *ʾby ʾhwd* instead of MT "Abihud" *(ʾbyhwd)*. That MT lists nine sons of Bela, two of which carry the same name—Gera (vv. 3, 5)—confirms that the text has suffered haplography. Cf. 1 Chr 7:37 *hôd*; Judg 3:15 *ʾēhûd*.

8:4. "these were the sons of Ehud." In MT and LXX this phrase occurs at the beginning of v. 6. Michaeli (1967: 64) and others have argued that it belongs here because v. 3 mentions Ehud (previous TEXTUAL NOTE) and v. 6 contains two successive introductory rubrics.

"Abishua" *(ʾăbîšûaʿ)*. So MT and LXX^{ALN}. LXX^{B} c_2 *Abeisamas*. Lacking in both Gen 46:21 and Num 26:38–40.

"Aḥiah" *(ʾḥyh)*. So LXX^{B} c_2 *(Achia)*, Syr., and v. 7. The name is not present in Gen 46:21, Num 26:38–40, some Tg. MSS of 1 Chr 8:4, and LXX^{AN} 1 Chr 8:4. MT "Aḥoaḥ" (*ʾḥwḥ*; cf. 2 Sam 23:9, 28; 1 Chr 11:29); LXX^{L} *Aōd*.

8:5. "Gera." So MT and LXX*. Lacking in Syr. LXX^{L} reads in v. 4 and in the beginning of v. 5: [4]*houtoi huioi* (lacking in e_2) *Aōd* [5]*Gēra* (y *-ram*) *kai Seppham* (y *-phan*) *kai Harouam*, "These are the sons of Aod: Gera, Seppham, and Harouam."

"Shephuphan." A few Heb. MSS, Tg., and LXX cursives reflect the final *mêm* of MT Num 26:39 "Shephupham" (cf. SP, Tg., and Vg. שופם; LXX *Sōphan*). LXX^{B} *Sōpharphak*; LXX^{AN} *kai Sōphan kai Achiran*. In Canaanite PNs, the terminations *-m* and *-n* sometimes interchange (Layton 1990b: 181).

"Ḥuram." So MT. LXX^{BN} *Hōim*; LXX^{A} c_2 *Hiōim*. Cf. Gen 46:21 "Ḥuppim" (LXX* *Hophim*); Num 26:39 "Ḥupham." It may be that Syr. *ḥwpm* corrects to the PN found in Num 26:39, but MT *ḥwrm* is probably a corruption of *ḥwpm* (Rothstein and Hänel 1927: 156; Noth 1928: 242). On the PN *ḥûrām*, see the 1st NOTE to 14:1.

8:6. "these were the ancestral heads." MT and LXX preface another introductory rubric, "these were the sons of Ehud," misplaced from the start of v. 4 (TEXTUAL NOTE).

"Ehud." Reading *ʾhwd* (cf. LXX^B^ *Aōd*; LXX^AN^ *Ōd*) instead of MT *ʾḥwd*.

"they exiled them" *(wayyaglûm)*. The *hipʿil* of *glh* with the object suf. should be translated with an active sense (*pace* NRSV; NJPS) even though the antecedent is unclear.

8:7–8. These verses are not found in Syr.

8:7. "Naaman, Aḥiah, and Gera." The appearance of practically the same names in vv. 4–5—Naaman, Aḥiah (MT Aḥoaḥ), Gera—has led some to view these names as a dittography.

"he was the one who exiled them" *(hwʾ hglm)*. So MT and LXX^L^. LXX^B^ *(Higaam)*, followed by NRSV, interprets *heglām* as a PN (cf. c_2 *Hichaam*; LXX^AN^ *Higlaam*).

"Uzza." LXX^B^ *Naana*; LXX^L^ *Hazan*; *by Nazan*.

"Aḥiḥud." A few Heb. MSS "Aḥihud." LXX^B^ *Iacheichōl*; LXX^AN^ *Iachichad*; b'y *Noua*.

8:8. "Shaḥaraim." LXX^B^ *Saarēl*; LXX^AN^ *Saarēm*; LXX^L^ *Seōrein*. One expects "Aḥraḥ" (v. 1).

"sired." The verb has no stated object. The textual corruptions in vv. 8–11 have given rise to many emendations, some of which are quite severe (e.g., Hogg 1899; Marquart 1902).

"the country of Moab." Literally, "the fields (*śdh*) of Moab."

"after he had sent them away" *(min-šilḥô)*. The syntax is rough. I am construing the prep. *min* in a temporal sense (Williams, §316).

"his wives." LXX* "his wife." Some (e.g., Curtis and Madsen 1910) omit and construe Ḥushim and Baara as the offspring of Shaḥaraim.

"them away . . . Ḥushim" *(ʾtm ḥwšym)*. LXX^B^ *auton Sōsin*; LXX^L^ *autous auton kai Ōseim*. Since Ḥushim is elsewhere a masc. name, Rudolph (1955: 76) emends to *ʾt-mḥšm*. But see the 1st TEXTUAL NOTE to v. 11.

"Baara" *(bʿrʾ)*. So MT. LXX^B^ *Ibaada*. One Heb. MS and c_2 *Baada* (= *bʿdʾ*) exhibit a *dālet/rêš* confusion.

8:9. "Ḥodesh." LXX* *Hada*; e_2 *Balaa*; Tg. *bʿrh*; Syr. *ḥrš*.

"Malcam." So MT and LXX^AN^. LXX^B^ *Melchas*; LXX^L^ *Melchom*. The PN may be understood as *malk* ("king") + enclitic morpheme *-am* (Layton 1990b: 176).

8:10. "Jeuz" *(yĕʿûṣ)*. Thus MT and LXX^A^. LXX^B^ c_2 *Idōs*; LXX^L^ *Iōas*.

"Sachiah" *(śkyh)*. So MT and LXX^L^. Many Heb. MSS, Tg. *šbyh*. LXX* *Sabia* (= *śbyh*?).

"these." So LXX* *(lectio brevior)*. MT and LXX^L^ add "his sons" *(bnyw)*.

8:11. "from Ḥushim" *(mḥšm)*. The reappearance of this name renders the emendation of Rudolph (1955: 78)—*mmḥšm* (6th TEXTUAL NOTE to v. 8)—unlikely.

"Abiṭub." Thus MT and LXX. A few Heb. MSS, LXX cursives, Tg., and Syr. have the more common "Aḥiṭub" or "Aḥiṭôb" (Tg.).

"Elpaal" (*ʾelpaʿal*). So MT. The reading of LXX[L] (*Eleiphaal*) suggests **ʾlypʿl*. LXX[B] imc$_2$ *Alphaad*. See also the 1st TEXTUAL NOTE to v. 12.

8:12. "Elpaal" (*ʾelpaʿal*). So MT. LXX[B] *Alphaad* (c$_2$ *Alphad*). Cf. LXX[L] *Eleiphaal*. See also the TEXTUAL NOTES to vv. 11 and 18.

"Eber." A few Heb. MSS have "Ebed." LXX* *Ōbēd*; LXX[L] *Heber*.

"Misham" (*mišʿām*). On the PN, "the (divine) kinsman saves," see Layton (1996). LXX[B] *Messaam*.

"Shemer." Reading with many Heb. MSS, LXX (*Sēmēr*), Tg., and Syr. *šmr* (Noth 1928: 259). MT "Shamed" (*šmd*) evinces a *dālet/rêš* confusion.

"and Lud." Thus MT and LXX[L] (*kai tēn Lōd*). Lacking in LXX*.

8:13. "Beriah" (*brʿh*). So MT. LXX[B] ic$_2$ *Beriga*.

8:14. "their kinsmen" (*ʾḥyhm*). Cf. LXX[B] *adelphos autou*; LXX[AN] *hoi adelphoi autou*; LXX[L] *hoi adelphoi autōn*. MT and Tg. "Aḥio" (*ʾḥyw*). That the name Aḥio is not impossible (contra Curtis and Madsen 1910) is evident from its many occurrences in the Elephantine papyri (*TAD* A4.4:7; B2.1:15; 2.2:18; 2.6:38; 3.1:22; 3.2:2, 12; 3.6:17). Cf. "Aḥio" in v. 31. But there are good reasons to doubt its originality here. The name lacks a connective *wāw* and descendants for this "Aḥio" are lacking in succeeding verses, whereas the other four individuals in vv. 13–14 all reappear later.

"Shashaq" (*šāšāq*). So MT. LXX[B] c$_2$ *Sōkēl*; LXX[AN] *Sōsēk*; e$_2$ *Sēsach*; *by Sisach*; b′ *Sitach*.

"Jeremoth" (*yrmwt*). Perhaps read "Jeroḥam" (*yrḥm*) as in v. 27.

8:15–16. These verses are lacking in LXX cursives b′ and e$_2$. Verses 15b–22 are lacking in Syr.

8:15. "Arad (and) Ader" (*ʿărād wāʿāder*). LXX[B] c$_2$ *Ōrēr kai Ōdēd*.

8:16. "Ishpah" (*yšph*). LXX[B] c$_2$ *Saphan*; LXX[AN] *Esphach*.

"Joḥa" (*yôḥāʾ*). Thus MT. LXX[B] c$_2$ *Iōachan*; LXX[N] *Iōachab*; LXX[L] *Iezia*.

"Beriah" (*brʿh*). So MT. LXX[ABN] c$_2$ *Ber(e)iga*. See v. 13.

8:17. "Ḥizqi." Probably a shortened form of a longer PN, *ḥizqîyāh(û)*, "Yhwh is my strength" (Layton 1990b: 122–27).

8:18. "Izliah" (*yzlyʾh*). LXX[B] c$_2$ *Sareia*.

"Elpaal" (*ʾelpāʿal*). So MT, LXX[AN], and Vg. LXX[B] c$_2$ *Elchaad*. LXX[L] *Eleiphaal* (= *ʾĕlîpāʿal*) may preserve an older vocalization. See also the TEXTUAL NOTES to vv. 11–12.

8:20. "Elioenai." Reading *ʾĕlyôʿênay*, a name that appears elsewhere in the Persian period (Ezra 10:22, 27; Neh 12:41; 1 Chr 3:23, 24; 4:36; 7:8; 26:3). See LXX[AN] *Eliōēnai*; Tg.[V] *ʾlywʿyny*; Tg.[CLAS] *ʾlywʿny*; Arm. *Helioune*; Vg. *Helioenai*. LXX[B] *Eliōliaa*; Josephus, *Ant.* 19.342 *Eliōnaion (ton tou Kanthēra)*. Claiming that the penultimate *yôd* is secondary, Allen (1974b: 76) thinks that the original form appears in MT 1 Chr 8:20 (cf. LXX[L] *Ēliōnai*) "Elienai" (*ʾĕlîʿēnay*). But the name *ʾlywʿyny* appears in an early Ptolemaic Jewish inscription (Lidzbarski 1902–15: 49; Horbury and Noy §3).

8:21. "Shimei" (*šmʿy*). Rudolph (1955: 78) proposes reading *šmʿ*, as in v. 13, but the former is simply a variant of the latter.

8:22. "Eber" (*ʿēber*). LXX[B] c$_2$ *Ōbdē*; LXX[AN] *Ōbēd* (see v. 12).

8:23. "Zichri" *(zkry)*. Thus MT and LXX. Syr. *zbdy*.

8:24. "Ḥananiah." LXX adds *Ambrei*; cec$_2$ *Amri* (= *ʿomrî).

"Anthothiah" *(ʿnttyh)*. Syr. lacks *-yh*. LXX^{B} c$_2$ *Anōthaith kai Athein*.

8:25. "Iphdeiah" *(ypdyh)*. LXX^{B} c$_2$ *Iephereia*; Syr. *pryʾ*.

"Penuel." So Qere, LXX^{AN} *Phanouēl*, Vg. *Phanuhel*. Kethib "Peniel;" LXX^{B} *Pheliēl*.

"Shashaq." LXX^{B} *Sōiēk*; LXX^{AN} *Sōsēk*; e$_2$ *Sēsach*; e *Sōkēm*. See also the 2nd TEXTUAL NOTE to v. 14.

8:26. "Shamsherai." LXX^{L} *Samsaia*; Syr. *šmyrʾ*.

8:26b–27. These verses are not found in Syr.

8:27. "Jaarshiah" *(yʿršyh)*. LXX^{B} *Iasaraia* (= *yʿšryh*) *kai Saraia* (dittography).

"Jeroḥam." LXX^{B} *Iraam*. See also the 3rd TEXTUAL NOTE to v. 14.

8:28–38. See also the TEXTUAL NOTES to the parallel verses in 1 Chr 9:34–44.

8:28. "these heads resided in Jerusalem." Some (e.g., Rudolph 1955: 78) think that this phrase has been misplaced from the start of v. 14, but see the NOTE to v. 28.

8:29. "father of Gibeon." So MT. Tg. "princes *(rabbānê)* of Gibeon."

"Jeiel" *(yʿyʾl)*. Reading with LXX^{L} *Ieiēl* (cf. b′ *Eeēl*) and the parallel in MT (Qere) and LXX^{AN} 1 Chr 9:35. MT 8:29 is lacking. Kethib 9:35 *yʿwʾl*; LXX^{B} 9:35 *Eiiēl*; LXX^{L} *Ieiēl*; f *Ieyiēl* (= *yʿwʾl?).

"resided." MT has the pl., but LXX and Syr. have the expected sg. Similar variants occur in 9:35.

8:30. "her firstborn son." So LXX* *(lectio difficilior)*. MT and LXX^{L} "his firstborn son."

"Ner." So LXX^{ALN} *(Nēr)* and 1 Chr 9:36. Lacking in MT because of haplography (*homoioarkton* before Nadab). See v. 33.

8:31. "Aḥio" *(ʾḥyw)*. LXX^{B} *adelphos autou*. See the 1st TEXTUAL NOTE to v. 14.

"Zecher" *(zkr)*. LXX^{B} ic$_2$ *Zachour* (= *zakkûr*?). The hypocoristicon of "Zechariah" *(zkryh)* in 1 Chr 9:37.

"and Miqloth." So MT 9:37 and LXX^{B} *(Makalōth)*, Syr., and Vg. MT 1 Chr 8:31 has suffered haplography (*homoioarkton* before "Miqloth" in v. 32).

8:32. "Shimeah." LXX^{B} *Semaa*; LXX^{L} gmnc$_2$ *Samaa*. MT 1 Chr 9:38 "Shimeam," but LXX *Samaa*.

"they also resided opposite (נגד) their kinsmen (אחיהם) in Jerusalem." So cursives djmpqtz and Syr. *(lectio brevior)*. MT and LXX^{ABL} add "with their kinsmen" (עם-אחיהם).

8:33. "Qish." So MT here and in 9:39. Some emend to "Abner," but Ab(i)ner was probably the cousin of Saul, not his father (1 Sam 9:1; 14:50–51; McCarter 1980b: 256). Unfortunately, the text of 1 Sam 14:50–51 is confused, so it is impossible to be sure. See also the 1st NOTE to 9:39.

"Abinadab" *(ʾbyndb)*. So MT here and in 9:39. In both cases, LXX has the more common *Ameinadab*. Syr. *yšwy* (cf. 1 Sam 14:49).

"Eshbaal" *(ʾešbāʿal)*. LXX^{B} *Asabal*; LXX^{L}, bcehimn *I(e)sbaal* (= *ʾîšbāʿal*).

8:34. "Merib-baal." LXX^{B} *Meribaal*; LXX^{AN} *Mephibaal*; LXX^{L} *Memphibaal*. Cf. LXX^{B} 1 Chr 9:40 *Mareibaal*; LXX^{N} *Mephibaal*; LXX^{L} *Memphibaal*.

"Micah" (מיכה). So MT 8:34 and 9:40. LXX^B c_2 *Michia*; LXX* 1 Chr 9:40 *Meicha*. MT 2 Sam 9:12 מיכא, but a few Heb. MSS מיכה.

8:35. "Melech" *(melek)*. A hypocoristic of the PN that appears in LXX^{BL} *Melch(i)ēl* (= מלכיאל).

"Taarea" *(tʾrʿ)*. MT 9:41 "Taḥarea" *(tḥrʿ)*.

"and Aḥaz." So MT. LXX^B *kai Zak*; LXX^L *kai Azaz*; LXX^{AN} *kai Chaaz*. Lacking in MT 1 Chr 9:41, but present in LXX^L *kai Azaz*.

8:36. "Jehoadah" *(yhwʿdh)*. So MT. LXX^B *Iad kai Iada* (dittography); LXX^A *Iōiada* (= *yĕhôyādāʿ*); LXX^L h *Iōda*. MT 1 Chr 9:42 "Jarah" *(yʿrh)*; LXX^B *Iada* (= *yʿdh*); LXX^L bn *Iō(a)da*.

"Moza" *(môṣaʾ)*. Thus MT and LXX^L *(Mōsa)*. LXX^{AB} *Maisa*; Syr. *mwṣyʾ*.

8:37. "Binea" *(binʿāʾ)*. A few Heb. MSS "Kinea"; LXX^{ABLN} *Ba(a)na* (= *baʿănāʾ*).

"Raphaiah" *(rpyh)*. So MT and LXX *(Rhaphaia)* 1 Chr 9:43 and LXX^{AN} 1 Chr 8:37 *(Rhaphaia)*. See also 1 Chr 3:21; 4:42; 7:2; Neh 3:9. MT 1 Chr 8:37 "Raphah" *(rph)*, a *hapax legomenon*, assimilates toward *rpʾ* in v. 2 (Allen 1974b: 96). LXX^B fc_2 *Rhaphai*.

8:38. "his firstborn" *(bkrw)*. So several Heb. MSS and LXX. There is no *wāw* before *bkrw*. MT (here and in 9:44) vocalizes "Bocheru," thus ensuring that Azel had six sons. See further in next TEXTUAL NOTE.

"Azariah." A reconstruction based on LXX^L (and Arm.), which reads a variant order of PNs here and in 9:44, *(Ezreikam prōtokos autou) kai Ismaēl kai Azarias kai Abdia kai Saaria kai Hanan*. The name "Azariah" (עזריה) was lost to the tradition underlying MT by haplography (either *homoioteleuton* after שעריה or before עבדיה).

8:39. "Esheq" *(ʿēšeq)*. LXX^B *Asēl*; LXX^{AN} *Eselek*; many cursives *Esēl*.

"Elipheleṭ" *(ʾĕlîpeleṭ)*. The PN ("my God is deliverance") also appears in MT 1 Chr 14:5 without the pronominal suf. ("God is deliverance") and in 14:7 with the pronominal suf. But see the TEXTUAL NOTES there.

8:40. "one hundred and fifty." LXX^{AN} "ninety."

"all." Lacking in MT.

9:1. "was genealogically registered, and their (records)." MT *hityaḥśû wĕhinnām*. LXX^{AB} *ho synlochismos autōn*, "their reckoning."

"the book of the kings of Israel and Judah (*sēper mlky yśrʾl wyhwdh*). And as for Judah (*wyhwdh*)." A restoration. Cf. LXX^{BL} *Basileōn Israēl kai Iouda*; Tg. *mlkyʾ dbyt yśrʾl wmlkyʾ dbyt yhwdh*. Given the pl. verb and the following pl. pronominal suf. on *bĕmaʿălām*, the antecedent should also be pl. But the Heb. can be taken another way. Indeed, almost all translations follow the lead of the medieval Masoretes, reading "kings of Israel" and construing "Judah" with the following pl. verb *(hoglû)*, hence "the book of the kings of Israel. And Judah was exiled," to avoid the apparent contradiction of the (northern) Israelites going into Babylonian exile. In this understanding, the reference to "the book of the kings of Israel" relates to the northern kingdom (cf. 1 Chr 8:1–40 [perhaps construing Benjamin as a northern tribe]), to Judah as representative of Israel (Curtis and Madsen 1910: 169), or to the people (north and south) as a whole (Japhet 1989: 276). But the use of "the book of the kings of Israel and Judah" is probably formulaic. Whereas the authors of Kings regularly speak of "the book of the kings of Israel" (2 Kgs 1:18; 10:34; 13:8, 12; 14:15, 28; 15:11, 15, 21, 31) and of "the book of the kings of Judah" (2 Kgs 8:23; 12:20 [ET 12:19]; 14:18; 15:6, 36; 16:19; 20:20; 21:17, 25; 23:28; 24:5), the authors of Chronicles speak either of "the book of the kings of Judah and Israel" (2 Chr 16:11; 25:26; 28:26; 32:32) or of "the book of the kings of Israel and Judah" (2 Chr 27:7; 35:27; 36:8). Only in one case is reference made to "the book of the kings of Israel" (2 Chr 20:34). Note that in each and every case, the author is referring to written records pertaining to southern (Judahite) monarchs. Hence, it may be best to follow the main contours of Oettli's proposal (1889) of a haplography *(wyhwdh)*, "the book of the kings of Israel and Judah. And Judah was exiled." Alternatively, one could read, "the book of the kings of Israel and Judah. And they were exiled to Babylon."

"they were exiled" *(hoglû)*. Reading the *hopʿal* pl. with MT. LXX[B] *meta tōn katoikisthentōn*, "with (them) were settled."

NOTES

1. "(and) Benjamin sired" (**ובנימן הוליד**). Within context, this is a most unusual beginning for a tribal genealogy. Most of the other lineages for Israel's sons begin: "(and) the sons *(wbny)* of PN" (2:3; 4:24; 5:1, 11, 18, 23, 27; 6:1; 7:13, 14, 20, 30). One lineage (Issachar) begins with the formula "Belonging to the sons (**ולבני**) of PN" (1 Chr 7:1), while the beginnings of two others are textually disputed (7:6 [TEXTUAL NOTE]; 7:12 [TEXTUAL NOTE]). The formula "PN sired" is, of course, found within other genealogies (e.g., Gen 4:18; 5:3, 4; 10:8, 13, 15, 24, 26[//1 Chr 1:10, 11, 13, 18, 20]; 11:27; 22:23; 25:3, 19; 1 Chr 2:10, 11, 36; Aufrecht 1988).

"Bela." Traditions (MT Gen 46:21; LXX Gen 46:21; Num 26:38–40; 1 Chr 7:6–11) offer only partially similar presentations of Benjamin's descendants. MT Gen 46:21 presents Benjamin with ten sons, while other texts (e.g., LXX Gen 46:21; Num 26:38–40) present some of the same names as Bela's sons and therefore as Benjamin's grandchildren. First Chronicles 7:6–11 presents a segmented genealogy of Benjamin that follows the offspring of each of Benjamin's three sons for a maximum of two generations. The list of Benjamin's descendants in 1 Chr 8 is largely unparalleled, but its beginning partially resembles LXX Gen 46:21 and Num 26:38–40 (see table). LXX Gen 46:21 mentions further progeny: a great-grandson of Benjamin (through Gera): Arad. First Chronicles 8:3–5 mentions one son of Gera—Ehud—as well as Ehud's six sons. Some of these sons (Naaman, Gera, Shephuphan, Ḥuram) have names that are identical or similar to the names in the other Benjaminite lists (TEXTUAL NOTES). In dealing with Benjamin's offspring one is, therefore, confronted not only with variant witnesses from different books but also variant witnesses within books. Aside from the differences between MT Genesis and MT Numbers, there are also substantial differences between MT and LXX Genesis. Chronicles further complicates the picture by presenting readers with two lists of Benjaminite progeny (1 Chr 7:6–11; 8:1–40.), each of

MT Gen 46:21	*LXX Gen 46:21*	*Num 26:38–39*	*1 Chr 7:6*	*1 Chr 8:1–2*
SONS OF BENJAMIN				
Bela	Bala	Bela	Bela	Bela
Becher	Chobor		Becher	
			Jediael	
Ashbel	Asbēl	Ashbel		Ashbel
Gera				
Naaman				
Eḥi		Aḥiram		Aḥraḥ
Rosh				
		Shephupham		
Muppim				
Ḥuppim		Ḥuppim		
Ard				
				Noḥah
				Rapha
SONS OF BELA				
		Ard		Addar
	Gēra			Gera
			Ezbon	
			Uzzi	
			Uzziel	
			Jerimoth	
			Iri	
	Noeman	Naaman		
	Agchis			
	Rhōs			
	Mamphin			
	Hophim			

which goes its own way. From a sociological vantage point, the discrepancies among the different biblical witnesses to the Benjaminite genealogies (MT and LXX Genesis, Numbers, Chronicles) may reflect shifting claims and competing assertions about Benjaminite blood lines over the course of time. In the ancient world, genealogies could be updated or modified to adapt to new circumstances ("Excursus: The Genealogies"). The cumulative effect of such activities is, however, a series of discordant Benjaminite lineages. One is reminded of Herodotus's habit of providing his readers with dual or multiple accounts given to him by his sources (e.g., *Hist.* 1.5.3). Herodotus does not attempt to reconcile all of the details in these contradictory traditions, although on some occasions he provides clues about his own judgment (e.g., *Hist.* 2.15–33). By relaying competing stories, Herodotus leaves his audience with the critical task, should they choose to exercise it, of sifting through and evaluating the evidence.

8:4. "sons of Ehud." Referring to the Benjaminite judge, Ehud *ben* Gera (Judg 3:12–30). One of the names (Naaman) appears as Benjamin's son in MT Gen 46:21. Another (Gera) instances papponymy, appearing as both the father (v. 3; MT Gen 46:21) and a grandson of Ehud (v. 5). See further the NOTE to 5:36.

8:6. "these were the ancestral heads of Geba's inhabitants." Literally, "these were they, heads of ancestral houses." The text does not clarify (TEXTUAL NOTE) whether the ancestral heads of Geba are the sons of Ehud or whether a third party is involved.

"Geba" *(gebaʿ)*, north of Jerusalem, was part of the Benjaminite inheritance (Josh 18:24; 21:17; cf. Judg 20:33; 1 Sam 13:16) and one of the sites associated with the returnees in the Persian period (Ezra 2:26). The name (גב[ע]) is found among the Samaria ostraca (Davies, §3.008.1). The mention of this site, along with a few others in the Benjaminite genealogy (1 Chr 8:12, 29), reflects postexilic interests (Zech 14:10; Neh 7:30; 11:31; 12:29; 1 Chr 6:45; 8:6; 2 Chr 16:6). In a number of biblical texts (e.g., Judg 19–20; 1 Sam 13–14; Isa 10:29) there is some confusion between Geba (גבע) and Gibeah (גבעה), confusion that is compounded in the versions. To complicate matters further, there are sites by names such as Gibeath-elohim and Gibeath-qiriath-jearim that are difficult to identify geographically (J. Miller 1999). Because of these and other difficulties, some view the two names as alternate designations of the same site (Arnold 1990: 37–38; Langston 1998: 83–92). Others prefer to keep the two separate, associating Geba with Čebaʿ, about 8–9 km north of Jerusalem (Kartveit 1989: 154), and Gibeah with T. el-Fûl, about 5 km north of Jerusalem (Lapp 1997).

"they exiled them." Both the subject and the object are unclear (TEXTUAL NOTE). The gap may reflect a haplography. In any case, the passage refers to an internal Benjaminite incident. Many of the tribal movements narrated in the genealogies result from population growth, warfare, or emigration, but the Benjaminite genealogy contains three cases of expatriation that apparently result from internal coercion (8:6, 7, 8).

"Manaḥath." According to some, Manaḥath is to be identified as el-Mâlḥah, some 4–5 km southwest of Jerusalem (Aharoni 1979: 248; Kallai 1986a: 393). The hypothesis of a connection to Manḫatu in the vicinity of Gezer, mentioned in the El Amarna letters (EA 292.30; Moran 1992: 335), is rejected by Niemann (1985: 156–58) on philological and historical grounds. Knauf (1992b: 493) prefers to see Manaḥath as Maḥnah, 7 km north of modern *ʿAjlûn.* See also the NOTE to 2:52.

8:7. "he was the one who exiled them" *(hûʾ heglām)*. The antecedent is unclear. One possible candidate is Ehud (v. 4; TEXTUAL NOTE). See also the 3rd NOTE to v. 6.

8:8–12. "Shaḥaraim" is not otherwise attested. The segmented lineage, which has no connection to the preceding lineage, has a maximum depth of two generations (v. 12). He and his many descendants have a long reach. One of Shaḥaraim's seed builds Lud and Ono (v. 12), which lie beyond the traditional territory ascribed to Benjamin (Josh 18:11–28). Shaḥaraim himself fathers children in the land of Moab.

8:8. "Moab." Many commentators attribute the mention of Moab to an earlier period (e.g., Judg 3:12–30; 1 Sam 22:3–5) purportedly referred to in a source within the Chronicler's employ. But the link to Moab is not altogether surprising in a Persian period context. In spite of earlier dire predictions about Moab's fate and Yhwh's relationship to it (e.g., Zeph 2:8–11), the literature from Yehud displays an interest in the connections between the eastern and western sides of the

Jordan (Dan 11:41; Ruth 1:4, 22; 2:2, 6, 21; 4:5, 10; 1 Chr 4:22; 18:2, 11; cf. 2 Chr 20:1, 10, 22–23). It should also be pointed out that "Paḥath-moab" appears as a prominent Jewish family or phratry in Ezra (2:6; 8:4; 10:30) and Nehemiah (3:11; 7:11; 10:15 [ET 10:14]).

"sent them away." The comment is parenthetical. Shaḥaraim fathered children after he divorced his wives Ḥushim and Baara. For other examples of the use of *šlḥ* in the context of divorce, see Deut 24:1; Isa 50:1; Jer 3:8. Tg. adds that "he remarried them," which harmonizes v. 8 with v. 11.

"Ḥushim" (also v. 11). See the second TEXTUAL NOTE to 7:12.

"Baara" *(bʿrʾ)*. So MT. The name is found among the Samaria ostraca (Davies, §§3.045.2//3.046.2; 3.047.1).

8:9. "Jobab" *(yôbāb)*. Also the name of a South Arabian people (Gen 10:29// 1 Chr 1:23), an Edomite king (Gen 36:33//1 Chr 1:44), a Canaanite king (Josh 11:1), and a son of Elpaal (1 Chr 8:18).

"Mesha" *(myšʿ)*. The name is famous because of the Moabite stela detailing the exploits of King Mesha (*KAI* 181; 2 Kgs 3:4), but it also occurs in the Judahite genealogy (1st NOTE to 2:42–45).

8:11. "Ḥushim: Abiṭub and Elpaal." There is a conflict with v. 8, as Ḥushim is already exiled, but the point of this notice is to mention Shaḥaraim's two sons through Ḥushim.

8:12. "Eber, Misham, and Shemer." A second and altogether different set of Elpaal's sons is given in vv. 17–18.

"he built." That is, Elpaal (v. 11). The Babylonian Talmud (*b. Meg.* 49) raises the question of how Elpaal (or his sons) could have built these towns, assuming that they had been in existence from at least the time of Joshua. Targum 1 Chr 8:12 states that the towns were destroyed in the Benjaminite-Israelite civil war (Judg 20:48) and later rebuilt. But see the next NOTE.

"Lud" and "Ono" appear among the sites associated with the repatriates (Ezra 2:33). Lud/Lod (Ezra 2:33//Neh 7:37; Neh 11:35) and Ono (Ezra 2:33//Neh 7:37; Neh 6:2; 11:35) are, in fact, only mentioned in late biblical literature. Ono (kafr ʿĀnā) was situated 9 km northwest of Lod (later Lydda; 1 Macc 11:34). It has been claimed that the author of Neh 6:2 assumes that the "Ono Valley" *(biqʿat ʾônô)* lies beyond the territory of Yehud (Blenkinsopp 1988: 266), but others (E. Stern 1982b: 245–49; Williamson 1985: 34, 253–55) suggest that Yehud included Lod and Ono within its northwest borders. Assuming, for the moment, that the sites in the list of (re)patriates refer to their destinations, as opposed to their ancestral homes, it is not necessary to hold that all of these places were located within the confines of Yehud. Some of the people in the list of Ezra 2//Neh 7 could have lived within communities that lay outside of Yehud's borders. How these Benjaminites came to settle so far to the northwest is, however, itself an interesting puzzle. It would seem that segments of the Benjaminite population (here associated with Elpaal) migrated to the northwest during the Persian era. Political stability, trade, and agriculture may all have been factors in this movement (Lipschits 1997). At least, this would explain the existence of a significant Jewish population in the Modein area in the Hellenistic era.

8:13. "Beriah." Neither this name *(bĕrîʿâ)* nor Shema appear in previous verses. In the segmented genealogy that follows (vv. 13–28), the author traces the offspring of Beriah, Shema, and their kinsmen Shashaq and Jeremoth (v. 14) for one generation. In earlier texts, Beriah is associated with Asher (Gen 46:17; Num 26:44–45; 1 Chr 7:30) and Ephraim (1 Chr 7:23). Sites mentioned in conjunction with the Beriah clan are Ayyalon, Gath, Beth-ḥoron, and Uzzen-sheerah (1 Chr 7:21–24; 8:13). Given the reoccurrence of the name Beriah (1 Chr 7:23), many scholars see a connection with the incident described in 1 Chr 7:21. If so, it would mark a reversal of the situation described there. In the view of Kallai (1986a: 306), land that earlier had been associated with or claimed by Ephraim came to be associated with Benjamin. Alternatively, Chronicles may preserve competing claims to the same territory by different groups.

"Ayyalon" *(ʾayyālôn)*, located about 20 km west-northwest of Jerusalem (1 Sam 14:31; 1 Kgs 4:9; 1 Chr 6:54; 8:13; 2 Chr 11:10; 28:18), was destined to be part of Dan's inheritance (Josh 19:42; 21:24), but is listed as uncaptured (Judg 1:35). See also the 1st TEXTUAL NOTE to 6:54.

"put Gath's inhabitants to flight." The statement is abstruse. Within biblical literature there is overwhelming evidence that Gath (T. ʾeṣ-Ṣâfī; Rainey 1975a; Schniedewind 1998) was a Philistine city (1 Sam 5:8; 6:17; 17:4, 23, 52; 27:2–4; 2 Sam 1:20; 1 Kgs 2:39–41; 2 Kgs 12:17; Amos 6:2; Mic 1:10, 14; cf. Josh 11:22; Amos 1:6–8). In Joshua, Gath is not assigned to any of the Israelite tribes. Only in some instances is the claim made that Israel controlled or won victories in Gath and its vicinity (1 Sam 7:14; 2 Sam 21:20–22 [1 Chr 20:4–8]; 1 Chr 8:13; 18:1; 2 Chr 11:8; 26:6). But some references to Gath may apply to a different city with that name situated at the western approaches to the Valley of Ayyalon, that is, Gath-gittaim (= Rās ʾAbu Ḥāmid?) west of Gezer and east of Ramleh (Kallai 1986a: 24–25). A few of the conquests of Gath mentioned above may refer to Gath-gittaim rather than to Philistine Gath (e.g., 1 Sam 8:13–14; 1 Chr 7:21; 8:13). In any case, the text does not claim that Beriah and Shema conquered Gath permanently, only that they scattered its citizens.

8:15. "Arad, Ader." Both of these are also names of towns (Num 21:1; 33:40; Josh 12:14; 15:21).

8:18. "Elpaal." If this is the same Elpaal as the Elpaal of vv. 11–12 (a son of Shaḥaraim and Ḥushim), then there are two different sets of children associated with Elpaal. See the TEXTUAL NOTES to vv. 11–12, 18.

8:24. "Anthothiah" *(ʿnttyh)*. The name (cf. "Anathoth"; 1 Chr 7:8; Neh 10:20) is taken from the Levitical Benjaminite town of Anathoth (2nd NOTE to 7:8).

8:25. "Penuel." On the site by this name, see the 1st NOTE to 4:4.

8:27. "Jeroḥam" *(yrḥm)* may be the same individual as Jeremoth *(yrmwt)* in v. 14, but the discrepancy in names remains unresolved.

8:28–38. "these were the ancestral heads." These verses are largely parallel to 1 Chr 9:34–44 (see NOTES). See further in SOURCES below.

8:28. "Jerusalem." The claim that all of these ancestral heads resided in Jerusalem is puzzling. Earlier statements identify ancestral heads of Geba (v. 6) and Ayyalon (v. 13). Elpaal builds Ono and Lud (v. 12). The tension results from the borrowing of 1 Chr 9:34–44 from its original location in 1 Chr 9. The duplication of the Saulide genealogy in the present context, without any significant reediting, creates a disjunction with the material in previous verses (see also R. Braun 1986: 123).

8:29–40. "father . . . Jeiel." Almost all scholars break up this genealogy into two (vv. 29–32, 32–40) or three (vv. 29–32, 33–38, 39–40) sections and label the second as the Saulide genealogy. Originally, the material may have pertained to two or three separate genealogies, but these lineages have been brought together and unified in the present literary context. Ner, who fathers Qish (v. 33), is undoubtedly the Ner who appears as Jeiel's fifth son (v. 30). Similarly, the "sons of Esheq" (v. 39) relate to "his brother," that is, to Azel (vv. 37–38). Miqloth (v. 32) and Ner (v. 33) are both descendants of Jeiel. Azel (vv. 37–38) and Esheq (v. 39) are both sons of Eleasah (v. 37). In brief, the entire section can be best viewed in its present context as one complex lineage.

8:29. "father." Probably in the sense of "founder" ("Excursus: The Genealogies").

"Gibeon." Also assigned to Benjamin in the tribal allotments (Josh 18:25; cf. 21:17) and in the Levitical town lists (Josh 21:17//1 Chr 6:45). With the discovery of dozens of seventh- to sixth-century B.C.E. jar handles inscribed "Gibeon" (גבען) at *el-Ǧîb* (Davies, §§22.001–061), the identification of Gibeon with this site, some 12 km northwest of Jerusalem, is secure. Gibeon figures noticeably in Nehemiah and Chronicles (Neh 3:7; 7:25; 1 Chr 8:29; 9:35; 14:16; 16:39; 21:29; 2 Chr 1:3, 13). In this context, one of Saul's ancestors, Jeiel, is presented as "the father" (= founder) of Gibeon. In Samuel Gibeah appears as the home of Saul (1 Sam 10:26) and as Israel's capital during Saul's reign (1 Sam 10.26; 15:34; 22:6; 23:19; Edelman 1991; 1996; 2003). The residents of Gibeon, according to 2 Sam 21:1–9, did not have good relations with the Saulides. On Gibeon's religious significance, see the 3rd NOTE to 16:39.

8:32. "resided opposite (נגד) their kinsmen in Jerusalem." The text intimates that certain Benjaminites (e.g., Miqloth and Shimeah) lived within Jerusalem near other Benjaminites. However obscurely expressed, the point is significant. Jerusalem lay near the border between Judah and Benjamin (Josh 18:28; 18:16), but the tribal allotments situate Jerusalem within Benjamin itself (Josh 18:28; Kallai 1986a: 136–37). The genealogies of Judah (2:3–4:23) note that David reigned in Jerusalem (3:4), but they do not contradict the claim that Jerusalem was part of Benjamin. Aside from the mention of Jerusalem with respect to David's rule, Jerusalem does not appear in the Judahite lineages.

8:33. "Qish." A case of neponymy (v. 30). See further the 2nd NOTE to 2:25.

8:35. "Melech" *(mlk)*. The hypocoristic name, "(God is) king," may be compared with the Phoen. and Pun. PNs *mlk* (Lemaire 2001: 10–11).

8:36. "Azmaveth" *(ʿazmāvet)*. The name, meaning "(the god) Death is strong," occasionally appears elsewhere, but especially in Chronicles (2 Sam 23:31//1 Chr 11:33; 8:36//9:42; 12:3; 27:25). For a different understanding of the name's meaning, see Noth (1928: 231). Note also the toponym in Benjamin, (Bet-)azmaveth (Ezra 2:24//Neh 7:28; Neh 12:29).

"Moza" *(môṣaʿ)*. Aside from the parallel in 9:42, the name appears elsewhere in Chronicles only in 2:46 (as a descendant of Caleb). But mention should also be made of *mōṣâ*, a Benjaminite site (Josh 18:26; Noth 1953: 112).

8:39–40. This material, unparalleled in 9:34–44, extends the Jeielite genealogy to two more generations by dealing with a collateral line, the progeny of Esheq, brother of Azel (v. 37). Hence, the material in 8:39–40 updates the genealogy found in 9:35–44 (and 8:29–38). Comprising both linear and segmented forms, the genealogy of 8:29–40 is one of the longest in the HB. With the material included in vv. 39–40, the lineage extends to seventeen generations. The final summary ("all these . . .") is editorial in nature.

8:39. "Elipheleṭ" *(ʾĕlîpeleṭ)*. The element *plṭ* is common in some Benjaminite PNs: *palṭî* (Num 13:9; 1 Sam 25:44); *palṭîʾēl* (2 Sam 3:15).

8:40. "archers." See the 2nd NOTE to 7:11.

"150." The number is quite low by the Chronicler's standards and pales in comparison with the size of the three Benjaminite phratries (7:7, 9, 11). The small number may be compared with some numbers in the list of Ezra 2//Neh 7.

9:1. "all Israel was genealogically registered." This statement concludes the genealogical survey of Israelite tribes (2:3–8:40). As such, it forms an *inclusio* with the introduction to Jacob's sons in 2:1, "these are the sons of Israel." Because the conclusion to the genealogies also contains references to the exile and the return (see the 3rd NOTE below), 9:1–2 mark off the genealogical prologue as a separate, self-contained section within the book. This use of genealogy as an introduction to the story of the monarchy is remarkable. The juxtaposition of genealogy with narratives is unusual, but perhaps not unprecedented in the ancient world ("Excursus: The Genealogies"). What is the literary effect of prefacing narratives about the monarchy with lineages of Israel's various tribes? In one sense, the genealogies in Chronicles provide both an introduction to the people of Israel—their origins, identity, relationships—and a variety of anecdotes about their development. References to individual monarchs and events during the monarchy are, of course, often found within the genealogies themselves. The genealogies record generations of priests and kings who served during the kingdom of Judah. In another sense, the Israel discussed in the genealogies outlives the monarchy discussed in the history (1 Chr 10–2 Chr 36). The account of the United Monarchy narrates, among other things, the consolidation of the Davidic kingdom, the establishment of Jerusalem, and Solomon's construction and administration of the First Temple. These normative institutions remain during the Judahite monarchy, but come to an end with the Babylonian exile. The people themselves survive, however, and return at a later time to rebuild (COMMENT on 9:2–34).

"the book of the kings of Israel and Judah" *(sēper malkê yiśrāʾēl wîhûdâ)*. The appearance of this expression reflects the popularization of the royal annals alluded to so often in the accounts of the divided monarchy found in Kings and Chronicles (2nd TEXTUAL NOTE to v. 1). In this author's usage, official documents purporting to recount the actions of various monarchs come to represent a much broader repository of information about the nation as a whole.

"exiled to Babylon." In Chronicles the people's very identity is bound up with its land. Living in an age in which Judaism had already become an international religion, the author proclaims that Judean distinctiveness derives from the land and Jerusalem's central position within that land. Hence, the author's coverage of the people's genealogical records ends with the Babylonian exile and resumes with the people's return to the land. Nothing is said either about the nature and extent of the Neo-Babylonian period or about the intervening years between the exile and the return (9:2). To be sure, the narration of smaller individual or group exiles makes it clear that the people can survive even if they do not inhabit their land (Ben Zvi 1993). But even for those Israelites who find themselves living within other states, Jerusalem remains critical to their identity. Deportation to and inhabitation of other states is linked to rebellion against Yhwh (1 Chr 5:25–26; 9:1–2; 2 Chr 6:36–39; 28:8–15; 30:6–9; 33:10–13). Living within foreign lands is more of an interlude to one's return home than privileged as a normal way of life. In the context of the Persian and early Hellenistic age, those who call themselves Israelites may find themselves scattered in different places, but even so, Jerusalem is indispensable to their identity and future hopes as a people. In this respect, the genealogical prologue (1 Chr 1–9) and the history of the monarchy (1 Chr 10–2 Chr 36), despite their different genres, reveal similar points of view. Both end with exile (1 Chr 9:1; 2 Chr 36:17–21), charge the deportation to infidelity (1 Chr 9:1; 2 Chr 36:12–16), and announce a return (1 Chr 9:2–34; 2 Chr 36:22–23).

"their transgression." The root *mʿl* is one of the Chronicler's favorites to denote individual and collective disobedience (1st NOTE to 10:13).

SOURCES AND COMPOSITION

A small portion of the material in the Benjaminite genealogy can be traced to earlier biblical sources, but the rest is unparalleled.

1 Chronicles 8	*Source*
8:1–3a	Gen 46:21; Num 26:38–40
8:3b	Judg 3:15
8:33	1 Sam 31:2 (cf. 14:49; 2 Sam 2:8–10.)
8:34	2 Sam 4:4; 9:12

If the Chronicler (and later editors) obtained additional information from oral or written sources to compose vv. 4–27, 28–32, 35–38, 39–40, those sources are now lost to us. Elsewhere the Jeielite genealogy serves as a prelude to the reign of Saul (1 Chr 9:35–44; 10:1–14). An editor has borrowed the genealogical material from that context to fill out the Benjaminite genealogy here. Three considerations point in this direction. First, as the TEXTUAL NOTES to vv. 28–38 demonstrate, 9:34–44 often bear the earlier reading when 8:28–38 and 9:34–44 are in conflict. One could argue, of course, that 8:28–38 have simply suffered more textual corruption than 9:34–44 have, but then one would have to contend that an earlier version of 8:28–38 was the source of 9:34–44 and that 9:34–44 accidentally came to be better preserved than 8:28–38. The more parsimonious explanation is to be preferred. Second, the summary statement about the inhabitants of Jerusalem (8:28) fits much more naturally in 9:34–44 than in 8:28–38, because 9:2–34 comprises a list of returnees from exile. In contrast, the statement about Jerusalem's inhabitants in 8:28 is awkward in the context of 8:1–27 because Geba, Manaḥath (v. 6), Moab (v. 8), Ono, Lud (v. 12), and Ayyalon (v. 13) figure earlier as the locales frequented or inhabited by the various Benjaminite clans (NOTE to v. 28). Third, the material in 8:39–40 is best understood as an early addition to 8:29–38, an interpolation that left the otherwise duplicate genealogy of 9:35–44 untouched. One could argue the contrary position that the writer of 9:35–44 omitted the material in 8:39–40, but one would have to explain why. It seems more likely that a later editor added 8:29–38 (or 8:29–38 with the expansion of 8:39–40) to fill out the Benjaminite genealogies of 8:1–28.

The addition of 8:29–40 to the Benjaminite genealogies creates a curious literary structure in the transition from the genealogical introduction to the narration of the monarchy. Jeielite lineages (8:29–40; 9:35–44) frame the list of Jerusalem's postexilic residents (9:2–34). To put matters somewhat differently, much of the material relating to the last section of the genealogies (8:1–40) and the first section of the monarchy (9:35–44; 10:1–14) pertains directly to Benjamin. However one should reconstruct the history of the composition of the genealogies and their relationship to the narratives about the Monarchy, the attention devoted to Benjamin is revealing (see COMMENT).

COMMENT

As scholars have long recognized, the Benjaminite genealogies in 1 Chr 8:1–40 present a special set of problems. The section does not exhibit a straightforward or coherent structure. The work shows no clear evidence that its authors aimed to compile one continuous lineage stretching from a distant progenitor (Benjamin) to a particular descendant living many centuries later. Like many other genealogies, the Benjaminite genealogies contain anecdotes about particular incidents, tribal movements, and persons. But tantalizing hints about shifts in population and deportations are undeveloped and go unexplained (vv. 6, 7, 8, 12, 13). Some of the difficulties are text critical in nature, but others are not. Obscure features remain. One approach to the issues is to create a continuous, uninterrrupted lineage by radically emending the text (e.g., Hogg 1899; Marquart 1902). Because such moves are so speculative, they fail to inspire confidence.

A second approach (e.g., R. Braun 1986; Kartveit 1989) attributes the heterogeneity to two major causes: the use of disparate sources and the redaction of these sources by a sequence of editors over a significant period of time. This theory has some validity. There is literary evidence to suggest, for instance, that the authors selectively drew from discrete biblical sources and that the Jeielite genealogy is a later addition to the text of 1 Chr 8 (see SOURCES). There are clear tensions both within the text (e.g., vv. 8 and 11; vv. 12 and 17) and between this text and the other Benjaminite genealogy (7:6–11). If this theory rightly points to the hand of more than one author, the theory also has its limitations. If one holds that the heterogeneity has resulted from the work of many different editors, this means that the contributions of each of these writers had the effect of multiplying incoherence in the text. Such a picture of editorial or scribal activity runs somewhat counter, however, to the evidence from Qumran and early Jewish literature about what editors and scribes sought to achieve by means of their embellishments, editorial comments, and interpolations (Kugel 1986; Vermes 1989; Tov 1994). Greater coherence and a more seamless text are among the chief goals of early Jewish scribal activity. To put the matter a different way, supposing that two or more editors contributed to the text, what is the effect of their cumulative activities? Why did they decide not to establish links between the various phratries they posit in Benjamin's past?

A third approach, not entirely opposed to the first two approaches, involves mining sections of the text for items of historical value in reconstructing Israel's past. These scholars (e.g., Yeivin 1971; Demsky 1971; Kallai 1986a, 1998) take the cryptic references to tribal movements, conflicts, and deportations in the Benjaminite genealogies as essentially preexilic records preserved by the Chronicler. The Benjaminite genealogical records bear witness to a long historical development, whether pertaining to early Israel or the late monarchy. That the genealogies in Genesis, Numbers, and Chronicles differ in so many details has only intensified the tendency to see each textual tradition as reflecting a particular historical period. But one must come to grips with the fact that the Chronicler wrote in the postexilic era, not in the preexilic era. Given the paucity of information in Kings about tribal movements, it is understandable why scholars turn to Chronicles and inquire as to how this work might reflect the past. But whatever stance one takes on this issue, it is necessary to ask how Chronicles engages the present. How is the Benjamin in Chronicles similar to or different from the Benjamin of earlier biblical presentations? Why do the authors of Chronicles take such an avid interest in Benjamin? What might be the effect in Persian period Judah of an expansive coverage of Benjamin's lineages?

A fourth approach, which I find quite promising, does not attempt to impose a larger structure upon the chapter. Instead, the Benjaminite genealogy is taken as a set of linear and segmented genealogies tied to different towns and to different social and historical circumstances (Rudolph 1955; Williamson 1982b). The geographical factor (what town one hails from) is as important a consideration in determining group identity as lineage (narrowly construed). The text refers to "the ancestral heads of Geba's inhabitants" (v. 6) and to the "ancestral heads of Ayyalon's inhabitants" (v. 13). Genealogy is tied to civic identity. The towns mentioned may have their own major families whose individual lineages can be sketched, but no large-scale attempt is made to systematize all of the separate lineages or to relate them all, each to the other. Only in one case, that of Elpaal, is there overlap between the lines (vv. 11–12, 18). The phratries have virtually no links between them. From the perspective of the authors, it is enough to subordinate the disparate lineages to a broader Benjaminite identity (vv. 1, 40).

The coverage devoted to Benjamin needs to be set against that of other texts. Like earlier biblical authors, these authors place the Benjaminites last and present certain Benjaminites as adept warriors (8:40; 2nd NOTE to 7:11). But Chronicles also modifies and contests earlier notions. Some scholars (e.g., Elliger 1962: 383) have argued that Benjamin's terminal position in Jacob's blessing (Gen 49:1–27) reflects Benjamin's historical status as the smallest and weakest of all the Israelite tribes. Indeed, in alluding to a festal procession of select Israelite tribes, the author of Ps 68:28 [ET 68:27] speaks of "little Benjamin" (בנימן צעיר) leading them. Geographically, the tribe is consigned to a small portion of land in the territorial allotments of Joshua, a wedge sandwiched in the midst of three other tribes (Josh 18:11–28): Ephraim to the north, Gad to the west, and Judah to the south. In the Deuteronomistic History, Benjamin has a mixed record. To take two notorious examples, the Benjaminite rape of a Levitical concubine leads to an Israelite civil war, which pits eleven tribes against one (Judg 19–21). Ironically, the very effort to save the integrity of the tribal union almost results in the decimation of one tribe. The book ends with a state of near anarchy as various Israelite tribes desparately arrange for an ambush of Shilonite women so that the remaining Benjaminite men can marry and repopulate their depleted ranks (Bal 1988; Exum 1990). In another case, two Benjaminite military commanders turn against their kin and king (Ishbaal) and assassinate him in the hope of currying favor with David (2 Sam 4:2–8). Benjamin in these sources is not one of the most acclaimed and celebrated of Israel's tribes.

This picture drawn from these biblical sources needs to be set against written and material evidence pertaining to the Neo-Babylonian era and the Persian period. The devastating impact of the Babylonian exiles is very much emphasized in 2 Kgs 24–25 and in a variety of other biblical texts (D. Smith 1989; E. Stern 2001: 303–50). Although destruction levels likely caused by the Babylonian invasions have been detected at many Judahite sites, there is also evidence of continuation of settlement at others, especially north of Jerusalem (A. Mazar 1990: 548–49; Ofer 1993a). Large areas of Benjamin seem to have been unaffected by the Babylonian campaigns (Lipschits 1998). Indeed, a Benjaminite town—Mizpah—becomes the adiministrative capital of Judah during Gedaliah's rule in the wake of the destruction of Jerusalem and the downfall of the Davidic dynasty (2 Kgs 25:22–24). It is interesting to note in this context that texts in the book of Jeremiah make no attempt to obscure the fact that only a portion of the people were exiled (Jer 40:7–12). Jeremiah purchases real estate (Jer 32:6–15) and wishes to remain in the land, despite the deportation of many Judahites and the assassination of Gedaliah (2 Kgs 25:25–26; Jer 39:14; 40:1–6; 42:10; Pohlmann 1978: 99–109; Seitz 1989: 279–81). An archaeological survey of the Benjaminite region conducted by Finkelstein and Magen indicates that the areas associated with Benjamin, excepting Jerusalem and its environs, did not undergo any significant population decrease until the late sixth century (Finkelstein and Magen 1993; Lipschits 1999: 180–84). The continuing importance of Benjamin is also suggested by Persian period biblical texts. The list of repatriates in Ezra 2(//Neh 7), for instance, mentions many Benjaminite names and toponyms (e.g., 2:20, 24, 25, 26, 28, 33, 34). Some fourteen out of a total of twenty-two names in Ezra 2:20–35 are Benjaminite in character (Blenkinsopp 1988: 83–87).

When seen against the backdrop of late Babylonian and early Persian developments, the keen attention paid to Benjamin in the genealogies makes eminent sense. In Chronicles a conscious effort has been made to contest claims of Benjamin's relative insignificance. Benjamin's final position is a badge of honor. Judah, which appears first, and Benjamin, which appears last, establish the larger context in which the other tribes are considered. Judah, Levi, and Benjamin receive the vast majority of coverage (74 percent) and the critical positions in the overall presentation (2:3–9:1). To be sure, Chronicles confirms the earlier picture of occasional internecine troubles. Notes about internal strife punctuate the lineages (vv. 6, 7, 8). But if allocation of coverage is one sign of authorial commitments, Benjamin does farely well, receiving approximately 15 percent of the total coverage (7:6–11; 8:1–28; 9:35–44).

Geographically, Benjamin's clans occupy towns that are not assigned to them in Joshua. Anecdotes provide important hints about holdings of Benjaminite ancestral houses (vv. 6, 10, 12, 13, 29, 32). Geba, Ayyalon, Gibeon, Jerusalem, Ono, and Lud all appear as founded or inhabited by Benjaminites. Geba, Gibeon, and Jerusalem are all traditional Benjaminite towns (Josh 18:21–28). But as the relevant NOTES point out, some of the sites mentioned in Chronicles are assigned to other tribes in Joshua, while others are not assigned to any tribe at all. At least a couple of sites (Lud and Ono) pertain to Benjaminite movements during the Persian period (Lipschits 1999). The individual Benjaminite phratries are not closely bound together; campaigns are undertaken by phratries and not by the tribe as a whole. The addition of the Jeielite genealogy (8:29–40) reveals that the concern about Benjamin was not confined to one particular writer. As opposed to the impression of decimation left by the book of Samuel, the Jeielite genealogy presents the line of Saul as enduring. This seventeen-generation lineage, extending perhaps to the late monarchy, is part of Israel's larger legacy.

In line with the importance assigned to Benjamin in the genealogies, Benjamin plays a sustained role in the monarchy. Benjaminites, including relatives of Saul, are among those who support David's rise to kingship (1 Chr 12:1–6, 17–19; cf. 21:6). Counter to some earlier biblical texts in which Benjamin is associated with the northern tribes, the Chronicler postulates close ties between Judah and Benjamin. In spite of the crisis created by the northern secession, Benjamin, together with Judah and Levi, remains loyal to the normative institutions established during the United Monarchy (2 Chr 11:1–4, 13–17; 13:4–12). For the Chronicler, the Judahite monarchy centered in Jerusalem represents the continuation of the ideals established during the time of David and Solomon (Knoppers 1990). During this period Chronicles consistently mentions Benjamin's involvement with Judah (2 Chr 11:12, 23; 14:7 [ET 14:8]; 15:2, 8–9; 17:17; 31:1; 34:9), as opposed to the irregular manner of Kings (1 Kgs 12:21).

As works written in the Achaemenid era, the Benjaminite genealogies must be judged on their own terms as declarations of the important role Benjamin plays within a larger Israelite identity. Creating a past, positing the existence of different phratries, and tracing the origins of the larger group into the Ancestral age confer a certain prestige upon the tribe. Because the past is related to the present, the genealogies provide a sense of continuity to those who identified with the Benjaminite lineages in Yehud. From the perspective of the ancient writers, the Benjaminite foundation or occupation of various sites in centuries past establish a precedent for claiming ancestral rights in the present. In appearance the Benjaminite genealogies present confusing and arcane details about various individuals, relationships, and lineages. The precise relevance of some of this information escapes us, but the due attention given to Benjamin's many descendants supports and ratifies the prominence of this group in Persian period Judah.

XII. The Genesis and Contours of the Return (9:2–34)

Repatriation

2 The first residents who (settled) in their properties within their towns were Israel, the priests, the Levites, and the temple servants. 3 In Jerusalem resided some of the descendants of Judah, some of the descendants of Benjamin, and some of the descendants of Ephraim and Manasseh.

Judah and Benjamin

4 From the sons of Judah: Uthai son of Ammihud son of Omri son of Imri son of Bani from the sons of Perez son of Judah. 5 Of the Shelanites: Asaiah the firstborn and his sons. 6 From the sons of Zeraḥ: Jeuel and their kinsmen—690. 7 From the Benjaminites: Sallu son of Meshullam son of Hodaviah son of Senaah, 8 Ibneiah son of Jeroḥam, Elah son of Uzzi son of Machir, and Meshullam son of Shephaṭiah son of Reuel son of Ibnijah; 9 and their kinsmen according to their lineages—956. All of these men were heads of their ancestral houses.

Priests and Levites

10 From the priests: Jedaiah, Jehoiarib, Jachin, 11 and Azariah son of Ḥilqiah son of Meshullam son of Zadoq son of Meraioth son of Aḥiṭub, ruler of the House of God, 12 and Adaiah son of Jeroḥam son of Pashḥur son of Malchiah, and Maasai son of Adaiel son of Jaḥzerah son of Meshullam son of Meshillemoth son of Immer; 13 and their kinsmen, heads of their ancestral houses—1,760, men of substance for the work of the service of the House of God. 14 From the Levites: Shemaiah son of Ḥashub son of Azriqam son of Ḥashabiah, of the sons of Merari; 15 and Baqbaqqar, Ḥeresh, Galal, and Mattaniah son of Mica son of Zichri son of Asaph, 16 and Obadiah son of Shemaiah son of Galal son of Jeduthun, and Berechiah son of Asa son of Elqanah, who resided in the villages of the Neṭophathites.

Gatekeepers

[17]The gatekeepers: Shallum, Aqqub, Ṭalmon; and their kinsman Shallum was the head [18]up until now in the King's Gate in the east—these were the gatekeepers belonging to the camps of the sons of Levi. [19]Shallum son of Qore son of Abiasaph son of Qoraḥ, and his kinsmen belonging to his ancestral house, the Qoraḥites, were in charge of the work of the service, guardians of the thresholds of the Tent. Their ancestors were in charge of the camp of Yhwh (as) guards of the entrance. [20]Phineḥas son of Eleazar was the officer in charge of them in times past. Yhwh was with him. [21]Zechariah son of Meshelemiah was the gatekeeper at the entrance of the Tent of Meeting. [22]All of them, the ones selected as gatekeepers at the thresholds, were 212. They were registered by their genealogies in their villages. They were appointed by David and Samuel the seer in their position of trust.

Their Duties at Tent and Temple

[23]They and their descendants were in charge of the gates of the House of Yhwh—that is, the House of the Tent—by guard units. [24]On four sides there were gatekeepers: to the east, the west, the north, and the south. [25]And their kinsmen in their villages had to come for the seven days at regular intervals (to be) with them. [26]Indeed, there were four chief gatekeepers in a position of trust who were Levites, and they were in charge of the chambers and the treasuries of the House of God. [27]They spent the night around the House of God, because they had guard duty and were responsible for opening (the Temple) every morning. [28]Some of them were in charge of the service utensils, for they had to be counted when they brought them in and when they took them out. [29]Some of them were appointed to be in charge of the utensils and to be in charge of all the holy utensils, the choice flour, the wine, the oil, the frankincense, and the spices. [30]Some of the sons of the priests prepared the mixture of spices. [31]As for Mattithiah of the Levites, he was the firstborn of Shallum the Qoraḥite in a position of trust, responsible for making the flat cakes. [32]Some of the sons of the Qohathites, their kinsmen, were in charge of the rows of bread, to prepare them for each sabbath. [33]These are the singers, the heads of the Levitical ancestral houses, in the chambers set free from other responsibility, because they were on duty day and night. [34]These were the heads of the ancestral houses of the Levites by their lineages; these heads resided in Jerusalem.

Textual Notes

9:2–18. The material in these verses is paralleled to some extent by Neh 11:3–19. The overlap between the two passages has been overstated, however, by many scholars (see the following TEXTUAL NOTES).

9:2. "the first" *(hrʾšnym)*. On this meaning of *rʾšn,* see also Gen 8:13; 25:25; Exod 12:15; Esth 1:14; Dan 11:29; etc. The translation of LXX *proteron,* "previously," provides another viable interpretation of *rʾšn* (Zech 1:4; 7:7, 12; Neh 5:15;

Qoh 1:11), one that is favored by some commentators (e.g., Keil, Japhet). The introduction provided by Neh 11:3 is different: "and these are the heads (*rʾšy*) of the province." Cf. MT Neh 7:5 *hʿlym brʾšnh*, "those who came up at first." See also the 1st NOTE to v. 2.

"residents" (*wĕhayyôšĕbîm*). LXX* *hoi katoikountes*, "the ones settling." Rudolph (1955: 82) proposes *haššābîm*, "the returnees," but MT Neh 11:3 evinces the same root as in 1 Chr 9:2, *yāšĕbû*, "they resided" (LXX *hoi ekathisan*). See also Neh 7:72 *wayyēšĕbû*, "and they resided."

"the priests and Levites" (הכהנים והלוים). So LXX^{L} (*hoi hiereis kai hoi leuitai*), as well as MT and LXX Neh 11:3. MT reads "the Levitical priests" (הכהנים הלוים). LXX^{B} c_2 "the sons of the Levites, the priests." The expression "Levitical priests," familiar from Deuteronomy (Haran 1978: 61–63), is also found twice in Ezekiel (43:19; 44:15). See 2 Chr 5:5; 23:18; 30:27, but all of the occurrences in Chronicles are textually disputed.

"temple servants." So MT and LXX, as well as MT Neh 11:3. Lacking in LXX* Neh 11:3. MT and LXX Neh 11:3 add "and the sons of Solomon's servants." Syr. 9:2 "proselytes" (cf. 1QS 14:3–5; Weitzman 1991: 172).

9:3. "and some of the descendants of Ephraim and Manasseh." So MT and LXX. Lacking in MT and LXX Neh 11:4.

9:4. "from the sons of Judah: Uthai" (*wmn-bny yhwdh ʿwty*). This reconstruction is based largely on MT (and LXX) Neh 11:4, *mn-bny yhwdh ʿtyh*, "from the sons of Judah: Athaiah." See also the pattern in 1 Chr 9:7, 10, 14. MT 1 Chr 9:4 (*ʿwty*), followed by LXX^{L}, has suffered haplography (*homoioarkton*) after *wmnšh* in 1 Chr 9:3.

"son of." So MT and LXX^{AN}. LXX^{B} "and son of."

"Ammihud." MT Neh 11:4 "Uzziah"; LXX* Neh 11:4 *Azed*.

"Omri." MT and LXX Neh 11:4 "Zechariah."

"son of Imri" (*bn ʾmry*). Lacking in LXX* due to haplography (*homoioteleuton*) after "son of Omri" (*bn ʿmry*). Neh 11:4 reads "Amariah" (*ʾmryh*; cf. *Samareia*) and adds "son of Shephaṭiah."

"Bani from" (*bānî min*). So Qere, Vg. (*Bonni de*). Tg. combines features of Qere and Kethib *bnymn* (McIvor 1994: 79). LXX* (*huioi*) *huiōn*; some LXX cursives *Bonni huiou*. MT Neh 11:4 again reads differently, "Mahalalel" (LXX *Malelēm*).

"son of Judah." So MT and LXX^{ALN}. LXX^{B} "and the son of Judah." Lacking in Neh 11:4.

9:5. "the Shelanites" (*haššēlānî*). A restoration. LXX^{B} *Sēlōni*. Cf. 1 Chr 2:3; Num 26:20. MT "the Shilonite" (*haššîlônî*). Later in MT Neh 11:5, "the Shilonite" (LXX *Dēlōne*).

"Asaiah" (*ʿśyh*). So MT. Neh 11:5 "and Maasiah" (*wmʿśyh*; LXX *kai Maaseia*).

"the firstborn" (*hbkwr*). Thus MT. LXX "his firstborn" (*prōtotokos autou*). MT and LXX Neh 11:5 "son of Baruch" (*bn-brwk*).

"and his sons." So MT. Lacking in LXX^{B}, probably due to haplography (*homoioarkton*) from *wbnyw* at the end of v. 5 to *wmn-bny* at the beginning of v. 6. Syr. *wbṣyʾ ʾḥwhyʾ* (= *wbṣyh ʾḥyw*). Neh 11:5–6 continues instead with an ascending genealogy, consisting of some six names, a reference to the descendants of Perez (cf. 1 Chr 9:6), and a numerical summary.

9:6. "from the sons of Zeraḥ. . . ." This verse is lacking in Neh 11:5–7. Cf. MT Neh 11:24 "Petaḥiah son of Meshezabel of the sons of Zeraḥ son of Judah" (LXX* *kai Pathaia huios Basēza*).

"Jeuel" *(yʿwʾl)*. LXX^{B} *Epiēl*. LXX^{AN} and some Tg. MSS "Jeiel" *(yʿyʾl)*; LXX^{L} *Ieēl*.

9:7. "Sallu" *(sallûʾ)*. LXX^{B} biyc$_{2}$ *Salōm*. MT Neh 11:7 *Salluʾ* (LXX *Sēlō*).

"Meshullam." So MT 9:7 and MT Neh 11:7 (LXX *Amesoula*). Neh 11:7–8 continues with a different ascending genealogy and a numerical summary. Neh 11:9a proceeds with some administrative information before the two texts (partially) parallel one another again.

"son of Hodaviah" *(bn hwdwyh)*. So MT. LXX^{B} c$_{2}$ *huios Hodouia*. For Hodaviah, Syr. has *hwdyʾ*. Neh 11:9 "and Judah" *(wyhwdh*; LXX *kai Ioudas)*.

"Senaah." Reading with LXX^{L} *Saana* and Tg.* *snʾh* (cf. Vg. *Asana*). LXX^{B} *Haana*; c$_{2}$ *Hanaa*. MT 1 Chr 9:7 *hassĕnuʾâ*. MT Neh 11:9 also reads *hassĕnuʾâ* (LXX *Hasana*) and adds "second in charge of the city" *(ʿl-hʿyr mšnh)*. Cf. Ezra 2:35(// Neh 7:38) *sĕnāʾāh*; Neh 3:3 *hassĕnāʾâ*. Zadok (1988a: 483–86) thinks that MT 9:7 offers an "eclectic" spelling, a combination of **snwh* and **snʾh*.

9:8–9. These verses are largely unparalleled in Neh 11 (see previous TEXTUAL NOTES).

9:8. "Elah son of" (אֵלָה בֶּן). So MT. Some follow LXX *(houtoi huioi)* and read "these are the sons of" (אֵלֶּה בְּנֵי), but MT's name is attested elsewhere (1 Kgs 16:6–14; 2 Kgs 15:30; 17:1; 18:1, 9; 1 Chr 1:52 [// Gen 36:41]; 4:15).

"Machir." So LXX^{B} *Macheir* (= *mkyr*). The difference with MT, "Michri" *(mkry)*—a *hapax legomenon*,—reveals metathesis.

"son of Shephaṭiah." Lacking in Syr.

"Ibneiah" *(ybnyh)*. LXX^{B} c$_{2}$ *Banaia*; LXX^{L} *Iechoniou*.

9:9. "956." Syr. "999."

"heads of their ancestral houses." Literally, "heads of the fathers for their ancestral houses" *(rʾšy ʾbwt lbyt ʾbtyhm)*. LXX is similar. It is possible that the text has suffered dittography.

9:10–11. "Jedaiah, Jehoiarib, Jachin, and Azariah" (ידעיה ויהויריב ויכין ועזריה). These are all traditional priestly names; the problem is determining their relationship. MT Neh 11:10–11a is slightly different: "Jedaiah son of Joiarib, Jachin, Seraiah" (ידעיה בן יויריב יכין שׂריה). The readings of LXX^{L} Neh 11:10–11, *Iadias* (e$_{2}$ *Iedias*) *huios Iōiareib (b Iōiareim) huiou Iachein huiou Saraia* (e *Sarea*), suggest "Jedaiah son of Jehoiarib son of Jachin son of Azariah/Seraiah" (ידעיה בן יהויריב בן יכין בן עזריה / שׂריה). Taking Jehoiarib/Joiarib as part of the problem, because he (later) appears as an ancestor of the Maccabees (1 Macc 2:1; Josephus, *Vita* 11), Hölscher (1923) and Rudolph (1949) propose deleting *y(h)wyryb* altogether or emending *y(h)wyryb* to *ywyqym* (see Neh 12:10) and changing *ykyn* to *bn*, thus "Jedaiah son of Jehoiaqim son of Azariah." But apart from the dubious emendation of Je(h)oiarib, it seems likely that this genealogy, even in its emended form, is too short to cover the time span from Azariah (or Seraiah) to the latter part of the sixth century. Williamson (1985: 343) suggests an alternative, based on 1 Chr 24:7, 17; Neh 12:6, 19 and the observations of Bartlett (1968) on priestly lists: "Jedaiah and Joiarib, sons of Seraiah." I prefer, tentatively, to read with MT *(lectio difficilior)*. The list sequence "PN_1 and PN_2 and PN_3 and PN_4 (son of PN_5)" is surprising at the beginning of a genealogy, but it is not unique. The same sequence appears in the material dealing with the Levites: "and Baqbaqqar, Ḥeresh, Galal, and Mattaniah son of Mica" (v. 15). Another list of names appears later in the section on gatekeepers (v. 17). Given the genealogy that accompanies Azariah's name in v. 11, the first three names can be construed as representing prominent priestly families (NOTES to vv. 10–11). If the list is to be emended, it might be preferable to read; "Jedaiah son of Jehoiarib son of Jachin son of Azariah." An original genealogy of priestly names may have become partially confused with a priestly list because of the similarity between names in this genealogy and those of prominent priestly families in Yehud (NOTES to vv. 10–11). Considering that the author traced the ancestry of this line to Azariah (Chronicles) or to Seraiah (Nehemiah), the resulting span of time (eighty years—twenty years per generation) would not be unreasonable.

9:10. "Jehoiarib" *(yhwyryb)*. So MT and LXX^{L}. LXX^{B} *Iōareim*; LXX^{A} *Iōareib*; b′ceghy *Iōiareim*; Syr. *ywndb*; Neh 11:10 *bn-ywryb.*

"Jachin." So MT 9:10 and MT Neh 11:10. LXX^{L} *Iōacheim*; Tg. *ymyn.* LXX^{L} *(be$_2$)* Neh 10:10 *huiou Iachein.*

9:11. "Azariah" *(ʿzryh)*. So MT and LXX. MT Neh 11:11 "Seraiah" *(śryh)*; LXX^{L} *(be$_2$ huiou Saraia* (e *Sarea*). Both readings are possible (1 Chr 5:27–41; Ezra 7:1–5), but "Azariah" is likely to be the earlier reading. In the development of the early Jewish scripts, *ʿayin* followed closely by (or joined to) *zayin* resembles a *šîn/śîn* (Tov 1992b: 249). The same ligature is found in Ezra 2:2 (שׂריה) and its parallel in Neh 7:7 (עזריה).

"Meraioth" *(mrywt)*. So MT 9:11 and MT Neh 11:11. Syr. *mzw.*

9:12. "and Adaiah." A few Heb. MSS, and Syr. "and Azariah." Neh 11:12 prefaces "and their kinsmen who did the work of the Temple—822." LXX Neh 11:12 lacks "822."

"and Adaiah . . . Malchiah." So MT. Lacking in LXX* Neh 11:12. MT Neh 11:12 is more expansive (see following TEXTUAL NOTES).

"son of Jeroḥam." So MT and LXX. MT Neh 11:12 adds three names in an ascending genealogy, "son of Pelaliah son of Amzi (אמצי) son of Zechariah." LXX* Neh 11:12 simply reads *Amasai huios Zachareia,* "Amasai [= עמשי?] son of Zechariah."

"son of Pashḥur." At this point, the texts of Neh 11 and 1 Chr 9 temporarily reconverge.

"son of Malchiah." So 1 Chr 9:12 and Neh 11:12. MT Neh 11:13 adds "and his kinsmen, ancestral heads—242." LXX* Neh 11:13 "ancestral heads—242."

"and Maasai" *(mʿśy)*. Thus MT. LXX^{B} *Maasaia.* The readings of MT Neh 11:13 "Amashsai" *(ʿmšsy)* and LXX Neh 11:13 *(Amaseia)* reveal metathesis (Noth 1928: 178; cf. Rudolph 1955: 84).

"Adaiel" *(ʿdyʾl)*. Thus MT and LXX^{L} (Adiēl). LXX^{AB} *Adaia.* MT Neh 11:13 "Azarel" *(ʿzrʾl*; cf. LXX *Esdriēl)*.

"Jaḥzerah" *(yḥzrh)*. A *hapax legomenon*. LXX^B *Iedeiou*; Syr. *ywḥnn*. Cf. MT Neh 11:13 "Aḥzai" *(ʾḥzy)*. Lacking in LXX* Neh 11:13.

"son of Meshullam." So MT and LXX. Lacking in Neh 11:13.

"Meshillemoth" *(mšlmwt)*. Reading with LXX^B c_2 *Maselmōth* and MT Neh 11:13 (Stamm 1965: 420b). MT "Meshillemith" *(mšlmyt)* manifests a *wāw/yôd* confusion. The name is not found in LXX* Neh 11:13.

"son of Immer." So MT, LXX *(huiou Emmēr)*, and MT Neh 11:13. Lacking in LXX* Neh 11:13.

9:13. "and their kinsmen, heads of their ancestral houses—1,760." MT and LXX Neh 11:14 "and their kinsmen, men of substance—128."

"men of substance for the work (*gbwry ḥyl lmlʾkt*) of the service of the House of God." Reading with LXX and Vg. (Kropat, §20). MT *gbwry ḥyl mlʾkt*. MT Neh 11:14 "Zabdiel son of Haggedolim was the official in charge of them" (see also the previous TEXTUAL NOTE). LXX* Neh 11:14 "and Badiel was the overseer." Earlier, Neh 11:12 mentions those "who did the work of the Temple" *(ʿśy hmlʾkh lbyt)*.

9:14. "from the Levites: Shemaiah son of Ḥashub [LXX *Hasōb*] son of Azriqam [LXX *Esreikan*]." So MT and LXX 9:14 and MT Neh 11:15. LXX* Neh 11:15 is similar, but reads *Ezerei* for Azriqam *(ʿazrîqām)*.

"son of Ḥashabiah." So MT and LXX 9:14 *(huiou Hasabia)* and MT Neh 11:15. Lacking in LXX* Neh 11:15.

"of the sons of Merari" *(mn bny mrry)*. So MT and LXX. MT Neh 11:15 "son of Bunni" *(bn bwny)*. Lacking in LXX* Neh 11:15. MT Neh 11:16 continues with other officials and their responsibilities for "the external work of the House of God." This additional material does not appear in LXX* Nehemiah.

9:15. "and Baqbaqqar." LXX^B c_2 *kai Bakar*. It is possible that MT has suffered dittography. In a somewhat different context (see 5th TEXTUAL NOTE to v. 15), MT Neh 11:17 has "Baqbuqiah" (lacking in LXX* Neh 11:17). Cf. 1 Chr 25:13 *buqqîyāhû*.

"Ḥeresh, Galal, and Mattaniah." Thus the order of MT and LXX. Some point to the evidence of Syr. and Arab. to read "son of Ḥeresh son of Galal son of Mattaniah." The names "Ḥeresh, Galal" do not appear in MT and LXX Neh 11:17.

"Ḥeresh." LXX^B *Rharaiēl*; LXX^L *Arēs*; Vg. *quoque carpentarius* reflects *ḥōreš*.

"Mattaniah son of Mica." So MT and LXX 9:15 and MT Neh 11:17. LXX* Neh 11:17 *Mathania huios Macha*.

"son of Zichri son of Asaph." Reading with MT and LXX *(huiou Zechrei huiou Asaph)*. MT Neh 11:17 (lacking in LXX*) "son of Zabdi son of Asaph, the head of the beginning [LXX^L the praise] who gave thanks in prayer, and Baqbuqiah the second among his kinsmen."

"Zichri." So MT and LXX*. A few Heb. MSS, Syr., Arab., and MT Neh 11:17 "Zabdi."

9:16. "and Obadiah" *(wĕʿōbadyāh)*. Thus MT. LXX^B *kai Abdeiah*. A hypocoristicon occurs in MT Neh 11:17 "and Abda" *(wĕʿabdāʾ)*. LXX^B Neh 11:17 *kai Ōbēb*.

"son of Shemaiah" *(šĕmaʿyāh)*. So MT and LXX *(huios Sameia)*. MT Neh 11:17 again has a hypocoristicon *(ben) šammûaʿ*; cf. LXX *huios Samouei*.

"son of Galal." So both MT 9:16 (cf. LXX *huiou Galaad*) and MT Neh 11:17. Lacking in LXX* Neh 11:17.

"son of Jeduthun." So MT and LXX, as well as Neh 11:17 (Qere). Syr. and Vg. 1 Chr 9:16 and MT Neh 11:17 (Kethib) "Jedithun." Missing from LXX* Neh 11:17.

"and Berechiah . . . Neṭophathites." So MT (and basically LXX). Lacking in Neh 11:17. MT Neh 11:18 adds "all of the Levites in the holy city—284." LXX* Neh 11:18 simply has "284."

"Asa." So MT, LXX^{ALN}, and Arm. *Asa* (maximum differentiation). LXX^{B} *Ossa*. Many Heb. MSS, Tg., Syr., and Arab. "Asaph."

9:17. "the gatekeepers: Shallum." So MT (and LXX). "Shallum" is lacking in MT and LXX Neh 11:19.

"(and) Aqqub (and) Ṭalmon" (ועקוב וטלמון). LXX^{B} *Akoum Tammam*. MT Neh 11:19 "Aqqub, Ṭalmon" (עקוב טלמון; cf. LXX* *Akoub Telamein*).

"Ṭalmon." Reading with Neh 11:19. MT 1 Chr 9:17 adds "(and) Aḥiman" (ואחימן; cf. LXX^{BL} *kai Aimam*), probably a dittography of "their kinsman" (ואחיהם), which follows. Alternatively, the name may have been lost by haplography *(homoioarkton)* in the sequence ואחימן ואחיהם ותלמן (Freedman, personal communication).

"and their kinsman" *(waʾăḥîhem)*. Thus MT. A few Heb. MSS, LXX *(kai adelphoi autōn)*, Tg., Arab., and MT Neh 11:19 "and their kinsmen" *(waʾăḥêhem*; LXX *kai hoi adelphoi autōn)*.

"Shallum was the head." Thus MT and LXX. Lacking in MT and LXX Neh 11:19.

9:18. "up until now in the King's Gate in the east." Lacking in MT and LXX Neh 11:19.

"they were the gatekeepers" (המה השערים). So MT. LXX^{AB} αὗται αἱ πύλαι, "these were the gates." Cf. MT Neh 11:19 "those standing watch at the gates (השמרים בשערים)—172." LXX* Neh 11:19 simply reads "172."

"belonging to the camps of the sons of Levi." So MT. LXX^{AB} τῶν παρεμβολῶν υἱῶν Λευει, "of the camps of the sons of Levi." There is no parallel in MT and LXX Neh 11:19.

9:19. "Abiasaph." So LXX. On MT's "Ebiasaph" *(ʾebyāsāp)*, see the 4th TEXTUAL NOTE to 26:1.

"camp of Yhwh." So MT. LXX "the camp" (= המחנה) has suffered haplography *(homoioteleuton)* before Yhwh (יהוה).

9:20. "in times past. Yhwh" *(lpnym yhwh)*. LXX^{B} *emprosthen kai houtoi*, "of old, and these"; cf. LXX^{A} *emprosthen tou Kyriou, kai houtoi*. On the use of *lpnym* (cf. Akk. *pānû*), see also Deut 2:10, 12; Josh 11:10; 14:15.

"Yhwh was with him" *(yhwh ʿmw)*. So MT. LXX^{AB} *kai houtoi metʾ autou* (= *wʾlh ʿmw*), thus introducing "Zechariah . . ." in v. 21.

9:21. "Zechariah." Perhaps add the connective *wāw* (haplography).

"Meshelemiah." LXX^{A} *Mosol(l)am* (= Meshullam).

9:22. "at the thresholds." So MT and LXX^{L}. LXX^{AB} *en tais pulais*, "in the gates"; Syr. *bmnynʾ* (= *bmspr*?).

"they" *(hmh)*. LXX[L] and Theodoret add *ērithmēsē kai*, "counted and."

"in their position of trust" *(bʾmwntm)*. Cf. LXX *tē pistōn autōn*, "in their charge."

9:23. "House of the Tent" *(lbyt hʾhl)*. Thus MT. LXX* *en oikō tēs skēnēs*. Contrary to Rudolph (1955: 88), there is no compelling need to emend to "close to the Tent" *(lĕʿummat hāʾōhel)*.

"by guard units" *(lmšmrwt)*. LXX *tou phylassein*, "for guarding"; Syr. *zbnʾ* (= [*ʾhl*] *mwʿd*). On this meaning of *mšmrwt*, see *HALOT* (649) and the last NOTE to 25:8.

9:24. "on four sides" *(lʾrbʿ rwḥwt)*. Perhaps preface *lʾrbʿt gbwry hšʿrym*, lost by haplography (*homoioarkton*; Rudolph 1955: 88).

"gatekeepers." Thus MT and LXX[L] *pylōroi*, "gatekeepers." Some repoint to "gates" (cf. LXX[AB] *hai pylai*, Syr., and Arab.).

"to the east." Reading *mzrḥh*, rather than MT's *mzrḥ*.

9:25. "at regular intervals." The Heb. *mēʿēt ʾel-ʿēt* literally reads "from time to time" (cf. *mēʿēt ʿad-ʿēt* in Ezek 4:10; *HALOT* 900).

9:26. "gatekeepers." Again (see 2nd TEXTUAL NOTE to v. 24), some repoint to "gates."

"who were Levites" *(hm hlwym)*. Perhaps read *hm mn-hlwym*, "who were from the Levites" (vv. 6, 7, 10, 14).

9:27. "they spent the night." LXX *parembalousin*, "they will encamp."

"around the House of God." MT literally reads "surrounding the House of God" *(sbybwt byt ʾlhym)*. Lacking in LXX because of haplography (*homoioteleuton* from *byt ʾlhym* in v. 26). Some would preface *wmhm* (cf. vv. 26, 28, 29).

"opening" *(hammaptēaḥ)*. MT is elliptical. LXX explicates *(anoigein tas thyras tou hierou)*, "to open the doors of the sanctuary."

"every morning" *(wlbqr lbqr)*. On the distributive, see Waltke and O'Connor (§7.2.3c).

9:29. "were appointed" *(mĕmunnîm)*. Interpreting the *puʿal* ptc. of *mnh* passively (Waltke and O'Connor, §25). NJPS "in charge of counting."

9:30. "prepared the mixture of spices." The Heb. has a cognate acc. construction, literally "pounded the pounding of the spices" *(rḥqy hmrqḥt lbśmym)*. Modern translations differ: "mixed the spiced ointments" (NAB); "compounded the ointment for the perfumes" (REB); "prepared the mixing of the spices" (NRSV). Depending on the ingredients, the preparation of spices could result in the making of an ointment or a perfume; cf. Akk. *rīqu(m), riqqu*, "scented material"; Phoen. *hrqḥ*, "apothecary" (*KAI* 49.22); Pun. *(h)rqʾ*, "the perfumer" (Tomback 1978: 306–7); Aram. *rqḥʾ zy mšḥ*, "perfume of oil" (Segal 1983: 64–85 [§45b.5]).

9:31. "the Qoraḥite." LXX* *koreitē*. Lacking in Syr.

"in a position of trust" *(beʾĕmûnâ)*. Understanding *ʾĕmûnâ* here and in vv. 22 and 26 (cf. 2 Chr 31:18) as a permanent official duty (cf. OSA *ʾmnt*, "security," "protection;" Arab. *ʾamāna*, "security"). This is preferable to construing *beʾĕmûnâ* as "because of their conscientiousness" (Jepsen 1974).

"making the flat cakes" *(maʿăśēh haḥăbittîm)*. LXX* *tēs thysias tou tēganou tou megalou hiereōs*, "the sacrifices of the frying pan of the high priest."

9:32. "some of the sons of the Qohathites" *(wmn-bny hqhty)*. LXX* *kai Baanaias* (LXX[ANS] *Banaias*) *ho kaatheitēs*, "and Baniah (= *wbnyh*) the Qohathite."

9:33. "and these" *(wĕʾēlleh)*. Perhaps add *haššōʿărîm (wĕ)* before the following *hamšōrĕrîm*, lost by haplography *(homoioteleuton)*, thus "these are the gatekeepers and the singers." Cf. v. 17. MT Neh 11:22 mentions an overseer of the Levites, who belonged to the Asaphite singers *(mibbĕnê ʾāsāp hamšōrĕrîm)*, while MT Neh 11:23 mentions a royal decree with respect to the daily duties of the singers *(hamšōrĕrîm)*. Not all of this material is found in LXX* Neh 11:22–23 (cf. Neh 11:15–18).

"the Levites" *(llwym)*. LXX[L] *tōn Leueitōn en tō p(l)astophoriō*, "the Levites in the chamber" (= *blškh*). There is no need to rewrite *llwym* as *wlʾ lhm* (contra Rudolph 1955: 90).

"set free from other responsibility" *(pṭwrym)*. So Qere, a few Heb. MSS, LXX*, and Tg. Kethib *pṭyrym*.

9:34. "heads of the ancestral houses of the Levites by their lineages" *(llwym ltldwtm)*. The parallel in 1 Chr 8:28 lacks reference to "the Levites."

NOTES

9:2. "the first" *(hrʾšnym)*. The most natural explanation of this comment is that it refers to those residents who were the first to settle "in their properties" after the return from exile (v. 1). Some commentators (Keil, Zöckler, Oettli, Benzinger, Kittel, Curtis and Madsen), who prefer to construe the list in vv. 2–34 as preexilic, understand "the first" as pertaining solely to a former (monarchic) situation (1st TEXTUAL NOTE to v. 2). But even allowing for such an interpretation, it would not follow that the catalogue only describes a preexilic situation. The reference to "former" residents could also mean that these people were back in their hometowns. Moreover, after the conclusion to the genealogies in v. 1a and the notice of the Exile in v. 1b, it would be odd for the author to switch back to providing genealogical and demographic information about the monarchic era.

"in their properties" *(baʾăḥuzzātām)*. Referring to one's traditional, landed estate (Gen 23:20; 49:30; 50:13; Lev 25:33; 1 Chr 7:28; 2 Chr 11:14; 31:1).

"Israel" appears as a blanket term covering Judah and Benjamin. The following verses (3–9) elaborate on who these Israelites were. In the context of the Persian and Hellenistic ages, the meaning and use of "Israel" become highly contested. Chronicles contains many plays on the different senses of the term: "Israel" to designate the people as a whole, "Israel" as the northern tribes, "Israel" as the southern tribes (Danell 1946; Japhet 1989; Williamson 1977b; 1989). In the Chronicler's treatment of the divided monarchy, for example, it is not uncommon to find "Israel" indicating Judah, or Judah and Benjamin (Knoppers 1989). Similar restricted usage can be found in some of the books of the Apocrypha (e.g., Jdt 4:1; 1 Macc 1:11, 20, 25, 30, 36, 43; 2 Macc 1:26; 11:6; Sus 13:48, 57). The use of "Israel" in reference to Judah and Benjamin is also found in Ezra (2:2; 3:1; 7:7;

9:1; 10:2, 25). By contrast, the late-third-to early-second-century B.C.E. Samaritan inscription recently discovered on the Aegean island of Delos makes reference to Mount Gerizim and uses "Israelites" to refer to the Samaritans (Bruneau 1982; White 1987). The Delos inscription, which may well be associated with a Samaritan synagogue on the island, demonstrates that more than one community claimed to carry on the legacy of Israel's past.

"the temple servants" *(hannĕtînîm)*. Literally, "the ones given (to the Temple)." Reference to these functionaries is found only in late sources (Ezra 2:43, 58, 70; 7:7; 8:17, 20; Neh 3:26, 31; 7:46, 60, 72 [ET 7:73]; 10:29 [ET 10:28]; 11:3, 21; Haran 1961a; Levine 1963). The term is found only once in undisputed contexts in Chronicles (see the NOTES to 6:33, in reference to *hannĕtûnîm,* and the TEXTUAL NOTE to 2 Chr 35:3; cf. 1 Esd 1:3). Some older commentators regarded the *nĕtînîm* as descendants, literally or figuratively, of the Gibeonites, who, having beguiled the Israelites into making a treaty, were consigned *(wayyittĕnēm)* to service duties by Joshua at Yhwh's chosen sanctuary (Josh 9:27). It is more likely that the similarity in usage (the verb *ntn* can designate "assign," "consign," or "dedicate") reflects an analogous conception of what functions the *nĕtînîm* played within the cult. At the beginning of the Second Commonwealth, as represented by Chronicles, Ezra, and Nehemiah, there is no stigma attached to the *nĕtînîm*; they participate freely in the operation of Temple worship and are party to Nehemiah's covenant (Neh 10:29 [ET 10:28]). In later sources, such as the Dead Sea Scrolls (4Q340; Broshi et al. 1995: 81–84) and the Babylonian Talmud (*m. Qidd.* 4.1; *m. Hor.* 3.8; *b. Hor.* 13a; *b. Qidd.* 70.2a), the *nĕtînîm* suffer a marked decline in status and become likened to and grouped with bastards (Levine 1973; Puech 1986; Broshi and Yardeni 1995).

9:3. "Jerusalem" is essential to Israel's national character in Chronicles (Beentjes 1996; Selman 1999). In line with the city's centrality to all Israelites, not only Judah and Benjamin come to reside in Jerusalem (vv. 3, 34) but also Ephraim and Manasseh.

"Ephraim . . . Manasseh." In mentioning the last two northern tribes, the list of 1 Chr 9 goes beyond that of the parallel in Neh 11:4 (TEXTUAL NOTE to v. 3). This is in keeping with the Chronicler's comprehensive notion of Israelite identity (Japhet 1989: 299–300). Nevertheless, the point should not be pressed too far. The succeeding verses, which deal only with Judah, Benjamin, and Levi, neglect Ephraim and Manasseh entirely.

"Perez." On this son of Judah and Tamar, see the NOTES to 2:4, 5, 9.

9:5. "Shelanites." Shelah was an offspring of the union between Judah and Bath-shua (NOTES to 2:3; 4:1–23).

9:6. "Zeraḥ" was another son of Judah and Tamar (NOTES to 2:4, 6–8). Tracing the various Judean immigrants to three of the major phratries (Perez, Shelah, Zeraḥ) in the genealogy of Judah (2:3–4:23) establishes their status in Yehud. The immigrants appear as repatriates with an excellent native pedigree.

"690." The quantities in this list (see also vv. 9, 13), although large, pale in comparison with the outlandish numbers that typify the Chronicler's account of the monarchy (NOTE to 12:38). The use of such high numbers to characterize the monarchy distances the portrayal of a past classical age from the portrayal of more recent times.

9:7. "the Benjaminites." Three tribes dominate the genealogy of the return: Judah, Benjamin, and Levi. This allocation of coverage is commensurate with the great attention devoted to Judah (2:3–4:23), Levi (5:27–6:66), and Benjamin (7:6–11; 8:1–40) in the earlier genealogies.

"Senaah." His family appears in the list of Ezra 2:35(//Neh 7:38) and among the rebuilders of Jerusalem's walls (Neh 3:3). In the parallel at Neh 11:9, Senaah has an important position—"second in charge of the city" (*ʿl-hʿyr mšnh*). See also the 4th TEXTUAL NOTE to v. 7.

9:8. "Jeroḥam." Only two of the names that appear in vv. 7–8—Sallu, Meshullam, Hodaviah, Senaah, Ibneiah, Jeroḥam, Elah, Uzzi, Machir, Shephaṭiah, Reuel, Ibnijah—also appear in the Benjaminite genealogies (7:6–11; 8:1–40): Uzzi (7:7) and Jeroḥam (8:27).

9:10. "the priests." The short priestly list of vv. 10–11 needs to be compared with the substantially longer genealogies in the later writings (1 Chr 5:27–41; 6:35–38; Ezra 7:1–5; 1 Esd 8:1–2; 2 Esd 1:1–3) and Josephus (*Ant.* 10.152–53). Although many scholars begin with the lineages of 1 Chr 9:10–11(//Neh 11:10–11) in reconstructing the history of the high priesthood, it seems best not to do so. First, on text-critical grounds 9:10–11 may be the most problematic of the various priestly lineages (TEXTUAL NOTES to vv. 10–11). Second, considering that Aḥiṭub (v. 11) is most likely the father or grandfather of Zadoq, the contemporary of David and Solomon, the lineage is highly telescopic. The ascending genealogy ends with Aḥiṭub and does not continue on to Aaron or Levi (see below and SOURCES AND COMPOSITION to 5:27–41). In this respect, the priestly genealogy of vv. 10–11 can be likened to the descending priestly genealogy of Josephus (*Ant.* 10.152–53) which begins with Zadoq (I). Third, neither this genealogy nor the other two priestly lineages in v. 12 are, strictly speaking, high-priestly genealogies (Knoppers 2003). To be sure, the first lineage has connections to the genealogy of 1 Chr 5:29–41 through Azariah, but this does not make the lineage a high-priestly genealogy. None of the figures listed in v. 10—Jedaiah, Jehoiarib, and Jachin—figure elsewhere in Persian period texts as high priests. Similarly, the lineage of Ezra 7:1–5 links Ezra to a line of priests that begins with Aaron "the chief priest" (הכהן הראש) without claiming that Ezra himself was a chief priest. The writers of 1 Esdras (9:39, 40, 49) correct this apparent discrepancy by elevating Ezra to the rank of high priest, but such a claim is not found in the text of Ezra itself.

"Jedaiah" recurs often as a priestly name in Persian period literature (Ezra 2:36// Neh 7:39; 12:6, 7, 19, 21; Zech 6:10, 14; 1 Chr 24:7). In David's time, he appears as the recipient of the second priestly lot (1 Chr 24:7). The family of Jedaiah is associated with the house of Jeshua in Ezra 2:36(//Neh 7:39). Cf. LXX Ezra 10:29. Jedaiah is mentioned as one of the exiled priests who came from Babylon in Zech 6:10, 14.

"Jehoiarib" appears elsewhere as a priestly name in the Persian period (Ezra 8:16; Neh 12:6, 19). Je(h)oiarib is the recipient of the first priestly lot in the time of David (1 Chr 24:7). Another Je(h)oiarib, a contemporary of Jedaiah, is said to have arrived with Zerubbabel (Neh 12:6, 19). A priestly ancestry from the Jehoiarib (Joarib) of David's era is claimed for Mattathias of the Maccabees (1 Macc 2:1; 14:29).

"Jachin." Aside from the parallel in Neh 11:10, Jachin (as a priestly name) only appears in 1 Chr 24:17, the holder of the twenty-first lot during the reign of David.

9:11. "Azariah" also appears as the son of Ḥilqiah in other priestly genealogies (2nd NOTE to 5:39).

"Ḥilqiah." See the 1st NOTE to 5:39.

"Meshullam" is probably to be identified with the Shallum who appears in other priestly genealogies: 1 Chr 5:38–39; Ezra 7:2; and Josephus (*Salloumos*; *Ant.* 10.153). After this point, the genealogy of 1 Chr 9:10–11//Neh 11:10–11 suffers a gap when compared with the more extensive genealogies of 1 Chr 5:29–41; Ezra 7:1–5; and Josephus (*Ant.* 10.152–53; NOTE to 5:38).

"Zadoq." Probably referring to Zadoq I (1 Chr 5:34; 6:38; Ezra 7:2; Josephus, *Ant.* 10.152), rather than to Zadoq II (1 Chr 5:38; Josephus *Ant.* 10.153 *Soudaios*). It seems that 1 Chr 9:10–11(//Neh 11:10–11) has suffered a major haplography from Meshullam to Zadoq (I) triggered by the repetition of Zadoq in the list (from Zadoq II to Zadoq I).

"Aḥiṭub" appears anomalously as the father of Meraioth (so also Neh 11:10–11) instead of as his grandson (1 Chr 5:33; 6:37).

"ruler." Only here (and in the parallel of Neh 11:11) is Aḥiṭub called a "ruler of the House of God" (cf. Jer 20:1; 1 Chr 5:35; 2 Chr 31:8, 13; 35:8). The use of *nāgîd* to denote a high priest is only attested in later sources (משיח נגיד; Dan 9:25–26; 11:22; Collins 1993: 355, 382).

9:12. "Adaiah" (*ʿădāyāh*). As a priestly (Gershonite) name, see 1 Chr 6:26. The name *ʿdyhw* also appears in a variety of extrabiblical inscriptions, including an early Persian period seal: "belonging to Pashḥur son of Adayahu" (Davies, §100.148).

"Jeroḥam" (*yĕrōḥām*) appears as a (Qohathite) Levitical name in 1 Chr 6:12, 19.

"Pashḥur." A priest with this name (patronymic Immer; see 6th NOTE to v. 12) is scolded and pejoratively renamed by the prophet Jeremiah (Jer 20:1–3, 6). This Pashḥur is to be distinguished from the Pashḥur who served as one of the officials (*śārîm*) of the Judahite king (Jer 21:1; 38:1; W. Holladay 1986: 570). The name Pashḥur is found on an ostracon in the Arad sanctuary, dating to the late eighth or early seventh century B.C.E. (Davies, §2.058). As the name of a priestly family in the Persian period, see Ezra 2:38; 10:22; Neh 7:41; 10:4 [ET 10:3].

"Malchiah" (*malkîyāh*) appears as the recipient of the fifth priestly lot in the reign of David (1 Chr 24:9). As a priestly name, see also Neh 10:4 [ET 10:3]; 12:42; 1 Chr 6:25.

"Maasai" (*mʿśy*). A hypocoristicon of *mʿśyh* or *mʿśyhw*, which appear often in the late monarchy and in the Persian period as priestly names (*mʿśyh:* Jer 21:1; 29:25; 37:3; Ezra 10:18, 21; Neh 8:4, 7; 12:41–42; 1 Chr 6:25 [TEXTUAL NOTE]; *mʿśyhw:* Jer 35:4; 1 Chr 15:18, 20).

"Immer" (*ʾimmēr*). Aside from its appearance in Jer 20:1, the name Immer is only attested in late sources (Ezra 2:37; 10:20; Neh 3:29; 7:40; 11:13; 1 Chr 9:12; 24:14). In Jer 20:1 the priest Immer appears as the patronymic of Pashḥur, officer-leader *(pāqîd nāgîd)* in the House of Yhwh. First Chronicles 24:14 situates Immer in David's time as the recipient of the sixteenth course. Ezra 2:37 and 1 Chr 9:12 intimate that Immer's priestly line was represented among the priests returning from Babylon.

9:13. "the work of the service of the House of God" *(mĕleʾket ʿăbōdat bêt ʾĕlōhîm)*. The expression, familiar from other contexts in Chronicles (1 Chr 23:24, 26, 28, 32; 28:20; 2 Chr 24:12), is to be contrasted with the parallel in Neh 11:12: "who did the work of the Temple" *(ʿōśê hammĕlāʾkâ labbayit)*. The usage in Chronicles is significant because it resembles that of the Priestly writers, who often speak of the Levitical responsibility for the work *(ʿăbōdâ)* of the Tent of Meeting (Num 1:53; 3:7–8; 8:15; 16:9; 18:4, 6, 21; Milgrom 1970: 60–82). But *ʿăbōdâ* in Chronicles bears broader connotations and is best translated as (cultic) service (1 Chr 9:19, 28; 25:1; 26:8; 28:14, 21; 2 Chr 34:13; 35:10). Moreover, in this case, the author is discussing the duties of the priests and not of the Levites! Similarly, in 1 Chr 28:13 both the priests and the Levites are mentioned in reference to "the work of the service of the House of Yhwh." Chronicles advances a different understanding of the relationship between the Levites and priests from that of earlier sources (Knoppers 1999a). The writer draws upon specialized terminology appearing in the Priestly source and Ezekiel, but employs it in new ways. Some key lines of authority observed by P and promoted by Ezekiel are blurred in Chronicles. To be sure, the Chronicler does not abandon all distinctions between the priests and the Levites (NOTES to 1 Chr 23:13–14, 28–32). But he does emphasize cooperation and complementarity in sacerdotal relations (see also vv. 19, 30).

9:14. "Shemaiah." Among the Levitical phratries, he represents Merari (3rd NOTE to 6:1). All three major lineages within the tribe of Levi seem to be represented in the return. In each case, the genealogy is telescopic.

"Ḥashabiah" (חשביה). A version of the same name (חשביהו) appears in a late-seventh-century letter and graffito from Meṣad Ḥashavyahu (Davies, §§7.001.7; 7.002.1).

9:15. "Baqbaqqar, Ḥeresh, Galal, and Mattaniah" are traced to Asaph, a figure from the Davidic age who represents the Gershonite line (NOTES to 6:16, 24).

9:16. "Obadiah" is linked to Jeduthun, another figure from the Davidic age (16:41). Jeduthun's own roots are obscure. Jeduthun lacks a patronymic and appears only in late sources, most often in Chronicles (Neh 11:17//1 Chr 9:16; 16:38, 41–42; 25:1, 3, 6; 2 Chr 5:12; 29:14; 35:15). The appearance of *ydwtwn* in a few Psalm superscriptions (Pss 39; 62; 77), while interesting, is unexplained (2nd NOTE to 25:3).

"Berechiah" is traced to Elqanah, perhaps representing the Qohathite branch of Levi (cf. 1 Chr 6:8–11; 15:23).

"villages of the Neṭophathites." Neṭophah was one of the sites in which the Levitical musicians resided (Neh 12:28). On the location of Neṭophah in northern Judah (2 Sam 23:28–29//1 Chr 11:30; 2 Kgs 25:23//Jer 40:8; 1 Chr 27:13, 15; Ezra 2:22//Neh 7:26), see the NOTE to 2:54.

9:17. "Shallum (and) Aqqub (and) Ṭalmon." These family names reappear in other gatekeeper lists from the Persian period, such as Ezra 2:42//Neh 7:45 (Shallum, Aqqub, Ṭalmon); Ezra 10:24 (Shallum, Ṭelem); and Neh 12:25 (Meshullam, Aqqub, Ṭalmon). It is entirely possible that the compiler of Neh 12:1–26 drew on other lists, such as the one reflected in 1 Chr 9:2–18//Neh 11:3–19 (Blenkinsopp 1988: 340–41).

9:18. "up until now" (עד־הנה). A reference to the contemporary operation of the Temple. Unfortunately, the text is not dated to provide a precise temporal context. The description of the gatekeepers' work (vv. 17–32.) alternates between present operations and past precedent.

"camps" *(maḥănôt)*. In older sources, the Deuteronomic work (Deut 23:15; 29:10 [ET 23:14; 29:11]) and the Priestly work (Exod 16:13; 19:16, 17; 29:14; Num 5:1–4), Israel is depicted as a camp, but the allusion here is to specific camps of Levi. Hence, the text seems to recall the camp of Levi situated near the Tent of Meeting (Num 1:53; 2:17 [P]). The author adapts Priestly usage and applies it to the gatekeepers' work at the Temple (cf. 2 Chr 31:2).

"sons of Levi." The gatekeepers are depicted as genuine Levites, as they are elsewhere in Chronicles (e.g., 1 Chr 26:1–19). The summary in 9: 34 also makes it clear that the priests, Levites, and gatekeepers all belong to the same tribe of Levi. But the situation in Nehemiah is not so clear. The list of Levites and its numerical summary in MT Neh 11:15–18 is followed by a list of gatekeepers (Neh 11:19), leaving the impression that these were distinct groups (Gese 1963).

9:19. "Qoraḥites." Their pedigree and notoriety are well known from other biblical sources (Exod 6:21, 24; Num 16:1–32; 17:5, 14 [ET 16:40, 49]; 26:9–11, 57–58; cf. Sir 45:18). The "sons of Qoraḥ" *(bny qrḥ)* also seem to be attested on one of the eighth-century Arad ostraca (Aharoni, §49.1; Davies, §2.049.1). In a few psalm headings, the Qoraḥites appear as singers (42–43; 44–49; 84–85; 87–88). In Chronicles, Qoraḥ's traditional genealogy is not questioned (1 Chr 6:7, 22) and the Qoraḥites appear at least once as singers (2 Chr 20:19). An additional connection with the Qoraḥ of Ḥebron is suggested by the Judahite genealogy (1st NOTE to 2:43). If some of the psalms' superscriptions associate the Qoraḥites with singing, Chronicles presents another function of the Qoraḥites: as gatekeepers (1 Chr 9:19; 26:1). This seems to be a new development. In the Priestly source, the Levites as a whole, along with the priests, bear responsibility for guarding the Tent of Meeting and its furnishings (Num 3:7–8; 18:1–5). In 1 Chr 23:32 all Levites—Qohathites, Merarites, and Gershonites—have responsibility for the "watch of the sanctuary." Here, the Qoraḥites are singled out as having this traditional responsibility. It may be, as some have suggested, that the author is thinking of the special responsibility that the Qohathites (Qohath was an ancestor of Qoraḥ) had of transporting and guarding the most sacred objects (Num 3:31).

"guardians of the thresholds" (שמרי הספים). Referring to doorkeepers, who serve at the palace or Temple (2 Kgs 12:10 [ET 12:9]; 22:4; Jer 35:4; Esth 2:21; 6:2; 2 Chr 23:4; 34:9; cf. 1 Chr 9:22 שערים בספים).

"the Tent" *(ʾōhel)*. The writer envisions or claims that the Tent of Meeting had become a constituent part of the Temple (see also v. 21: *lĕʾōhel môʿēd*; 1 Chr 6:17; 23:32). This is congruent with the Chronicler's presentation of Solomon's reign in which the Ark and the Tent of Meeting, along with its sacred furnishings, are brought into the Jerusalem Temple (2 Chr 1:3, 6, 13; 5:5; Friedman 1992). Associations between the Tabernacle (or Tent of Meeting) and the Jerusalem Temple also occasionally appear in the Apocrypha (Jdt 9:8; Sir 24:10–11; cf. 2 Macc 2:4–5), but these associations are not as strong as those made in Chronicles.

"their ancestors." The author validates the activities of the Persian period Levitical gatekeepers by appealing to ancient genealogy and to two related ancient precedents: (1) the work of the Levites as guardians of the "thresholds of the Tent" and of "the camp of Yhwh;" and (2) their appointment by David and Samuel (v. 21). The appeal to genealogy is particularly interesting because it mirrors, to some extent, the pattern of ancient Greek genealogists, who attempted to link contemporaries or near contemporaries to the heroic age and the mythical past (see COMMENT). Intervening links were not nearly as important as postulating a genealogical tie to the distant past. In this case, the genealogies have a maximum depth of only three generations. Connections direct and indirect are made to Levi, Qoraḥ, and Phineḥas.

"Phineḥas." It is surprising to see him cast as a gatekeeper (2nd NOTE to 5:30). In speaking of his role as "the officer in charge of them in times past," the author may be thinking of the famous incident of Num 25:2–8 in which the community of Israel gathered by the "entrance of the Tent of Meeting" and Phineḥas, acting as if he were the officer on duty, took a spear in his hand and killed an Israelite man and a Moabite woman caught having sexual intercourse within "the domed Tent" *(haqqubbâ)*, that is, within the Tent of Meeting (Cross 1973: 55).

9:22. "appointed by David and Samuel the seer." In Chronicles there is a link between David and Samuel, who is most often called "the seer" (1 Chr 9:22; 26:28; 29:29; cf. 2 Chr 35:18). It is common for Chronicles to tie the reign of a given king to a prophet or seer (Micheel 1983). But only here is Samuel given partial credit for appointing the gatekeepers. On the role and importance of gatekeepers, see the last NOTE to 15:18.

9:23. "the House of Yhwh, that is, the House of the Tent." The phrase "the House of the Tent" is unique in the HB. The author seems to be positing a link not only between the reestablished Jerusalem cult of the Persian period and the Jerusalem Temple cult of the monarchy but also between the Jerusalem cult of the Persian period and the Tabernacle cult of the Sinaitic period. In this manner, the author attempts to establish the high antiquity of a relatively new system of worship. A similar rhetorical strategy is found in the speech of King Abijah to Jeroboam and the representatives of the northern kingdom (2 Chr 13:4–12). There the Judahite monarch posits an identification between the cult of the first Temple and that of the Sinaitic era (Knoppers 1993a).

"by guard units" (למשמרות). It is possible that both here and in 1 Chr 26:12, משמרות designates service units. But elsewhere in Chronicles this term often refers to guard duties (NOTE to v. 27). The usual term for divisions is מחלקות (Japhet 1968: 344–48). The form משמרות here may be the pl. of משמר (cf. Neh 4:3, 16 [ET 4:9, 22]; 7:3; 12:25; Milgrom 1970: 12). The author is claiming another important link with Israel's normative past. The organization of the Levitical gatekeepers into guard units is attributed to Davidic mandate (COMMENT on 26:1–19).

9:24. "on four sides" (לארבע רוחות). The terminology recalls what used to describe the four perimeters (ארבע רוחות) of Ezekiel's temple: רוח הקדים, "the east side;" רוח הצפון, "the north side;" רוח הדרום, "the south side;" רוח הים, "the west side" (Ezek 42:16–20). Similarly, the expression refers here to the four major gates of the Temple (NOTES to 26:13–18). Since the Davidic age gave rise to the plans for the Temple and its proper administration (1 Chr 17:1–14; 21:28–22:19; 28:2–29:9), the gatekeepers recieved their appointment before the Temple was even built.

9:25. "for the seven days at regular intervals." That is, they were expected to journey to Jerusalem so many times a year ("at regular intervals"), and they served as gatekeepers for one week at a time. How often they came depended on how many teams there were and whether they adhered to a strict rotation.

9:26. "chief gatekeepers" (גבורי השערים). The reestablishment of services for the Temple (1 Chr 9:23–33) includes the appointment of four chief gatekeepers, who were responsible for the Temple chambers and treasuries. No such "chief gatekeepers" are mentioned in the charter text of 1 Chr 26:1–19. On the paramilitary duties of the gatekeepers, see the COMMENT on 1 Chr 26:1–19.

"the chambers" *(hallĕšākôt)*. Referring to the chambers of the Temple (2 Kgs 23:11; Ezek 42:13; 44:19; Ezra 10:6; 3rd NOTE to 23:28). Verse 33 mentions singers and Levitical clan chiefs, who also had access to the Temple chambers.

"the treasuries" *(h'ṣrwt)*. Aside from palaces, the other major repositories of wealth in the ancient world were temples. In this respect, temples were important not only as places of worship, but also as banks. Considering the high value of the precious items donated to and deposited in ancient Near Eastern sanctuaries, it comes as no great surprise that these structures attracted the attention of foreign invaders. This was also true of the Jerusalem Temple, which suffered a series of despoliations over the centuries, culminating in the sack of 586 B.C.E. by the Babylonians. Unlike Kings, Chronicles consistently portrays a Babylonian destination for both the Temple furnishings (2 Chr 36:7, 10) and the Temple and palace treasures (2 Chr 36:18; cf. 2 Kgs 24:13; 25:13–17). In this respect, the Chronicler's handling of the national treasuries differs from that of the Deuteronomist (Knoppers 1999e). In Chronicles, Ezra, and Nehemiah, there are clear lines of continuity between the preexilic and postexilic Jerusalem communities.

9:27. "guard duty" *(mišmeret)*. One of the traditional Levitical duties was to defend the sanctuary against lay encroachment (Num 1:53; 3:25–26, 36–37; 18:3, 22–23). Similarly, 1 Chr 23:32 speaks of a Levitical "watch *(mišmeret)* of the Tent of Meeting." So also in Ezekiel's allotment of sacerdotal responsibilities, the Levites are to perform guard duty at the Temple (Ezek 44:14). On *mišmeret* with the sense of guard duty, see also Exod 12:6; Num 8:26; 31:30, 47; 2 Kgs 11:5–7; 1 Chr 9:27; 12:30; 23:32; 25:8.

9:29. "all the holy utensils" *(kol-kĕlê haqqōdeš)*. Referring to the *sancta*, the sacred objects associated with the proper functioning of the sanctuary (Num 3:31; 4:15; 7:9; 31:6; 1 Chr 23:26).

"the choice flour" *(hassōlet)*. Those Priestly passages that speak of the choice flour (for the cereal offering) do so in the context of offerings for priestly ordination (Exod 29:1–30), priestly offerings (Lev 6:1–7:10), and lay offerings submitted to the priests (Lev 2:1–7; 7:11–21; 14:21–32; 23:9–21; cf. Num 6:1–21; 15:1–16; 28:1–31). In these Priestly texts, the Levites are never mentioned. The references in Ezekiel (46:11–14) to the choice flour for the cereal offering and to the unleavened wafer(s) also do not mention the Levites. In Chronicles, however, the Levites bear some responsibility for these sacrificial ingredients. On the meaning of *sōlet*, see the 2nd NOTE to 23:29.

"the wine." That the Levites are in charge of the Temple wine may seem surprising in light of the prohibitions expressed by some earlier texts. Leviticus 10:9 forbids the drinking of wine by Aaron and his sons in the Tent of Meeting (Milgrom 1991: 611–14), while Ezek 44:21 declares that "no priest will drink wine when he enters the inner court." Wine is also, of course, forbidden to Nazirites (Num 6:3, 20; cf. Jer 35:1–6). A related question is whether wine was forbidden to worshipers at the Temple. Was a distinction made between the laity and the priesthood? In this regard, the point is not intoxication (1 Sam 1:13–14; Isa 28:7), but lubrication. The authors of Deut 14:26 answer the question in the positive. They permit Israelites to spend their money near the central sanctuary on "cattle, sheep, wine, or other intoxicant" so that they may eat there "in the presence of Yhwh your God." In any case, the wine need not have been imbibed. It could have been used as a libation (cf. Exod 25:29; 30:9; 37:16; Num 4:7). The use of libations, such as beer and ale, was common in the various cults of the ancient Near East. For example, a late-first-millennium (B.C.E.) text from Seleucid Uruk lists a number of food offerings, including approximately "half a ton of bread and fifty-four containers of beer or wine" (Robertson 1995: 446). The mention of wine storehouses in late biblical literature (Song 2:4; 1 Chr 27:27; 2 Chr 11:11) is interesting, but does not shed any direct light on this specific issue. More relevant is the mention of wine, along with sacrificial ingredients, in the storerooms of the Second Temple (Neh 13:5).

"frankincense" *(lĕbônâ)*. Along with the fine flour and the oil *(šemen)*, frankincense could be used in offerings, for instance, in cereal offerings (Lev 2:1–16; 6:8–17; Isa 1:13; 43:23; 66:3; Jer 17:26; cf. Num 5:15) and in the rows of bread (Lev 24:7; cf. Neh 13:5, 9). Frankincense *(Boswellia carterii)*, a balsamic gum extracted from the wood of certain trees and shrubs, is not native to Palestine and had to be imported. The different species of *Boswellia* are found in India, the Somali coast, and southern Arabia. According to Isa 60:6 and Jer 6:20, frankincense was imported from Sheba.

9:30. "prepared the mixture of the spices" *(rḥqy hmrqḥt lbśmym)*. The text is alluding to the work outlined both in Exod 30:22–30 (P), in which various aromatic spices were to be mixed with olive oil to make "holy anointing oil, a blended concoction" *(šemen mišḥat-qōdeš rôqaḥ mirqaḥat)*, and in Exod 30:34–37 (P), in which various herbs were to be blended with frankincense to make "blended incense, work of a perfumer" *(qĕṭōreṭ rōqaḥ maʿăśēh rôqēaḥ)*. See also Exod 37:29; 1 Sam 8:13; Qoh 10:1 [Seow 1997: 312]; Neh 3:8).

"the spices" *(habbĕśāmîm)*. Some scholars identify *beśem* with *Commiphora opobalsamum*, the so-called balm, or balsam, of Gilead (Song 5:13; 6:2), which in biblical times was grown in the Jordan Valley and perhaps also in Gilead. Biblical writers also employ *bĕśāmîm* to refer to a variety of spices, not all of which can be identified (Exod 25:6; 30:23; 35:8; Isa 39:2; Ezek 27:22; Song 4:10, 14; 8:14; Esth 2:12; 2 Chr 9:1, 9, 24; 16:14; 32:27; *BP* 2.5).

9:31. "making the flat cakes" *(maʿăśēh haḥăbittîm)*. A *hapax legomenon* in the HB, *ḥăbittîm* most likely designates what may be made on a *maḥăbat*, a "griddle" (Lev 2:5; 6:21; 7:9; Ezek 4:3; 4th NOTE to 23:29).

9:32. "the rows of bread" *(leḥem hammăʿărāket)*. This expression (1 Chr 9:32; 23:29; 2 Chr 13:11) or a shortened version of it (*hammāʿreket*; 1 Chr 28:16; 2 Chr 2:4; 29:18) appears six times in Chronicles and once in Nehemiah (10:34 [ET 10:33]). In P the relevant expression is "the bread of the presence" (*leḥem happānîm*; Exod 25:30; 35:13; 39:36; Lev 24:5–9), a phrase that also appears in 1 Sam 21:7 and 1 Kgs 7:48(//2 Chr 4:19). The bread of the presence, along with its accompanying table, is a feature of both Tabernacle and Temple worship. In P, the bread of the presence is discussed solely in the context of the obligations and rites of Aaron and his descendants (Exod 25:30; 35:13; 39:36; Lev 24:5–9). According to Lev 24:9 the bread of presence belongs to Aaron as one of the "most holy things" *(qōdeš qŏdāšîm)*. As such, the bread could only be handled and eaten by Aaron and his sons in the holy place. The instruction to (re)place the bread of the presence every sabbath is, according to Lev 24:8–9, "an everlasting covenant" *(bĕrît ʿôlām)*. The table on which the bread rested was also off limits to the Levites while the Tabernacle was not in transit because it too belonged to the category of "most sacred objects" (*qōdeš haqqŏdāšîm*; Num 4:4–7). The situation is, however, different in Chronicles. Here, some of the Qohathite Levites bear responsibility for the rows of bread (Knoppers 1999a).

9:33. "the singers (*hamšōrĕrîm*), the heads of the Levitical ancestral houses." The author does not elaborate on the identity of these Levites, who take charge of the musical liturgy in the Temple "chambers" (2nd NOTE to 23:28). The reference to their being on duty day and night resonates with the description of their duties under David in 1 Chr 23:30–31: "to stand every morning to give thanks and to praise Yhwh, and likewise in the evening, and whenever burnt offerings are offered to Yhwh for the sabbaths, new moons, and festivals, with the number [being set] according to prescription, perpetually before Yhwh." See also the 2nd NOTE to 6:16.

9:34. "heads of the ancestral houses of the Levites." In his summary, the writer is careful to state that these Levitical leaders, like some of the people from Judah, Benjamin, Manasseh, and Ephraim (9:3), resided in Jerusalem. The statement in 1 Chr 8:28 is not so specific.

SOURCES AND COMPOSITION

The focus of the following remarks will be on the relationship of 1 Chr 9 to other relevant texts. Two portions of the material in 1 Chr 9 are attested in other biblical contexts:

1 Chronicles 9	*Parallel*
9:2–18	Neh 11:3–19
9:34–44	1 Chr 8:28–38

The relationship between 1 Chr 9:34–44 and 1 Chr 8:28–38 has already been discussed in our study of 1 Chr 8:1–9:1. The material of 1 Chr 9:19–34, which largely deals with the responsibilities of the gatekeepers in cultic affairs, likely stems from the authors of Chronicles. It is appropriate to speak of authors, rather than of an author, because it seems likely that the material in vv. 19–33 stems from more than one hand (most recently, Dirksen 1998b). The description of responsibilities within these verses resonates with other passages in Chronicles that relate Levitical duties. Hence, there is no compelling need to posit an extrabiblical Temple source for this material (*pace* Japhet 1993a). As for the parallels between 1 Chr 9:2–18 and Neh 11:3–19, these are distinct enough to suggest some sort of relationship between the two passages. Both list residents of Jerusalem and follow a similar order. An analogy between the two texts and the parallels between Ezra 2 and Neh 7 has been suggested by Ackroyd (1973a), but the differences between 1 Chr 9:2–18 and Neh 11:3–19 are too great to sustain the comparison. Indeed, there are more differences between the two lists than there are parallels. How then should one understand the relationship between the two texts? In past discussions, the nature of the relationship has been imagined in every conceivable way. Bertheau, Myers, and Williamson posit an original source from which the authors of both Neh 11 and 1 Chr 9 each selectively drew. Some (Benzinger 1901; Noth 1943; Rudolph 1955: 85, 94; Gese 1963: 224; Willi 1972: 56) see 1 Chr 9 as a later addition to the text. Others see the list as original to Chronicles, but dependent on the longer list in Neh 11 (Curtis and Madsen 1910; R. Braun; Japhet 1993a). Hölscher (1923) argues the opposite point, namely, that the longer formulation of Neh 11 depends on the shorter formulation of 1 Chr 9.

The aforementioned scholars legitimately propose a number of theories to address a complex issue. Space constraints do not allow us to deal with all of the pertinent questions in this context, but it is possible to offer some observations. (For a more comprehensive overview and treatment, readers are referred to my specialized article [Knoppers 2000c].) Largely overlooked in the studies on the relationship between the two texts is the testimony of LXX Neh 11 (see the TEXTUAL NOTES). As Alt (1951) and Tov (1997: 257) have noted, the shorter witness of LXX Neh 11 represents, in many respects, an earlier text than the longer witness of MT Neh 11. Being less prone to various kinds of expansion, such as the filling out of genealogies (MT Neh 11:7, 13, 14, 15, 17), explanatory comments (MT Neh 11:16,17, 18, 19), summaries (MT Neh 11:3, 12), and descriptions of functions (MT Neh 11:17), LXX Neh 11 represents a typologically earlier text than MT Neh 11. Taken together, the evidence provided by MT and LXX Nehemiah is important because it shows a development within the textual tradition of a single book. This means that one needs to consider not only the use of a source by one or more authors but also the contextualization and supplementation of that source within the history of a book.

Two other factors also support the notion of development. First, some of the minuses in LXX Neh 11 when compared to MT Neh 11 are shared, in part, by MT and LXX 1 Chr 9. Second, MT and LXX 1 Chr 9 share some readings with MT Neh 11 while differing from LXX Neh 11. Conversely, there do not seem to be any significant cases in which LXX Nehemiah and LXX Chronicles agree with each other in places where they differ from MT Nehemiah or MT Chronicles. As for the priority of Chronicles as opposed to Nehemiah (or vice versa), it may be better to think of both works as developing older, shared materials. In this context, it is pertinent to point out that MT and LXX 1 Chr 9 have a number of pluses that both MT and LXX Neh 11 do not have and that MT and LXX Neh 11 have a number of pluses that both MT and LXX 1 Chr 9 do not have. This evidence makes any relationship of direct dependence unlikely because one would have to contend that the authors of Chronicles (or Nehemiah) both excised a substantial amount of material from their source and added their own material. It is possible, of course, that there have been some corrections from one text to another, but the two texts do not seem to be intimately related. One hastens to add that most of the material lacking in Chronicles when compared to Nehemiah (and vice versa) pertains to much more than headings and summaries, in which one might expect editors to be most active. It also involves genealogical information, titles, functions, and numerical totals. Why would an editor cut much of this material and not replace it with his own? It makes more sense to imagine that each editor has gone his own way with earlier material. Moreover, even in those cases in which MT and LXX 1 Chr 9 and MT and LXX Neh 11 all overlap, the readings of Chronicles and Nehemiah contain some important variations in genealogical relationships, titles, and functions (see TEXTUAL NOTES). Again, these variations are much more economically explained by positing writers who each supplemented a source with their own information than by positing one author who configured relationships one way and another author who later abridged, altered, and reconfigured these relationships. In short, the differences between the lists in Chronicles and Nehemiah are substantial. In their present form, 1 Chr 9:2–18 and Neh 11:3–19 provide further evidence for the existence of different literary editions within discrete biblical books. Both (sets of) editors have contextualized and supplemented the catalogue according to their own interests (see NOTES). Given the evidence furnished by LXX Neh 11, one must also allow for development within each textual tradition.

COMMENT

Like most other biblical texts dealing with the Judahite deportations to Babylon in the early sixth century B.C.E., 1 Chr 9 follows the path taken by the deportees into captivity and, after the decree of King Cyrus in 538 B.C.E., back to Judah. The authors do not address the plight of those who remained in the land during the exile (cf. Lamentations). A similar pattern is found at the end of Chronicles. The history of the Judahite monarchy ends with the Babylonian exile (2 Chr 36:6–21) and resumes with the decree of Cyrus allowing the people return to their land (2 Chr 36:22–23). History stops, so to speak, with the deportees' absence from their traditional territory (3rd NOTE to 9:1). By the same token, the genealogies resume in capsule fashion after the exile (1 Chr 9:1) with the first returnees (9:2). The quick literary transition from rebellion and deportation to return and restoration downplays and masks the enormous problems posed by the razing of Jerusalem, the destruction of the Temple, the deaths of many, the overthrow of the Davidic kingdom, and the deportation of the elite. The attempt to underscore the continuity between the late monarchic and the Persian period communities may be seen as an attempt to overcome or, at the very least, contain the negative legacy of the exile.

Like the authors of MT and LXX Neh 11, the authors of 1 Chr 9 address the identity, pedigree, and destination of the returnees. The text validates repatriated leaders in Persian period Yehud by recourse to genealogy (sixteen times in vv. 4–31). The attraction to lineage is particularly interesting because it mirrors to some extent the interests of some ancient classical writers ("Excursus: The Genealogies"). In the surviving fragments of Greek genealogists, great effort is expended in linking a contemporary or near-contemporary person to the heroic age and the mythical past. According to Herodotus, Hecataeus of Miletus was supposed to have been able to trace his family back sixteen generations to a god (*Hist.* 2.143). But such long genealogies appear to have been rare. In many cases, lineages achieved a depth of only a few generations. Intervening links to the more recent past, though helpful, were not nearly as important as postulating a linear tie to an ancient hero who could be linked, in turn, to the mythical age. Similarly, most genealogies in 1 Chr 9:1–34 are telescopic in nature and achieve a depth of only two to three generations, yet some of the connections—whether direct or indirect—are ancient: Perez, Zeraḥ, Judah, Zadoq, Aḥiṭub, Levi, Merari, Asaph, Qoraḥ, Phineḥas, and Eleazar. Other connections are not as archaic (e.g., Immer, Pashḥur), but are sufficiently entrenched to establish the lineage of the officials mentioned. Those recent immigrants who settled "in their properties" (v. 2) are given the patina of a native pedigree.

But when one compares the material dealing with the return in 1 Chr 9 with that in the parallel of Neh 11, one immediately notices how much more attention is given to cultic affairs in the former than in the latter. Chronicles supplements information about Judahites, Benjaminites, priests, and Levites with information about the functions of the priests, Levites, gatekeepers, and singers. Such close coverage of the Jerusalem cult parallels the keen attention paid to public religion during the Davidic monarchy, but the point that must be addressed is the nature of this cultic interest. Curtis and Madsen (1910: 173) speak of "somewhat contradictory and confused" statements in 1 Chr 9:17–34. "Conditions of the writer's own time (v. 18a), of the Davidic period (v. 23), and of the Mosaic period are not sharply distinguished." One may push the issue further. Why deal with the Mosaic and Davidic periods at all? In presenting the first stages of the return, would it not make more sense to concentrate simply on the individuals themselves—their identity, pedigree, and destination? This is largely what the catalogues in MT and

LXX Neh 11 offer. Evidently, connections to the late monarchy were not sufficient to address the challenges faced by the authors of Chronicles in Yehud. Such connections would not give the authors sufficient leverage in making the case for the importance and primacy of the Jerusalem Temple to their readers. Judaism could claim ancient roots, but the Second Temple was by its very nature a new sanctuary and not an old one. In the ancient Mediterranean world the status of a sacred precinct was, of course, very much bound up with its heritage. Innovation, invention, and novelty were not prized as traits of fine religious practice. Given the destruction of the Jerusalem Temple in the early sixth century, defenders of the new cultic establishment built in the late sixth century found it necessary to buttress its position.

Complicating any attempt to defend the Second Temple's status was an important contrast between it and the First Temple. The sanctuary of Zerubbabel and Jeshua, unlike the sanctuary of Solomon, was authorized, endowed, and supported by a foreign power (2 Chr 36:22–23; Ezra 1:1–4, 7–11; 5:13–16; 6:1–12; 7:11–24). The editors of Ezra (1:1–4; 7:27–28; 8:36; 9:9) and Nehemiah (2:8–9, 18; 5:14; 11:23; 13:6) champion this record of foreign patronage, but it is conceivable that there were other Judeans who did not. Even among Yahwists, the Jerusalem Temple had competitors ("Introduction," VI.C). During the late Achaemenid era the Jerusalem Temple did not command the exclusive allegiance of all Yahwists. In a time in which Judaism had become an international religion, the authors advance a case for the centrality of Jerusalem. The coverage of the return begins and ends with Jerusalem (1 Chr 9:3, 34). The authors of Neh 11 provide significant attention to the population of villages (Neh 11:25–36), but this material is not found in Chronicles. To be sure, the writers acknowledge that the repatriates also settled in other towns (1 Chr 9:2, 16, 22), but their focus is on one particular town. The priority given to Jerusalem mirrors the priority given to Jerusalem in the United Monarchy. David's first major public action upon becoming king of Israel is to capture Jerusalem (1 Chr 11:4–9; cf. 2 Sam 5:6–10). Subsequently, much energy is devoted to bringing the Ark into Jerusalem and establishing proper services there (1 Chr 13; 15–16). Because David serves at the behest of all the tribes and leads a united nation (1 Chr 11–12), Jerusalem becomes the patrimony of all Israelites. For this reason Chronicles mentions people from Ephraim and Manasseh, as well as people from Judah and Benjamin, as inhabiting Jerusalem in the Persian period (1 Chr 9:3; Japhet 1989).

In line with the primacy given to Jerusalem in the coverage of David's reign, detailed attention is given to the proper (re)constitution of its cult in the Persian period (vv. 17–33). The authors do not claim that Zerubbabel and Jeshua's temple was actually an old temple. Nor do they directly address the issue of the Temple at all. Instead, its cultus is described in such a way that it becomes virtually indistinguishable from the formative cults of the Sinaitic and Davidic eras. For example, in speaking of the gatekeepers' work at "the King's Gate in the east," the text mentions that they belong to the "camps" (מחנות) of the sons of Levi" (v. 18). By alluding to the camp of Levi situated near the Tent of Meeting (Num 1:53; 2:17), the writers adapt Priestly usage and apply it to the gatekeepers' work at the Temple (cf. 2 Chr 31:2). The text speaks of the Qoraḥites as "guardians of the thresholds (שמרי הספים) of the Tent" (1 Chr 9:19). At first glance, this seems to be a straightforward reference to the Levites' ancient service at the Tent of Meeting. But all of the references in other biblical books are to doorkeepers, who serve at the palace or Temple (2 Kgs 12:10 [ET 12:9]; 22:4; Jer 35:4; Esth 2:21; 6:2). This is also true in Chronicles (2 Chr 23:4; 34:9). Similarly, Chronicles speaks of "their ancestors" as being "in charge of the camp of Yhwh (as) guards of the entrance" (שמרי המבוא; 1 Chr 9:19). Most references to such an entrance (מבוא) deal with an urban (Judg 1:24), palatial (2 Kgs 16:18; 2 Chr 23:15), or sanctuary (Ezek 44:5; 46:19) setting. The Priestly writers do not speak of the entrance, at least using this terminology (המבוא). One could argue, as Curtis and Madsen do, that the writers are confused, but there may be a better explanation. Because the authors wish to link the present state of Temple worship directly to ancient precedent, they repeatedly equate the activities of Levites and priests in late Achaemenid times with those of their ancient predecessors in earlier sources.

For the same reason, the authors go into some detail about the preparation of sacrificial ingredients. As the NOTES make clear, the terminology—"the holy utensils, the choice flour, the wine, the oil, the frankincense, and the spices" (v. 29)—recalls that used in the Priestly source concerning the Tent of Meeting. The antiquarian allusions even include the Temple itself, which is described as "the House of Yhwh, the House of the Tent" (לבית-יהוה לבית-האהל; v. 23). Most scholars would distinguish between these institutions, even as they would hold that one was modeled on the other. But the text underscores the continuity between them by claiming that the Second Temple, much like the First Temple (2 Chr 1:3, 6, 13; 5:5), honored the Tent of Meeting (see also 1 Chr 9:21). In brief, the chapter depicts the Persian period cultus by alluding to two critical developments in the organization of the Israelite cult: the era of Moses and Aaron and the era of David and Samuel (v. 22). For the authors, it is far more important to claim continuity with pivotal developments in Israel's classical past than it is to rehearse the period between the United Monarchy and the Persian period. In this manner, the writers establish the high antiquity and prestige of a relatively new system of worship. When seen against the backdrop of many centuries of continuous orthopraxis, the disruptions of the early sixth century seem less momentous. In Chronicles the exile itself becomes only an interruption in the ongoing story of Israel and its national institutions.

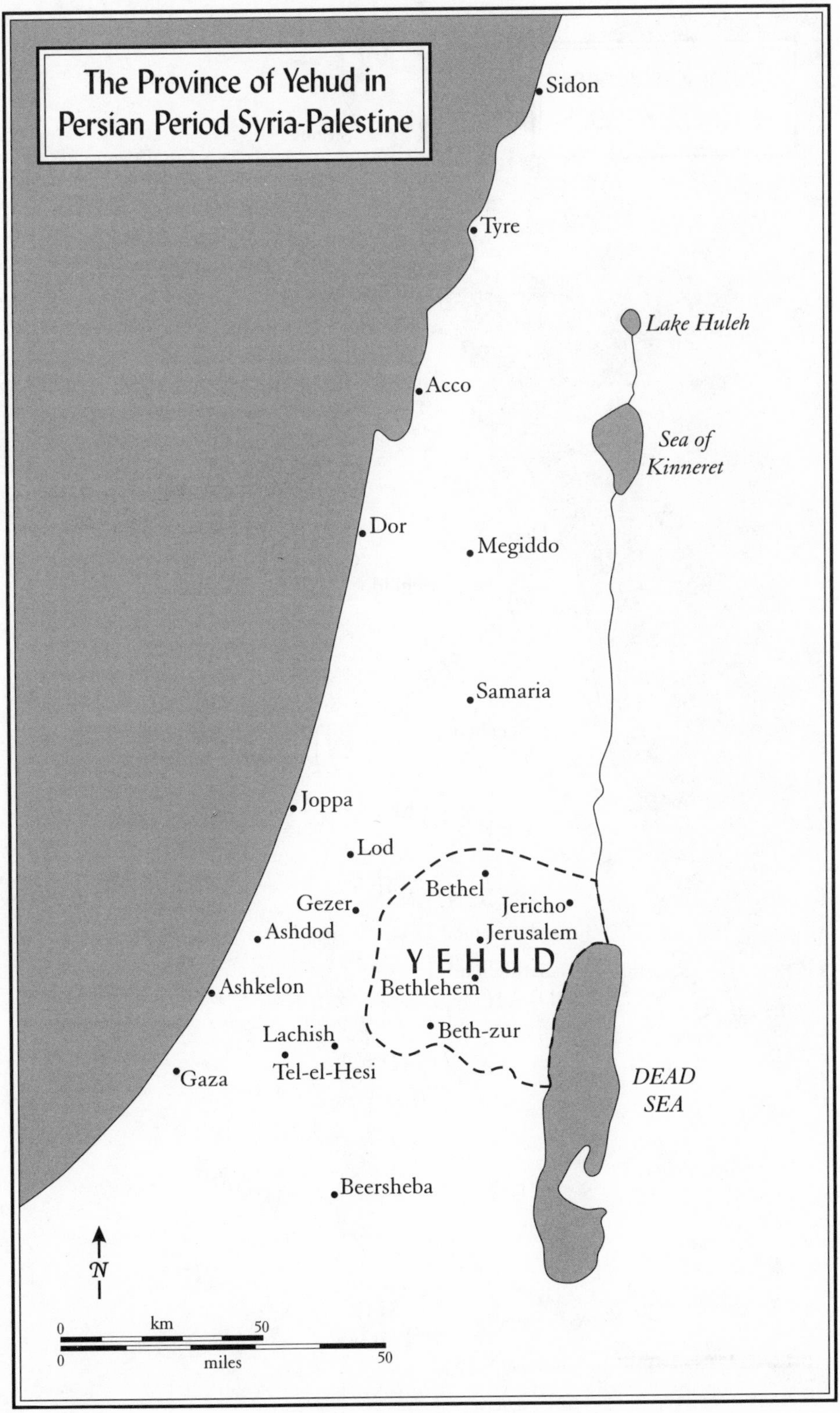

The Province of Yehud in
Persian Period Syria-Palestine
Sidon
Tyre
Lake Huleh
Acco
Sea of
Kinneret
Dor
Megiddo
Samaria
Joppa
Lod
Bethel
Gezer
Jericho
Ashdod
Jerusalem
YEHUD
Ashkelon
Bethlehem
Beth-zur
Lachish
Gaza
Tel-el-Hesi
DEAD
SEA
Beersheba
N
0
km
50
0
miles
50

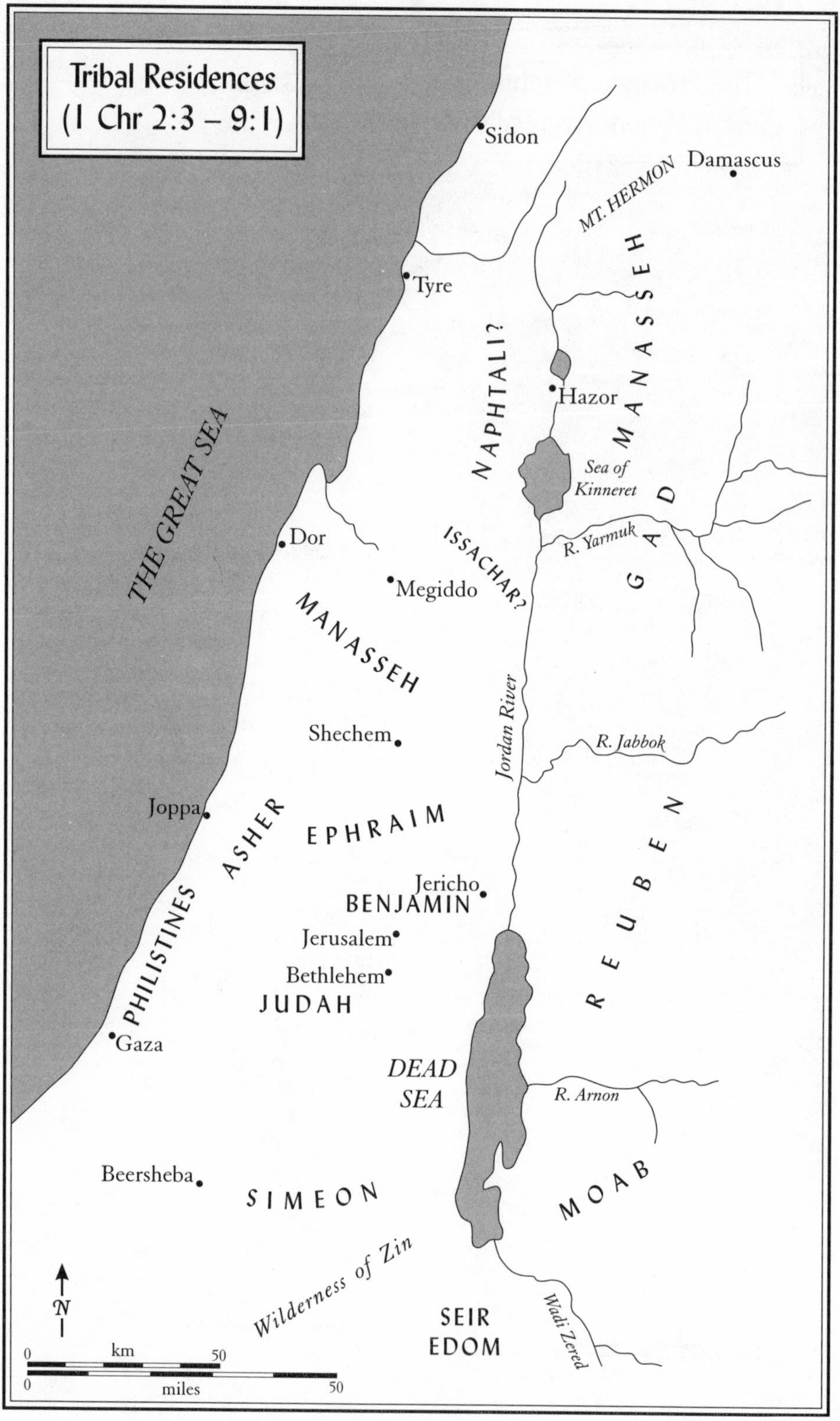
Tribal Residences
(1 Chr 2:3 – 9:1)
Sidon
Damascus
MT. HERMON
Tyre
NAPHTALI?
MANASSEH
Hazor
Sea of
Kinneret
THE GREAT SEA
Dor
ISSACHAR?
R. Yarmuk
GAD
Megiddo
MANASSEH
Jordan River
Shechem
R. Jabbok
Joppa
ASHER
EPHRAIM
REUBEN
Jericho
BENJAMIN
PHILISTINES
Jerusalem
Bethlehem
JUDAH
Gaza
DEAD
SEA
R. Arnon
Beersheba
SIMEON
MOAB
Wilderness of Zin
N
SEIR
EDOM
Wadi Zered
0
km
50
0
miles
50

Selected Sites Relating to the Judahite Genealogies – 1 Chr 2:3 – 4:23

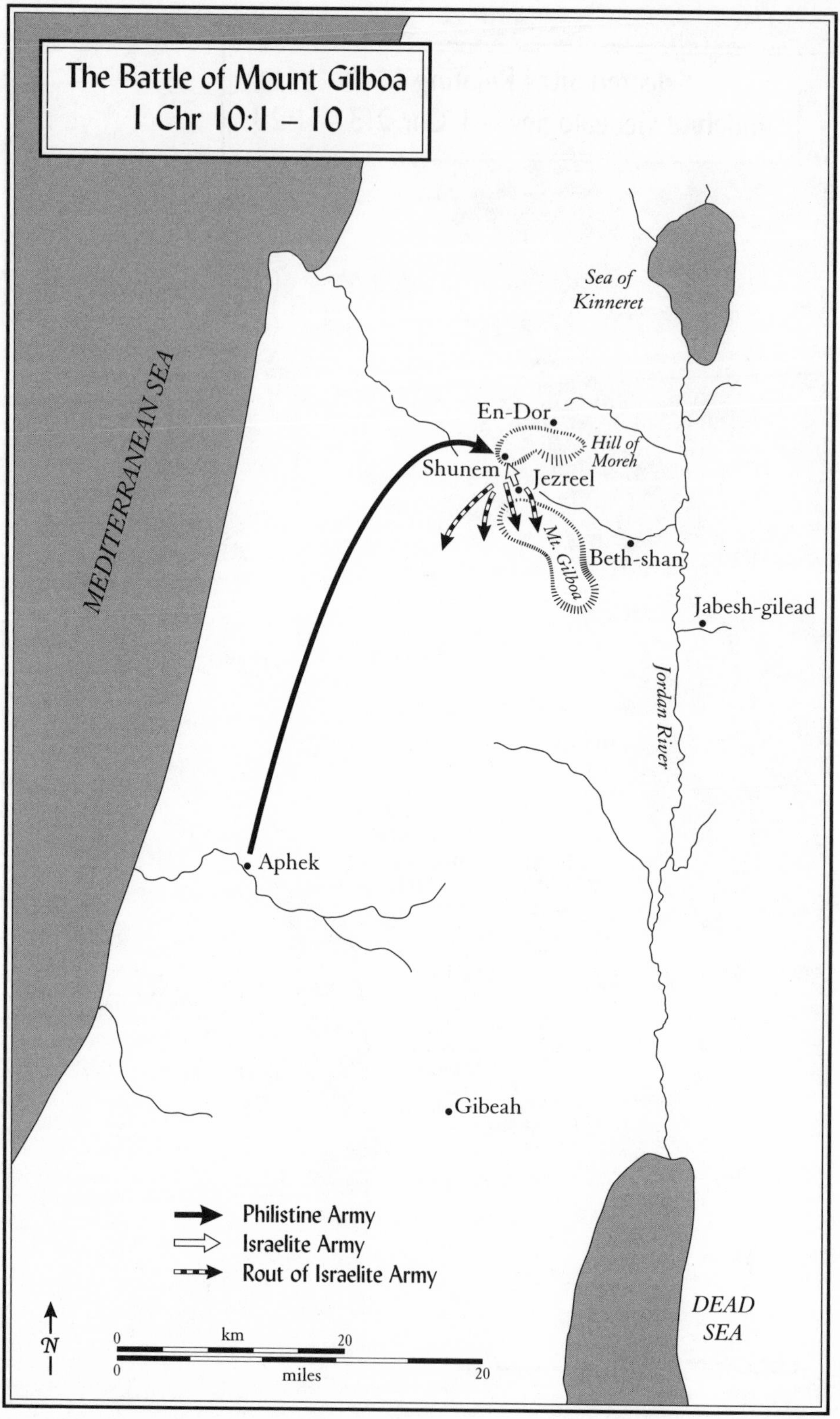

The Battle of Mount Gilboa
1 Chr 10:1 – 10
Sea of Kinneret
MEDITERRANEAN SEA
En-Dor
Hill of Moreh
Shunem
Jezreel
Mt. Gilboa
Beth-shan
Jabesh-gilead
Jordan River
Aphek
Gibeah
DEAD SEA
Philistine Army
Israelite Army
Rout of Israelite Army
N
0
km
20
0
miles
20

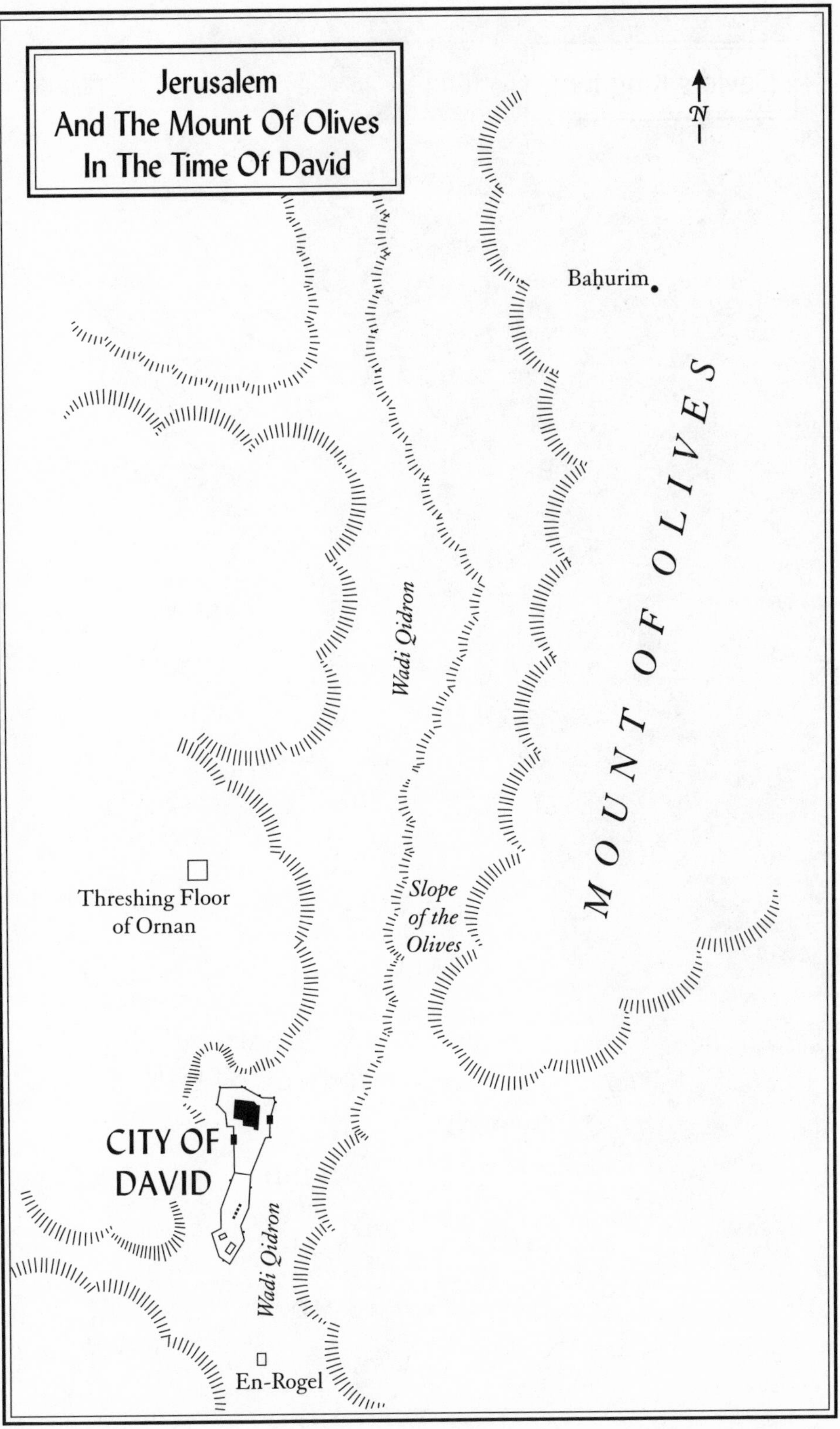

Jerusalem
And The Mount Of Olives
In The Time Of David
N
Baḥurim
MOUNT OF OLIVES
Wadi Qidron
Slope of the Olives
Threshing Floor of Ornan
CITY OF DAVID
Wadi Qidron
En-Rogel

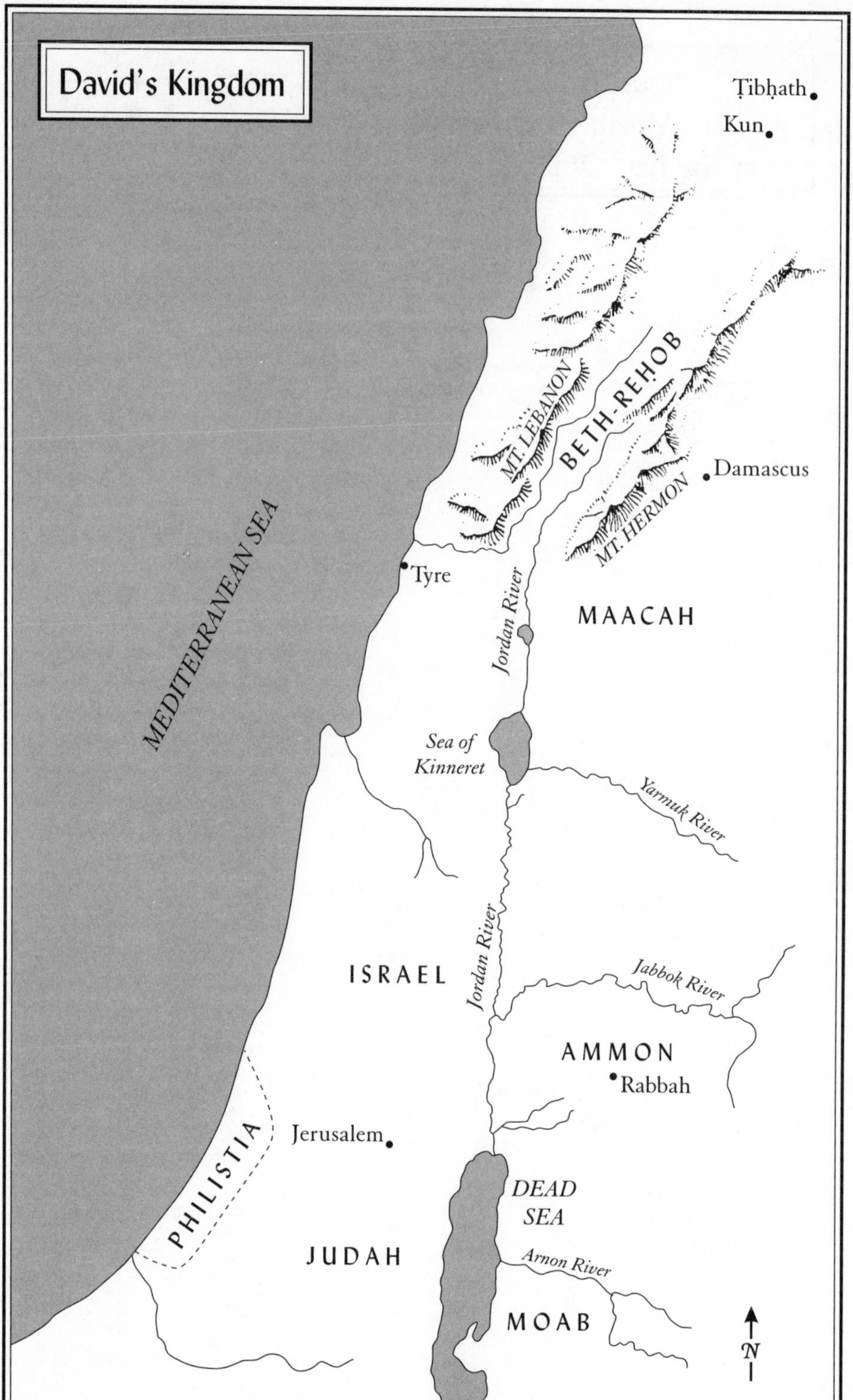

David's Kingdom
Ṭibḥath
Kun
MT. LEBANON
BETH-REḤOB
Damascus
MT. HERMON
MEDITERRANEAN SEA
Tyre
Jordan River
MAACAH
Sea of Kinneret
Yarmuk River
ISRAEL
Jordan River
Jabbok River
AMMON
Rabbah
Jerusalem
PHILISTIA
DEAD SEA
JUDAH
Arnon River
MOAB
N

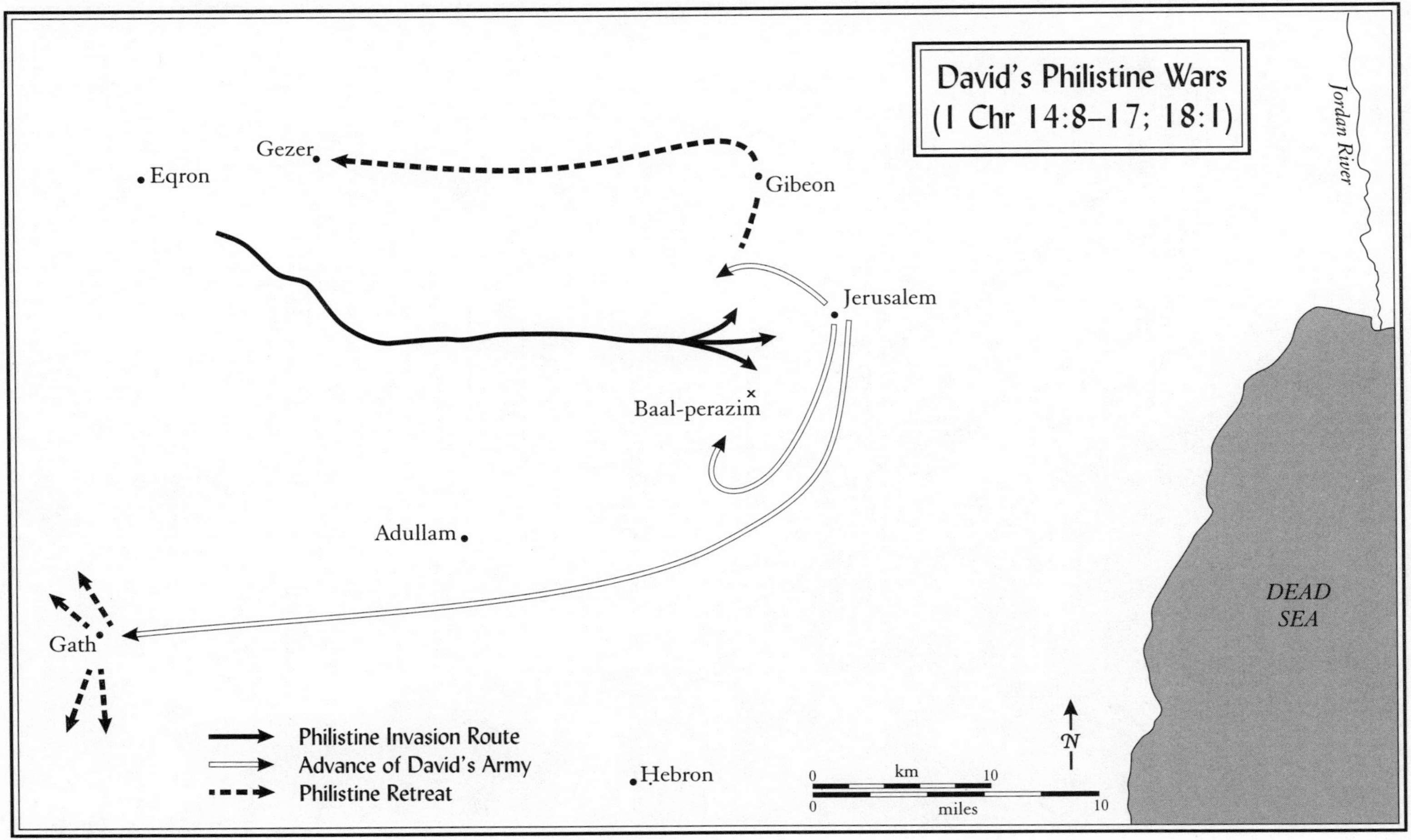
David's Philistine Wars
(1 Chr 14:8–17; 18:1)
Jordan River
Gezer
Eqron
Gibeon
Jerusalem
Baal-perazim
Adullam
Gath
DEAD
SEA
Hebron
N
0
km
10
0
miles
10
Philistine Invasion Route
Advance of David's Army
Philistine Retreat

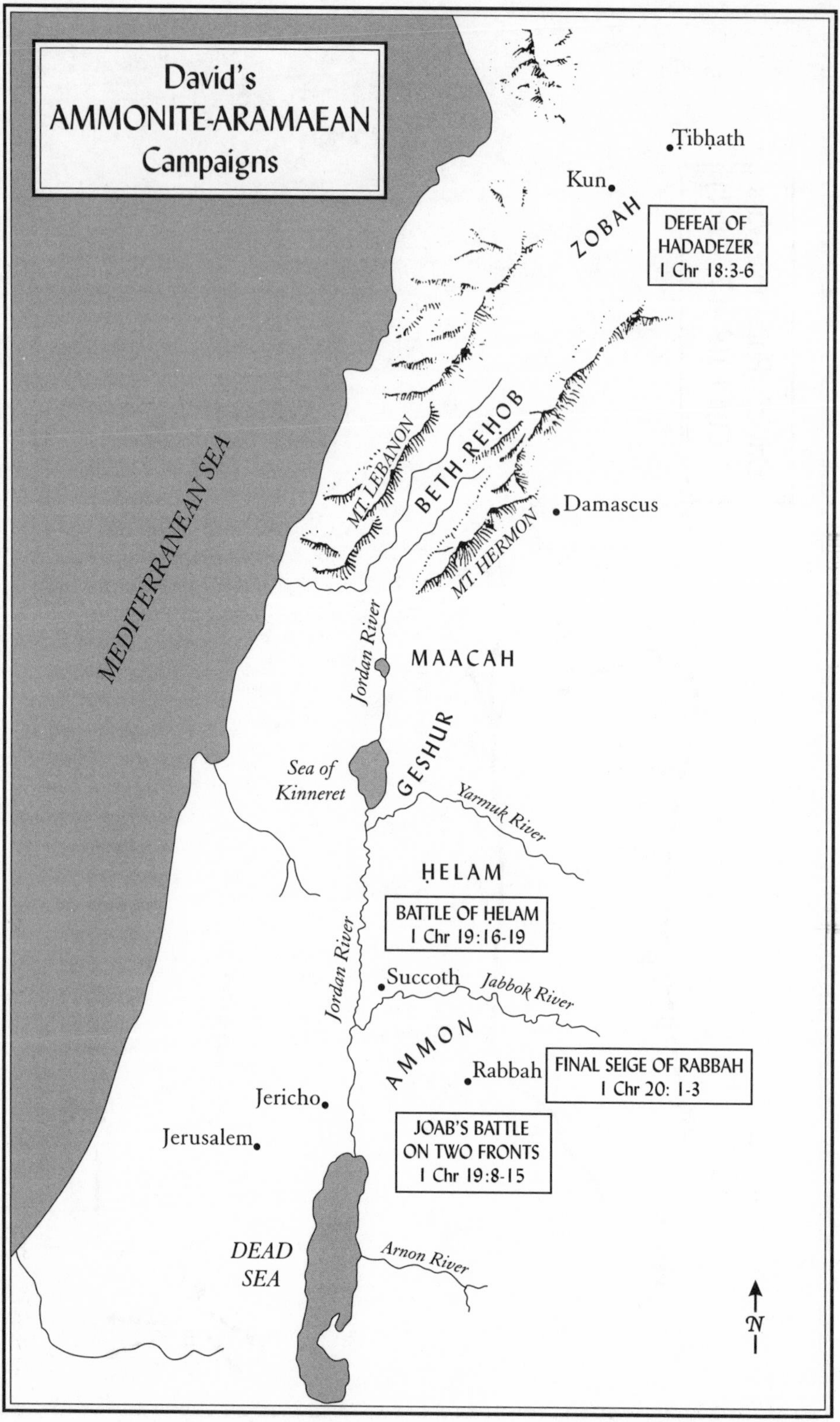

David's
AMMONITE-ARAMAEAN
Campaigns
Ṭibḥath
Kun
ZOBAH
DEFEAT OF
HADADEZER
I Chr 18:3-6
MT. LEBANON
BETH-REḤOB
Damascus
MT. HERMON
MEDITERRANEAN SEA
Jordan River
MAACAH
GESHUR
Sea of
Kinneret
Yarmuk River
ḤELAM
BATTLE OF ḤELAM
I Chr 19:16-19
Jordan River
Succoth
Jabbok River
AMMON
Rabbah
FINAL SEIGE OF RABBAH
I Chr 20: 1-3
Jericho
Jerusalem
JOAB'S BATTLE
ON TWO FRONTS
I Chr 19:8-15
DEAD
SEA
Arnon River
N